WESTERN EUROPEAN LABOR
AND
THE AMERICAN CORPORATION

CONTRIBUTORS

John A. Belford

Roger Blanpain

Louis Buckley

Robert Copp

L.H.J. Crijns

Owen Fairweather

P.P. Fano

Allan Flanders

Franz Gamillscheg

Cyril Grunfeld

Peter Henle

J.B. McCartney

J.D. Neirinck

Guy Nunn

Julius Rezler

Lee C. Shaw

John C. Shearer

Samuel C. Silkin

Clyde W. Summers

G.M.J. Veldkamp

WESTERN EUROPEAN LABOR
AND
THE AMERICAN CORPORATION

Edited by Alfred Kamin

Professor of Law, Loyola University of Chicago

●

Foreword by Otto Kahn-Freund

Professor of Comparative Law, University of Oxford

The Bureau of National Affairs, Inc.   ●   Washington, D.C.

HD)
8376.5
.W46
1970

Printed in the United States of America
Library of Congress Catalog Number 72-83775
Standard Book Number 87179-026-2

TO SARA

NOTES ON CONTRIBUTORS

JOHN A. BELFORD has been Vice President of Massey-Ferguson Limited since 1960. He is in charge of corporate direction of personnel and industrial relations functions in the company's world-wide operations in Canada, the United States, Mexico, Brazil, United Kingdom, France, Germany, Italy, Spain, South Africa and Australia. His responsibilities have required extensive travel and involvement with overseas operations. Mr. Belford was born in Ottawa in 1918, is a graduate of McGill University, and served as a Major in the Canadian army in World War II. He joined Massey-Ferguson in 1957 as Director of Personnel and Industrial Relations. Mr. Belford is a member of the Advisory Committee of the Industrial Relations Centre, University of Toronto.

ROGER BLANPAIN has been Professor of Law of University of Leuven (Louvain) since 1965 and Director of the University's Institute for Industrial Relations since 1966. He was born in Belgium in 1932 and obtained his law degree from University of Leuven in 1956, his master of arts degree from Columbia University in 1957, and his doctor's degree from Leuven in 1961. He has written extensively in legal and industrial relations periodicals on Belgian labor law and has made comparative labor law studies for the European Economic Community and the European Coal and Steel Community. Among his published books is a treatise on Belgian labor law, *Handboek van het Belgish Arbeidrecht* (in Flemish), 1968. He is president of the Belgian Association for Industrial Relations and a member of the International Society for Labour Law and Social Legislation.

LOUIS BUCKLEY joined the faculty of Loyola University of Chicago in 1967 as Associate Professor of Industrial Relations. In 1969 he became Professor of Economics. He was born in Galesburg, Ill., in 1906 and received his B.A. degree in 1928 and his M.A. degree in 1930 from Notre Dame University. He pursued further graduate studies at the University of Wisconsin and the University of Illinois from 1933 to 1938. He is a member of the Industrial Relations Research Association and the American Economic Association; he served as president of the Catholic Conference on Industrial Problems from 1948 to 1958. He is author of "Economics and Guidance" in *Foundations of Guidance and Counselling: Multidisciplinary Readings,* Smith and Mink, eds. (Philadelphia: J. B. Lippincott Co., 1969) and many articles in professional journals.

ROBERT COPP has been Overseas Liaison Manager, Labor Relations Staff of the Ford Motor Company, Dearborn, Mich., since 1965. He was born in Wilkinsburg, Pa., in 1921. From the University of Michigan he received the degrees of A.B. in 1947 and LL.B. in 1950. He has been with Ford Motor Company since 1950 in a variety of industrial relations positions. He served as Labor Relations Manager, Ford International Staff from 1962 to 1965. He was Chairman (1966-1968), Personnel and Employee Relations Committee, National Foreign Trade Council, Inc., New York. He is a member of the Business Research Advisory Committee on Foreign Labor and Trade, Bureau of Labor Statistics, U. S. Department of Labor. He is a member of the Industrial Relations Research Association.

LEO H. J. CRIJNS* has been the Adviser of the Director General of Social Affairs of the European Communities since 1968. He was born in Nuth in the Netherlands in 1923. He received his doctorate in economic and social sciences from the University of Leuven (Louvain) in 1951, and served in the Ministry of Economic Affairs at the Hague from 1948 to 1954 and as Secretary General of the Man and Society Foundation at Nimegue, the Netherlands, from 1954 to 1958. Dr. Crijns was Head of the Labor Problems Division, Directorate General for Social Affairs, EEC Commission, from 1958 to 1968.

OWEN FAIRWEATHER was born in 1913. He was graduated with a B.A. degree from Dartmouth College in 1935 and from the University of Chicago Law School with a J.D. degree in 1938. He commenced the practice of law with Pope and Ballard, Chicago, and became a partner of that firm. In 1945 he participated in the organization of the firm of Seyfarth, Shaw & Fairweather, which in early 1957 became Seyfarth, Shaw, Fairweather & Geraldson. He has acted as a management representative for many companies in the negotiation of labor agreements and the handling of matters before the National Labor Relations Board, the courts, arbitrators, and fact-finding tribunals. Mr. Fairweather was a coordinator of *Labor Relations and the Law in the United Kingdom and the United States* (1968) and *Labor Relations and the Law in Belgium and the United States* (1969), both published by the University of Michigan.

P. P. FANO* has been Director of the Italian Branch Office of the International Labour Organization since 1960. He was born in Ferrara, Italy, in 1905. After receiving his law degree from Rome University in 1929, he practiced law in Rome until 1938, when he moved to the United Kingdom. He returned to Italy in 1943 on behalf of the International Transport Workers Federation to help the resistance movement and the rebuilding of free trade unions. In 1945, Mr. Fano was a member of the Italian delegation at the Paris session of the International Labour Conference. Thereafter he joined the staff of the International Labour Office. He has carried out I.L.O. advisory missions to governments in Latin America, the Middle East and the Far East and has represented the organization at meetings of various international bodies.

ALLAN FLANDERS became a full-time member of the Commission on Industrial Relations in 1969. He was born in Watford, England, in 1910 and studied philosophy, political history, and economics in Germany. Subsequently he worked as a journalist, tutor in adult education, and engineering draughtsman, in which position he held union office. He was research assistant to the Trades Union Congress from 1943 to 1946. Mr. Flanders became Senior Lecturer in Industrial Relations at the University of Oxford in 1949 and held this position until his appointment this year to the Commission on Industrial Relations. His principal publications are *Trade Unions; The System of Industrial Relations in Great Britain* (with H. A. Clegg); *The Fawley Productivity Agreements; Industrial Relations: What is Wrong with the System?; Collective Bargaining: Prescription for*

---

* These contributors wish to state that the views expressed by them in this volume are entirely personal and are not necessarily those of the governmental bodies or international organizations which each of them serves or has served.

Change; Experiments in Industrial Democracy (with R. Pomeranz and J. Woodward); and *Readings in Collective Bargaining.*

FRANZ GAMILLSCHEG has been Professor of Law at the University of Göttingen since 1958. He also serves as Director of the University's Institute for Labor Law. He was born in 1924 at Hall (Tyrol) and studied at Berlin, Tübingen, and Paris. From 1951 to 1958, he was associated with the Max Planck Institute of Foreign and Private International Law and was Privatdozent at Tübingen. He is a member of the International Society for Labour Law and Social Legislation, the German Labor Courts Association and the German Council on Private International Law. His publications include the following books: *The Influence of Dumoulin on the Development of the Conflict of Laws; International Labor Law; Civil Liability of the Salaried Employee; Disparities in Treatment on account of Trade Union Membership;* and *Labor Law: Cases and Problems.*

CYRIL GRUNFELD has been Professor of Law, London School of Economics and Social Science, since 1966. He was born in Cardiff, Wales. After service in the British army he received his LL.B. degree in 1946 and his M.A. degree in 1948 from Cambridge University (Trinity Hall). He was called to the bar in 1948 by the Inner Temple. His teaching positions at London School of Economics and Political Science prior to his elevation to a chair in 1966 were: Assistant in Law, 1946-1947; Assistant Lecturer, 1947-1949; Lecturer, 1949-1956; Reader in Law, 1956-1966. He is a co-editor of *Modern Law Review* and the *British Journal of Industrial Relations.* His publications in book form are Chitty, *Contracts* (21st ed.), II, Ch. 4; *Anti-Trust Laws* (Friedmann, ed.); *Trade Unions and the Individual in English Law* (Institute of Personnel Management); and the treatise *Modern Trade Union Law.*

PETER HENLE* has been Chief Economist of the Bureau of Labor Statistics, U.S. Department of Labor since 1961. He is a graduate of Swarthmore College (B.A., 1940), and in 1947 received his M.A. degree from The American University, Washington, D.C. Mr. Henle came to the Bureau of Labor Statistics after 15 years of service on the research staff of the AFL and the AFL-CIO. In 1956 he became Assistant Director of Research in the merged AFL-CIO. His governmental responsibilities include providing policy direction to the Bureau's program of economic analysis, stimulating special studies of economic and social issues, and managing a comprehensive system of program planning activities. He has also been serving as Chairman of an interagency staff group for the President's Committee on Corporate Pension Funds and Other Private Retirement and Welfare Programs.

OTTO KAHN-FREUND has been Professor of Comparative Law, University of Oxford, since 1964. He was born in Germany in 1900 and studied at Goethe-Gymnasium, Frankfurt-am-Main and the Universities of Frankfurt, Heidelberg, Leipzig, and London. He received his degrees of Doctor of Laws (Frankfurt) in 1925 and Master of Laws (London) 1935. From 1935 to 1964 he was on the faculty of the London School of Economics and Political Science, where he became a professor of law in 1951. He is a co-editor of *Modern Law Review.* From 1965 to 1968 he was a member of the Royal Commission on Trade Unions and Employers' Associations. He is a Past President of the International Society for Labour Law and Social Legislation. Professor Kahn-Freund is a co-author of *The System of Indus-*

trial Relations in Great Britain (Flanders and Clegg, eds. 1953) and *Law and Opinion in England in the Twentieth Century* (Ginsberg, ed. 1959). He wrote "Labor Law and Social Security" in: *American Enterprise in the Common Market* (1960).

ALFRED KAMIN has been Professor of Law, Loyola University of Chicago, since 1963. He was born in Chicago in 1910, graduated from Chicago-Kent College of Law in 1932 and admitted to the bar of Illinois in the same year. He was professionally active on behalf of labor unions in Chicago during the rise of industrial unionism and thereafter until 1963 practiced as attorney for many national and local labor unions. In 1949-1951 he was Chairman of the Labor Law Section of the Illinois State Bar Association and in 1952-1953 served as Chairman of the Section of Labor Relations Law of the American Bar Association. He is co-editor of *Labor Relations and the Law*, adopted by many American law schools. He was Director of the 1968 Loyola Summer Institute on Business and Law on the topic "The Supranational Corporation and Western European Labor," the basis for this book.

J. B. McCARTNEY has been Senior Lecturer of the Faculty of Law, The Queen's University of Belfast, since 1968. He was born in County Antrim, Northern Ireland, in 1917. Prior to receiving his LL.B. degree from The Queen's University in 1958, he was an electrical engineer and trade union officer. He has been on the faculty of The Queen's University since 1960. His articles on labor law and other legal subjects have appeared in the *Irish Jurist* (Dublin) and the *Northern Ireland Legal Quarterly*. He is the author of "The Contractual or Non-Contractual Nature of Collective Agreements in Great Britain and Eire" and "Strike Law and the Constitution of Eire," in *Labour Relations and the Law* (Kahn-Freund, ed. 1965). He is Secretary of the Irish Society for Labour Law and Social Legislation.

JOSÉ D. NEIRINCK* has been Deputy Chief of Cabinet of the Deputy Prime Minister of Belgium since July 1968. He was born in Belgium in 1920 and was educated at the University of Ghent, from which he received the degree of Drs. Social Science. He was Social-Economic Adviser at the Planning and Documentation Office, Belgian General Federation of Labor (FGTB), from 1947 to 1954; Deputy Executive Assistant and later Executive Assistant to the Minister of Labor and Social Welfare of Belgium, 1954-1958; and Deputy Governor and Director-General of the Belgian National Social Security Service and Vice President of the National Pension Fund for Employees from 1958 to 1963. From 1963 to 1968, Dr. Neirinck was Director-General of Social Affairs of the European Economic Community. In English he has written, with Dr. G. M. J. Veldkamp, *The Rome Treaty Social Policy and EEC Applied Labour Economics*, No. 3 of the Chronique de Politique étrangère, 1969, published by the Royal Institute of Foreign Affairs (KIIB-IRRI), Brussels.

GUY NUNN is Assistant Director, International Affairs Department, United Automobile, Aerospace & Agricultural Implement Workers of America. He has been associated with UAW since 1948. From 1949 to 1966, Mr. Nunn was Director of the UAW Radio-TV Department. He received his B.A. degree from Occidental College, Los Angeles, in 1936 and an M.A. degree from University of Oxford in 1939. Before joining the UAW staff, he was employed as a field examiner of the National Labor Relations

Board (1940), labor economist, Federal Reserve System (1941), Regional Director, War Manpower Commission, Minorities Branch (1942). He has written for many American magazines, such as *New Republic, The Nation, Atlantic, Collier's* and *The Saturday Evening Post.* He is the author of a novel, *White Shadows.*

JULIUS REZLER has been Professor of Economics at Loyola University of Chicago since 1969. From 1957 to 1969 he was Professor of Industrial Relations and from 1965 to 1969, Director of the Loyola Institute of Industrial Relations. He was born at Miskolc, Hungary, in 1911 and holds the following degrees: M.A., University of Budapest, 1935; Ph.D., University of Szeged, 1938; Dr. Political Science, University of Pecs, 1941. He was visiting Professor of Economics at University of Texas, 1952-1953 and Associate Professor of Economics, St. Francis College, Brooklyn, N.Y., 1954-1957. He was Fulbright Professor at Xavier Labour Relations Institute, Jamshedpur, India, 1961-1962. He is the author of *Automation and Industrial Labor* (New York: Random House, 1969) and many articles in professional journals.

LEE C. SHAW is a partner in the Chicago law firm of Seyfarth, Shaw, Fairweather & Geraldson. He was born in 1913 in Red Wing, Minn. He attended the University of Michigan and University of Chicago and received his B.A. degree from the latter in 1936. He was graduated from University of Chicago Law School with the degree of J.D. in 1938 and was admitted to the bar of Illinois in the same year. He has spent most of his legal career in representing companies and employer associations in the negotiation of collective bargaining agreements, trial of arbitration proceedings, and trial of cases before the NLRB and the federal courts. His public activities include service as a member of President's National Labor-Management Panel. He has written extensively on labor relations law.

JOHN C. SHEARER is Professor of Economics and Director, Manpower Research and Training Center, Oklahoma State University. He was educated at Cornell University, the New York State School of Industrial Relations (B.S., 1952), and Princeton University (A.M., 1958; Ph.D., 1960). He also studied as a Fulbright fellow in industrial relations, economics, and social administration at the University of Manchester, England. He has taught at Marietta College, Ohio; Carnegie Institute of Technology; the Latin American Institute of Economic and Social Planning, Santiago, Chile; and Pennsylvania State University. He has served as a consultant to the Organization of American States, the United Nations, the Ford Foundation, the Inter-American Development Bank, the Council for International Progress in Management, and the International Manpower Institute.

SAMUEL C. SILKIN has been a Labour Member of Parliament for the constituency of Dulwich (South London) since 1964. He was born in 1918 and received his B.A. degree from Cambridge University (Trinity Hall) in 1941. He was called to the bar by the Middle Temple in the same year. He was appointed Queen's Counsel in 1963 and Recorder of Bedford in 1965. He became Chairman at its inception in 1966 of the Parliamentary Labour Party's European Affairs and Common Market Group, and served as Chairman of the Select Committee on Parliamentary Privilege in 1967. Mr. Silkin was elected in 1965 to the Assemblies of the Council of Europe and the Western European Union. He was elected Chairman of the Legal

Committee of the Council of Europe in 1966 and in July 1968 became the leader of the British delegation to the Council. He was the British nominee for the position of Secretary-General of the Council of Europe in 1969.

CLYDE W. SUMMERS, Garver Professor of Law at Yale University, received his undergraduate and law degrees from the University of Illinois (B.S., 1939; J.D., 1942). He taught at the College of Law of the University of Toledo from 1942 to 1949 and then spent six years as professor of law at the University of Buffalo before joining Yale's law faculty in 1956. He holds Master of Laws (1946) and Doctor of Juridical Science (1951) degrees from Columbia University. A specialist in labor law, he held a Guggenheim fellowship in 1955-1956 to study labor relations in Sweden and a Ford Law Faculty fellowship in 1963-1964 to study comparative labor law and labor relations in the countries of the European Economic Community. He was Visiting Professor of Law at University of Leuven (Louvain), 1965-1966. Since 1951 he has been a labor arbitrator for the American Arbitration Association. Professor Summers is the author or editor of 10 books.

GERARDUS M. J. VELDKAMP* is Chairman of the Netherlands Royal Commission for the Codification of Social Security Laws. He was born at Breda, the Netherlands, in 1921. He studied at the College of Economics at Tillburg, from which in 1949 he obtained his doctorate in economic sociology. From 1941 to 1950 he was employed by the Board of Labor at Breda and from 1950 to 1952 he was scientific adviser to the Minister of Social Affairs and Public Health. From 1952 to 1961 he served as 'Secretary of State for Economic Affairs, and from 1961 to 1967 was Minister of Social Affairs and Public Health of the Netherlands. Dr. Veldkamp is a leader of the Catholic People's Party and holds numerous decorations of his own country and other nations. He is the author of many works on social insurance policy and legislation.

FOREWORD

In the course of the last few years the growing interest in the comparative study of labor relations and of labor law has led to a number of publications, both in North America and in Western Europe. Increasing awareness of the significance of such studies has mainly two sources. One is the rise of the large economic empires known as "multinational corporations," and the other is the emergence of common market organizations aspiring to the unification or harmonization of rules of economic behavior, whether legal or customary.

To this body of literature the present volume makes a significant contribution, and its organizer and editor, Professor Alfred Kamin, deserves the gratitude of all those interested in such studies for having devised an interesting and illuminating scheme of work and for having assembled a distinguished team of contributors.

The principal value of a work of this nature is that it reduces those misunderstandings and misapprehensions which arise from the use of identical or similar words for different things. As Professor Clyde Summers points out, it is dangerous for an American to believe that words such as "labor union" or "collective bargaining" signify in a European country what they mean in America, and, equally important, that they mean the same things everywhere in Europe. To create a world market for words is easy; to export institutions is dangerous and difficult. The present volume deals with technical terms which were to a large extent imported into the United States from Europe — hence the look of disbelief on the face of American observers when they see that in the course of crossing the Atlantic these words have changed their meanings.

Another service which the book may perform for the benefit of employers and unions and of governments is to administer a warning against attempts to transplant bargaining methods and habits of handling industrial relations from one country to another. Industrial relations are determined by power and by levels of wealth and productivity. But they are also embedded in their cultural environment, in traditions — very old traditions, sometimes — and their adaptation to economic change is itself a process whose tempo and whose character depend on the imponderables of the atmostphere of civilization. This is an important aspect of multinational and supranational government, enterprise, or unionism. The present volume is likely to reinforce this lesson. It is also a lesson to the comparative lawyers not to overrate the practical utility of their discipline.

Still another use to which the book may be put is a measure of sound reflection on the eternal dilemma between evolving highly sophisticated patterns of labor relations for a minority and concentrating one's energy on getting at least some social improvement for the largest possible number of workers. The European observer of the American scene is sometimes left wondering whether transatlantic misunderstandings would not be reduced if this dilemma was made a little more articulate. The solidarity of the working class is the traditional concept which gave to the European union movement its ethos and its impetus. This is not to say that the corporate self-assertion of the craft union or of the plant unit is alien to any European traditions; far from it. But the tendency of the continental unions, in alliance with political parties, to obtain what can be obtained for all workers and to use legislation as the chosen instrument for this purpose, is as significant an expression of this fundamental attitude as is the promotion or the acceptance of industry-wide bargaining by British trade unions. The contrast to the situation in North America is fairly obvious. Today the American system of plant bargaining is regarded by many with admiration on account of its comprehensiveness and of its effectiveness. Occasionally the European observer asks himself what proportion of the working class of the United States benefits from these institutions.

All those interested, whether as practitioners or as teachers, in questions of this nature will welcome the appearance of this book. It is in the nature of a symposium to present its subjects from many different points of view and in many different styles. No contributor can be expected to agree with the methods, approaches, or views of all or — for that matter — of any of his colleagues. It is the conspectus which matters, the possibility which a volume like this opens of looking at familiar problems, as it were, through many eyes at the same time. This is an intellectual experience which is bound to stimulate further thought, and — who knows? — here and there improved action in practice.

The writer appreciates the honor of having been asked to help to launch the ship, and he now breaks his bottle of champagne against its bows and wishes it a good passage.

Otto Kahn-Freund

Brasenose College
Oxford
May 1969

EDITOR'S PREFACE

Comparative studies in labor relations law and practice, using American experience as a paradigm, but not a paragon, are not just desirable intellectual exercises but indeed a national imperative.

The American presence in Western Europe is a major political and economic reality of our time, as inextricably woven into the U. S. economic fabric as into the European. Samuel C. Silkin comments in Part VII of this book "that there are those who when asked who the superpowers of the world will be in the next generation reply, 'The United States, the U. S. S. R., and U. S. investment in Europe.'" In "The American Challenge" (New York: Atheneum, 1968), J. -J. Servan-Schreiber commences his book with a similar observation: "Fifteen years from now it is quite possible that the world's greatest industrial power, just after the United States and Russia, will not be Europe, but *American industry in Europe.* Already in the ninth year of the Common Market, this European market is basically American in organization."

American investment and management in Western Europe are by no means accepted by the European citizenry as an unmixed blessing. Vocal criticism, indeed hostility, is increasingly directed to the U.S. invasion of the West European economy, especially in the crucial sectors of aerospace, electronics, and chemicals. Not all critics are content, as is Servan-Schreiber, with a laudatory appraisal of American research, technological, and managerial efforts in Europe as a "challenge" to Europeans that calls for solution through European political unity.

Nor are all European observers as gentle as a reporter to the Consultative Assembly of the Council of Europe in an "Introductory Report on Disparities between the USA and Europe in the scientific and technological fields — Ways and means of remedying them." In this "informal exchange of views between a United States Congressional delegation and the Members of the Consultative Assembly in May 1968" (Assembly Document 2368), the reporter, a Mr. Gustafson, analyzes the American advantages over Western Europe, such as a domestic market of 200 million to absorb the enormous costs of the burst of recent technological developments, a strong U. S. capital market, and a greater American capacity to take risks in research and development for a period of years before reaping the benefits. He observes:

"Since the ability to take risks is to no little extent dependent on

xv

the firm's turnover, it should be noted that out of 460 international companies surveyed by the review Fortune in 1965 with a turnover of more than $250 millions, 60% were American.

"Further, the two leading American firms had a turnover almost equal to the first 500 French firms. The 19 biggest American companies had a turnover equal to the GNP of the U.K. The net profit of the four leading American firms would be enough to finance the Belgian budget."

Mr. Gustafson continues:

"As regards direct US investments in Europe I wish to repeat the proposals in last year's paper (Assembly Document 2200, pp. 16-17):

"American companies in Europe should, wherever possible, develop into multi-national companies.

"The multi-national corporation should:

"(a) Operate research and development facilities within the host country, thereby strengthening its technological base and, combatting any 'Brain-Drain';

"(b) Permit the development of early reciprocal participation by Europeans and Americans in their new products; this would make it less likely, for example, that new products of American technology would be developed initially in the US home market and only later made available in Europe;

"(c) Wherever possible, place nationals from the host country in responsible management positions;

"(d) Decentralize decision making."

More typical of European reactions are the views expressed by McMillan and Harris in "The American Take-Over of Britain" (London: Leslie Frewin, 1968). These authors vigorously express their distaste for "the American Way" and include an attack on the application of American labor policy and practice to British workers (pp. 127-146). After presenting a fully documented case, they conclude (at 229):

"What concerns Britain and Europe is the fact that US-owned concerns can change their ownership without the slightest consultation with their subsidiaries, or with the governments of the countries in which the subsidiaries are situated. This ought to produce a twentieth-century equivalent to the battle cry: 'No taxation without representation.' It is another compelling argument for the Americans to share control of their subsidiaries with the nationals of the states in which they operate.

"Appeals for 'fair play' by themselves are not likely to alter American attitudes. But if they are faced by aggressive business techniques, such as bidding for some of the bright young American executives in England and the threat of legislative action by the governments of the European Economic Community as well as the UK, a more accommodating view may be taken. The Americans, like other folk, much prefer half the loaf to none at all.

"For Britain at least, the way ahead is clear. The status of a cringing satellite does not become England. Yet that is what England will become if she remains hobbled to the US."

McMillan and Harris quote, with obvious relish, Senator Fulbright's observations:

"One reason why Americans abroad may act as though they 'own the place' is that in many places they very nearly do: American companies may dominate large segments of a country's economy; American products are advertised on billboards and displayed in the shop windows; American hotels and snack bars are available to protect American tourists from foreign influence; American soldiers may be stationed in the country and, even if they are not, the population are probably well aware that their very survival depends on the wisdom with which America uses her immense military power.

"I think that any American, when he goes abroad, carries an unconscious knowledge of all this power with him, and it affects his behavior just as it once affected the behavior of Greeks and Romans, of Spaniards, Germans, and Englishmen, in the brief high noons of their respective ascendancies."

This book explores a principal ramification of American involvement in Western Europe: the labor relations of American firms that operate there. By using the domestic labor policies of such American firms at their home bases as a referent, we hope the American reader will come quickly to grasp the essentials of other industrial relations and labor law systems. This method of presentation should also enable readers outside North America to understand the basis of American managerial experience at home in labor matters, however erroneous might be efforts to export industrial relations systems from one nation to another.

The labor relations systems of Western Europe were mature long before the development of a significant American presence in Europe after World War II. It is now evident that American labor relations laws and our techniques for resolving labor problems are not effective programs for dealing with European workers and labor organizations. Indeed, it is suggested by many that American labor relations advisers have much to learn from the European experience. The essential task is one of reciprocal accommodation between the expectations of American investment, engineering, and management and the realities of economic, political, and social life in each of the host nations.

This book is based on the Summer Institute on Business and Law, sponsored by Loyola University of Chicago, through its School of Law and School of Business Administration, held at Highland Park, Ill., July 7-12, 1968. The theme of the conference was "The Supranational Corporation and Western European Labor." With but one exception, every contributor to this volume attended the morning plenary sessions of the conference and participated in the afternoon seminars. Virtually all contributors made substantial revisions in their conference papers to include reevaluations and insights stimulated by questions raised and challenges hurled by their fellow conferees — businessmen, labor leaders, arbitrators, government officials, practicing lawyers, and professors of law, economics, and industrial relations. Thus, by their activities in the afternoon seminars, all of the conferees contributed to this book, and even those who did not formally serve as reporters or commentators are its coauthors. The conferees who have no by-lines in the Table of Contents are listed in Appendix 1.

The volume follows in the main the presentations made at the six plenary sessions of the Loyola conference. The papers delivered at these plenary sessions served as the basis of Parts I, III, IV, V, VI, and VII. With one exception, each of these parts follows the same general format. A perspective on the subject of the part is first presented in American terms and expectations by an American (in Part I, a Canadian) with intensive experience in Western Europe. Supplementary or critical comments by Europeans and a sprinkling of American experts then follow the contribution of the principal reporter. Part VII presents commentaries by Europeans only on the American presence in their respective countries and in the general area. Parts II and VIII are explained in the introductory notes that precede each part.

Several of the contributors have appended reading lists to their articles. Such lists and many footnote references suggest the abundance of published materials on West European labor relations systems available in English. What will, I am sure, prove to be the most significant study of an industrial relations system in the twentieth century is the entire output of the British Royal Commission on Trade Unions and Employers' Associations, 1965-1968, under the chairmanship of the Rt. Hon. Lord Donovan. In reaching the conclusions of its report, the Commission evaluated more than just the existing British system. They considered a host of proposals, offered by expert witnesses, that were borrowed from industrial practice or labor law outside the United Kingdom and restated in British terms. I urge readers, especially those interested in pursuing further comparative studies, to acquire from Her Majesty's Stationery Office, before they go out of print, not only the final report of the Royal Commission (London: HMSO Cmnd. 3623, 1968) but the Minutes of Evidence (69 parts), the 11 Research Papers, and the supplementary written evidence of the Ministry of Labour, the Chief Registrar of Friendly Societies, the Confederation of British

Industries, the Trades Union Congress, and others in three separate volumes. To complete the file, the researcher should also obtain a copy of the Conservative Party paper "Fair Deal at Work" (Conservative Political Centre, 32 Smith Square, London S.W. 1) and the January 1969 White Paper, "In Place of Strife" (London: HMSO Cmnd. 3888).

There is one obvious deficiency in comparative labor relations research. It is difficult to comprehend the collective bargaining process of another nation without examination of the end product of that process — the collective labor agreement. There is no center in the world, so far as I can ascertain, that gathers and translates collective agreements. I have had no difficulty in securing British and Irish union-employer or union-association contracts. Study of these documents taught me much about the industrial relations systems of the United Kingdom and the Republic of Ireland. Perhaps some day soon, one of the public or private international organizations listed in Appendix 3 will remedy this barrier to comparative industrial relations research by making available English translations of continental collective bargaining agreements and doing the reverse with similar Irish, British, and North American documents.

Another difficulty in comparative studies was suggested by Professor Kahn-Freund in his inaugural lecture at the University of Oxford on May 12, 1965: "In my own teaching of comparative law I have often felt that, like Bagehot's monarch, I had a duty to warn and a duty to encourage. To teach students not to be lured by homonyms and not to be afraid of synonyms . . . ."

Homonyms are indeed deceptive. "Moonlighting" is one thing in the United States and quite another in Ireland. "Arbitration" can mean anything from a final and binding private adjudication, as it does in the United States, to a mere unenforceable recommendation to the parties by a government official for settlement of a labor dispute, as in Luxembourg. The Federal Labor Court of West Germany has little in common with the Labour Court of the Republic of Ireland. The "union shop," familiar to Americans, is called a "post-entry closed ship" in Britain. What Americans would call a "closed shop" would be a "pre-entry closed shop" in the United Kingdom. In the United States the term "socialist" is a pejorative. In Europe the word is quite respectable and encompasses major, and sometimes dominant, political parties. The issuance of a negotiation license under the Irish Trade Union Act 1941 or the certification of a trade union by the British Registrar of Friendly Societies is altogether different from the certification of a bargaining representative under Section 9 of our National Labor Relations Act. The

British shop steward performs functions far beyond the scope of authority of his American counterpart. Indeed, as several contributors to this volume point out, the very term "collective bargaining" varies in meaning from nation to nation.

Still other problems in comparative research inevitably arise from language barriers. It was my deliberate choice in planning the 1968 Loyola Summer Institute that whatever continental scholars would be invited should be able to write and speak English acceptably. My American parochialism may have barred participation by eminent European scholars who speak little or no English. But past experience had persuaded me that "headphone" international conferences inevitably prove to be dreary and wearying affairs. The best of interpreters, even those armed in advance with textual copies, succeed only in reducing a brilliant and subtle paper to a succession of drab clichés. Leisurely translation of papers written in another language is often better — if the translator is entirely at home with the concepts and terminology in the field. But where in America — outside of a handful of bilingual or multilingual scholars and practitioners — does one find such translators? If they can be found, they should be used as speakers and contributors and not as mere linguistic intermediaries.

Insuring the use of reasonably idiomatic English in the final draft of articles written by our continental contributors, to whom English is only an auxiliary language, was my editorial responsibility. I feel confident that my extensive correspondence, even occasional transatlantic phone calls, with these distinguished statesmen and scholars has eliminated any error, real or apparent, stemming from translingual communication. If such error should appear anywhere in this book, the responsibility is mine alone.

ALFRED KAMIN

August 1969

ACKNOWLEDGEMENTS

This book is based upon the proceedings of the Summer Institute on Business and Law of Loyola University of Chicago, held July 7-12, 1968 at Highland Park, Ill. Acknowledgements of aid in the preparation of this volume thus include those who made possible the original gathering of the contributing authors and other invitees.

First and foremost, I wish to thank the Very Reverend James F. Maguire, S.J., President of Loyola University of Chicago, and his associates and staff for their unstinting support of the conference and for their encouragement of this publication. I am also grateful to William L. Lamey, Dean, Loyola University School of Law, and F. Virgil Boyd, Dean of the University's School of Business Administration, for their active cooperation in planning the 1968 Summer Institute and participating in the multitude of necessary arrangements.

Generous assistance was given us by scholars, public officials, business executives and labor leaders in Ireland, Britain and the six Common Market countries.

Some of those in Britain who gave much help in various forms and to whom I now express my appreciation are the following: The Rt. Hon. Sir Eric Sachs, M.B.E., Lord Justice of Appeal, for his warm sponsorship during my visits to London when the Loyola Conference was being planned; the Rt. Hon. Lord Donovan, Chairman of the Royal Commission on Trade Unions and Employers' Associations, for arranging private meetings for me with Commission members and for his insightful correspondence relating to our 1968 Summer Institute and this book; Roger Rideout, Reader in Law, University College, London, for his valuable comments on our conference plans; Sir Edward Brown, M. P., and Stephen Abbott, of the Research Department of the Conservative Party, for explaining to me the particulars of the party's position on British industrial relations problems; H. Nightingale, of the British Institute of Management, and Leslie Hodgson, General Secretary of the General Federation of Trade Unions, for their counsel on questions facing British industrial management and trade union leadership; and Norman M. Selwyn, Lecturer in Law at University of Aston, for his fruitful invitation to me to address a seminar of the Industrial Law Society of Birmingham held at the University in September 1967.

I acknowledge with thanks the help of Alice-Leone Moats, the American journalist and novelist, who arranged and ably interpreted a lengthy conference in Rome with Vittorio Foa of the Secretariat of the Italian General Confederation of Labor (CGIL), and Marco Vais, head of the Confederation's legal department. Of course, I am also grateful to Messrs. Foa and Vais for their generosity in receiving me and adding to my education about the Italian labor movement.

The 1968 Loyola Summer Institute and this volume were aided by several Belgian citizens and residents: Alfred Braunthal, Assistant General Secretary of the International Confederation of Free Trade Unions, supplied the Loyola conferees with helpful literature on labor-management relations in Western Europe; Piet De Somer, Rector of the University of Leuven, and Zeger Van Hee, then Dean of the Law School of the University (and now Professor of Law), opened many doors for me by their invitation to lecture on American labor law at the University in January 1968; Albert Verscheuren, Director of the Federation of Belgian Industries, Ignaas Lindemans, head of the Studies Department of the Christian Trade Unions of Belgium (CSC-ACV), and Jozef Baeten, legal adviser to CSC-ACV, were most helpful to us in securing literature and information on West European industrial relations methods.

All of us connected with the 1968 Summer Institute and the preparation of this volume are beholden to Jean Rey, President of the Commission of the European Communities, for his abundant aid and cooperation in our University's undertaking in developing the materials discussed at our 1968 conference and published here.

This volume offers the first American publication of materials relating to the industrial relations system of the Republic of Ireland. For their generous contributions to our efforts, I am especially obligated to Mr. Justice Brian Walsh, of the Supreme Court of Ireland, and Cathal Loughney, Director of the Irish Industrial Development Authority. I wish also to express my gratitude to C. B. MacKenna, Regius Professor of Laws, and A. K. Asmal, Lecturer in Law, of Trinity College, Dublin, for their generous invitation to address a seminar on American labor law held at the college in September 1967, from which I learned much more about Ireland than did my auditors about the United States.

We are indebted to Victor G. Reuther, Director, International Affairs Department, United Automobile, Aerospace and Agricultural Implement Workers of America, for supplying our conference with the working papers of the Sixth World Automotive Conference held at Turin, Italy, in May 1968 and for other assistance in the preparation of this book. And we are similarly grateful to Paul Jennings, President, International Union of Electrical, Radio and Machine Workers, AFL-CIO, for data relating to the International General Electric Conference held at Bogotá, Colombia, in April 1969.

My personal thanks — which they will fully understand — for help in the completion of this book go to Drs. William Swisher, Ernest G. McEwen, Allen H. Babbitz, and Robert P. Miller, of Evanston, Ill.

Students of the School of Law of Loyola University of Chicago assisted in the Loyola Summer Institute and in proofreading of galleys of this book. My special thanks are due Anne H. Miller, Keith Davidson, Daniel J. Farrell, and Patrick Filter, now members of the bar of Illinois; Dennis M. Sheehan, my administrative assistant; Kathleen A. Johnston, Robert O. Kuehn, and Richard J. Prendergast, Jr., now candidates for the Illinois bar; and Wendell A. Sebastian, who is entering his final year at the School of Law.

We wish to express our appreciation to American Photocopy Equipment Company, Evanston, Ill., for furnishing equipment and materials to make videotapes of our Summer Institute.

Finally, we are grateful to the following labor unions, business corporations, and individuals, whose generous financial contributions made it possible for certain scholars to take part in our Institute and contribute to this volume: Amalgamated Meat Cutters and Butcher Workmen of North America, AFL-CIO: Patrick E. Gorman, Secretary-Treasurer; Taylor Forge, Inc. (a subsidiary of Gulf + Western Industries): R. M. Odegard, President; American Federation of Grain Millers, AFL-CIO: R. O. Wellborn, General President, and H. A. Schneider, General Secretary-Treasurer; Local 1031, International Brotherhood of Electrical Workers, AFL-CIO: Maurice Perlin, President; and Philip D. Goodman, Management Attorney, Chicago.

TABLE OF CONTENTS

The Supranational Corporation

The modern corporation, "an artificial being, invisible, intangible, and existing only in contemplation of law," is no more inhibited by the concept of nationality than it is by the idea of mortality. Professor Raymond Vernon has observed (*Daedalus,* Winter 1969, at 116):

> "Just as the simple Darwinian model of the firm as a profit maximizer seems somewhat at variance with the behavior of the large modern enterprise when viewed from close up, so also do other time-honored concepts seem out of place, including the concept of unambiguous national identification. Most sovereign states will permit the corporations created under their laws to own other corporations or to be owned by them. Each parent, sibling, or offspring in the group may have its own juridical identity, its own assets, and its own liabilities. Accordingly, the 'firms' that are heavily engaged in foreign investment actually consist of a group of corporations of diverse corporate nationality."

John A. Belford, Vice President of Massey-Ferguson Limited, a Canadian-based corporation that manufactures farm machinery and other products, opens this book, as he did the Loyola conference, with a frank exposition of Massey-Ferguson methods for supervising and guiding the labor relations policies of 33 factories in 10 countries, employing over 45,000 people. Some of the Loyola conferees characterized Mr. Belford's paper as an essay on "corporate imperialism." Special attack was made on his statements:

> "The written policy must recognize that at times within certain jurisdictions a point of [corporate industrial relations] policy cannot be invoked because of law or other environmental conditions. In these circumstances, it is management's task to identify the element in the environment that frustrates application and to surmount it if possible . . . . the essence of management is to make things happen by coping with the environment. By 'cope,' I mean not only to engage and contend successfully with the environment but also to influence it — by management example and responsible participation in affairs of the community."

The European contributors to this volume construed these comments as a plea for intervention by the multinational corporation in all levels of domestic politics of the host nation. Conferees from EEC countries also chided Mr. Belford for discussing corporate needs without reference to the needs of the rank-and-file personnel

at the diverse operating sites. Mr. Belford, however, stood by his remarks and is one of the two contributors who elected not to revise
his conference paper for publication in this volume.

Guy Nunn, Assistant Director, UAW International Affairs Department, discusses developing, albeit embryonic, forms of supranational unionism to deal with corporations doing business on a
world scale. Mr. Belford argues that today's product market is global; Mr. Nunn agrees and looks ahead to a day when the world must
be considered an integrated labor market.

Some American unions now pursue comparatively modest and
limited techniques at home to deal with large corporate units. Coordinated or coalition bargaining, the subject of a recent book by Wm.
L. Chernish (*Coalition Bargaining,* Philadelphia: University of
Pennsylvania Press, 1969) and two recent decisions by U. S. courts of
appeals *(General Electric* v. *NLRB,* 71 LRRM 2418, 2nd Cir.
1969, and *Minnesota Mining & Mfg. Co.,* 72 LRRM 2129, 8th Cir.
1969), is a process far less sophisticated than the world-wide economic trade union tactics envisioned by Mr. Nunn and his colleagues in the United States and overseas. But there have been more
developments since the Loyola conference was held in July 1968.
Daniel Benedict, Assistant Secretary General of the International
Metalworkers' Federation, told a workers conference at Bogotá, Colombia, in April 1969:

> "The growth of giant multi-national concerns also means that
> [employer] decisions will often seem to fly beyond any local control
> whether it be on the part of a local trade union, of the community or
> even of the national parliament when the center of decision making is
> thousands of miles away from the subsidiary plants and when that
> far-off head office transfers investments from one country to the other,
> increases production programs in one area and reduces them in anoth-
> er, passes research and development programs on new or modified
> products from one country to the other and does the same with the
> hiring and firing of thousands of workers. . . . this is a far vaster chal-
> lenge. This requires a trade union organization that is effective at the
> shop level, at the national level . . . as well as effective organization
> on a world scale."

The Bogotá conference was the first International General
Electric Conference, sponsored by the International Metalworkers'
Federation through its Committee on Multi-National Electrical and
Electronics Companies. Union representatives at the conference
came from Argentina, Brazil, Colombia, France, Ireland, Italy,
Venezuela, Mexico, and the United States.

THE SUPRANATIONAL CORPORATION AND LABOR RELATIONS

By John A. Belford

In the legal or statutory sense, the truly supranational corporation is not a reality at this stage of the evolution of international law. Nevertheless, within the framework and restrictions of national statutory requirements, there are companies operating internationally or multi-nationally like Massey-Ferguson that aim to run their affairs from a policy and strategy base that overrides any single national locus.

CRITERIA OF THE SUPRANATIONAL CORPORATION

It is difficult to set out a definitive list of the criteria that distinguish these companies. I suggest that such a list might include the following:

1. The operations and organizational segments disbursed around the globe have more than simply a fiscal and custodial responsibility to a common parent company: they also work within common policy and strategy, directed from what — to use an American term — we can call the "world-wide corporate management;"

2. Corporate management eschews any parochial, national point of view and has no special operating responsibility in any one country;

3. Nationality, as such, is irrelevant to executive appointments in the corporate management group;

4. The operating manager, wherever he exercises his responsibility, accepts prime accountability to serve the interests of the world-wide enterprise. However, sometimes he does this best by making a case for priority consideration of local community interests;

5. Facilities world-wide are rationalized and integrated; and multiple sourcing and a high degree of commonality of design within product groups is achieved;

6. Within the world-wide enterprise, the authority for the allocation of limited financial and manpower resources among competing operations rests with the corporate management;

7. Marketing programs in each location are an aspect of a global marketing strategy;

8. Management resourcing and succession planning are integrated world-wide;

9. Basic organization and senior executive appointments in all operations are subject to corporate authorization.

APPROACH IN MASSEY-FERGUSON

These precepts of the supranational corporation operate in Massey-Ferguson, a company described in June 1968 in *Business Week* as follows:

"To an American executive mired in the problems of operating abroad, Canada's Massey-Ferguson Limited might seem to be begging for trouble. Consider this state of affairs:

"MF" sells tractors, combines, hay balers and other farm machines in about 170 nations. It manufactures in 44 factories scattered in 15 countries subject to a rich stew of labor unrest, political turmoil, and monetary troubles. And it borrows long-term funds in nine different currencies and deals in many others.

"MF's increasingly ardent love affair with global business comes at a time when some American corporations that went overseas with high hopes have begun to feel like rejected suitors. World monetary problems, distribution woes, restrictions on U.S. financing, and political and labor unrest have spelled red ink or, at best, marginal profits for these companies.

"The result is a company with both global discipline and a global attitude. Such phrases as 'foreign' and 'domestic' get a Boston censor's treatment in Toronto. 'All of us here have worldwide responsibilities,' says Thornbrough. 'We could move headquarters overnight anywhere in the world with telephones and a good airport.'

" . . . MF is one of North America's first and 'purest' examples of truly multi-national corporations."

Business Week quotes our president,

"We have developed a deliberate, integrated approach to the world market, because for us the world is just that — a single market."

The general manager of each operations unit is directly responsible to his group vice president — farm machinery, industrial & construction machinery, or engines. Together with the group vice presidents and their immediate staff, corporate management comprises general staff divisions for finance & administration, research & development, personnel & industrial relations, logistics, and manufacturing, each with world-wide responsibility. There is no vice president in charge of "foreign" or "overseas operations."

Apart from his general responsibilities as a senior executive of the corporate management and a member of the corporate coordinating committee, each division head — generally a vice president of the parent company — is responsible to the president for the development of functional policy and its communication and interpretation to operations units; for the auditing of operating performance; for functional services, advice, and counsel to the president and to operations units; and for participation in operating activities as required.

Massey-Ferguson's commitment to supranationalism, in the sense we are using that term, raised important questions about local operating autonomy and the role of central or corporate management in all functions, including personnel & industrial relations. It was quite clear that centralized administration of industrial relations was not feasible; but more important, even if it were, it was a basic point of our philosophy that it would not be as effective as decentralized executive management.

Centralized technical assistance and advice on industrial relations in a world-wide company is theoretically practicable without universal policy. Such a centralized group provides a means of utilizing specialist talent most economically. It can also provide the agency for the coordination of the assignments of specialists from one operating unit to another as need arises. But the effective centralized direction, control, and audit of performance cannot be real and valid without policy.

Without basic corporate policy — a "grand design" for the enterprise as a whole — and consistent functional policies subsidiary to it, a truly integrated world-wide enterprise cannot be built. Apart from this general consideration, there are particularly compelling reasons for common industrial relations policies at all locations in the international enterprise. With the shrinkage of time and space by modern communication and transportation technology, it is important that the company should take a consistent position on principle in its relations with individual employees and with employee representatives at all locations. We cannot assume that the right hand will not know what the left hand is doing. Consistent and comprehensive policy avoids, for example, the company taking a strike in Coventry on an issue of principle conceded to a union in Detroit. I was in England several years ago when a well-known North American-based international company was struck on a union security issue. The company chose to take the strike rather than to concede officially that union membership should be a condition of employment for a single recalcitrant employee. (No conscientious objection was involved.) While the British subsidiary of this company was suffering strike on this issue, a full union shop was a feature of their agreement in their Canadian subsidiary, a Taft-Hartley union shop was in effect in the United States, and a full closed shop was in effect in Australia.

DEFINITION OF POLICY

The most useful form for policy that I know — certainly in the industrial relations function — is a statement of objectives and principles, objectives being the conditions we aim to achieve and principles being the basic assumptions that guide management action directed to the achievement of the objectives. Each functional policy enunciates attainable objectives, the achievement of which would serve the purpose of the corporation; and its principles aim to distill the lessons of management and research experience as a guide to management action.

To be fully effective, the policy statement must meet certain standards which have been enumerated before. Among these are the following:

1. It must be applicable universally within the enterprise. In the international company it must be applicable in all countries.

2. It must be in writing. Although it has been stated that if the policy is not in writing there is no policy, I concede that in many circumstances policies can be operative and, in substantial measure, effective without being in writing. However, the more complex and extensive the enterprise, the more important that its policy should be written. This is especially so in the international company.

3. It should be in broad terms permitting application to meet varying conditions and provide the framework for local tailormade practices and programs. It should not inhibit innovation and experimentation.

4. It should be justifiable on an assessment of its contribution to the basic objectives of the enterprise.

5. It should be authorized by the highest authority in the corporation.

6. It must be regarded as inviolate so far as this is within the power of management.

POLICY DEVELOPMENT

We have found that the best policy is developed with the active participation of operations executives. This in no way diminishes the accountability of the corporate executives for sound policy development. But the participation of operations management brings to bear the experience, the expertise and the special insights of local management in a variety of countries; it provides the first step in the extremely difficult problem of communicating policy; and it serves to commit local management to, and identify them with, the policy position.

We have found that the technical problems in policy development fall mainly into four areas: meaningful definitions; selectivity; distinction in the hierarchy of objectives; and differentiation between practice and procedure on the one hand, and true points of policy on the other. I know of no way to develop these skills in an organization except by doing. One clear lesson we have learnt is that this is not a "one-man job."

In our experience, the enumeration of policy objectives — although not without its tribulations — is a more straightforward process than the codification of principles. Selecting objectives for functional policy is facilitated by applying a three-part test: Will its achievement serve basic corporate objectives? Is it operationally meaningful, and not merely platitudinous? Can it be expressed as a durable purpose of management activity?

The codification of principles is more difficult. Here we are attempting to distill management and research experience. Ideally, the principles of an industrial relations policy should epitomize the basic assumptions on which management operates. This, in itself, is demanding enough: and is a process about which we still have much to learn. But more than this, we quite often find that no matter how well-founded and universally acceptable an assumption may be, there are environmental factors in one jurisdiction or another which make the related point of policy either inapplicable or inconsistent with another point of policy. For example, our employee benefit policy provides that no feature of any employee benefit plan should be a disincentive to work.

Our general personnel policy provides that personnel practices and programs (including benefits) should conform with public policy and employee and community values. There are some jurisdictions in which Massey-Ferguson operates where it is impossible to provide employee benefits that meet community standards and, at the same time, avoid creating a disincentive to work. In this sense, then, working to policy in no way relieves operations management of decision-making responsibility. Indeed, to the contrary, it increases responsibility by imposing a more highly disciplined, analytical approach to problem-solving and decision-making in industrial relations.

The written policy must recognize that at times within certain jurisdictions a point of policy cannot be invoked because of law or other environmental conditions. In these circumstances, it is management's task to identify the element in the environment that frustrates application and to surmount it if possible.

A good example of surmounting the environment is provided in our Australian operations. Local management recognized that under the industry-wide Australian arbitration system, three points of our industrial relations policy could not be invoked. Our policy provides that:

- collective agreements are to be for fixed terms and must proscribe interests disputes for their duration;
- interests disputes should be resolved by negotiation, conciliation, mediation, third party fact-finding or economic action; and rights disputes should be resolved by acceptance of management decision or by arbitration or by other forms of adjudication;
- management should take the initiative in industrial relations and the collective bargaining structure should facilitate such initiative.

They could not effectively work to these principles under the Australian system. Accordingly — and this is significant — our local Australian management on their own initiative devised a strategy and plan to, in effect, contract out of the industry-wide arbitration system by means of a form of company contract known under the Arbitration Act as an "industrial agreement." This has now been effectively achieved.

Under the agreement, management can take the initiative in collective bargaining; wage rates and work conditions are negotiated with the local union — the distinction between rights and interests disputes is spelled out in the agreement and rights disputes are subject to ultimate arbitration. The agreement is for a fixed term and proscribes claims or demands and, therefore, interests disputes during its term; it is silent on strikes; and the agreed functions of management and the union are spelled out in appropriate clauses in the agreement.

Our Australian management regard this agreement as a major contribution to the local competitive position and the Australian Operations Unit. Over the period of the last four years, during which the Australian economy and the engineering industry have suffered serious labor disruptions, our company in Australia has lost no time through industrial disputes. The local union enthusiastically supports the industrial agreement.

Our experience with industrial relations policy convinces us in a number of ways that working to policy is good business. Sound policy orients all operating management to the defined objectives of the enterprise. It gives practical effect to the philosophy of *management by objectives*. Good policy provides operating management with a basis for consistency and integrity in its relations with employees, employees' representatives and government agencies. At the same time, it permits flexibility. Contrary to the opinion of some people who have not worked to written policy, policy is not restrictive. Rather, it serves to *free up* operating management by providing a framework within which to act promptly and decisively on problems as they arise. When policy is developed — as it should be — with the participation of operating management, it helps to build a concerted management group of all management at all locations. Finally, it provides an instrument for control at the corporate or operating-unit level — control, in the sense of measurement of results against a standard.

RESULTS OF INDUSTRIAL RELATIONS POLICY

As a direct result of working to policy, a number of innovations have been introduced by local management in various jurisdictions. I have already referred to Australia. In the United Kingdom, for example, local management planned and introduced such features as:

- term agreements with a moratorium on claims during their currency;
- arbitration of agreement interpretation disputes;
- contractual predetermination of the yield on new incentive standards — in our view a major defense against an endemic U.K. problem, incentive wage drift;
- formal union security agreements with "management" security *quid pro quo* (e.g., union contractual obligation to work with nonunion members; prescribed notice of industrial action.)

But just as important — probably more important — than the substance of the agreements is the policy base for management stance and action in labor disputes. Here I refer to research in support of the company position; the policy bar against conceding under pressure of wildcat, unofficial, or illegal strike action; and, above all, the willingness to pay a price currently to serve long-range interests in industrial relations. Our 1968 strike in Canada of 10 weeks' duration is an example.

LESSONS OF LABOR RELATIONS IN THE SUPRANATIONAL CORPORATION

It is said that antidotes to management obsolescence include being informed on modern developments, learning from experience and adapting to changing conditions. The lessons we have learned about labor relations in the multi-national setting can be simply stated — but were not, on that account, easy.

What I shall enumerate are, in my view, equally valid in any national environment or under any industrial relations system:

1. For industrial relations administration to have direction and consistency — to be a planning and executive function and not a fire-fighting one — to be fully integrated as a part of general management, it must work to clear and explicit policy;

2. Successful industrial relations requires the acceptance by management that it is just as accountable for the quality of labor relations in the plant as it is for the other major responsibilities of management such as engineering, marketing, and finance. This implies management planning, initiative, and decision-making in labor relations rather than expedient response to the demands or claims initiated by the trade unions.

3. Because manpower problems are indivisible, the senior industrial relations executive in any jurisdiction should have responsibility and accountability for personnel administration as well.

4. The top executive for industrial relations within national operations should bring to his task that understanding and feeling for the local problem that is rarely found in other than a citizen of the country of the operation. Let me draw an analogy: it is rare to find a marketing executive who can meet the challenge of the U.S. market in a highly competitive industry unless he has been trained in, nurtured by, and has grown up with the American market. The same applies to industrial relations executives in all countries. It is easier to impart professional competence and policy orientation than it is to induce cultural understanding and sensitivity.

5. The industrial relations executive, assuming he is professionally qualified and understands the policy, must exercise decision-making line authority in his field. In industrial relations today, the commercial vulnerabilities are too great, the problems too complex, and the policy implications too subtle to dilute accountability

for industrial relations among other functional executives. The status and rank of the senior industrial relations executive must be commensurate with this authority and responsibility. In all Massey-Ferguson's major operations units the senior industrial relations executive is an officer of the company or a member of the board of directors.

6. In day-to-day management, the relationship between the operations and corporate executives should be that of colleagues. This applies, in my view, to all the functions of management, not only industrial relations. When such a "colleague" relationship exists, it is natural and comfortable that corporate management should participate in a staff capacity in the major and critical industrial relations episodes in operations. This not only focuses available talent resources on the high payoff or vulnerability situations; but also fosters corporate-operations unit communications in a very real and intimate way. Nothing binds men better than having gone through crises together and having supported one another in decision-making and risk-taking.

7. To make its greatest contribution, industrial relations (linked as it must be with personnel administration) must be an integral part of general management and directed by executives who, first and foremost, are members of the senior management of their company and only secondly specialists in their field. In this regard, I probably cannot do better than quote Auguste Detoeuf: "The three roads to ruin in this world are women, gambling and technicians. Of these, women are the pleasantest, gambling is the quickest and technicians are the surest."

I have not presumed here to review in detail the points of industrial relations policy that have been confirmed by our international experience over several years. Policy must be tailor-made to accord with the style and basic philosophy of management and the needs of the company. Otherwise, however compelling, however valid, it will be ineffective.

The global company operating today with a supranational approach is working in a difficult and uncomfortable environment. From this, the most fundamental lesson of all is confirmation that the essence of management is to make things happen by coping with the environment. By "cope," I mean not only to engage and contend successfully with the environment but also to influence it — by management example and responsible participation in affairs of the community.

If management is irresponsible — by which I mean passive —

the economy and society as well as the enterprise will suffer. The manager who is discouraged and immobilized rather than challenged and activated by the environment is in the wrong business.

WORLD COUNCILS OF EMPLOYEES: A CHALLENGE TO THE SUPRANATIONAL CORPORATION?

By Guy Nunn

The increasingly international, multi-national, or supranational character of investment in basic industry is by now too obvious to require documentation. The trend has been especially marked in the world auto industry and the agricultural equipment industry. The president of Massey-Ferguson frankly conceded, well over four years ago, that "It is now possible to take a transmission from Detroit, an engine from Italy, other components from England — and build a tractor to prescribed specifications in France, or the other way around."

Nearly six years ago, the chairman of the board of General Motors was calling attention to what he called a "new kind of capitalism. It is the emergence of the modern industrial corporation as an institution transcending international boundaries . . . no longer adequately described as Dutch, German, French, Italian, British or U.S." Mr. Donner didn't have to nudge anybody for attention. General Motors was already well on its way toward its present employment of nearly half a million workers in 22 countries outside North America.

In 1950, only one combustion-powered vehicle in five, worldwide, was produced outside the United States and Canada. Today's production of 24 million or so units per year is 60 percent abroad. About a dozen corporations, all deeply international in structure, now account for close to 99 percent of world automotive production. They might easily be reduced to half a dozen in the next 10 years.

Is there a world trade-union attitude toward this process? Viewed strictly as a process, there is certainly no serious trade-union opposition. Most unions — and especially those with strong international relationships and contracts — favor maximum freedom in international trade, the reciprocal export of capital and technology as between industrially advanced nations. They see in the new multi-national corporations a possibly hopeful source of rapid industrialization for still-developing nations.

But while most unions, and especially those in the metalworking industries, support the expansion and integration of markets and

13

the creation of wider trading areas, some are profoundly itchy over some possible social dangers presented by the emergence of supranational corporations whose economic authority often transcends that of half the world's national entities. They are concerned as well over the possibility that radically deficient wage structures might conceivably become a massive factor in a highly competitive world market.

The United Automobile Workers is perhaps the most deeply concerned of all the international unions over this possibility. Although wage costs account for an astonishingly low percentage of total production costs (about 17 percent by UAW estimate), it has taken 30 years of tough bargaining to eliminate wage differentials on identical jobs within the relatively homogeneous economies of the United States and Canada.

Other unions, especially those of Western Europe, are almost equally concerned. This concern was expressed a few years ago, in the creation within the International Metalworkers' Federation, which embraces close to 11 million workers in some 60 countries, of a World Automotive Department. Walter Reuther is the president of the World Automotive Department, to which are presently affiliated national unions representing some two million auto workers in the free world. Within that Department there have been created world corporation councils, Ford, Chrysler, General Motors, Volkswagen, Fiat, Toyota, etc., whose function is to pool information and to coordinate collective bargaining internationally. The affiliated unions are also grouped regionally (Latin America, Asia, Africa, Western Europe, North America) and are committed to seeking common wages and working conditions within these broad marketing areas.

In June 1968, in Turin, Italy, the IMF's World Automotive Department held a large international congress which adopted a good many specific resolutions and this general declaration:

> Reaffirming the Declaration of Detroit of June 3, 1966, the Second Convention of the IMF World Automotive Department declares its dedication to an intensified defense and promotion of the rights and interests of automobile workers throughout the world.
>
> The past two years have seen a vast proliferation of the multinational corporation, in supranational aggregations of economic power capable of a high degree of market control, exerting enormous political and commercial influence, maximizing the economies of standardization and product interchangeability, yet deeply resistant to efforts to standardize and harmonize the wages and working conditions of those they employ.
>
> The dangers to working people inherent in the development of multi-national corporations relentlessly in pursuit of profit have, if

anything, multiplied during the past two years. Productive capacity threatens to outrun both demand and purchasing power. The growth of excess capacity sharpens the temptation by producers to pit the workers of one country against those of another, the more so since the product is frequently identical and its components are available from multiple sources. The way is now open to scores of multi-national corporations, using "world-wide sourcing," to exploit investment opportunities involving minimal economic and social responsibility, while selling their products in the dearest accessible markets.

In the world automotive industry, as in others, we have noted a persisting tendency amongst employers to harass, intimidate and subvert unions of workers in the less industrialized nations and to thwart the realization of industrial democracy and social progress in the interest of keeping wage costs low and profits high. We have noted, too, in South Africa and elsewhere, the willingness of multi-national corporations to conform their employment and wage policies to forms of discriminatory domestic racism which are not only morally repugnant but illegal in the nations from which such corporations have emerged.

These and other evils which flourish in the shadow of the increasing de-nationalization of investment capital can only be combatted, we affirm, through the development of an effective world-wide solidarity of purpose and action amongst unions representing the workers involved in each industry. We are encouraged by, and welcome improvements in, the steady progress which national unions in the world automotive industry have been making toward the perfection of methods of mutual assistance, information-sharing, and the fixing of common goals.

As an integral part of the International Metalworkers Federation, we share fully the Federation's determination to strengthen international economic cooperation and economic growth as the foundations of full and stable employment and continuing social progress. Within this context, we pledge ourselves to work toward protection against inflation and corrosion of living standards of workers and pensioners, a general reduction of the work week to forty hours or fewer at full wages or salaries, longer vacations with higher vacation pay, the elimination of all wage inequalities based on sex, age, race or nationality, income guarantees for workers disabled or disemployed, and a more equitable distribution of income, within each nation, through a rising worker share of the fruits of economic activity.

We insist categorically upon recognition within each nation of the right to bargain collectively on wages, working conditions, and grievances, and upon the right to strike. We seek, within each nation, the progressive democratization of economic life through equal participation by workers and their unions in the solution of economic and social problems.

Internationally, we commit ourselves to seeking the upward harmonization of both wages and job-related social benefits to the maximum extent possible, and in the shortest time possible, within the limitations which may be imposed by differing national or regional levels of technological development. We applaud the success of U.S. and Canadian auto workers in having negotiated elimination of the last vestiges of wage differentials between these two countries, where tariffs and technological variations affecting costs have disappeared.

As offsets to the increasing dehumanization of industrial employment, we are determined to achieve a general reduction of working time through a compensated shorter work week, more paid holidays, adequate relief time, longer vacations and early retirement — along with the elimination of excessive overtime work and a guarantee of adequate premium pay for such overtime as may be justified.

Parity in power and influence with the new breed of multinational corporations can no longer be achieved or maintained by workers organized purely on a national scale. Only by a pooling of our strength, through the IMF, and by the perfection of our techniques of mutual assistance, can we begin to deal on equal terms with these giants in the extraction of profits. We here pledge to ourselves, and to workers the world over in the automotive industry, our determination to oblige this industry, already dominant in profitablity and in the application of advanced productive technology, to become an international pace-setter, as well, in the enlightened acceptance of its responsibilities to the workers and the people at large of whatever the nation in which they may be functioning. We offer this pledge not alone in the interests of common progress and prosperity for all peoples, but as a manifest of our determination to give bone and sinew to the concepts of justice, peace and freedom.

Obviously that statement is rather rhetorical, and rhetoric never took a nickel an hour from anybody. It does suggest, however, the IMF's general line of intent, which is, so far as possible, to get wages and working conditions out of competition in the world market. It's not going to be easy, but it is also not impossible. A universal work week of 40 hours or less is a probability within five years or fewer, whether through national legislation or collective bargaining. Within the Common Market — and as between it and the Outer Six — the movement toward wage harmonization is quite marked. The Japanese auto union council (and Japanese metalworkers generally) now claim to have won approximate parity in wages with auto workers in Western Europe.

The most serious obstacles to realization of the IMF's minimum goals appear to lie in the underdeveloped nations. This is not because the multi-national corporations have been especially retrograde there as employers. On the contrary, foreign firms, being "guests," in a sense, in the local economy, have tended, with some exceptions, to conduct themselves somewhat more benevolently than their equivalent domestic employers. In general, the problem lies with the weakness of unionism overall in developing countries, in government opposition to pattern-breaking wage agreements, and in the fear that the outside corporation will pull out if pressed too hard.

These are very serious obstacles, and they will not easily be overcome. As a starter, the World Automotive Department of IMF has begun sending technicians and experts of different kinds to work with fledgling unions in still-developing countries. It has also sent money, office equipment, mobile health clinics, and other forms of material assistance, but these seem to produce more gratitude than action. Perhaps it should be surprising if this were not the case. In automobile manufacture, at least, the creation of basic production facilities in underdeveloped countries is still grossly uneconomic. The domestic market can rarely sustain even a typical assembly operation. It is fair to say that virtually every nation in the southern hemisphere except Australia would do far better to import fully finished units manufactured elsewhere. Every nation, however, seems to want a domestic auto industry, even, God help them, the Russians, who ought to know better. A predictable result is overcapacity. But a possible result is that, as has begun to happen in Mexico, the host government may force the investing foreign corporation to build basic facilities as a condition of staying in business at all, and compel the corporation, as a means of finding enough market to make the new basic facilities viable, to invade its own home market, in competition, so to speak, with itself. Precisely that suggestion, in any case, was recently made by the Mexican government to U. S. car makers. The UAW has no objection in principle at all, but it is fair to say that we now have a more than theoretical interest in Mexican auto industry wages.

The 1968 Turin auto worker conference took a practical step which, while exceedingly simple, may eventually make possible a kind of "international" bargaining with the multi-national corporations which simply has not yet taken place.

That step was to agree to establish, as quickly as possible, common terminal dates for all contracts in all countries with a given multi-national corporation. This, it is hoped, will tend to maximize the leverage which a strong union might exert on a corporation at its headquarters in support of demands by weaker unions representing workers at a corporation affiliated abroad.

This, it seems obvious, should greatly enhance the ability of the established headquarters unions to lend strength to weaker unions in corporation affiliates in other countries, and it seems equally clear that the sooner bargaining is "denationalized" the more quickly it should be possible to move, purposefully, toward at least regional wage harmonization.

At the same time, the IMF hopes, the pursuit of ultimate world-wide wage parity, by planned stages, can be carried on across the entire world automotive spectrum. It goes almost without saying that corporate resistance to staged steps toward parity will be less, in each case, if every multi-national corporation has the assurance that all others in competition with it will be obliged eventually to accept the same set of changes. In Western Europe, at least, the Europe-wide wage contract is well over the horizon.

Mr. George Ball, in his recent book and in earlier reflections on the international economic future, speculates on the desirability, and perhaps the inevitability, of some form of international corporate law, or charter-issuing authority, to govern the conduct of multi-national corporations. While neither the IMF nor its automotive department as yet endorses such an idea, let alone any specific formulation of it, both are insistent that should such an authority be created, eventually, by treaty, acceptance must be required of every multi-national corporation within its purview of a set of minimum stipulations. These should include honoring the right of employees everywhere to organize, to bargain collectively, and to strike, and adherence to all provisions of all ILO Conventions (whether or not such Conventions have been ratified by the country in which the multi-national corporation may be operating). They should require harmonization of wages and social benefits to the highest level allowed by the technical development of the industry in each country and abstention from investment in countries whose national laws may (as in the case of South Africa) require racial discrimination in wages or employment.

Naturally, no one expects that the achievement of even approximate regional wage parity is just around the corner. But it should be reachable in most of the metalworking industries within perhaps a decade, and the auto industry is, of all the metalworking industries, the best-qualified pace-setter. It is generally high in productivity and profitability; it is capital-intensive, with a future of declining labor costs per unit; and it is managed, in the main, by cadres sufficiently sophisticated to recognize twentieth century imperatives when they see them.

PART II

Social Policy of the European Community

In Part I our contributors discussed the realities and the potential of supranational business and labor organizations. In this part the author discusses the social realities and potential of a supranational or international quasi-governmental body created by a multilateral treaty between six nations of Western Europe. Since the resignation of former French President Charles de Gaulle, increasing attention is being given to the use of the European Economic Community as an instrument for innovating social and economic changes.

Interest is heightened by the possibility of favorable action on the applications for EEC entry of the United Kingdom, the Republic of Ireland, Norway, and Denmark. Frequent references are being made to the dictum of Professor Walter Hallstein, first President of the EEC: "We are in politics, not business."

Most American writings on EEC have dealt with the Community as a common products market. Not enough attention has been paid to the labor market aspects of EEC. J. D. Neirinck was Director-General for Social Affairs of the Commission of the European Communities when he wrote his first draft of this part. He explains Common Market governing structure and operative machinery and analyzes the social objectives of the Treaty of Rome. He discusses with remarkable candor some of the obstacles, essentially nationalistic in origin, to the resolution of social problems in the Community. He would allocate a significant role to private collective bargaining in achieving Community-wide solutions. Because of the frequent references in this part to various sections of the Treaty of Rome of 1957 establishing the EEC, the editor has added Appendix 2, which contains the unofficial English translation of the Treaty's relevant portions.

SOCIAL POLICY OF THE EEC

By J. D. Neirinck

INTRODUCTION

Before tackling the themes of the conference I want to provide you an outline of the structure of the institutions which actuate the European Common Market. Then I shall rapidly indicate some of the main subjects with which the European Economic Community is concerned.

They are no more than a few essential glimpses of an organization that has to deal with innumerable questions, and to do so has to produce scores of documents every day — many of them at a highly specialized level.

We shall deal with Europe as a problem, the subject of our daily self-interrogation when faced with the difficulties and contradictions arising in its path — faced with the political choices which it imposes and to which, sometimes, "politics" makes a negative response, as we see today. The Common Market represents:

(1) Six Member States.

(2) A powerful (but fragile) administration, with its headquarters in Brussels.

(3) 184 million inhabitants (10 percent more than in 1957).

(4) A community gross product which has gone up by 50 percent between 1957 and 1967.

(5) Private consumers' expenditure up by 103 percent in 10 years.

(6) Industrial production up by 71 percent.

(7) Agricultural production up by 29 percent.

(8) Wages which have almost doubled, by going up 97 percent between 1957 and 1966.

That is what the Common Market is, among other things: figures, figures, and more figures — that you will spare me — and I will spare you. It is also a world of countless problems to be solved.

INSTITUTIONAL FRAMEWORK

When the Treaty of Rome came into force 10 years ago, in the face of the skepticism and inertia of a section of public opinion, the

21

enthusiasm of the supporters of Europe prevailed. In a climate of euphoria we had a glimpse, despite all the obstacles, of the possibility of a united Europe, in which the institutions of the Economic Community in particular would play a truly executive role. According to the first President of the EEC Commission, Professor Hallstein, the Commission was to be a kind of guardian of the treaty.

This "vestal virgin" role is not as idyllic as one might imagine. It has been subjected to many limitations as it has clashed with political realities of great complexity. It is a fact that the states in the Community have preserved their structures and sovereign prerogatives intact. In the long run, this means that their will is the arbiter and interpreter of the situation. The Community's efforts to bring political aspirations, legislation, prospects, and projects closer together meet with the resistance of the states, which are naturally inclined to maintain what they have acquired or to develop along the lines of their own traditions.

During the crises that have shaken the Community structure, we have been forced to realize that the Commission was not — to put it in terms of dialectic procedure — the synthesis of the conflicting aspirations of the states, but more often than not one of the terms of the antithesis, the term "Community" as opposed to the term "Member States." This opposition makes itself felt in the Council of Ministers of the Community, where most of the decisions are taken, on the basis of the Commission's proposals. In other words, the Commission proposes and the Council disposes.

Community Machinery

Let me outline briefly the pattern of Community machinery. For the layman it is of somewhat bewildering complexity, because it differs from the machinery of power as we know it on the national level.

The tasks of the European Communities are carried out by four institutions: the European Parliament, the Council, the Commission, and the Court of Justice. The Parliament consists of 142 members selected by the six national parliaments from their own members. The Council is made up of the representatives of the governments. Each of the member governments is represented by one of its ministers. The composition of the Council therefore varies according to the subjects dealt with. Hence, while the Foreign Minister is, in a way, considered to be the "main" representative of his country in the Council, the Ministers of Agriculture, Economic Affairs, Finance, etc., also often attend meetings, either on their own or together with the Foreign Ministers.

On 1 July 1967 the executive bodies of the EEC, ECSC, and Euratom merged to form a single Commission, which consists of 14 members appointed by unanimous agreement of the governments. Throughout their term of office, the members of the Commission must act completely independently of both the governments and the Council of Ministers. The Council does not have the power to end their term of office. Only the Parliament can do this; by a vote of censure, it can bring about the automatic resignation of the Commission.

The Council and Commission are aided by the Economic and Social Committee, an advisory body made up of representatives of the various categories of economic and social life, in particular employers and workers. In a large number of cases the Committee must be consulted by the Council or Commission before decisions can be reached.

The Court of Justice, consisting of seven judges appointed for six years by common agreement among the governments, ensures that the law is observed as the Treaty is implemented.

The Council and Commission have certain means of action at their disposal in order to carry out their tasks. First of all, they may issue regulations. Under the terms of the Treaty, a regulation has general application. It is binding in every respect and is directly applicable in each Member State. The Council and Commission may also issue directives to one or more Member States. A directive is binding upon the Member State concerned in respect of the results to be achieved, but the form and manner of implementing it are left to the national authorities. They also make "decisions," which may concern a government, a firm, or an individual. A decision is binding in every respect upon those to whom it is addressed. Lastly, the Council and Commission may issue recommendations and opinions, but these have no binding force.

The Commission's Role

When I say that the concept of the Commission as the guardian of the Treaty should be regarded with some reserve, I mean to stress the limitations of its supranational character. When the Community was born, the champions of Europe undoubtedly envisaged a supranational authority which would, at the very least, have prepared the ground for the "withering away" of nation states. The time was not ripe; and today we are witnessing, not a total extinction of this hope, but at any rate its reduction to a condition of suspended animation.

However, there is a more limited field in which the Commission may indeed be said to be the guardian of the Treaty. The Commission ensures that its own measures and the decisions of the other Community institutions are properly carried out. If there is any failure to do so, it is up to the Commission as an impartial body to make an investigation, give an objective opinion, and tell the defaulting state what steps it must take to put its house in order.

The Treaty lays down a detailed procedure for stopping infringements. The Commission may conclude that an infringement has occurred — either following an investigation carried out by its own staff, or on the application of a government, or as a result of complaints made by individuals. When the Commission so finds, it invites the Member State concerned to submit to it any observations or grounds for justification within a specified period. If the state maintains the measure in question and if its observations do not cause the Commission to change its viewpoint, the Commission addresses a reasoned opinion to the state to which the latter must conform by the deadline fixed by the Commission. If the state does not do so, the Commission may bring the case before the Court of Justice, whose judgment is binding on both the state and the Community institutions.

I wish to make it clear that, although the Commission as such does not have supranational power, the Member States, when establishing Community regulations or taking decisions, either through the Council or by delegating this power to the Commission, surrender their sovereign rights in precisely defined areas to the Community which they have created. In this way a new autonomous public authority has been created, independent of the public authority of each Member State. The legal rules adopted by the Community institutions in carrying out their duties under the Treaty ("secondary Community law") constitute a new legal order independent of international law and the domestic law of the states.

The Community lives, it has been said, through the power of the law, the written law, but it needs the spur of political action in order to develop. Written law provides no guarantee against the erosion of positions, against the upsetting of the delicate balance of the forces concerned, or against shifts of power. And we have seen that at present the Community is undergoing a process involving such factors as these. Consequently, the executive body of the EEC has gradually changed. Its mission has become more difficult, and it carries less weight, since it has become aware that it is no longer the driving power behind the policy of European unification. It is reproached for lacking boldness, for taking the advice of the governments too much, for having recourse to compromises. Likewise, the states tend more and more to seek compromises among themselves.

As for the Commission's executive powers, both the Treaty and regulations based on the Treaty give the Commission the duty and competence to draw up the instruments to implement the "European laws" contained in the Treaty or adopted by the Council.

The Commission's Right of Initiative

The Commission is the initiator of Community policy. This is certainly its most important, and perhaps its most original task.

The Common Market Treaty is frequently described as an "outline treaty," unlike the Euratom and Coal and Steel Community Treaties, which may be called "law-giving treaties." The Euratom and Coal and Steel Community Treaties lay down in detail the rules to be applied in relatively restricted areas. The Common Market Treaty, apart from its "automatic" clauses on customs and quota disarmament, simply gives general indications on the guidelines for the Community's policies in the main economic fields, leaving to the Community institutions, in particular the Council and the Commission, the duty of working out the rules to be applied by the Community and the power to do so.

Everything, in a way, that concerns economic union has been left unwritten in the Treaty, but the "blanks" may be filled in by the Community institutions without any need to conclude new treaties or to obtain further parliamentary ratification. The measures which the institutions have the power to take are true "European laws," directly applicable in all the Member States and liable to bring about profound changes in the spheres they cover. The provisions on agriculture, for example, constitute a body of rules whose scope is certainly as wide as that of the whole Coal and Steel Treaty.

The Commission/Council Relationship

The first job of the Community's institutions is to prepare the structure of the economic union of Europe. Once this structure is in place they will also have to work out the Community's future policy, and implement it day by day. The treaty endows the Commission with this role as architect of the structure to be set up and as initiator of the common policy.

Any provision of general scope or of some importance must be adopted by the Council of Ministers but, except for one or two specific exceptions, the Council can act only on a proposal submitted by the Commission. The Commission therefore has the permanent duty of taking the initiative. If it does not submit proposals, the Council is paralyzed and the Community's progress is blocked, whether in respect of agriculture or transport, commercial policy or harmonization of laws.

The submission of a proposal is the starting point for the dialogue between the national governments represented in the Council, where they express their national viewpoints, and the European body, i. e., the Commission, whose purpose is to represent the Community interest and to seek European solutions to common problems.

Article 149 of the Treaty, which continues to be one of the keystones in the Community's institutional system, stipulates that "When, pursuant to this Treaty, the Council acts on a proposal of the Commission, it shall, where the amendment of such proposal is involved, act only by means of a unanimous vote."

Accordingly, when the Council is unanimous it can make a decision without referring to the Commission, even when it decides against the Commission's proposal. When, however, a majority decision is provided for by the Treaty and the Member States have divergent opinions, they are bound by the Commission's proposal, for by a majority vote they may only adopt the Commission's proposal itself, without making any change. In such a case the Commission alone may amend its proposal. The Council can reject the proposal only if a majority is opposed to it; otherwise it must adopt the proposal as submitted. The Commission thus has the power to negotiate in the Council.

The European Parliament

In the European legislator's mind, the Commission's independence was to be guaranteed by its responsibility to the European Parliament. The Parliament's composition makes it an essentially Community body. There are no national sections, only political groupings organized at the European level. The Parliament keeps a permanent watch on the Commission, making sure it adheres to its role as representative of the Community interest. It is always ready to demand correction if, in the Parliament's opinion, the Commission is allowing itself to be unduly influenced by one or more of the governments.

The Parliament must be expressly consulted on the Commission's main proposals before the Council takes action on them. In this connection the parliamentary committees play an important part. As a rule the Parliament holds eight sessions a year, of a week each. Between sessions most of the parliamentary committees meet at least once. When such a committee is dealing with any of the subjects coming within its competence it invites the relevant member of the Commission to give an account before it of decisions taken by the Commission and of decisions submitted to the Council, or of the attitude adopted by the Commission before the Council. In this way the committees follow what is happening in detail, and their activity has certainly helped to develop the European Parliament's influence on current events. The written questions that the members of the Parliament can submit to the Commission (and also to the Council) are likewise a method of parliamentary control, and one which is being used more and more. Over 300 written questions were put to the Commission in 1967.

An extension of the European Parliament's powers and a strengthening of its representative character — for example, through its election by direct universal suffrage — are absolutely necessary, simply because of the extension of the Community's responsibilities. Parliamentary control should ensure the Commission's independence.

Despite the work of the Parliament, which follows the Commission's proposals in very great detail, its influence is still far from sufficient. It suffers from being a Parliament "twice removed," that is, one not based on universal suffrage. The fact, of course, that the political groupings are organized on a European basis must be considered a highly significant and promising point in its favor. But one cannot help regretting that the Parliament's debates make too little impression on the public — that the European parliamentarians, apart from some rather rare exceptions, do not draw the attention of their national parliaments to matters of European interest more often and more vigorously.

This is one of the weaknesses of the institution, a weakness which is generally recognized but is not of a congenital nature. One day, presumably, it will be remedied, in particular through election by universal suffrage, an idea which is gaining ground but for the time being is a fine example of European wishful thinking.

Let me just quote a few words — to me very significant — from the Strasbourg maiden speech of the French leader of the left, M. Mitterand, at a session of the European Parliament in January

1968. He made a number of points, which incidentally did not always find wide acceptance among some members, on European policy and on the role of the Parliament. He argued, in particular, that the European Parliament must be truly representative of the national parliaments, at any rate until the stage of direct universal suffrage has been achieved.

He also argued that "the Parliament must not be a meeting of experts, of specialists, but a political assembly having the power to establish the lines of force and determine the pattern of the Community. . . ." "The Parliament," he went on to explain, "has the right and duty to address the governments and the Council of Ministers and to speak to them openly, just as it has the right and duty to address public opinion and the peoples . . . in order to inform them and stir them to action. . . ."

The Economic and Social Committee

The Economic and Social Committee, an advisory body, is made up of representatives of industry, agriculture, transport, the workers, merchants and craftsmen, the liberal professions and the general interest. There are 12 representatives each from Belgium and the Netherlands, 24 each for Germany, France, and Italy, and five for Luxembourg. Committee members are appointed by the Council by unanimous decision for a period of four years. The Committee contains specialized sections, similar to the parliamentary committees, to study the particular problems of the fields covered by the Treaty: social affairs, agriculture, transport, etc. The Committee's opinions are transmitted to the Commission and the Council. The aim of this institution is to provide some control over the main Community activities.

How the Commission Functions

Since the recent merger of the executive bodies of the EEC, ECSC and Euratom, the Commission has had 14 members. They are appointed by the Member States, but once they take office they may, in the words of the Treaty, "neither seek nor take instructions from any Government or from any other body." They give a solemn undertaking to this effect. Each member of the Commission has special responsibility for one of the Commission's main sectors of activity and has under his authority the corresponding Directorate-General.

The members of the Commission constitute its political component, the administrative component being a staff of officials now divided into 20 Directorates-General and seven joint services: Secretariat, Legal Service, Statistical Office, etc. Despite the distribution of tasks among the 14 members, the Commission functions as a unit and makes its decisions collectively. All the measures that the Treaty or the implementing regulations specify, such as regulations, decisions, and proposals to the Council, must be adopted by the Commission as a body. It is therefore not possible for the Commission to delegate to one of its members, in the sphere for which he has special responsibility, power conferring on him particular independence comparable, for example, with that of a minister in his department.

Since all the members of the Commission endorse all its affirmative decisions, there is a danger of its agenda becoming so overloaded as to paralyze it. To prevent this the Commission makes great use of "written procedure." The members receive notice of intended proposals. If they do not express criticisms or opposition within a specified time (generally a week), a proposal is deemed to be adopted. Only matters of especial importance are placed on the agenda of the Commission's meetings. These take place once a week and last the whole day.

Although the Commission's decisions can be adopted by majority vote, most of them receive the unanimous approval of all the members. The solidarity and profoundly united outlook of the members, overriding differences of character and training, impress all who can observe the Commission's activities. When the policy guidelines must be established, the Commission first consults others as widely as possible, seeking the opinions of governments, government departments, employers' associations, and trade unions, and then adopts its position solely with the help of its staff. This is often a time of numerous and protracted working sessions, spaced out by weeks of reflection between the presentation of successive versions.

When the Commission decides on the detailed practical arrangements for implementing a policy already laid down, or makes essentially technical decisions, it always seeks the cooperation of experts from the six countries. The Commission's staff calls a meeting, over which it presides, of government experts selected by each of the national administrations concerned. These experts do not commit their respective governments formally, but as they are sufficiently aware of positions and desires of their governments they can usefully guide the Commission's staff in its search for technically suitable solutions that will be generally acceptable to the six governments.

The meetings also enable a dialogue to be conducted at the administrative level between European officials and officials of the six governments. In addition, numerous meetings are arranged regularly by the Commission in order to consult the leaders of the professional organizations (unions, employers' associations, farmers' organizations, dealers' groupings, etc.) that cover the six countries of the Community.

At the final stage the Commission itself is informed of the results of all this preparatory work and makes the ultimate decisions.

This is the process by which proposals to be submitted by the Commission to the Council are worked out. It also follows the same procedures in the issuance of its own regulations or decisions when such are permitted without Council participation.

The Working of the Council of Ministers

On receiving a proposal from the Commission, the Council has the preparatory work for its discussions done either by an *ad hoc* committee of senior officials (e.g., the Special Committee for Agriculture), or by one of its permanent working parties (one for each of the Community's main activities). The activity of these committees and working parties is coordinated by the Committee of Permanent Representatives, which functions as a kind of committee of "stand-ins" for the ministers. The Commission is represented at all the meetings of the working parties, the special committees, and the Committee of Permanent Representatives, so that the dialogue begun at the level of national experts can be pursued at the level of officials selected for this purpose by their governments.

The Council's decisions can be made only by the ministers themselves. However, in the case of matters of secondary importance on which the six permanent representatives and the Commission's representative have already agreed unanimously, the Council decides without any discussion. All important matters, on the other hand, in particular those of political significance, are discussed in the Council by the ministers and by the members of the Commission who are taking part, as is their right, in the Council meeting.

This brief survey of the Community institutions gives an idea of the complex system of wheels within wheels to which are geared not only the economic market but also the very life of Europe in all its social, cultural, and political aspects. My object in pointing out certain difficulties in the way of the Community's development was to illustrate better the extent of the efforts made each day to palliate the shortcomings of the Treaty, the reservations of the parties concerned, and the unwieldy nature of the machinery.

SOCIAL OBJECTIVES OF THE TREATY

Social progress is a principal objective of the Treaty of Rome. In the preamble, the Treaty's signatories declare their decision "to ensure the economic and social progress of their countries by common action in eliminating the barriers which divide Europe" and by "directing their efforts to the essential purpose of constantly improving the living and working conditions of their peoples." Article 2 asserts that "[i]t shall be the aim of the Community . . . to promote . . . an accelerated raising of the standard of living . . . ."

Detailed provisions of the Treaty establish the machinery through which its social objectives shall be attained. Title III of the Treaty, entitled "Social Policy," contains many, but by no means all, of these provisions. The drafters recognized the difference between the wish for social progress and the fulfillment by action in Article 117: "Member States . . . consider that such a development will result not only from the functioning of the Common Market which will favour the harmonisation of social systems, but also for the procedures provided for under this Treaty and *from the approximation of legislative and administrative provisions.*" Within the limitations of this paper, I shall now discuss some of the most important aspects of EEC social objectives: free movement of labor; social security for migrant workers; the European Social Fund; equal pay; and paid holidays.

Free Movement of Labor

The Treaty provisions on free movement of labor within the Community gave the Commission a task that has yielded tangible results because objectives are clearly defined.

Article 48 of the Treaty states that freedom of movement means "the abolition of any discrimination based on nationality between workers of the Member States as regards employment, remuneration and other working conditions." It therefore implies the right to move freely from country to country in the Community and to reside within any given EEC country in order to take any job actually offered, and the right to remain in the country of immigration after having worked there.

On proposals from the Commission, the Council in 1964 had already abolished a large number of restrictions upon EEC nationals. It is, indeed, fair to claim that genuine Community law had been developed through legislation in 1964 adopting and implementing Regulation No. 38 with an accompanying directive, to govern the free movement of labor and its concomitant problems.

Proposals for a final regulation and directive were submitted to the Council of Ministers in April 1968, as a last step toward the full implementation of free movement of labor. Complete freedom of movement was achieved through adoption of the regulation of October 15, 1968. The new regulation abolishes all restrictions and discriminatory practices. It also provides for the rapid and efficient registration and clearance of job vacancies and applications.

To be more precise, the principle of the priority of national labor markets is discarded, labor permits are no longer required, and workers from one Member State are treated on an equal basis in all other Member States. This new principle of equality ensures to migrant workers the same treatment as to taxation and social benefits as is given to national workers.

Migrant workers are entitled to vote in the election of workers' representatives and members of works committees and to stand for election themselves, without any discrimination whatsoever.

The residence permit is called "Identity card for nationals of an EEC Member State." This means a real simplification of formalities which will stimulate Community migration.

The Tripartite Consultative Committee on Free Movement — its members are representatives of the governments, employers, and trade unions — and the Technical Committee, manned by experts from national employment departments, cooperate in all activities concerning free movement of labor and also provide help in forecasts of manpower requirements and resources.

Social Security for Migrant Workers

The abolition of discrimination based on nationality concerning employment, remuneration, or other working conditions also called for the solution of the problem of social security for migrant workers. In fact, this problem arose in the six Community countries even earlier than the question of true freedom of movement. Thus between 1946 and 1958 they concluded among themselves 80 bilateral agreements and a few multilateral agreements; but the scope of these agreements was limited, being based on differing national legislation, and the provisions they made for the workers concerned were inadequate. The European Coal and Steel Community did the preparatory work for the coordination of the various national laws. There are not just six labor codes but more like 50, since miners, farmers, railway workers, and the like have special systems.

Article 51 of the Treaty provided the legal basis for EEC Regulations Nos. 3 and 4, which were adopted unanimously by the

Council of Ministers and made effective on January 1, 1959. In general, these regulations are more favorable than the bilateral or multilateral conventions. Three basic principles lie behind Regulations 3 and 4. First, equality of rights as between nationals of the country concerned and nationals of other Community countries. Second, the adding together, for the right to benefits and their calculation, of all periods of employment and of insurance: for example, for purposes of retirement, account will be taken of years of work in more than one country. Third, Article 51 of the Treaty allows the "export of benefits" to any other Member State.

Accordingly, family allowances will be paid in Italy to the wife of a worker employed, say, in Germany if she has not been able to join him with her children. In this case, the rate of benefit does not exceed that of the country of residence of the worker's family. Otherwise, the principle is that the legislation of the country in which the worker is employed governs the benefits.

Of course, the basic regulations had to provide for health care for workers and their families who fall sick during residence in a Community country other than their own. Later this advantage was extended to nonmigrant workers and their families on holiday in the other Community countries. Considerable improvement has been made since the implementation of the basic regulations by means of amendments.

The regulations have also been supplemented in the case of certain categories of wage earners, for whom special rules seem desirable. Special regulations for seasonal workers and frontier commuters were adopted in 1963. A regulation extending the basic provisions of Regulations 3 and 4 to seafarers was adopted in 1968. Similar solutions are being sought for self-employed persons in order to promote the realization of two other important principles of the Treaty: the right of establishment and freedom to supply services. Because of the great number of amendments, legislation on social security for migrant workers has become rather unwieldy. In order to facilitate its application, a revision of the texts of Regulations 3 and 4 incorporating all changes incurred is being undertaken.

The interpretation and practical application of the regulations are in the hands of an administrative committee, which has certain powers of decision. Its members are the heads of social security departments in the six countries and representatives of the European Communities; meetings are also held periodically with workers', employers', and farmers' representatives.

It is estimated that there are about two million beneficiaries of these social security provisions, if we add to approximately 900,000 insured migrant workers their families, incapacitated persons, old-age pensioners, and, for sickness insurance, people on holiday abroad.

European Social Fund

The only financial instrument at present available to the EEC in the social field is the European Social Fund. It constitutes an adjunct to the free movement and vocational training policies, since under Article 123 of the Treaty the Fund has "the task of promoting within the Community employment facilities and the geographical and occupational mobility of workers." The primary object was to deal with any detrimental effects on firms and their workers which might arise from the functioning of a wider and more competitive market.

At present there are three cases in respect of which the Fund may make grants: first, in the retraining of unemployed workers, or workers in a situation of prolonged underemployment; second, in resettling workers who must move to find new jobs; and third, where a firm undergoing fundamental structural changes must re-train or suspend its workers, to ensure that workers receive 90 percent of their previous wage during the period of conversion.

After the expenditure has been incurred, the Fund repays half of the sums applied for these purposes by a Member State or a public body, provided that the workers have since been employed or reemployed for at least six months. In the third case, the conversion scheme of the employer must have been approved in advance by the Commission. In its examination of refund applications, the Commission is again assisted by a tripartite committee. The Fund is maintained by annual contributions from the Member States, though the apportionment is not the same as that for the Community's general budget. By the end of 1966, the Fund had contributed a sum equivalent to nearly $43 million to the retraining of more than 200,000 workers and the resettlement of nearly 300,000 workers.

No payment has so far been made for structural changes in industry. By 1968 we had received only one application soliciting the Fund's participation in the financing of a conversion scheme, and this had to be turned down. We have had to conclude that structural changes in industry are made under circumstances different from those provided for in the Treaty, and that the very strict conditions imposed by the Treaty and the Fund regulation have in many cases prevented firms from applying for aid from the European Social Fund.

For example, the stipulation imposed by present regulations that funds must go to the conversion of old firms, not to the establishment of new ones, is not realistic, and excludes most of the operations which are of such value to the Community as to justify an intervention of the European Social Fund. These operations most often take place in single-industry regions, or regions with an obsolete industrial structure, or in economic sectors which have run into serious difficulties. In all these cases the public authorities endeavor to forestall social repercussions caused by closures by encouraging new firms to set up and provide jobs for the workers threatened with redundancy.

Therefore, it seems to be advisable to abandon the notion of structural change of an industrial firm introduced by the Treaty and to authorize the Fund instead to intervene in cases where new firms are being set up with the encouragement of public authorities.

The results of the Social Fund's operations have in general been satisfactory as far as its interventions in favor of measures of readaptation and resettlement of workers are concerned, but have been less favorable with regard to promoting structural changes in industry. Considering all aspects of the operation of the Fund, it has been increasingly evident for some time that changes are necessary. The Fund was founded at a time when many Europeans feared that the gradual establishment of the Common Market would have a marked effect on the level of employment by eliminating less competitive undertakings, and so it was given the primary aim of tackling unemployment, mainly by means of retraining and the placing of workers in new jobs.

It is true that there are several hard-core areas of unemployment, but on the other hand we have the problem of a shortage of skilled manpower in the European Community. The growth of the economy and technological developments have meant that the main problem in the employment field has switched from the elimination of unemployment to the maintenance of a high level of employment. The main concern now is, therefore, to meet skilled manpower requirements and to provide retraining for special groups within the labor force — for instance, farm workers faced with structural changes — so that these workers will be in a position to take up new jobs in industry and services.

The Commission has therefore proposed that the Social Fund should in the future take part in the retraining of workers actually at work — and not just of the workless and the underemployed —

with the aim of enabling them to acquire qualifications corresponding to the new demands for manpower. In this way, unskilled workers or workers with inadequate skills — and therefore threatened
with redundancy and unemployment at some future date — could
take up work at a higher level and with a good prospect of stable
employment.

On the other hand, the Community economy is still subject to
a measure of regional disequilibrium, which it becomes all the more
vital to rectify the closer the Community approaches conditions of
free movement for workers, services, goods, and capital. A fundamental solution of the unemployment problem is linked to the development of underdeveloped or declining areas, and the Commission
has, therefore, submitted proposals to the Council with a view to
extending the Social Fund's activities in regional matters.

These proposals would allow the Fund to contribute toward
the cost of guaranteeing the income level of workers in declining
regions made redundant by closures and reengaged by another company setting itself up in the area. Furthermore, the proposals
provide that the Social Fund should contribute toward the cost of
building vocational retraining centers in areas where they are at
present lacking. Finally, the Fund would have the power to make
advance payments toward the cost of retraining programs aimed at
stimulating regional growth or for migrant workers, instead of, as
at present, making reimbursements after such costs have been incurred.

Equal Pay and Paid Holidays

The principle of equal pay for men and women is declared in
Article 119 of the Treaty. Recommended by ILO Convention No.
100, equal pay was already a principle enshrined in the laws or even
the constitutions of the EEC countries, particularly in Italy, the
Federal Republic of Germany, and France. However, in practice
there were still great disparities; in the Benelux countries the gap
in some industries has been as wide as 30 percent. Relying on Article
119 of the Treaty, in July 1960 the Commission addressed a recommendation to the Member States, calling on them to eliminate all
discrimination in pay between men and women workers by June
1961. At the end of that year, the Member States found that it had
been impossible to comply with the time limit, and they agreed on
progressive equalization measures in three stages. Progress has been
made, but disparities have not yet been completely eliminated. The
disparities are less pronounced in identical jobs done by both sexes

than in industries where more women than men are employed, for example, textiles. Even if the principle of equal pay is being followed theoretically, discrimination still exists in practice, mainly because of inadequate job descriptions which are taken as criteria in the collective bargaining process.

The second rule laid down in the Treaty concerns holidays with pay. Article 120 says with forceful brevity: "Member States shall endeavour to maintain the existing equivalence of paid holiday schemes." A Commission survey confirmed in 1960 that, while annual holidays (vacations) were longer in some countries, the total of national holidays spread out through the year was greater in other countries, and together they came to about 20 to 30 working days a year. Since 1958, the law and collective agreements have generally made progress: the number of paid annual holidays — including the national holidays — has now reached or is very close to the average of 30 days in all Community countries.

CURRENT PROBLEMS OF SOCIAL POLICY

Government circles often show a lack of political good will in the matter of a Community social policy. There are many reasons for this attitude, and I shall mention only a few of them. Justification to a degree may be found in the objective obstacles to achieving a common social policy within the European Community. These obstacles may cause the government to be somewhat reluctant to face problems which do not appear to merit priority attention at the purely national level, or which at any rate the government is not ready to face.

General Political Climate

The absence or insufficiency of political willingness may also be due to the cost of the social policy. It is bound to be expensive. Measures of a social nature, even where they are mere improvements to existing systems, must involve some additional expenditures on the part of the public authorities or private firms.

The harmonization of social conditions in the European Community — the celebrated Article 118 — fundamentally depends on close cooperation between the governments, and between the governments and the Commission. When France temporarily stopped its participation in Community activities in the 1965 crisis, it gave this article a very narrow interpretation. If, therefore, only one of the governments is unwilling, it is not possible, for instance, to ask the two sides of industry to collaborate even in studies arising from the social harmonization program. The social field is not the only one to experience a situation in which a veto by one Member State paralyzes the activity of the five others and the Commission.

But the objection of one Member State does not prevent the Commission from proceeding on its own responsibility to all the consultations which it thinks fit and necessary either in the institutional organs, such as the advisory committees or *ad hoc* working parties, in order to obtain any data it considers essential for information and assessment, notably for the purpose of the cooperation which it has a legal and political obligation to promote.

There are other difficulties and responsibilities that must be pointed out. For example, policies of trade unions or social partners very often precede legislative measures in the social field, at the national level, that is to say. At the Community level, there are as yet no real trade union* organizations. There are, it is true, European secretariats, liaison offices, and workers' and employers' organizations covering the six countries. These bodies undoubtedly constitute the core and the embryo of future Community trade unions and union federations, but for the time being they do not have the structure, the powers, or the means necessary to play such a part. The sum total of trade union powers, what we might call trade union "sovereignty," like political sovereignty remains the attribute of the individual Member States. I would add that certain labor organizations, which are quite strong within some of the countries, are not yet represented at the institutional level of the European Communities.

The time has come, in my view, for the labor and employers' organizations to advance beyond mere service as liaison bodies and secretariats and with courage and resolution to tackle the problem of setting up a European center and transferring to this organization some of the powers of the national organizations, thus making a start on effective trade union integration. The labor movement's powers and its role in the Community will then become very different. And no one will have to ask whether or not the two sides of industry should be consulted, because, in such a case, the two sides of industry will have ceased to have a mere advisory function and will be playing a really active part as promoters and builders of a European social policy.

---

*Ed. Note: Mr. Neirinck here uses the term "trade union" in the broad European and British sense wherein both workers' and employers' organizations are embraced.

Recent Trends in Socio-Economic Development

It may be of interest to indicate here the trends in the development of social structures in 1967; I have tried to isolate the common points in the development and the problems which often arise at the same time in the same way in different Community countries. This analysis shows that integration has become a firmly based reality, and demonstrates the possibility, even the need, for future action at Community level to promote social progress. These conclusions are borne out by an information memo on social events in the Community in 1967.

Employment: Improvement in Stability

In 1967 there was an economic decline attributable to an unfavorable cyclical change and structural modifications. Some of the closures and mergers of enterprises that occurred are linked with the increased competition in the Common Market, while others can be put down to structural changes in demand or to keener competition on the world market.

Adverse structural and economic changes together caused a substantial rise in the number of unemployed, from 1,440,000 in October 1966 to 1,700,000 in October 1967. Short-time working also increased considerably. The impact of the economic slowdown was not, however, uniformly felt throughout the Community. Unemployment usually developed in areas which were characterized by weak economic structures or dependent on a single activity. Similarly, not all categories of workers suffered equally. The least-skilled workers were the earliest and hardest hit by unemployment.

Security of employment has been more efficiently organized within groups of enterprises or branches of industry, e.g., shipbuilding in Italy and iron and steel in France. A transfer system guarantees work for people whose jobs are threatened by rationalization plans. These transfers may take place between branches. Such was the case with the Lorraine iron miners, for whom new jobs were found in the iron and steel industry of the region, and with unemployed managerial staff in France, who were helped by the government to enter the civil service.

A variety of measures to stimulate employment have been undertaken. A trilateral conference on employment was held in Italy, at which the government and both sides of industry spent several months examining the current situation and future prospects. This was followed by a trilateral conference on employment for women. Similar action to study the position of working women was taken in

France and Belgium, but there only by the trade union organizations. The advisory body of the three Dutch trade union organizations asked for the establishment of a "labor market council," in which the unions and the authorities would work together under government chairmanship to promote a consistent employment policy.

In 1967, too, the governments did more to divert industry toward certain areas. Examples are the decree implementing the Belgian law on aid to regions threatened with decline, and the loans granted in the Netherlands to encourage the establishment of industries in areas particularly affected by unemployment.

Attractive arrangements have been made in France to encourage internal migration. Compensation is paid to unemployed workers for expenses incurred by them in obtaining information on vacancies, and to workers obliged to live away from home.

Vocational Training: an Instrument for Mobility and Social Progress

The greatest difficulties encountered in the employment market arise from the differences between qualifications offered and qualifications required, as well as from the sheer inadequacy of vocational training. We can assume that this state of affairs is likely to last. Full employment, or a very high level of employment, cannot be achieved in a situation of immobility. It can be achieved in a dynamic process involving the movement of manpower according to the overall requirements of production. Maintenance of employment at the level of the individual enterprise, or even of the individual industry, will often be impossible.

Technological progress and industrial reorganization are already forcing many workers to change their jobs, and will force even more of them to do so in the future. This can only take place without too much difficulty if with multicraft training their professional qualifications enable them to adapt themselves with relative ease to the technical patterns of their work. Vocational training systems must be overhauled to facilitate the training of workers not just for a specific job but for a set of unspecified functions.

Many reforms, some of them still on the drawing board, have begun to affect the systems of vocational training in the Community countries along these lines. Measures have been taken to encourage vocational training of older workers or to retrain them for other jobs. At the state level, grants are made in Belgium to help older workers to adapt themselves to industrial change, and in Germany a draft law has been tabled which provides for grants, courses, etc., to help workers obtain higher qualifications. At the industrial relations level, a "social agreement" and an "agreement applicable to engineers and executive staff" have been introduced in the iron and steel industry in Lorraine.

Labor Relations and Conditions:
New Rights and Responsibilities

The worker's place in the enterprise and in society has continued to evolve; formerly a mere cog in the wheel of production, he is now becoming a responsible member of the production unit, and as such is more frequently consulted on decisions, particularly those concerning him most directly and immediately affecting his job. But the consultation of workers on decisions has wider connotations. Workers are consulted on the establishment of general lines for the development of an industrial sector (iron and steel and metal products in Belgium, for instance), or even the entire economy. This is the case in Germany, where the government has begun to hold regular discussions with the unions and certain groupings of enterprises concerning the main problems of economic policy. Such talks have resulted in agreements on a series of macroeconomic guidelines which will provide foundations for the decisions of the parties concerned. Thus it is hoped to achieve concerted action. This procedure evidences the general trend toward basing collective bargaining on objective data.

The protection of certain categories of low-grade or underprivileged workers was improved in 1967 in a number of countries. Examples are laws and draft laws to safeguard juvenile labor in Italy, France, Germany, and Luxembourg and the rights of women workers in Belgium.

As a counterpart to the rights being created, a new sense of solidarity inspires labor relations. One of its most pronounced manifestations is in the "social peace pacts" which are now frequently found in collective agreements.

More specific obligations sometimes see the light. They may result from agreement, as in the case of the limitations placed on the Italian workers' right to strike in order to ensure safety of persons and machinery. Or they may result from unilateral action. In the absence of laws specifying the conditions of exercise of the right to strike laid down by the Italian constitution, Italian railwaymen have themselves established the rules which they intend to follow.

This trend is not without risks and drawbacks. Labor organizations are sometimes "overtaken on the left" by extremist groups and are not always able to control the situation immediately. Besides the Belgian examples of Zwartberg (coal mines) and Herstal (strike of women at the national armaments factory), mention should be made of the various unofficial strikes which took place in 1967 in Germany.

Industrial relations is a field the Commission believes it must aid by the compilation and coordination of statistics and by other encouragement. It has therefore asked a group of experts to make comparative studies of labor laws and collective agreements. Certain aspects of labor relations have already been investigated or will soon be dealt with, such as procedural rules for the settlement of disputes, workers' voice in formulation of management policy, the legal and practical aspects of collective bargaining in the member countries, the legal grounds and scope of collective agreements, the right to strike, and rules governing dismissal.

How far these studies, now virtually completed, which the Commission has carried out in consultation with experts from governments and both sides of industry, have affected developments in the member countries is, of course, difficult to ascertain.

The inquiry into the law and practice of collective bargaining agreements in the EEC may perhaps have made Dutch wage negotiators more aware of the fact that their government's "interventionist" wages policy was a system that was not being followed in the other member countries. In Luxembourg's law of June 12, 1965, on collective bargaining agreements, traces of the EEC inquiry can be detected. And the Belgian bill on collective bargaining agreements and joint committees (1967) was clearly inspired by the EEC's work, for in both the introduction and in the grounds stated for certain clauses, mention was made of the situation and developments in the other member countries. The dialogue in each EEC country about law and practice in the other member countries cannot but help the development of the law and reform of practice. Furthermore, common ideas and a convergent approach lead to harmonization.

The Commission has also suggested that a central EEC records office be set up, where the major provisions of collective bargaining agreements in the member countries would be registered. Here it has not been possible as yet to reach agreement with all those concerned: governments, employer associations, and labor unions. Difficulties of a technical nature are being investigated further so that when the time comes the Council will have to decide only the political aspects.

The statutory provisions on which collective bargaining is predicated and the implementation of these provisions differ considerably from one country to the next. This does not alter the fact, however, that they have a number of important factors in common, including intent and effect, so there is value in seeking Community solutions. The Commission hopes that the provision of well-presented comparative statistics and technical assistance will stimulate developments that might eventually result in various forms of collective bargaining at Community level.

Toward an Incomes Policy?

The logical outcome of the trend toward basing collective bargaining on objective data would be the establishment of an incomes policy. Such a policy is also envisaged in the Community's medium-term economic program, but the idea is often criticized by the trade unions. Its implementation comes up against a real obstacle in the lack of data on the trend of nonwage incomes. The figures indicating this trend are out of date and incomplete. And since they are often extracted from documents written for particular purposes, such as taxation, it is justifiable to doubt their accuracy.

The primary argument for an incomes policy is the need to encourage formation of the capital essential for productive investment by increasing the workers' share in the national income. However, in doing so inflationary tensions must be avoided; hence the idea of reserving part of the wage increases to form an investment fund. Some Dutch measures, the French ordinances on profit sharing by workers, and certain attitudes adopted by employers in Italy as a result of the trilateral conference on employment constitute steps in this direction.

Social Development and Future Activity of the Community

I shall supplement this outline of recent trends in social development by discussing some of the main features of the Commission's social policy. These will show how the Community's work is designed for application to various critical points in the social structures.

The Community's social policy is being developed in a general socio-economic setting. Levi Sandri, vice-president of the Commission and president of the Social Affairs Group, said in his "Report on the Development of the Social Situation in the Community in 1967" to the European Parliament, ". . . the single Commission proposes to fix a certain number of objectives for priority action, bearing in mind both national and Community requirements." In this spirit agreement has recently been reached between the Commission and the Council on a program of work to encourage collaboration among the Member States, and between them and the Commission, in achieving social harmonization, more particularly as regards social security,* employment, and industrial health and medicine.

In the near future, priority will be given to structural changes. The EEC will concentrate first and foremost on the social problems arising from the common policies themselves. There are prospects for development in particular in the sectors where the European Community is planning further activity: industrial policy, energy policy, regional policy, scientific research policy, the European-type company, and medium-term economic planning.

The social policy should help to solve one of the major problems confronting the Six in the coming years: that of structural changes within enterprises and industries. The structural aspect is the basis of the second medium-term economic policy program which the Commission is shortly to submit to the Council. Structural matters will also play a leading part in the development of the common agricultural policy. The same will apply to the industrial policy, whether it affects the structural adaptation of enterprises or the social side of the common policy in such matters and the agricultural sector and fisheries. Attention will also be paid to the social aspects of regional policy, energy policy, and scientific and technological research policy.

The Commission's concern in the social field will call for solutions to problems of employment which the Commission and the two sides of industry have always emphasized and whose importance the Council has recently acknowledged. To this end the European Social Fund, in order to become an indispensable instrument of employment equilibrium, is to receive a thorough overhaul in order to improve its efficiency and scope.

Among future social tasks are those connected with labor relations. In view of the priority given to matters of structural change, employers and employees are directly involved. In all the Community countries there is a growing tendency toward concerted action between the employers' and employees' unions on the one hand and between both sides of industry and the authorities on the other.

---

*Ed. Note: See G.M.J. Veldkamp, "Toward Harmonization of Social Security in the EEC," p. 351, *infra*.

From such action a common will should emerge, associating economic progress with social progress.

The Commission regards standards of living as a main task, and special attention is to be devoted to social security. The various governments are confronted with a major problem. The great increase in expenditure on social services means that measures to increase both the number of beneficiaries and the amount of payments will be possible only in the context of a general program in which all requirements must be fairly balanced and all legitimate interests safeguarded.

Freedom of movement for workers throughout the Community was an accomplished fact by July 1, 1968, two years in advance of the original date, and the coordination of social security systems for migrant workers has been improved and simplified. At the same time, work on industrial health and safety has been stepped up and its scope expanded. The activities of the former Coal and Steel Community in the social sphere will, of course, continue, since the ECSC has not lost sight of its role as European pioneer of "sectoral" policy!

THE CREATION OF A EUROPEAN-TYPE COMPANY

The representatives of the six Common Market countries recently signed a convention on the reciprocal recognition of companies and bodies corporate provided for by the Treaty of Rome. This convention constitutes a first step toward the harmonization of company law in the Community and the creation of a "European" company. The convention is based on the principle that all companies under civil or commercial law, as well as bodies corporate under public or private law, are recognized as such throughout the Community provided their registered offices are within the Community and provided there is a substantial link between these companies and the economy of a Member State.

The creation of a European type of commercial company is one of the important tasks now facing the Community. The Council is already deliberating on the proposals submitted to it by the Commission. There are, however, many questions to be settled in this very complicated undertaking.

The Community enterprises must be able to stand up to intra-Community and international competition. They must be able to adjust themselves to the European market, to the oft-changing conditions of the world markets, and to technical progress. This requires the expansion of many enterprises, increases in capital, and association with other firms. While enterprises can amalgamate with others inside their own countries, mergers between firms in different Member States and the transfer of companies' registered offices from one State to another have so far been impracticable for reasons of company and tax law. Hence, alongside the forms of commercial companies already existing in the Member States, a new legal form will have to be created, namely, the European commercial company.

A panel of experts was asked to draw up a scheme for such a European company. Their recommended scheme contains all the rules with which the European company that utilizes the form of a "Ltd." or limited-liability company should comply. These rules presuppose the existence of a European register of businesses, which is just as necessary to the case as the European Court of Justice. They are supplemented by proposals relating to the cooperation of the workers within the departments of the company, according to the principle that this cooperation must, as far as possible, be maintained where it already exists and not be introduced where it does not already exist. The commentary explains the various provisions of the European company's articles of association and provides guidance for the drafting of certain rules of criminal and tax law to supplement the articles.

The articles of the European limited-liability company would be included in a convention contracted among the Member States and put into effect through ratification by the national parliaments. By laying down rules for uniform interpretation, the scheme takes account of the aim of making the entire area of the Community subject to uniform law. Generally speaking, eligibility to found European companies would be restricted to limited-liability companies which have carried on economic activity during the three business years preceding registration of the European company.

The present discussions are concerned with a basic problem. The choice between the coordination of national bodies of law on companies, prescribed by the Treaty, and the creation of the European company by means of an intergovernmental convention entails an economic study of the effects of the two approaches in the light of the desired aims. Some people, prompted by misgivings about the European company, have asked that a comparative examination be made beforehand. Others prefer the lines indicated by the Treaty, such as freedom of establishment, right to transfer the head office without losing legal personality, and conclusion of a convention on international mergers. From the political point of view, various circles think that the consequences of creating large European enterprises which have European articles but remain subject to national legislation and jurisdiction have not yet become sufficiently clear.

Creation of a European-type company is of paramount importance to development of European social policy. Indeed, as I have emphasized throughout this paper, when supranational methods have been adopted, achievements are positive, but when the method of intergovernmental cooperation must be used, achievements are meager. The most successful results were achieved in EEC where the Treaty provided for the Community-type procedure. Professor Gérard Lyon-Caen has wisely stressed in his lectures on European social law that the innovation of a European-type company could well give a new impetus to harmonizing social systems.

MANPOWER POLICY

In its First General Report, in 1958, the EEC Commission stated that its treatment of the employment problem must implement the provisions of the Treaty and provide a general picture of employment and labor market trends within the Community. Action by the Commission is based on two articles in the Treaty. Article 118 is a general clause requiring the Commission to promote close collaboration among Member States in the social field, particularly in matters relating to employment. Article 49(d) specifically concerns freedom of movement for workers. Under the latter, the Commission is to propose to the Council measures designed to bring about freedom of movement, including provisions that will enable the employment offices to be organized as efficiently as possible to balance the supply of and demand for labor without impairing living standards or opportunities of employment.

From the very outset, the Commission's work in this field has moved along two separate lines. First, regular inquiries have been instituted with a view to taking short- or medium-term measures relating to employment in specific regions and industries and for specific groups of workers. These inquiries are economically and demographically oriented and take account of technological change. They are designed to reveal in broad outline which are the declining industries, which are growing, differences in growth rates among the various branches of activity and areas, the pattern and development of employment for men and women, and the extent of migration within individual countries and from one country to another. The regions and industries that are chosen for study either exhibit special internal problems or affect the establishment of the Common Market.

Second, a draft was made of regulations for freedom of movement for workers, and measures were proposed to enable employment offices to meet the demand for manpower as efficiently as possible within individual member countries and at the Community level. An early task was to find out how the placement techniques of these offices could be improved and harmonized. Work was also begun on the alignment of existing job classifications and the coordination and improvement of employment statistics.

We hear it said repeatedly that it was quite a few years before any clear line of action was discernible in the Commission's approach to employment. This was partly due to the Treaty, which lays down no directives for an employment policy and leaves the matter wholly within the jurisdiction of the Member States.

Although employment is mentioned in several Treaty clauses, in addition to Articles 49(d) and 118, nothing more than general pronouncements or objectives can be inferred. In the preamble, for instance, the Member States affirm that the essential objective of their efforts is the constant improvement of the living and working conditions of their peoples. Article 39 states that one of the objectives of the common agricultural policy is to ensure the optimum utilization of all factors of production, especially labor. Articles 48 to 51 cover the free movement of workers and refer only incidentally to employment. Under Article 75, provisions on the principles governing transport are to be laid down by the Council in all cases where the implementation of such provisions might seriously affect living standards and employment and also the use of transport facilities, taking into account the need for adaptation to economic developments resulting from the establishment of the Common Market.

Article 92, which deals with government aids affecting competition, includes one provision to the effect that aid designed to promote the economic development of regions where living standards are abnormally low, or where there is serious underemployment, may be deemed compatible with the Common Market. In Article 103 short-term economic policy is stated to be a matter of common interest; the Member States must regularly consult each other and the Commission on what measures should be adopted in the light of prevailing circumstances. Although employment is referred to in Article 104, no policy guidelines can be based on this clause. Nor can they be derived from Article 118, already mentioned, which stipulates that the Commission must promote close collaboration among member countries in the social field, particularly as regards employment. Articles 123 to 128 are about the European Social Fund, which was set up in order to improve job opportunities for workers in the Common Market and thus help to raise the standard of living. This Fund has clear-cut powers which leave no scope for an independent policy on employment. Articles 129 and 130, on the European Investment Bank, provide for a financial contribution to the balanced and stable development of the Market, by authorizing the Bank to grant loans and guarantees for specified economic projects. Important as these provisions are, they offer no opportunity for the formulation of a policy on employment.

The rapid economic expansion that was under way in 1958, in what was to become the EEC, produced a manpower surplus in Italy and serious shortages in the other member countries. And there was also the continuing flight of workers from the land. These were the circumstances which provided the Commission with the surest grounds for action on employment under the terms of the Treaty.

The Commission consequently instituted its policy by drafting regulations on freedom of movement for workers, promoting cooperation among employment services, preparing job descriptions for trades most closely concerned in freedom of movement, and planning surveys of employment in agriculture.

The Community institutions have always emphasized that the EEC is an economic union characterized by the pursuit of common policies. Moreover, the Treaty makes specific provision for common policies in certain sectors and for coordination in others. In the economic field the Commission has always endeavored to establish a general policy to serve as a framework for the elaboration of Community policies in the sectors concerned and for the harmonization of national policies.

General Community policy is closely bound up with the establishment of close cooperation among Member States in the social field. As the Commission has explicitly and repeatedly affirmed, the cooperation it is required to promote is by no means confined to providing assistance in the form of an "extra" to the economic objectives of the Treaty. On the contrary, this cooperation is a specific and essential element in the coordination of economic policy that is to be aimed at in every member country.

In its Third General Report, in 1960, the Commission stated that the first aim of coordination of social policies should be the optimum utilization of manpower reserves in the Community. This view was based on the imbalance then affecting the Community's labor market — local shortages of manpower, with structural unemployment and underemployment in certain regions and industries.

The Commission thought it necessary to pursue an employment policy that would contribute to more-balanced economic growth by taking steps, including social measures, for which the Treaty provided a clear basis. These measures included direct action in respect to free movement of workers and the European Social Fund.

The question of labor supply also came up in the Commission's urgent recommendations to the Council in 1960 for the coordination of short-term economic policies. Since the Treaty's aims include a high rate of employment as well as balance-of-payments equilibrium, confidence in the currency, and stability of prices, the Commission considered it essential to lay particular stress on the labor-market situation within the scope of the policy measures it proposed.

Reports on Employment Development

The Commission has made a special survey of employment developments in the Community every year since 1960. This annual report is preceded by a survey designed to make available such information as might serve as a basis for an employment policy.

In compiling its report on employment in the period 1954-1958, the first report of its kind, the Commission came up against great difficulties, caused particularly by the variety of definitions and statistical methods used in the member countries. The difficulties have now been diagnosed though not yet eliminated.

These annual reports are drafted with the aid of experts from Ministries of Labor, the Commission's Short-term Economic Policy Committee, and representatives of both sides of industry. They discuss trends and problems over the preceding year and make a forecast for the following year.

Both the overall trend and developments in individual industries, regions, and trades are analyzed. As regional unemployment progressively assumed greater proportions, the analysis of this particular problem was correspondingly expanded over the years. The macroeconomic forecasts cover employment and the labor market, especially the expected trend of manpower requirements, and reserves.

The reports conclude by summarizing the measures adopted in the member countries to counteract difficulties that have arisen or to extend existing provisions and machinery. The Commission adds its views and proposals, and reports on what the Member States and the Commission itself have done to strengthen Community cooperation on labor market questions.

The annual reports are intended chiefly for the Council. It cannot be said, however, that the Council paid much attention to them in the early years; official note was always taken of them, and sometimes there was a short discussion. This situation changed when unemployment took a turn for the worse in the autumn of 1966. Since then, interim reports on the unemployment trend have been issued at the Council's request, and discussions in the Council have become more thorough. In June 1967, for instance, the Council decided to have a careful discussion on the underlying trend of labor supply at least once a year.

Other Studies

In addition to its general survey, the Commission has also undertaken studies on the structural aspects of labor supply. Mention should also be made of the employment statistics published by the Statistical Office of the European Communities — an indispensable source of material on the subject. The following issues of the Social Statistics Series cover unemployment: 1963, No. 4 (1958-1962); 1965, No. 4 (1963-1964); 1967, Supplement (1965-1966). The statistics given relate to the structure of the population and the labor force, the structure of employment, the working week, unemployment, unfilled vacancies, placement services, and foreign labor. The studies on the structure of employment concentrate either on specific industries or on specific groups of workers.

Industry Studies

The first industry study made by the Commission in conjunction with experts was devoted to employment in EEC farming. This was published in the Social Policy Series, Nos. 7 and 8 of 1964. The first part deals with structure and the second, with developments and prospects. The importance of this inquiry cannot be overemphasized since, because of the social and economic structure of the industry and the seasonal character of the work, agriculture is the one sector of the economy in which it is the most difficult to ascertain the employment situation. This study is now being supplemented by others covering sugar beets, rice, grapes, and olives. The purpose of these reports is to give a better picture of seasonal unemployment in order to improve continuity of employment for workers in these departments of agriculture.

Another survey, related to those just discussed, is devoted to the regional aspects of employment in farming. The first part, dealing with a number of important agricultural areas in Germany, France, and Italy, is already finished. A second part, on other farming areas in these countries, is still being prepared. The third part will cover agricultural areas in Benelux.

A survey of underemployment in general was instituted at the same time as the first structural inquiry concerning agriculture. The report was published as No. 9 (1965) in the Social Policy Series. This study, confined to Belgium, is methodological and documentary.

Other industry studies deal with construction, textiles, shipbuilding, electrical engineering, and synthetic manufactures. The industries covered were deliberately selected from those in decline and those which are growing; and I would mention that the seriously threatened mining industry was the responsibility of the ECSC High Authority until the Communities' Executives were merged.

Although the framework of the five studies is broadly the same, account is naturally taken of the special situation of each industry. They survey the current situation, developments in the size of enterprises and the location of industry, changes in the structure of labor and employment, unemployment and recruitment, the adequacy of vocational training and a forecast for the medium term.

Studies Covering Specific Groups

Studies covering specific groups of workers deal with young people, old people, the handicapped, and women. The last of these — a structural inquiry into employment and skills of working women — is the furthest advanced. It served originally as basic material for the first medium-term economic policy program but was subsequently expanded and given a more general scope. It is based on monographs for the individual countries and deals in turn with demographic aspects, the structure of and changes in the population in paid employment, the classification and vocational training of female workers, attitudes toward the working woman, and measures adopted in this field. The concluding chapter will contain forecasts on the supply of and demand for female workers in both numbers and skills.

Comparability of Statistics

Finally, attention is paid to the comparability of the instruments essential to this matter, particularly employment forecasts. Both in the framework of medium-term economic policy and for the execution of some of the surveys mentioned above, work on labor supply was hampered by methodological differences among member countries. which made comparisons at EEC level virtually impossible. In 1967 the Commission therefore began a survey designed to lay the technical foundations for Community-level comparison. An attempt can be made at a later stage to arrive at more uniform methods for working out forecasts. The survey gives an overall view of existing methods of estimation — total working population, activity rate and numbers actually working — and a number of theoretical and practical conclusions. Enough progress has been made to enable the first internal discussions to start in 1968.

Cooperation Among Employment Services

Another factor besides work on vocational training which helps to improve the overall balance of the labor market is cooperation among employment services. A circumstantially documented report, published as No. 16 (1967) in the Social Policy Series, deals with employment services in the Community countries. It outlines the history and work of these services, the major statutory and administrative provisions involved, organization, structure, and methods of operation; finally, there is a set of conclusions. The report was based on monographs on the individual countries written by experts at the request of the Commission.

This report was the first step toward close cooperation among the member countries in the field of labor supply within the meaning of Article 118 of the Treaty of Rome. Discussion of its conclusions resulted in a plan for cooperation among employment services of the member nations that the Council approved in June 1967 and is now being implemented. For the time being. cooperation includes the exchange of information on matters of labor supply, the examination and comparison of training programs of Member States and further training of the staffs of these services, and the exchange of trainees.

In its efforts to coordinate the administrative rules made by the member countries to match demand for and supply of manpower within the Community, the Commission has also given attention to harmonization of classifications of trades in the member countries. This problem also arises in connection with freedom of movement for workers. For instance, Article 36 of Regulation No. 38/64 provides for the elaboration of a comparative glossary of those trades in which migration is most frequent. It was thought that such a glossary would be desirable in view of the differences in terminology and the diversity of operations encountered in the different countries. A first list, with short descriptions of 68 trades, had been drawn up in conjunction with the International Labor Organization and published in 1962. A new edition came out in 1965 in the form of a comparative manual. It describes 119 trades in agriculture, manufacturing, textiles, metal manufacture, construction and the hotel industry.

This manual was distributed to all employment offices in the member countries. It has proved to be particularly useful as a source of information for prospective migrants, who can now find out beforehand how their crafts or occupations are carried on in other Community countries.

Vocational Guidance

Of more general importance is vocational guidance, a matter to which the Commission has also turned its attention in order to promote cooperation among government agencies in the member states. The function of vocational guidance as a part of national policy on education, vocational training, and labor supply has become substantially more important in recent years, both in the member countries and elsewhere. Its usefulness is constantly increasing because population growth, economic expansion, the continuing advance of technology, and social progress are bringing about rapid and radical changes in the classification of workers and in the nature and degree of skills required of them. The aim is to provide information and to facilitate a freer and more efficient choice of occupation. Vocational guidance also makes it easier for people to change jobs and place of work, two kinds of mobility that have become indispensable to improving overall balance on the labor market.

Since 1960 the Commission has endeavored to promote cooperation on vocational guidance among government agencies in the member countries. The main aim originally was to improve the exchange of information, but the scope of the work was expanded through the recommendation on the extension of vocational guidance services that the Commission addressed to the Member States in July 1966. For increasing stimulation of the quantity and quality of work, such extension proved to be more and more desirable.

The first reactions to the recommendation in most government services were favorable. They enabled the Commission to issue a summary of progress in this field, and to note experience gained, difficulties to be overcome, and gaps still to be filled.

On the basis of the recommendation the Commission worked

out a program for cooperation that was adopted by the Council in June 1967. What was advocated in the recommendation was laid down in the program. The main objects are to expand vocational guidance services for young people and adults; to adapt services and funds to the requirements of the population, particularly in rural areas; and to ensure greater continuity and improved coordination of the work of the agencies responsible for vocational guidance. The Commission organizes fact-finding courses for civil servants and businessmen, at which the problems are discussed and various information centers in the member countries are visited. The first annual report on vocational guidance in the Community is to be issued in 1968, in the context of the program of cooperation among the member countries.

In its 1962 memorandum on the action program for the second stage, the Commission expressed the view that the Community's essential task in the social field in the years ahead would be concerned with vocational training and employment policy. The implementation of a Community policy on vocational training would enable a common employment policy to be defined and put through. With the various parts of the Community suffering at the time from either shortages or surpluses of manpower, especially shortages of skilled manpower, and with so much technological progress and other change, it was felt that an effective vocational training policy, coordinated with other Community machinery (the European Social Fund and freedom of movement), would exercise a decisive influence on the geographical and occupational mobility of labor within the Community. However, it was thought that coordination alone would not be enough: the various instruments would have to be applied in conformity with a Community employment policy designed to make the best use of the manpower available. Such a policy would naturally also have to be coordinated with other aspects of Community policy, especially regional policy. The difficulties in the textile, shipbuilding, and a few other industries, which subsequently grew worse and worse, together with the technological and structural changes mentioned, prompted a series of industry surveys as an integral part of the medium-term economic policy program.

All in all, these activities might be taken to show that a start has been made with a Community employment policy. It is difficult to see, however, that this is in fact the case. First of all, the Commission has no powers to pursue such a policy. If it did have such powers, the basis would still be too narrow.

In the technical and economic structures in all the member countries, the situation has so many interdependent factors that employment can no longer be treated in isolation. Employment policy is part of economic policy, monetary policy, agricultural and industrial policy, regional policy, and the educational system. It is not even a result of these factors but is interwoven with them, just as the different kinds of policy are themselves interdependent. In the short run, then, we cannot expect any Community employment policy to emerge.

Another question is whether the Commission's policy should be directed toward offsetting the injurious consequences of technological advance and economic growth or whether it should be designed to prevent them. The Commission intends to do the one but not to leave the other undone. As the Commission itself states in its social report for 1967, it will do everything in its power to counteract the ill effects of economic reorganization and to guarantee security for workers so that they may benefit from the modernization of industrial and agricultural structures.

MEDIUM-TERM ECONOMIC PROGRAMMING

In its action program for the second stage in the implementation of the Treaty of Rome (January 1, 1962), the Commission stated the view that the Community would need a forward program of development in the years to come. This in no way implied any kind of centrally imposed plan to which individual firms would be obliged to conform and which would impair the free operation of the market as an efficient instrument for distributing the factors of production. On the contrary, the program would constitute a framework within which the Member States and Community institutions would coordinate their action. In short, it would be a general program laying down medium-term guidelines for measures at domestic and Community level and intended partly to guide the private sector in matters, for instance, of economic and social infrastructure, energy, agriculture, and transport.

In July 1963 the Commission submitted to the Council a recommendation on the Community's medium-term economic policy. This recommendation was based on two articles in the Treaty — Article 105, whereby the Member States cooperate to coordinate their economic policies and the Commission submits the appropriate recommendations to the Council, and Article 145, whereby the Council ensures that the general economic policies of the Member States are coordinated.

The Commission believed that two sets of measures would have to be introduced. First, future developments had to be investigated.

This meant that consultation had to be arranged, on the basis of all available data, in order to work out Community forecasts for periods of five years. Second, the quantitative results thus obtained should be used to draft a program to coordinate decisions in the member countries and at the Community level concerning medium-term economic developments. With a view to the implementation of these proposals, the Commission suggested that the Council set up a Medium-term Economic Policy Committee. In April 1964, after endorsement by the European Parliament and the Economic and Social Committee, the Council decided to set up this Committee. It is composed of representatives from the Member States and the Commission, with one of the Member States in the chair. An independent group of experts on medium-term forecasts was also attached to the Commission.

A draft medium-term economic policy program was submitted to the Council by the Commission in April 1966 and was approved by the Council in February 1967 after the customary procedures. This program gives an overall picture of expected developments from 1966 to 1970. The projections relate to trends in population and employment, the industrial origin of GDP (agriculture, industry services), and the allocation of resources to consumption or investment.

The major part of the program is devoted to guidelines for the various fields of economic policy. Supply is discussed first, then demand. In the case of supply a set of measures are considered which, though they relate to different components of economic policy, complement each other and are aimed at getting the most out of the available factors of production. Among the points covered are policy on employment and vocational training, investment policy, competition policy, and regional policy. On the demand side the program is concerned with various policies designed to produce rapid economic expansion together with internal and external monetary stability — public finance policy, monetary, credit, and capital market policies, incomes policy, and external trade policy.

Meanwhile, in 1968, the Medium-term Economic Policy Committee drafted a second program, which includes scientific and technical research policy, structural adaptation of firms and structural policy for specific parts of industry and agriculture, and, finally, the encouragement of saving and investment and an incomes policy.

Social aspects are woven into the fabric of the first program. Because economic and social policies are linked in this way, medium-term economic policy will also help to attain the social objectives of the Community. What is essential is to bring about a continuous improvement in the living and working conditions of all groups in the population, as far as is economically possible. Improvement of this kind requires not only optimum growth and monetary stability but also a better distribution of incomes and property. If the Common Market is to grow toward economic union, regular information on social developments in the member countries must be made available and the member countries must cooperate closely in the social field.

Although it was not possible to take all aspects of social policy into account in drafting the first program, a comparative inquiry was carried out regarding a number of social policy points in the member countries, in particular employment and vocational training. Aspects of social security, certain labor questions, and incomes policy in general were also dealt with.

The first medium-term economic policy program gave special consideration to the supply of labor and vocational training. The working population of the Community increased by 2.1 million between 1960 and 1965; growth between 1965 and 1970 is expected to slow down to about 1.7 million, which amounts to a mean annual rise of 0.4 percent between 1965 and 1970 as against 0.6 percent between 1960 and 1965.

Increasing Manpower Supply

In theory there are several ways of stepping up the supply of manpower. The first is to keep the school-leaving age as it is at present. In all Community countries this stands at 14 to 15. Changing the age at which young people start work affects the number of workers. The Medium-term Economic Policy Committee ignored the idea of halting the trend toward staying on at school longer, but the Commission considered that the school-leaving age should be statutorily raised to 16 as quickly as possible. It was therefore assumed that the average age for starting work would be higher than before.

A second possibility lies in the statutory pensionable age. This varies between 60 and 65 in the six Community countries. For obvious reasons, it cannot be raised. The Committee believes that this does not necessarily mean that other ways may not be sought of allowing people who are still willing and able to go on working after retirement age to find an appropriate place in the production process. Nevertheless, it is considered that no significant increase in the numbers available should be expected from such a move.

Another possibility would be to increase the number of women at work. In all EEC countries except the Netherlands there is one woman to every two men in the labor force. The question was whether the Committee should recommend a policy of encouraging women to go out to work or should adopt a neutral position. The first program opts for neutrality. Nevertheless, certain obstacles still have to be dealt with; for instance, the tax on joint incomes should not be unduly progressive, vocational training and retraining policy should be geared to requirements, arrangements should be made for looking after children, and the social insurance laws should be adapted in order to make part-time jobs more attractive.

Then there is the working week. It makes a considerable difference whether a 50- or 45- or 40-hour week is worked by the same number of workers. With a constant supply of manpower, the total volume of work may vary appreciably depending on the actual number of hours worked per year. The first program states the view that the increase in productivity expected between 1966 and 1970 will justify devoting part of the expected social benefit to shortening the working week. It also points out that a substantial proportion of the decisions on hours worked are reached independently in collective bargaining agreements, which raises the question of how economic policy can ensure that the medium-term trend in hours worked coincides with the principles that have been laid down. This means that any reduction in the working week in the coming years should be introduced in such a way and so gradually that an adequate growth rate can be maintained and internal and external equilibrium is not disturbed.

These were the main recommendations likely to have an impact on the amount of manpower available. Migration policy is another means of satisfying demand for manpower. The main objective is to facilitate the placing of Italy's surplus labor in the other member countries. Freedom of movement for workers, however, is not enough to ensure the optimum employment of labor in the Community. There will have to be still closer cooperation between employment services. And more must be done to promote the training of Italian workers who are willing to emigrate to other Community countries. Further efforts will also have to be made to ensure that social security arrangements for migrant workers are as flexible as possible. Despite this, the five Community countries concerned will have to satisfy their labor requirements by bringing in even more workers from nonmember countries than in the past.

Between 1960 and 1965 there were about 3.5 million foreign workers in the Community, about half of them from nonmember countries, particularly Greece, Morocco, Portugal, Spain, and Turkey. Now, more than half the foreign workers in the Community come from nonmember countries. Before 1970 it is expected that between 550,000 and 800,000 more workers from outside the Community will be needed. The Commission believes that this growth rate requires the member countries to coordinate at the Community level their recruitment policies in nonmember countries. Furthermore, the employment services should not be permitted to recruit workers from nonmember countries in the territory of another member country. Finally, efforts will have to be made to render the immigrant groups more stable by giving them more help in the host country, particularly by finding satisfactory solutions to the housing difficulties which often prevent families from being united.

Upgrading Skills

The question of skills is, of course, another facet of this problem. Workers should be trained so that they can adapt at any time to the structural and other changes that will be a feature of most occupations in the years to come. This will require increased efforts by all member countries in the field of vocational guidance and training for young people and vocational training, retraining, and further training for adults, in accordance with the general principles we have referred to for the implementation of a Community policy on vocational training.

Under the first medium-term economic policy program, measures must be adopted for the training of young people once an idea is gained of how the pattern of employment by occupation will look in the longer term. Moreover, young people should be given training not so much to prepare them to specialize in a given craft as to provide them with a broad grounding of basic technical knowledge. Assessing future opportunities of employment from the structure of occupations will at best result in a scale of priorities, and multiskill vocational training can be given only after a fundamental choice has been made among the various trades where work is expected to be available. A longer-term survey of training requirements at all levels — if possible, supplying quantitative data as well — can make a contribution to the formulation of policy, and the first program again emphasizes the need for EEC cooperation.

Whereas vocational training for young people should be regarded as an instrument that has its effects in the longer term, vocational training and retraining for adults is aimed at the medium or short term. The first program therefore emphasizes the urgency in all member countries of measures to encourage the mobility of adult workers. On the one hand, there is the question of superfluous manpower in certain industries such as mining, agriculture, textiles, and shipbuilding, and on the other, the chronic shortage of sufficiently skilled workers in rapidly expanding industries such as electrical equipment.

The first program favors encouraging interindustry and geographical mobility, and it also stipulates that provision should be made for new jobs in places with a high concentration of potentially available workers. The regional policy that the Commission is introducing goes more thoroughly into the matter of the link with industrial-structure policy.

Incomes Policy

The second medium-term economic policy program goes more thoroughly into EEC incomes policy. For instance, it deals with wage incomes in the private sector, primary nonwage incomes, and transfer incomes. It also discusses the need for a policy to encourage the acquisition of property by workers. The main points here are the encouragement of voluntary saving, wage increases in the form of investments, and profit sharing. The draft emphasizes that an incomes policy must take account of all primary and secondary incomes. In order to increase the efficiency of the decisions that those concerned (government, management, and labor) reach independently in the matter of incomes, it is recommended that target figures be worked out. The figures arrived at, and any alternatives that are prepared, must be checked against actual developments in view of the discrepancies that may arise between the real situation and the agreed plan. Regular confrontation at the EEC level of the views and systems relating to incomes policy in the member countries is also considered to be essential. Great importance is attached to better statistics, particularly for nonwage incomes, and to the distribution of incomes among the various social groups.

According to the second program, optimum economic expansion presupposes a policy on incomes and property as a link that will promote rapid growth with high employment, price stability, and equilibrium in external trade. It is emphasized that the distribution of incomes should be improved to benefit the underprivileged parts of the population and that property-owning by workers should be stimulated.

The first and second programs are still confined to general guidelines and recommendations in accordance with the Council decision in February 1967. This applies to the treatment of social matters, too.

The programs include an explanation of the main lines of economic policy that the member countries and the Community institutions are planning to pursue during the period under review, and are designed to promote policy coordination. Medium-term economic policy, then, is not intended as a substitute for the policies of the member countries or for Community policy — particularly on agriculture, transport, competition, and social affairs. Nor is it any part of the object to set quantitative targets, based on a fully econometric model, that would have to be reached at all costs; this would be incompatible with the economic systems in the EEC countries. No such idea is to be found in the Treaty of Rome, so EEC programs for medium-term economic policy are obliged to be indicative and to delineate broad policy lines alone.

EUROPE AS A SOCIAL ENTITY: A FIRST STEP TOWARD EEC COLLECTIVE AGREEMENTS

The life of the European Communities has been marked by a series of crises: crises in the ECSC, crises in Euratom, and crises in the EEC in 1963, 1965, and 1967. Nevertheless, great progress has also been achieved year after year: the accelerated establishment of the customs union, the formulation of common policies, and action by the Community in the framework of its association with certain African states and Madagascar and, more generally, on behalf of the developing countries.

As it has never ceased to affirm, the Commission's role is to stimulate and speed up this Community development. The Commission does not regard itself as the opponent of the Member States but, on the contrary, as their constant, trusting collaborator under the permanent supervision of the European Parliament. Nor does the Commission regard itself as the opponent of the nonmember states, but rather as associated in growing cooperation with them. Completion of the common policies, merger of the Treaties, enlargement of the Community, and expansion of its world function: these are the aims it has set itself in order to form a united and democratic Europe, a force for progress and peace in the world.

In the last analysis our Europe remains a market, even if it forms a Community. We cannot hope that mere market machinery, even though Community-inspired, will have the same effects as domestic structures like those of the state.

The general survey I have given of the principal aspects of Community policy must obviously stop at the threshold of the customs union. However, it is clear that, as time goes on and the EEC, in its capacity as a common market, gradually adopts more common policies towards the outside world, the Community will become internally more closely knit. Thus, the adhesion of new countries and the equilibrium resulting from it ultimately pose a problem that is less geographical than political: that of the supranational character which Community policy might come to have. And it is obvious that the institutional framework of this desired democratic Community goes beyond that of the Common Market as it exists at present.

I believe profoundly that a great change of heart is taking place today in Europe — and not only in the Europe of the Six — and in the United States, too. This change I see in the growing need felt among men to seek means of combining their efforts, often outside the conventional structures for doing so such as the traditional state, which is being transcended by the implementation of the Treaties of Paris and Rome. I would even say that instances of creative collaboration can be seen in the student demonstrations against university authority, even if the demonstrations are tinged with a certain anarchism and with what I might call "collectivized individualism."

None of these attempts to join forces can develop in a closed system — the closed system of the six Community States — and without any democratic control. The Community is too promising for it to remain in close confinement or abandoned to irresponsible enterprises. To be sure, individualism manifests itself in all our countries; it is in any case essential to national and social life. But beyond the divergencies, there is in the youth of much of the world an immense desire to pool resources in a common endeavor, even if the means are different and the ideologies on which they are based appear to be antagonistic. Here, underlying the political phenomenon, we have a cultural phenomenon, no doubt felt especially keenly by intellectuals — and students are young or future intellectuals — who have often, in the course of history, revealed themselves as the spokesmen of their nations.

If, then, we rise above economic preoccupations and consider Europe — not the still rickety Europe of today but the idea of Europe, the idea in which there is inherent a ferment of universality — then, I think, the most profound aspirations of this Europe and the United States are essentially the same.

Over the years, ingenious legal arguments have been advanced to the effect that there is no basis for a social policy in the Treaty of

Rome. This is a more or less stock criticism reiterated by certain national officials present regularly at meetings at the Community's headquarters. At other times the thesis is maintained that the Commission's recommendations on short-term economic policy do not leave room for a Community social policy, or that this is only a byproduct of economic policy.

Those of us who advocate a pragmatic approach to European social policy — a policy which, moreover, must not create problems but must try to solve those in existence — are pleased to report a recent event of importance in the field of labor relations which passed almost unobserved. I refer to the agreement of June 6, 1968, on the harmonization of working hours of agricultural workers steadily engaged in growing crops. This first agreement between COPA, the European agricultural employers' association, and the agricultural unions of the EEC nations is a practical illustration of the sense of Community responsibility in labor and management. It concerns only working hours and affects only permanent agricultural employees. In form it is a simple recommendation and not a collective agreement, but its restricted scope does not detract from its pioneer value.

The background of the measure deserves attention. When, the Commission submitted its proposals in June 1960 for establishment of the common agricultural policy, it envisaged this as resting on four pillars: structural policy, market policy, commercial policy, and social policy.

For social policy, the Commission formulated an action program in 1963. It referred the social problems of paid agricultural workers to the Joint Advisory Committee for an opinion on the priorities to be observed and the methods of implementing the program. The Joint Committee issued its opinion in December 1964; it emphasized that working conditions were primarily a matter for labor and management to decide and that it was also up to them in the first instance to agree on suitable measures for ensuring that social requirements were given priority in the matter of working hours. The basic objectives are the achievement of a 45-hour week for permanent workers engaged in crop-raising and a 48-hour week for those in livestock-raising. The Committee added, however, that the prerogatives of management and labor do not absolve either the governments of the Member States or the institutions of the EEC from their own responsibility in the matter.

As a result of the Joint Committee's opinion, the EEC Commission, placing its faith in management and labor, asked them in February 1966 to make their own arrangements regarding working hours. By the end of 1966 they had overcome their final hesitations and negotiations began. These took only about a year and a half. The signatories to the agreement undertook to pass the text to their affiliated national organizations and to urge them to take as a basis the standards laid down in it when formulating, renewing, or reviewing collective agreements at all levels affecting the category of permanent paid workers engaged in growing crops. The two sides of industry were conscious of the complexity and the technical difficulties inherent in any negotiations outside the national context, and made their innovations in a European Community spirit. Thus, this first step having been taken, the way is open not only to other collective recommendations but also to true European collective agreements.

To conclude, I would point out that management and labor had recourse to a flexible procedure — flexible because it is not binding — which is repeatedly used by the Commission and for which the Commission is often reproached, especially by labor unions, with lack of boldness: the Recommendation!

PART III

Labor Disputes and Collective Bargaining in Western Europe

The processes of collective bargaining in West European countries vary significantly from one country to the next. In this part, Owen Fairweather, a Chicago management attorney who has had extensive experience in representing the interests of clients engaged in operating West European facilities, supplies an overview of collective bargaining institutions and practices of all the nations studied at the Loyola conference, except the Republic of Ireland. (J. B. McCartney of Queen's University, Belfast, remedies this gap in his article in the next part.) Dr. Leo H. J. Crijns, Director of the Division of Labour of the Directorate General of Social Affairs of EEC, supplies further particulars about private bargaining in the Six. P. P. Fano, Director of the Italian Branch Office of the ILO, discusses Italian bargaining practice and cautions us about the validity of statistical data emanating from Italian labor organizations, particularly about membership enrollments. Robert Copp, of the Ford Motor Company home office at Dearborn, gives a case history of Ford of Britain negotiations in 1967 and supplies an exciting postscript on what strikes this editor as the unfortunate coincidence of a constructive labor agreement and an intraparty crisis of the Labour Government, which had sponsored a White Paper early in 1969 calling for legal restraints on "unofficial" strikes. Ford of Britain's efforts to secure judicial enforcement of its labor agreement are further discussed from a different perspective by Professor Cyril Grunfeld in the next part. This part concludes with a discussion of the French General Strike of 1968 by Lee C. Shaw, a Chicago employer attorney with much experience in the representation of American companies with French branches. Although Mr. Shaw's contribution at first blush seems an exercise in contemporary journalism, it furnishes a valuable discussion of long-term French labor and social problems and the deficiencies of efforts to deal with them by fragmented, plant-localized collective bargaining. The influence upon labor policy and wage levels of the French Government, as an employer in enterprises in what most Americans would call the "private sector," will surprise many readers. Those who wish to study further the phenomenon of *étatisme*, or state control, may wish to read John Ardagh's *The New French Revolution* (New York and Evanston: Harper & Row, 1969).

WESTERN EUROPEAN LABOR MOVEMENTS AND COLLECTIVE BARGAINING—AN INSTITUTIONAL FRAMEWORK

By Owen Fairweather

Before reviewing how employees bargain with their employers in Western European countries, we must examine certain basic contrasts between the labor relations systems of the United States and these countries.

First, in the United States a union selected by a majority of the employees in an appropriate unit has the legal right and obligation to represent the minority who are not members of the union and who might have preferred a different union or no union representation at all. This right to exclusive representation of all by the union selected by the majority is a concept unknown in any European country.

Second, in the United States a union selected by the majority has a legal monopoly over all bargaining with the employer. This means that no bargaining can occur between the employer and the employees through any other institution.

In the European countries under study the employer often bargains with employees through councils to which the employees elect representatives. These alternate bargaining institutions, sometimes referred to as representation plans, are either legally required or established unilaterally by the employer.

Similar institutions existed in the United States prior to 1935, and their formation was encouraged by the law, specifically Section 7 (a) of the National Recovery Act (NRA), the basic labor relations legislation which preceded the Wagner Act. When the Wagner Act became law, the National Labor Relations Board declared in its first decision that representation plans, very similar to the works councils of Europe, were illegal because they were institutions through which the employer could bargain with employees and thereby infringe upon the monopoly over bargaining granted by law to the union.[1]

Third, collective bargaining in Europe is usually between rep-

---

[1] *Pennsylvania Greyhound Lines, Inc.,* 1 NLRB 1 (1935).

resentatives of an employers' association and representatives of a confederation of unions, sometimes on a national basis but usually on a regional basis. The resulting wage and benefit levels are then extended by some legal procedure or fixed custom to all employers in the industrial segment to prevent one of the employers from having the advantage of lower wage costs than the others. As economic conditions improved after World War II, many European employers bid for employees by paying wages that were higher than those fixed in the national and regional agreement. This was not difficult for a reasonably profitable employer to do, as the wage levels fixed by the regional or national agreement were established at a level that permitted marginal firms to survive. The extent to which wages actually paid by employers exceeded the negotiated level became known as "wage drift." The more sprawling the economic segment covered by a single agreement, the greater was the wage drift because the greater was the variation in the profitability of the subdivisions of the segment. As wage drift increased, the real wage and benefit levels would be established either unilaterally by the employer or through bargaining at the plant site. This shift in the power center of collective bargaining from employer-association bargaining to plant-level bargaining[2] has been occurring in all European countries in different degrees. In the industrial sector in the United States there has been very little association bargaining. Hence, the transfer of the power center is taking place in Europe but not in the United States.

Fourth, the individual contract of employment between employees and the employer is important in all European labor relations systems. In the United States, by contrast, a collective agreement negotiated between an employer and a labor union supersedes the individual employment contract.[3]

In most European systems, rights obtained by the union or confederations of unions in bargaining at a national or regional level with employer associations or in plant bargaining are enforced in actions on the individual employment contract, on the theory that the right obtained by collective action becomes a right incorporated into the individual employment contract.

Fifth, the number of employee benefits that are established by law is greater in Europe than in the United States. European un-

---

[2] But see Allan Flanders, "Labor-Management Relations and the Democratic Challenge," p. 487, *infra.* for a demonstration that in Britain, at least, the shift has been to fragmented bargaining with separate work groups in each establishment. — Ed.

[3] *J. I. Case Co.* v. *NLRB,* 321 U.S. 332 (1944).

ions are more closely allied to political parties and find that benefits can be won more quickly in the political arena than across the collective bargaining table.

UNITED KINGDOM[4]

In the United Kingdom there are about 596 labor unions, whereas in the United States there are only 184 unions. However, let us not be misled by numbers. In the United Kingdom in the private manufacturing sector there are five large unions — the Amalgamated Engineering and Foundry Workers Union, the Transport and General Workers, the National Union of General and Municipal Workers, the Electrical Trades, and the Amalgamated Society of Boilermakers, Shipwrights, Blacksmiths and Structural Workers.

The word "amalgamated" is often found in the title of these major U. K. unions, reflecting a trend toward merger of unions originally based upon crafts. Through the process of merger unions are becoming more industrial in character.[5]

In a survey conducted by our law firm, we found that a management in a typical manufacturing plant dealt with about seven unions — in sharp contrast to the one union typical in the United States. Furthermore, the seven is only an average. Ford Motor Company, for example, negotiates with the branch officials and stewards of 21 unions at its Dagenham plant.[6]

Because there is little regulatory law in the U. K., there is great diversity in the manner in which collective bargaining takes place. However, one bargaining relationship is so important that it should be described briefly with the caveat that it is not necessarily typical. This is the bargaining between the Engineering Employers Federation, representing employers operating 4,500 plants, and the Confederation of Shipbuilding and Engineering Unions, representing 34 unions that, in turn, speak for over two million employees in the plants of "federated" employers.

The agreements that are negotiated between the two committees establish the minimum wage pattern for "federated" employers and many other employers employing another 1-1/2 million employees.

---

[4] See generally, Seyfarth, Shaw, Fairweather & Geraldson, *Labor Relations and the Law in the United Kingdom and the United States,* Vol. 1, Michigan International Labor Studies (1968).

[5] See Trade Union (Amalgamations, etc.) Act, 1964, ch. 24.

[6] See Robert Copp, "Negotiating a New Wage Structure at Ford of Britain," p. 109, *infra.* — Ed.

The agreements that the two committees negotiate do not resemble U. S. labor agreements. Obviously, it would be quite impossible to negotiate one labor agreement that would regulate the day-to-day administrative details in over 4,500 plants. The agreed level is only the minimum, or floor, to be built upon by additional bargaining at the plant site. The agreements set forth only the broadest guidelines. There is not one agreement to be replaced at the end of its term by a new agreement, but rather a series of separate agreements superimposed one on the other which are then collected into the "Engineering Handbook," containing over 300 printed pages. Furthermore, these agreements are not enforceable in a court of law and are not interpreted by arbitrators.

One might assume that the unions, bound together for coördinated bargaining at the national agreement level, would remain cohesive at the plant level, but this is not the case. Each union, through its own staff representatives, usually known as "branch officials," attempts to negotiate separate agreements at the plant level.

On the shop floor each union functions through its own shop stewards. In theory, the stewards are elected to assist employees with grievances and complaints and to present new demands, but in some instances the stewards generate many of the claims because they are plant politicians who must make a showing to be reelected each year.

The ability of the branch officials of the union to direct the stewards varies from plant to plant. In the United Kingdom there is one branch official for each 2,500 union members, whereas in the United States there is one staff official for each 300 members. British union branch officials are relatively overworked and, compared to U. S. standards, underpaid, and their contact with the stewards in a particular plant is often infrequent. Limited contact is one of the reasons behind the conflict that exists in the United Kingdom between many stewards and the union branch official, fed, of course, by the same rank and file rebellion against authority that is observed everywhere.[7]

The formation of stewards councils composed of stewards of the various unions who have members in a particular plant encourages their independence. Since the council is composed of stewards of different unions, the branch official of any one union has little influence compared to the council's elected chief steward, known as the "convenor."

---

[7] For an additional explanation of the conflict, see comments of Allan Flanders, p. 494, *infra*. — Ed.

In addition to a stewards council, in many plants there is another institution known as the "works council" or "joint consultation council." These councils are an outgrowth of the Whitley Committee recommendations in 1914.[8] Employees are elected to these councils as representatives of the employees of a department. Theoretically, discussions at these council meetings should not involve grievances or collective bargaining matters. But these limitations are rarely respected, and the council may become an important part of the collective bargaining process.

Because of rivalry, conflict often arose between the stewards councils and the consultation councils. Some joint consultation councils ceased to function, but others were captured by the stewards. When this happened, the stewards would represent not only the members of their own union but also members of other unions working in the department, creating a dual representation function that enlarged the gap between the branch officials and the stewards.

The labor agreements at the plant level are negotiated with branch officials, individual stewards, stewards councils, or joint consultation councils. They do not resemble U. S. labor agreements any more than the central agreements do. They usually have no fixed term and, if they are in writing, are found in various memoranda, letters of understanding, or minutes of meetings; but more often they are oral understandings encrusted with "past practice."

Because the central agreements contained in the Engineering Handbook cover over 4,500 plants in engineering, they establish only general guidelines. The details must be filled in at each individual plant. This process generates disputes. Hence, one of the central agreements establishes a "Procedure for Handling Questions Arising." Such claims are not limited to complaints that a given action by the management violates a specific provision of an agreement between the parties. They may include a demand that a certain new agreement should be reached granting a new benefit or changing an established practice.

It would be quite futile to try to divide the types of questions being processed through the "Procedure for Handling Questions Arising" into interpretative matters (sometimes called "rights disputes") and collective bargaining matters (sometimes called "interest disputes"). The combination of the central agreement, local written and oral understandings, and past practices makes it difficult to determine whether a given dispute is a claim for a new concession or a

---

[8] Pelling, *A History of British Trade Unionism,* p. 160 (1963); Allan, *Trade Unions & The Government,* pp. 60-61 (1960).

claim that there has been a failure on the part of management to comply with one of the many agreements. This Procedure, which ends before an employers court at York, is not within the scope of this paper, but since it is also a bargaining procedure, it must be noted.[9]

Unions in the United Kingdom have gained extensive control over the jobs of the members through *de facto* closed or union shops, created not by agreement between the employer and the union,[10] as they were before 1947 in the United States, but by the refusal of employees to work with a member found by a trial committee of the union to be in bad standing. If the employee summoned before a union trial board is expelled, the other members will refuse to work with him, and the employer will then be faced with an unauthorized wildcat strike he does not know how to stop unless he terminates the employment of the expelled member, which he often does. By doing so, he builds union control over members to the point where employees prefer to disobey the foreman rather than to disobey the steward. If he disobeys the latter, he not only will lose his job but will be unable to work at his trade in the locality and, in some instances, anywhere in England.

There is no legal obligation in England requiring either unions or employers to bargain in good faith. For example, the employer can attempt to lure an individual striker across a picket line by offering him a "perk," such as lower rent on a company-owned house or other financial inducement. The discipline of the unions over the members is so strong, however, that once a plant is "blacked" it usually remains "black" regardless of these inducements.

A Royal Commission on Trade Unions and Employers' Associations has taken testimony and received written reports in London for more than three years. Its report was published in 1968.[11] I recommend it as a route to deeper insight into the U. K. labor relations system.

BELGIUM[12]

In Belgium, 65 percent of the eligibles belong to unions. This

[9] See Mr. Fairweather's chapter, "British and American Grievance Handling" in *Developments in American and Foreign Arbitration* (Washington: BNA Books, 1968), p. 1. — Ed.

[10] But see McCarthy, *The Closed Shop in Britain* (1964), p. 20: "The crucial variation . . . relates to the role of the employer in imposing the closed shop. At one end of the scale is *the closed shop which is the subject of a written collective agreement.*" (Italics supplied) — Ed.

[11] Cmnd. 3623, H.M.S.O., London (1968).

[12] This section is based mainly on our firm's study. *Labor Relations and the Law in Belgium,* Volume II, Michigan International Labor Studies (1969).

is higher than the 41 percent belonging in Germany, the 33 percent in the U. S., and the relatively much lower 20 to 25 percent who belong to unions just across the border in France. This high percentage is maintained in a country whose Constitution outlaws a closed, union, or agency shop agreement. Individuals have a protected right to join and the corollary right to withdraw from a union at any time. While in the United States an employee's right to join a union is completely protected from interference, he does not have the corollary right to withdraw if withdrawal is restricted by the negotiated agreement. The cumbersome union-shop deauthorization procedures of U.S. law are little used. [13]

In Belgium, there are three national union federations. Since they structurally resemble U. S. unions with industry sections, it is accurate to say that there are only three unions in Belgium in contrast to 596 in the United Kingdom and 184 in the United States. The largest is the Confederation of Christian Trade Unions, politically affiliated with the Catholic party; only slightly smaller is the General Federation of Belgium Labor, politically affiliated with the Socialist party; and the third, much smaller, is the General Federation of Liberal Trade Unions, affiliated with the Conservative party.

Why are there only three labor unions in Belgium? This happened because unions in Belgium did not have any legal personality; they could not sue or be sued, and the Belgian legislature, which is composed largely of lawyers, concluded that if unions had no legal personality they just did not exist in law and no regulatory legislation concerning them could be enacted. This type of legal sophistry never troubled U. S. legislators.

In 1927, a Catholic priest, Father Rutten, proposed to the Belgian Senate a statute granting to the two large unions the right to have representatives make safety inspections in mines. He pointed out that the two largest unions had a legal status in Belgium because they were "most representative societies" under Article 389 of the Treaty of Versailles. This legal status, borrowed from international relations, became a domestic labor law doctrine in Belgium limiting union recognition, first to two unions and finally three, and avoided the problems generated by multiple unionism so obvious in the United Kingdom.

These three unions appoint the employee representatives on 86

---

[13] In fiscal 1967, the National Labor Relations Board conducted only 65 union-shop deauthorization elections in which about 5,000 employees were eligible to vote. *Thirty-Second Annual Report of National Labor Relations Board* (1968), p. 237.

joint labor-management commissions that negotiate agreements, usually applicable to the different industrial and service segments of the economy but sometimes in segregated geographic areas. Each union can appoint employee representatives to these commissions in proportion to its membership strength. An equal number of employer representatives are nominated by the dominant employers' association for the particular segment. Each commission has a president and staff appointed by the Minister of Labor, but the president has no vote or arbitration authority.

Once an agreement is reached between the two sides of the commission, it can be submitted to the Minister of Labor with the request that it be confirmed by the King. When it is confirmed, it becomes a decree binding on all employers in the industrial segment, irrespective of the employer's membership in the association that nominated the employer members of the commission.

Negotiations also take place between the employers' association and representatives of the three unions outside the commission. These agreements are often as important as agreements made within the commission.

The difference between the laws of the United States and Belgium produce quite different reactions at bargaining tables in each nation. Even though the substance of agreements is not within the scope of this paper, the effect of these differences merits some attention.

In 1953, the cement industry in Belgium negotiated a fixed-term agreement with the unions, containing a no-strike clause. The membership in the unions immediately dropped from 65 percent to 45 percent. The members reasoned that a union which relinquished its right to strike for a term of years became impotent. So why pay dues? Exercising their constitutional right, the members withdrew.

After the union leaders lost nearly a third of their members, they asserted that no-strike agreements would never again be negotiated. The employers countered with a plan designed to stabilize the union's membership. They agreed to pay each employee who remained in the union for the full year a special bonus, known as a "members only" bonus. This "members only" bonus plan spread from industry to industry and increased in amount as more employers sought to negotiate long-term agreements containing an industrial peace pledge.

Fabrimetal, the employers' association in metal fabrication, was asked by the unions to pay a similar bonus. It took the position that a bonus to cause employees to remain union members was inconsistent with the freedom of association and disassociation principle of the constitution. However, it countered with a proposal to pay the three unions proportionate shares of one half of 1 percent of the wages and salaries, up to a certain limit, paid by the member companies, on condition that labor peace was maintained. This payment permitted the unions to finance benefits for union members that prevented a membership loss during a long-term contract and also created for the employers a financial sanction that could be quickly applied if the union breached its no-strike pledge. Unions cannot be sued for damages in Belgium,[14] but this quick-acting sanction by the employer for a breach by the union is quite effective.

A plan to pay 1/2 of 1 percent of wages directly to the unions might at first shock a U. S. observer, until he is reminded that in the United States at least 1 percent of the wage bill is similarly paid directly to the union after being "checked off," a practice that would be illegal in Belgium. However, in the United States the employers, in return for this arrangement, do not obtain the right to stop this payment if there is a breach of the no-strike clause.

A plant of over 150 regular employees is required by the law to have an "enterprise council" (conseil d'entreprise). Blue collar and white collar workers and "young people" are represented by individuals elected from slates proposed by the unions, and each union is given a share of the total seats proportionate to its membership.

The law specifies that a council cannot be formed unless a union sponsors the employee delegate slates. This rule distinguishes the Belgian factory councils from the joint consultation councils or Whitley Committees so often organized by employers in the United Kingdom and, prior to 1935, in the United States. The requirement that employee delegates to the factory council must be sponsored by the unions in Belgium minimizes the friction that usually exists between a council and a union.

It has been said that these "enterprise councils" are consultative bodies and do not deal with collective bargaining matters. However, Belgian law requires that these bodies negotiate the work-shop regulations that are posted in the plants and filed with the government. These regulations cover the following:

(1) The working hours, lunch periods, and rest periods.

---

[14] The terms of the collective agreements are not directly enforceable by the employee, but because they become an implied part of his employment contract he can bring an action for enforcement of the incorporated terms in a tripartite labor court.

(2) Any special rules concerning shift work.

(3) Where incentive work is involved, the manner by which work performance time will be measured and incentive earnings calculated.

(4) Payment procedures and paydays.

(5) The length of notice to be given an employee before dismissal and the exceptions to such requirement and the length of notice that an employee should give the employer before quitting.

(6) The rights and duties of supervisors.

(7) The disciplinary sanctions and fines that the employer may impose and the procedure open to the employee subjected to discipline.

(8) First-aid procedures.

(9) The dates of annual vacations and holidays.

The required list does not exclude negotiation on other matters. It can be seen that the matters which must be negotiated between employee delegates on the council and management representatives are matters which would be negotiated with union representatives in the United States.

The voting procedures at council meetings do not provide that a deadlock will be broken by the employer. This means that the council is a forum for bargaining. Disputes that arise out of the negotiation of regulations are referred to the appropriate regional joint labor management commission (Commission Paritaire) or to the Minister of Labor for resolution.

A national inter-industry agreement, negotiated between the Federation of Belgian Industries (FIB) and representatives of the three unions in 1947, established the procedure for electing a trade union delegation. Membership on this delegation is proportional to the expressed union affiliation of the employees.

Under this agreement a delegation shall be established if there are over 50 employees in the plant, 25 percent of them have expressed a desire to have a delegation, and 10 percent of them are members of a union.

The trade union delegation does not normally bargain with the employer; rather, it assists individual employees in processing complaints through a grievance procedure and, if need be, to a labor court. It also presents claims to the management that the company has failed in some respect to comply with a labor law, a work-shop regulation, a provision of a collective agreement or joint labor-management commission (Commission Paritaire) agreement, a royal decree, or an individual contract of employment. The delegation cannot discuss matters within the province of the enterprise council or the committee on safety and hygiene.

Because each of the three unions has representatives on the delegation, the enterprise council, the joint labor-management commission, or the committee bargaining with an association on a proportionate basis, the Belgian employer, or his association, usually bargains with a single committee. In this respect the single-committee arrangement more closely resembles U. S. bargaining than does the plurality of bargaining that often exists in the United Kingdom.

Belgian law also requires that a safety and hygiene committee be organized at each plant to determine by inspection whether the legal requirements concerning safety and sanitation have been met. This institution concerns itself with matters which in the United States would be within the province of a union-sponsored safety committee. Matters assigned by law to this committee cannot be handled by either the enterprise council or the trade union delegation. It represents another example of how Belgian law has dispersed the bargaining process through different institutions and at different levels, where in the United States a monopoly over all bargaining with the employer has been granted to the union selected by the employee majority.

WEST GERMANY[15]

Like Belgium, and in contrast to the United Kingdom, the bargaining process in West Germany has been surrounded by much regulatory law.

Under West German law, a union must meet certain standards before it may be recognized as a union for the purposes of collective bargaining. Membership in the union must be voluntary but not open to persons whose interests are aligned with those of the management, and it must be independent of any ties to a political or religious organization. This does not mean that German unions are not politically active. If the membership of a union is confined to employees of a single firm, it is conclusively presumed to be incapable of being truly independent.

The union must accept the principle that conciliation proce-

---

[15] This section utilizes material in Seyfarth, Shaw, Fairweather & Geraldson, *Labor Relations and the Law in West Germany and the United States*, Vol. III, Michigan International Labor Studies (publication pending).

dures must be exhausted before strike action can occur. Before a strike may lawfully take place, 75 percent of union members must approve of the action by a secret ballot. Even after a strike is sanctioned by secret vote, it must be approved by the governing authorities of the union or strike benefits will not be paid. Finally, before bargaining starts, a union must be authorized by its members to enter into a collective agreement, should one be reached in negotiations. In the United States, the members of unions do not grant this authority to the bargaining committee in advance and currently are rejecting more than one out of every seven agreements after the union and management representatives have concluded direct negotiations.[16]

The 16 largest German unions are members of the German Confederation of Labor Unions. The largest union is the Metal Workers Union (I.G. Metall) with over two million members. Under German law, the Minister of Labor can extend a collective agreement to employers who are not members of the Employers' Association by issuing a Declaration of Universal Application upon the request of either party to protect association members from the unfair competition of low-wage-paying competitors. The I.G. Metall agreements, negotiated separately in each Land or state, actually affect three and one-half million employees.

Leaders of West German unions frequently complain that the 41 percent of the eligible employees who are union members bear the cost of negotiating collective agreements, while the benefits gained are granted to nonmembers by the employers, often by an "extension agreement" negotiated with the works council. In 1960, one union requested that it be granted the right to levy "solidarity contributions" from nonmembers working in the plant — an arrangement that would be parallel to the U. S. agency shop. Not only the huge German Confederation of Employer Associations (Bundesvereinigung der Deutschen Arbeitgeberverbände (BDA)), an affiliation of 37 national and various regional employer associations, but also the German Federation of Labor Unions rejected the idea. They felt it would be tantamount to compulsory membership in the union and incompatible with the constitutional concept of freedom of association and disassociation.

Usually unions bargain with associations of employers on a district basis coinciding with the boundaries of each Land or state, but sometimes the bargaining is on a national basis. Membership in the appropriate employer association is voluntary, but once an em-

---

[16] Federal Mediation and Conciliation Service, *Twentieth Anniversary Report, 1947-1967*, (1968), pp. 5-6.

ployer joins he is obligated by the bylaws not to enter into a private agreement with the union, can be enjoined from doing so, and must pay damages if he does. Under German law, the lockout has the same legal status as the strike (which is not true in the United States[17]) and the lockout has been effectively used as a power weapon by the employer association bargaining committees. One lockout in one region alone in 1966 put over 300,000 employees out of work in a single industry. When American employer associations attempt to bargain with construction trades unions, for example, the membership unity often breaks down at the critical moment, and the resulting fiasco results in a wage-cost rise which inflates building costs. Such employer associations should study the organization of German associations which have developed a cohesion through power given by their charters and bylaws.

West German unions do not have any legal rights at the plant level. A works council, required by law, is the bargaining institution at that level. In an attempt to control and direct the activities of the works council members, the unions submit lists of candidates for election. If one quarter of the members of the works council concur, a representative of the union can sit in at meetings of the works council as an advisor. (A similar advisor arrangement is found in France.) Unions also appoint shop stewards and plant committees, but in contrast to Belgium there is no required recognition of union committees at the plant level. Employers confine their bargaining at the plant level to bargaining with the legally created works council.

The number of employee representatives on the works council is determined by a formula. Where there are over 50 employees but less than 150, there would be three; over 150 but less than 300, five; over 300 but less than 600, seven, etc. There is also a formula to determine the number that should represent blue collar and white collar employees.

The law states that "the employer and the works council shall refrain from doing anything likely to imperil . . . the tranquility of the undertaking," and more specifically that the employer and the works council shall not engage in "industrial warfare against each other. . . ." The works council was designed as an instrument of peace and cooperation, and the unions say that, for this reason, it is not a good representative of the employees' interests.

The works council members are elected for three years. The council must meet at least once a month with the employer, and every three months the council convenes a works assembly of all the

---

[17] But see *American Shipbuilding Co.* v. *NLRB*, 380 U.S. 300 (1965).

employees in the plant and presents a report to them. The time lost by members of the works council is paid by the employer. Works assemblies take place during working hours without loss of wages or salary.

The works council hears employee grievances, determines whether all laws and agreements are being complied with by the employer, and negotiates with the employer in three areas referred to as "social," "personnel," and "economic-managerial."

"Social matters" include hours of work, plant rules, incentive rates and other compensation systems, vacations, and holidays. When agreements in this area are reached, they are often reduced to writing as "works agreements." If agreements are not reached, the State Conciliation Committee can issue a binding decision.

"Personnel matters" involve the hiring, regrading, transfer, and dismissal of employees. Concerning these matters the works council has a right to be heard. If no agreement is reached, the employer may take the contemplated action, but the works council can appeal to the Labor Court, which has power to rescind the action, a procedure similar to U. S. arbitration.

"Economic-managerial matters" are questions such as reduction, cessation or removal of operations, the introduction of new work, new methods, etc. In this area there is no compulsory arbitration or appeal to the Labor Court, but a dispute may go to a mediation committee. In "economic-managerial matters" the law reserves to the management the right to make the final decision; whereas in the United States unions take many similar matters to impartial arbitrators with claims that the employer is contractually restricted from contracting out work, discontinuing work, etc. This area of American managerial decision has also been circumscribed by bargaining obligations and certain other restrictions of the National Labor Relations Act.

Another feature of the labor relations system of West Germany that requires mention is what has been called "codetermination." There are two statutes that establish the requirement of codetermination; one is confined to mining and the iron and steel industry, and the other covers the rest of German industry. Codetermination in the first of these two statutes is slightly more extensive than in industry generally, but only the second type will be described. The managerial structure of a German corporation involves two boards — a board of supervision and the management board, neither of which is the precise equivalent of a corporate board of directors in the United States. The board of supervision does not take part in the direct management of the business, but it does appoint and remove those who do — specifically the members of the management board.

In general industry, one third of the members of the board of supervision are employee representatives and the other two thirds are shareholder representatives. The one third representing employees can make themselves heard on any given issue, but they have no real power. They are elected directly by the employees in the plant by a secret ballot.

A difference between the Belgian and the West German system deserves comment. In Belgium, in addition to the works council, known as the conseil d'entreprise, there is a trade union delegation representing the unions in proportion to their membership strength in the plant. Hence, in Belgium, the unions have a more important role at the plant site than they do in West Germany, where the works council is the sole bargaining institution at the plant site. German unions may sponsor candidates for the works council, but they have no independent voice at this level.

FRANCE[18]

In France, like the other countries on the continent, there is a constitutional provision guaranteeing that employees are free not only to join but to disassociate from a labor organization. As a result, closed shop and union shop contracts are not permitted, only 20 to 25 percent of the eligibles are union members, and only about 10 percent pay union dues.

The Confédération Générale du Travail (CGT) is the largest union federation in France. It is under the control of the Communist party, although signs of more conservatism in its leadership show up year by year.[19] The Confédération Française Démocratique (CFDT) is next largest. It espouses the philosophy of the Catholic Church. The Confédération Générale du Travail-Ouvrière (FO), Socialist-oriented, is next. It was split off from the large Communist-dominated federations in 1947. The smallest federation is the Confédération Générale des Cadres (CGC) which broke away in 1952 and represents engineers, technicians, supervisors, and, to some extent, top management personnel.

---

[18] This section of the article utilizes materials in Seyfarth, Shaw, Fairweather & Geraldson, *Labor Relations and the Law in France and the United States*, Vol. IV, Michigan International Labor Studies (Publication pending).

[19] The role of the CGT in the French General Strike of 1968 is discussed by Lee C. Shaw, pp. 123-124, *infra*. — Ed.

The basic law regulating collective bargaining in France, enacted in February 1950, ranks the various agreements. A local plant agreement may not diminish the terms of the regional agreement, and a regional agreement may not undercut a national agreement. This ranking of agreements by law in France has occurred in Italy by negotiated agreement.

National or regional bargaining may be between one or more labor unions on the one hand and one or more employer associations on the other. An employer who is a member of the association is bound to the terms of the agreement, and the Minister of Labor may extend it to employers who are not members. Regional agreements tend to become the pattern even if not formally extended. Every national or regional agreement must include:

(1) a no-discrimination clause;

(2) minimum wage scales;

(3) premiums for hazardous work;

(4) a guarantee of equal pay for equal work;

(5) rules on hiring and severance

(6) the term of notice to be given to employees before severance;

(7) provisions recognizing shop steward and enterprise committees (like the U. K., Belgian and German committees);

(8) vacations and holidays;

(9) a conciliation procedure for settling disputes;

(10) an apprentice program;

(11) special benefits for women and children; and

(12) a procedure for revision and termination of the agreement.

National and regional agreements may include provisions regulating (1) overtime, shift, night, Sunday, and holiday premiums, (2) incentive rate establishment procedures, (3) length-of-service and attendance bonuses, (4) expense reimbursements, (5) the arbitration of disputes, and (6) a pension plan supplementing state benefits.

No employee may be paid less than the minimum wage fixed by governmental decree for each department or geographical area. The differential between the minimums for the highest and lowest zones has been about 12 percent, and the wages established by agreements have reflected parallel differentials. Employee dissatisfaction with this differential arrangement mounted year by year, and these regional differentials in the minimums were eliminated during the general strike negotiations between the government and the three large unions in May of 1968.

Although the important agreements were those negotiated at the national level for textiles, for example, or at the department level for the metal fabrication industry, a trend toward plant- or company-wide bargaining started in 1955. Renault that year negotiated an agreement with an independent union representing production employees and the four major federations, with the largest federation signing months after the others. A number of large companies briefly followed Renault's lead. But by 1956 the trend toward individual company agreements had ended, though Renault still negotiates its own agreement and recognizes a union committee as the representative rather than the legally required Comite d'Entreprise. Renault was thus behaving much more like an American company than were the other employers in France.

However, the general strikes of May 1968 also resulted in many plant-by-plant negotiations because the pattern-setting Grenelle agreement was not generous enough to satisfy some of the local plant leaders.

In January 1968 the first step in developing a "people's capitalism" in France was taken. The law now requires that a company employing over 100 persons shall agree to a profit-sharing plan modeled on one of two principles: to give to its employees a proprietary interest in the enterprise by distributing shares of stock or, as an alternative, to set up a profit-sharing plan generating payments to a fund based on productivity improvement and a share in net profits after a 5-percent return on invested capital has been earned. There are two ways such funds may be invested. If invested with the company, employees with over three years' service are to receive an ownership certificate to a share proportionate to the wages or salaries they receive. This ownership interest vests after five years, so the employee can take his share with him if he quits. If not invested with the employer, the funds are to be paid into a government-operated investment fund, not yet set up at this writing. The payouts from these funds are exempt from personal income tax. If the details of the plan cannot be agreed upon between the parties, the Minister of Labor has the power to prescribe a plan.

Patronat, the French central employers association, was less than enthusiastic about the new law, and the trade unions were indifferent. The industrial events of 1968 may mean that this new law will be rapidly implemented and more participation of the employee and his representatives in plant-level bargaining and managerial planning will follow.

Since profit-sharing plans by their very nature must function at the plant level, more bargaining will shift from the regional and national conference tables to the plant level — a current trend in the United Kingdom and Italy but not in West Germany or Belgium.

At the plant level, bargaining usually occurs through three different channels. The first is through the legally required enterprise committee (Comite d'Entreprise), similar in its makeup to the Belgian and German councils. The second is through the shop stewards (Delegues du Personnel), who under law may be elected in plants of 50 or more employees. The shop stewards assist employees in the presentation of their complaints and grievances and are granted time off with pay (up to 15 hours per week) to perform their functions. Finally, there are union members who sit as advisors in the enterprise committee meetings as the direct representatives of the unions. The law requires that the employer pay these advisors up to 20 hours per month for time in meetings.

Members of the enterprise committee are nominated by the unions and elected for two-year terms. Certain places on the committee are assigned to employees elected from slates sponsored by the different unions, as in Belgium. This proportional representation system was designed to prevent the CGT from getting control of all the works committees and delegations of personnel (stewards). This would have occurred if the union whose slate was chosen by a majority were to fill all the seats on the committee.

French unions are undermanned and under-financed. The Confédération Générale du Travail is the best financed because of its size. It has recommended that each member pay one hour's wages per month. Union dues are generally collected at the plant gate and range from 60 cents to 80 cents per month.

ITALY

Most Italian union members belong to a union affiliated with one of three federations. Each federation has industrial sections or "categories." The Italian General Confederation of Labor (Confederazione Generale Italiana del Lavoro or CGIL) is the largest. It is Communist controlled and affiliated with the World Federation of Trade Unions. This union is particularly dominant in industrialized northern Italy.

In 1949, in protest against Communist control, the Catholic labor leaders and the Socialist leaders withdrew from the General Confederation of Labor and formed the two other federations. The larger of these is the Italian Confederation of Labor Unions (Confederazione Italiana Sindicati Lavoratori (CISL), considered to be the labor branch of the Christian Democratic Party (Catholic). The other federation thus created is the Italian Union of Labor (Unione Italiana del Lavoro or UIL), allied with the moderate Socialist Party. Both of these labor federations are members of the non-Communist International Confederation of Free Trade Unions (ICFTU).

There is also a tiny federation with which the other unions will not cooperate on joint bargaining — the Italian Confederation of National Workers' Unions (Confederazione Italiana Sindicati Nazionali de Lavoratori or CISNAL), affiliated with political parties described as neo-Fascist.

Each sector or "category" within one of the federations selects the employee representatives that sit across the bargaining table from employer representatives selected by the appropriate employers' association. In the private sector, such an association would be one of 103 national associations and 107 regional associations affiliated with Confindustria. For government-owned industrial enterprises, other than those in petro-chemical, there is a comparable employers' association called "Intersind."

The "metal-mechanical" category is the largest. It includes the steel, automobile, shipbuilding, electrical equipment, and other metal-fabricating industries. This conglomerate group resembles the mixture represented by the Engineering Employers Federation in the United Kingdom. The General Confederation of Labor (CGIL), through the Metal Employees and Workers Union (Federazione Impiegati Operai Metallurgici or FIOM), dominates the bargaining in this category, although representatives of the two other unions sit on the employee side. Because of its sprawling character, the unions have made an effort to break the category down into "sectors" to achieve better bargaining results with the more prosperous "sectors." These divisive efforts have been strongly resisted by Confindustria. The failure of these efforts to divide up the category led to major changes in the form of bargaining that started in 1962.

The category unions, until recently, had no legal or *de facto* status at the plant level. Employee representation at this level was performed by an Internal Commission (Commissione Interna) which is a representation council resembling the Whitley Councils in the United Kingdom, the enterprise councils in Belgium and France, and the works councils of West Germany, but with no counterpart in the United States. The unions sponsored the slates of candidates in hotly contested elections. The attitude of a union toward an internal commission would vary with its success in electing its slates and with the extent to which the internal commission attempted to engage in plant-level collective bargaining, an activity bitterly opposed by all the unions.

In 1954, the monopoly of the internal commission over the plant-level employer-employee communication and over a substantial amount of bargaining began to break down. The union confederations began to foster "factory unions" — an effort initiated by the non-Communist unions to counteract the successful takeovers of internal commissions by the General Confederation of Labor. By setting up a plant committee that could engage in organizational activities, a non-Communist union could improve its ability to elect its slate of candidates to the internal commission. However, these "factory unions" soon began to generate plant-level agreements between employers and one of the unions, negotiated not jointly with the other unions but separately by a staff member from the local office of the union. By 1960 there were 587 such plant-level agreements covering 700,000 workers, providing benefits exceeding those of the national agreements. The greatest number of such agreements were concluded in the metal-mechanical category, followed by textiles and chemicals.

A rival method to internal commission bargaining consequently developed. Friction grew between the two methods. Intersind, the employers' association representing state-controlled enterprises, reached an agreement with the major union confederations on July 5, 1962, formally recognizing direct plant-level bargaining by union representatives. This move by Intersind generated pressure for a similar agreement in the private sector with associations affiliated with Confindustria. After a series of strikes for 40 days, an agreement was reached in the metal-mechanical category in February 1963.

Since 1963, the first level of bargaining in the metal-mechanical category is national. The second is at the subdivision level within the category (a breakdown previously resisted by Confindustria) — iron and steel, electrical engineering, shipbuilding, smelting, automobiles and general engineering, where the minimum wage rates for employees in the various work categories and working hours would be fixed. The third level is the plant. Here the bargaining is over piece rates, job evaluation, productivity bonuses, and wage rates for classifications not fixed at the second level. The 1963 agreement also required that plant-level bargaining conform to any limitations placed upon its scope in the national agreement.

Some bargaining still goes on between employers and the internal commissions, but the Italian courts have ruled that only union-employer agreements at the plant level are valid. This has the effect of favoring union-negotiated plant-level agreements and assigning communication and consultation to the internal commission.

Matters covered by the three-year national agreements are not subject to strike action. Matters covered at the second or third levels are subject to such action if the prestrike procedures of the national agreement are completed — an open-end type of arrangement that also resembles the British Engineering Employers Federation "Procedure for Handling Questions Arising." Another similarity to U. K. bargaining is that at the national and regional levels the three unions are confederated, whereas at the plant level they are not.

Article 39 of the Italian constitution says that individuals are free to join and to withdraw from unions. This typical continental principle prevents closed, union, or agency shops and mandatory and escape-proof checkoff arrangements. Article 40 of the constitution specifically protects the right to strike.

Unions may sue and be sued, and the law provides that the agreements they negotiate in concert at the national and regional levels become "compulsory norms" applicable to the entire industry segment or category. These norms, of course, are tending to be minimum rather than average or median, as the center of meaningful bargaining shifts to the plant level where the important extras are negotiated.

The difference in the financial strength of U. S. and Italian unions is revealed in part by the differences in dues structure. The present minimum *annual* membership dues of one of the category unions of a large federation is 4,000 lire ($6.45), equal to 53 cents per month, somewhat lower than in France, of which 11 cents per month goes to the parent federation. Hence, union dues are about 10 percent of what they are in the United States, whereas the average wage level is about 30 percent of that in the United States. The financial problems of Italian unions were so complicated by the casual attitude of the members toward their dues obligations that dues checkoff agreements, based on voluntary and withdrawable authorizations, are spreading.

In addition to dues, Italian unions receive financial assistance from the political parties to which they are allied, as well as a government subsidy allegedly to reimburse them for assisting in the administration of various governmentally financed social welfare plans.

THE IMPACT OF THE EUROPEAN ECONOMIC COMMUNITY ON UNIONS

Unions in the six countries now in the European Economic Community derive substantial power from their domestic political influence. Many employment benefits ordinarily contained in collective agreements in the United States are mandatory under statutes passed by the legislators in Europe in response to the political influence of unions. But unions have little voice in the affairs of the European Economic Community. When the Treaty of Rome was signed, trade unions were granted representation on the Economic and Social Committee, but this group has only consultative status and can be convened only by the Council of Ministers or the Commission. Organized labor has only one third of the membership of the Economic Committee; employers' organizations have another third, and the remaining seats are divided among other special-interest groups, such as farmers and consumers. Unions gain added influence in their home countries because they control the administration of the EEC Social Fund, which provides financial and training assistance to unemployed workers or those whose jobs are threatened by employment shifts caused by tariff changes.

Because of the tendency to exclude labor from the EEC decision-making process, dissatisfaction among union leaders has mounted. Some seek reappraisals of means to safeguard union interests in the EEC. Some union leaders have recognized the need for greater cooperation among the unions of the six countries.

Soon after the EEC Treaty was signed, trade unions in the EEC countries established liaison offices in Brussels. The Common Market trade union body is the European Community Trade Union Secretariat (ECTUS).[20] Also concerned with EEC labor problems are two other noncommunist labor bodies, the International Confederation of Free Trade Unions (ICFTU) and its European Regional Organization (ERO).

The extent and pace of a common influence of the 19 million trade unionists in the Six on future EEC developments are uncertain because they are split into three major ideological groupings — Socialist, Catholic, and Communist. Internationally, the Socialist ideology is represented by ICFTU, the Catholic by the IFCTU (International Federation of Christian Trade Unions), and the Communist by the WFTU (World Federation of Trade Unions). Communist influence is very strong in the largest French and Italian un-

---

[20] See Eric Wigham, "Britain's Entry the Kiss of Life for European Trade Unionism," *The Times* (London), May 22, 1967.

ions, but is of little significance in unions in West Germany and Belgium.

The strong ideological differences that divided European Catholic and Socialist-oriented unions at the beginning of the 20th century have been greatly reduced. The recent apparent cooperation between the Communist-controlled largest union in France and the others suggest lessening of inter-union frictions. It seems that European unions are becoming more "bread and butter" oriented, as U. S. unions have been since Gompers. On our side of the Atlantic we see a counter trend in the Auto Workers' withdrawal from the AFL-CIO in protest against that organization's "bread and butter" emphasis. Walter Reuther believes that labor organizations should be active in such community affairs as housing and race relations and should work more actively in the political arena to obtain employee benefits through legislation — somewhat of a shift to the classic European model of trade unionism.

Author's Recommended Reading List

Citrine, N. A., *Trade Union Law* (London: Stevens & Sons Limited, 1960).

Clegg, H. A., *A New Approach to Industrial Democracy* (Oxford: Basil Blackwell, 1963).

Cox, R. W., "Social and Labour Policy in the European Economic Community," *British Journal of Industrial Relations,* Vol. 1, No. 1, pp. 5-22 (London: London School of Economics and Political Science, 1963).

European Information Service, *The Cost of Labour in Europe,* Summary No. 2, July 1962 (London: Industrial Welfare Society, 1962).

Helin, Guy, *The Right to Strike and Conciliation Procedure in Belgium and Abroad* (Brussels: Fédération des Industries Belges, 1960).

Kahn-Freund, Otto, *Labor Relations and the Law, A Comparative Study,* British Institute Studies of International and Comparative Law No. 2 (London: Stevens & Sons Limited, 1965).

Kahn-Freund, Otto, *Labor Law: Old Traditions and New Developments,* (Toronto: Clarke, Erwin Co., 1968).

International Confederation of Free Trade Unions, *Workers' Participation in Industry,* Study Guide No. 3 (Brussels: International Confederation of Free Trade Unions, 1954).

"Labor Relations in France," *California Management Review,* Vol. 3, Summer 1961, pp. 46-63.

"The Law and the Strike; A Comparative Study of the Law of the Strike: Britain, France and the United States," *Symposium on Labor Relations Law,* California, 1961, p. 16.

Meyers, Frederic, *Ownership of Jobs: A Comparative Study,* (Los Angeles: Institute of Industrial Relations, University of California, 1964).

McPherson, William H., "European Variations on the Mediation Theme," *Lab. L.J.,* August 1955, pp. 525-536.

McPherson, William H., *Grievance Settlement Procedures in Western Europe,* (Proceedings of the 15th Annual Meeting, Industrial Relations Research Association, Pittsburgh, December 1962) (Urbana: University of Illinois, 1963).

Ross, Arthur M., "Prosperity and Labor Relations in Western Europe: Italy and France," 16 *Ind. & Lab. Rel. Rev.* 63-85 (October 1963).

Stagner, Ross, "Union-management Relations in Italy: Some Observations," *Current Economic Comment,* May 1957, pp. 3-15.

"Symposium: Comparative Labor Law and Law of the Employment Relation:" *Rutgers L. Rev.,* Vol. 18, No. 2 (Winter 1964).

COLLECTIVE BARGAINING IN NATIONS OF THE EUROPEAN ECONOMIC COMMUNITY

By L. H. J. CRIJNS

There is no uniformity in labor movements or collective bargaining practice in the six EEC countries. Instead we find a great variety of institutions, organizations, legal systems, and bargaining methods.

In the Netherlands there are three central workers' organizations — the Nationaal Verbond van Vakvereniginen (NVV), with about 570,000 members; the Nederlands Katholiek Vakverbond (NKV), with about 410,000 members; and the Christelijk Nationaal Vakverbond (CNV), with about 235,000 members. These three federations meet regularly in a Consultative Council. Together, they have approximately 1.2 million members. The number of union members as a proportion of total civilian employment is about 34 percent. There is also the Nederlandse Vakcentrale, which represents only 1 percent of the unionized workers.

In Belgium there are also three national federations — the Confédération des Syndicats Chrétiens (CSC), with about 800,000 members; the Fédération Générale du Travail de Belgique (FGTB), with about 700,000 members; and a small Liberal organization, the Centrale Générale des Syndicats Libéraux de Belgique (CGSLB), with about 120,000 members. These three organizations have about 1.6 million members. The degree of unionization is very high in Belgium — about 65 percent, the highest of all the EEC countries.

In France there are three central organizations — the Communist Confédération Générale du Travail (CGT), the Catholic Confédération Française Démocratique du Travail (CFDT, formerly CFTC), and the Socialist Confédération Générale du Travail-Force Ouvrière (CGT-FO). There is also a separate organization for civil servants and white collar workers, the Confédération Générale des Cadres (CGC). The exact numerical strength of these organizations is unknown. According to figures available, the three big federations have between 1.7 million and 3.4 million members in all. The Communist CGT appears to have as many as the CFDT and the CGT-FO together. Union membership can be estimated at about 20 percent of all persons in employment — the lowest figure in the EEC.

In Italy there are three major organizations (plus a number of small federations hardly worth mentioning) — the Communist Confederazione Generale Italiana del Lavoro (CGIL), the Catholic Confederazione Italiana Sindacati Lavoratori (CISL), and the Socialist Unione Italiana del Lavoro (UIL). Their exact strength is unknown, but an item in "Il Corriere della Sera" on 19 April 1964 put the CGIL's at 4 million members, the CISL's at 2.4 million and the UIL's at 1.5 million. At any rate, it is generally recognized that the Communist federation has about as many members as the other two combined. The degree of unionization is approximately 40 percent.

In Germany there are an estimated 7.8 million union members, 6.5 million of whom belong to the Deutscher Gewerkschaftsbund (DGB). Then there is the Deutscher Beamtenbund (DBB), with about 650,000 members; the Deutsche Angestelltengewerkschaft (DAG), with about 480,000; and the Christlicher Gewerkschaftsbund (CGB), with about 165,000. Unionization is about 30 percent.

Lastly, Luxembourg has three workers' organizations — the Socialist Confédération Générale du Travail (CGT), the Confédération Luxembourgeoise des Syndicats Chrétiens (CLSC), and the Communist Fédération Nationale des Ouvriers du Luxembourg (FNOL).[1]

EMPLOYERS' ORGANIZATIONS

There are fewer employers' organizations in the EEC nations. In the Netherlands there are two — the Verbond van Nederlandse Ondernemingen (VNO) and the Nederlandse Federatie van de Katholieke en Protestants Christelijke Werkgevers Verbonden (F.K.P.W.V.). Close consultation is maintained between these federations.

Generally speaking, there is a single employer's federation in each of the five other countries — in Germany the Bundesvereinigung der Deutschen Arbeitgeberverbände (together with the Bundesverband der Deutschen Industrie), in Belgium the Fédération des Industries Belges, in France the Conseil National du Patronat Français, in Italy the Confindustria, and in Luxembourg the Fédération des Industriels Luxembourgeois. Apart from these central organiza-

---

[1] It should also be mentioned that the free unions in the member countries are affiliated with the ICFTU and the denominational unions with the IFCTU, through a Community secretariat. The Communist unions are members of the WFTU, with which the EEC has no links.

tions, practically all the countries have separate bodies for agriculture, small business, and so on.[2]

Both the workers' and the employers' federations are subdivided according to industry. The Deutscher Gewerkschaftsbund, for instance, consists of 16 separate industrial organizations. In Belgium there are about the same number in the CSC and the FGTB. In Italy and France the number of organizations for individual industries is between 35 and 45. It is nearly always in the same industries that both unions and the employers' organizations have the highest membership or carry the most weight. Examples are metalworking, chemicals, textiles, construction, and mining.

LEVEL OF NEGOTIATIONS

At what level are wages negotiated? In Germany, for instance, the Deutscher Gewerkschaftsbund has little influence on wage determination. Wage policies are developed in the industry-level organizations. While some collective bargaining agreements cover the whole of the Federal Republic (for example, for the printing and allied trades and for the shoe industry), the general rule is one agreement for each Land or state. Agreements confined to a single firm are not very common. The Volkswagen works agreement is atypical.

German unions try to negotiate at a level as close as possible to the individual plant, whereas the employers prefer wage negotiations at top levels, such as for a whole industry. Most employers want to block union efforts to obtain maximum terms from the most profitable firms and then extend them to the entire industry concerned, even to marginal enterprises.

In France, negotiations can be carried on at the national or regional or firm level. There is no general rule. In the metalworking industries regional agreements are made. In the chemical industry national agreements are typical. There are about 250 single-plant agreements in France. An example is that of the Renault motor works, which caused a stir a few years ago by being the first to introduce four weeks' paid vacation each year — an advance that was

---

[2] The chief employers' organizations at EEC level are the Union des Industries de la Communauté Européenne (UNICE) for industry, the Comité des Organizations Commerciales des Pays de la CEE (COCCEE) for commerce, the Union Artisanale de la CEE (UACEE) for small business, the Comité des Organizations Professionnelles Agricoles (COPA) for agriculture, the Comité de Liaison des Transports Routiers Professionnels de la CEE for road haulers for hire and reward, the Comité de Liaison des Transporteurs Routiers pour Compte Propre de la CEE for road haulers on own account, the International Union for Inland Navigation, and the International Union of Railways.

extended to 75 percent of industry within a year and is now the general custom throughout the country.

In Italy the central organizations have always had a great influence on wage negotiations. Since 1954, however, the setting of wage differentials has been left to the single-industry organizations. A new tendency has been observed since 1963. The industry-wide agreements now leave room for additional agreements at the firm level embodying specific terms of employment. This is done, for instance, in the metalworking and mechanical engineering industries.

In Belgium, most collective bargaining is carried out by joint committees composed of equal numbers of worker and employer representatives. There are about 75 such committees. The majority of workers are covered by agreements concluded at the national level, though there are regional ones and agreements for separate firms.

In the Netherlands most of the collective bargaining is done at the industry or national level, with some at the regional level or for individual firms like Philips.

Another feature of some collective bargaining agreements in the six nations is that their terms can be made binding on a whole industry. The aim is to ensure that the negotiated terms are also observed by employers who are not members of the employers' organizations. There is seldom any need for this procedure in Germany, where all employers, whether or not they belong to the organizations, generally fall in line with the collective bargaining agreements. In France official request may be made to have agreements declared generally binding, but a series of conditions must first be fulfilled. In Belgium either or both of the parties to an agreement can apply to have it declared binding, but the option often is ignored — for instance, in such major industries as mining, metal processing, chemicals, and textiles. In the Netherlands the government can declare that a collective agreement has generally binding force once the College of Government Mediators has recommended such action to the Minister of Social Affairs. Binding wage agreements can also be made and enforced where there is no collective bargaining agreement. In Italy a collective bargaining agreement cannot at present be declared generally binding, but there is a tendency in the courts to impose the terms negotiated in collective bargaining agreements on everybody in the industry concerned.

CONTENT OF AGREEMENTS

The content of labor agreements often varies. Some deal with only a few employment matters, while others are quite voluminous.

Agreements may deal with all or some of the following: wages, working hours, paid holidays, public holidays, extra allowances, recruitment, promotion, dismissal, and industrial health and safety. Agreements may also be either general or very specific, as, for example, where they establish wage differentials according to major occupational group or function. In France there is a legal prohibition against linking wage increases to rises in the cost-of-living index. While there is no prohibition of such agreements in Germany, trade unions are opposed to such clauses. In Italy cost-of-living allowances are handled as indemnities (indennità di contingenza) that are calculated each three months. In the Netherlands there are no agreements with automatic upward adjustments based upon increases in the official index, but contracts running for periods in excess of one year have provisions for reopening for such adjustments in wages. In Belgium clauses for automatic cost-of-living adjustments are ordinarily found in labor agreements.

Sometimes there are separate agreements dealing only with wages and other agreements covering conditions of employment that, unlike wages, are not subject to frequent change, such as paid vacation and holidays. Sometimes a collective agreement will remain in force for years, with intervening agreements on specific points taking the form of appendices or addenda.

Until recently a significant difference between collective agreements in the Netherlands and in the other EEC countries was that agreed-upon wages in the Netherlands were at the same time the minimum and the maximum. Uniformity was imposed under a 1945 decree providing that negotiated wage agreements could be made effective only after government approval had been granted by the College of Government Mediators (College van Rijksbemiddelaars).

In the five other countries contractually established wages have constituted minimums only. Employers may not pay lower wages but are free to pay more, and in fact they nearly always do. In Germany, for instance, a special survey in 1962 showed that the difference between actual wages and agreed-upon wages was about 13 percent and in some parts of industry as much as 30 percent or more.

In the Netherlands collective bargaining agreements usually last a year, though there is a growing tendency to write them for longer terms (as at Philips and in the metalworking industries). In Germany agreements cannot last longer than 18 months and usually run for a year. Since 1963, an increasing number of agreements in Italy have been made for three-year periods. In Belgium agreements generally last a year. In France there is no regular custom, but agreements frequently are concluded for indeterminate periods. Wage increases in France usually antedate labor agreements; actual gains are consolidated later when the collective agreements or annexes to the agreements catch up.

THE ITALIAN LABOR MOVEMENT AND COLLECTIVE BARGAINING

By P. P. Fano

TENETS AND STRUCTURE OF THE LABOR MOVEMENT

Since the fall of fascism, the Italian Government has not interfered in the development of the labor movement. Legislation concerning labor-management relations has been minimal.

The Italian Constitution, adopted in 1947, proclaims and guarantees freedom of association and the right to engage in collective bargaining and strikes. The Constitution also contemplates the possibility of ordinary legislation to impose some objective conditions for the exercise of these rights. Despite the passage of two decades, such legislation has never been passed for want of a sufficient measure of agreement on its content. The only controlling legal norms applicable to trade union rights and collective bargaining now in effect are those embodied in ILO conventions ratified by Italy. They are of a general character.

In these circumstances, the Italian labor movement is autonomously organized. Employers' and workers' organizations have pragmatically built up a system of industrial relations based on mutually agreed practices and institutions. Although this process of self-determination has upon occasion deeply tested the sense of self-discipline and responsibility of both labor and management, by and large it has proved to be workable and successful.

The Italian labor movement has never been independent of political influences. In its origins in the latter part of the nineteenth century, it was promoted and shaped by the socialist, the Catholic, and the republican political movements, and it remained divided along these party lines until fascism deprived it of its freedom.

Italian labor organizations were united only for a few years immediately after the Second World War when it had seemed inevitably necessary that workers who had combined to resist the fascists and the Germans in the factories and in the maquis, irrespective of political affiliations, should continue in unity to meet the problems of postwar reconstruction.

Italy's first postwar government was formed by a coalition of all the anti-fascist parties, including the Communists. The labor movement was entirely contained in the Italian General Confederation of Labor (CGIL), which had been organized by a group of trade union and political leaders of every shade of anti-fascist opinion.

The honeymoon was full of misgivings while it lasted. By 1948 the Communists were forced out of the government. At about the same time, the democratic sectors of the labor movement became weary of the relentless attempts of the Communists to take over complete control of the organization and to implicate it in political agitations and departed from the Italian Confederation of Labor.

Today, the Italian labor movement is divided into three major confederations of trade unions and a number of independent unions which cater mainly to white-collar workers in the public services and the liberal professions. There is, in addition, a fourth confederation of trade unions, with a very limited following, that looks back nostalgically to the fascist corporative system.

The three major confederations of trade unions are the already-mentioned General Confederation of Labor (CGIL), which includes a Communist majority and a left-wing Socialist minority, the Catholic-oriented Italian Confederation of Trade Unions (CISL), and the Social Democratic Italian Union of Labor (UIL). None of these organizations has formal ties with the political parties, although many of their leaders are active in the political arena.

The principles underlining the policy of the Italian General Confederation of Labor are based on traditional Communist tenets: class warfare, the nationalization of the key sectors of the economy, and ultimately the overthrow of the capitalist economic and political system. Yet the approach of this organization to the practical problems of collective bargaining and labor relations in general is more flexible, realistic, and tolerant of the existing systems than would seem permissible by its ideology.

Within the framework of the Communist-controlled World Federation of Trade Unions, with which it is affiliated, the CGIL has distinguished itself by claiming the freedom to adapt its policies to the peculiar political, social, and economic situation obtaining in Italy and to cooperate closely with the democratic sectors of the labor movement, even at the cost of deviating from the official lines of international communism.

This disposition to compromise, corresponding to "the Italian way to communism" adopted by the Italian Communist Party, enables the CGIL to play a full role within the existing capitalistic system and to keep within its ranks its more moderate socialist wing. In the long run, it also tends to integrate the Confederation into the existing social system, and for this very reason the official policies are opposed by a group of its members who reject any compromise with the capitalistic society. All these different tendencies are present in the policy-making bodies of the organization, but the communist leadership plays the decisive role.

There are no significant basic ideological differences between the Catholic-oriented Italian Confederation of Trade Unions and the Social Democratic Italian Union of Labor. Both stand for interclass collaboration and recognize the role of free enterprise, subject to state intervention whenever the economic and social development of the country makes it desirable. They are both affiliated with the International Confederation of Free Trade Unions in Brussels. Their refusal to amalgamate can be explained only by the traditional influence of party politics.

It is not easy to make an objective assessment of the respective strength of the three confederations. In 1967 the CGIL claimed 3.3 million members, the CISL 2.5 million members, and the UIL 1.5 million members. These figures, whose aggregate amounts to almost 60 percent of the total number of wage earners and salaried employees, must be taken with caution.

Another indication of number of adherents among the industrial workers to each of the three confederations may be gathered from the results of the elections for members of the works committees. These committees are not formally a part of the trade union structure. Their function consists mainly in representing the workers at the plant level in connection with individual and group grievances. Works committees are elected by all the wage earners and the salaried employees in the plant, irrespective of their affiliation with a union. Nevertheless, the confederations are entitled to submit their separate lists of candidates, and from the successes of these candidates lists some idea of relative trade union strength may be gathered. In 1967, in 1585 industrial undertakings, 53 percent of the votes were cast for the candidates of the CGIL, 30 percent for those of the CISL, and 11 percent for those of the UIL. Only the remaining 6 percent went to other lists.

The organizational structures of the three big confederations are similarly molded. Each is characterized by a high degree of centralization fashioned to a degree from the fact that the reconstruction of the free trade union movement after the last war proceeded from the top down. Centralization also was made inevitable because collective bargaining has been carried out predominantly at the national level.

The unions affiliated with the confederations are organized nationwide by widely defined branches of industry, agriculture, and services, each including both manual and nonmanual workers. They have regional sections throughout the country.

The establishment of trade union sections at the plant level has so far been successfully resisted by the employers, but recent collective agreements have opened the door to collective bargaining at that level. The labor movement is pressing the question of trade union recognition at the plant level with increasing determination. Plant rules regarding the posting of trade union informational material inside the establishment, leave of absence for trade union officials to carry out their duties, and employers' checkoff of trade union dues have recently been liberalized.

The activities of the unions are guided strictly by the policies laid down by the respective confederations, and the confederations themselves almost invariably take an active part in collective bargaining together with the unions concerned.

For some years after the split of the labor movement, relations among the confederations were competitive, tense, and recriminatory. More recently, rivalry has abated and interconfederational relations have become closer. Although each may put a different emphasis on certain problems, give a different interpretation of the facts, and even disagree eloquently on principles of general policy, the three confederations and their respective unions almost invariably succeed nowadays in coordinating their claims and their tactics before going together to the bargaining table and, if need be, in organizing joint strikes. Sometimes, but not often, the common front is broken by the refusal of one of the organizations to sign an agreement which is acceptable to the others.

THE EMPLOYERS' ORGANIZATIONS

Because collective bargaining is conducted separately for the private and the government-controlled sectors of the economy, the employers in each sector are represented by different organizations.

In the industrial sector, the General Confederation of Italian Industry represents about 200 private employer associations embodying over 87,000 enterprises that operate in nearly all branches of industry and employ about 2-1/2 million workers. Private agricultural and commercial entrepreneurs are organized separately in other associations.

Enterprises in which the government owns the controlling majority of the shares are represented by Intersind, an association of some 140 undertakings operating mostly in the iron and steel industry, engineering, air transport, shipbuilding, road building, banking, and telecommunications and employing altogether about 300,000 workers. Another association, ASAP, represents the government-controlled petroleum and chemical industries.

State-controlled industries operate in fields which overlap with private enterprise and are required to conduct their business on a competitive basis and at the same time to set an example of progressive labor-management relations. The imposition of the role of exemplar is regularly exploited by employees and their unions to obtain from government-controlled industries concessions that can be used as precedents in bargaining with private employers. Such efforts seldom succeed, as labor policies in private and government-controlled industries do not tend to vary significantly and collective bargaining agreements governing the conditions of employment in both sectors are substantially equivalent.

COLLECTIVE BARGAINING

Under the Italian legal system collective agreements are considered private contracts, binding only the members of the organizations who have signed them. But there are no rules, legal or otherwise, governing trade union recognition for the purpose of collective bargaining, compelling parties to negotiate, or regulating their conduct during negotiations. In this situation, complicated by the plurality of the workers' organizations, a practical system has been evolved whereby all of the various unions with members in an industry are associated in the negotiation of the collective agreements affecting that industry.

The employers are legally bound by a collective agreement insofar as they are members of an association that is a party to the agreement and only in respect to the workers who are affiliated with a union that is also a party to the agreement. The agreements are applied in practice to all the workers in the industry concerned, irrespective of their trade union affiliation.

The basic collective agreements in the Italian industry are of two sorts. The first aims at uniform regulation of such nationwide and industry-wide employment benefits as equal pay for men and women, the sliding scales for the automatic adjustment of wages to changes in the cost of living, regional wage differentials, the organization and operation of the works committees, and procedures regarding individual and group dismissals. These agreements are negotiated between the General Confederation of Italian Industry, on the one hand, and the confederations of trade unions, on the other.

The second type of agreement determines conditions of employment the nation over for individual branches of industry, such as metals, engineering, textile, and chemicals. These lay down national standards for each industry regarding wages, salaries, piece-work rates, hours of work, overtime, annual holidays, separation allowances, job classification, and apprenticeship and include provisions concerning, welfare, special allowances, facilities for trade union leaders, and contract duration. These agreements are negotiated by the employers' association and the national unions concerned, with the assistance of their respective confederations.

Until a few years ago the application of the national agreements at the plant level and the granting of more favorable conditions than those called for in such an agreement was left as a general rule entirely to the discretion of the management, except in a number of instances when plant agreements of limited scope were negotiated by the works committees, which are not part of the trade union machinery.

The unions always objected to the exclusive role of management in the administration of the agreements at the plant level, but did not press the issue so long as working conditions and productivity remained fairly stable and uniform in the enterprises throughout the life of the agreements. In recent years, because of technological changes and industrial reorganization, working conditions began to undergo frequent changes, and productivity started to vary significantly from one plant to another. The unions promptly claimed the right to negotiate supplementary agreements at the plant level to complement the national standards or adapt them to the different circumstances obtaining in the various plants.

The question came to a head in 1962 in connection with the renewal of the national collective bargaining agreement for the metal trades and engineering industries. Overcoming strong resistance by both the government-controlled and the private enterprises, the Italian unions obtained a number of concessions which, with the necessary adaptations, have since been included in the national agreements covering many other branches of industry. Under these concessions, authorizations are contained in national agreements allowing the local representatives of the employers' and workers' organizations to negotiate, within the limits laid down in the national agreement itself, supplementary plant agreements concerning collective productivity bonuses, piece-work rates, and criteria of job classifications. Agreements of this kind were negotiated with some difficulty in 1967 in about 1,200 plants, principally in metal trades and engineering, food processing, chemicals, glass and ceramics, textiles, and building industries.

Settlement of Disputes

National collective bargaining agreements make provision for dealing with individual and group grievances arising in the undertakings in connection with the implementation of the agreements. The general rule is that these grievances must be taken up first by the works committee and the management. If no solution is reached at that level, the grievance must be referred for a further attempt at conciliation to the employers' and the workers' organizations concerned. In the last resort the workers may ask the local office of the Ministry of Labor to interpose its good offices, or they may take their grievances to the courts.

In a number of industries in which piece-work rates, productivity bonuses, and job classification have become matters for collective bargaining at the plant level, the employers' and workers' organizations are authorized by the national agreements to set up joint investigation and conciliation committees at plant level to deal with grievances arising from such matters. The worker members of these committees must be selected from among the employees of the plant concerned.

There are no rules, legal or otherwise, concerning the settlement of collective disputes of any nature, but some national collective agreements provide that collective disputes concerning their application are to be examined by the employers' and the workers' organizations who are parties to the agreements.

In particularly critical collective labor disputes it is customary for the Ministry of Labor to make its services available at the request of one of the parties or on its own initiative.

There are no rules concerning the calling or conduct of strikes, except that in most cases collective agreements contain an explicit guarantee of industrial peace for the duration of the contract.

Occupation of the premises by the workers during strike action, especially in connection with collective dismissals, is not infrequent and, although illegal, it is often tolerated by the authorities. Special arrangements are normally made for the safeguard of the installations during work stoppages. Wildcat strikes are rare, and when they occur they are promptly endorsed by one or another of the unions or by all.

Special forms of strikes, call "hiccup" or "checkered," are sometimes called by the unions. The former consist of work stoppages lasting for only a fraction of the working day; the others affect the various undertakings concerned at different times.

Participation in strikes, especially when they are jointly organized by the three confederations, is generally high. A recent trade union source puts it, for 1967, at 85 percent of the workers concerned. This seems an exaggeration. But the fact remains that since 1962 the number of hours lost in strikes has been greater and has involved a higher proportion of the working population in Italy than in any other country of the European Economic Community. On the other hand, the average length of the strikes is generally less in Italy than in the other countries of the community, mainly because of a lesser power of resistance of the Italian labor movement.

The impact of the modernization of Italian industry in industrial relations may be gleaned from the fact that in recent years wage claims have less frequently been a cause of strikes than modification of working rules, introduction of new job classifications, or layoff of personnel after labor-saving innovations.

THE ROLE OF THE LABOR MOVEMENT
IN ECONOMIC PLANNING
AND THE QUESTION OF ITS UNIFICATION

The atmosphere of understanding which has developed between the major labor organizations has been carried a step further by the call made upon them by the government to cooperate in the realization of the first national economic development program for 1966-1970.

The program does not rely on coercive measures for its implementation. It seeks most of all the voluntary compliance on the part of private employers and the labor movement with government guideposts which include, among other things, a selective investment policy, a wages and incomes policy, and financial and fiscal incentives.

The program does not rely on coercive measures for its implementation. It seeks most of all the voluntary compliance on the part of private employers and the labor movement with government guideposts which include, among other things, a selective investment policy, a wages and incomes policy, and financial and fiscal incentives.

In order to obtain their cooperation the government has consulted the employers' and workers' organizations in the preliminary phases of the elaboration of the program and is currently asking them to take part in joint tripartite meetings to discuss the measures which should be taken to stimulate its implementation. Meetings of this kind have been held recently in connection with employment policies and public and private capital investments in new industrial enterprises in the south.

Besides the important role that the labor movement has been called upon to play well beyond its traditional field, it is interesting to observe that on many of the questions raised by the national development program the big three labor confederations have consciously tried, and on various occasions have succeeded, to harmonize their views and present a common front.

In the light of so many instances of a coordinated policy and unity of action on the part of the three confederations, the question is now being squarely posed of their organic unification. Exploratory consultations to this end are currently being held among their leaders. So far, these consultations have not gone beyond an expression of a general willingness to pursue them further. Of the three organizations the Communist-dominated CGIL is the one which is pushing hardest for amalgamation. Within the others, opinions on this issue are divided and there is a good deal of suspicion as regards the intention of the Communists. On the other hand, the powerful Association of Italian Catholic Workers (A.C.L.I.), a non-trade-union organization, is conducting a nationwide campaign in favor of reunification.

What the outcome will be no one can tell, except that the eventual unification of the labor movement would require a complete reappraisal of the respective roles of the trade unions, on the one hand, and of the political parties, on the other.

In the light of Italian traditions, this is a very difficult problem. If it could be resolved and the three confederations could reunite, it is obvious that the bargaining power of labor would improve. On the other hand, the demagogic claims that are made sometimes by sectors of a divided labor movement for reasons of interunion competition will lose their *raison d'être* and the employers will not be the worse for it.

Author's Recommended Reading List

Adams, John Clarke, "Italy," *Comparative Labor Movements* (ed. Walter Galenson) (New York: Prentice-Hall, 1952).

Guigni, Gino, "Recent Developments in Collective Bargaining in Italy," *Int. Lab. Rev.*, Vol. LXXXXI, No. 4 (April 1965).

Gualtieri, Humbert L., *The Labor Movement in Italy* (New York: S. F. Vanni, 1946).

Horowitz, D. L., *The Italian Labor Movement* (Cambridge: Harvard University Press, 1963).

La Palombara, Joseph, *The Italian Labor Movement: Problems and Prospects* (Ithaca: Cornell University Press, 1957).

Neufeld, Maurice F., *Italy: School of Awakening Countries* (Ithaca: New York State School of Industrial and Labor Relations, Cornell University, 1961).

Reynaud, Jean-Daniel, "The Future of Industrial Relations in Western Europe: Approaches and Perspectives," International Institute for Labor Studies, Bulletin No. 4, February 1968.

Sanseverino, Luisa Riva, "Collective Bargaining in Italy," *Contemporary Collective Bargaining in Seven Countries* (ed. Adolf Sturmthal) (Ithaca: Institute of International Industrial and Labor Relations, Cornell University, 1957).

Sanseverino, Luisa Riva, "The Influence of International Labor Conventions on Italian Labor Legislation," *Int. Lab. Rev.*, Vol. LXXXIII (June 1961).

Labor Unions and National Politics in Italian Industrial Plants (Ithaca: Institute of International Industrial and Labor Relations, Cornell University, 1954).

NEGOTIATING A NEW WAGE STRUCTURE AT FORD OF BRITAIN

By ROBERT COPP

As a practical extension of what Mr. Fairweather has written for this volume — a pragmatic illustration of how these things work in one company in the United Kingdom — I shall describe labor relationships at Ford Motor Company and how they worked in the negotiation of a new wage structure in 1967. I will also comment briefly about the way in which Ford coordinates the labor relationships of its overseas affiliates in terms of some of the things that Mr. Belford has written for us.

This discussion has a good deal more topicality about it than we anticipated at the time that we decided to include a brief discussion of these negotiations in the Loyola conference, because, since the publication of the Report of the Royal Commission on Trade Unions and Employers' Associations,[1] many practitioners and commentators in Britain have cited Ford Motor Company Limited as one of the models of what the Royal Commission was talking about.

As Mr. Fairweather has pointed out, the conventional collective bargaining arrangements in the United Kingdom involve employer associations and confederations of trade unions. In the engineering industry (of which the motor industry is a part in its collective bargaining structure) these parties are the Engineering Employers' Federation and the Confederation of Shipbuilding and Engineering Unions. However, three major U. S. firms — General Motors, Massey-Ferguson, and Ford — do not conduct their collective negotiations as federated companies or as members of the Engineering Employers' Federation. And so Ford will illustrate more an exception to the system generally prevailing in the United Kingdom than an illustration of it.

The Ford Company in Britain did not recognize trade unions until 1944, when Ford undertook to operate for the Aircraft Production Ministry a Rolls-Royce aircraft engine plant at Manchester. It was government policy that management of these plants should deal with trade unions, and the company's relationships with trade unions really date from that time.

---

[1] Report of Royal Commission on Trade Unions and Employers' Associations, 1965-1968 (Cmnd. 3623), issued June 13, 1968.

109

As a result of the acquisition of other firms during the 1950s, the Ford management faced both a diversity of employment conditions and a variety of unions. Rationalization began with a Procedure Agreement in 1958 which, in effect, extends recognition to 21 unions and establishes a National Joint Negotiating Committee of representatives of the 21 unions and the management. This body, the National Joint Negotiating Committee, negotiates the basic wages and conditions of employment, and handles dispute settlement at the final level.

As the almost classic Chapter 3 of the Report of the Royal Commission (which outlines the present collective bargaining system in Britain) points out, there is both a formal and an informal system of relationships. In a sense, Ford is illustrative of this — the formal structure being the National Joint Negotiating Committee (which consists of national officers of the 21 unions) and the informal structure being the shop-steward organization, somewhat formalized in about 20 plant-level joint works committees.

The wage structure was one of the growing problems in relationships at Ford that had to be faced in 1967. Most important, Ford in Britain has never used a payment-by-results or incentive system. From the beginning, the wage system has been a day-rate system, but the structure was almost too simplified. It consisted of four wage grades: one for females (observing the traditional female differential in Britain) and three others for male operatives — an unskilled grade, a semiskilled production grade (in which about 80 percent of the employees were classified), and a skilled grade. The proliferation of company operations and the growing technological complexity of these operations all prompted the management, beginning about five or six years ago, to take a much closer look at this oversimplified wage structure. The management had adopted a merit pay plan, which as operations grew in complexity, was used less for merit than for the recognition of job differentials. There was a three- or four-year internal management discussion as to whether something should not be done about the wage structure before a decision was taken in June 1967 to propose study of possible revisions to the Ford National Joint Negotiating Committee.

The unions were generally receptive. They agreed that they would cooperate and attempt to induce their members and the shop stewards to cooperate in the massive job of job evaluation, if the unions' national officials could be assured that no one would lose as a result of this exercise. The company quickly undertook to make this commitment.

The management departed somewhat from its normal approach

in these matters in retaining a firm of outside consultants, Urwich, Orr & Partners, Ltd. There were two reasons for this. First, in order to assure the cooperation of the trade unions, one had to involve a disinterested third party. The consultants served most effectively in this role — the unions never complained that the management was trying to put something over on them. Second, Urwich, Orr & Partners, Ltd. brought to the exercise a great deal of expert information about wage payment systems, primarily in the United Kingdom — information that, despite all of its resources, the corporate labor relations staff in the United States was not in a position to provide.

A massive operation, the exercise went through several stages. First was the information stage. The managing director of the company tape-recorded a report which told all shop stewards on the same day throughout 20 Ford plants in Britain what the exercise was all about. The employee newspaper explained the exercise to all employees. This was part of a general effort right at the threshold to tell employees what was going on. Of course, this had already been done with the trade unions through the National Joint Negotiating Committee.

Next, the consultants and the Ford of Britain labor relations staff identified 56 benchmark jobs. They undertook the training of 100 company job evaluators and identified some 3,000 different job titles in the company. The 100 trained job analysts or job evaluators then wrote some 1,800 profiles or job descriptions, using a 28-characteristic format provided by the consultants. Close to a half million pieces of paper resulted from this exercise before it was done.

Again, in order to keep shop stewards and in-plant management involved, divisional review committees were established in eight operating components of the company. The coordinating of the actual checking of the job profiles was done by a central review committee on which the National Joint Negotiating Committee had its own member privy to all of the decision-making process.

Once the fact-finding exercise of describing these 1,800 jobs was completed, there came the task of ranking them. From this evolved eventually the idea of a five-grade wage structure, followed by the grading of specific jobs.

By February 1967, a scant nine months after the project had really started, the ranking and grading proposals had been completed and the board of directors of the British company approved the proposal in principle. The corporate staffs in Dearborn, Mich., reviewed it primarily in terms of costs, and the British management presented it to the National Joint Negotiating Committee on April 10, 1967. During the ensuing three months, there was a good deal of internal discussion by the 21 union representatives with their respective executives as to the acceptability of the proposals. In July 1967, the proposals were agreed to.

The company, under the 1967 incomes policy of the United Kingdom, had said that the proposals would have to be accompanied by appropriate and meaningful productivity bargaining. This proved to be a six-month exercise of varying but generally acceptable results.

Furthermore, in a major exercise like this the parties could not hope to resolve all of the disputes in one meeting of the National Joint Negotiating Committee, so the parties agreed to a separate expedited procedure to deal with the individual grading complaints and disputes. One of these disputes received a good deal of press publicity in 1968.

The sewing machinist classification (these are the operators who sew the soft trim materials made into seat cushions, inside padding, the cloth headlining in the vehicle, and so forth) had, as a result of the evaluation process, been graded in the lower of two semiskilled grades. The operators contended that they were highly specialized people, that the evaluation was wrong, and that they ought to be in the higher paid of the two semiskilled classifications. The dispute originally arose in terms of grading. Without even pursuing their complaint through the special procedure, the operators (nearly all of whom were women) began unofficial strikes, first in the Dagenham (London) plants and shortly thereafter in the Halewood (Liverpool) plants, on this issue of grading. But one of the union officials on the National Joint Negotiating Committee opportunistically seized upon this dispute and turned it around to achieve another objective that he was working on as well — equal pay for women.

The company had suggested in July 1967, when it made its basic proposals to the National Joint Negotiating Committee, that it might be appropriate to consider the female differential written into the proposals. The differential had been set at about 75 percent of the male rates at Ford of Britain and, in the new proposals, was revised to 85 percent of the male rates. But the trade unions showed no real interest in discussing any further reduction in the female differential until early June 1968.

The dispute quickly shut down assembly operations at Ford of

Britain because these trim components are essential to the final assembly of the vehicle. Mrs. Barbara Castle, the First Secretary of State for Employment and Productivity, appointed a Court of Inquiry about a week after the strike began. Usually, in Britain, when a Court of Inquiry is appointed, the employees promptly return to work. But in this dispute the ladies and their representatives wanted certain commitments both from the management and from the court, primarily that they were going to get "something" out of this, before they would return to work. In a Friday meeting, eight ladies (an ad hoc committee of the operators) met with Mrs. Castle, and she was able to convince the ladies that the company would give sympathetic attention to their claims if they would just return to work. After weekend meetings of the employees, they did return to work on the following Monday.

One of the principles observed by Ford Motor Company Limited and other Ford companies is that managements normally do not bargain with unofficial or wildcat strikers or their representatives. Within two hours after the ladies resumed work on the Monday morning, the National Joint Negotiating Committee met and the management proposed to reduce the female differential from 85 percent to 92 percent of the male rate. The original issue about the grading and the company's concern about the violation of procedure in undertaking the unofficial strike were referred to the Court of Inquiry.[2]

LESSONS LEARNED

Now, what have we learned from this negotiation of a new wage structure?

The first lesson — and I am glad to have it reinforced by Mr. Belford — is that management must take the initiative in seeking reform and change. The management at Ford of Britain may have delayed too long in its internal discussions about undertaking the task of revising its wage structure and securing agreement to the changes. But whatever the case, the management seized and pursued the initiative in this set of negotiations.

---

[2] In its Report (Cmnd.3749), issued August 13, 1968, the Court of Inquiry concluded that the dispute was about grading (not equal pay) and recommended that the grading question be reviewed by an ad hoc committee, which subsequently affirmed the original grading. In commenting on violation of procedure by members of two unions, the court said that it was "far from satisfied that all reasonable measures had been taken to resolve the problem before the machinists went on strike and the two unions supported their action."

Second, we learned the effectiveness of laying the ground work (in terms of communication and consultation) for a major move like this in employee relations. The negotiations were atypical of much of British industry in the degree of consultation with the trade unions at the National Joint Negotiating Committee, in the involvement of a trade union nominee in the actual job evaluation process, in consultations at the joint works committee level in the plants and, most notably, in terms of direct employee communication.

Third, the whole exercise proved the value of using and reinforcing existing collective bargaining institutions. The Ford National Joint Negotiating Committee, composed, as it is, of national trade union officials, tends to be somewhat isolated from the shop floor level, where the employees are represented by shop stewards meeting periodically in their plant-level joint works committees. The management at Ford of Britain conscientiously attempted to reduce this distance and remoteness by keeping the National Joint Negotiating Committee intimately informed about what was going on. And, by using that committee as the forum in which the major decisions were made, the management enhanced and reinforced that major part of the collective bargaining machinery at Ford of Britain. Likewise, the National Joint Negotiating Committee remains the ultimate agency for the resolution of any disputes that arise under the new structure or under its implementation.

Fourth, the exercise was most useful in refining some notions about a rather cloudy area — the distinctions between *consultation* with the employees and their representatives and *negotiation* of matters properly negotiable or subject to agreement.

Finally, for us at the parent company labor relations staff, the lesson we learned again from this generally successful exercise was that negotiations like this are best left in the intelligent hands of the local management. The British management wrote the show and played the parts. This responsibility of the local management remains a cornerstone of Ford's overseas labor affairs policy.

On the whole, we remain quite satisfied with the institutions that Ford Motor Company Limited has developed for its collective bargaining and cooperation with the trade unions. We feel that they have the potential to realize most of the objectives that the Royal Commission seeks for the improvement in industrial relations in Britain. And, finally, we in the corporate staff intend (for the foreseeable future, at least) to leave the achievement of those objectives in the intelligent hands of local management at Ford of Britain.

Ford of Britain: A 1969 Postscript

In the preceding article I described how Ford of Britain concluded a major wage-structure-reform agreement effective in July 1967. The agreement included a union undertaking that it should "subsist" for two years. Because collective labor agreements are not legally enforceable in Britain, commitments about duration are seldom meaningful. I did not mention in my original article that shortly after devaluation of the pound sterling in November 1967, Ford of Britain began to receive a variety of union demands for a further wage increase, for layoff benefits, for improved pensions and sick absence payments, for a liberalized vacation bonus, and for other changes.

Commencing September 23, 1968, the layoff-benefit demand was pressed by an overtime ban that seriously affected production. Management decided to begin negotiations in order to secure a lifting of the ban. The ban was lifted about November 30, 1968, upon Ford's declaration of a willingness to confer with the National Joint Negotiating Committee. However, the management decided to pursue a "package" concept in the negotiations so that it could achieve some of its own objectives — most notably restraints on wildcat strikes — in an overall settlement.

A settlement was reached on February 11, 1969, to be effective March 1. The settlement agreement was approved by a majority of the trade union representatives on the National Joint Negotiating Committee. It provided an 8-percent general wage increase for most employees, layoff benefits based on 66-2/3 percent of pay, and an annual vacation bonus liberalized from five pounds (about one day's pay) to a maximum of 25 pounds (about one week's pay).

The layoff benefits were new at Ford of Britain but had been provided earlier in varying forms elsewhere in the industry. Under the 1969 agreement, the layoff benefits were to be paid entirely by the company. The government does not permit supplementation of state benefits for unemployed persons, but does provide modest weekly National Assistance payments to the nonworking spouse and children of an unemployed person, which (for a married employee) would raise his "total benefit" above the 66-2/3 percent of pay provided by the company. In each layoff, the company agreed to pay its benefit for up to 10 days for employees with more than two years of service and for up to five days for employees with at least six months but less than two years of service. The plan applied to layoffs or short-time working, of at least a full shift's duration, caused by failure of supplies for whatever reason external to the company or by a temporary shortage of work resulting from trade recession. The company benefit was not to be paid for any layoff or short-time working caused directly or indirectly by any disruptive concerted action within any of the company's plants or establishments.

Because disciplinary action for participation in unconstitutional actions is neither customary nor accepted in Britain, sanctions for individual participants in wildcat strikes and similar forms of concerted "unconstitutional action" were built into the new layoff benefits and into the added portion of the vacation bonus. A participant in such unconstitutional action would forfeit his eligibility for layoff benefits for six months after the incident and would forfeit the 20 pounds added portion of the annual vacation bonus.

RESISTANCE TO ORIGINAL SETTLEMENT

The settlement was accepted by a majority — but not all — of the 19 unions.[3] The joint union negotiating committee has, since its inception nearly 15 years ago, allotted one vote to each of the constituent unions, irrespective of each union's membership at Ford, and has traditionally taken its decisions by majority vote of the unions. A clear majority of the unions voted for the February 11 settlement, but the representative of Transport and General Workers Union, the largest union in Ford of Britain, abstained and the representative of the Amalgamated Union of Engineering and Foundry Workers, the second largest, voted against it. The representatives of the two large unions objected primarily to the specified built-in sanctions against unconstitutional action.

Plant-level resistance to the sanctions arose among militant shop stewards, who quickly perceived how the reduction of benefits would undercut their power to seek local management concessions by calling wildcat ("unofficial") strikes or imposing unofficial overtime bans. Several shop-steward caucuses successfully generated support for wildcat strikes opposing the settlement, and a major wildcat strike began in one plant on February 21 and quickly spread to other plants. Although union members customarily do not ratify settlements in Britain, the management proposed a company-wide secret ballot on acceptance of the settlement, but the unions declined the proposal.

---

[3] By union amalgamations after the 1967 settlement, the unions represented on the National Joint Negotiating Committee had been reduced to this number.

ATTEMPT TO SECURE LEGAL ENFORCEMENT

After the two largest unions declared the wildcat strike "official" as to their members, who together constituted a majority of the hourly employees of Ford of Britain, the management decided to test the common notion that collective labor agreements are not legally enforceable in Britain. Mr. Justice Geoffrey Lane of the High Court issued an *ex parte* temporary injunction against the two largest unions, the effect of which was to restrict the spread of the strike. But, after hearing arguments by union counsel, Mr. Justice Lane on March 6, 1969, declined to extend the injunction. He ruled that the settlement memorandum duly signed by company representatives and by the chairman and secretary of the unions' negotiating committee was not an enforceable contract. He noted that the individual unions had nowhere explicitly bound themselves to accept majority-vote determinations by the negotiating committee and that the defendant unions had not individually signed the settlement memorandum. Furthermore, he found no evidence of an intent of the parties that their agreements should be enforceable — an expression of intent that he deemed essential to overcome the general assumption about nonenforceability of collective labor agreements in Britain.[4]

GOVERNMENT CONCILIATION AND STRIKE SETTLEMENT

Provoked by their distaste for legal intervention in labor relations, top union officials intervened to seek a negotiated settlement. What followed was under the watchful eye of Mrs. Castle, First Secretary of State for Employment and Productivity, whose efforts in another Ford matter I have earlier described. Mrs. Castle's concern arose both because of the balance-of-payments impact of the loss of export income from the strike (Ford of Britain exports 43 percent of its production) and because, as one of the administrators of the Prices and Incomes Act, she deemed the sanctions, or something like them, as essential *quid pro quo* for the 8-percent general wage increase for most employees in the settlement.

In the revised settlement that resulted after a strike of nearly four weeks, the principle of unconstitutional-action sanctions was retained, but the restraints will operate on a plant-level basis rather than an individual-offender basis. The company will set aside week-

---

[4] As this is written, the only available citation to the judgment of Mr. Justice Geoffrey Lane is the Law Report of *The Times* of London, March 7, 1969, p. 8.

ly per-capita contributions for a company-wide layoff-benefit account and for 30 plant-level vacation-bonus accounts. But the company will cancel these contributions for a plant in any week in which an unconstitutional incident occurs in the plant. Weekly per-capita contributions amount to four shillings ($0.48) for the layoff-benefit account and 10 shillings ($1.20) for the vacation-bonus account.

The contribution for the layoff-benefit account is based on provision of layoff benefits at levels established in the original settlement and on recent layoff history at the company. Any surplus in the company-wide benefit account at year-end will be transferred into the 30 plant-level vacation-bonus accounts, with pro-rata reductions applicable to plants that experienced unconstitutional incidents during the accumulation year.

The contribution for the plant-level vacation-bonus accounts is set at a level to provide an annual bonus of 25 pounds (about one week's pay) for employees in plants with incident-free records during the qualifying year. The settlement provides a minimum annual vacation bonus of 15 pounds for employees with a full year's service. How much more than that an individual employee's bonus will amount to is dependent upon his plant's experience in terms of unconstitutional action and his plant's share of any year-end surplus in the layoff-benefit account.

The amount of the general wage increase in the original settlement, 8 percent for most employees, was a secondary but important issue in the strike-settlement discussions. The unions again raised their demand for "parity" with higher earnings in many other companies in the motor industry which result from loosely administered incentive systems. Ford of Britain has always paid time or day rates. Although the original wage settlement was unchanged in the strike settlement, in the circumlocutions often characteristic of labor agreements in Britain, the Ford management acknowledged its readiness to respond to a union request to commence discussions on the subject of parity of rates within the motor industry in Britain.

Because collective labor agreements are not legally enforceable, the 1969 Ford of Britain agreement, effective from March 1, 1969, will be of indefinite duration. In the strike-settlement discussions, however, senior officials of three large unions undertook not to subject the company to any economic demands before July 27, 1970, a date one year beyond the declared, but unenforceable, duration of the "two year" major wage structure agreement of July 1967 described in my original paper.

GENERAL STRIKES

By Lee C. Shaw

I. THE FRENCH GENERAL STRIKE OF 1968

The Events

The May 1968 general strike throughout the industrial centers of France was similar to the general strike of 1936. Then the threat of fascism provided the communists and the socialists with a common cause and united the communist and socialist unions in joint demands for wage increases, the 40-hour week, paid vacations, nationalization of key industries, and national economic planning. Union demands in May 1968 were comparable to those of 1936.

The 1936 settlement — the so-called "Matignon Agreement" — with the Leon Blum government was estimated to increase labor costs by 43.5 percent. About 15 weeks after the settlement the franc was devalued. The Blum government fell soon after the Matignon settlement because of the financial crisis created by this inflationary increase in labor costs.[1]

In 1968 unions and many employees contended that the Gaullist government had neglected domestic social programs which had produced a reservoir of pent-up demands for the unattained and lost goals of the 1930s. Some French businessmen agreed that the French worker had been treated unfairly as compared with his counterpart in other West European countries.

Economic Factors

Wages

Except for Italy, French wages are the lowest in the six-nation Common Market. The Common Market Executive Commission has reported that in 1967 the average French industrial worker made the equivalent of 79 cents per hour. This compares with 68 cents in Italy, 96 cents in the Netherlands, $1.00 in Belgium, $1.15 in West Germany, and $1.29 in Luxembourg. Wages have been rising more slowly than in all the other countries of the Common Market except Luxembourg. Between April 1964 and October 1966 (the latest pe-

---

[1] *The Times* (London), May 25, 1968.

riod surveyed), the average increase in France was 15 percent. It was 20 percent in West Germany, 18 percent in Italy, 23 percent in the Netherlands, and 24 percent in Belgium. Even after the substantial wage increases granted in May and June of 1968, French wages were the lowest in the Common Market countries, excepting only Italy.

Another standard — that of wage increases in Western Europe in the decade 1958-1968 — shows France behind her neighbors. French wages during the period rose 87 percent, while in Italy wages rose 95 percent, in West Germany 99 percent, and in Holland 103 percent. Also in this period, France's cost of living went up approximately 45 percent, the largest increase in the Common Market. West Germany's cost of living, for example, increased only half as rapidly.[2]

The average workweek in France is also the longest — 47 hours (time and one-fourth between 40 and 48 hours, and time and one-half after 48 hours).[3] By early 1968 the amount of overtime work available had been reduced and there was spotty unemployment.

While money wages in France rose steadily over the past decade, real wages leveled off during the year preceding May 1968 mainly because of special price increases in the nationalized industries effected in the summer of 1967. In addition, social security was raised in October 1967 by about $600 million, and the increase was charged to employees rather than to employers because employers traditionally pass all increases directly on to consumers through higher prices.[4] These factors, combined with a decline in total hours worked, led to a decrease in the wage package in real terms.

This slowly rising wage structure, unsatisfactory to the work force, was not compelled by the economic condition of France and could have been avoided, according to a *New York Times* editorial (May 26, 1968). The country had been kept on a "tight belt" not simply to speed investment and economic progress, but also to advance de Gaulle's personal foreign policy, including his nuclear striking force and his determination to build a large gold hoard (over $5 billion) in the summer of 1968 to support his attack on what he considered to be a world monetary system controlled by the United States.

[2] Editorial, "Grass Roots Rebellion," *The New York Times*, May 28, 1968.
[3] Vicker, Ray, "French Chaos Weakens the Franc," *Wall Street Journal*, May 23, 1968, pp. 1, 22.
[4] *Id.* at p. 37.

The question facing de Gaulle was whether to give domestic matters priority over foreign policy, something he had been reluctant to do in the past.

Inflation and Devaluation

Since World War II, French economic policy has been to allow a high rate of inflation at home and to redress the imbalance periodically by devaluation. Pierre Uri, one of the architects of the European community, characterized the improvement in the French balance of payments as the most creditable achievement of the de Gaulle regime. He attributed the result to the particularly rapid development of export sales to Common Market countries (French exports increased by more than 300 percent from 1958-1968) and to a considerable inflow of American investment. Uri remarked:

> "It appears ironic that the French surplus relies on the construction of Europe, which the General opposed before his return to power, and on American expansion in Europe, which, once in power, he tried to block."[5]

The Power Play

The events of May brought together the leaders and the rank and file of ideologically distinct and rival unions. While this was significant, one must remember that only 20 to 25 percent of all French employees belong to unions and of those not more than 10 percent are believed to be up to date in the payment of union dues. The majority of the striking employees were not union members, and it appears that the real cause of the strike was a feeling of frustration on the part of the French workers.

Labor relations aspects of the crisis of May and June of 1968 are best understood if two important features of French social, economic, and political life are kept in mind: (1) the role played by the Communist Party and the communist-dominated CGT (the largest of the French unions); [6] and (2) the dominant role played by the French government, the country's major employer. [7]

The interplay of the strategies of the French communist Politburo and of the communist-dominated CGT on the one hand, and

---

[5] Uri, Pierre, "No Bouquets for the Fifth Republic," *The Times* (London), May 21, 1968, p. 17.

[6] *Labor Digest*, No. 72, U. S. Department of Labor (1965).

[7] A third feature could be added: the pervasive role of history in the lives of the French people. Social historians will be hard put to avoid making comparisons between 1968 and 1936. It is generally agreed that one has to go back to 1936 and the Popular Front for a parallel to the 1968 strike.

the defensive response of the government on the other, resulted in the pattern settlements which went a long way toward meeting the demands of the unions and employees generally, and at the same time repelled a most serious challenge to a fundamentally capitalistic society based on concepts of private property.

The Spreading Strike

Among the first enterprises seized or shut down by the employees during the week of May 13 were:

(1) Sud-Aviation at Chateau-Bougon near Nantes and at Toulouse (the latter being the location at which the Concorde supersonic airliner is being assembled).[8]

(2) The Renault factories at Cleon near Rouen and at Boulougne-Billancourt just southwest of Paris, at Flins, at Sandouville near Le Havre, at Lemans, and in Orleans.[9]

(3) The Berliet Works (trucks) and Rhodiacéta (textiles and synthetic fibers) at Lyons, the French National Railroads (SNCF), and the naval shipyards at Le Havre.[10] The strike spread from these large enterprises to small factories, and by May 31 most factories were shut down. Ports were closed, railroads and busses stopped running, and utilities were affected by periodic blackouts.

On May 23 the French police, speaking through the major police unions, expressed sympathy for the strike movement. Although they did not threaten to strike, the police warned the government not to "systematically" put the police in opposition to "workers fighting for their demands." [11]

The farm population also decided to protest the government farm policy which had sought to move them off the land. On May 25 they established roadblocks disrupting highway traffic and called for strong government protection of their interests in Common Market negotiations.[12]

Also on May 25, the reporters and newscasters of the government-owned television network struck. For the preceding few

[8] Tanner, Henry, "French Workers Occupy Plant," *New York Times*, May 16, 1968, pp. 1, 4.

[9] Tanner, Henry, "Pompidou Asserts Mounting Unrest Imperils France," *New York Times*, May 17, 1968, pp. 1, 14; Mortimer, Edw., "Pompidou Consults Security Chiefs," *The Times* (London), May 18, 1968, p. 1.

[10] Mortimer, Edw., note 9, *supra*.

[11] Hess, John L., "Regime is Warned by French Police," *New York Times*, May 24, 1968, pp. 1, 8.

[12] Pare, Eric, "Farmers of France in Massive Protests," *New York Times*, May 25, 1968, pp. 1, 17.

days the only programs had been news, and then even the news disappeared. The striking journalists had said they would work in the public interest as long as there was hope that they could cover the news objectively. By the time of the general strike, they said this hope had vanished.[13]

By the end of May it was estimated by the National Statistical Institute in Paris that nearly 20 million people throughout France were affected by the strike.[14]

Communist Influence

In the political life of France, as in its labor relations, the communists are engaged in a crafty and mischievous power play in response to de Gaulle's equally crafty and mischievous policy of fraternizing with communism abroad while curbing it at home. Although the CGT is about the same size as its two rival unions (the Confederation Francaise Democratique du Travail, CFDT; and the Force Ouvriere, FO), since the days of the Fourth Republic (1945-1958) the two rivals have received most of the government's subsidies for the training of union officials and have named French labor delegates to international bodies such as the European Economic Community. Some observers believe the communists have been more concerned with political goals than with satisfying the bread-and-butter demands of the labor movement. It is too early to reach this conclusion, but both political and union power demands were involved in the current events.

The CGT [15] and the two other national labor federations (CFDT and FO) originally refrained from calling a *general* strike and were content to let the rank and file at each plant decide what action was most appropriate.[16] However, once the strikes spread, the CGT urged all employees to endorse the strike movement. At the same time the CGT took pains to urge supporters to limit demands to traditional union goals such as higher pay and shorter hours. It did not suit the communists and their allies to join in the anarchy advocated by extremist student groups.[17] While undoubt-

---

[13] Tanner, Henry, "Regime Lifts Minimum," *New York Times*, May 26, 1968.

[14] "Strikes Affect 20 Million," *The Times* (London), May 22, 1968, p. 1. *Cf.* "Paris Exchange is Closed," *Wall Street Journal*, May 22, 1968, p. 4.

[15] Mortimer, Edw., "Paris Students March," *The Times* (London), May 18, 1968, p. 1.

[16] Hargrave, Charles, "Red Flag Flies Over the Shipyards of France," *The Times* (London), May 20, 1968, p. 8; Mortimer, Edw., "Warning by DeGaulle Against Continuation of Disorders," *The Times* (London), May 30, 1968, p. 1.

[17] See Ricklefs, Roger, "De Gaulle Works on Plan to Boost Power of Students, Workers as Crisis Deepens," *Wall Street Journal*, May 22, 1968, p. 4.

edly willing to take credit for the achievement of mere improvement in the economic status of French workers, Georges Séguy, Chief Executive of the CGT, told an American correspondent he did not care to be "the Brigitte Bardot of this strike."[18]

One journalist referred to the role of the communists in the strikes as follows: "The communists have climbed on the bandwagon but only to put the brakes on."[19] There are many reasons why the French communists appeared to support the established order, and why the CGT leadership spoke publicly against the "troublemaking and provocative elements in the University."[20]

A French journalist explained the role of the communists as follows:

> "It is not at all astonishing that in these conditions the CGT militants were all instructed to come out against the 'irresponsible elements' and to remind their Comrades that the principal objective of the workers' movement was to better the lot of the workers. Militants carried out their task and their consciences were not excessively disturbed; most of them have known extreme poverty and find it absurd to ally themselves with young people bored with the consumer society."

He concluded, "France reached the point where those who formerly we called reformists had become revolutionary, and those who had the reputation of revolutionaries were behaving like firm partisans of the maintenance of order."[21]

On May 29 the leaders of the historically moderate CFDT supported the CGT in taking the position that the present government was incapable of satisfying the workers' demands. The CFDT wanted to see Pierre Mendès-France returned to power.[22]

As the strikes spread and negotiations began, the CFDT proved to be the most militant union. It was the CFDT, and not the CGT, that pressed for more union activity at the plant level. When de Gaulle finally announced his determination to stay in power, the socialists reacted in blind rage but Séguy quietly backed down.

---

[18] "Voice of French Strikers: Georges Séguy," *New York Times*, May 23, 1968, p. 15.

[19] "A Revolution Set Alight by Students, Snuffed Out By Communists," *The Economist*, May 25, 1968, p. 21.

[20] Ullman, Marc, "Why the French Communists Support the Established Order," *The Times* (London), May 29, 1968, p. 11; *Cf.* Hargrave, Charles. "De Gaulle Winning Move May be a Referendum," *The Times* (London), May 21, 1968.

[21] Ullman, Marc, note 20, *supra*.

[22] Mortimer, Edw., note 16, *supra*.

Role of the Government

The role of the French government is twofold: First, it is the employer, not only of most employees in transportation, coal, and utilities, but also of some in manufacturing, such as those at the Renault auto works. Second, it must be concerned with the state of the economy as a whole.

The terms and conditions of employment in the publicly owned industries and at Renault and other related companies have in the past set the pattern for employment conditions in private industry.

Equally important, of course, is the role of the government in broad economic planning. A delicate balance had to be struck between reaching an agreement on wage increases and the welfare of the economy. Well before the current crisis, many sectors of French industry were in serious trouble. The foreign editor of *Paris Match*, Rene Dabernat, reports that in 1967 "the electrical equipment industry, a good barometer for measuring competitiveness, suffered a real setback, with French exports in this field dropping by 23.6 percent on the German market and 45.9 percent on the Italian market. Sales in France of similar equipment made in Germany and Italy rose by 26 percent and 51 percent, respectively." [23]

The inflationary settlements which have come out of the 1968 negotiations will make it even more difficult for French manufacturers to compete with manufacturers located in other countries. Unless imports are restricted and subsidies paid for exported products, the future would not appear to be bright for the French balance of trade.

May and June Negotiations

The three major unions — the CGT, the CFDT, and the FO — announced on May 22 that they were ready to take part in negotiations with the government. In a joint statement the CGT and the CFDT announced that they would not accept unilateral government decisions. [24]

The largest employer association, the Conseil National du Patronat Français, participated in the national negotiations and later in negotiations at the regional level. But these tripartite negotiations had to be ratified by employees at the plant level.

---

[23] De Gaulle Crisis Measures Inadequate," *The Times* (London), May 29, 1968.

[24] "French Unions Ready to Negotiate Over Crisis," *The Times* (London), May 23, 1968.

At the same time these national negotiations were going on, the workers and their local trade union representatives were formulating their demands at the plant level. Workers were demanding a variety of concessions ranging from substantial wage increases to the lowering of the retirement age from 65 to 60 for men and 55 for women; longer vacations; a universal 40-hour week without loss of pay; and a restoration of the 1967 cuts in social security.

On May 22 the CGT and the CFDT jointly announced that the unions would negotiate for unspecified pay raises; a monthly minimum wage of 600 francs (1,000 francs for certain operations such as Renault); guaranteed jobs; progressive reduction of hours of work without loss of pay; and the extension of union bargaining rights in industry. The socialist FO repeated the last two demands and called for wage increases with priority for the lowest-paid workers. The FO wanted a monthly minimum wage of 650 francs, social and economic measures to ensure jobs for all, expanded unemployment protection, and an improved National Health Service.[25]

The Grenelle Protocol

The government, the unions, and the Patronat came to an understanding set forth below on May 25, now known as the "Grenelle Protocol"[26] after the location of the Social Affairs Ministry on the Rue de Grenelle in Paris:

(1) *Minimum Wage*: An increase effective June 1, 1968, in the minimum wage to an average of three francs an hour from an average of 2.2 francs, an increase of about 36 percent.[27] *There will be no regional variations as in the past.* This is roughly the equivalent of an increase in the minimum wage from 45 cents an hour to 60 cents an hour. This generally met union demands, although in some higher-paid industries workers insisted on much higher minimums. On May 31 this minimum wage was extended by government decree to agricultural workers for increases up to 57 percent.

(2) *General Wage Increase*: A 10 percent increase in wages in two steps was offered — 7 percent on June 1, 1968 and 3 percent on October 1, 1968 — based on rates as of January 1. Raises granted earlier in 1968 were included in these percentages. For example, many manufacturing concerns had granted a 3 percent increase in

---

[25] *Ibid.*

[26] See, for example, Ricklefs, Roger, "French Workers Spurn Big Package Offer," *Wall Street Journal*, May 28, 1968.

[27] Training allowances, housing loans, and other benefits are calculated on the basis of the minimum wage.

February 1968; this was considered to be an offset against the 7 percent due June 1, 1968.

(3) *Cost of Living*: The CGT demanded that wages be pegged to the cost of living. This demand was particularly objectionable to French employers. The government agreed to discuss this matter in March 1969 and to determine at that time whether a catch-up increase was needed.

(4) *Hours*: A general progressive reduction of hours to 40 per week with no reduction in take-home pay was agreed upon in principle, the details to be negotiated. directly by employers and unions. It was contemplated that the reduction would take place over a period of two to five years and would result in a substantial wage increase.

(5) *Social Security*: In 1967 the government had decreed various reforms in the French social security program, the most unpopular of which was a cut in medical benefits. The share of the workers' medical bills paid by social security decreased from 80 to 70 percent. The government agreed in the Grenelle Protocol to raise this to 75 percent and to consider other revisions. An outright repeal of the 1967 social security amendments was rejected.

The unions proposed a reduction in the retirement age from 65 to 60 for males, and 65 to 55 for females. The Grenelle negotiations did not produce an agreement on early retirement, but it accepted the need for further study of this proposal in the near future. Several firms indicated a willingness to reduce the retirement age to 60. At Sud-Aviation and Nord-Aviation this reduced age of retirement will be extended to all operations, if a lesser workload makes it necessary. Studies to this end were to commence immediately at Ciotat shipyards and Renault.

Larger family allowances were granted, as well as increased allowances for old-age pensions and for the handicapped.

(6) *Strike Pay*: Strikers were to receive half pay for working time lost due to the strikes.

(7) *Codetermination*: The CFDT's demands for greater participation in management decisions were tabled for later consideration.

(8) *Union Rights:* More union activities within plants and offices were to be allowed. The government promised passage of an enactment on the exercise of trade union rights in the shop. The employers conceded that the bill should contain:

—recognition of the trade union branch;

—protection of shop stewards;

—prerogatives for negotiation by the trade union branch;

—collection of dues, and dissemination of trade union papers and pamphlets in the shop;

—freedom to put up posters of trade union information;

—plant space and paid time for shop stewards to carry out union functions; and

—right to hold meeting of union members once a month in the factory.

The Grenelle minutes therefore recorded the employer's agreement on the recognition, protection, and means of expression of shop stewards in the factory.

This success was all the more striking because the subject "recognition of the trade union branch in the shop" had hitherto been taboo.

(9) *Miscellaneous Items*: These included an agreement not to introduce tax-withholding procedures and an unspecified reduction of income tax on wage earners later in 1968.

On May 26 an overwhelming majority of French workers rejected this package.[28] Groups of strikers met in factory assemblies and voted almost unanimously by raising their hands against the settlement. The first results came from the publicly owned automotive plants of Renault and the privately held Citroen works in the Paris region; from the Berliet motor-truck plant and from Rhodiacéta, a plastic fiber manufacturer, in Lyons; and from the Michelin Tire factories in Clermond-Ferrand in central France. The 10-percent general increase was not satisfactory to many plant employees.

One local observer stated that "when the government caved in to the workers' leaders during the negotiations, the workers felt cheated because victory came too soon and too easily. So they set themselves new and much more ambitious goals and stayed, as it were, on the barricades."[29]

The press commented editorially that the workers' appetites, like their grievances, seemed to have expanded as a result of the concessions they had wrested from the government, from industry, and from their own trade unions:

---

[28] Tanner, Henry, "French Strikers Turn Down Pact," *New York Times*, May 28, 1968, pp. 1, 16.

[29] Tanner, Henry, "The Question: How Long Will Agony Last," *New York Times*, May 30, 1968, p. 11.

"The spectacle of an authoritarian regime that has lost its authority and is now only too willing to make a deal with the trade unions after years of notorious unwillingness to bargain, has provoked dissatisfaction and contempt among the rank and file." [30]

Beginning of the End of the Strikes

On May 30 President de Gaulle announced his decision to remain in power if supported by the people, and to determine the degree of support he said he would dissolve Parliament and call for general elections. On May 31 Séguy, of the CGT, announced that the strike was no longer general, and that his union would seek settlements industry by industry.[31] The CGT also then announced that it would not obstruct the elections, and the path was cleared to move the revolution from the picket line to the ballot box.[32]

On the morning of May 31, French police cleared strikers from post offices, communication centers, and gasoline depots with little or no opposition.[33] In the meantime negotiations were proceeding on national (in a few instances) and regional levels, and on the plant level with the larger companies. The wage settlements will be discussed in some detail later, but by the end of June most plants had reached an agreement ranging from the Grenelle 10 percent to the highway transport workers' 26 percent, with a majority in the 11-to-14-percent range.

The Settlements After Grenelle

Wages. In the government-owned industries (gas, electric, railroads, airlines), the increase in wages ranged from 10 to 21.1 percent, with the lowest-paid workers receiving the highest increases. (Unless otherwise indicated, the wage increases reported do not include the amount of increases granted to offset a reduction in the workweek).

In the public-employee sector, comprising some two million civil service employees, soldiers, teachers, and postmen, the increase was 8.5 percent, not including the 2.25 percent granted February 1, 1968.

In the Paris bakery industry, with employment of approximate-

---

[30] "French 'Miracle,'" *New York Times,* May 29, 1968.

[31] Hess, J. L., "Cabinet Aides in France Open Talks with Unions," *New York Times,* June 1, 1968, pp. 1, 9.

[32] Tanner, Henry, "Elections June 23," *New York Times,* June 1, 1968, pp. 1, 8; "General De Gaulle Gains Union Pledge," *The Times* (London), June 1, 1968, p. 1.

[33] "Police Act to Break up Strikes," *The Times* (London), June 1, 1968, p. 1.

ly 20,000, the increase was about 12 percent, but the retail saleswo-
men, who were often paid below the SMIG rates, received an increase of as high as 72 percent.

As a general rule, the various agreements tended to favor the
lowest-paid workers and therefore to have a leveling effect on the
wage structures.

In the automotive industry, the Renault wage increases were
reported at between 10 and 15 percent. The Peugeot settlement followed the wage settlement at Renault. The Citroen settlement was
13 percent plus 1.6 percent for reduction of work time for the manual workers, and 11 percent plus 1.6 percent for reduction of work
time for the professional workers.

The application of the 7-percent plus 3-percent increase agreed
at Grenelle for the year 1968 often materialized in increases of 11,
12, or 13 percent, depending on the plant; thus, it was 13.8 percent
at J. J. Carnaud, a light steel works in the Department of Basse-
Indre. The 3-percent stage agreed upon at Grenelle, set for October 1, was sometimes predated, partly or fully, by two, three, or
four months. Such was the case in the Sociétés Aéronautiques
(aircraft companies), in the east, and Hérault, in the Department
Haut-Rhin.

The coal industry granted an average increase of 13 percent,
and this was in addition to the 3.1-percent increase in January 1968.

The Reduction in the Workweek. In the steel industry in eastern France (Siderurgie de l'Est), on continuous operations, the
workweek was reduced from 48 to 42 hours with a minimum compensation starting from 66 percent of income forfeited. Other examples of compensation for reduced working hours were:

—Renault: one hour on resumption of work and 30 minutes
as from September 1, 1969 — 100 percent compensation.

—Peugeot: 46-1/2 hours before the strike, 45-1/2 hours as
from January 1, 1969, return to 45 hours on January 1, 1970,
with reductions at the rate of one fourth hour every three
months — 100 percent compensation.

—Sociétés Nationales Aéronautiques (national aircraft companies): one half hour immediately and one half hour in the
first quarter of 1969 — 100 percent compensation.

—Dassault: ceiling at 48 hours with pay for 49 hours and reduction by one hour on July 1, 1968, one hour on January 1,
1969, one hour on July 1, 1969 — 100 percent compensation.

—Métallurgie de la Loire: working weeks from 45 to 48 hours,
one half hour before December 1968, one half hour between

January 1 and October 1, 1969; working weeks longer than 48 hours, one half hour before December 1968 and one hour between January 1 and October 1, 1969 — 66 percent compensation.

In various other settlements the workweek was reduced, but there is no information as to the amount of the offsetting wage increase. For example, in the food industry workweeks of more than 52 hours were to be reduced one hour in 1968 and another hour in 1969; the French National Railways reduced hours from 46 to 44.5 as of July 22, 1968; the electric and gas companies reduced immediately from 45 to 44 hours; and in the public sector the previous 45-hour week was reduced to 44, and the former 48 hours to 46.5.

Strike Pay. The Grenelle Protocol agreement was to make up 50 percent of wages lost because of the strikes. In the public and nationalized sectors and in most of the petroleum industry, there was to be a 100 percent makeup. Peugeot agreed to an 80 percent makeup for the month of May and 25 percent for the month of June up to and including June 19. Citroen, on the other hand, agreed to the Grenelle Protocol settlement of a 50-percent makeup.

Miscellaneous. There were additional fringe benefits in vacation pay and casual-days pay averaging an additional two or three days. In many of these industries this resulted in 29 days of vacation time per year. A few of the settlements increased four weeks of vacation to five weeks.

From the foregoing reports, two points are clear: (1) the settlements varied considerably in both wages and reduction of hours and (2) the Grenelle Protocol agreement was a minimum pattern-setting agreement which was enlarged in the national, regional, and plant agreements.

In the Peugeot settlement the unions won a substantial victory for union representation at the plant level. For example, at Sochaux, the main plant, each union now selects one delegate who in turn has 12 assistants selected by the unions. Formerly these assistants were elected by the workers. The delegate is paid for 20 hours per week for union time, and each assistant receives five free hours. In addition the union has a room in the plant for conduct of its union business.

At Renault in Billancourt the shop steward will have 100 hours at his disposal per month, and a telephone is to be made available to each union organization with both internal and external communications.

Impact on Management

Within hours of the start of the national strike, the Conseil National du Patronat Français (the French employers association) declared that "French industry is threatened by a paralysis which could harm not only the immediate future but the prospects of our economy and the conditions of life of every one of us." [34]

The Patronat denounced attempts to place "impossible" burdens on business and said that only a policy of vigorous expansion could provide the means of satisfying the aspirations of the workers.[35] French employers appear most concerned about the unlawful seizures of factories and offices.

General de Gaulle, in his speech on May 23, offered the workers "participation in professional responsibilities and at all levels of the economy." [36] Exactly what is meant by "participation" in management was not made clear. It could range all the way from the student anarchists' demands for "new forms of management" to the lesser problems of codetermination as practiced now under the labor laws of West Germany. Some thought that it might mean a measure similar to the July 1967 profit-sharing law.[37] This law, opposed by both business and labor, requires management and labor to agree on one of three plans for profit-sharing as follows: (1) distribution of company stock to employees; (2) a fund set up by the firm to be invested on behalf of the employees; or (3) shares in a government administered, open-end investment fund, yet to be set up.

While it was free to moralize, the French Patronat was not in a strong bargaining position. The government is the largest employer and hence sets the pattern at enterprises such as Renault. In addition, the government has the authority to raise minimum wages by decree, and inevitably any substantial raise in the minimum wage must spread in some measure to the higher-paid classifications. One of the government participants in the negotiations asserted that the economy could absorb the wage increases without increases in consumer prices. This obviously means that costs would have to come from the profits of the employers. The French Government, it must be remembered, has the power to freeze or restrict price increases.

While one could not predict the extent of participation that

---

[34] Stafford, P., "Economy 'may be paralysed,' " *The Times* (London), May 23, 1968, p. 1.

[35] *Ibid.*

[36] See "De Gaulle's Address to Nation," (text), *The New York Times*, May 25, 1968, p. 1; *Cf.* Ricklefs, Roger, "De Gaulle Works on Plan to Boost Power of Student Workers as Crisis Deepens," *Wall Street Journal*, May 22, 1968, p. 4.

[37] Stafford, note 34, *supra.*

might emerge from the 1968 negotiations and legislation, the historical precedents for the 1968 national strike merit examination. In 1936 the unions demanded the nationalization of numerous industries. The socialist CFDT has favored workers' control (*autogestion*) in the past, but the communist CGT has not warmed up to it. De Gaulle's offer of participation in the management of French enterprises may be related to the CFDT's program. He avoided, however, spelling out what he meant. Thus the term could be variously interpreted to mean the relatively weak forms of codetermination found in West Germany in industries other than mining and steel, or it could represent creeping socialization and nationalization whereby managerial control is gradually transferred and the property relationship is changed.

One must remember that de Gaulle made these statements during the critical strike days when he was obviously trying to appeal to the strikers not to attempt to overthrow the government. In view of his overwhelming victory in the June 1968 elections, only time will reveal whether the participation he talked about in May will become a fact.

One knowledgeable American correspondent stationed in France flatly stated that de Gaulle's reforms would include not only profit-sharing but decision-making as well:

> "Ironically as it may sound in view of the election result, the Gaullists actually need all the political help they can get in the coming weeks. The President is publicly committed to give the country sweeping domestic reforms, and some of the reforms that he envisions are profoundly unpopular with many of the conservatives who voted for him and his followers . . . .
>
> "The President has gone on record in favor of 'participation' in politics, in the universities and in business. So far he has spoken only in general terms. But it is known that what he means, in business, is that workers and employees must share not only in the profits but in the decision-making of management . . . .
>
> "Specialists are known to have started working on an outline of these reforms. When they are ready, the President may well decide to carry out the referendum he was forced to abandon during the May rebellion." [38]

At least one government official believes in joint management as well as in sharing the profits. René Capitant, the new Minister of Justice, made the following statement on the radio on June 10:

> "I would like to see in all companies workers grouping themselves and forming an association which I would love to see in the form of a co-operative society or a mutual association.

---

[38] "Now De Gaulle's Real Job Begins," *The New York Times,* July 7, 1968.

"They would not be subordinates of a boss any more but would be their own managers, they would form a co-operative society of production in which they would govern themselves. This co-operative society of production would associate itself with a corporation of capital to get the financial means they need. All companies which are today the exclusive property of capital would then change and emerge into a joint property of a corporation or an association of capital on one side and of a co-operative society of workers on the other. These two associations would then set up a management which would be elected by both groups and responsible to both, who would then split the benefits."

This extreme concept of M. Capitant may have been a trial balloon to find out how French management would react. Reaction came and it was strong. Ten days later the Conseil National du Patronat Français (CNPF) published its opinion of M. Capitant's proposals, taking a very strong stand against any such idea. It quoted M. Chalandon, Minister of Industry, who has said that he does not think that industry could be split in two. It also quoted M. Edgar Faure, Minister of Agriculture, who mentioned that participation could only be considered in the European context. The CNPF hoped but was not quite sure that M. Capitant spoke on his own and not as a representative of the government. It foresaw the ruin of efficiency and of the national economy if M. Capitant's ideas were ever put into effect.

To add a personal observation, I believe the great unknown of such an idea is its effect on the shareholder. Since his dividend consists of what is left when everybody else has been paid, one really wonders what he could get out of such a system, especially in the coming years when France will have to make up the losses attributable to the May-June strike. After all, the investor still decides where to put his money.

A poststrike Gallup poll showed that Frenchmen did not have a passionate interest in "participation." It may all end by being only an assurance of providing more economic and social information to the workers.

Effect on Gross National Product*

Paul Huvelin, head of the employers' association, estimated that the Grenelle wage increases alone would cost France $2 billion a year and that the strike would reduce the country's gross national

---

*Ed. Note: It cannot be overemphasized that Mr. Shaw's paper was delivered in July 1968 and could not foresee the fast-moving events that culminated in President de Gaulle's resignation and the election of M. Pompidou to succeed him in June 1969.

product by 2.5 percent.[39] It was early evident that the Grenelle formula would be the minimum settlement in the private sector.

Spokesmen from the Organization of Economic Cooperation and Development believed that the French gross national product could expand by an additional 2 percent to accommodate these wage increases. They pointed out that one of the main reasons for France's troubles was that productivity had been growing faster than employment for several years, and in 1968 the economy was running at about 75 percent of its capacity.[40]

René Dabernat, of *Paris Match*, has written that "from an international point of view, the strikes sound the death knell of France's position as a creditor country which was a lever for General de Gaulle's pressure against the United States, Britain and all the countries that signed the Stockholm monetary agreement." [41]

Impact on Common Market Relations

On July 1, 1968, the tariffs between Common Market members were eliminated and a free trade area established. On the same day the first-round cuts of the Kennedy Round of tariff negotiations were implemented. The troubles in France created doubt that either or both would go through on schedule.

French businessmen were saying that the wage raises and efforts to reduce unemployment were inconsistent with the tariff cuts. In addition, the inroads upon France's balance-of-payments position which the strikes and settlements would produce could only be aggravated and increased by the tariff cuts.

On June 20, 1968, Premier Pompidou said that France would meet the Common Market tariff-cut deadlines but would ask for delays in the Kennedy Round cuts.[42] The next day it was leaked that France might introduce large-scale import restrictions in the form of either duties or quotas, and might also grant export subsidies, to cope with the economic effects of the crisis on the country. In addition, France attempted to put pressure on other Common Market countries to obtain a one-year postponement for introducing free trade. It was felt that France could not afford the political stigma of failing in her obligation and was trying to get the proposals for

---

[39] It may be recalled that the Matignon settlement of 1936 gave the workers wage increases ranging from 7 to 15 percent and the 40-hour week. The cost of the total package, as noted earlier, was estimated at 43.5 percent.

[40] See also Stafford, note 34, *supra*.

[41] "France Counts the Cost," *The Times* (London), May 30, 1968.

[42] "French Aid for Exports," *The Times* (London), June 20, 1968, p. 19.

postponing the July 1, 1968, cuts to come from other nations.[43] Since France had been given preferential treatment throughout the formative period of the Common Market, her partners were irritated by this move just as free trade was about to become a reality.

On June 26, 1968, however, France shocked the economic world by announcing that she would meet the July 1 deadline for Common Market tariff elimination *but* at the same time would put quotas on the importation of automobiles, textiles, and durables such as electrical household appliances.[44] These were part of a series of measures to boost exports while reducing imports for a six-month period.

The reaction to France's moves was immediate and volatile. Condemnation and protests were sent by Britain, the United States, Germany, Japan, and Switzerland. The United States representative indicated that his country would take retaliatory moves.[45] In addition, the Common Market challenged the legality of the unilateral French measures and called for a meeting of the Common Market Council of Ministers to decide whether to retaliate.[46]

De Gaulle ordered the suspension of steel import quotas until France received the approval of its Common Market partners. This came on July 6, 1968. With very little amendment, the French proposal on steel quotas and manufacturing subsidies was adopted for a period of six months. Clearly, France's five economic partners realized that France needed their assistance if the franc was not to be devaluated.

II. THE WEAPON OF THE GENERAL STRIKE

The important concessions won by French workers in their general strike did not go unnoticed in the other countries of Europe or in the United States. Nor was the political reaction by the French voters to the student riots and the strikes ignored outside France.

One had to conclude that both the de Gaulle administration and the workers won substantial immediate victories. It remained to be seen what the effect of the inflationary labor settlements would be

---

[43] "France Puts on the Pressure to Delay EEC Free Trade," *The Times* (London), June 22, 1968, p. 11.

[44] "France Puts Import Quotas * * * ," *The Times* (London), June 27, 1968, p. 21.

[45] Jay, Peter, "Angry Protests Follow French Move," *The Times* (London), June 28, 1968, p. 23.

[46] "EEC Challenges France's Right to Act Alone," *The Times* (London), June 29, 1968, p. 15.

on the business community and on the French economy. It also remained to be seen what form of labor-management codetermination the French Government would propose and what the reaction would be to the government's proposal.

Observers asked whether the strategy of the general strike would spread to other countries. Would it be attractive to American labor organizations? Coalition bargaining and industry strikes, such as the 1967-1968 copper strike, seem to some a step in the direction of a general strike. However, nothing that has happened indicates that unions in the United States or their members have any thoughts at the present time along this line. Why this lack of interest by U. S. unions in what appeared to be such a successful use of economic force in France? After considering some of the legal implications, I will note some of the practical differences between labor relations in France and the United States that may explain the difference in approach by the American unions.

The Legal Considerations Involved in the General Strike

In France the right to strike "is now firmly embedded in modern French constitutional documents." [47]

> "No-strike clauses in French collective agreements . . . do not run until the termination of the contract, but either provide only a specified period of notice or run until the contractual conciliation procedures have been exhausted." [48]

In France a no-strike clause, as such, cannot effectively take away the constitutional right to strike; however, it can defer the exercise of that right for a reasonable period of time, such as one month. Many French agreements provide that a strike shall not occur within one month of the date of a notice to reopen, and the parties pledge to refrain from strikes or lockouts "over a contractual issue" until the agreement's conciliation procedures are exhausted.

French employees who strike in violation of a reasonable deferment established by contract may be discharged. If all employees strike, it is obviously impracticable to discharge the entire work force.* It would appear that the strike leaders could have been sin-

---

[47] Wilson, "At the Crossroads in Jurisprudence of the French Law of Lockout," 15 *Int. and Compar. L.Q.,* 286, 288 (1966).

[48] Meyers, "A Comparative Study of the Law of the Strike," *Symposium on Labor Relations* (1961), p. 522.

*Ed. Note: See similar comment by Allan Flanders in "Labor Management Relations and the Democratic Challenge," *infra.* p. 487.

gled out for discharge for instigating a strike in violation of the contract.

In France the law of January 11, 1950, specifically provides that every person and every organization covered by a labor agreement "shall be bound by such collective agreement." (Sec. 31(e)). Further, "groups of employees or employers which are bound by a collective agreement . . . shall abstain from doing anything likely to impair the loyal execution of the agreement." (Sec. 31(g)). And finally, "groups capable of suing and being sued . . . may bring an action for damages . . . against any . . . who have violated the obligations contracted." (Sec. 31(r)).

In France, workers who participate in illegal strikes may be sued for breach of their contracts of employment, and unions may be sued for authorizing strikes in breach of labor agreements. The French employers who were struck in May had a cause of action at law for damages against both the striking employees and their unions because the required notice was not given.

As far as we know, none of the struck French employers filed lawsuits against the employees or the unions for damages incurred as a result of the strikes in violation of the agreements. Nor did the employers discharge strikers on a general or selective basis.

In the United States there is no constitutional right to strike.[49] There is statutory protection for lawful strikers to the extent that they cannot be discharged for engaging in a lawful strike.[50] However, it is clear that employees may be discharged for striking in violation of a "no-strike clause." [51]

In the United States, where lawsuits have been filed against unions for damages during the period of an unlawful strike, the union is usually successful in persuading the employer to withdraw his lawsuit as part of the strike settlement. This does not mean that such lawsuits do not exert some pressure on the union to settle.[52]

So far as lawsuits for damages are concerned, there would appear to be very little difference between the two countries. In both instances there is a cause of action for damages, but at the same time

---

[49] *Dorchy* v. *Kansas,* 272 U.S. 306 (1926); *International Union, U.A.W., AFL* v. *Wisconsin Employment Relations Board,* 336 U.S. 245, 23 LRRM 2361 (1949).

[50] 29 U.S.C. §158(a) (3).

[51] *NLRB* v. *Rockaway News Supply Co.* 345 U.S. 71, 31 LRRM 2432 (1953), applying doctrine enunciated in *NLRB* v. *Sands Mfg. Co.,* 306 U.S. 332, 4 LRRM 530 (1939).

[52] Torff, *Collective Bargaining: Negotiations and Agreements* (New York: McGraw-Hill Book Co., 1953), pp. 99-101.

the economic pressure of the strike either discourages the filing of a lawsuit or results in its dismissal.

In the United States over 90 percent of labor agreements contain binding no-strike commitments. Employees who engage in unlawful strikes have been discharged, and such discharges have frequently been upheld by arbitrators. In some instances the employer has discharged only the local union leaders on the theory that they have a special duty to honor the no-strike pledge. By and large, arbitrators have sustained these selective discharges unless it appeared that the local union leaders were not instigating or supporting the unlawful stoppage of work.[53]

Reasons Why the General Strike Will Not Be Used in the United States

There are several practical reasons why general strikes are more likely to occur in France than in the United States.

The French Government is the largest single employer of French workers. The U. S. Government is a large employer of white-collar workers, but until recently there has been relatively little bargaining between the government and its employees.[54] Unlike France, the U. S. Government does not own or operate manufacturing plants, transportation facilities, utilities, or mines.

The French Government has the authority to fix wages and prices. In the United States there are minimum wage laws that establish a floor. However, that floor is relatively unimportant in the manufacturing, construction, transportation, and mining industries. Under the Davis-Bacon [55] and Walsh-Healey [56] Acts, the Federal Government does establish rates for federal construction and supply contracts, but they must be based upon the prevailing rates in the private sector.

These contrasting roles of the U. S. and French Governments suggest practical reasons why French unions are politically motivated and also why such important pattern-setting bargaining occurs between unions and the government. These contrasting government roles also help explain why government negotiating in the United States is relatively unimportant and, further, why unions in this country look primarily to their negotiations with private concerns

---

[53] *Ibid.* See also Stessin, *Employee Discipline* (Washington: BNA Books, 1960), pp. 211-218.

[54] See, for example, Anderson, ed., *Public Employee Organization and Bargaining* (Washington: BNA Books, 1968).

[55] 41 U.S.C. §35-45.

[56] 40 U.S.C. §276a-276a-5.

to establish wage levels, fringe benefits, and conditions of employment.

The size and complexity of American industry and the large number of unions involved makes it far more difficult for unions in the United States to combine their efforts to effect a general strike. In France there are only three or four unions, and, consequently, it is more feasible for them to take concerted action.

Whatever the reasons may be, American unions, by and large, respect their no-strike pledges.   Perhaps union leaders recognize that if strikes frequently occurred in violation of contract provisions, not only would the employers use their legal recourse in suits for damages, but Congress would enact legislation that would greatly restrict the bargaining rights set forth in existing law. In brief, there is a recognition in the United States that the right to bargain is a statutory right which can be modified by Congress if it is abused.

Unions in the United States are very strong and have been highly successful at the bargaining table within their respective industries. American unions and their members do not need a general strike to achieve their goals. In this country many of the large unions have substantial strike funds. Recently in the copper industry strikers were paid strike benefits of $25 per week for over eight months. Thus, company or industry strikes — or the threat of strikes — normally result in substantial gains for the union and its members.

Apparently the unions and the employees in France were convinced that they needed a general strike to persuade the government and the employers they were entitled to a bigger slice of the pie. French unions are comparatively weaker than U. S. unions and do not have the funds to pay strikers. Thus it is difficult for French unions to engage in long strikes on an industry, plant, or regional basis. The general strike has such a paralyzing effect that it succeeds or fails in a relatively short period of time.

Conclusion

We are inclined to talk about union power and union objectives when we are discussing strikes and collective bargaining. However, in the final analysis the attitudes of union members and employees generally and their willingness to strike is probably the most important factor in prophesying whether there will be general strikes in the United States.

Union members in this country have every reason to feel that their union leadership will adequately and effectively represent them at the bargaining table and during the term of the agreement. This confidence in their union leadership may explain the lack of frustration among at least the great majority of union members. Indeed, many of them privately concede they never had it so good.

When the racial crisis occurred in our large cities in 1967, neither union members nor union leaders gave thought to taking advantage of the situation and engaging in strikes for the purpose of winning concessions at the bargaining table.

In France, during those hectic days in May when the students of the Sorbonne took the law into their own hands, both union members and union leaders used the attack on the government launched by nonunion forces and proceeded to paralyze French industry. Their strikes were primarily bread-and-butter strikes for higher wages, reduced hours of work, and a greater voice in the day-to-day activity in the plants. There was a definite undercurrent of frustration on the part of the French worker which exploded into plant seizures, picketing, marching, and rejection of the first settlements reached by the government and the union leadership. Apparently the French worker looked on the government as a natural enemy and also as the logical authority to improve the workers' standard of living.

In the United States the unions look to employers and not to the government for improvements in their compensation and conditions of employment. They look to their own employers or in some instances to the larger manufacturers in their industry to achieve their objectives.

For all of these reasons, it is most unlikely that a general strike will occur in the United States. The reader may speculate as to whether general strikes will take place in Britain, Ireland, West Germany, Italy, Belgium, or the Netherlands.

PART IV

Labor Relations and the Law in Western Europe

The role of law in labor relations in Western Europe is discussed in this part by five prominent labor law teachers on law faculties in the United States, the United Kingdom, Belgium, the Federal Republic of Germany, and Ireland. The European participants at the Loyola Summer Institute, even the four Europeans who contributed to this part, were astounded at the significant role played by American lawyers in shaping and implementing governmental, corporate, and trade union labor relations policies. Professor Gamillscheg came closest to accepting a limited role for lawyers in the *enforcement* of the terms of labor agreements against alleged violators. Seminar debate centered on the American policy, encapsulated in Section 301 of the Labor Management Relations Act, 1947 (29 USC §185), that opened the courts to actions for violation of collective labor agreements and for this purpose made unions juridical entities with capacity to sue or be sued. Professors Grunfeld and Blanpain were skeptical about the transportability of this American policy to their countries. Mr. McCartney, however, while deploring the practice of suing unions for alleged contract violations, expressed doubts that British legal doctrine really precludes the judicial enforceability of collective labor agreements. He elaborated on the views expressed in his article, "The Contractual or Non-Contractual Nature of Collective Agreements in Great Britain and Eire," in *Labour Relations and the Law,* Kahn-Freund, ed. (London: Stevens & Sons; Boston: Little, Brown & Co., 1965).

LABOR RELATIONS AND THE ROLE OF LAW IN WESTERN EUROPE

By Clyde W. Summers

It is a truism that collective bargaining takes many forms and is shaped by the industrial structures and social institutions of which it is a part. In the United States the bargaining structure of the trucking industry is quite unlike that in the auto industry; the content of agreements in construction differs widely from that in meat packing; and grievance procedures and arbitration in the garment industry bear little resemblance to those in steel. We readily recognize these differences and accept them as natural. But all of these differences fall within the framework of certain working principles which characterize our collective bargaining system. Understanding the bargaining process in one industry in this country provides at least a beginning base for understanding that in another industry.

The collective bargaining process in Western Europe, however, is not so easily understood. It is not bound by those working principles which we take for granted and unconsciously assume are inherent in any system because they are so familiar. Instead, it is framed by principles and practices which we instinctively disbelieve, and easily forget, because they are so different. Knowledge of our own system may be as much a handicap as a help. Labor relations policies developed for an electronics plant in Boston may be self-defeating when exported to a Brussels branch. Experience in handling grievances in an auto plant in Michigan may have little usefulness in the English Midlands. And methods of counteracting strikes in an oil refinery in Naples cannot be borrowed from methods that are successful in New Jersey.

It is true that collective bargaining structures and institutions in Western Europe may have many obvious similarities to our own. This, however, only increases the danger of misunderstanding, for these similarities tempt us to carry over our parochial preconceptions and to discount the differences. Some of those differences are so basic and pervasive that even generic terms such as "collective agreement," "union," and "strike" do not convey common concepts. We quickly recognize the familiar terms but only slowly appreciate their different meaning.

The purpose of this paper is to identify and underline certain of those basic differences in areas ranging from union recognition to

145

grievance adjudication. Both the legal rules and working principles will be marked out with bold strokes which oversimplify and overstate. This is deliberate, for comprehensiveness or pedantic precision would obscure the basic framework and dull your awareness that you are dealing with a foreign body of law in a foreign land. My goal, therefore, is emphasis, not academic accuracy.

UNION RECOGNITION

Section 9 (a) of the National Labor Relations Act provides that the union selected by the majority of the employees in a bargaining unit shall be the exclusive representative for all the employees in such bargaining unit for the purposes of collective bargaining. The principle articulated by this section is so deeply embedded in our labor law and collective bargaining system that we have difficulty conceiving of a system working without it.

The principle of sole bargaining representative, however, does not exist in Western Europe. Indeed, the basic legal rule is just the opposite: Each employee is free to choose his own representative or to bargain for himself. The union acts as agent only for its members, and its collective agreement binds only its members. This means that an employer in bargaining for a single category of employees may be confronted by several unions, each with separate demands, for except in Germany the labor movement lacks unity. In France, the Catholic and Communist unions often cannot agree, and if the employer reaches an agreement with one, the other may, for political reasons, refuse to sign. All the employees can claim the benefits of the agreement, but the nonsigning union remains free to criticize and disrupt. At one time Ford Motor Co. in England * bargained with 22 different unions, and at the present time a typical British assembly plant has three of four industrial-type unions and a dozen or more craft unions, all competing for membership with overlapping jurisdictions. The employer has no union with full authority and sole responsibility to which he can turn but must try to make peace with a balkanized work force.

The fragmenting effect of multiple unionism may be avoided at the national level by various forms of coalition bargaining. In Holland, for example, there are three union confederations, Socialist, Catholic, and Protestant; and there are also two employer confederations. All five have representatives on the trade councils, each of which acts as the permanent negotiating committee for a particular

---

* See Robert Copp, *Negotiating a New Wage Structure at Ford of Britain,* *supra,* p. 109.

industry and negotiates a single national agreement for that industry. In Belgium, structures for unified bargaining at the national
level have been created by law. A *commission paritaire*, or joint
committee, is established for each industry by royal decree. These
joint committees have representatives from the employers association
and from each of the three major union federations, Socialist, Catholic, and Liberal; and they can conclude collective agreements only
by unanimous vote. The result, of course, is a single agreement for
the industry binding all of the unions and all employers in the employers association.

In other countries, coalition bargaining is less tightly structured. In most Italian industries representatives of the three major
labor federations — Communist, Socialist, and Catholic — meet
with the representatives of both public and private employers at the
same bargaining table and negotiate a single national agreement. In
England, where they are so fragmented, unions commonly bargain
at the national level through structures such as the Confederation of
Shipbuilding and Engineering Unions in the auto industry. Even in
France, where the labor movement is deeply split, the Communist
and Catholic unions frequently sign the same agreement.

These unified bargaining structures might lead us to conclude
that differences in basic legal principles do not cause differences in
working systems. Even without our legal rule that the majority
union is the sole representative, multiple unions do not lead to multiple bargaining and multiple contracts, for some unifying agency or
procedure produces a single representative which negotiates a single
contract. This, however, is only to see the shell of the system. The
unification is only at the national level; and the national agreements, as we shall see, are of limited practical importance. At the
provincial or plant levels, where terms and conditions are actually
fixed, the problems of multiple unionism remain real and the lack of
an exclusive representative with which to deal alters the entire
structure of labor relations.

European labor law has another legal rule, that of the extension of the collective agreement, which is commonly considered an
analogue to the rule of exclusive representation. Under this rule an
agreement made between a representative union and an employers
association can be made binding on the entire industry. For example, in Belgium an agreement negotiated by one of the governmentally created joint committees can, upon the request of the
parties to the agreement, be made binding by royal decree on all
workers and employers in the industry, regardless of whether they
are members of the union or the employers association. In France,

the collective agreement must have been made by organizations "the most representative," but these words do not require that the union have a majority, only that it have been certified as meeting certain statutory standards. In Germany, the agreement must cover employers who employ at least half the employees in the trade and district to which the contract is to be extended.

It is true that this rule of extension is like our rule of exclusive representative in that it makes the contract binding on those who are not members of the union or the employers association and who did not agree to be bound by the contract. However, the two rules may play quite different roles. First, except in Holland, agreements are not automatically extended to bind others, but are extended only selectively by administrative decree. In Belgium fewer than half are made enforceable by royal order; in France fewer than one fourth are extended; and in Germany the power is only rarely used. Second, extension is designed primarily to reach out and bind unaffiliated employers rather than workers. The purpose of extension is to establish the terms of the collective agreement as the minimum terms for the industry and to prevent unorganized employers from undercutting those standards. Extension is functionally much more analogous to an industry minimum wage order than to the rule of exclusive representation.

THE EFFECT OF THE COLLECTIVE AGREEMENT

Closely tied to our rule of exclusive representation is the working principle in the United States that the collective agreement fixes both the minimum and the maximum terms and conditions of employment. It is as much a breach of contract and an unfair labor practice for an American employer to agree with an employee individually to pay him more as it is to pay him less than the rate specified in the collective agreement. Although the collective agreement can, by explicit language, permit variations upward, such agreements are so uncommon that we compulsively assume otherwise.

This marks the second basic difference between American and European collective bargaining, for the basic working principle in every Western European country except Holland is that the collective agreement establishes only minimum terms. In England, it does not even do that, for the collective agreement is considered to have no legal binding effect. Its terms only establish a custom or practice which is read into the individual's contract of employment in the absence of contrary express terms, and the individual remains free to make his own contract of employment for better or for poorer terms. The same is true in Belgium unless the agreement has been made enforceable by royal decree. The dominant rule on the continent, however, is that the collective agreement fixes minimum terms and an individual cannot make a binding agreement to accept less.

Because the collective agreement sets only minimum terms, those terms can be varied upward by an almost infinite variety of agreements and informal arrangements. In Italy, formal plant agreements are made supplementing the national agreements and substantially improving on national minimum terms. In other countries local or plant agreements may be less formal but no less important. The plant agreement, likewise, sets only a minimum, and within the plant groups of employees in a department or in a certain trade may negotiate for still better rates or additional benefits. Finally the individual himself may bargain for special terms beyond those obtained at other levels.

These methods of improving on the minimum are not theoretical, but real; they are not exceptional, but commonplace. The result is that the terms set out in the collective agreement have little relation to the actual terms in force. Although precise data are impossible to obtain, it is estimated that the actual wages in the German steel industry are 30 percent above those provided in the collective agreements. In the British shipbuilding industry weekly earnings have averaged 50 percent above those in the industry agreement. In the Paris area the wages in construction and some other industries are more than double those negotiated at the bargaining table. Practically all of this difference is the result of informal agreements or understandings which are not a part of the structured collective bargaining system. Much of it is the result of individual bargaining and employer unilateral action.*

The spread between contract terms and actual terms has critical consequences which pervade every aspect of labor relations. Two of those consequences should be noted here. First, the negotiation of collective agreements, from the standpoint of both the employees and the employer, may be of limited importance. A new industry agreement which increases the minimum rates by 10 percent has limited effect where wages are already 30 to 50 percent above that minimum. The union, by making such an agreement, wins little loyalty or support among the workers; it therefore directs more of its attention to other functions whereby it may serve or represent its members. Similarly, the employer finds that the collective agreement

---

* See discussion of the phenomenon of wage drift in Allan Flanders, *Labor-Management Relations and the Democratic Challenge, infra,* p. 487.

settles little, and he must confront his labor relations problems at other times and in other forums. In some countries, such as Belgium, there is an effort to make the collective agreement more relevant by providing for increases in actual rates as well as for increases in minimum rates. The negotiated increase, however, is still not a maximum increase, and the same market and institutional forces operate to cause the actual increases obtained from some employers to be greater than those negotiated.

The second critical consequence of the spread between contract terms and actual terms is that the actual wages are immediately responsive to the labor market, with the collective agreement having relatively little retarding effect. When the labor market is tight, wages can be bid up by individual bargaining regardless of the terms of the collective agreement. When the labor market loosens, the spread between negotiated rates and actual rates can shrink or disappear. The collective agreement provides little stability until wages approach the contractual minimum.

CENTRALIZATION OF BARGAINING

The most deceptive difference between European and American collective bargaining is that in Europe collective bargaining is so much more centralized in form, but so much less centralized in substance. What first appears to be a highly integrated and nearly monolithic system proves, upon closer examination, to be an atomistic arrangement with little or no cohesion.

The formal European structure is characterized by industry-wide agreements negotiated between national employers associations and national unions. For example, in Holland a single collective agreement covers the whole heavy-metal industry, and this is negotiated by the employers associations and the national unions for that industry. The scope of the industry-wide agreement varies widely from country to country. In Italy the metalworking industry is divided into six technological sectors (iron and steel, electrical engineering, shipbuilding, smelting, auto, and general engineering), and a national agreement is negotiated for each sector. In France and Germany collective agreements are customarily not national but regional in scope. For example, the steel industry has separate agreements for the Paris, Moselle, Loire, and other regions in France, and for the Saar, Rhineland, Lower Saxony, and other regions in Germany. The industries can be narrowly defined, so that in Belgium, which is smaller than Pennsylvania, there are some 80 industry joint committees established by law, a number of them covering fewer than 2,000 employees, and in France so-called "regional" agreements may be for a single town. Regardless of how fragmented the industry may be, the basic characteristic remains: the collective agreement is a multiple employer contract covering all members of the employers association, and by extension it may be made binding on all the employers in the industry, sector, or region.

Although this is the dominant pattern, collective agreements can be made at levels both above and below the industry level. Interconfederation agreements may be made at the national level covering all industries and all unions to deal with special problems, largely as a substitute for legislation. For example, in Belgium and Italy the national union and employer confederations have made agreements establishing work councils at the plant level, defining their composition, their method of selection, and their functions. In countries other than England this is done by law. In Italy such interconfederation agreements establish for all employers rules governing layoff and discharge, again subjects which in other countries, except England, are regulated by law.

Formal collective agreements may also be made by individual employers outside the multiple employer structure. Renault has, for a number of years, negotiated company-wide contracts independent of the employers association which represents other auto firms. Such single-employer bargaining has become increasingly common, particularly with the larger firms, which do not feel the need or desire to cooperate with other employers. In Italy there is a movement toward "articulated bargaining," which is a combination of association and single-employer bargaining. In 1962 a precedent-making agreement in the metalworking industry provided that the national agreements for each of the six sectors would provide minimum wages, job classifications, and working hours. These, however, would be supplemented by formal plant agreements for piece rates, job evaluation, and productivity bonuses, to be negotiated within the framework of the national agreements. It should be noted that the plant agreements were to be negotiated not by local unions in the plant but by provincial unions for the area. Despite the trend toward single-employer bargaining in other countries and toward articulated bargaining in Italy, the dominant pattern is still the industry-wide agreement.

Although the negotiation of collective agreements is centralized in employer associations, the determination of terms and conditions of employment is not centralized. As has already been emphasized, the collective agreement does not fix the terms and conditions of employment; it only establishes minimum terms. The negotiation of the agreement is not the end of the bargaining process; it is but the first step. Bargaining for more than the minimum may take place at the plant level with local union officers or the works councils, at the department level with shop stewards, militants, or informal groups, and at the individual level with single employees. Commonly it takes place at all of these levels simultaneously or in sequence. It is at these lower levels that the actual terms and conditions are fixed.

This multilevel bargaining process becomes disjointed, indeed atomized, because neither the unions nor the employers associations which negotiate the industry agreement have effective control over the lower levels where the ultimate decisions are made. Local unions in the American sense normally do not exist. Although active union members or "militants" may assert leadership in local bargaining, they do not do so as representatives of the national union nor are they bound by policies of the national union. For example, local bargaining in England is largely in the hands of shop stewards who are elected at the shop level. Although they are union officials, they act as agents of shop-floor democracy, are subject to little influence and control by the national union, and often view themselves as competing with or hostile to the union hierarchy. Even when local unions do exist and control local bargaining, as in Belgium, their autonomy is almost unlimited. They decide their own demands, call their own strikes, and make their own settlements. The national union is seldom consulted and often not even informed. Indeed, the national union often does not even know the terms of the local agreement or the wages actually being paid. The most integrated system is the "articulated bargaining" being developed in Italy with formal agreements negotiated at the plant level. But the Italian unions have no effective local organization, and the actual terms are determined through shop-floor bargaining by works councils or informal groups over which the union has little control.

Employers associations have little more control over their members. Although employers will maintain a united front in negotiating an industry agreement, and generally will not make separate formal agreements individually, they act quite independently in making informal plant-level agreements. The individual employer may make settlements with local groups without ever notifying the association. In many instances the individual employers refuse to tell their association the rates they are actually paying or the other terms and conditions actually in effect. When qualified workers are scarce, employers compete with each other for the available workers by informally negotiating better terms, either with local groups or with individual workers.

Because the bargaining process in Europe is so disjointed, it has a fundamental difference from the bargaining process in the United States which is obvious but easily overlooked. We consider that one function of collective bargaining is to standardize terms and conditions of employment, both among workers in the same firm and between workers in competing firms. One of the articulate policies of many American unions is to prevent any employer from getting a competitive advantage at the expense of his workers. The American union, often prodded by employers with whom it bargains, attempts to impose equivalent terms on all competing employers. Collective bargaining in Europe is built on the opposite premise. The industry agreement establishes minimum terms which are in fact applicable only to marginal employers and which are generally set within the limits of the less efficient employers' ability to pay. Further negotiations at the local level then attempt to obtain better terms from the more profitable employers. Thus, collective bargaining is not a process for establishing a uniform standard but a process for creating a system of differentials. And those differentials may be substantial. Two employers in the same city bargaining with the same union and competing in the same product market may have wage differentials of 20 or 30 percent or more. Even within a single plant there may be significant differentials in the wages of individual employees performing similar work because of group or individual bargaining.

ECONOMIC CONFLICT

The legality of various forms of economic action, such as strikes and lockouts, varies so widely in Western Europe that any generalizations are impossible. These differences are of critical importance because they significantly affect, or reflect, the climate of labor relations and the practical working of the collective bargaining system. For simplicity and emphasis, we will distinguish among three patterns or models.

First, the German model is most nearly like our own in multiple-employer bargaining units. The German Constitution guarantees the right to strike, but this is not an absolute right and has been restricted by judicial decision. One limitation is that the strike can be used only as a last resort. It cannot be used if any other legal method is available to achieve the objective, and it cannot be resorted to until all peaceful means of reaching a settlement, such as conciliation or mediation, have been exhausted. Another limitation is that the dispute must be of such nature that it can be settled by a valid collective agreement. Thus, a political strike is illegal, as is a strike for an invalid union security clause. More important, this principle prohibits strikes by the works council or by local groups at the shop level to obtain better terms than those in the industry agreement, for such organizations are not considered trade unions and such an understanding reached at this level is not considered a collective agreement in the legal sense. When the strike is legal, the strikers are protected against discharge, for the strike is considered as temporarily suspending their individual contracts of employment and discharge for striking would be an unjustifiable dismissal, making the employer liable in damages.

The employers' right to lock out is substantially equal to the unions' right to strike; and the lockout can be used either defensively or offensively. German law, in principle, prohibits sympathetic action. However, because collective bargaining is structured on a regional basis, if the union calls out the workers in selected enterprises the employers association can respond to such selective strikes by locking out the workers in other enterprises in the region. In practice, strikes or lockouts in Germany have been relatively infrequent, and they customarily take the form of area-wide shutdowns which may last from several days to several months. Local or wildcat strikes are not only illegal but uncommon.

The second, or English, model* is characterized by a lack of any substantial legal limits on collective economic action. There are almost no legal restraints on the use of the strike weapon, either at the national level in the making of an industry agreement or at the local level in compelling concessions on the shop floor. Similarly, there are no legal restraints on lockouts, although these are not commonly used. Strikes or lockouts may, however, breach the individual contract of employment and make the individual workers or the employer liable in damages. Because the law views every strike or lockout as terminating, not suspending, the contract of employment, failure to give reasonable notice of an intent to strike or lock out is a breach of the employment contract. Slowdowns, refusals to work overtime, and other restrictive devices are likewise breaches of contract, making the worker individually liable in damages. Such suits, however, are rare, so these legal rules have little practical importance.

The legal rule that a strike terminates the contract of employment, rather than suspends it, means that the employer can dis-

---

* See Cyril Grunfeld, *Labor Relations and the Role of Law in Great Britain, infra,* p. 169.

charge and refuse to reinstate any and all strikers. This nearly makes it academic whether a strike breaches the contract of employment, for the striker is vulnerable to discharge regardless of the legality 'of the strike. In practice, unofficial stoppages or wildcats at the shop level are commonplace. They may be called by shop stewards to enforce particular demands or may be spontaneous reactions to specific grievances. They come without notice, and often involve only a small number of workers walking out for a short time. Local unofficial action may also take the form of a slowdown, refusal to work overtime, refusal to perform certain tasks, standing in place, or working to rule. In practical terms these devices are no more subject to legal sanctions and leave the workers no less protected in their jobs than regular official strikes. Unofficial action then becomes a normal weapon of economic conflict.

The third, or French and Italian, model is built on legal rules, many similar to our own. However, differences occur at such strategic points that economic conflict takes a radically different and unfamiliar form. In France and Italy the right to strike is constitutionally guaranteed, though subject to some judicially imposed limitations. If the strike is legal, it does not terminate, but only suspends, the individual contract of employment. The striker cannot be dismissed, even with notice, and is entitled to his job when he offers to return to work. If the strike is illegal, he can be summarily discharged. To be legal, the strike need not be authorized by a union but may be spontaneous or called by an informal group. No notice is required, nor is there any requirement that peaceful processes of settlement be exhausted unless a collective agreement is in effect. The strike is illegal if it is for a political purpose or to compel the discharge of a nonunion worker. It is also illegal if it takes the form of a slowdown, a "skippy" strike in which the workers perform only a part of their tasks, or a "zeal" strike in which the workers obstruct production by insisting on perfection.

In principle, sympathy strikes are illegal, and the secondary boycott is practically unknown. The strike must be for an interest common to those who participate, and this requirement has been so strictly applied as to bar a group of employees from striking in support of the demands of an individual in the same plant who has been discharged. At most, the right to strike extends to actions in support of other workers generally in the same establishment.

These legal rules are quite familiar, but economic conflict takes a wholly unfamiliar form because of other legal rules as to union strike action and the employers' permissible response. On the one hand, repeated short-term and selective strikes are legal. The union can, without notice, call a two-day or even two-hour stoppage. At the end of the stated time, all the strikers can insist on the right to return to work, and every few days the process can be repeated. In the 1962 metal industry dispute in Italy this pattern of recurrent stoppages continued for more than six months until an agreement was reached. To this device can be added the selective stoppage of a single department walking out with all others remaining at work and insisting on being paid. The strike may rotate among the various departments so that the burden of the conflict is shared by all workers.

The employers' response to such fragmented strike action is severely limited. He cannot use the lockout, for it does not enjoy the constitutional protection of the strike. He cannot refuse to allow the strikers to return to work until the dispute is settled, and because of the short period of the stoppage he has no practical possibility of hiring replacements. When one department walks out, he cannot send the other employees home, for by law he is barred from laying off any employee without giving notice of termination of two weeks or more. Those who report for work during the stoppage must be paid unless the employer can show that the strike constitutes *force majeure*. To do this he must show that the strike makes it impossible to provide work, and some have said that it must be "absolutely impossible" to do so.

The practical result of the legal rules in France and Italy is that economic conflict is highly fragmented, with frequent strikes of short duration and settlement coming after extended periods of repeated disruption. Short-term and selective strikes are particularly advantageous, if not essential, to French and Italian unions, which are poorly organized and without any substantial treasuries to support strikes of long duration. Though the legal rules make the employer highly vulnerable, this is offset by the unions' institutional weakness.

Two general observations should be made about the weapons of economic warfare under all three models. First, in all the countries of Western Europe the employers associations have substantial resources, both organizationally and financially. When a sympathetic lockout is illegal or impracticable, employers carrying the brunt of the union attack often are supported by strike payments or loans. The employers associations in France and Germany are particularly strong and effective. Second, other than in Germany, the legal rules governing strike action are particularly adapted to decentralized bargaining, for they give local groups effective bargaining power. Unauthorized strikes called by shop stewards, local militants, or even autonomous groups get as much legal protection as authorized strikes by the national union. The use of fragmented economic action enables such legal groups to exert the maximum pressure with the minimum resources and to bargain effectively for special conditions and terms better than those in the industry agreement.

GRIEVANCE STRUCTURES

Every country in Western Europe has developed structures at the plant level for representing employees in settling local disputes or grievances. The creation of these structures may be required by law, as in France, Germany, and Holland; they may be created by national interconfederation agreements, as in Belgium and Italy; or they may be largely the product of spontaneous growth in the work place, as in the case of shop stewards in England. Regardless of how they are created and their functions defined — or left undefined — they are of central importance in the administration of labor relations at the plant level.

At first glance these local bodies, or works councils, look much like American grievance committees, and in many respects they serve many of the same functions. This outward appearance, however, can be quite misleading, for there are three significant differences in the role they play in labor relations and in the collective bargaining process.

Lack of Integration With the Union Structure

First, these local bodies are not an integral part of the union structure which negotiates the collective agreement. They are essentially independent of union institutional control. In most countries the works council members are elected not by the unions but by a vote of all employees in the plant. Indeed, in all countries but England the works councils are required, either by law or by interconfederal agreement, to be established in every plant of a certain size regardless of whether any of the employees in the plant are union members. In France nominations in the first instance can be made only by the unions, but election is still by all employees in the plant, under a system of proportionate representation. In Germany and Italy even the nominations may be made by petition independent of the union. A member of the works council is, therefore, elected as a representative of the employees as a whole and not as an officer of a union.

The unions, of course, play an active part in the works council elections. Each union customarily nominates a slate of candidates and campaigns to get its slate elected. As a result, many of those elected to the works councils are active members or even union officers. In theory, any union which had majority support in the plant would be able to control the works council and make it an arm of the union. However, such an integration of the union and works council seldom happens; those who are elected consider the works council as an independent body and feel they owe their first loyalty to it rather than to the union. Indeed, once they are elected their sense of responsibility to the works council often leads them to take positions hostile to the union. The works council, therefore, acts largely independently of the union, and its relation to the union is more often one of competition and tension than of coordination and support.

In Belgium the works councils are more closely linked institutionally with the unions. They are created by a national agreement between the employers' confederation and the three major union confederations; only union members can be nominated, and only union members can vote. Each works council member, in a sense, sits as a representative of his union. Even so, the works council is not an integral part of the union structure but is a separate structure and acts quite independently of the union. Although there may be no tension between the union and the works council, there is no dominance or control.

In England the shop stewards are union officials and might be considered an integral part of the union structure. Their function commonly includes recruiting members, collecting dues, and acting as a channel for union communications. This, however, does not mean that the shop steward is a subordinate union official who is subservient to the higher echelons which negotiate the collective agreement. On the contrary, he is not elected as a part of the union hierarchy but by a "show of hands" in the work place. His constituency is the workers on the shop floor; it is from them that he derives his authority; it is their interest which he serves; and it is to them that he owes responsibility and loyalty. Particularly in their bargaining activities and settlements of grievances, shop stewards act almost completely independently of those levels of the union which have negotiated the collective agreement. They are often ready to circumvent procedures established by the agreement, call strikes in violation of government or union rules, and make settlements in violation of union policy if this is necessary to satisfy the demands of those who elected them. The union has no practical method of control over these activities of the shop stewards; and indeed, many union officers look upon workplace bargaining with suspicion and upon shop stewards as a challenge to their authority.* The practical result is that although shop stewards in England are union officers, they are, in their bargaining function, nearly as independent as works councils in other countries.

This independence of works councils and shop stewards is difficult for Americans to comprehend fully for it seems so contrary to the nature of unions. But it must be remembered that European unions are umbrella-type organizations which spread to cover an entire industry at the top level but have little organizational structure underneath. Regional and branch organizations serve as administrative units and perform political and social functions, but the local union, as we know it, simply does not exist. The umbrella organization negotiates collective agreements, but the subordinate units do not undertake to administer or elaborate those agreements. This is in contrast to American unions, which might be characterized as pyramid-type organizations, built up from a base of local unions whose primary function is to represent employees in the making of collective agreements and the settlement of grievances. Works councils on the Continent, and shop stewards in England, perform this function of representation at the local level. But unlike our local unions they are not the base upon which the union structure is built. Instead, they have little or no linkage to the organizational structure which makes the collective agreement.

In every country the unions are seeking to extend their influence and control to the local level. In France, Germany, and Italy the unions have tried to develop a system of shop stewards to parallel or supplant the works councils. None of these efforts to channel grievances through the union stewards instead of the works council has had much success. In Germany the shop stewards do little more than serve as a first step for the grievance and then pass it on to the works council. In France the employers have rigidly resisted any intervention by union representatives, spurning them as outsiders and insisting that matters be handled by the works councils. In Italy, the system of articulated bargaining looks toward locally negotiated plant agreements administered by local representatives, but as yet the unions have not developed local organizations capable of carrying out this function. Unions in Belgium and England seek to integrate their plant representatives or shop stewards more completely into the union structure, but the gap between the national officers

* See Allan Flanders, *Labor-Management Relations and the Democratic Challenge, infra*, p. 488.

who negotiate the agreements and the locally elected representatives who bargain at the plant level remains largely unbridged.

Breadth of Functions Beyond
Administering Collective Agreement

The second significant difference between West European works councils and American grievance committees is that the function of works councils is not limited to administering or enforcing the collective agreement but extends to bargaining for better terms on the one hand and to protecting legal rights or providing social benefits on the other hand. In theory, at least, it extends to participating in the business and financial decisions of the enterprise.

We have emphasized earlier that the collective agreements negotiated at the national or regional level establish only minimum terms. The works council often takes the lead in bargaining at the plant level for terms better than those in the collective agreement. Because the terms thus negotiated at the local level may be 20 to 50 percent higher than those provided in the formal agreement, this function of the works councils may be of far greater immediate importance to the workers than administration of the formal agreement. Studies in England have shown that more than half the shop steward's time and effort is spent in negotiating wage rates. The works council may be legally forbidden to negotiate wages or other terms regulated by the collective agreement, as in Germany and Italy; or the plant agreement it negotiates may not have the legal status of a contract, as in France and Germany; but the legal rules and theories give way before the economic and institutional imperatives. The works council, in one form or another, negotiates terms and conditions of employment which are of more practical relevance in the work place than those negotiated by the union in its formal agreement.

The works' councils, of course, handle problems which we would term grievances, including matters that some American employers would insist were management prerogatives. Thus, works councils on the Continent are by law or agreement not only authorized to deal with disputes over layoffs, discharges, changes in work rules and schedules, and the application of piece rates; they are also to be consulted on plans for curtailment of production, changes of production processes, plant transfers, and plant mergers. Although the functions of shop stewards in England are not formally defined, they often deal with an equally wide range of issues. On the Continent, works councils in addition supervise the enforcement of applicable labor laws, such as statutory holidays and vacations, legal limitations on overtime, statutory protection against mass dismissals and individual discharges, and legal prohibitions against discrimination because of race, religion, nationality, or political beliefs.

The authority of the works council, as described in legal provisions, extends considerably beyond that of an American grievance committee or local union to include the right to participate in decision-making on economic, financial, and technical aspects of the firm. In Germany, for example, the works council can appoint representatives to the economic committee of the enterprise, which is legally entitled to demand information concerning the financial conditions of the firm, its profit and loss situation, and its financial plans. The committee can advise management on all important economic matters, such as product and price changes, changes in technology and organization, and changes in management structure. This function of the works councils, however, is often more theoretical than real, and the economic committees exist only on paper, if at all. At best the workers' representatives have only an advisory function, and the right of decision remains in management. This advisory function becomes entirely empty because European management has a very broad concept of business secrets and refuses to give these bodies sufficiently detailed or comprehensible information to enable them to make meaningful suggestions.

Beyond this, works councils on the Continent often administer the welfare institutions in the plant, and, indeed, this is often more important than grievance handling. Thus, they administer benefit plans such as emergency loan funds, vacation homes, health centers, medical services within the plant, canteens, and various cultural and athletic activities. In this, as in the functions previously described, the works council plays much more the role of the local union than the grievance committee in the United States. For just that reason, it is important to remember that the works council is not a local union and is not an integral part of the union structure. Nor does the union earn any loyalty or support from the workers because of the functions performed by the works council. On the contrary, such performance detracts from the union's relevance to the workers and undermines its effectiveness.

In Belgium and France, however, these functions of worker representation are divided and performed by two different bodies. In general, the enforcement of the collective agreement and labor legislation is performed by so-called union or worker delegates — the works council proper. The social welfare activities, employee-management cooperation, and economic advisory functions are performed by so-called enterprise councils or committees, which have representatives from both employees and management. In addition, safety committees, made up of representatives elected by the employees, are required by law in most countries to be established at the plant level. These committees are considered to be one of the important agencies of worker representation and, like the works councils, are not an integral part of the union structure but are organizationally independent.

Lack of Developed Procedures

The third distinctive character of the works-council structure is that the council generally lacks developed procedures. Grievances do not move up a prescribed series of steps, nor are there provisions for written statements of the grievance and written answers. The individual generally takes the matter up directly with his immediate superior, and if he fails to obtain satisfaction he goes to a member of the works council who may take it to various levels of management; but there is no orderly sequence of appeals. In Germany the individual may go to the union steward, who will refer his grievance to the works council, and if the works council fails to settle the matter it may be taken up by the union secretary. But again, this is not an orderly or prescribed procedure.

In England there is more semblance of procedure. In some plants there may be a hierarchy of shop stewards with "general" stewards and "convenor" or "senior" stewards, and the collective agreements may contain procedural provisions concerning stewards. Moreover, because no clear distinction is drawn in England between disputes on rights arising out of an agreement and disputes on interests for new terms, the contractual procedures for settling disputes generally become potentially applicable. These procedures may include a series of steps culminating in a joint committee of the national unions and employers association. However, where grievances or disputes arise at the shop level and are handled by the shop stewards, these procedural provisions are in fact largely irrelevant. Few such disputes go above the plant level, and within the plant the procedures are quite informal and governed more by practice than by contractual provisions. Formal procedures simply do not thrive in the climate of plant-level labor relations, so that grievance handling by shop stewards in England is, in practice, as lacking in orderly procedures as grievance handling by works councils on the Continent.

ENFORCEMENT OF THE COLLECTIVE AGREEMENT

A full and precise analysis of the enforceability of the collective agreement would lead us into a thicket of legal theories, one through which European scholars love to thread their way but which would leave us snarled in brambles. To avoid the worst of that thicket, I focus on two practical questions: First, how are disputes as to the interpretation and application of the collective agreement resolved? Second, to what extent does the existence of the collective agreement bar strikes and lockouts? My concern here is with conclusions, not with the theories used to reach those conclusions.

First, disputes as to interpretation and application of the agreement are seldom settled by arbitration. There are, however, exceptions. In Italy, mass layoffs and individual dismissals are governed by interconfederal collective agreements, and those agreements provide that disputes as to their application shall be decided by an arbitration tribunal presided over by an impartial chairman. In Germany, disputes as to certain working conditions, such as shift hours, incentive rates, assignment of vacations, and rules governing employee conduct, may be submitted to *ad hoc* arbitration panels chaired by a neutral third person. Some British disputes procedures provide for resort to arbitration, but this is rarely used to resolve grievances over the application of an agreement. All other disputes arising under an agreement are resolved either by the courts or by economic force.

In France, Belgium, and Germany these disputes generally go to specialized labor courts, which may be constituted in various ways. In France the labor courts are composed entirely of lay members, with an equal number being elected by the workers and the employers covered by the particular court. Appeals from the labor court are to the courts of appeal, which have special sections for handling such cases, and ultimate appeal is to the Supreme Court. In Belgium the labor courts of first instance are composed of lay judges, but the labor courts of appeal have lawyers as chairmen. Again, ultimate appeal is to the regular courts. Germany has a more comprehensive, three-level system of labor courts. All courts are composed of a chairman, who is a lawyer and normally a judge, and one employer and one employee representative nominated by the organizations on each side. England, Holland, and Italy have no labor courts, so resort must be to the ordinary courts.

Disputes are brought to the courts not in the form of grievances by the union claiming violation of the collective agreement but in the form of a suit by the individual claiming violation of his contract of employment. The collective agreement is interpreted and applied because it is read into the individual's contract, either by force of custom, as in England, or by force of law, as in Germany. The union is normally not a formal party to the suit but often is the active advocate. Although the labor courts or ordinary courts in adjudicating these individual suits serve somewhat as the substitute for our grievance arbitration, their function is much broader than interpretation and application of the collective agreement. They may determine the existence and validity of agreements. Also, they may entertain suits based on informal local agreements or individual agreements which have provided for better terms than those in the collective agreements. More important, labor courts have jurisdiction to enforce various employment rights which are created by statute, such as protection against unjust discharge, right to notice of termination, limitations on mass dismissals, and rights to paid holidays and vacations.

Two practical distinctions between the labor courts and grievance arbitration should be noted. One is that in Western Europe the individual controls his grievance; it cannot be settled by the union without his consent, for he can bring an individual suit on his individual right. The most the union can do is refuse to support his case in court. The other practical distinction is that cases are seldom brought to court to correct continuing violations. Almost all suits are brought by employees after termination of employment to collect past underpayment of wages or damages for wrongful dismissal. In short, suits in the labor courts or other courts, unlike grievance arbitration, are not a part of the ongoing administration of the collective agreement.

Court suits are not the only method of giving meaning to the collective agreement; recourse may be had to economic force. Indeed, this is the chief instrument used in England by shop stewards to contest employers' actions under formal or informal agreements. Suits to enforce individual contracts of employment are rare because they are too slow and too expensive, and the remedies are too limited. But recourse to economic force depends at least in part on the extent to which it is legally permissible during the contract.

The effect of collective agreements on the right to use economic force covers a wide spectrum in Western Europe. At one end of the spectrum are Germany and Holland, where the law implies into every formal collective agreement a "peace obligation." During the term of the agreement neither party may resort to economic force concerning any matter regulated by the agreement. The obligation, however, does not extend to disputes on matters not regulated by the agreement, leaving a substantial loophole because of the lack of comprehensiveness of most formal agreements. The peace obligation binds the union not to engage in or tolerate any economic action and makes the union liable in damages. The union, however, is not liable for unauthorized strikes by local groups which it is unable to control. Union members also are bound by the peace obligation, violation of which makes them subject to discharge. France and Italy too have implied peace obligations. However, these do not apply throughout the contract term but only during the period required for conciliation procedures. Belgian law imposes a peace obligation nominally equivalent to that imposed by the German; the union is obligated not to engage in or tolerate any economic action during the agreement on any matter regulated by the agreement. However, this obligation has only moral force because the union lacks legal personality and cannot be sued. The employer's only remedy is to discharge the strikers. This brings us to the other end of the spectrum, which is represented by British law. In England the collective agreement is generally considered as creating no binding legal obligation between the union and the employer, but only moral obligations. There are strong arguments that this traditional view is not correct, that the collective agreement is a legally enforceable contract between the union and the employer. Regardless of which view is taken, however, there is no implied peace obligation, and in the absence of an express no-strike clause the union is legally free to strike at any time. Again, the employer's only remedy is discharge of the striking employees.

Apart from the legally imposed peace obligation, the parties may by their contract restrict economic action during the contract term. No-strike, no-lockout clauses are not strangers to any of the collective bargaining systems in Western Europe. However, they are not widely used nor readily accepted by unions in any of the countries. Such clauses are legally enforceable in all countries except, of course, Belgium and perhaps England. Probably more important than the presence of legally imposed or contractually accepted peace obligations and their enforceability is the actual propensities of unions to strike during the contract term. Although generalizations are dangerous, it might be ventured that strikes during the contract term are rare in Germany and Holland, occasional in Belgium, frequent in France and Italy, and commonplace in England. Again it should be emphasized that these are not strikes called by the contracting unions at the industry level but rather strikes called by works councils, shop stewards, or other local groups primarily for the purpose of obtaining concessions at the local level.

CONCLUSION

There is no need to summarize, nor is any summary possible, for collective bargaining systems are too complex to capsulize. I would only conclude as I began by trying again to make explicit my premise and my purpose. The collective bargaining systems of Western Europe have many superficial similarities to that of the United States. However, they have critical differences which reach to the very roots of these systems and which cause them to function quite differently from our own. Those differences are easily discounted or overlooked, and we may fail to realize fully that we are dealing with systems that are foreign to our experience and to our preconceptions. My purpose has been to emphasize those differences, to mark them out in such bold relief that you will see clearly their importance. Of necessity, I have greatly oversimplified and overstated. Important details have been omitted and significant variations from country to country have been glossed over. But I hope that this stark outline will make clear the contrast between European and American systems of collective bargaining.

Author's Recommended Reading List

Aaron, B., ed., *Dispute Settlement Procedure in Five Western European Countries* (Los Angeles: Institute of Industrial Relations, Univ. of Calif., 1969).

Barkin, Solomon, ed., *International Labor* (New York: Harper & Row, 1967).

Flanders, A., *Collective Bargaining: Prescription for Change* (London: Faber & Faber, 1967).

Flanders, A., *The Fawley Productivity Agreements* (London: Faber & Faber, 1964).

Flanders, A., *Industrial Relations: What's Wrong With the System* (London: Faber & Faber, 1967).

Galenson, W., *Trade Union Democracy in Western Europe* (Berkeley: Univ. of Calif. Press, 1961).

Grunfeld, C., *Modern Trade Union Law* (London: Sweet & Maxwell, 1966).

Kahn-Freund, O., ed., *Labour Relations and the Law, a Comparative Study* (London: Stevens & Sons, 1965).

McPherson, W. H., and Myers, F., *French Labor Courts: Judgment by Peers* (Urbana: Institute of Labor and Industrial Relations, Univ. of Ill., 1966).

Sturmthal, A., *Workers Councils* (Cambridge: Harvard Univ. Press, 1964).

Turner, H. A., and Roberts, G., *Labor Relations in the Motor Industry* (New York: A. M. Kelley, 1968).

Turner, H. A., *Trade Union Growth, Structure and Policy* (London: George Allen & Unwin Ltd., 1962).

Guigni, G., "Recent Developments of Collective Bargaining in Italy," 91 *Int. Lab. Rev.* 273 (1965).

Konowitz, L., "The Strike and Lockout Under French Law," 9 *St. Louis Univ. L.J.* 211 (1964).

Ross, A., "Prosperity and British Industrial Relations," 2 *Ind. Rel.* 63 (1963).

Ross, A., "Prosperity and Labor Relations in Western Europe: Italy and France," 16 *Ind. & Lab. Rel. Rev.* 63 (1962).

Ross, A., "Prosperity and Labor Relations in Europe: The Case of West Germany," 76 *Q.J. Econ.* 331 (1962).

Summers, C., "American and European Labor Law: The Use and Usefulness of Foreign Experience," 16 *Buffalo L. Rev.* 210 (1966).

Summers, C., "Labor Relations in The Common Market," 43 *Harv. Bus. Rev.* 148 (1965).

Weber, A., "The Structures of Collective Bargaining and Bargaining Power: Foreign Experiences," 6 *J. of Law & Econ.* 79 (1963).

"Labour Law in Europe, With Special Reference to the Common Market," *Int. & Comp. Law,* Supp. Pub. No. 5 (1962).

LABOR RELATIONS AND THE ROLE OF LAW IN GREAT BRITAIN

By Cyril Grunfeld

INTRODUCTION

In round figures, the employees in the United Kingdom number about 23-3/4 million out of a population of 55 million. Slightly under two thirds of employed persons are men and slightly over one third women. The general distribution of the labor force is, broadly, as follows:[1]

	(Millions)
Manufacturing	9.0
Building and construction	1.75
Transport and communication	1.75
Distributive trades	3.0
Financial, professional, and scientific services	3.25
Central and local government service	1.5
Agriculture	0.5
Other industries, including gas, electricity, and coal mining	3.0

Confining our attention to the private sector of manufacturing, the pattern of distribution of its labor force is universally recognizable among advanced industrial countries: Of some 200,000 different establishments in the United Kingdom about 150,000 employ 10 or fewer employees; 6-1/2 million out of the nine million employees in manufacturing are in factories of 100 or more people, while there are about 70 establishments at each of which more than 5,000 are employed, nearly half of them in the motor industry. Over the general field of employment, the proportion of white-collar employees, usually administrative, technical, supervisory and clerical, shows a small but steady annual increase. At the present rate of increase, they will be the majority of the labor force in the foreseeable future.[2]

For present purposes, the key characteristic of British labor relations is that similar procedures, institutions, and rules of law apply to both the establishment and the interpretation and enforce-

---

[1] Report of Royal Commission on Trade Unions and Employers' Associations (Cmnd. 3623), paras. 25, 26 and 192; also, Ministry of Labour Gazette, April 1968.

[2] Bain, *Trade Union Growth and Recognition*, Royal Commission Research Paper No. 6.

ment of agreements about terms and conditions of employment, both to disputes arising out of collective bargaining and also to day-to-day disputes in the running of plants, both to disputes of interest and to disputes of right. Disputes have not been classified into distinct categories each with its own special treatment under the law.

THE PARTIES TO COLLECTIVE BARGAINING

The central method in Great Britain of establishing and changing terms and conditions of employment, including procedures for their interpretation and enforcement, is that of voluntary collective bargaining at both industry and plant levels; and the Royal Commission on Trade Unions and Employers' Associations (hereafter, the Royal Commission) has affirmed "that collective bargaining is the best method of conducting industrial relations"[3] in Britain.

Although only 42 percent of the labor force is unionized (over 50 percent of manual workers and about 30 percent of white-collar workers), collective bargaining directly affects, it is estimated, some 65 percent of employees,[4] since collectively agreed terms are normally applied to all the relevant employees in a plant, unionists and nonunionists alike. One might add at this point that nearly a further 18 percent of employees have minimum wage rates, standard hours, vacations with pay and certain cognate terms established through the machinery of the 57 Wages Councils and the two Agricultural Wages Boards at present in being.[5] For the remaining 17 percent or so of the labor force no authoritative account has yet been given of how their terms of employment came to be settled, save that clearly some, like senior management and domestic servants, bargain, where they do, individually, while others, like the armed forces, have special procedures.

At the industry level, collective bargaining is predominantly between unions or federations of unions and employers' associations, like the Engineering Employers' Federation. Nevertheless, in each industry, important companies will be found outside the associations of employers. Examples in the key engineering, or metal-using, industry, which employs a third of the labor force in manufacturing, are Ford Motors and Vauxhall (General Motors). Also, where a single employer monopolizes an industry or occupational area, industry-wide bargaining is of necessity conducted with all the unions concerned by a single employing organization, as notably in the case

---

[3] Royal Commission Report, para. 203 (1).
[4] Royal Commission Report, para. 38.
[5] I.e., in Great Britain excluding N. Ireland.

of employment by central government and by the nationalized industries like the National Coal Board and British Railways Board. Industrial agreements may be national in scope or confined to regional or district coverage.

Employers' associations number about 1,350, of which more than half have only regional or district coverage.[6] At the apex of the employers' organizations stands the Confederation of British Industries, whose function is advisory and coordinating and also that of acting as national spokesman and representative of employers (i.e., principally, senior management). The CBI does not exercise any control over the collective bargaining of employers' associations at industry (or any other) level.

At the last recorded count at the end of 1966, there were 574 trade unions in Britain with a total membership exceeding 10 million. The number of unions is declining steadily each year, chiefly through mergers. Even so, the total of 574 unions is somewhat misleading since one half of all trade unionists are in the nine largest unions, while the top 38 unions contain 80 percent of total union membership.[7] At the apex of the British trade union movement stands the Trades Union Congress, to which only some 160 unions are affiliated but these embrace nearly 90 percent of total union membership.[8]

The TUC, like the CBI, has no power of direct control over the affairs of its members, including collective bargaining and direct industrial action. Within its sphere, however, it is a more substantial and influential body than the CBI, not only advising and coordinating but providing also many important services — conciliatory, arbitral, informational, educational — for its members and, today, vetting wage claims on a voluntary basis as part of the general incomes policy at present being pursued, to which I shall return later. So far, the trade union movement in Britain has not divided along religious, racial, or political lines and has avoided any serious fission between blue-collar and white-collar employees. The TUC is the recognized national spokesman for industrial labor. Like the CBI it is regularly consulted by the government, and its members and union nominees are to be found throughout the extensive network of advisory, consultative, administrative, and adjudicatory bodies which permeate the running of the country and implement the generally held belief in the virtue of a widely participative democracy.

---

[6] Royal Comission Report, para. 29.
[7] Ministry of Labour Gazette, November 1967.
[8] TUC Annual Report, 1968.

More than 80 percent of the Labour Party's national funds come from the unions.[9] A union that wishes to give financial support to "party-political activities" — candidature for Parliament and local government authorities, maintenance of elected members, and meetings and literature for these purposes — whether of the Labour Party or any other party (though, in practice, until now, of the Labour Party) has to obtain a majority vote of its members to establish a political fund. The political-fund rules subsequently incorporated in its rule book must permit dissentient members to contract-out of the obligation to contribute to the fund.[10] At present, 113 unions, including most of the largest, have such funds. About 1-1/2 million of their eight million members do not pay political fund contributions.[11]

An accurate picture of how the Conservative Party is financed is still awaited, but under the Companies Act 1967, companies must now reveal their political contributions, and it is becoming clear that large sums are donated by employers and management either from personal or from corporate funds.

At *plant* level, bargaining is normally conducted between management and shop stewards, who are often local union officials chosen by employees in the workplace to represent them in collective dealings with management. In the case of multi-union plants, the shop stewards of the respective unions may form a joint committee for bargaining purposes, electing one of their number as convenor. There are about 175,000 shop stewards throughout industry. Behind them normally stand the supportive services of the very much smaller number (about 3,000) of full-time district, regional, and national officials of their unions.[12]

THE PRECONDITIONS OF COLLECTIVE BARGAINING

For the establishment of voluntary collective bargaining, three conditions have usually to be fulfilled: freedom to join a trade union, recognition of the union as bargaining agent for its members, and bargaining by management and union in good faith. A word about each of these conditions in the British context.

Freedom of Association

English law does not guarantee freedom of association. For

---

[9] Harrison, *Trade Unions and Labour Party since 1945,* p. 72.
[10] The law governing the political activities of British trade unions is analyzed in Grunfeld, *Modern Trade Union Law,* Part Four (1966).
[11] Royal Commission Report, para. 923.
[12] Royal Commission Report, para. 99.

over 150 years British employees have simply associated, overcoming opposition by establishing stable, financially sound organizations and deploying the economic power implicit in the collective withdrawal or calculated application of their labor. The legality of their associations was finally recognized in the Trade Union Act 1871. The way in which the law regards the strike and other forms of direct action, whether for organizational or other ends, will be described later.

Occasionally, but relatively rarely now, an employer will insist on a "yellow-dog" contract. Such a contract remains lawful, if archaic; and the Royal Commission has recommended that yellow-dog contracts be declared void. Far less rarely, especially in the case of white-collar employees, an employer will dismiss or not engage an employee who wishes to belong to a union. This remains the employer's right in English law, but the Royal Commission's recommendations about "unfair" dismissal will, if legislated, affect dismissal for favoring trade unionism. Not infrequently in the case of white-collar employees, independent trade unionism has been forestalled by the creation of "staff associations." Views about these vary, but they are beginning to come under pressure as the desire to participate in the decisions that affect one's livelihood and one's life strengthens and spreads through society.

A government contractor or subcontractor who wishes to insist on a yellow-dog contract or who wishes, in practice, to refuse to employ trade unionists, will fall foul of the standard "fair wages" clause which is included in all government contracts with outside contractors and requires that "The contractor shall recognise the freedom of his workpeople to be members of Trade Unions." [13] This fair-wages clause, recommended by the House of Commons' Fair Wages Resolution of 1946, is also used today by the leading local authorities and nationalized industries in their contracts with outside contractors. The sanction is the formidable commercial one of termination of the contract or removal from the official list of approved contractors or both. Violations have been rare.

Union Recognition

There is at present no scheme of law to compel an employer or management to accept a union as bargaining agent for its members. However, with certain exceptions, manual-worker unions have se-

---

[13] The bulk of the fair wages clause is concerned with observance of the terms and conditions of employment laid down in relevant industrial collective agreements.

cured recognition for bargaining purposes over the greater area of industry. The present position is the result of a protracted conflict moving from one industry to another over more than a century. In the first half of the period, the law was interventionist and repressive. Repression stimulated a proportionate reaction in the shape of stronger union organization and the creation of a political party. From the Trade Disputes Act 1906 until 1964, English law largely stood aside from industrial conflict, including conflict over union recognition. The methods of conciliation, arbitration, and investigation were strongly developed to help to prevent or settle open conflicts; and the vital role of the Industrial Relations Department of the Ministry of Labour (now the Department of Employment and Productivity) will be referred to at the end of this paper. But since 1964, a new legal situation has begun to emerge, which I shall analyze briefly later.

For white-collar unions, recognition continues to be an active general problem.[14] Fully recognized in the spheres of central and local government, there are many areas in the major private sectors of industry and commerce where recognition continues to be denied by management. In banking, the efforts of the Industrial Relations Department, at the instance of the National Union of Bank Employees, have only in 1968, after more than a decade, arrived at a successful conclusion. But there is considerable concern that all white-collar unions might not be prepared quietly to wait one or two decades for concession of a right increasingly regarded as one that ought to be accorded to a union with substantial membership in any class of employees.

Both the Royal Commission and the Conservative Party, in its electoral program contained in the booklet "Fair Deal at Work," propose indirect legal pressures against managements resisting recognition. The union concerned would in the last resort be given the right to bring its current wage or other claim before an arbitration tribunal, which would have the power to make an enforceable award. It would be a process of compulsory *ad hoc* recognition claim by claim until, possibly, management saw the light. There is still no proposal for direct compulsion.

Bargaining in Good Faith

English law knows of no "unfair labor practices." Once a union is *de facto* recognized, management may be expected to bargain in good faith and to be kept to this expectation by the same

---

[14] See Bain, *Trade Union Growth and Recognition*, above noted.

economic pressures that led to recognition. The rules of the game have been formulated and enforced by the industrial parties themselves within a general legal and administrative framework consisting of the law relating to strikes and other forms of direct action, the expertise and work of the Industrial Relations Department and the outside authorities and experts on whose services the Department frequently calls, and, one might add, the Disputes Committee of the TUC. Into this general framework of collective bargaining has recently been inserted the structures of incomes and prices policy, which will be described in a later section.

LEGAL BASES OF BARGAINING POWER

For unions and, indeed, for unofficial work groups the principal *legal* basis of bargaining power is the "right to strike," though in practice less dramatic forms of direct action may be equally effective. First, I shall give a brief and, necessarily, simplified theoretical analysis of the law of strike action together with other forms of direct action, and then, I should like to describe the way in which the law has been developed and applied by the British judiciary in the period 1964-1968.

The Rules in the Abstract[15]

In Britain, the "right to strike" is not a legal phrase of art, but a political phrase. In English law, it has a three-tier meaning. It includes the legal immunity of the rank-and-file employees on the job for withdrawing their labor; the legal immunity of their official and unofficial leaders in threatening or directing a collective withdrawal of labor; and the legal immunity of trade union funds from actions for vicarious liability in tort for what the authorized officials or members may have done.

The Employees on the Job

The foundation of the right to strike in Britain is the power of each employee to withdraw his labor lawfully in concert with others. Until judicial doubts expressed in and after 1964, this power was orthodoxly believed to be based on each employee's acknowledged right to terminate his employment lawfully at any time by giving and working out the due period of notice (generally, since the Contracts of Employment Act 1963, a minimum of seven days); and

---

[15] For a basic analysis of the law of strike action in Britain, see Grunfeld, *op. cit.*, Part Five. The deficiencies in strike law as seen by the Royal Commission are discussed in the Report in chapter XIV.

so a strike notice of the appropriate length given for all would establish strike legality. However, certain of the judges in *Rookes* v. *Barnard*,[16] *Stratford* v. *Lindley*,[17] and *Morgan* v. *Fry* (at first instance) [18] appeared to be of the opinion that a strike notice was the notice of an intention not to turn up to work in *breach* of contract because the *industrial* intention of a strike is not to terminate but to suspend the contractual employment relationship. But suspension by one side only is not recognized in English law; therefore, since the true intention of a strike notice was not to terminate, and since it was ineffective to suspend, its effect, if carried out, must be to break the contracts of the employees concerned. In other words, if these opinions represented the correct state of English law, there was no right to strike at the rank-and-file level.

The Court of Appeal in *Morgan* v. *Fry*[19] have just drawn back from the abyss. Lord Denning M.R. has said that, when due strike notice is given, there is to be *implied* an agreement by both sides to suspend the employment relationship; Davies L.J. agreed. *A fortiori* it would be a lawful withdrawal of labor if the strike notice specifically stated that the strikers were terminating their contracts: their contracts would then be terminated. Clearly, for the time being, the right to strike has been preserved, whatever its legal basis, at least until the House of Lords passes on the issue.

The Royal Commission, who seem to have anticipated the Court of Appeal decision,[20] propose no changes in the present, problematical state of the law. If fundamental changes are to be made, the Commission recommend that the entire subject be referred to an expert committee, possibly the Industrial Law Committee that is recommended to be attached to the pivotal new Commission on Industrial Relations.[21] The Conservative Party do not refer to the problem.

If employees have agreed to observe due procedure before striking, due strike notice will not legalize a strike or any other form of industrial action in breach of contract like a concerted go-slow or collective ban on compulsory overtime. In these situations, each employee always has been and will continue to be in breach of his or her contract of employment. But, in the period since the war, Brit-

---

[16] [1964] A.C. 1129.
[17] [1965] A.C. 307.
[18] [1967] 2 All E.R. 386.
[19] [1968] 3 All E.R. 452.
[20] Royal Commission Report, para. 949.
[21] The "Industrial Relations Commission" in the Report. The change of name was made to avoid a confusion of initials between the new body and the Industrial Reorganization Corporation.

ish managements as a whole have shown no inclination to sue individual workers for damages for breach of their contracts of employment. This reluctance will not necessarily continue.[22]

Union Officials and Unofficial Strike Leaders

In practice, the real importance of deciding whether employees who strike, go slow, or ban overtime are in breach of their contracts of employment has lain in determining whether a foundation has been laid for the legal liability of their leaders. In broad terms, it is a civil wrong to cause damage by threatening an unlawful act, to induce an unlawful act and so cause damage, or to conspire by means of an unlawful act to cause damage. Breach of contract, including breach of contract of employment, is an unlawful act, certainly in the first two cases and probably in the third as well.

The *threat* by official or unofficial leaders of an unlawful strike or other industrial action has been legalized, where a trade dispute is contemplated or furthered, by the Trade Disputes Act 1965, the validity of which the Commission has confirmed as "necessary for the protection of trade union officials in the reasonable performance of their functions." [23] Unofficial leaders are proposed by a majority of the Royal Commission to be excluded from the 1965 Act. The Conservative Party has pledged itself to repeal the 1965 Act.

Under Section 3 of the Trade Disputes Act 1906, *inducing* breach of contracts of *employment* is not actionable if done in contemplation or furtherance of a trade dispute. A majority of the Commission has recommended that this protection should no longer extend to unofficial leaders of unlawful strikes and other forms of industrial action. This would mean that, whereas management can now only sue unofficial leaders in such circumstances for damages for breach of their own contracts of employment, they would in future be able to sue them in tort for damages and, more important, for an interlocutory (i.e., emergency) injunction ordering them to stop leading the unlawful action, with a discretionary fine or imprisonment as the sanction in default. The minority of the Commission considered such a legal move against unofficial strike leaders to be premature. It thought that no change in the law directed against unofficial leaders should be contemplated until one could see the effect of the new law of unfair dismissal (dismissal being a significant

---

[22] If the Royal Commission's recommendations about the Industrial (Labor) Tribunals are implemented, employers as well as employees will have access to a speedy, informal, and inexpensive procedure to enforce contractual obligations; though practical considerations of labor-management relations will doubtless decide whether use is made of the new law-enforcement facilities.

[23] Royal Commission Report, para. 852.

cause of unlawful, unofficial strikes) and of the improved labor relations and disputes procedures at "factory" level which form part of the general transformation of the industrial relations scene which the main sections of the Report of the Royal Commission envision.

Even official strike leaders may find themselves stripped of the protection of Section 3 as a logical projection of the judgments in *Rookes* v. *Barnard*.[24] For, where a union official employs democratic procedures, in which the rank and file participate, to decide on unlawful strike action, the leader may be held to have combined, i.e., *conspired*, with the employees on the job to damage the employer by means of unlawful acts, namely, the democratically resolved withdrawal of labor, etc., in breach of contracts of employment; and so, Section 3, which is confined to "inducement," would be circumvented. This possibility the Commission unanimously, and without differentiating between official and unofficial acts, decided should be removed where a trade dispute is present, another task, possibly, for the new Industrial Law Committee. The Conservative Party do not refer to the problem in their pamphlet "Fair Deal at Work."

The Union Funds

Under Section 4 of the Trade Disputes Act 1906 a trade union may not be sued in respect of torts committed by its servants or agents in trade-dispute situations or, indeed, in respect of a fairly wide range of non-trade-dispute torts. The Royal Commission has recommended that the immunity of trade union funds be confined to trade-dispute torts, adding two detailed proposals to reinforce the scope of a "trade dispute" at points where the Irish and English courts had begun to sap the walls of the definition.

Even if this recommendation is enacted, a "trade dispute," which is the key concept defining the coverage of the Trade Disputes Acts 1906 and 1965, will not include a dispute the predominant purpose of which is to pursue a personal vendetta, or racial discrimination, or a purely political objective, or any other nontrade object, nor will it include a pure union-employer dispute nor, again, a pure inter-union dispute as, arguably, where one union challenges an "established" union in a plant or enterprise in respect of the latter's recruiting or bargaining "rights."

The Conservative Party proposes not to reinforce the definition of a "trade dispute" but, on the contrary, to redraw its scope more narrowly in certain important respects. They wish to take out of the

---

[24] [1964] A.C. 1129.

protection of the Act any direct industrial action to enforce a closed or union shop, or to prevent an employer from employing certain types of labor on work they are qualified to undertake, or to pursue a jurisdictional, demarcation, or other inter-union dispute "in which the employer has no interest to support or oppose either side." [25] They also propose outlawing sympathetic union action, but the judiciary in its decisions since 1964 may already have largely anticipated this proposal.

Sympathetic Union Action: the Secondary Boycott

The most important form of sympathetic action, the secondary boycott, usually involves causing a breach of *commercial* contract between the employer in dispute and an outside supplier or customer, since it is an industrial stratagem whereby an employer's supplies are stopped or his outlets of distribution are sealed off. Consequently, the secondary boycott is not covered by Section 3 of the Trade Disputes Act 1906 (inducing breach of contract of *employment*) and attracts the tort of *inducing* breach of commercial contract where the union (or unofficial) leaders bring direct pressure to bear on the supplier or customer and the tort of *procuring* breach of commercial contract where pressure is brought to bear indirectly through the unlawful acts of the employees of the supplier or customer, e.g., by inducing those employees to disobey orders to deliver supplies to the employer in dispute.

The Royal Commission recommends that Section 3 of the 1906 Act should be altered to include inducing breach of commercial as well as employment contracts, though the majority advise withholding this protection from unofficial boycott leaders. One need not be a clairvoyant to foresee that the courts are likely to insist on the distinction between "inducing" and "procuring" breach of commercial contract. But, with the proposed amendment, it might be theoretically possible to trace out for union officials the steps to take to impose a lawful secondary boycott. As already mentioned, the Conservative Party would withdraw all forms of sympathetic action from such protection as the 1906 and 1965 Acts afford by excluding such action from the definition of a "trade dispute."

Picketing

The prime objects of picketing are to make known the existence and the facts of a dispute and peaceably to persuade persons to abstain from working or supplying or giving their custom to the em-

---

[25] "Fair Deal at Work," p. 30.

ployer in dispute. The law of picketing is to be found partly in Section 2 of the 1906 Act ("peacefully obtaining or communicating information, or . . . peacefully persuading any person to work or abstain from working" in contemplation or furtherance of a trade dispute), partly in the law of tort relating especially to nuisance, partly in the criminal law concerning physical violence to person or property or the threat of violence, and partly in the criminal law about public places, like public nuisance, conduct likely to cause a breach of the peace[26] and obstruction to the highway.[27] Pickets may also be protected by Section 3 of the 1906 Act if, where there is a trade dispute, they succeed in persuading workers to stop work in breach of their employment contracts. On the other hand, pickets who, for example, induce a lorry driver not to deliver his goods will commit the tort of indirectly procuring breach of the commercial contract between the lorry driver's employer and the employer in dispute.

The Royal Commission has recommended that, where there is a trade dispute, pickets should be immune from liability for causing a breach of commercial contract between the employer in dispute and his "customer," which presumably is intended to include a supplier. The Conservative Party say nothing about picketing.

Other Forms of Direct Action

Work to rule ("meticulosis")[28] is lawful at present. Go-slow ("working without enthusiasm")[29] or a ban on contractual overtime are breaches of contracts of employment. Many other restrictive practices could be brought under the headings of disobedience, misconduct, or breach of duty of fidelity. The Royal Commission sees the best solution in its major proposals for the general reconstruction of industrial relations and their continued investigation. The Conservative Party appear to be of the same mind.

Only a word is necessary about the legality of direct action by management. Lawful action is simple to plan if deemed necessary For example, legally sufficient notice to each member of the labor force concerned may establish a lawful lockout; and virtually any employee, including a shop steward, may be lawfully dismissed with due notice or wages in lieu; though the Commission's proposal about "unfair" dismissal could be relevant here.

---

[26] As in *Piddington* v. *Bates*, [1960] 3 All E.R. 660.

[27] As in *Tynan* v. *Balmer*, [1966] 2 All E.R. 133.

[28] The word coined by white collar workers in the national health service when applying pressure for higher wages during the 1961-1962 "pay pause."

[29] The phrase coined by the draftsmen in a dispute this year.

Industrial Conflict and the Judiciary, 1964-1968

In 1964, the House of Lords awarded substantial damages to an employee who was dismissed when management was threatened with a strike in breach of procedure. The employee had left and refused to rejoin his white-collar union, which had recently secured a 100 percent union shop. The legal basis for the award was conspiracy to injure by means of an unlawful threat.[30] On the other hand, in 1968, the Court of Appeal refused a remedy in damages to an employee dismissed under threat that his fellow employees would not work with him where the threat notice was about three times as long as the week's notice of termination required by the men's contract. The employee dismissed had left the established union and joined a small breakaway union. The threat was held not to be unlawful apparently because, though to stay at work and refuse orders to work with the dismissed man would be unlawful, the length of the threat notice gave the men time to adopt the lawful but severer course of withdrawing their labor had management not given way.[31]

In 1965, the House of Lords awarded an injunction to stop a secondary boycott the purpose of which was to persuade an employer to recognize a smaller union with only three members in his labor force, where recognition had already been given to a larger union which organized 45 of the work force of 48. The decision itself was in accordance with established common law but contained judicial statements pointing to an enlargement of labor liability.[32] In 1968, the Scottish Court of Session granted an injunction against a secondary boycott in a straight recognition dispute. Again, the decision could be justified on orthodox grounds but contained some liability-enlarging indications.[33]

Yet again, in 1968, the English High Court granted an injunction to stop the secondary boycotting of heating-oil supplies to a hotel in a recognition dispute in which one large union was "muscling in" on the territory of two other large unions. In this case, *Torquay Hotel Ltd.* v. *Cousins,*[34] the implications of a *quia timet* interlocutory injunction were brought out in respect of stopping the likelihood of disrupting contracts which *might* be made and in respect of forbidding picketing, not at present a common law nuisance, which *might probably become* a nuisance if the injunction were not granted.

---

[30] This was *Rookes* v. *Barnard*, above, note 16.

[31] *Morgan* v. *Fry*, above, note 18.

[32] *Stratford* v. *Lindley*, above, note 17.

[33] *Square Grip Reinforcement Ltd.* v. *MacDonald*, 1968 SLT 65.

[34] [1968] 3 All E.R. 43. In part affirmed, appeal dismissed, and leave to appeal to House of Lords denied by Court of Appeal. [1969] 1 All E.R. 522.

In 1966, an injunction was awarded against union officials in the construction industry to stop their interfering with the performance of a labor-only contract on the ground that such a contract is a commercial contract, not a contract of employment, so that inducement of its breach was not protected by Section 3 of the Trade Disputes Act 1906.[35] The decision was a sustainable one on traditional lines, but, once more, judicial statements were made exploring wider avenues of labor liability, as occurred also recently in *Daily Mirror Newspapers Ltd.* v. *Gardiner,*[36] a trade association case.

Take the torts of intentionally and knowingly inducing or procuring a breach of contract. Before 1964, the law appeared to be that the defendant must have had sufficient knowledge of the contract in question to be able to intend its breach. The modified formulation in 1966 was that absence of knowlege would not exonerate if the means of finding out existed but were disregarded.[37] Again, "inducement" to break a contract used to be contrasted with "mere exhortations" to act where the acts could be effected lawfully or unlawfully. Now the suggestion is that, if the sympathetic workers are willing to act, informing them of the dispute would be enough to constitute inducing their subsequent acts in breach of contract.[38] Again, breach of contract was regarded as essential for the commission of these torts; but the judicial talk now is of unjustifiable interference with contractual relations though no actual breach has occurred.[39]

Stamp J., in the *Torquay Hotel* case, preferring what a High Court judge had previously said *obiter* to what the Court of Appeal had said, opined that, though a trade union could not be sued in damages because of Section 4 of the 1906 Act, the wording of that section did not prevent the issuance of an *injunction* against a union. Where a union is seeking recognition in a situation in which another union has already been recognized, the current disposition of the courts is to regard this as a pure inter-union dispute [40] and therefore not a trade dispute for the purpose of the protection of the Trade Disputes Acts 1906 and 1965. Also, breach of procedure is described as a "flagrant violation of a pledge not to strike," [41] while failure to give the correct strike notice or refusal to obey orders are

---

[35] This was *Emerald Construction Ltd.* v. *Lowthian*, [1966] 1 All E.R. 1013.
[36] [1968] 2 All E.R. 163.
[37] In *Emerald Construction Ltd.* v. *Lowthian*, above, note 35, also in *Daily Mirror Newspapers* v. *Gardner*, above, note 36.
[38] In *Square Grip Reinforcement Ltd.* v. *Macdonald*, above, note 33.
[39] The dicta are in *Stratford* v. *Lindley, Torquay Hotels Ltd.* v. *Cousins,* and *Emerald Construction Ltd.* v. *Lowthian,* above, notes 17, 34, and 35.
[40] In *Stratford's* case and the *Torquay Hotels* case.
[41] Lord Denning, M.R. in *Morgan* v. *Fry* in the Court of Appeal.

just breaches of contract. Also, there are the perplexities concerning the right to strike, already referred to, which the Court of Appeal decision in *Morgan* v. *Fry* cannot be confidently said to have settled.

Every lawyer will recognize in these judicial stirrings the symptoms of a judicial inclination to intervene in labor relations on a new scale with a view to redrawing more narrowly the scope of legally permissible industrial action. To what degree of intervention the British judiciary will go and whether its consequences for labor relations will be good or bad remain to be seen.

CONTENT AND ENFORCEABILITY OF COLLECTIVE AGREEMENTS

Content

The subject matter of collective agreements is not controlled by the State though it is today directly influenced by the prices and incomes policy and legislation, of which more later. On the other hand, the content of collective bargaining has for many years been strongly, if indirectly, affected by the existence of a comprehensive national health service and social security scheme, which covers all employees, irrespective of whether they are employed under a collective bargaining regime or within a Wages Council industry or in agriculture or are among the 17 percent or so yet unaccounted for in detail by industrial relationists.

The social security and health (medical, ophthalmic, and dental) services are paid for partly out of general taxation and partly by the weekly national insurance contributions of employer and employee: where the employees are on the basic pension scheme, the employer's contribution is 18s. 1d. ($2.17) a week, while the employee's contribution while in work is 19s. 1d. ($2.29). In the event of *sickness*,[42] an employee with a wife and three children will at present receive benefits at a flat rate of £9 18s. ($23.76) a week. By way of comparison, the *average* gross earnings for manual workers in the engineering industry range from about £16 ($38.40) a week for unskilled laborers to about £27 ($64.80) a week for the best-paid skilled workers. The flat rate of sickness benefit is payable in the first instance for a maximum period of one year.

In addition, under the National Insurance Act 1966, an earnings-related sickness benefit supplement may be claimed by

---

[42] The principal Act regulating sickness and unemployment benefit is the National Insurance Act 1965, replacing the original Act of 1946 which inaugurated the comprehensive national insurance scheme.

those whose gross earnings were in the range £9-30 ($21.60 — $72.00) a week. Such a person may claim supplementation amounting to one third of the difference between £9 and actual earnings at the time of falling sick. The supplementation is payable only from the thirteenth day of illness and thereafter for six months. Flat rate plus supplementation must not exceed 85 percent of gross earnings.

Both the flat-rate and earnings-related supplementation of *un-employment* benefit are the same as for sickness benefit.

Absence from work due to industrial injury or disease [43] entitles an injured worker with a wife and three children to £12. 13s. ($30.36) a week. This is payable for six months from the date of the accident, as is also the earnings-related supplement for those whose weekly earnings were £9-£30 and which is calculated in the same way as for the sick and the unemployed. Permanent disability attracts a lump-sum gratuity or, in effect, an industrial pension for severer forms of disability calculated according to medical assessment. A totally disabled worker, unemployable, suffering special hardship, and requiring constant attendance, with a wife and three children, will receive in all about £24 ($57.60) a week. In the event of a fatal industrial accident, the widow will be entitled to £8. 5s. ($19.80) a week for herself and three children. All the above amounts include, in respect of the children, normal family allowance.

Claims for sickness, unemployment, and industrial injury, etc., benefits are processed in the first instance by civil servants (insurance officers) subject to an appeal to a local appeal tribunal consisting of a lawyer-chairman and two lay members, one from each side of industry, with a final appeal to the National Insurance Commissioner (or one of his deputy commissioners), who is a permanent judicial appointee roughly on the level of a County Court judge. The High Court (and above) has only a very limited power of review in respect of an error of law on the face of the record.

It is open to management and unions or shop stewards to negotiate benefit schemes above the "floor" of the national provision against sickness, unemployment, and industrial injury. Little has been done in respect of unemployment and injury. On the other hand, sick-pay schemes are fairly widespread, more particularly for white-collar employees. Their starting point is the national insurance scheme of benefits.

---

[43] The principal Act is the National Insurance (Industrial Injuries) Act 1965, replacing the original 1946 Act of the same title.

Since 1965, redundancy too has been made the subject of national, almost universally applicable arrangements. Redundancy here means, broadly, unemployment due to cessation of a business, or to moving the place of business, or to the employee becoming surplus to the requirements of a business. Who shall be redundant and how they shall be made redundant remain matters of unilateral decision by management or of joint determination by management, shop stewards, and union officials. How much shall be paid to the redundant employees may be settled by collective agreement if its terms are at least as favorable as those now formulated in the Redundancy Payments Act 1965. To date, management and unions have been generally content to depend on the statutory provisions.

Since the Redundancy Payments Act came into force in December 1965, about £100-million ($240-million) had, up to mid-March 1968, been paid out in redundancy payments, each of which has averaged around £200 ($480). This is a tax-free lump sum to which the redundant employee is entitled in addition to his flat-rate unemployment benefit and, where appropriate, earnings-related supplementary benefits. The employer, in his turn, is entitled to recover a rebate, which was recently reduced to a flat 50 percent of the redundancy payment made.[44] The rebate is paid from a Redundancy Fund made up of exclusively employer contributions, which have just been raised to 1s. 3d. (15¢) a week for adult male workers and 7d. (7¢) for adult female workers.

The Act is very technical and has given rise to many disputes. These disputes are processed by the Industrial Tribunals, originally set up under the Industrial Training Act 1964, consisting of a lawyer-chairman and two lay members drawn from either side of industry. By March 1968, the Tribunals had handled some 18,000 claims. Appeals on points of law lie to the High Court and thence to the Court of Appeal and House of Lords. So far a case law of about 750 reported decisions (mainly of the Industrial Tribunals) has been produced.

The Royal Commission envisages a greater role for the Industrial Tribunals in the future under the name of Labor Tribunals. They would become in effect a national system of labor courts and their jurisdiction would extend to all disputes arising out of the individual labor relationship based on the individual contract of employment. They would take in the administration of the projected law on "unfair" dismissals and, also, the notice of dismissal provisions of the Contracts of Employment Act 1963, failure to observe

[44] Redundancy Rebates Act 1969.

which at present goes unredressed for want of a speedy, informal, inexpensive procedure.

The British employer is at present formally free in law to dismiss an employee, whatever the motive, provided only that the correct procedure is followed, namely, due notice is given or due wages paid in lieu of notice. The Contracts of Employment Act has established statutory minimum periods of notice of dismissal: seven days after six months' continous employment, two weeks after two years' and four weeks after five or more years' continuous employment. These are minimum periods which may be improved on but not undercut whether by individual or collective bargaining.

Finally, collective bargaining is also affected by the existence of a national pensions scheme,[45] which provides a basic £4. 10s. ($10.80) a week for a retiree or his widow and £7. 6s. ($17.52) a week for a man and wife. Mention should also be made of the legislation about maximum working hours for women, young persons (those between school-leaving age 15 and 18) and, to a small extent, men, and of the comprehensive legislation on safety, health, and welfare in industry, agriculture, shops, and offices.

The above, then, in general terms is the environment of statutory provision within and subject to which collective bargaining takes place in Britain at both industry and plant levels.

The content of industry-wide collective agreements generally does not go significantly beyond basic rates of pay, night-shift premiums, basic holiday arrangements, general principles to be observed in introducing redundancies, and private procedures both for reaching agreement at industry level and for dealing with disputes of all kinds which may arise in the establishments within an industry.[46]

The theory of "managerial prerogative," that within the plant matters not dealt with in the industry agreement shall be decided unilaterally by management with or without joint consultation, has been challenged by the reality of workplace bargaining power generated by the postwar run of full employment. A contributory factor also has been the shift in the center of gravity of employers' power from the associations to managers by reason of the growth in size and importance of factories and companies.

Thus, at the plant level, the content of collectively bargained

---

[45] The principal Act is again the National Insurance Act 1965.

[46] The main source of information concerning the nature of current British industrial relations is the Report of the Royal Commission, Research Papers, and the 68 parts of the Minutes of Evidence.

agreements or arrangements, formal or informal, reflects actual local needs and demands: actual earnings (which may be 40-50 percent above the industrial basic rates including overtime), the decision about how much overtime is to be worked, going piecework rates, lieu bonuses for timeworkers, merit ratings, *ad hoc* rates (e.g., for dirty work or an emergency), teabreaks, demarcation, recruitment, promotion and grading, disciplinary rules and dismissal procedures, operational rules for redundancy, working practices, safety conditions, and the introduction of new machinery and processes. On the other hand, disputes procedures have not been developed at the plant level to displace or adapt the general industrial procedures, which have tended to be too slow and to take the dispute away from the plant too quickly — unless the unofficial strike be regarded as a form of specialized local procedure filling the vacuum created by lack of adequate plant-adapted procedures.

The way in which British industrial relations have tended to fall between the two schools of the formal, limited, industry-wide system of collective bargaining and the more realistic, informal system of bargaining in the "factory" has been described by the Royal Commission as follows:

> "Procedure agreements fail to cope adequately with disputes arising within factories . . . The assumption that industry-wide agreements control industrial relations leads many companies to neglect their responsibility for their own personnel policies. Factory bargaining remains informal and fragmented, with many issues left to custom and practice. The unreality of industry-wide pay agreements leads to the use of incentive schemes and overtime payments for purposes quite different from those they were designed to serve." [47]

The recommendation at the heart of the Royal Commission's report is that employers' associations and company management should now recognize and institutionalize plant bargaining whenever this is appropriate. Industry-wide bargaining should confine itself to dealing with the length of the standard working week and of annual holidays, with explicitly minimum pay rates, and to setting out what matters companies should be expected to settle for themselves and to providing guidance on how this should be done; industry-wide agreements should deal with actual pay structures only in those cases where effective, not merely minimum, pay structures can be so established.

> "In order to promote the orderly and effective regulation of industrial relations within companies and factories [the Commission] recommended that boards of companies review industrial relations

---

[47] Royal Commission Report, para. 149.

within their undertakings. In doing so, they should have the following objectives in mind:

"(1) to develop, together with trade unions representative of their employees, comprehensive and authoritative collective bargaining machinery to deal at company and/or factory level with the terms and conditions of employment which are settled at these levels;

"(2) to develop, together with union representatives of their employees, joint procedures for the rapid and equitable settlement of grievances in a manner consistent with the relevant collective agreements;

"(3) to conclude with union representatives of their employees agreements regulating the position of shop stewards in matters such as facilities for holiday elections; members and constituencies; recognition of credentials; facilities to consult and report back to their members; facilities to meet with other stewards; the responsibilities of the chief shop steward (if any); pay while functioning as steward in working hours; day release with pay for training;

"(4) to conclude agreements covering the handling of redundancy;

"(5) to adopt effective rules and procedures governing disciplinary matters, including dismissal, with provision for appeals;

"(6) to ensure regular joint discussions of measures to promote safety at work." [48]

In pursuit of the above objectives, "companies should welcome the exercise by employees of their right to join trade unions as a prerequisite of orderly and representative joint institutions. They will need to develop positive management policies on such matters as recruitment, promotion, training and re-training," [49] and to these ends, the Commission urges the maintenance of "competently-staffed and adequately-equipped personnel departments." [50]

The objectives commended to industry by the Commission apply to nonfederated firms, like many American-owned firms, only to the extent that they do not already pursue them.

An Industrial Relations Commission (renamed the Commission on Industrial Relations) is proposed by the Royal Commission to assist and, so far as possible, accelerate the reorientation of the British system of industrial relations. Among its wide range of duties described and explained in the Report, the new body will monitor the industrial relations aspects of those company collective agreements that will be required to be registered with the Department of Employment and Productivity if the Royal Commission's recommendation passes into law.

---

[48] *Id.*, para. 182.
[49] *Id.*, para. 184.
[50] *Id.*, para. 179.

Enforceability of Collective Agreements

In Britain, as is widely known, collective agreements are not legally binding contracts between the employer or employers' association and trade union parties. Without going into technical refinements, employers and trade unions have not sued each other in the courts for breach of collective agreement since collective bargaining began in this country and have consistently expressed an unwillingness, if not an aversion, to doing so. Accordingly, following common-law principle, there being no intention to create legal relations, the collective agreement is merely a "gentlemen's agreement."

Though not directly enforceable, however, the collective agreement is not devoid of indirect legal consequences.

First, its terms, at least those that are appropriate, may be incorporated in the individual contracts of employment of the employees concerned. Incorporation may be by express agreement that the collectively bargained terms shall form part of the contract of employment; alternatively, the collectively bargained provisions, by becoming the new "custom" of the place of work, may be incorporated as customary implied terms. Precisely when such implication occurs the courts have never yet had cause to consider. Equally unknown at present is which collectively bargained terms the courts would regard as "appropriate" for enforcement, *qua* customary implied terms, at the level of the individual labor relationship and, more particularly, whether the disputes-procedure provision would be so regarded.

Britain since the war has not been a badly strike-prone country in terms of number of working days lost or number of stoppages per annum, as the table on page 190 indicates.

On the other hand, the special national feature of strikes in Britain in recent years has been that 95 percent of the number of stoppages have been unofficial strikes, that such strikes have been showing "a strong general upward trend,"[51] and that the vast majority of unofficial strikes have been in breach of procedure.

"It is imperative," the Royal Commission concluded in its discussion of the legal enforcement of collective agreements, "that the number of unofficial and especially of unconstitutional strikes should be reduced and should be reduced speedily. This is not only a serious, it is also an urgent problem."[52] But the Commission recognized the unfairness and probable futility of attempting to impose general legal sanctions for breach of the present inadequate proce-

---

[51] Royal Commission Report, para. 370.
[52] Report, para. 500.

Stoppages in Years 1948-1967

Year	Number of stop-pages begin-ning in year	Number of workers involved in stoppages			Aggregate number of working days lost in stoppages		
		Beginning in year		In progress in year (000)	Beginning in year		In progress in year (000)
		Directly (000)	Indi-rectly (000)		(a) (000)	(b) (000)	
1948	1,759	324	100	426	1,935	1,938	1,944
1949	1,426	313	120	434	1,805	1,818	1,807
1950	1,339	269	33	303	1,375	1,382	1,389
1951	1,719	336	43	379	1,687	1,710	1,694
1952	1,714	303	112	416	1,769	1,797	1,792
1953	1,746	1,329	41	1,374	2,157	2,173	•2,184
1954	1,989	402	46	450	2,441	2,480	2,457
1955	2,419	599	60	671	3,741	3,788	3,781
1956	2,648	464	43	508	2,036	2,051	2,083
1957	2,859	1,275	81	1,359	8,398	8,399	8,412
1958	2,629	456	67	524	3,461	3,474	3,462
1959	2,093	522	123	646	5,257	5,280	5,270
1960	2,832	698	116	819	3,001	3,049	3,024
1961	2,686	673	98	779	2,998	3,038	3,046
1962	2,449	4,297	123	4,423	5,757	5,778	5,798
1963	2,068	455	135	593	1,731	1,997	1,755
1964	2,524	700	172	883	2,011	2,030	2,277
1965	2,354	673	195	876	2,906	2,932	2,925
1966	1,937	414	116	544	2,372	2,395	2,398
1967	2,116	552	180	734	2,765	2,783	2,787

dures contained in many industrial agreements. The remedy prescribed is, therefore, in two distinct stages, of which the second, it is hoped, will not be called for:

(1) "The reform, mainly through factory and company agreements, of the existing procedures."[53] This reform is envisaged as part and parcel of the general reorientation and modernization of industrial relations, which are at the heart of the Commission's findings.

(2) *If,* notwithstanding adequate jointly agreed procedures, unconstitutional strikes continue to disrupt a crucial industry or section of it — the key export industry of car manufacturing springs first to mind — then the Minister of Employment and Productivity should

---

[53] Report, para. 507.

be empowered, after consulting both sides and the Commission on Industrial Relations, to apply to the existing Industrial Court for an order making the procedure agreement in question legally binding at the level of the individual labor relationship. The sanction would be an action for damages by employer against employee for "the loss suffered by the plaintiff."[54] Certain criteria are laid down for the Industrial Court's guidance, but further details are left for future consideration should the need for trying legal sanctions become convincing if the reorganization of the structure of industrial relations fails to have the hoped-for effect. The new Commission on Industrial Relations is given a watching and advising brief in these matters.

Two further relevant recommendations are worth noting: first, that the regional industrial relations officers of the Department of Employment and Productivity (DEP) should be able rapidly to investigate and assist with unofficial and unconstitutional stoppages; and second, that unofficial strikers and their leaders should be deprived of the protection of the Section 3 of the Trade Disputes Act 1906, and the corresponding provision in the Trade Disputes Act 1965, and so exposed to the possibility of an action for damages and a final or interlocutory injunction (*quia timet* or otherwise) for inducing breach of contract or for conspiring or threatening to induce breach of contract.

Compare the Conservative Party's proposals, which refer particularly to the unconstitutional strike. Their recommendation is that "a collective agreement should be enforceable except in so far as the parties specifically agree that the whole, or parts of it, should *not* be legally binding."[55] If the procedure agreement is binding and is broken, whether by official or unofficial action, the *trade union* will be liable for damages subject to an as yet unspecified statutory limit because, otherwise, "an established and responsible trade union could be 'broken' by a single judgment."[56] The union's liability will depend on its failure to convince a tripartite industrial court that its officials had done "all in their power" to prevent the breach or, after the event, to get an immediate return to work. The union would have the right to recover the damages for the individual members concerned, though the anonymous individuals who produced "Fair Deal at Work" recognize the improbability of such an action.

---

[54] Report, para. 516.
[55] *Fair Deal at Work*, p. 32.
[56] *Fair Deal at Work*, p. 33.

"Extension"

Under the "claims" procedure established by Section 8 of the Terms and Conditions of Employment Act 1959, it is possible to extend an industry agreement negotiated with an employers' association (not a single company or corporation) to a nonfederated employer at the instance of either the association concerned or a trade union party to the agreement. In practice, it has been the unions that have initiated on average about a dozen claims a year to enforce the *minimum* rates continued in industry agreements against nonfederated employers. The net effect of a successful claim is that the Industrial Court's award makes the basic industrial rates or other terms statutory implied terms in the contracts of employment of the workers of the respondent employer. It may be noted that, before the claim is sent to the Industrial Court, it is first vetted by the DEP, whose officers, where there is a prima facie case, try to effect a voluntary settlement.

The Industrial Court has a similar jurisdiction in respect of government contractors and subcontractors as a result of the Fair Wages Resolution of the House of Commons, but few references occur annually; and the same may be said of the Court's jurisdiction under the statutes compendiously known as the "fair wages legislation." [57]

PRICES AND INCOMES POLICY

Without comparable restraints on prices and unearned incomes, an earned incomes policy would never have taken off and attained even the low altitude it has so far achieved in Britain. About prices and unearned incomes I shall say no more. The restraints on them have been imperfect, but well meant and sufficient to keep the earned incomes policy moving along. What I want to try to do is to outline the structure of the earned-incomes policy and indicate how it has been fitted into the general framework of voluntary collective bargaining, concluding with a few words about the net success of the policy to date.

In aiming at an adequate growth economy without either intolerable inflation or, by British standards, massive, e.g., 3-1/2 percent, unemployment, the British Government has pursued a highly structured incomes policy since mid-1966. The policy is based on the provisions of the Prices and Incomes Acts 1966-1968 and on the

---

[57] The Road Haulage Wages Act 1938, Part II; Civil Aviation Act 1949; Housing (Scotland) Act 1950; Television Act 1954; Sugar Act 1956; Housing Act 1957; Road Traffic Act 1960; Films Act 1960.

work of the National Board for Prices and Incomes, the Department of Employment and Productivity, and the Incomes Policy Committee of the TUC, on the less formalized work of the CBI, and on the cooperation of both sides of trade and industry, subject to mounting resistance on the trade union side. The operation of incomes policy may be divided into three phases: notification, negotiation, and implementation.

Notification

The Acts provide that notice of "any pay claims or other claims relating to terms and conditions of employment made on behalf of employees"[58] must be given "the appropriate Minister," [59] generally the Secretary of State for Employment and Productivity, within seven days of the day on which "the claim is presented to the employers or employers' organization concerned."[60] Responsibility for giving notice is imposed jointly and severally on both sides, including apparently unofficial leaders. Failure to give notice renders those concerned liable to a maximum fine of £ 50 ($120) on summary conviction. This criminal sanction, like all the sanctions in the Acts, is in reality a background power designed to keep faith with the cooperating majority by whipping in the odd straggler. It has not yet been invoked and it may be taken as axiomatic that, if the government has to have recourse to legal sanctions on more than the odd occasion, the incomes policy will have collapsed. In practice, notification of claims has been made voluntarily to the DEP.

The TUC, meanwhile, has established an important filter for claims under consideration by TUC affiliates before they are formally made. An Incomes Policy Committee of the TUC General Council has been set up, and affiliated unions have been asked to notify the Committee at least of significant claims under consideration (i.e., claims which might set a pattern for increases over a substantial area) before they are presented to management. The Committee has then tried to ensure that the union in question receives its observations within five weeks. According to the 1966 Annual Report of the TUC:

> "The action taken by the Committee has fallen into four categories. On some claims, for example those which concern groups of workers whose pay is low or which relate to minor changes in conditions, they have informed the union that they do not wish to make any observations: even in these cases, however, they have not so far

---

[58] Prices and Incomes Act 1966, §13 (1).
[59] Id., §13 (2).
[60] Ibid.

explicitly approved or endorsed any claims. In the second place they have on a number of claims confined themselves to asking the unions in general terms to bear in mind the prices and incomes policy during the course of negotiations: the proportion of claims in this category has steadily declined. Third (and this category has grown at the expense of the second) they have made specific and pointed comments on claims or aspects of claims which they regard as conflicting with the income policy, and in some of these instances have explicitly asked the union to reconsider the claim before submitting it to the employers. Fourth, the Committee have in 18 cases asked the union or unions concerned to send representatives to meet a panel of the Committee to discuss their claims."[61]

In 1968, the TUC Annual Report stated: "While all notified claims have been considered by the Committee, they have continued to examine in greater depth claims which they regarded as important because of the number of workers involved, the likely extent of their repercussions on other parts of the collective bargaining system, or because they contained novel features (for example, the abandonment of national bargaining in favor of company negotiations)."[62] Between July 1967 and May 1968 the General Council of the TUC were notified of 376 claims covering 9-1/2 million workers, a smaller number of claims than in the 1966-1967 period though covering the same number of workers. Despite formidable opposition from the Amalgamated Engineering and Foundry Workers' Union, the second largest in Britain, in the September 1968 Annual Conference of the TUC its *voluntary* wage-vetting policy was approved by a bare majority of 34,000 in a total vote of about 8-1/2 million.

Voluntary notification to the DEP of actual claims made has chiefly come from employers and employers' associations. Both the CBI and the TUC are kept informed by their members and by the DEP and are not infrequently asked by the latter for preliminary advice. During 1967, over 6,000 such voluntary notifications were received by the Department, the legal sanctions being kept completely invisible in the background. Departmental emphasis is on "claims and proposed settlements which might be significant (e.g. because of the nature of the claim, or the possible repercussions on the pay of other groups) and in any case, . . . all those involving more than 100 workers."[63] Contact between the CBI and TUC has been institutionalized by the creation in 1967 of a Joint CBI —

---

[61] TUC Annual Report, 1966, para. 306.
[62] TUC Annual Report, 1968, para. 313.
[63] *Productivity, Prices and Incomes Policy in 1968 and 1969* (Cmnd. 3590), para. 48.

TUC Committee which meets monthly "to discuss matters of mutual concern." [64]

Negotiation

In the phase of negotiation, the Prices and Incomes Acts have no application, and the traditional system of collective bargaining operates, theoretically unfettered, complete with the law of industrial conflict. The DEP appears to have been examining ways in which the "public interest," or the "interest of the consumer," might be given effective representation in the phase of negotiation itself; but, so far, the Department has seemingly experienced a strong negative reaction on the part of both sides of industry.

Implementation

The real nub of the incomes policy lies in the phase of implementation of a negotiated settlement, or an arbitration award, or, indeed, under the latest Act, a wages recommendation of a Wages Council or an award of an Agricultural Wages Board.

Within seven days of the settlement, the employers must give the DEP its details, subject to a maximum fine of £50 in default. Notification *may* be given by a union concerned. The more important theoretical sanction for nonnotification of a settlement is that implementation is in such case forbidden on pain of a maximum £100 ($240) fine on summary conviction or £500 ($1,200) fine on conviction on indictment.

When due notification has been given, the Minister has 30 days in which to decide whether there should be a referral of the settlement to the National Board for Prices and Incomes. During this period discussion with the parties will be undertaken by the headquarters staff and regional industrial relations officers of the DEP. The guiding criteria of these discussion, the criteria of the incomes policy, are listed below.

If the Minister decides not to refer, the settlement may be implemented in its original form or, frequently, with amendments thrashed out in discussions during the 30 days' standstill period.

If, on the other hand, a reference to the Board is the Minister's verdict — and only roughly 1 percent of notifications have been so referred — the parties must desist from implementing their settlement until the Board reports or until the lapse of three months, whichever is the longer. If the Board reports favorably, the parties

---
[64] TUC Annual Report, 1967, para. 342.

may go ahead; but if there is an unfavorable report in whole or in part, then the parties will be required to conform with it. If they do not, the Minister may make a standstill order to have effect (under the 1968 Act) for up to 11 months (six months for a Wages Council recommendation and three months for an agricultural award) from the date of publication of the reference to the Board. Violation of the order, whether by employers, unions, or unofficial action, renders those involved liable to the £100 and £500 maximum fines, but not, be it noted, to imprisonment in the first instance. Prosecutions may only be instituted with the consent of the Attorney General, while the law of strike action has been carefully insulated from the illegalities of the prices and incomes legislation.[65]

These statutory arrangements will remain in force, under the 1968 Act, until the end of 1969. The criteria of incomes policy to guide the Prices and Incomes Board, the DEP officers, and the TUC Incomes Policy Committe as well as both sides of industry are broadly similar to those operative since mid-1966. They allow for increases above a general ceiling of 3-1/2 percent in the following circumstances:

"(i) Where employees concerned, for example by accepting more exacting work or a major change in work practices, make a direct contribution towards increasing productivity in the particular firm or industry. Even in such cases some of the benefit should accrue to the community as a whole in the form of lower prices;

"(ii) Where it is essential in the national interest to secure a change in distribution of manpower (or to prevent a change which would otherwise take place) and a pay increase would be both necessary and effective for this purpose;

"(iii) Where there is general recognition that existing wage and salary levels are too low to maintain a reasonable standard of living;

"(iv) Where there is widespread recognition that the pay of a certain group of workers has fallen seriously out of line with the level of remuneration for similar work and needs in the national interest to be improved." [66]

It may be added, in conclusion, that, once a standstill period has ended, and this, it will be seen, may be 12 months from the original settlement or arbitration award, the parties may implement their originally agreed terms or the original award notwithstanding the disfavor of the Board; but back-dating will not be permissible.

The effect of incomes policy so far cannot be stated with fine accuracy. Perhaps the following general observations may be made.

The average annual rise in actual earnings does not appear to

---

[65] Prices and Incomes Act 1966, §16 (5).

[66] Prices and Incomes (General Considerations) Order 1968 (S.I. 616), para. 34.

have been substantially reduced since mid-1966. This appears to have been due in part to the problem of control over plant negotiation being at present far more intractable than in the case of negotiations at industry level. The fundamental reconstruction of industrial relations proposed by the Royal Commission would thus favor the effectiveness of an incomes-policy apparatus in the future, as the Commission itself has pointed out.

On the other hand, it would be a bold man who asserted that the average annual increase of earnings since mid-1966 would not have been greater or that it would not have taken place sooner in the absence of incomes policy. Moreover, in its Third General Report, the National Board for Prices and Incomes has satisfied itself, after a highly sophisticated calculation, that the average increase in earnings in recent years "may have been just under 1 percent less than otherwise it would have been."[67] The policy, indeed, bears all the earmarks of a large-scale delaying action in the hope that the post-devaluation surplus-to-be will enable an ordered growth of incomes to replace the present restraint with exceptions.

A major positive effect of incomes policy has been the stimulation through criterion (i) above of "productivity bargaining," including the establishment of improved wage structures and the bargaining-out of restrictive practices and overmanning. In the last 18 months or so, over 900 productivity bargains have been submitted to the DEP representing almost the entire breadth of industry. This effect must have been at least a factor in the substantial rise in industrial productivity recently reported. In a sense, therefore, incomes policy has been helping to prepare the ground for the central changes which the Royal Commission has urged, as witness the recent acceptance in principle by both sides of the engineering industry of the need to go over to plant bargaining.

Incomes policy has also had the effect of drawing attention to and defining more closely the lowest-paid workers, which seems to have drawn in its train the serious reconsideration of the demand for equal pay for women doing equal work with men.

However, the roughest going is yet to come. Devaluation and its attendant deflationary measures confront the unions with an unavoidable minimum price rise of the order of at least 3 percent and the concurrent demand to hold the earnings level stable, subject only to the 3-1/2 percent ceiling and exceptions criteria set out above. More unions have consequently joined the AEF in open opposition to the statutory incomes policy. At the 1968 Annual Conference of

---

[67] National Board for Prices and Incomes, Report No. 77, para. 32 and Appendix A.

the TUC, the resolution deploring the *statutory* incomes policy was carried by a majority of no less than nearly 6-3/4 million in a total vote of about 8-1/2 million.[68]

THE "PROCESSING" OF LABOR DISPUTES AND INDUSTRIAL CONFLICT

Labor disputes and industrial conflict may be "processed" through one or more of three filters: voluntary procedures, government-provided procedures and assistance, and sanctions.

Voluntary Procedures

Tens of thousands of labor disputes, ranging over every conceivable cause of a dispute, are successfully settled each year in British industry through the procedures established in industry or company agreements. Some of these procedures, including that in the engineering industry where it has not been replaced by company agreements, have been going for more than half a century and are no longer well adapted to modern industrial conditions. Out-of-date procedures were regarded by the Royal Commission as a significant source of unofficial strikes, and reforming them, we saw, has been recommended as an urgent objective of the reconstruction of industrial relations. As far ahead as one can see into the future, the main brunt of labor relations disputes will and must be borne by voluntary procedures.

Government-Provided Procedures and Assistance

All government-provided assistance and procedures begin with the headquarters and regional officers of the Industrial Relations Division (IRD) of the Department of Employment and Productivity. These permanent civil servants maintain a close relationship with industry at national, regional, and local levels and are justly regarded as experts in the field of industrial peacemaking.

Where a dispute has broken out, say, in a local plant, the regional industrial relations officer (RIRO) will not normally offer his conciliatory services if the employees and their leaders are acting unofficially or in breach of procedure. The general convention is to respect the established parties in industry and their agreed procedures. Since, however, unofficial, unconstitutional action is now con-

---

[68] At the same Annual Conference, a resolution condemning the statutory incomes policy was carried by a majority of nearly four million in a total vote of nearly 6-1/4 millions.

sidered a major source of industrial dislocation, the Royal Commission has recommended in such cases a more interventionist role for the RIROs as well as their headquarters superiors.

Be that as it may, statistics show that industry has been taking increasing advantage of the conciliatory expertise of the Industrial Relations Division, the number of conciliations now running at over 400 a year. This of course is a very small number compared with the total number of disputes settled each year without outside assistance. But, since they represent the cases that proved intractable for voluntary procedures alone, their qualitative importance in reducing industrial dislocation is far greater than their quantity suggests.

Conciliation is one part of the IRD's work. Another major part is to act as adviser on and organizer of a series of other settlement-finding procedures, notably (a) voluntary arbitration, whether before a single *ad hoc* arbitrator, an *ad hoc* board of arbitration, or the permanent Industrial Court; (b) a committee of investigation to find and publicize the facts and make recommendations in respect of smaller, difficult disputes; and (c) a court of inquiry to find and publicize the facts and make recommendations concerning major disputes. Currently, there occur about 60 to 70 voluntary arbitrations each year, while the annual committees and courts of inquiry until recently could together be counted on the fingers of one hand. Recently, however, the court-of-inquiry procedure has been more frequently resorted to.[69]

The above do not exhaust the IRD's armory. An open-minded flexibility is the hallmark of government-provided procedures and assistance. Thus, as the occasion seems to demand, the Minister for Employment and Productivity, the Prime Minister, the TUC General Council (whose Disputes Committee, incidentally, deals principally with inter-union disputes), a Law Lord, or any other influential person may be pressed into service to resolve a particularly damaging conflict. The government may also adapt traditional procedures to new uses, as when, in effect, a standing court of inquiry was set up for the motor industry called the Joint Labour Council for the Motor Industry under the chairmanship of Sir Jack Scamp.[70]

Finally, mention should be made of the other side of the DEP's work, namely, encouragement of long-term improvements in labor-management relations in, for example, the fields of training, man-

---

[69] Recent developments in the use of the court of inquiry procedure are analyzed in McCarthy and Clifford, *The Work of Industrial Courts of Inquiry*, 4 BRIT. JO. OF IND. RELATIONS (1966), p. 39.

[70] Sir Jack Scamp's Council has now been wound up and may be replaced by a new joint council with wider powers.

power planning, personnel management, dismissal, redundancy, and other procedures, and the institution from time to time of a major inquiry into the conditions of an industry, like the Devlin Inquiry into the port-transport industry which led to a rationalization of employers and negotiations for the final decasualization of dock work.

The formal source of the DEP's powers in labor disputes are the Conciliation Act 1896 and the Industrial Courts Act 1919.

Sanctions

One may have unilaterally imposed sanctions, as where management dismisses the employees concerned in a dispute or their leaders. The efficacy of this type of sanction will naturally depend on the balance of power within a plant, which may also reflect the weakness or strength of organized labor in the locality or in the country as a whole.

Again, one may have collectively agreed sanctions, e.g., loss of bonuses for three or six months, in the event of taking part in unconstitutional or unlawful industrial action.

Third, one has legal sanctions in the form of an appeal to the courts for damages and/or an injunction, but more particularly, at present, for an interlocutory injunction, on the ground that the strike or picketing or secondary boycott is unlawful, or for damages for the dismissal of an employee under union pressure. Notwithstanding the case law developments since 1964, management, with one possible exception, has not yet tried in appropriate circumstances to obtain a "labor injunction" in respect of a straight wage dispute and strike, official or unofficial, in breach of procedure. It should be noted that there is a wide "trade dispute" disqualification for receipt of unemployment benefits in respect of unemployment caused by a strike or lockout.

In the event of a dispute interfering with the supply of essentials, the government may have recourse to emergency powers under the Emergency Powers Acts 1920-64. The Conservative Party propose an extension of these powers to include a compulsory 60-day cooling-off period in the event of an Industrial Court finding that the "national interest" was endangered. During this period, the DEP could conduct a secret ballot among the strikers to decide whether the employer's last offer should be accepted. The Royal Commission turned down a similar proposal made by the Society of Conservative Lawyers.

CONCLUSION

I have dwelt on the Royal Commission and Conservative Party proposals because, in my opinion, labor relations and labor law in Britain have reached an historical turning point. The Labor Government is now engaged in a series of consultations with the CBI and TUC, and its White Paper on implementing the recommendations of the Commission is expected to be published at the end of 1968 and probably to be followed by legislation. More importantly, it is expected that the restructuring of industrial relations, which has already begun, will be pursued with greater vigor and purpose and with the new machinery which the Royal Commission has urged.

On the other hand, in the general election of 1970-1971 there may take place a large swing to the political right, and the question will arise of putting into effect the Conservative Party's proposals in "Fair Deal at Work" with its central assertion of managerial prerogative and industrial discipline.

Only one or two developments seem reasonably certain at the moment. One is that British industrial relations are likely to convert to plant bargaining on a comprehensive scale over the next five to eight years. In this respect, the industrial relations scene will become a more familiar one to American management and labor leaders. The other development that seems fairly likely is that the law will play an increasing role in processing labor disputes whether at the level of individual or of collective labor relations. But British labor law, even after a further decade of change, will probably retain a strongly British flavor.

Postscript: June 1969

It should be evident to the readers of this volume that there is no single cause for the relatively inferior performance of British industry as a whole in the postwar period. Within the wide span of locatable causes, official or unofficial strikes, in accordance with or in violation of agreed procedure, do not constitute a predominant factor. A significant cause of the relative failure of British industry to respond to the changes and challenges of postwar trade may be summarized, crudely it is true, as a relative inability of British management to adapt to the new demands of international competition or to appreciate even the professional training it needed to solve the economic and human problems confronting it. Another major element has been a similar deficiency on the part of full-time union officials, including a failure to apply themselves adequately to the novel problem of the shop-floor power generated by full employ-ment. Still another factor in Britain's postwar industrial perform-ance was the absence of active and timely steps by the government to ginger up business men and industrial management and the unions when the defaults of these groups in doing it themselves became apparent. Nor did the government institute timely reforms in education and training to give management, unions, and the labor force a chance to meet effectively the competitive drive of the other industrially advanced nations.

If these relative shortcomings stemmed from any common source, they came from the complacency and inertia induced by the memories and unthinking expectations resulting from British world hegemony now irreversibly past. In addition, from that past were inherited institutions and commitments, notably the sterling area and the overseas defense expenditures, no longer capable of being sustained by Britain's shrunken economic strength, while the con-duct of the Second World War involved loss of the earnings from some £4,000 million of overseas investments which thereafter had to be set off by a great increase in exports without a commensurate increase on the importing side. However, in one respect there had not been a relative failure of performance in keeping in reasonably good repair the social and political foundations of the nation.

This, I would suggest, is the correct kind of perspective within which the 1968-1969 debate about labor relations and legal and oth-er reforms as well as the practical consequences of that debate should be viewed.

Following the publication of the Donovan Commission Report, the Trades Union Congress and the Confederation of British Indus-try issued a joint statement in October 1968 in which they declared that, subject to natural reservations on both sides, there was much of value in the Report of the Royal Commission. They went on to say that many improvements could be made in the system of volun-tary collective bargaining without waiting for legislation. They put particular emphasis on a more rational approach to factory and workplace relations and to pay structures, a greater readiness on the part of managements to recognize the function of trade unions, including the role of shop stewards, the improvement of disputes procedures, and a more flexible use of manpower and the develop-ment of new attitudes toward industrial training, including appren-ticeship training. In addition, they both considered that the Com-mission on Industrial Relations might be set up immediately and that management of large firms might also immediately notify the Department of Employment and Productivity on a voluntary basis of the procedural aspects of their main collective agreements and industrial relations policies.

After discussions with the CBI and TUC, the government in January 1969 issued its White Paper entitled "In Place of Strife — A Policy for Industrial Relations."[71] Its contents were largely based on the recommendations of the Donovan Report, save that, on the one hand, it did not propose to withdraw the protection of the Trade Disputes Acts 1906 and 1965 from the leaders of unofficial strikes, as a majority of the Commission had recommended, while, on the other hand, it did not propose, despite observations in the Donovan Report to the contrary, to confer on the Minister of Employment and Productivity discretionary power to require a secret ballot before any significant official strike and a "conciliation pause" of 28 days before or at the outset of a significant unofficial strike, with penalties imposable on individuals violating the "pause."

The reactions of both the CBI and TUC did not deviate a hair's breadth from character and self-interest. The CBI considered that the White Paper was too weak in its proposed legal regulation of trade unions, collective agreements, and unofficial strike action; in other words, it did not come close enough to the Conservative Party's "Fair Deal at Work."

The TUC General Council, for its part, issued a statement in January 1969 containing the following observations:

> "The T.U.C. General Council have examined with care the proposals made by the Government for changes in the system of industrial relations and in the law relating to trade unions. A number of the suggested changes — those which relate to the establishment of a Commission for Industrial Relations and to the registration of procedure agreements, to the assurance to work people of the right to join trade unions and to trade unions of the right to recognition, to the maintenance and indeed the extension of the protection now afforded to trade union activities by the Trade Disputes Act 1906, to the protection of work people against unfair dismissal, to the extension of the jurisdiction of the Industrial Tribunals, to the provision of better information for collective bargaining purposes, and to the removal of some obstacles to workers' participation in management — could in principle help to improve industrial relations and to promote trade union objectives. The General Council will wish to clarify certain aspects of these proposals in their further discussions with the Government. The General Council however are opposed to, or at least have reservations about, the Government's other proposals, and they wish to leave the Government in no doubt about the nature of those reservations and the strength of their objections."

---

[71] Cmnd. 3888 (London: H.M.S.O., 1969).

The TUC's comments went on to specify their reservations and objections.

The CBI then took counsel with its members, while the TUC organized six "post-Donovan Conferences" which, in March 1969, produced interesting reports on blue-collar and white-collar labor relations in the private and public sectors of employment, and on the engineering, shipbuilding, construction, and wages council industries. In the same month, the management of Ford Motors brought an ill-conceived action to enforce their procedural agreement with their unions after a carefully thought-out package deal, including built-in sanctions against unconstitutional strikes, had come to grief on the shop floor. The details of this *cause célèbre* are outlined by Mr. Robert Copp in Part III, *supra*. The British judiciary, in the person of Mr. Justice Geoffrey Lane, declined the invitation to hold collective agreements to be legally binding contracts and to thrust the law into labor-management relations in a major area, without the thorough parliamentary discussion and consultation with both sides of industry which ought prudently and properly to precede such an innovation. Instead, the learned judge affirmed the orthodox view that collective agreements are at common law binding in honor alone. But the readiness of some of the elite of British management to take the two biggest unions in the country to court for alleged breach of a procedure agreement hoisted the storm cones.

In late April 1969 the government announced its intention to implement its White Paper in two stages, beginning with a short Industrial Relations Act in the pending parliamentary session that would include the prestrike secret ballot, the 28 days' conciliation pause backed by penal sanctions, and legalization of the secondary boycott by making inducement of breach of commercial contract not actionable where there is a trade dispute. The proposed act would also have liberalized the disqualification conditions for the receipt of unemployment benefits where unemployment resulted from a strike or lockout, established the relatively simple recognition machinery suggested in the Donovan Report as well as the White Paper, and inaugurated a development fund to facilitate union mergers and other improvements in trade union structure. The cat was among the pigeons, but, in the event, proved to be no match for them.

Precisely why the government adopted this line of march to implement its White Paper remains a matter of uncertainty and speculation. It has been suggested that there was a desire to place the regulatory elements of the new law on the statute book before they could be opposed at the TUC and Labor Party annual conferences due to be held in September 1969; but this would have been a gross and quite unbelievable error of judgment. Another suggestion was that it was a show of strength against the inflationary forces in society designed to impress the members of the International Monetary Fund (IMF), but, given the known sophistication and worldliness of those gentlemen, this was most unlikely. The more likely explanation, in my opinion, derived from the still-precarious state of the economy. After all, the current statistics showed that Britain was not a particularly strike-prone country. But, whereas a strong economy could take in its stride the 1969 level of unofficial strikes or even, say, a three-month official strike in the steel industry, such an official strike or a continuance of, *a fortiori,* an increase in the existing level of unofficial strike activity were deemed sufficiently serious threats to the British economy and, possibly, to managerial morale to make it desirable to cast about for means of avoiding them. Hence, as I see it, the issue of disorder in labor-management relations was forced, with consequences of great short- and long-term importance.

The opposition among the unions to the proposed legislation was virtually unanimous and centered on the introduction of penalties for individual employees breaching a conciliation pause as well as on the practical futility, in the British context, of both the conciliation pause and the secret prestrike ballot. Arguments about the residuary and discretionary character of the proposed ministerial power as well as about the other richly pro-union provisions in the package were brushed aside. There was reason to suppose that the vehemence and obduracy of the union leaders were derived in part from the largely unspoken fear that this relatively mild, if possibly fruitless, attempt to discipline unconstitutional strikers and to halt a catastrophic official strike would turn out to be only the hors d'oeuvre to the main course of legal regulation which the anticipated Conservative Government of 1971 would thus be encouraged to force down the unions' throats. For these reasons, massive resistance to the government line was generated not only on the industrial side but also on the political side within the Parliamentary Labour Party.

Meanwhile, negotiations continued between Prime Minister Harold Wilson and Barbara Castle, Minister of State for Employment and Productivity, on the one hand, and the TUC General Council and its acting General Secretary Victor Feather, on the other. As part of these negotiations, for the first time in about 40 years a special TUC Congress was convened and took place in

Croydon on June 5th. Its report, "Industrial Relations, A Programme for Action,"[72] formed the *quid pro quo* of the subsequent settlement between the government and TUC. On June 18, 1969, in return for the abandonment by the government of its proposed legislation, the TUC General Council unanimously agreed to play a far more active and, indeed, interventionist role in employer-union and interunion disputes, both official and unofficial, than ever before in the past. In this, they were prepared to press member unions, on pain of suspension or expulsion from the TUC, to discipline individual member employees in accordance with their rule-book powers. The misgivings expressed about the immunity in practice from such pressure of the biggest unions, like the Transport & General Workers' Union or the Amalgamated Union of Engineering & Foundry Workers, took insufficient account, in my opinion, of the effectiveness of internal public opinion within the trade union movement in the TUC; and the General Council immediately began to honor their undertaking with some success, and proceeded to organize a panel of about 200 full-time officials throughout the country to operate on a regional basis. Nevertheless, in trying to bring more order into industrial relations, TUC representatives did not blind themselves to the merits of individual cases, including the culpability of management in particular circumstances. They planned also to seek long-term improvements, especially of wage structures and disputes procedures.

The CBI, which earlier in the year had refused an offer by the TUC to act jointly with them in investigating and helping to prevent or settle industrial disputes, announced in June 1969 that they, in their turn, would act "independently in collaboration with our members to deal as best we can with industrial situations that arise." But, this "does not . . . preclude consultation with the TUC," with whom, as I mentioned in my main paper, the CBI has been holding regular monthly meetings. Plainly, the CBI, notwithstanding its published reasons, was rightly anxious that sympathetic attention should be paid to management's views in the course of future investigatory and conciliatory activity.

To sum up, as of June 1969 the concrete achievements of the Donovan Report and the government White Paper since the summer of 1968 were: (1) the establishment of the Commission on Industrial Relations (CIR) under the chairmanship of George Woodcock, former General Secretary of the TUC, which began paying attention in the first place to specific procedural and recognition problems; (2)

---

[72] A draft of "T.U.C. Programme for Action" was published in full in the *Times* (London) for May 19, 1969, p. 3.

companies employing 5,000 or more employees began voluntarily registering their procedural agreements with the Manpower and Productivity Service of the Department of Employment and Productivity; (3) an agreement between the Engineering Employers' Federation and the Confederation of Shipbuilding and Engineering Unions to recast the bargaining structure of the engineering and shipbuilding industries on a predominantly company or plant basis within a general industrial framework and to reconsider the 50-year-old York procedure; and (4) the TUC's "Programme for Action" and the vigorous steps taken to implement it, as well as the belated but welcome entry of the CBI on the task of improving and modernizing British labor relations by painstaking voluntary methods which, in my personal opinion, were far more likely to produce positive and durable results than the attempted imposition of penal sanctions.

Meanwhile, the government planned to go ahead in the following parliamentary session with a comprehensive bill on industrial relations which, however, in pursuance of the government-TUC agreement, would not contain penal sanctions in respect of worker or union conduct in the area of labor-management relations. Furthermore, the Chancellor of the Exchequer, Mr. Roy Jenkins, stated in his letter to the IMF that, at the end of 1969, the statutory framework of prices and incomes policy would be maintained but in attenuated form, for example, allowing for a maximum standstill period of only four months in the implementation of a negotiated agreement. The criteria to be applied to price and income increases by the National Board for Prices and Incomes were to be published later in a new White Paper, which could continue the salutary pressure on management and unions created by the Prices and Incomes Acts 1966-1968 toward furthering or reinforcing the beneficial effects of productivity bargaining in labor relations. Finally, the Chancellor stated in June 1969 that an error, which originated in 1964, in calculating the volume of exports might have concealed the fact that the British economy, taking both invisible and visible exports into account, could conceivably have been in balance since the beginning of 1969. Further details were awaited as this postscript was being completed.

LABOR RELATIONS IN BELGIUM

By Roger Blanpain

FOREWORD

The labor relations system of Belgium has obvious similarities to structures and processes of other countries, yet has special characteristics of its own. But similarities can be extremely deceptive and special national characteristics difficult to grasp. This paper will focus attention on the fundamentals of Belgian labor: policies, practices, and attitudes.

In Part I, I supply some information and data on the Belgian economy, wages, and companies, on social security benefits, and on the categories and aspirations of the Belgian labor force. Part II deals with the main characteristics of the Belgian labor relations system, its ideological implications, its political influences, and other features. Part III gives a description of the Belgian trade unions: trade union freedom; trade union structure; the most representative trade unions; union democracy and administration; and problems arising from the absence of legal personality of trade unions. The attitudes of the trade union movement towards the free-enterprise system are also examined. In Part IV the institutionalized relations between employers and trade unions will be discussed at the establishment or enterprise level through the union delegation, working council, and safety and health committees; at the level of the industrial sectors through the joint committees; and finally at the national level through the National Labor Council.

Part V deals with restrictions on free collective bargaining, the binding effect of the collective agreements, and the implications of cumulative bargaining.

Finally, the freedom to strike and the settlement of industrial disputes will be examined in Parts VI and VII, respectively.

In the course of the academic years 1966-1967 and 1967-1968, the Institute for Labor Relations of the University of Leuven (Louvain) organized two seminars for foreign investors in Belgium, in which more than 60 managers participated. In the following pages observations and commentary made during the seminars are used. References to these unique materials on labor relations in English will be indicated as "Louvain Seminar" in the footnotes.

INTRODUCTION

Belgium covers an area of 11,779 square miles, slightly larger than the state of Maryland, and has some 40 miles of coastline on the North Sea and 860 miles of land frontiers (bordering the Netherlands, West Germany, Luxembourg, and France). The country has a population of 9.4 million and about 792 inhabitants per square mile, or more than twice the density of the state of New York.

Belgium is composed of two cultural-linguistic communities, one speaking Flemish (Dutch) and the other French. The Flemish, who outnumber the French-speaking Walloons, live mainly in the north and west, while the Walloons live in the south and east. Both Flemish and French are official languages. The capital, Brussels, is administratively bilingual.

Belgium is a constitutional hereditary monarchy with a two-chamber parliament elected every four years, or more frequently if either chamber should be dissolved earlier. The entire Chamber of Deputies (212 seats) and 106 senators are elected by direct popular vote of all persons 21 years of age and over and are based on proportional representation. Certain additional senators are designated by provincial governments, and others are appointed by cooption. The three major political parties are the Social Christian Party, the Socialist Party, and the Party of Freedom and Progress.

THE BELGIAN ECONOMY

The Belgian economy system is a market economy with active governmental intervention in cyclical and structural evolution.[1] The Belgian economy is quite open to the rest of the world and two thirds of its exports are destined for E.E.C. (Common Market) countries.

The average annual growth rate of the gross national product at constant prices attained 3.7 percent over the period 1954-1966. This growth depended mainly on an increase in product per man-hour, the growth of active population being 0.5 percent per year and working hours decreasing at an average rate of 0.5 percent per year.

In 1965, the average revenue per capita attained 70,000 Bel-

---

[1] Van Rompuy, *Evolution and Structure of Wages*, Louvain Seminar 1967-1968 (see foreword to this article). The public sector (mainly classical public utilities) is rather small (7 percent of the labor force).

gian francs ($1,400), as against 63,000 B.F. for the E.E.C. countries and 142,000 B.F. for the United States.

Although wage determination is free, through collective or individual bargaining, government policy has a direct influence on labor costs, especially by fixing social security contributions of employers and employees. Belgian wages have been increasing since World War II. Until 1960 they were the highest in Western Europe, but they were then surpassed by Germany. Over the period 1959-1966 the increase in the E.E.C. countries showed a rather converging pattern; it was greater in the Netherlands (5.9 percent), Western Germany (5.4 percent), and Italy (4.7 percent) than in Belgium (4.4 percent).

The following tables show average gross wages of male and female workers in Belgium and average hourly wages of workers in selected countries of Western Europe.

Average Gross Wages of Male and Female Workers

Category	Year		
	1953	1960	1965
(1) Manufacturing industry			
(In Belgian Francs per day)			
A. Male manual workers	193	249	358
B. Female manual workers	110	142	222
(In Belgian Francs per month)			
C. Male nonmanual workers	9,580	12,360	16,430
D. Female nonmanual workers	4,630	5,960	8,280
(2) Commerce (nonmanual workers)			
(In Belgian Francs per month)			
A. Male	8,460	11,070	14,545
B. Female.....................	4,245	5,505	7,355
Relations (in %)			
1B to 1A......................	57	57	62
1D to 1C......................	49	48	50
2B to 2A......................	50	50	50

Source: National Office of Social Security. Gross wages are the conventional compensation for a basic unit of performance per hour, per day, or per month.

Average Hourly Wages of All Workers in Western Europe
(Additional charges to employers included)

Country	Year		
	1953	1961	1966
	(In Belgian Francs)		
Belgium	28.2	41.8	68.7
Western Germany................	24.5	48.1	72.8
France	n.a.	40.2	52.4
Italy	23.2	34.4	55.3
Netherlands	n.a.	35.5	59.3
Great Britain	25.7	42.2	58.7

Source: Belgian Federation of Industries.

The majority of the Belgian companies can be labeled "small business." Indeed, 95.54 percent of all employers employ fewer than 50 persons and 67.17 percent fewer than five persons. Nevertheless, 44.84 percent of the workers are employed in enterprises having more than 200 employees (1.05 percent of the total number of enterprises), 21.15 percent of the workers in enterprises utilizing between 50 and 199 employees (3.41 percent of the total number of enterprises), and only 34.01 percent of the workers are employed in enterprises with fewer than 50 employees (95.54 percent of the employers). These characteristics are illustrated by the following table.

Size of Enterprises and Employed Personnel (1965)

Number of employees	Companies		Total of paid employees	
	Number	Percent	Number	Percent
Under 5	93,497	67.17	161,581	7.77
5 to 9	19,229	13.81	125,328	6.02
10 to 19	11,624	8.35	157,610	7.57
20 to 49	8,643	6.21	263,189	12.65
50 to 99	3,126	2.25	216,722	10.41
100 to 199	1,613	1.16	223,414	10.74
200 to 499	993	0.71	301,211	14.47
500 to 999	296	0.21	199,433	9.58
1,000 and over......	186	0.13	432,647	20.79
Total..........	139,207	100.00	2,081,135	100.00

Social Security Benefits

Belgian legislation provides for a compulsory social security system, which covers pensions, unemployment, health, occupational diseases, and family allowances. The social security system is administered by the O.N.S.S. (Office National de Sécurité Sociale), to which the employer is obliged to pay the required contribution both on his own behalf and on behalf of the employees. Besides social security contributions, there are contributions for annual vacation, work accidents, short leave, paid holidays, guaranteed salary in case of sickness or accident, indemnity in case of closing down of enterprises, and occupational medicine.

The mounting costs of social security and other social benefits during the past decade are shown in the following table. Additional social security benefits are provided in some industrial sectors through collective agreements, such as in the metal, textile, and dock industries.

Evolution of Social Security Costs, 1958-1968

Year	Manual workers			White-collar workers		
	Employers' contribution	Workers' contribution	Total	Employers' contribution	Workers' contribution	Total
1958.................	31.45	8.45	39.90	24.85	5.55	30.40
1959.................	31.25	8.35	39.60	24.50	5.50	30.00
1960.................	31.60	8.65	40.25	24.40	5.45	29.85
1961.................	33.80	8.90	42.70	27.00	5.75	32.75
1962.................	34.95	8.85	43.80	28.20	5.55	33.75
1963						
First and second trimester	37.00	9.05	46.05	29.15	5.50	34.85
Third and fourth trimester	37.25	9.05	46.30	29.35	5.50	34.85
1964						
First trimester	40.00	9.25	49.25	30.65	5.40	36.05
Second, third, and fourth trimester	40.50	9.75	50.25	31.40	6.20	37.60
1965.................	42.68	9.93	52.61	32.48	6.08	38.56
1966.................	44.01	10.13	54.14	33.31	6.05	39.36
1967.................	45.56	10.30	55.86	34.31	6.08	40.39
1968.................	47.38	10.54	57.92	36.55	6.58	43.13

The following tables give an overall picture of the financial obligations for social security and other social benefits in 1968.

White-Collar Workers*

	Percent of wages (gross)
Employers' contribution	
Social security	16.53
Annual vacation	12.40
Work accidents	1
Short leave	1
Holidays....................	3.74
Guaranteed salary...........	1
Closing down enterprise	0.03
Occupational medicine	0.20
	36.55
Employees' contribution	
Social security	6.58
Grand total...............	43.13

*Includes also supervisory personnel.

Manual Workers

	Percent of wages (gross)
Employers' contribution	
Social security	23.17
Annual vacation	12.40
Work accidents	3.75
Short leave	1
Holidays	5.23
Guaranteed salary...........	1.60
Closing down enterprise	0.03
Occupational medicine.........	0.20
	47.38
Employees' contribution	
Social security	10.54
Grand total...............	57.92

Labor Force

The labor force comprises almost 40 percent of the Belgian population (3.8 million). Of these, 2.1 million were subject to social security, compulsory for civilian employees. About two thirds are blue-collar workers and about one third white-collar workers, as is shown in the following table.

Categories of Employees (1965)

Blue-collar workers	
Male	1,133,695
Female	352,913
Total.................	1,486,608
White-collar workers	
Male	379,324
Female	223,902
Total.................	603,226
Total employment	2,089,834

Employment in each industrial sector is as follows: manufacturing, 34 percent; services, 24 percent; commerce, banking, and insurance, 15 percent; construction, 8 percent; transport, 7 percent; agriculture, forestry, fishing, 7 percent; mining, quarrying, 3 percent; and electricity, gas, sanitation, 1 percent.

Unemployment is about 3 percent. Employment of foreign workers has been considerable. Preference in this employment goes to workers from other Common Market countries, who have the benefit of the Community arrangements for labor mobility, with continuity of social insurance benefits, including pension rights.[2]

Categories of Employees

Belgian employees are divided in two main categories: blue-collar and white-collar workers. The distinction between blue-collar and white-collar workers has legal significance. The criteria used in drawing the line between the two categories depend on the essential characteristics of the work performed. Predominantly manual work is blue-collar and predominantly intellectual effort is white-collar. This distinction, stemming from the dark ages, is completely archaic but remains the "summa divisio" of Belgian employees. The vast difference in the legal and practical status derived from this distinction appears especially in the areas of guaranteed salary and job security.

In case of sickness or nonwork accident, blue-collar workers get a guaranteed weekly salary of 80 percent for 30 days and 100 percent in case of work accidents. White-collar workers are granted 30 days at 100 percent payment for occupational and nonoccupational

---

[2] See J. D. Neirinck, *Social Policy in the EEC,* page 21, *supra.*

disability. In all instances the employer pays. When the 30-day period has expired, social security payments commence. But there remains a more significant difference in the period of notice the employer has to give in case of termination of the contract of employment. Blue-collar workers must get advance notice of 14 days if they have less than 10 years of service. This term is doubled if the worker has more than 10 years and quadrupled if he has more than 20 years of service. White-collar workers get a minimum term of notice of three months for each five years of service. This means that highly qualified blue-collar workers with 30 years of service must receive 56 days' notice of termination of employment, while white-collar workers of equal service records, doing routine office jobs, must have a minimum of 18 months' notice.

An examination of collective agreements and political discussion shows clearly that there is no significant tendency to make uniform the labor standards statutes affecting blue- and white-collar workers. Although this has been repeatedly promised by succeeding governments, uniformity seems distant. Uniformity would practically mean that manual workers would achieve the status of white-collar workers. The latter, of course, do not want to relinquish the advantages of their long notice terms. Thus virtually everybody is resigned to the unlikelihood of extending these longer terms of notice to the blue-collar workers in the near future.

Almost all important structures within the labor relations system are built upon the distinction between blue- and white-collar workers. There are different union delegations for blue-collar and white-collar workers, different joint committees, and different chambers of the labor courts. But most of all, the trade union structure has taken into account the stated distinction. White-collar workers are not organized by industry but each national federation of trade unions has its own white-collar workers' union. The unions recognize that the differences in structures are so deeply rooted in daily life that it is almost impossible to abolish them.

Leading Personnel — Supervisors

Leading personnel and supervisors, even head-managers, are classified under Belgian law as white-collar workers. This means that they benefit in principle from the whole range of protective labor legislation, such as the long terms of notice which sometimes may be two or even three years.

However, under some statutes different criteria are specified for leading personnel and supervisors. For example, according to Article

35 of the Coordinated Act concerning the Individual Contract, white-collar workers whose annual income exceeds 180,000 B.F. a year ($3,600) are excluded from certain important provisions of the law.[3]

The Act of September 20, 1948, concerning the organization of industry declares that employees who are "leading" personnel are neither eligible to serve as nor have the right to vote for working council representatives. The term "leading personnel" is not defined in the Act. In practice, in the case of first elections, it is left to the employer to draw up the list. In the case of second and later elections, it is up to the working council to decide who are or are not leading personnel. The labor court is available in the last resort to settle eventual conflicts. The compilation of the list of eligible voters is a practical matter to be settled between the employer and the trade unions.

The Act of July 15, 1964, on working time excludes leading personnel from its scope of application. This means, for example, that they are not bound by the rules on overtime limits, as are the white- and blue-collar workers in general. The Act of July 9, 1926, concerning labor courts indicates that cases of certain categories of supervisory personnel are to be settled by the court of commerce.[4] Finally, it should be stressed that leading supervisory personnel are not involved in collective bargaining, nor are they represented in union delegations.

Aspirations of Employees:
Job Security and Guaranteed Income

Belgian workers are no different from their counterparts elsewhere in their desire for good wages, good working conditions, good management, steady work, promotional opportunities, proper conduct of foremen, information about the general course of business, and a chance to perform useful work. However, the aspirations of Belgian workers for job security and guaranteed income should be especially emphasized. These aspirations are so dominant that they have heavily influenced postwar labor relations.[5] Different statutes

---

[3] This financial ceiling is widely criticized as being too low. It is argued that the reasons are outdated by which employees with a higher annual income allegedly need less protection than low-income employees and should therefore take care of themselves.

[4] It should be pointed out, however, that the new procedural code, published in the *Belgian Official Journal* on October 10, 1967, and which will be in effect not later than three years after this date, does not stipulate this exclusion. Cases of all employees without exception are to be treated by the new labor courts.

[5] Goris, *How to Lead a "Conseil d'entreprise,"* Louvain Seminar 1966-1967.

and attitudes reflect these strong aspirations. Some of the legislative measures to improve job security and guaranteed income deserve mention.

Guaranteed income in varying amounts to blue-collar and white-collar workers have already been mentioned. Job security is mainly protected in two ways. The law provides for a suspension of the individual labor contract in case of sickness,[6] military service, pregnancy, annual vacation, and the like. This means that during such periods the employee may not be dismissed. Furthermore, the employment contract may be terminated either for just cause without notice or through respecting a term of notice.

Terms of notices with which the employer must comply are shown as follows:

Length of Notice Period

| Length of service | Blue-collar employees | White-collar employees | |
		Up to 120,000 B.F.	More than 120,000 B.F.
5 years	14 days	3 months	Minimum of
10 years	28 days	6 months	3 months
15 years	28 days	9 months	for each 5
20 years	56 days	12 months	years of
30 years	56 days	18 months	service
40 years	56 days	24 months	

Belgian notice periods are far more liberal than in neighboring countries, especially for white-collar jobs above 120,000 B. F., for which it is not exceptional to see terms of notice fixed by the courts at two or even three years.[8] However, an employer cannot be obliged to retain a worker in service; he has the absolute prerogative of dismissal. But a question of indemnification arises if the employer does not respect the legal provisions concerning the dismissal of an employee. It should be added that, in contrast to countries like

---

[6] An employee may be dismissed if the sickness lasts longer than six months. In that case, wages corresponding to the length of the notice period must be paid.

[7] The governing statute declares:

"Where the annual remuneration exceeds 120,000 B.F. ($2,400) the notice to be given by the employer shall be of such a period as is fixed by the contract or by the court, but it shall not be less than the relevant period prescribed in Section 1." (This is three months for each five years' service).

[8] A termination notice must be given only in the case of a contract for an indefinite period. A conventional protection of job security exists if the contract is for a definite time; the job security equals, in principle, the duration of the contract it-

the Netherlands, the law does not require that dismissal be authorized by a government agency, nor does the employer have to justify
it.

Employment and job security form the primary target for the
trade unions, and naturally the workers themselves feel very strongly about these issues. Dismissals are deeply resented and in many
cases may cause strikes. The working council, the union delegation,
and the trade unions want to be informed if the employer plans to
dismiss personnel. It is widely felt that an employer has a social and
moral obligation to keep his workers occupied even if the enterprise
is temporarily less active than usual. In many sectors collective
agreements provide that dismissals can take place only after consultation with the trade unions and only for economic or technical reasons. White-collar workers successfully claim that employees with
more than 15 years' service should not be dismissed except for economic or technological reasons. In many agreements severance pay
is stipulated. Many collective agreements involving blue-collar
workers stipulate additional guaranteed salary benefits beyond the
statutory guarantees in case of sickness. Aspirations of workers for
job security and guaranteed salary curtail managerial freedom more
than might be assumed from the short notice terms for blue-collar
workers. Full employment is such a concern that even the government is held responsible, with significant election consequences, if
the percentage of unemployment increases or enterprises are closing
down.[9]

THE BELGIAN LABOR RELATIONS SYSTEM

It is commonplace that no labor relations system can be
grasped completely without taking into account the cultural and historical environment in which the system has its roots. This is certainly the case for a country like Belgium, in which the Communist
Manifesto was published in 1848, where the socialist movement has
had a large following, where the Catholic religion had a deep im-

---

self. The following indemnification has to be paid in the case of a breach of contract:

"In the case of a contract for a definite time, its termination before the
end of the period without just cause shall entitle the injured party to a compensation equal to the salary and perquisites for the remainder of the term, up
to a maximum of twice the salary and perquisites corresponding to the notice
which would have been allowable if the contract had been without a specified
term." (Art. 21, Act on White-Collar Workers Contracts).

[9] In 1967 the Prime Minister himself intervened personally and directly when
a decision to close down an enterprise was made by management and workers had
occupied the plant.

pact, and where Liberalism was a strong force in the 19th century.

Labor relations, generally in Europe but especially in Belgium, are still marked by ideological differences. The different trade unions pursue conflicting principles on such issues as the role of the state in public life, the role of private enterprise, nationalization of industries, and the programs and goals of the educational system and seek to influence the views of Belgian society as a whole on such issues. Ideological conflicts are so deeply rooted that trade unions themselves are integrated parts of larger movements. Political parties and cultural organizations, which share and defend the same beliefs, also belong to these larger movements. Although lately ideological differences are emphasized less sharply than before and a pragmatic approach prevails in some matters, opposed ideologies still remain influential factors in the development of the dynamics of our society and our system of labor relations. They explain many realities which otherwise would be completely misunderstood or not grasped at all. An example is the prevalent pluralism of trade unions, which contrasts with the unity of employer associations in Belgium.

The close links of major trade unions with the major political parties, and the parliamentary membership and even government membership of a large number of actual or former trade union leaders, also are characteristic of Belgian labor relations. It is a truism that if both the Socialist and the Christian trade unions support an issue, they can have it pushed through parliament rather easily. This explains the constant political influences upon Belgian labor relations. The political power of trade unions explains the extensive protective labor legislation, the absence of legislation regulating trade unions, and the existence of the almost absolute freedom to strike. Labor relations in Belgium are largely dominated by the two major trade unions, which are almost omnipresent. On the national, interprofessional or interindustrial level, they participate in the shaping of national economic and social policies, through formal consultation, generally at the request of the public authorities. On the industrial level they are represented in the joint committees in which industry-wide collective agreements are made with binding effect for the industry as a whole. On the level of the enterprise they are represented through union delegations, working councils, and safety and health committees, all of which are more fully described below.

Another feature of Belgian labor relations is organized participation in public life and even collaboration between trade unions and employer associations, especially the Federation of Belgian Industries, on national and industry-wide levels. This working relationship is the result of a long evolution in which the events of World War II played an important and special role. At war's end, prominent leaders made a secret agreement in which they established the main principles on which a modern labor relations system would be realized. This working relationship led in 1960 to agreements, called "programmation," by which social progress, taking into account economic possibilities, is jointly planned by employers and trade unions at the national interindustrial level as well as at the industrial level. The program is discussed in greater detail later in this paper.

Collective labor relations in Belgium rely almost entirely on practices and *de facto* agreements between the social partners. There is no significant legislation on collective bargaining, strikes, settlement of industrial disputes, and the like.[10] It should be added that Belgian trade unions have no legal personality, which means among other things that they cannot be sued and in fact are not sued in court for breach of collective agreements. To strict legalists who look for certainty of principles and structures, labor relations in Belgium may appear chaotic. But in general, the pragmatic approach which prevails seems to have quite satisfactory results, as might be gathered from the rather low number of lost working days through strikes. Lawyers do not play any substantial role in the negotiation and administration of collective agreements or in the settlement of industrial conflicts.[11] It might be added that unions are rather jealous of their system and openly and frankly resist any imported changes. Nevertheless, the system is by and large quite elastic and leaves to management a great deal of freedom in exercising its managerial functions.

TRADE UNIONS

The most important trade unions are the Confederation of Christian Trade Unions (A.C.V.-C.S.C.) and the Socialist Trade Union Movement (A.B.V.V.-F.G.T.B.). Less important is the Liberal Trade Union Movement (A.C.L.V.-C.G.S.L.B.). Of the total

---

[10] On December 5, 1968, a law on joint committees and collective labor agreements was enacted. The law will be effective whenever the King commands the necessary measures by Royal Decree, expected as early as 1970. The new law will not significantly alter the labor relations system described in this article.

[11] Belgium has no counterpart of the labor-lawyer experts, representing management, unions, and government agencies or practicing as professional labor arbitrators, such as the European visitors met at Highland Park, Ill., at the 1968 Loyola conference. The work of such lawyers is fully described in Kamin, "The American Labor Lawyer," *Federation News* (London), October 1965.

active salaried population of 2,863,500 in 1965 (1,974,600 male workers and 888,900 female workers), about 1.7 million were organized, as follows: Christian trade unions, about 840,000; Socialist trade unions, about 775,000; Liberal trade unions, between 80,000 to 100,000.

Almost 65 percent of Belgian workers belong to trade unions, thus putting Belgium first in the degree of unionization in the E.E.C. countries. Italy has 43 percent, Germany and Luxembourg 37 percent, and the Netherlands 34 percent. In France 26.5 percent of the eligible workers are union members.

In the most important sectors of industry, such as metals, chemicals, cement, petroleum, and mines, almost 90 percent of the blue-collar workers are organized. White-collar workers tend to organize less (approximately 40 percent), while staff or supervisory personnel are rarely organized although they have a legal right to do so and to bargain collectively.

Belgian trade unions are not organized on a craft or occupational basis. Industrial unions prevail. Both the Socialist and Christian unions have divisions for white-collar workers only, whatever may be the sector of industry to which they belong.[12]

The F.G.T.B. is based on the principles of democratic socialism.[13] These principles correspond with those of the Belgian Socialist Party. Its declared goal is a system of social and economic democracy under which the production apparatus will be at the service of the whole community. Fourteen national unions are affiliated with the F.G.T.B. Each union is an independent organization with its own structure, governing bodies, and statutory rules. To become affiliated, the union must give assurance that it will accept the basic principles of the socialist F.G.T.B. and that it will carry out all the decisions made by the governing bodies of the F.G.T.B. The industrial unions in the Socialist Trade Union Movement are completely free in their organizational activities and cannot be forced to give an account of conduct that accords with the basic F.G.T.B. principles and governing rules. On the other hand, the F.G.T.B. is the only

---

[12] The Christian trade unions have a Flemish branch of white-collar workers (Landelijke Bedienden Centrale or L.B.C.) and a Walloon branch (Centrale Nationale des Employes or C.N.E.). The total membership of both language groups was put at over 90,000 in 1964. The Socialist union's white-collar division (B.B.T.K. or Bond der Bedienden, Technici en Kaders van België and in French: Syndicats des Employés, Techniciens et Cadres de Belgique) claimed over 60,000 members in the same year. The four teachers unions of the Christian Trade Unions are not classified as "white-collar" organizations.

[13] Gogne, *The F.G.T.B. Trade Union Movement*, Louvain Seminar 1966-1967.

Socialist union body authorized to make decisions on the general or national level in defense of the general interests of the workers. The Socialist Trade Union Movement is decentralized at regional and local levels. The F.G.T.B. participates in the "Socialist Common Action," which was created in 1950. The Socialist Common Action coordinates the various branches of the socialist movement — Coop-Health Institutions, F.G.T.B., and Socialist Party — and is the discussion center on the principal problems of concern to the whole socialist movement.

The Christian workers in Belgium are grouped in a national organization called the Christian Labor Movement. The aim of this organization is to defend the interests of the workers in accordance with Christian social doctrine and the principles of democracy. It is composed of specialized national organizations for economic, cultural, and educational action such as the Confederation of Christian Trade Unions (C.S.C.), mutual insurance companies, cooperative societies, Workers' Youth, Women's Guild, and the Workers' Associations.

The C.S.C. is the nation-wide organization entrusted with the direction of the activities of all Christian trade unions in Belgium. The C.S.C. in the main has the same structure as the F.G.T.B. It is composed of 17 national unions based on industry, which are also decentralized on a regional and a local level.

The Christian, Socialist, and Liberal Unions are recognized by the government as being the "most representative unions." They are considered to be representative of the totality of the workers. Other minority trade unions are almost totally excluded from any possible trade activity. Only the three unions mentioned are represented in the different economic, social, and financial institutions and bodies. They alone have the right to present candidates for social elections (working council, health and safety committee) at the plant level or for nomination in the joint committees at the industry level. In practice, only the C.S.C. and the F.G.T.B. are the significant "partners" with which the employers must deal on all levels.

Trade Union Freedom

Freedom to join or not to join a union is guaranteed by the Act of May 24, 1921. According to Article 1 of this Act, "no person shall be compelled to join or refrain from joining any association." However, a punishable infraction of the law depends upon proof of "criminal" intent to infringe upon the freedom of association. This act requires a "dolus specialis," which is extremely difficult to prove.[14] Only about 10 prosecutions have been undertaken since 1921.

In practice, yellow-dog contracts as well as union-security clauses, such as closed shop, union shop, agency shop, and maintenance of membership, are almost unknown in Belgian labor relations.[15] With few exceptions, checkoff is not practiced because unions do not want employers to know how many members they have. Unions prefer to collect dues from the members themselves at the place of work in Walloon country or at their homes in Flanders, in order to maximize personal contact and learn first hand of complaints of members.

Other devices exist to persuade employees gently to join the representative unions. For the last 10 years, most collective agreements have contained a clause providing benefits only for union members. This clause is usually accompanied by a no-strike clause, through which trade unions guarantee "social peace" during the life of the agreement. Unions have successfully argued that a situation under which non-dues-paying, nonunion members also benefit from trade union accomplishments financed by the dues and contributions of members is no longer acceptable, and thus it is just and equitable that a special benefit in the form of dues reimbursement, paid by the employer, should be reserved solely to the union or to the union members. Although this union solidarity demand has been vigorously resisted by many employers, almost one million workers are covered by such clauses. The amount of the benefit or partial dues reimbursement varies from 250 B.F. ($5.00) a year to 1,500 B.F. ($30.00). Union dues in Belgium are quite low by American standards.

The building trades unions reject the idea of reserved benefits

---

[14] Art. 3 provides as follows:

"Any person who, for the purpose of compelling a particular individual to join or refrain from joining an association, resorts to violence, molestation or threats, or who causes him to fear the loss of his employment or injury to his person, family or property, shall be punished by imprisonment from one week to one month and a fine of 50 to 500 francs, or by one of these penalties."

Art. 4 reads as follows:

"Any person who, with the intent to attack freedom of association, makes the conclusion, the execution or (even with due regard to customary notice) the continuance of a contract of work or service conditional upon the affiliation or nonaffiliation of one or more persons to an association, shall be liable to the same penalties."

See Blanpain, *La Liberté syndicale en Belgique* (Louvain: 1963).

[15] Special devices exist in some sectors. In the port of Antwerp 12,500 "dokkers" are eligible for a job only if they are holders of a "working card." Trade unions dispose of 90 percent of those cards. A similar system is practiced in the diamond industry.

for union members. However, the administrative formalities and red tape in the Belgian construction industry are so complicated that unionization is virtually a necessity for workers, as is the formation of associations for employers. The availability of special financial allowances paid through a special social fund provided for by collective agreement in case of layoff for bad weather is alone sufficient to convince building tradesmen of the merits of unionization.

Trade Union Structure

The C.S.C. and the F.G.T.B. have essentially the same structure. Both are federations of national trade unions, organized on behalf of industry, trade, or service.[16] Fourteen national unions are affiliated with the F.G.T.B., 17 with the C.S.C. I regard as superfluous an analysis of the Liberal Union Movement, which has little practical influence.

The C.S.C. (Christian) unions are divided among the following groups: food industry; utilities, chemical industry, leather industry; diamond; paper and printing industry; building and timber industry; metal industry; coal mining; public offices; railroad, telephone, and telegraph industry; stone, cement, and glass industry; textile and garment industry; teamsters; clerical workers; teachers in primary schools; teachers in technical schools; teachers in public high schools; and teachers in free high schools.

Each national trade union is autonomous in defending the interests of its members and discharging essential trade union functions. The national trade unions have provincial, regional, and local sections. The F.G.T.B. and the C.S.C. have 24 and 33 regional federations, respectively. The regional federations coordinate the activities of the different trade unions operating within the region. For the most part, they are charged with administrative and financial duties such as recruiting of new members, collection of dues, legal assistance to members, and propaganda.

Jurisdictional or demarcation disputes between national trade unions belonging to the same national federation are resolved through a binding decision taken within the central committee of the federation. There are no jurisdictional disputes between the parallel organizations of C.S.C. and F.G.T.B. Both deal with the employer or employer association in a common front. Both are equally recognized by the employer side of the bargaining table. Of course, each

---

[16] Excluding unions of white-collar workers, discussed in note 12, *supra*. In the public sector there is one national union that embraces public employees in state, provincial, and local governments.

movement seeks to attract as many members as possible. The relative strength of each union is reflected in the elections of working councils and health committees discussed later in this paper.

Most Representative Unions

Belgian labor relations cannot be understood without a full grasp of the practical meaning and consequences of what we call the "most representative trade union." As noted earlier only three unions, the Christian, the Socialist, and the Liberal, are recognized to be most representative by the government as well as by the employers' associations.

The most representative trade unions enjoy a legal and practical monopoly in representing the interests of the workers at the national level, the industry level, and the level of the enterprise or undertaking. They are the only ones to be represented in the officially organized joint organs, composed of employers and employee representatives, in which a great deal of collective bargaining is done. At national interprofessional level or interindustrial level this is the National Labor Council, at industry-wide level the joint committee, and at the enterprise level the working council and the health and safety committee.

The most representative unions, practically speaking only the Christian and Socialist Unions, must be dealt with as the authorized and duly empowered bargaining spokesmen of employees. They cannot be excluded at the level of the enterprise by means of devices known to American or Canadian law, such as an election among eligible employee voters by which a majority union would be sole and exclusive bargaining representative of the employees or in which union representation would be altogether rejected.[17]

Union Democracy and Administration

There is nothing in Belgian labor law comparable to the American Landrum-Griffin Act. Belgian unions are completely free and sovereign in all matters. Trade union leaders are not directly elected but are appointed by cooption, when vacancies occur, by those already in power.

---

[17] In the 1967 elections of working councils in undertakings of 150 employees or more, F.G.T.B. received over 50 percent of the votes, C.S.C. received over 40 percent, and the Liberals less than 6 percent. The results in elections of health and safety committees were similar. Hence, I pay little attention in this paper to the Liberals.

The C.S.C. describes the existing system as follows:

"In the heroic times of the trade union movement, trade union leaders were nominated directly by the members, who selected for positions of leadership the most eloquent among their comrades and those who displayed the greatest dynamism and the liveliest zeal for trade union interests. These were the times of direct democracy in the management of trade union affairs. But with the further development of membership, the growing complexity of trade unions, and the centralization of trade union action caused by changes in industrial life, it proved no longer possible for the leaders to be elected directly by the members. First of all, not all members attend meetings; furthermore, ordinary members are not always capable of forming a sound judgment of the aptitudes required of possible leaders. Direct election, therefore, was replaced by appointment, by delegation and by co-optation.

"Full-time officers are nominated by the Committee of the organization in whose service they are employed and their appointment has to be confirmed either by the Central Committee (Trades Centers and Regional Federations) or the Council (C.S.C.). They are paid by their organization and relieved of all other professional activities.

"At the top of the trade union hierachy, we find those full-time officers who are entrusted with the direction of the Trades Centers, the Regional Federations and the C.S.C. They are recruited from among full-time officers of the second echelon and their nomination must also meet with the approval either of the Central Committee, or the Council of the organization concerned."

For the most part, rank-and-file members are not involved in the elaboration of union programs or in the establishment of the dues schedules. They have no right to examine financial documents and reports, which are kept secret. Trade unions claim that, notwithstanding the aforementioned procedures, there is a high degree of informal democracy; that trade union leaders come to the forefront through their zeal for the trade union cause and are readily accepted by the members; that union funds and especially the strike fund must be kept secret; and that employers above all should not know the financial strength and possibilities of the unions in cases of economic showdowns.

Whatever the merits of this reasoning, trade union members have a rather strong weapon in that in Belgium, the majority-union system is unkown and dissatisfied members may shift to the Socialist, Liberal, or Christian union. Ideology is incidental. Many employees join and remain with a particular union, less for adherence to the fundamental principles of "Rerum Novarum," "Quadragesimo Anno," or the Marxist-Socialist doctrine than for the practical bread-and-butter services rendered by the union.

Trade Unions and Legal Personality

Belgian trade unions have no formal legal status or corporate capacity. Collective agreements are not legally binding between the collective contracting parties and as such are not judicially enforceable. Lacking corporate capacity, unions cannot be sued if they do not fulfill their peace obligations, even when the obligation is explicitly stated in the collective agreement.[18] Nor may the union in its own name sue the employer or the employer association for failure to perform obligations under the collective agreement.

This situation may seem deplorable — and it is, according to many observers — but it will not change within the near future. It is also for this reason that employers — looking for some guarantees regarding the execution and administration of collective agreements — have geared the payment of "benefits" reserved to union members, discussed earlier, directly to the faithful performance of the collective agreement and the maintenance of social peace during the life of the agreement.

Trade Unions and Free Enterprise System

The major Belgian trade unions strongly advocate a thorough reform of the existing free enterprise system. They proclaim that the status of the enterprise system in its present structures and functions can no longer be determined through the liberal individualistic philosophy of the nineteenth century. The fact of "property," it is claimed, is no longer sufficient to justify the authority of the employer over the enterprise. For trade unions, the enterprise is a community of capital, labor, management, and public interest. Consequently, it is asserted that because the actual legal structure of the enterprise does not respond to this reality, a new structure must be found to close the gap between law and reality; a new structure in which the different components mentioned should be adequately integrated and represented in the decision-making.

Belgian trade unions, including the socialist F.G.T.B., do not now favor the nationalization of private enterprises.[19] Nor do trade union officials today demand active codetermination which would involve trade union representatives in the financial and economic de-

---

[18] There are some exceptions. For example, the Act of September 20, 1948, inaugurating the working councils, stipulates that the trade unions may sue employers in cases of disputes concerning elections.

[19] Although the F.G.T.B. in 1956 proposed the nationalization of some basic industries, such as power and energy suppliers. The reason for this evolution is that private property is asserted to be only of secondary importance. Management is the significant source of power and authority.

cision-making process of the enterprise. They do not wish to contribute to the fragmentation of the authority required for the efficient operation of the company. Another argument made by labor leaders is that sharing responsibility in management decisions might weaken the spirit of vigilance over and the right of challenge to management decisions. Indeed, the F.G.T.B. states that in the Belgian economy the most important decisions are not made by the enterprise itself but are "dictated" by dominant financial pressure groups not active and visible in front-line management.

According to trade unions, the profit motive should be replaced by the idea of serving the general welfare. Therefore, unions in Belgium demand complete and detailed information on all aspects of the employers' activity, participation in decisions affecting the wages and social and labor conditions of employees through the process of collective bargaining and some right of control on corporate financial and economic decisions. According to the Christian C.S.C., the enterprise should be governed by a large council, composed of capital, labor, and the public interest. This council would make the so-called "vital decisions," such as nomination of management, closing down of the enterprise, major changes in production, augmentation of capital, and the like. The idea of codetermination led to the creation of working councils, which will be discussed later.

THE INSTITUTIONALIZED RELATIONS
BETWEEN EMPLOYERS AND TRADE UNIONS

Interaction between organized labor and employers has resulted in degrees of institutionalization of labor relations at different levels. This working relationship between labor and employers is the result of a long historical development which started at the end of the last century.

At the level of the enterprise or establishment, three different bodies, representing both the personnel and the trade unions, may operate. These are the union delegation, the working council, and the safety and health committee.

Joint committees function at the industry level. The National Labor Council, created in 1952, functions at the national interprofessional or interindustrial level. These unique institutions are the consequence of acceptance by employers that trade unions are their natural partners both inside and outside the business undertaking. It must be stressed that not all of these institutions are commanded by law. For example, the union delegation is entirely the product of collective bargaining. Even in legally obligatory bodies, working rules and practical matters are generally regulated by the collective partners in accordance with the immediate and long-range needs of the enterprise or the industry, rather than by legal mandates.

Representation at Enterprise Level

The "triad" of the union delegation, the working council, and the safety and health committee that functions at the enterprise level is the result of compromise between the competitive attitudes of the major unions. The Christian unions favor the idea of collaboration between worker and management through the working council, and the Socialist trade unions emphasize the competition between labor and capital through the union delegation. A typical Belgian solution solved the problem. Not two but three organs were created where many agreed that one could do the job. It follows that there is a great deal of overlapping in practice regarding both the jurisdiction and the composition of the different bodies. In many cases the same employees are simultaneously members of the union delegation, the working council, and the health and safety committee.[20]

The Union Delegation

The union delegation is the product of collective bargaining. The delegation was first sketched in the pact of social solidarity clandestinely signed by union leaders and the representatives of the employer associations at the end of the Second World War. The pact, which was very explicit, was a blueprint describing the main points of social reform to be developed in the postwar period. To assure union recognition at the plant level, a union delegation was to be created in every enterprise with more than 20 employees.

In June 1947, a national interindustry collective agreement was concluded between the social partners in which the main principles concerning the inauguration and the work of the union delegations were formulated. Each joint committee was asked to adapt these principles to the specific situations of the industry sector. More than 40 agreements were concluded in different industries and many more at the level of the enterprise or establishment.

The employer is not legally obliged to recognize a union delegation in his enterprise,[21] but unions will ask him to do so if they

---

[20] Declercq, *Representation of Personnel in the Enterprise*, Louvain Seminar 1966-1967.

[21] Nevertheless, a legal obligation may result from a collective agreement concluded in the competent joint committee and rendered binding by Royal Decree. See discussion accompanying note 26, *infra*.

have sufficient strength in the establishment to press such a claim. Union delegates are employees. They are sometimes elected by their fellow workers, but more frequently they are appointed by regional trade union officers. The number of the delegates varies with the size of the enterprise. In most cases there are separate delegations for manual workers and for white-collar workers. That union delegates are elected on different lists or are designated by different unions does not mean that the union delegation does not act as a whole. Generally, a chief delegate is chosen from the strongest union in the enterprise and acts as a spokesman for the group. When unions have about equal strength, two chief delegates usually are named.

The union delegate is the Belgian equivalent of an American shop steward, but he has little of the authority and power of a British shop steward. He presents and discusses grievances and otherwise supervises the application of collective agreements and labor law standards in the enterprise. It is sometimes claimed that in his actions within the enterprise, the union delegate is actually less autonomous than before, by becoming to a greater degree the mere deputy of the union in the enterprise, and that consequently he relies more heavily than in the past on the regular union business agent. However, in my view, the trade union succeeds or fails with the union delegation. This body is the favorite of all trade unions. They have such strong feelings about their delegates that they strongly resist the termination or disruption of their employment. In practice, union delegates enjoy almost complete stability of employment.

Working Council

The employer is legally obliged to establish a working council when his enterprise regularly employes an average of 150 persons, including supervisory or leading personnel. The council is composed of a number elected of employee representatives and an equal number of employer representatives chosen by the employer from among his supervisory personnel.[22]

Elections must be held every four years under legally detailed procedures. Only the three representative unions have the right to present candidates in the election at the level of the enterprise. The

---

[22] The size of the working council is determined by the total number of persons employed in the establishment. The minumum number of members is six in enterprises of 150 to 500 employees. The maximum number of working council members is 18 in establishments with more than 6000 employees. In all cases an equal number of substitute delegates also are elected.

available seats of delegates and substitute delegates are divided between blue-collar workers and white-collar workers according to
their respective numerical strength in the establishment. All workers, whether members of a union or not, participate in the elections
with the exception of leading or supervisory personnel, who have
neither the right to vote nor the right to be candidates.

The purpose of the working council is to promote "collaboration" between the employees and the employer. The Act of 1948
enumerates functions of the working council. The council has the
right to receive from the employer regular information on corporate
financial and economic data, including productivity ratings of the
various categories of workers. Every three months an oral progress
report must be given, and at the end of the year the employer must
supply a written progress report, together with such accounting information as the balance sheet and profit and losses. However, since
the law is vague, and even requires some information which is impossible to compile, and since the employer is naturally reticent in
giving financial and economic information, I say without hesitation
that this part of the law has been unsuccessful. It is equally true
that, notwithstanding a great effort by trade unions, many worker
delegates are not able to understand fully the information that is delivered to them. It is also true that some are not really interested in
the overall financial picture of the undertaking, as long as their own
jobs and earnings are not affected.

In principle, the Act upholds the right of the workers' delegates
to ask an auditor to check the financial and economic information
given by the employer. In practice, however, this provision has little
effect, for the task of the auditor is limited to a declaration as to
whether the information given by the employer is complete and correct. Without the consent of the employer, the auditor cannot give
any further information to the employee members of the working
council. But, above all, since an auditor's practice is usually confined
to employers, ordinarily he will decline a union's commission for an
independent audit. It is not surprising that, in order to get complete
financial and economic information, the trade unions today urge the
promulgation of uniform legal rules of accounting and a thorough
reform of the statute regarding certified auditors.

The working council also has an advisory function concerning
working conditions, productivity, and the examination of general
criteria related to hiring and, more importantly, firing of employees.
The role of the working council is limited to giving suggestions. The
right of ultimate decision remains completely with management.
Unions accept the advisory role, but criticize the fact that many

measures that result in changed working conditions at the job, such as automation and other work revisions to increase productivity, are taken without previous consultation with the enterprise council.

Finally, the working council has a function of codetermination in the making of work rules which generally bind the employer and employees,[23] fixing of dates of annual vacations for employees, and the direction of the welfare works of the enterprise in cultural and social activities, recreation, sports, and the like.

Workers' delegates enjoy a great stability of employment and can only be dismissed for just cause — e.g., fighting, stealing, or other offense familiar to those who read American grievance arbitration cases — or for technical or economic reasons, which must meet criteria recognized by the joint committee.[24] The remedy for illegal discharge of a delegate or substitute is not reinstatement with possible back pay but the payment of an indemnification according to established scale: two years of wages when the delegate has less than ten years of service in the enterprise, three years when the delegate has from ten to twenty years' service, and four years when he has more than twenty years' service. The working councils have been most effective in protecting their delegates and substitutes and also in handling disputes concerning layoff and firing of rank-and-file personnel.

It is generally agreed that the working council has not had the success visualized by its creators. To what degree has the working council realized the idea of codetermination proposed by social reformers as an ultimate goal? My answer is not at all. First, economic and financial information and even suggestions are in many cases almost farcical, and the workers are not really interested in them. Information and suggestions are considered only as debating

---

[23] Article 6 of the Act of April 8, 1965, specifies at least 15 aspects of employment that must be covered by work rules. Typical of such matters are the time of commencement and termination of the regular working day, the time and duration of breaks, and the days when work is normally interrupted; methods of measuring and checking work done with a view to fixing remuneration; method, time, and place of payment of remuneration; periods of notice required and serious grounds for termination of the contract by either party, without notice, subject to judicial opinion, provided that such causes are not laid down by law; rights and obligations of supervisory personnel; sanctions, amounts of fines, and uses to which they shall be put, together with offenses in respect of which they are imposed and procedures for employee redress of such disciplinary measures; first-aid information; date of annual collective vacation leave; the names of members of the works council, the health and safety committee, and the union delegation; names of physicians to treat work injuries.

[24] If the joint committee cannot agree upon the adequacy of the technical economic reasons for termination of employment of workers' delegates, the controversy is adjudicated by the labor court.

points when jobs and livelihoods may be in danger. Comparatively speaking, it is my impression that in many ways American workers get more effective codetermination through collective bargaining than their Belgian counterparts get through formal and legal co-determination procedures.

The Safety and Health Committee

A health and safety committee must be established by the employer when the enterprise employs more than 50 persons. The safety committee has a format much like the working council: elected employee members who enjoy equivalent job-stability guarantees and supervisory personnel nominated by the employer. The physician head of the medical service, a nurse, or even a social worker may assist at the meetings, as an expert without the right to vote. The safety committee must examine accident reports, attend to the application of the safety and health legislation, and develop means of propaganda and other proper measures to improve the safety and health of the workers in the establishment. The safety committee has no right of decision since the responsibility for safety and health rests with the employer. But the employer must eventually explain to the safety council and the state inspectors why a proposal agreed upon in the safety committee was not applied. Observers agree that the activities of the safety committees have been successful.

This short description of the different organs and institutions at the enterprise or plant level leads to these conclusions:

1. In practice the employer must deal with trade unions, whether he wishes to or not. He can refuse to recognize a union delegation in his enterprise and engage in an ensuing struggle, but he is legally obliged to establish a working council and a safety committee in which only union candidates can be elected.

2. The representative trade unions, through their political influence, have succeeded in establishing a shared legal monopoly in the plant or establishment. Only their candidates may appear on the election lists. In some cases, however, unions do not find candidates easily.

3. Leading personnel do not participate in the elections, nor can they be elected. Since the term "leading personnel" is not clearly defined, many disputes occur between unions and employer and even among the personnel themselves. The fact that leading personnel are not represented as such in the working council has, in my opinion, greatly hampered the unionization of this category of employees.

4. The requirement that the delegate must be elected by all workers, including nonunion personnel, means that sympathetic, but not necessarily competent, people are entered on the lists.

5. In practice, the union delegation, working council, and safety committee have overlapping compositions, functions, and jurisdictions. The different structures are not rigidly fixed by law or collective agreement. Working councils and safety and health committees can be reduced to lifeless formalities if they are not supported by strong unions at the plant level. This is true even of the union delegation in many cases.

6. The three organs, especially their union delegations, can be and are the machinery for collective bargaining. The working council has to agree on the work rules and on the scheduling of annual vacations of employees. But above all — and this differs from industry to industry — many collective agreements are concluded on the level of the enterprise between the employer and the union delegation with the expert aid of the business agents of the different unions involved. This is the case, for example, in the chemical industry, where collective bargaining is done mostly at the plant level.

7. It is fair to draw an overall conclusion that the system is flexible and permits a great deal of constructive freedom of maneuver, depending on human relations, strength and aggressiveness of unions, and the employers' attitudes.

Bargaining Structures at Industry Level: the Joint Committees

Joint committees have played an important role in Belgian labor relations since their inauguration in collective bargaining, the settlement of industrial disputes, and the implementation of social legislation and labor standards.

The first joint committees were established on an informal basis in the mining and metal industry after the First World War. This number expanded slowly according to union strength and the pace of recognition of unions by associations of employers, which were then also organizing. Only after the economic crisis in the 1930s were a large number of joint committees set up.

In their pact of social solidarity after the Second World War, employer representatives and trade union representatives expressed their intention to conduct their relations on a basis of mutual respect and reciprocal recognition of each other's rights and duties. They explicitly agreed upon the restoration of the joint committees at the level of the industry. At present, more than 80 such joint committees exist, covering almost all industrial sectors and employers and employees.

It was only after the Second World War that the joint committees were endowed with a legal status according to the decree of June 9, 1945. This decree was not intended to innovate, but only to confirm the *de facto* exercise of power and authority of existing institutions by conferring legal status upon them. Essentially, this means that the committees were and still are built directly upon the trade unions and the employer associations.

Establishment and Composition of the Joint Committees

Joint committees are established by Royal Decree at the request of, or at least after consultation with, the most representative employer association and trade unions in every branch of industry, commerce, and agriculture and for every liberal profession.[25] The Royal Decree defines the territorial and industrial coverage of each committee. Generally, the coverage is the entire industry throughout the nation, but on occasion regional committees are set up which operate under the supervision of the national committee for the particular industry. A single, but multiproduct, enterprise may fall within the scope of several joint committees. In many branches of industry, different committees are set up for manual and white-collar workers, respectively. This is the case in the most important sectors, such as textiles, metals, chemicals, petroleum, and mining.

Joint committees are composed of an equal number of labor and management representatives. These are formally named by the King of Belgium pursuant to actual selection by the Minister of Employment and Labor from the most representative unions and employer associations. As might be expected, there are occasional disputes and displays of pressure regarding the distribution of union designees to joint committees. Each joint committee is staffed by an independent chairman, a vice-chairman, and a secretary of the Ministry of Employment and Labor, in most cases civil servants, also designated by the King.

Under Article 10 of the Royal Decree of June 9, 1945, the principal duties of the joint committees are to fix wages and condi-

[25] In practice, the creation of a joint committee has always been the result of negotiations between employers and trade union representatives. See further: Lagasse, "The Law of Collective Bargaining and Collective Agreements in Belgium," *Labour Relations and the Law: A Comparative Study*, Kahn-Freund, ed., 1965; Delperee, "Joint Committees in Belgium," *International Labour Review*, March 1960.

tions of employment, primarily by means of concluding collective agreements; to prevent and settle industrial conflicts by way of conciliation; and to assist the government in the drafting and adoption of labor legislation.

Several legislative acts have subsequently endowed the joint committees with additional powers. Under the Act of July 15, 1964, the joint committees may fix working time below 45 hours a week. By the Act of August 19, 1948, as modified, concerning the safeguarding of essential services in peacetime, the committees are required to define those services and operations that must be maintained in the event of industrial disputes. The services and equipment exempted from shutdown because of labor disputes are discussed later in this paper. Under the Act of September 20, 1948, the joint committees enumerate the economic or technical reasons to justify dismissal of a member-employee of a working council. These acts confer upon the joint committees the right to be consulted or to submit proposals before the Executive can enforce labor law measures.

All decisions of the joint committees, whether agreements or proposals to the Executive, must be unanimous. Mere opinions or advice do not require unanimity.

Collective agreements concluded within the joint committees can be rendered obligatory by Royal Decree. This makes the agreement binding upon all employers and employees who fall within the jurisdiction of the joint committee.[26] Deviations and exceptions are possible only if they contain more advantageous conditions for the employees. One of the consequences of royal enforcement is that the rules stipulated in the agreement are sanctioned penally. Employers and employees who do not live up to these regulations may be heavily fined. Governmental inspection of terms and conditions of employment is quite intensive to insure compliance with such a Royal Decree. A request to secure a Royal Decree must be made to the Minister of Employment and Labor, either by the joint committee or by an organization represented in the committee. The Minister may refuse to grant enforcement. The Act of 1945 does not stipulate the reasons for which enforcement may be refused. It is, however,

---

[26] See, for example, the Royal Decree of January 11, 1965, imposing funded income guarantees and regulatory rules and bylaws upon the entire cement industry of Belgium to conform to the collective agreement of October 1, 1964, made by the National Joint Committee for the industry; see also Royal Decree of December 20, 1968, making obligatory upon all employers within the Province of Hainaut in the brickwork industry the provisions of the collective labor agreement made on October 22, 1968, by the Regional Joint Committee (Commission Paritaire Régionale) of the brickwork industry for that province.

an accepted rule that only juridical reasons may be invoked. The Minister must explain his rejection on the rare occasions of its occurrence. This means that enforcement may not be refused for such reasons as government policy, economic considerations, or intervention in wage increases. Therefore, complete freedom in wage determination exists in Belgium.

The National Labor Council

The National Labor Council, created by the Act of May 29, 1952, had many predecessors. In 1892 a tripartite Supreme Council of Labor was set up. It was composed of representatives of management and labor and specialist-experts. This consultative body played a substantial role in the preparation of a significant number of labor-standards acts voted on by Parliament until 1918.

Taking into account the growing importance of trade unions, the Council was reorganized in 1935 and became more involved in the formulation of social and economic policy.[27] In this prewar period, trade unions and employer associations started significant direct negotiations at the national interindustry level, which culminated in agreements such as the national agreement of 1936 concerning wages, annual vacations, working time, and freedom of trade union activity.

After the war of 1940-1945, an informal General Parity Council was created. This council was composed of trade union leaders and employer representatives under the chairmanship of the Minister of Employment and Labor. The General Parity Council prepared a number of important measures requiring implementation or decrees. The program gave expression to the new social ideas and programs that originated even while the war was still a reality. It also concluded nationwide interindustry collective agreements. From the General Parity Council there emerged in 1952 a public body, now called the National Labor Council. The president of the Council is chosen for his economic and social knowledge and independence of trade unions and employer associations. The 22 council members are divided equally between the most representative trade unions and the most representative organizations of employers in industry, agriculture, and commerce. The president and members are designated by Royal Decree.

The main function of the Council is to give advice to the legislature or the Executive, on its own initiative or on request, about

---

[27] Lagasse, note 25, *supra.*

general social problems concerning employers and workers. In practice the Council has great prestige and is frequently consulted by the Executive. The government would find it very difficult to push a bill on social matters through Parliament if there were serious opposition in the National Labor Council. Although not authorized expressly in the Act of 1952, the National Labor Council has concluded some important collective agreements.[28]

COLLECTIVE BARGAINING

Although collective bargaining may be generally described as the procedure by which wages and conditions of employment of workers are regulated by agreement between their representatives and employers, the differences in approach, procedure, and scope among different countries are so extensive that a general definition is almost meaningless.[29]

Trade unions in Belgium, and generally employers and employer associations, believe in free collective bargaining without any intervention whatsoever by the government in the establishment of wages and conditions of employment. But the broad statement must be qualified. Through their links with political parties, trade unions have succeeded in pushing through Parliament detailed legislation conerning individual labor relations between employer and employee, as well as social security. Many questions that are the subject of collective bargaining in the United States or in Great Britain are governed by law in Belgium. Acts concerning individual labor contracts for blue-collar and white-collar workers regulate, among other things, the different forms of contracts, damages for breach thereof, layoff, period of notice prior to dismissal, illness, working time, overtime, female and child labor, safety and working conditions, holidays with pay, paid annual leaves, and the like. There are also very detailed social security regulations dealing with unemployment, sickness and health insurance, pensions, occupational diseases, and family allowances.

With so much social and labor-standards legislation, there is, of course, less room for collective bargaining. The process of private bargaining must take into account the existing legal rules. While

---

[28] De Broeck, *Bargaining Structures*, Louvain Seminar 1966-1967.

[29] Allan Flanders recently published a critique of *Industrial Democracy*, by Sidney and Beatrice Webb. " . . . the very term 'collective bargaining,' which we owe to them, has been a persistent source of confusion in understanding and evaluating the social system it was meant to describe." "Collective Bargaining: A Theoretical Analysis," 6 *British Journal of Industrial Relations* 1 (March 1968).

these are mostly protective minimum standards that could be improved by collective bargaining, nevertheless, collective bargaining does not cover as many items as a system with fewer legal regulations. Many agreements on the national level concern only wages, premium pay for night, dangerous, or unpleasant work, and job classifications for individual employees. In some sectors of the economy, especially the expanding ones, agreements might stipulate other items, but legally they build upon some existing legal provisions. For example, the petroleum sector is covered by different national agreements which cover the following items for blue-collar workers: (1) job-classification; (2) working time; (3) wages, premiums, and cost-of-living clause; (4) overtime; (5) absence with pay (civic and other obligations); (6) vacation (legal vacation); (7) additional pension; (8) sickness indemnity (improvement of legal system); (9) job stability (improvement of legal system); and (10) grievance procedure (union delegation). From items (4) through (9) the collective agreement provides some improvements over existing legal benefits not dependent on the agreement.

The large financial commitments to social security and other social benefits, namely, 57.92 percent of gross wages for blue-collar workers and 43.13 percent for white-collar workers, inevitably affect the collective bargaining process. Indeed, these percentages of wages have a legal destination that cannot be modified by collective bargaining. While the government does not formally intervene in the setting of wages and benefits, it intervenes indirectly by fixing the social security contributions and compels the parties to bargain within a limited scope.

Staff Personnel and Collective Bargaining

Staff personnel or cadre employees are not involved in collective bargaining. This is not so much the consequence of the absence of bargaining machinery, since the joint committees for white-collar workers may represent all white-collar employees. But an examination of collective agreements concluded in joint committees shows clearly that in almost all cases wages and employment conditions of supervisory personnel above the level of foreman are omitted. It is also established that at the enterprise level the union delegation does not include representatives of cadre or leading personnel. The main reason is that leading personnel either are not unionized or do not affiliate with a representative trade union. Accordingly, individual contracts or, more likely, unilateral employer determination establishes the wage and labor conditions of staff personnel.

Collective Bargaining and the Law

In Belgium, as well as in most European countries, the collective labor agreement falls into several legal categories. The obligatory part concerns the rights and obligations between the contracting parties, such as the trade union and the employer association. Examples are the peace obligation, the no-strike clause, and the obligation to mediate collective disputes. The normative part is the set of labor and working conditions upon which the parties have agreed. These conditions will be the rules or norms governing relations between employees and employers, such as wages, working hours, and job classifications. The normative part is further split into two parts: The first part concerns individual normative rules, which concern only the individual relation between the employer and employee, such as the individual's wages and job classification. Then there are the collective normative rules, which are intended to regulate collective labor relations at the level of the enterprise or at the level of the industry, such as status of union delegation, social funds, and the like.

Belgian law regulates only the binding effect of the individual normative rules, those rules concerning the individual relation of employer and worker. According to the Acts of March 4 and 11, 1954, those stipulations of the collective agreement have the following bounds: "Matters not covered by any joint industrial agreement rendered binding by Royal Decree shall, in the absence of any explicit stipulation by the individual parties, be governed by collective agreements and joint committee agreements or by custom."

This means that the individual normative rules of a collective agreement have first a general and second a supplementary binding effect. The agreement affects all employers and employees operating within the territorial and industrial scope of the agreement, unless the individual parties decline the application of the collective agreement. Thus, a decision on wages made in the national joint committee for all the white-collar workers and their employers in the metalworking industry is binding for all the white-collar workers and their employers throughout the whole nation in that sector which falls within the scope of the joint committee, unless an employer agrees with an individual employee not to follow the collective agreement but to provide different individual terms.

The obligatory stipulations, such as rights and obligations between contracting parties, peace clauses, and the like, paradoxically produce only moral obligations since the contracting parties do not have the legal capacity to conclude binding agreements whose performance can be enforced through judicial proceedings.

Collective normative rules also give rise to moral obligations only, as they are not regulated by the Acts of March 4 and 11, 1954.

The normative part of the agreement, collective as well as individual rules, can have a more binding effect through the intervention of the government by Royal Decree. But only agreements concluded within the framework of the joint committees may be so extended. Once the Royal Decree is published, every clause in the working rules or in the individual labor contract that is contrary to a stipulation of a collective agreement rendered binding is deemed to be null and void.

Such an agreement is binding upon all the employers and workers operating within the industrial, territorial, and personal scope of the joint committee, effective on the date of publication in the "Moniteur," or on a later date if one is indicated in the Royal Decree. It is more or less accepted practice that a collective agreement extended by Royal Decree is effective retroactively to the date on which the bargaining commenced which resulted in the agreement.

It should also be stressed that the individual contract and working rules may provide stipulations which provide for better or higher wages and conditions for the workers. This examination of the binding effect of the collective agreements in Belgium enables us to establish a list of the legal sources in a hierarchical order which regulates the individual labor relation:

1. The imperative statutes and treaties.
2. The collective agreement rendered binding by Royal Decree.
3. The work rules.
4. The individual labor contract.
5. The collective agreement.
6. The suppletive statutes.
7. The customs.

These legal considerations concerning the binding effect of the collective agreements lead to some unusual results. An employer can be bound by an agreement although he did not take part in the negotiations. This may happen even if he is not a member of the employer association that concluded the agreement. And since the agreements provide only for minima, there is always room for improvement and consequently for more bargaining.

National Interindustry Bargaining

Before World War II, there began the practice of concluding nationwide interindustry agreements. This practice was continued and even expanded after the war. More than 30 such agreements were concluded. These agreements were of course not all of equal importance, but some have really influenced the overall picture of labor relations in the postwar period up to now.[30] An example is the aforementioned pact of social solidarity by which the employers and labor representatives expressed their willingnesss to cooperate loyally and constructively. The pact contained a number of principles and stipulated the renewal of the joint committees, the idea of the union delegation and similar matters.

Another important interindustry agreement, which has been in force since 1947, concerns the institution and working of the union delegation. Since 1958, interindustry agreements have also dealt with supplementary holidays, productivity, and the working council.

An unusual interindustry agreement is the "Pact of Social Programmation," which was concluded on May 11, 1960. Trade unions and employer associations laid down three fundamental principles:

1. A concerted policy of economic expansion must enable workers to share in a regularly improving standard of living;

2. This participation of the workers in the improvement of their standard of living must be realized through collective agreements, concluded at national interindustry level, by which the share of workers in the growth of the national wealth is programmed for a fixed period. National agreements by industry sector and agreements at the plant level must program supplementary advantages. The programmation will, however, take into account governmental social security benefits, financed through employer contributions.

3. This programmation is possible only if industrial peace is observed during the life of the collective agreements.

Social programmation dealt specifically with family allowances and annual vacation. Further agreements, concluded in the same spirit in 1963 and 1966, stipulated the third week of annual vacation at double pay. Negotiation at the national industry-wide level since 1960 has been incorporated into social programmation.

---

[30] Lagasse, note 25, *supra.*

Industry-wide Bargaining

Most industrial sectors are covered by national agreements. These national agreements assume varying documentary forms. In some sectors, such as the chemical industry, they will almost be meaningless, since the major collective bargaining is done in that sector at the plant or establishment level. In the construction, petroleum, textile, and metal industries, the national agreements are more elaborate. Nevertheless, national agreements generally leave room for matters to be determined at the level of the enterprise. They are "minimum agreements" which can be improved. Statistics show differences in wages, according to regions, plant size, or other factors.

In some national agreements, the textile and metal industries, for example, the national trade unions have agreed that no general claims should be made at the level of the enterprise. This means that the national agreement is in principle final. But many companies that were paying better wages or want to attract labor may permissibly pay above the national scale.

In the metal industry important changes in collective bargaining for blue-collar workers have occurred since the programmation idea started in 1960.[31] Before 1960, the metal industry was characterized by traditional union activity in an atmosphere of struggle and strong employer opposition to unions. Union claims were supported primarily by means of strikes or threats to strike. Union activity was for the most part concentrated at the plant level. Where the workers were sufficiently organized, advantages were extorted "with the fist." The chief aim of programmation was to generalize through national agreements the benefits that had been obtained only in some enterprises. The activity of the different joint committees was of course very limited. Nevertheless, national agreements were reached on certain matters, namely, the union delegation, cost-of-living clause, absence with pay for civic or family obligations, and a 45-hour work week. No national agreement was reached on wages.

In 1960 the programmation on the national level started in the steel industry as well as in the metalworking industry. Following social programmation, agreements were achieved in the metalworking industry for varying periods from August 1960 to December 1963. In 1964 no national agreement was concluded, bargaining occurring mainly at the establishment level. But two-year national

---

[31] Houthuys, *Application and Recent Evolution of Collective Bargaining in the Metal Industry*, Louvain Seminar 1967-1968.

agreements were made for the calendar years of 1965 and 1966 and for the calendar years of 1967 and 1968.

The national agreements in steel and metal industry cover wages and benefits and working time, among other things. Except for the year 1964, essential bargaining since 1960 has been concluded at the national level. The national agreements contain an explicit statement that no claim of a general or collective nature may be made by the trade union at the level of the enterprise. This clause, however, does not exclude individual wage adjustments for age, job hazard, or personal merits, changes in a wage structure resulting from a change in the organization of work, or restudy of unusual and significant wage cases.

In return for the social programmation, employers get "social peace" during the life of the agreements. This means that trade unions accept as their responsibility the enormous task of safeguarding social peace during the fixed agreement period. According to the peace obligation, trade unions are required to prevent wildcat or unofficial strikes and to get the workers back to work should one occur. If workers continue to strike, trade unions may not award allowances to strikers. In return for safeguarding social peace, trade unions receive from the employers, through the employer association, which collects the money, a financial "subvention" of 0.5 percent of gross wages. If the trade unions support striking employees, the subvention is diminished by $2.50 daily for each striking employee. The reduction becomes $5.00 daily per striker if the strike continues for more than 20 days.[32]

Social programmation is a recent phenomenon in labor-management relations. It is difficult to forecast whether it will continue to develop smoothly in the future. Much will depend on the approach and attitudes of the involved parties and on practical experience.

Solution of two problems will largely determine whether the system will continue. One problem is raised by management and the other, by labor. The problem that concerns management is union insistence upon cost-of-living clauses. The automatic adaptation of wages to rises in the cost of living was long ago obtained by trade

---

[32] If the strike is caused by an employer's failure to live up to the collective agreement, there would be no reduction of the employer's contributions to the trade unions. If the contracting parties disagree on the question of whether an employer violated the collective agreement, the dispute is settled by "definite and final advice" given by three mediators. One is designated by each of the two parties; the third is the president of the national joint committee. Out of the "peace money," the benefit reserved for trade union members is paid; the remainder is used by the unions for labor education and the like at its discretion.

unions. In the system of social programmation, cost-of-living adjustments are being resisted by the employers. The employers' argument is that since programmation fixes social burdens, its meaning is lost if wages must be adjusted every time there is a rise in the cost of living. Another uncertainty within the system is, of course, the likely rise of social security contributions, upon which government may decide unilaterally.

The problem unions face is union activity at the plant or enterprise level. Social programmation at the national level means the setting of wages and labor conditions on the basis of the potential and possibilities of the "average" enterprise. Consequently, in theory at least, all enterprises should bear the same burdens. From labor's point of view, there is fear that the rules fixed at the national level will become too rigid and especially that wages will not be able to be adjusted upward in accordance with special regional or plant circumstances. Unions feel that national agreements do not take into account the discrepancy between prosperous and less well-to-do enterprises. Consequently, trade unions propose more flexibility in the programmation and the possibility of bargaining on some matters at the enterprise level.[33]

Bargaining at the Level of the Enterprise

Although programmation on the national level may have resulted in a general reduction of the bargaining activity at the plant level, many individual establishment collective agreements are still concluded. National agreements do not cover all terms, and there are minima which can and should be improved. In some industries, of which the chemical industry is a prime example, the real bargaining is done at the enterprise level, and bargaining at the national level is insignificant.

Experienced Belgian employers are wary of reaching an agreement with only one of the trade unions even if that union has organized a large majority of the workers in the establishment. The other union will not accept exclusion and will not rest until it has been recognized as full spokesman. As a rule, it is better for employers to avoid interfering in trade union competition and to accept negotiations only on common proposals. However, employers are more inclined to fall into line with the program urged by the strongest trade union. This applies equally when negotiations are undertaken on the level of the industry.[34]

---

[33] Van Uytven, *Psychology of Collective Bargaining*, Louvain Seminar 1967-1968.

[34] *Ibid.*

Since collective agreements establish only minimum standards, an employer might be compelled to afford better conditions to attract workers. He may respond similarly if the plant traditionally has been a high-wage establishment or the undertaking is situated in a highly industrialized, high-wage region. In such cases there is considerable individual bargaining, or "workplace" bargaining, with small groups within the enterprise.

This description of collective bargaining in Belgium may lead to the conclusion that there is no bargaining system at all. However, one should not conclude that there are no rules. Through programmation, employers and trade unions have sought to fix the social burdens for definite periods. Nevertheless, industry-wide collective bargaining in practice always leaves room for bargaining at the plant or enterprise level, according to union strength and the economic potential and requirements of the enterprise. A cautionary note is required. I have described the system of collective bargaining in effect early in 1969. On December 5, 1968, legislation was enacted, and a Royal Decree is in the offing under which there will be changes in collective bargaining law as early as 1970. Among the reforms will be the right to conclude legally enforceable agreements only by the most representative unions, thus barring the right of independent unions to conclude enforceable labor agreements; limited juridical identity of unions as organs capable of suing or being sued under some circumstances; revision of legal doctrine concerning the binding effect of normative provisions of labor agreements; and other significant reforms.

ECONOMIC CONFLICTS — THE FREEDOM TO STRIKE

Since the Act of 1921,[35] an almost complete freedom to strike has existed in Belgium. Employer lockouts are similarly free, but in practice they do not occur. Strikes are by no means a rarity. A strike might amount to an offense only if it infringed upon the freedom of association or if ordinary offenses, such as violence, were committed during its course.

The Act of August 19, 1948, dealing with essential supplies and services in peacetime, stipulates a procedure by which public interest and equipment are protected in case of a strike. It is, however, up to the joint committees to decide what supplies and services have to be maintained. Their decisions are put into operation by a

---

[35] Abolishing the provisions of the Penal Code outlawing strikes. Cf. Lagasse, "The Law of Strikes and Lock-outs in Belgium," in *Labour Relations and the Law; A Comparative Study*, Kahn-Freund, ed., 1965.

subcommittee designated by the joint committee. Workers can be requisitioned; selection is by agreement between the employer and the union. If no decision or proper action is taken by the joint committee, the government can intervene and requisition workers. Experience has shown that the joint solutions have not been satisfactory. Most *a priori* decisions of joint committees are incomplete and become quickly out of date. The government is sometimes reluctant to intervene and leaves it up to the parties to settle their differences.

It cannot be stressed enough that the freedom to strike is absolute, even if no notice is given or if the strike is in breach of a collective agreement, and that the trade union involved cannot be sued since it lacks legal personality. Trade unions are convinced, however, that immoderate use of strikes may lead to their ineffectiveness. Consequently, they look upon strikes only as an ultimate solution to settle labor disputes. They will use their absolute freedom to strike only when necessary, and they act to control wildcat strikes. It should be noted that both the C.S.C. and the F.G.T.B. have substantial strike funds at their disposal.

In practice, well-established trade unions are often the only stabilizing force in labor relations between employer and trade unions. In a system allowing absolute freedom to strike, even to engage in wildcat strikes, many employers prefer strong unions that can control the action and emotions of the workers to having no unions and the possibility of uncontrollable and undisciplined wildcat or unofficial strikes.

Statistics show that the freedom to strike has been used moderately. Time lost due to work stoppages as a percentage of total time worked over the period 1945-1964 was 0.48 percent. The meaning of this figure is that, on the average, for every 10,000 workers working at their jobs, there were only 48 workers idle due to a work stoppage. This figure is low. It has been correctly observed that far less productive work time is lost because of strikes than by reason of the well-known coffee break or unemployment. Statistics also show that strikes have a rather short duration, generally from one to five days, and that the majority of strikes are engaged in to improve wages and employment benefits. In the E.E.C. countries the number of lost work days because of strikes is on the decrease, Italy being an exception.[36]

---

[36] I.L.O. *Year Book of Labor Statistics, E.E.C. Commission Report on the Evolution of the Social Situation in the Community.* Strikes are practically unknown in the Grand Duchy of Luxembourg. There were only five strikes during the period 1953-1959.

Workdays Lost
(Annual average)

	Period	
	1951-1954	1961-1964
Germany	1,277,627	593,648
Belgium	578,037	263,612
France	4,097,577	3,247,580
Italy	4,814,822	14,250,508
Netherlands	46,904	28,624

Although doctrine and jurisprudence are fundamentally divided on this matter, the latest tendency in the labor court decisions is toward the view that, in the present socio-economic circumstances, strikes only suspend the performance of the individual labor contract and that the failure to carry out the individual labor contract is not sufficiently serious in itself to justify a break or dismissal without notice or indemnity. In fact, whatever the theory may be, it is accepted custom that all strikers resume their jobs after the strike.

No one disputes that a striker has no right to remuneration for the period when he is on strike. Ordinary employees who do not report for work have no such right. If employees report for work at a struck plant, the employer must provide them with work and pay them, unless he can prove that the strike, as a *force majeure*, an unforeseeable, insurmountable event, prevented his giving them work. In practice, however, trade unions will seek to preclude this possibility and try to keep all workers, even nonunion workers, by paying strike benefits to the nonunionists as well as to union members. Statistics show that 50 percent of the strikes are successful for the employees involved. This indicates a relative equality of economic power.

SETTLEMENT OF INDUSTRIAL DISPUTES

The academic classification of labor disputes into individual and collective disputes or into disputes of "rights" and disputes of "interests" are not relevant in Belgian labor relations. Indeed, while individual conflicts can be decided by the labor courts so also may some collective disputes, such as disagreement over election procedures for choice of working-council delegates. All individual disputes are subject to negotiations, even under pressure of strike, and so are all collective conflicts. The differences between conflicts of rights, such as disputes over interpretation and application of collective agreements and conflicts of interests involving the conclusion of new agreements, further lose practical importance in Belgium because trade unions have no legal personality and as a result cannot conclude legally binding or judicially enforceable agreements.

According to the Act of 1926, Belgian labor courts have jurisdiction over individual disputes between employer and employee concerning the application of the individual labor contract or employer compliance with protective labor legislation. Labor court litigation involving individual claims of workers resembles many of the cases reported by the The Bureau of National Affairs, Inc., in its *Labor Arbitration Reports* for the United States. Typical issues are the correctness of wage payments, the propriety of docking a worker for late reporting where he insists that his tardiness was caused by some unusual traffic conditions, and the adequacy of the cause asserted by the employer for dismissal without minimum statutory notice (or contractual notice if it is more generous to the worker than the statute). The labor courts have no power to order reinstatement of a dismissed employee.

In practice the labor court is not the instrument to settle individual disputes which come up during active employment. This is for two reasons: first, the procedure takes too long, and second, a suit against the employer before the labor court is looked upon as an act of war. Consequently, the great majority of cases which are presented to the court usually concern grievances which arise after the individual employment contract has been terminated. In an exceptional case an active employee might be the nominal plaintiff to test whether a collective agreement made in a joint committee applies to a particular plant or establishment. Despite the availability and jurisdiction of labor courts, it may be generalized that, for all practical purposes, no adequate machinery is available to settle individual disputes when there is no active union delegation in the establishment.[37] It may also be generalized that despite the availability of the labor courts and their authority in exceptional cases to determine some collective conflicts, most collective conflicts are in fact resolved through negotiation and conciliation, as are indeed many disputes involving claims of individual employees.

Belgian labor courts can be traced as far back as August 16, 1790, under the French regime. The principal legislation of July 9, 1926, has been amended repeatedly. The most recent statutory

---

[37] In many of the small enterprises employing fewer than 50 persons (34 percent of the labor force), there are no union delegations. See Table III in the body of this paper and accompanying text.

changes concerning labor courts were enacted on October 10, 1967, and will become effective not later than October 10, 1970. The new law will not affect the basic principles of labor court functions and jurisdiction which are detailed in this article.

Regional labor courts are established throughout Belgium. Each court is divided into two sections,[38] one for adjudicating claims of blue-collar workers and the other for determining claims of white-collar workers. The judges are laymen. Half the judges represent employees and half represent employers. Each section of the court is assisted by a lawyer possessed of a university degree. In case of an equal division of votes the legal "assessor" has the deciding vote. Labor courts of appeal are similarly composed, but the president of the appeals court is always a lawyer.

Arbitration of industrial disputes, whether of basic agreements or grievances, is unknown in Belgium. The trade unions, the C.S.C. and the F.G.T.B., reject both compulsory and voluntary arbitration because in their view the freedom to strike would thereby become meaningless.

Industrial disputes are thus prevented or settled through conciliation. The conciliation is either the result of negotiation between the parties or mediation through government officers. Both systems of conciliation, which in practice intersect, are characterized by pragmatism and successful achievement in protecting social peace.

The formal systems in labor agreements in most sectors of industry entail common features. On the level of the enterprise, the union delegation has authority to take up both individual grievances and collective disputes. If talks between the union delegation and the employer are not successful, the business agent of the trade unions will be called in, while the employer might be assisted by a representative of the employer association. In most agreements it is stipulated that there will be no strike or lockout until all conciliation procedures have been exhausted. These conciliation procedures are either official or conventional at the level of the industry. Some of the conventional conciliation procedures are part of programmation agreements, according to which trade unions guarantee social peace. In many industries conciliation machinery is set up within the joint committees, where appointed subcommittees, composed of equal numbers of representatives of the employer association and the trade unions, seek to reconcile the parties.

---

[38] Each labor court has a special section to decide questions as to whether the claimant is a white-collar or blue-collar worker so that assignment may be made to the appropriate permanent section of the court. The special section also resolves conflicts concerning working councils and health and safety committees.

Government officials are social inspectors, and recently six official full-time mediators were appointed. These official mediators, who act under the direct responsibility of the Minister of Employment and Labor, are at the same time presidents of the most important joint committees. If the conflict is not settled within the joint committee, they act as mediators and try to bring the parties to an agreement. If a potential or actual labor dispute might have far-reaching national consequences, the Minister of Employment and Labor or even the Prime Minister himself may try to reconcile the parties.

OUTLINES OF COLLECTIVE
LABOR LAW IN THE
FEDERAL REPUBLIC OF GERMANY

By Franz Gamillscheg

SOURCES OF LABOR LAW

The entirety of collective labor law in West Germany is extensive and detailed. In the brief space available in this volume, at best only an overview is possible.[1]

My country's legal system is bottomed on civil law. But contrary to the expectations of many students who are not familiar with a civil law system, the existing statutory law is full of gaps. While there is a law on collective agreements[2] and another on works councils,[3] there are no statutes on trade unions or on strikes and lockouts. On the other hand, collective labor relations, as in Britain, for example, are not left primarily to social controls, but are specifically regulated by law. In Germany collective agreements are legally enforceable contracts, like any other contracts. They confer rights on individual workers which may give rise to enforceable claims of contract breach.

Where there is no written applicable statutory law, operative

---

[1] The most thorough expansion of German labor law is *Lehrbuch des Arbeitsrechts,* by Hueck and Nipperdey (7th ed., 1967) (hereinafter cited as Hueck-Nipperdey). Another valuable treatise is also entitled *Lehrbuch des Arbeitsrechts,* by Nikisch (3rd ed., 1966) (hereinafter cited as Nikisch). Unfortunately neither work is available in English. However, in 1963, the Federal Ministry of Labor and Social Structure published in English a series of monographs in 50 booklets under the collective title *Social Policy in Germany.*

[2] The Collective Agreements Law (Tarifvertragsgesetz) of April 9, 1949, as amended by the law of November 1, 1952. Additionally on December 23, 1955, the Federal Republic of Germany ratified ILO Convention No. 98 on the Application of the Principles of the Right to Organize and to Bargain Collectively, promulgated on July 1, 1949, and ILO Recommendation No. 91 concerning collective agreements, dated June 29, 1951.

[3] The Works Council Law (Betriebsverfassungsgesetz) of October 11, 1952. Codetermination in production companies of the coal and steel industry is governed by the Law on Co-determination of Employees in the Boards of Supervision and Managing Boards of Enterprises of the Mining and Iron and Steelmaking Industries (Gesetz über die Mitbestimmung der Arbeitnehmer in den Aufsichtsräten und Vorständen der Unternehmen des Bergbaus und der Eisen und Stahl erzeugenden Industrie) of May 21, 1951. In practice we shorten this to an informal reference to the Law on Co-determination. The rights and duties in collective bargaining of federal civil servants (öffentlicher Dienst) are set forth in a statute of the Federal Republic and the different Länder (states) Personalvertretungsgesetze.

rules are laid down by the courts — most authoritatively by the
Federal Labor Court, the Bundesarbeitsgericht, often referred to by
American and British writers as the Supreme Labor Court. On infrequent occasions the Federal Constitutional Court (Bundesverfas-
sungsgericht) may also decide important labor cases.[4] Thus we have
in Germany a jurisprudence based on case law resembling that of
the common law countries. This system has much to commend it in
that it has the advantage of flexibility to accommodate to social
changes or changes in public opinion. Indeed, we now live in a period of such great change that new questions arise concerning matters once presumed to have been permanently settled in a prior case.

On the other hand, German jurists are not accustomed to the
case law system, and much uncertainty is produced. That a case law
system exists at all in Germany is denied by many legal writers.
Certainly there has not yet been articulated in Germany anything
akin to the doctrine of *stare decisis* enunciated and applied by the
courts of Britain and the United States. Thus, there are as yet no
guarantees of reasonable and necessary continuity and stability of
the rules of law promulgated and refined by the courts of West Germany.

But to the credit of German courts, I must observe that basic
reversals or overturnings in German jurisprudence are rare and that
none of any importance has yet occurred in collective labor law.

The legal starting point of this case law is Article 9 of the Constitution of the Federal Republic of Germany, enacted March 23,
1949.[5] This article guarantees the freedom of the individual worker
to join the trade union of his choice.[6] This is strict law, directly
binding upon the executive, legislative, and judicial branches. It is
unlawful for the employer to discriminate against anyone because he
is a member of an organization. There is no recorded case where an
employer has openly refused to hire people because they were union
members; if such a thing were to happen it would no doubt gener-

---

[4] Thus, the Federal Constitutional Court decided that a union cannot be
barred from distributing propaganda materials before staff council (Personalrat)
elections, Entscheidungen des Bundesverfassungsgerichts Band 19, p. 303 *et seq.;*
and that a union's declination of the strike as a weapon in bargaining does not justify
denial of the union's rights of a coalition, *id.,* Band 18, p. 18 *et seq.* The question
of reserving employment benefits for union members only (see text accompanying
note 17, *infra*) is now pending before the Federal Constitutional Court.

[5] Grundgesetz für die Bundesrepublik Deutschland of May 23, 1949. Article 1,
Section 3, thereof declares: "The right to form associations to safeguard and improve working conditions and economic conditions shall be guaranteed to everyone
and to all trades and professions. Agreements which restrict or seek to hinder this
right shall be null and void; measures directed toward this end are illegal."

[6] For further details see Hueck-Nipperdey, §§8-10; Nikisch, §§58, 59.

ate a storm of public indignation. A dismissal of an employee for joining a union is null and void; the employee can gain reinstatement in the plant.[7]

Nonunion enterprises are unknown in Germany. Not only is such the law, but it represents public opinion as well as the convictions of most employers. Within the last 50 years we have lived through two military defeats, one revolution, and four political systems, and the system that followed every major change was in open contradiction to that which preceded it: in 1918, in 1933, and in 1945. In the dark months of 1918 and 1919, and the equally somber years of 1945 through 1949, trade unions and employer associations had to collaborate to keep things going and to prevent the country from perishing in anarchy. So despite the natural antagonism and conflict of interests, in the light of these historical experiences trade unions and management both recognize the rightful existence and necessity of the other side.

This basic understanding is reflected in the interpretation that Article 9 of the Constitution has received in jurisprudence. Though Article 9 speaks expressly only about the right of the individual workers in all trades and professions to form and join associations to safeguard and improve working and economic conditions, the protection is extended to the existence, the well-being, and the activity of the union itself. Thus, any interference by the state with union activities, as long as these activities are in conformity with the general law, would be illegal. For example, if Italian workers employed in Southern Germany should choose to form a union of their own, no local authority, such as the Foreigners Board, would have the right to forbid it.

The protection accorded by the Constitution also affects the relations between employer and union. It has recently been decided that the union has a clear right to distribute its propaganda materials on the plant premises.[8] In that case the employer had prevented the distribution, declaring that the plant was his property and that nobody had the right to do anything in his plant he did not agree with. The Federal Labor Court decided that he had to tolerate such union activities basing its decision on the constitutionally protected right under Article 9 of unions to existence and activity.[9]

---

[7] Hueck, *Kündigungsschutzgesetz* (Law on the protection against dismissals) (6th ed., 1968), No. 22 to §12 (no case reported).

[8] Decision of Federal Labor Court (Bundesarbeitsgericht), February 14, 1967, Arbeitsrechtliche Praxis (Report of the Court Decisions in Labor Law), No. 10 to Article 9 GG.

[9] In the seminar session of the Loyola conference immediately following the presentation of this paper, Mr. Arnold Ordman, General Counsel of the National

The deduction of union dues from salaries and remission to the union is becoming widely practiced.[10] In several cases this has increased union income by 40 percent. But the checkoff device has not significantly altered the serious income difficulties of many labor unions, which I discuss later in this paper. Such help is the object of many an existing collective agreement, but has never yet been imposed by strike action. The members must agree before such deductions are regularized. Under these constitutional protections, trade unions and employer associations could develop and together become one of the strongest pillars in the so-called pluralistic society.

Structure of Labor Movement

Though there is complete freedom to form individual unions, there exists a practical unity in the labor movement.[11] During the Weimar period — 1918 to 1933 — the labor movement was divided into socialist, Christian, liberal, national, and anarchist branches. Then came Hitler, who dissolved them all and put their leaders into concentration camps or forced them into emigration. In 1945, in the light of this experience, the newly resurrected socialist and Christian unions merged into the principal union existing now, the Deutsche Gewerkschaftsbund (DGB), referred to by British and American writers as the German Trade Union Federation.[12] The Deutsche Gewerkschaftsbund was expected to remain politically neutral; but, in fact, it has inclinations toward the Social Democratic party. The DGB is the top-level labor organization. It consists of 16 member unions with about 6-1/2 million members. The 16 unions are organized along industrial rather than professional lines; every branch of industry has its own union. Thus, the most important of the 16 unions in DGB, the Industrial Union of Metal Workers with a total of nearly two million members, organizes all employees in the

---

Labor Relations Board, advised me that the problem of distribution of union literature on an employer's premises has been the subject of much American litigation. After the conference Mr. Ordman was kind enough to mail me the Labor Board decisions in *Stoddard-Quirk Mfg. Co.*, 138 NLRB 615, 51 LRRM 1110 (1962), *Solo Cup Co.*, 172 NLRB No. 110 68 LRRM 1385 (1968), and the text of the U.S. Supreme Court decision in *Food Employees, Local 590 v. Logan Valley Plaza, Inc.*, 391 U.S. 308, 68 LRRM 2209 (1968). It was impressive to see that those cases invoke American federal constitutional guarantees of freedom of speech and assembly or association, much as does the Federal Labor Court decision reported in note 7 above.

[10] Hueck-Nipperdey, p. 96. The late Professor Nipperdey, eminent scholar and first president of the Federal Labor Court, was of the opinion that the checkoff was unlawful.

[11] For a thorough history of trade unions and employers' associations see Hueck-Nipperdey, §7; Nikisch, §58I.

[12] Hueck-Nipperdey, §11; Nikisch, §61.

metal industry, regardless of their particular professions, laborers as well as white-collar workers. For example, a mason, a printer, or a clerk employed by Volkswagen belongs to the metalists and not to the building or the printing unions. This system enables us to function effectively with the very small number of 16 DGB unions.[13] The employers in a given industry need deal with their particular union only and not with a multitude of craft, occupational, or professional unions whose members are employed in their plants.

The Deutsche Gewerkschaftsbund unions are not the only unions, however. For white-collar employees there is the rather important Deutsche Angestelltengewerkschaft (DAG). Staff personnel has its VELA (Verein Leitender Angestellten). And then there still are the Christian unions that were revived in the 1950s but have not yet risen to a position of any practical importance, except perhaps in the Saarland. Mention should also be made of the Civil Service Associations, although extended discussion thereof is irrelevant to the purpose of this paper.

Unions that recruit their members only from the employees of a single enterprise or establishment do not exist. Germany has no counterpart of the independent industrial union that still seems to be a significant aspect of American unionism.[14] They would not be rec-

---

[13] Besides the large Industrial Union of Metal Workers, the 15 other unions in DGB, which include workers, salaried staffs, and some establishment officials, are:

(1) The Industrial Union of Workers in Quarrying, Building and Public Works Contracting.

(2) Industrial Union of Mining and Energy.

(3) Industrial Union of Chemical, Paper and Pottery Workers.

(4) Industrial Union of Printing and Paper Processing Workers.

(5) The Union of the Railwaymen of Germany.

(6) The Union of Educational and Scientific Workers (Association of German Teachers). In its membership figures for 1962 this union claimed as members no "workers," about 2,500 salaried staff employees, and 86,000 establishment officials.

(7) The Union of Horticultural, Agricultural and Forestry Workers.

(8) The Union of Salaried Employees in Trade, Commerce, Banks and Insurance.

(9) The Woodworkers Union.

(10) The Artists Union, which has such subdivisions as stage, variety, film, radio, musicians, commercial artists, and the like. I was informed at the Loyola conference that the organization of performing artists and other artistic talent in the United States consists of similar autonomous subdivisions of one principal union affiliated with the AFL-CIO.

(11) Leather Workers Union.

(12) Union of Food, Drink, Tobacco and Catering Trade Workers.

(13) The Union of Workers in Public Services, Transport and Communications.

(14) The German Postal Workers Union.

(15) Textile and Clothing Workers Union. My American readers will note that there is no separate union divisions for workers in ladies clothing and those making men's clothing.

[14] In *America's Forgotten Labor Organization* (1962), Dr. Arthur B. Shostak

ognized as "unions" in the sense of Article 9. Though no statute or judicial decision covers the subject, there is general agreement that such unions would probably lack the necessary independence from the employer, and so be unable to further the interests of their members.[15]

The internal operations of the union are legally unrestricted. There is no law imposing any rules relating to democratic structure, union elections, meetings, procedures, finances, and the like. No need for such a law has yet been felt.

Unions and employers must respect the freedom of the individual worker. While he is genuinely free to join a union, he must be no less free to remain aloof, and coercion to make him enter one is not allowed. As a matter of fact, only about 30 percent of the eligible manpower is organized. This percentage varies from industry to industry. It is relatively high in the chemical and metal fields and in the mines and particularly low where the labor force consists mainly of women or white-collar employees or in agriculture.

The nonmember is well protected by German law. There is no closed shop or union shop in Germany. A collective agreement that contained such a clause would be illegal and void; no such agreement has been concluded since 1945. Of course, if an employer, in tacit consent with his union, chooses to engage only organized manpower, practically nothing can be done about it. But a dismissal motivated by the employee's leaving his union would be void. We call that the "negative liberty of coalition."[16] Recently the Federal Labor Court has decided that it is illegal in a collective agreement to provide that certain minor financial benefits may be reserved only to union members.[17] I doubt the correctness of the decision, which seems to be an exaggeration of the principle of equal treatment. My views are also borne out by the Belgian experience.[18]

COLLECTIVE BARGAINING AND COLLECTIVE AGREEMENTS

The main task of trade unions and employer associations is the conclusion of collective agreements. About 6,000 collective agree-

---

found that there were as many as 1400 single-firm independent unions in American industry with a total membership of 400,000 persons. He also found that such unions thrive in Canada, Israel, Indonesia, Japan, and elsewhere.

[15] Hueck-Nipperdey, p. 99; Nikisch, p. 9.

[16] Hueck-Nipperdey, §10; Nikisch, §59II.

[17] Arbeitsrechtliche Praxis, No. 13 to Art. 9 GG. On the same question, see Gamillscheg, *Die Differenzierung nach der Gewerkschaftszugehörigkeit* (1966); Zöllner, *Tarifvertragliche Differenzierungsklauseln* (1967).

[18] *Cf.* Blanpain, *supra* p. 209.

ments are registered every year with the Federal Ministry of Labor at Bonn. Generally, employers are willing to negotiate with their partners of the other side. The American problem of "bargaining in good faith" is virtually unknown in Germany. The Federal Labor Court once decided that a minority union could not assert a right to be included in and invited to negotiations that were going on between the employers and a DGB union.[19] But the union that sought participation was a very small one, and the case has little significance. The unions with which an American investor will have to deal — the Deutsche Gewerkschaftsbund unions and the Deutsche Angestellten Gewerkschaft — are powerful enough to compel anyone to open up negotiation whenever such unions choose.

The statutory authority to conclude a collective agreement is conferred by the Collective Agreements Law of 1949 upon unions, employer associations, and individual employers. In addition, federations of trade unions and federations of employer associations have such authority and capacity.

Collective agreements are binding contracts, and not mere gentlemen's agreements. They create legal obligations concerning the mutual relations between unions and employer associations.[20] Most unions are not registered and have therefore no legal personality, but this is pure theory. For all practical purposes they are treated as if they were legal entities; they can sue and be sued.[21]

The most important obligation imposed on a union and employers in every collective agreement is the so-called duty of peace: so long as the agreement is in force, no labor dispute may be commenced by either party over a question that has been settled in the agreement. In 1958, the metal workers' union was ordered to pay damages for breach of the duty of peace:[22] damages that have been estimated at about 100 million Deutsche Marks. This was an enormous sum, but the employers were wise enough to decline it in exchange for the conclusion of an arbitration agreement.[23]

---

[19] Arbeitsrechtliche Praxis, No. 5 to Art. 9 GG.

[20] Hueck-Nipperdey, §§12-18; Nikisch, §69.

[21] Aside from litigation in labor matters, this was not certain until quite recently; now the Federal Court of Justice has decided that the lack of legal personality did not prevent unions from suing: Neue Juristische Wochenschrift 1968, p. 183s. After the Loyola conference was concluded, I received from Professor Kamin a reprint of his article, "The Union as Litigant: Personality, Preemption and Propaganda," 1966 Supreme Court Review 253. It seems universal in industrialized countries that unions generally seek the immunities that attach to absence of legal personality, and that lawmakers, whether legislators or judges, usually find some legal basis for imposing a juridical personality upon such labor organizations.

[22] Federal Labor Court, 31 October 1958; Arbeitsrechtliche Praxis, No. 2 to §1 TVG Friedenspflicht.

[23] Recht der Arbeit 1964, p. 216.

Rules in a collective agreement dealing with labor conditions — wages, hours of employment, and so on — though set up by private parties, are as effective as law. They establish binding minimum standards of direct and compulsory application to the labor contracts of those who fall within the personal and territorial scope of the agreement. A convention between employer and employee that deviates from these standards to the detriment of the employee is void and automatically superseded by the standard contained in the collective agreement. If, for instance, the wage is fixed in the collective agreement at 3.50 Deutsche Marks and 3.30 has been agreed upon in the individual labor contract, the contract of employment is valid, but the 3.30 clause is superseded by the 3.50 provision. The employee can sue his employer for the difference; even the employee's capacity to renounce is limited.[24]

Another difference from the American model is evident when we consider the scope and personal and geographical limits of the collective agreement.[25] While in the United States unions may lawfully compete at every plant in a general preference contest for the exclusive power of representation of all employees in the "appropriate unit" in negotiating and administering labor agreements, in Germany the union's power is limited and fixed by law to that of representing only its members. No representation elections take place in the plants. If there are competing unions, the employer has to make agreements with those unions that are strong enough to force him to do so. For instance, where a body of white-collar employees might be divided in their allegiances between the Deutsche Gewerkschaftsbund union (DGB) and the Deutsche Angestellten-Gewerkschaft (DAG), most collective agreements bear the signature of both unions, which generally act in common. In the case of the operative workers, the problem of competing unions does not arise, because the Christian unions, as I have noted, are practically nonexistent.

I have observed earlier in this paper that only about 30 percent of eligible German manpower is organized. The 1949 law on collective agreements provides that only members of the union that has concluded the agreement can claim its benefits, so the employer is legally free to agree with nonmembers on conditions that are below the collective standard. That is the law, but not the practice. In practice, employers avoid making any distinction between member and nonmember. It would burden them with a great deal of administrative work, poison the climate between the workers, and, last but

---

[24] Hueck-Nipperdey, §§26-32; Nikisch, §§73, 74.
[25] Hueck-Nipperdey, §§23, 33; Nikisch, §§71, 86.

not least, make the nonmember enter the union, which employers consider to be contrary to their own interests. So in reality the collective agreement fixes the conditions for all. When a man is hired, he is not asked whether he is a member of a union, but in most cases the parties acknowledge that he is hired under the terms contained in the pertinent collective agreement. If he is a union member, that contract guarantees what is already due by law; if he is not, the clauses in the individual employment contract refer to the content of the collective agreement. This being so, no special need is felt for extension of collective agreements[26] to the nonmembers by act of state. Only about 2 to 3 percent of all collective agreements are thus extended; the practice is seen especially in the building industry and in the retail trades.

Let me make my last observation on the personal scope of the collective agreement. During the recent years of prosperity and full employment the nonmember has become the central problem of, if not a mortal danger to, trade unions.[27] Inasmuch as he gets everything the member gets, the nonmember asks himself why he should feel obliged to pay dues and take part in all sorts of union activities. Of course, only the member and not the nonmember is supported by the union in the event of a strike. But strikes have been rare, so this factor has had little or no impact on the general apathy of nonmembers. Some of the 16 unions of the Deutsche Gewerkschaftsbund are actually in financial difficulties. As a consequence of the recession in 1967 the membership of the Deutsche Gewerkschaftsbund fell for the first time since 1949; but more recently the membership has again been rising.

The geographical scope of collective agreements depends on the parties. Many of the 6,000 or so collective agreements concluded every year cover the entire Federal Republic. A recent example is the collective agreement on protection against the consequences of automation in the metal industry, whether it affects a region or district, a community, or a single plant. The parties may make agreements to cover specific localities or certain Länder (states), as well as the Federal Republic as a whole. Apart from what the parties decide, geographical coverage depends on several factors. The first is the competence or jurisdiction of the union and the employer association: the union of railwaymen cannot, of course, make agreements relating to the terms of employment in the textile industry. The second is geographical limits: a local administration of the IG Metall

---

Hueck-Nipperdey, §§34-36; Nikisch, §§87, 88.

This was the background of the unions' claim for certain benefits for their s only, discussed in text accompanying note 16, *supra*.

(Industriegewerkschaft Metall) cannot make collective labor law for the whole republic, but the central bodies can very well conclude agreements for a limited area or a single plant. And the third is the extent to which the parties exercise their freedom to restrain the field of application: for instance, they may except one or several marginal enterprises that would not be able to bear the burden of the new tariffs.

While social legislation in our country is as comprehensive as that to be found in any industrialized nation in the world,[28] the various social codes are minimum legal guarantees that are often enlarged by private collective agreements. For example, under the Federal Law on Holidays of January 8, 1963, the minimum number of annual paid holidays is 15 days for employees under age 35 and 18 days for those over 35. In practice, collective agreements provide in most cases for 21 days or more for weekly wage earners and 24 days or more for salaried employees.

Much as in the United States, collective agreements in the Federal Republic are for fixed periods. Basic agreements covering general employment conditions and standards are of long duration, three years or more. Agreements for specific standards covering wages and direct economic benefits are of shorter duration.

Economic action by strike or lockout at the end of the shorter period fixing wages or other economic benefits is lawful despite the general peace obligation applicable to the long-range terms and conditions of employment.

While I have previously said that the union in effect represents all employees, members and nonmembers alike, the same cannot be said about the employer association. Here the situation is different. While about 80 percent of the employers are organized in about 785 employer associations, big enterprises sometimes stay aloof. Volkswagen, for instance, is not a member of an association and has its own conventions with the Industriegewerkschaft Metall. Such was the case with the German Ford Motor Corporation in Cologne. But

---

[28] A quick glance at the English translation of just a few titles in the monograph series described in note 1, *supra*, will furnish some idea of the range of social legislation in the Federal Republic: "Employment of Seriously Disabled Persons;" "Employment of Women;" "Promotion of All-the-Year-Round Employment in the Building Industry;" "Vocational Guidance and Placing in Apprenticeship and Trainee Occupations;" "Unemployment Benefit and Assistance"; "Notice of Dismissal and Protection Against Dismissal"; "Annual Holidays" (called Paid Vacations in America); "Workers' Inventions and their Recompense"; "Safety and Health Protection at Work"; "Noise Abatement and Measures to Combat Pollution of the Atmosphere"; "The Protection of Working Mothers"; "Children's Allowances"; "Superannuation Insurance for the Professions"; and "Pensions for Retired Farmers."

when the union demanded that all extras paid by Ford above associ-
ation-established tariff be included in the collective agreement and
threatened a strike, Ford, in response, hastened to join the association. It thus came under the protection afforded by the union's duty
to keep peace during the currency of the agreement concluded between the union and the employer association.[29] Little wonder that
the union felt somewhat cheated by such tactics.

STRIKES AND LOCKOUTS

Labor disputes are recognized as an appropriate means of furthering economic interests for both sides.[30] In this respect they share
the protection that Article 9 of the Constitution grants to the liberty
of coalition. The sequence of logical arguments runs as follows: The
liberty to join a union must be safeguarded; this liberty is of no
value when the union is too weak to achieve its aims; only the liberty to strike gives it the necessary strength; so the strike must be
equally protected by the Constitution.[31]

And yet strikes have seldom occurred. In 1964 we had 5,629
persons on strike and 16,711 working days lost. The total for the
years 1949-1964 was 1,666,614 strikers and 11,482,299 days lost, a
yearly average of 104,163 strikers and 717,644 lost days. Compare
this with 1927, when there were about 500,000 strikers and 33 million days lost. These figures should be viewed against the background of an economic growth that has permitted industry to make
almost all concessions demanded of it. But it must also be acknow-
leged that, especially during the first decade of reconstruction, unions were reluctant to provoke economic controversy and disruption
and thus refrained from making unrealistic and exaggerated bargaining demands.

Restrictions on Strikes

In the absence of a statute on strikes, case law jurisprudence
has created the legal framework within which strikes must be confined. According to these rules, a strike can be legal or illegal.
When illegal, the union is required to pay damages. I have mentioned already the 100-million-Marks case of the Industriegewerk-

---

[29] The Labor Court at Cologne issued an injunction forbidding a strike as a
violation of the union's duty of peace. *Betriebsberater* 1964, p. 844.

[30] The best information in this field is found in Brox-Rüthers, *Arbeitskampf-
recht* (1965). The second part of volume II of Hueck-Nipperdey, containing the
law of industrial disputes and the Works Councils, is expected to be published in
1969.

[31] Rüthers, *Streik und Verfassung* (1960).

schaft Metall for trespass on the trade ("Eingriff in den Gewerbebe-
trieb").[32] If a strike is proclaimed before expiration of the collective
agreement, a lawful claim for breach of contract may be enforced.

No such remedies are available in consequence of a legal strike.
A strike is legal when the parties, union and employers, are no
longer bound by the duty of peace in a current collective agreement.[33] The strike must be organized by a trade union, and the aim
of the strike must be the improvement of working conditions through
negotiated collective agreements. No other aim is lawfully justified.

Wildcat strikes are illegal and make the participants liable for
damages. In a recent case the Federal Labor Court held 66 participants in such a strike jointly liable to pay damages of about 400,000
Deutsche Marks.[34] A wildcat strike may become legal if, after it begins, it is taken over by a trade union which continues it as its own
for lawful objectives.

A political strike that is directed against the government or the
parliament with the intention of creating pressures on political matters is illegal and regarded as a tort in contravention of public policy. This was clarified by a decision rendered in 1952.[35] At that time
a draft of the Law on Workers' Councils was presented to the Diet.
The draft did not satisfy the Deutsche Gewerkschaftsbund unions.
To demonstrate their indignation, the printers' union struck for two
days, during which no newspapers could appear. The union was
held to be responsible for all damages. That a political strike is no
proper instrument of politics was confirmed in the summer of 1968
by the Deutsche Gewerkschaftsbund itself, when its leaders refused
to strike on behalf of the emergency laws.

The legality of sympathetic strike action has not yet been decided by the Federal Labor Court. Not all demands for changes in
working conditions will lawfully justify strikes. In the law on
Works Councils the enumerated rights of participation granted to
such bodies are limited and cannot be enlarged by strike or by collective agreement. Though this point has not yet been decided by
the courts, it seems to be the rule the courts would adopt.[36]

It has also been held that the strike must be the ultimate reme-

---

[32] See text accompanying notes 21 and 22, *supra.*

[33] See case cited in note 21, *supra.*

[34] Arbeitsrechtliche Praxis, Nos. 32 and 33 to Art. 9 GG. Arbeitskampf.

[35] Federal Court of Justice (Bundesgerichtshof), Arbeitsrechtliche Praxis, No. 2
to §2 AGG; *cf.* Court of Appeals Düsseldorf, *Recht der Arbeit* 1953, p. 393.

[36] In support of my assertion see Hueck-Nipperdey, §15V; Nikisch, Vol. III
(1966), §111V. For contrary views see Court of Labor Appeals, Berlin, *Sammlung
Arbeitsrechtlicher Entscheidungen* 1965, p. 12.

dy, reserved until all peaceful means to reach understanding have been exhausted. Above all, the other side must not be taken by surprise.[37] No strike is allowed for the purpose of enforcing claims that could be enforced by a court. For example, if someone does not receive his full salary, he must go to court and not solicit his union to proclaim a strike. Nor may a strike be organized by the Works Council in the plant.[38] The members of the council are of course free to take part in any strike called by the union.

When all these rules are observed, the participant in a strike is acting legally. He cannot be dismissed for breach of contract, even if the period of notice has not expired.[39] He is not liable for damages. His right to a salary under the labor contract is suspended for the duration of the dispute. However, if an employee is guilty of any penal offense during a strike, such as duress or battery in connection with picketing, he may be dismissed for this misconduct.

The employer is not without economic defenses. If he cannot dismiss the striker for breach of contract, the same result can be achieved by means of a lockout. In this case the employee bears the risk of definitely losing his job under a rule promulgated by the Federal Labor Court in 1955.[40] Prior to that time, the lockout had been used only as a weapon against those who did not strike and were willing to work. Now the employer is also entitled to declare the lockout against the individual striker, and this declaration terminates the labor contract and imposes on the striker the risk of permanently losing his job.[41] This weapon is even more potent than the summary dismissal, for the courts have held that a lockout is something different from a dismissal, so that none of the legal limitations on the power of dismissal, in respect, for instance, to expectant mothers, apply to a lockout. The wisdom of these rules, I openly declare, is doubtful, and a reversal of jurisprudence is not improbable here, but of course I am no prophet.

The state takes a neutral position in labor disputes and is urged to keep out of them by both sides. Hence no support is given to strikers through social unemployment insurance; they must rely entirely on their own organizational resources and solidarity.

Neither is there any forced official conciliation. During the

---

[37] Federal Labor Court *obiter*, in decision cited in note 16, *supra*.

[38] §49 BVG, Works Council Law, note 3, *supra*.

[39] So the Federal Labor Court held in its leading case: Arbeitsrechtliche Praxis, No. 1 to Art. 9 GG Arbeitskampf.

[40] *Ibid*.

[41] Views contrary to the holding discussed in the text accompanying note 39, *supra*, are increasingly expressed. See, *e.g.*, Brox, *Festschrift Nipperdey*, Vol. II, page 55 *et seq.* (1965).

Weimar regime, the prospect of a settlement imposed by the state discouraged the parties from coming to an agreement; each side would take an extreme position in the expectation that the official conciliator would eventually impose a solution. In the end, such awards ironically bore the name of collective agreements, even though they had been rejected by both sides; social autonomy was in full dissolution. That is why, since 1945, nothing similar has been reintroduced. It is the prevailing opinion that the legislature is without authority to impose compulsory arbitration or conciliation. Until now, no situation has yet arisen where one has had the feeling that state intervention would be indispensable. Of course the parties are free to conduct economic arbitration involving disputes of interests. But such arrangements are private and entirely voluntary.[42]

LABOR COURTS IN THE FEDERAL REPUBLIC OF GERMANY

Works Councils and codetermination [43] are beyond the scope of this paper. I conclude with a brief description of the procedures in the Federal Republic for the resolution of private disputes or disputes of rights.[44]

Germany does not utilize the system of private arbitration of disputes of rights, disputes known best to American readers as "grievances," by an impartial nongovernmental designee, paid privately by the parties in equal shares for his fees and expenses. Disputes arising under labor agreements are decided by labor courts. Courts of first instance are local labor courts, of which there are slightly over 100 in the Federal Republic. Parties may appear in their own behalf or may be represented by lawyers. If one party has a lawyer appearing and the other can afford none, the court will appoint counsel for him without cost. Despite the fiction that trade

---

[42] These observations apply to the Federal Republic of Germany, which has no effective legal provisions for conciliation and arbitration. Virtually all the constitutions of the Länder of the Federal Republic provide for voluntary conciliation and arbitration of disputes of interest. Compulsory concilation in certain restricted matters is specified only in the Land of Rhineland-Palatinate and in the South Baden area of the Land of Baden-Württemberg.

[43] The best and latest published information on Works Councils is found in Nikisch, Vol. III (1966). See also Dietz, *Betriebsverfassungsgesetz* (4th ed., 1967). American and British readers of this volume will find useful Monograph 23 of Social Policy in Germany, described in note 1, *supra*: Klein, "Co-determination and the Law Governing Works Councils and Staff Representation in the Public Service" (1963).

[44] The best analysis of these procedures currently to be found is Hueck-Nipperdey, Vol. I, §§91-104.

unions are not juridical entities, trade unions and employer associations freely participate in labor court proceedings.

Land (state) labor courts, 12 in number, are intermediate courts of review to which appeals may be made from judgments of local labor courts.

From decisions of the Land labor courts appeals may be taken to the Federal Labor Court, which in labor matters is the court of last resort. In this "Supreme" Court the parties must be represented by lawyers. Appeals to the Federal Labor Court are available when either the issue involves 6,000 Marks or the appeal has been permitted by the Land labor court or when the decision of the Land labor court deviates from a prior decision of the Federal Labor Court.

A local labor court will consist of one learned judge and usually two lay members, equally representing workers and employers. The number of lay members may be increased to four in special cases. Land labor courts similarly have either two or four lay members. The composition of the various labor courts may strike American readers as unusual. The British Restrictive Practices Court, however, also has lay members.

The Federal Labor Court operates in five parts or senates. A panel includes three federal judges and two lay members separately representing workers and employers. In cases of unusual importance a Grand Senate of the Federal Labor Court consisting of six federal judges and four lay members, two representing workers and two representing the employers, will be convoked.

This description lets me conclude where I started this paper. In the civil law system of Germany, labor jurisprudence emerges from the case law developed by these labor courts no less than from the written statutes.

Author's Recommended Reading List

Carey, James B. and others, *Trade Unions and Democracy, A Comparative Study of U.S., French, Italian, and West German Unions;* Planning Pamphlet No. 100, National Planning Association (October 1957).

Erdman, E. G., "Organisation and Work of Employers' Associations in the Federal Republic of Germany," 78 *Int. Lab. Rev.* 533 (1958).

Jungbluth, Adolf, "The Role of the Labour Manager in Undertakings under Co-management in the Federal Republic of Germany," 78 *Int. Lab. Rev.* 368 (1958).

Lepinski, Franz, "The German Trade Union Movement," 79 *Int. Lab. Rev.* 57 (1959).

Nipperdey, H. C., "The Development of Labour Law in the Federal Republic of Germany Since 1945," 70 *Int. Lab. Rev.* 26, 148 (1954).

Ramm, Thilo, "The German Law of Collective Agreements. Its Developments and Its Problems" and "The Restriction of the Freedom to Strike in the Federal Republic of Germany," in *Labour Relations and the Law: A Comparative Study*, Kahn-Freund, ed., (London: Stevens & Sons, 1965).

Shuchman, Abraham, *Codetermination, Labor's Middle Way in Germany* (Washington: Public Affairs Press, 1957).

Spiro, Herbert J., *The Politics of German Codetermination* (Cambridge: Harvard University Press, 1958).

"Labour Law in Europe, with Special Reference to the Common Market," *Int. & Comp. L.Q.*, Supp. Pub. No. 5 (1962).

IRELAND AND LABOR RELATIONS LAW

By J. B. McCartney

INTRODUCTION

Northern Ireland, consisting of the six counties of Londonderry, Antrim, Down, Armagh, Tyrone, and Fermanagh, came into existence in 1921 as a separate political unit within the United Kingdom. What has since 1949 been called the Republic of Ireland, consisting of the remaining 26 counties of the island, became a political entity in 1922 as the Irish Free State.

What is important for our discussion is that in both governments the case law and statutes of the former United Kingdom of Britain and Ireland were expressly continued in force.[1] In the Republic, the constitutional proviso was added that English laws in force in 1922 should be effective "[s]ubject to this Constitution and to the extent to which they are not inconsistent therewith."[2]

The present Constitution of the Republic, drafted in 1937, is a fertile source of labor law in the South. It has been observed that "Ireland is the first common law country with a written constitution to apply for membership in the EEC."[3] What is of greater interest to the labor law student is that the British Trade Union Acts of 1871 and 1906, with only insignificant amendments to the former, and the interpretations thereof by English courts prior to 1922, still constitute the principal source of labor law in the Republic.

The Northern Ireland Parliament, popularly called Stormont, has power to make laws for the peace, order, and good government of Northern Ireland in relation to all matters except those especially reserved to the Parliament of the United Kingdom. Under the constitutional practices which have developed since Northern Ireland became a separate political unit, the U. K. Parliament does not legislate on matters within the powers of the Northern Ireland Parlia-

---

[1] Government of Ireland (Companies, Societies, etc.) Order, 1922, S.R. & O. 1922, No. 184.

[2] Article 50, Section 1 of the Constitution of Ireland, 1937. Under Article 73 of the 1922 Irish Free State Constitution, the "laws in force" at the date of its coming into effect were continued in full force and effect, subject to their being consistent with the Constitution and subject also to their subsequent repeal or amendment. Delany, *The Administration of Justice in Ireland*, p. 13 (1962). See also *Irish Transport and General Workers' Union* v. *Transport and General Workers Union*, [1936] I. R. 471.

[3] Temple Lang, *The Common Market and the Common Law*, p. 39 (1966).

ment unless the government of Northern Ireland expressly requests that this be done. Thus, the Northern Ireland Parliament has enacted the equivalent of almost all the post-1922 legislation in Britain in all fields of labor law, though often with its own variations that may constitute traps for the unwary. For example, despite the repeal of the 1927 Trade Disputes Act by the Westminster Trade Union Act of 1946, a trade union member in Northern Ireland must still "contract in" to pay the political levy; the Terms and Conditions of Employment Act of Northern Ireland of 1963 is wider in scope than Section 5.8 of its 1959 counterpart in Britain; the Northern Ireland Redundancy Payments Act of 1965 differs in application, e.g., regarding dock workers, from its counterpart 1963 and 1965 legislation across the Irish Sea. Some modern legislation in Britain has no counterpart in Ireland. For example, there is no equivalent in Northern Ireland or in the Republic of the Trade Disputes Act 1965, which patched over the legal gap made evident by *Rookes v. Barnard.*[4]

Of the preexisting statutes regulating the affairs of trade unions, only that of 1871 was amended in the Republic in 1935 in a minor respect by extending the landholding rights of a trade union. But there have been important additions in the Trade Union Acts of 1941, 1942, and 1952.[5] Other significant changes in the labor relations laws of the Republic were made by the Industrial Relations Acts, 1946 and 1955, which, *inter alia,* repealed and replaced the Conciliation and Arbitration Act, 1896, the Industrial Courts Act, 1919, and the Trade Boards Act, 1909 to 1913. These laws are discussed in substantial detail later in this article.

In both parts of Ireland labor-management relations, especially in the fields of wage negotiations and grievances, are mainly matters for free collective bargaining rather than legal determination. The conceptual differentiation of "interests" from "rights," or "economic" strikes from other strikes, is as unknown in both parts of Ireland as in Britain. However, there are, again as in Britain, quite a number of statutes on a variety of aspects of individual terms and conditions of employment and on collective relationships including disputes, as well as on safety and health and welfare in employment. Social security provisions are, however, mainly state-provided, though some — like the new redundancy payments — are provided by industry under legislative schemes.

Whether the role of law, the courts, or the Parliament on ei-

---

[4] See discussion in Grunfeld, *Modern Trade Union Law,* pp. 435-39 (1966).
[5] See Shillman, *Trade Unionism and Trade Disputes in Ireland,* Ch. 8 (1960).

ther side of the Irish Sea has been one of "abstention" [6] is a matter of opinion, to resolve which would require a fuller consideration of the normative effects of the law than has yet been written. Certainly, the absence from the Republic of many of the factors which, for most of the period from 1915 to 1959, in practice precluded the courts in Britain from opportunity to intervene is reflected in the vastly greater number of actions in the Irish courts on the Trade Disputes Act, 1906 — the basic statute on strikes. Consequently, for authority on much of this Act, English writers, lawyers, and judges often rely on Irish decisions.[7]

There is little published material on labor law in the Republic. Most of it is listed in this paper. The only labor law publications in Northern Ireland appear in the *Northern Ireland Legal Quarterly*. Some of the latter was reproduced in 1968 in a pamphlet, "Recent Developments in Labour Law in Northern Ireland." [8]

There is a comprehensive range of statistics in the trade, industry, and labor fields in the Republic from both official and other sources and a more restricted one in the North. The government in the Republic regularly utilizes for a number of purposes the services of a wide variety of both independent and state-controlled bodies which it subsidizes. Those in the field of this volume come within the purview of the Departments of Industry and Commerce and of Labour. The Northern Ireland Government may rely on its own ministries for the services it requires, but more frequently it utilizes the results of studies made for Westminster, such as those of the Donovan Commission. At times it utilizes outside bodies such as the Northern Ireland Economic Council. The relevant Stormont departments are the Economic Section of the Prime Minister's Department and Cabinet Offices, the Ministry of Commerce, and the Ministry of Health and Social Services which includes the Labour Department.

Invaluable guides to these services are the *Ulster Year Book*,[9] for the North, and the *Administration Yearbook*,[10] for the Republic.

Bills for reform of trade union law and labor relations law are

---

[6] Cf. Kahn-Freund, "Labour Law" in Ginsberg, (ed.), *Law and Opinion in England in the Twentieth Century*, pp. 227-44 (1959) and same author in Flanders and Clegg (eds.), *The System of Industrial Relations in Great Britain*, pp. 42-127 (1953).

[7] See Wedderburn, *The Worker and the Law*, p. 255 (London: MacGibbon and Kee, 1965).

[8] *Northern Ireland Legal Quarterly*, 19 University Square, Belfast 7.

[9] Government Bookshop (H.M.S.O.), Linenhall Street, Belfast. Despite its title it is published triennially.

[10] Institute of Public Administration, 57-61 Landsdowne Road, Dublin 4.

imminent in both jurisdictions. Northern Ireland, as the result of the step-by-step policy with Britain, will closely parallel whatever legislation springs from the Donovan Report.[11]

Proposals for reform were announced by the Minister for Labour in the Republic in April 1966 and have been under discussion with trade union and employer organizations since. The Minister stated on May 21, 1968 that legislation was being drafted then.[12] An attempt to provide some legislative solution to the difficulties created by the Supreme Court's ruling in the Educational Company case [13] has been promised since 1963. A bill was prepared in that year but has not been presented, the difficulty of outflanking the constitutional obstacles being the probable reason.

THE RIGHT TO ORGANIZE AND BARGAIN COLLECTIVELY

In the Republic of Ireland a number of legal and nonlegal factors affect the right of an employee to join a trade union and engage in collective bargaining. They are (1) Article 40.6 of the 1937 Constitution, (2) an absence of any general legislation, (3) some special legislation applying to state-controlled public corporations, (4) a Fair Wages Resolution, which has not the force of legislation, and its occasional legislative embodiment in particular situations, (5) the Republic's adherence to the relevant I.L.O. and other conventions, and (6) the pressure which a trade union by itself or with the assistance of others can apply. In practice only the last of these is presently effective.

The pertinent provisions of the 1937 Constitution are the following:

"40.6.1°. The State guarantees liberty for the exercise of the following rights, subject to public order and morality:

* * *

"iii. The right of the citizens to form associations and unions. Laws, however, may be enacted for the regulation and control in the public interest of the exercise of the foregoing right.

"2°. Laws regulating the manner in which the right of forming associations and unions and the right of free assembly may be exercised shall contain no political, religious or class distinction."

These provisions, and their predecessors in Article 9 of the

---

[11] *Report of the Royal Commission on Trade Unions and Employers' Associations,* 1965-1968. Cmnd. 3623.

[12] For details of the original proposals and subsequent discussions with the trade union side, see Annual Reports of the Irish Congress of Trade Unions (I.C.T.U.) for 1966, 1967, and 1968.

[13] See notes 19 and 51 *infra* and accompanying text.

original Constitution of 1922, have been invoked in a number of cases.[14] All were instances of activity or, in one case, of legislation [15] that was designed to force the plaintiff into a union or a particular union, and, with only one peculiar exception, all were held to be interferences with the quoted constitutionally guaranteed rights. But there has been neither legislation nor decisions of the courts requiring employers in general to permit their employees voluntarily to join unions despite a number of strikes over employers denying this right to their employees or their right to collective bargaining.

In the recent cases concerning the dispute with the E.I. Co. at Shannon (a wholly owned subsidiary of General Electric Co.), a whole range of protections of the right to organize and collectively bargain was at stake; but none was in issue in the courts, and the decisions turned on whether the picketings were protected by the Trade Disputes Act, 1906.[16]

Some statutes of the Republic relating to public corporations operating state-controlled enterprises require such corporations to bargain with representative unions. C.I.E., the nationalized transport undertaking, is one such corporation. The Meskell[17] case decided by the High Court in 1968, and now pending in the Supreme Court, concerns the dilemma in which C.I.É. was placed, on the one hand, by such bargaining provisions in the several road and rail statutes, [18] under which it had entered into a closed-shop agreement with four unions, and, on the other, by the Supreme Court decision

---

[14] The cases are discussed in McCartney, "Strike Law and the Constitution of Eire," in Kahn-Freund (ed.), *Labour Relations and the Law*, p. 154 (1965); see also XXX Irish Jurist, p. 54 (1964).

[15] *N.U.R.* v. *Sullivan and I.T. & G.W.U.*, [1947] I.R. 77 (High Court); 91 (Supreme Court). (The delay in publishing the Irish Reports frequently results in the publication of the proceedings in the High Court and the Supreme Court as a continuous one.) In the N.U.R. case a statute (Trade Union Act, 1941, Part III) providing for a trade union tribunal empowered to grant exclusive organizing and recruiting rights for classes of workmen to particular unions was held to be repugnant to Article 40 of the Constitution.

[16] Judgments, so far unreported, of (a) Henchy J. on March 19 and 29, 1968; (b) O'Keefe J. on April 5, 1968; (c) Supreme Court of April 9, 1968; see also recommendations of Labour Court on April 26, 1968. See *Irish Times* for March 20, 29, and 30, April 6, April 4-10 and April 19-27, 1968. All except the Labour Court hearing concerned applications for labor injunctions. There is no equivalent to the Norris-LaGuardia Act in either part of Ireland. For further discussion, see my article in Part VII, *infra*.

[17] *Meskell* v. *C.I.É.*, unreported judgment of Teevan J. given on April 26, 1968, a year after the hearing. See *Irish Times* of April 13, 1967, April 14, 1967, and April 27, 1968. In the writer's opinion the decision is wrong so far as the grounds for the decision as stated in the Irish Times of April 27, 1968, are concerned and the Supreme Court should overrule it.

[18] Section 55 of the Railways Act, 1924, and Section 10 of the Railways Act, 1933, as extended to C.I.E. by Section 46 of the Transport Act, 1950.

in the *Educational Company* case,[19] that the closed shop was an infringement of the "necessary correlative" constitutional right of employees to eschew unionism.

The Irish Republic is a signatory to a number of declarations and conventions which require it to guarantee the right to organize and to bargain collectively. Most important are the I.L.O. conventions Nos. 87 and 98[20] and the European Convention on Human Rights.[21] The United Nations' Universal Declaration of Human Rights [22] is in point also.

However, Articles 15.2.1° and 29.6 of the 1937 Constitution were interpreted by the Supreme Court[23] to be insuperable obstacles to the importation of provisions of such treaties or conventions into the domestic law of the Republic, unless by legislation. The conventions, though ratified, are not self-executing. No such legislation has been introduced, and thus, so far as the citizen is concerned, the conventions remain unenforceable in practice — though many conventions of other types have been embodied in legislation and though the Republic has from the beginning permitted individual citizens to petition the European Commission under Article 25 of the European Convention.

Though Northern Ireland has a written constitution,[24] it is not of the type in which fundamental freedoms are enshrined, and consequently it does not guarantee a right to organize or freedom of association. Nor is there any relevant general legislation on such rights. Northern Ireland also has requirements similar to those of the Republic in its statutes relating to state enterprises; [25] but again these have no application to private employment.

Similarly, the United Kingdom, of which Northern Ireland is a part, has ratified the I.L.O. Conventions of 1948 and 1949 on freedom of association and the right to organize and bargain collectively. But in the United Kingdom, as in the Republic of Ireland, such conventions are not self-executing upon ratification but require spe-

---

[19] *Educational Co.* v. *Fitzpatrick,* [1961] I.R. 343, 345, 370.

[20] Freedom of Association and Protection of Right to Organize Convention, No. 87, 1948. Right to Organize and Collective Bargaining Convention, No. 98, 1949. See *International Labour Code 1951,* Vol. 1, pp. 677 *et seq.* and corresponding articles in 1966 ed.

[21] European Convention for the Protection of Human Rights and Fundamental Freedoms, 1950, Art. 11. See Council of Europe, Collected Texts on European Conventions on Human Rights (1966).

[22] Arts. 20 and 23.

[23] *Re O'Laighleis (Lawless),* [1960] I.R. 93 and 109.

[24] Government of Ireland Act, 1920, as amended.

[25] E.g., the Ulster Transport Authority and its predecessor the Northern Ireland Road Transport Board.

cific legislation. No such protections have been established by legislative act of either Westminster or Stormont.[26]

The provisions of the Fair Wages Resolution of the Northern Ireland House of Commons (Stormont) of 1947 [27] is identical with that of Westminister in 1946 [28] and its scope of application similar. The Resolution is in some respects a counterpart of the American Walsh-Healey Act [29] in providing that contractors in government contracts shall pay wages and observe hours of work not less favorable than those established by collective bargaining, or in the absence of collective bargaining to pay prevailing wage rates and observe prevailing hours and conditions of employment.

However, unlike the Walsh-Healey Act, the Fair Wages Resolution is not a statutory enactment, but merely a direction to the executive by the legislature.

Inter alia, the Fair Wages Resolution provides that contractors to government departments must permit their employees to join trade unions if they wish, as a condition of the contract with the department concerned.[30] This has been extended to cover local-authority contracts and nationalized-industry contracts,[31] and is a condition of receiving some kinds of grants, subsidies, loans, guarantees, and licenses. The principle has been embodied in some statutes.[32]

The provisions are rarely enforceable by individual employees and only occasionally by their unions. Enforcement usually is by complaint to the appropriate government department or other body, which attempts persuasion. Failing that, there may be reference to the Industrial Court. The only sanction is the employer's fear of losing a future opportunity to contract with a branch of the government of Northern Ireland.

The provisions of the Resolution have no application outside these fields. Even within their very considerable scope they have very doubtful effect in practice because of lack of policing, due

---

[26] Cf. Wedderburn, *The Worker and the Law,* p. 18 (1965).

[27] 11 February 1947. (1946-47) XXX N.I. H.C. DEBS. 3876.

[28] 14 October 1946. 427 H.C. DEBS. 619. See Ministry of Labour's Industrial Relations Handbook, H.M.S.O. 1961.

[29] 41 U.S.C. Sections 35-45 (1964 ed.)

[30] Par. 4 of the Fair Wages Resolution, 1946 specifies: "The contractor shall recognize the freedom of his workpeople to be members of trade unions." See Wedderburn, *Cases and Materials on Labour Law,* p. 330 (1967).

[31] E.g., Electricity Board for Northern Ireland; Ulster Transportation Authority.

[32] E.g., Transport Act (Northern Ireland) 1948; Housing Act (Northern Ireland) 1939; Civil Aviation Act, 1949; Television Act, 1964 — the latter two being U. K. statutes which apply to Northern Ireland.

mainly to inaction by workers and their unions — which in turn results from widespread ignorance of the provisions and the scope of their application. Undoubtedly they have some normative effect, but I suspect that that too is rather small. No study of the effectiveness of the Resolution and its extensions appears to have been made.

Since the 1922 Treaty, Dail Eireann, the lower house in the parliament of the Republic, has not passed a Fair Wages Resolution.[33] The government has, however, followed a practice similar to that in Northern Ireland and in Britain, based on an amended version of the Westminster 1909 Resolution, an ancestor of the 1946 Resolution. The amendment, put into effect by the Government Contracts Committee in 1923, added the following words to those of 1909:

> "and for this purpose also regard shall be had to the conditions of employment generally in the contracting firm."[34]

A similar field of extension exists to that in the North, though neither, it would appear, is as wide as in Britain. Sporadic attempts at securing enforcement and at extending its scope to other fields, e.g., to industries protected by tariffs, have been made in the Republic by the trade union movement and by the Labour Party.

In both the North and the South of Ireland, those employers who are affected by the Resolution, or by any of its administrative or legislative extensions, are required to observe for all their employees terms and conditions not less favorable than those established by collective bargaining between representative unions and employer associations in that industry or district of it. They must also ensure that their subcontractors conform to the Resolution as well. Only in the case of a few enactments which expressly provide that the statutory commands are implied terms of his contract, and so enable a worker to sue for breach, is failure to observe the conditions of the Resolution enforceable other than by administrative refusal of contracts or licenses.[35]

While one can conceptualize comfortably about separate rights to organize, to recognition, and to collective bargaining, the latter two are so much necessary ingredients of the right of organization that any attempt to separate them in practice quickly produces an atmosphere of unreality, as in the E.I. dispute of 1968.[36] Of what use, normally, is the right to join a union if the latter is not permit-

---

[33] Dail Eireann Debates, answer to Question No. 23 on November 15, 1962.

[34] Dail Eireann Debates, answer to Question No. 22 on November 22, 1962.

[35] Cf. Wedderburn, *The Worker and the Law,* pp. 126-29 (1965).

[36] My principal comments on the E.I. litigation are reserved for my article in Part VII of this volume.

ted to bargain for its members? What does recognition of a union mean without the right to bargain? These questions are answered by specific legislation in some countries, especially in the United States, Canada, and Sweden. But constitutions, statutes, and case law do not yet answer these questions in either part of Ireland. The answers are to be found not in law but in practice, and in the remainder of this article I shall discuss mainly the practice of unions, individual employers, and employer associations in union recognition and collective bargaining. Consideration will also be given to the procedures developed in Northern Ireland and in the Republic for dealing with the realities of labor controversies, which of necessity arise in industrialized nations committed to democratic principles.

LABOR UNIONS, EMPLOYER ASSOCIATIONS: THEIR STRUCTURES AND REGULATION

Labor Unions

Contrary to the situation in many continental European countries and except for the years 1944-1957, when there was a breakaway Congress of Irish Unions (C.I.U.) resulting from a split based partly on national politics and partly on personality, there has been a single [37] national trade union center in Ireland since the Irish Trade Union Congress was formed in 1894.[38] Since the split was healed, the title has been the Irish Congress of Trade Unions (I.C.T.U., or Congress). There is no division at the Congress level on ideology, religion, character of employment, or other grounds. Ninety percent of all organized workers in Ireland (94 percent of those in the Republic and 85 percent of those in Northern Ireland) are in Congress-affiliated unions. Fewer than 60,000 are in unions outside Congress.

The Irish Congress of Trade Unions is an all-Irish body, with its headquarters in Dublin; but there is a partly autonomous Northern Ireland Committee with an office in Belfast, established mainly to enable the Northern Ireland Government to recognize an all-Ireland Congress. It is one of the few national trade union centers that is not affiliated with any of the three international trade union bodies.[39] It does, however, nominate workers' delegations to I.L.O.

---

[37] There is a tiny Irish Conference of Professional and Service Associations, some 20, founded in 1945. Not only is it tiny but some of its member unions are affiliates of Congress also, and some are not regarded by Congress as unions at all.

[38] See Bleakley and Roberts, *Trade Union Organization in Ireland,* (1958-59).

[39] World Federation of Trade Unions, International Confederation of Free Trade Unions, and the International Federation of Christian Trade Unions, now

In proportion to its work force, Ireland has one of the highest degrees of trade union organization (52 percent) in the capitalist world. The last full analysis was published in 1967 by Congress Research Service in its periodical, *Trade Union Information*. According to those figures, there are now some 610,000 organized workers of all kinds in Ireland,[40] 346,000 in the Republic and 246,000 in Northern Ireland, approximately three fifths and two fifths, respectively, of the total. These represent organizational rates for all workers of 56 percent and 48 percent, respectively,[41] and increases in membership of 11 percent and 15 percent, respectively, over the 1960 figures. The rates for white- and blue-collar workers are similar; but organization of women, which is still rather low compared with that of men, is estimated at about 40 percent in the Republic and 25 percent in the North. Thus, about 66 percent of male employees in the Republic and about 60 percent of those in Northern Ireland are in unions.

Such a high rate of unionism has been achieved without legislative encouragement or assistance in most cases and is probably not unconnected with national history, culture, and temperament. I believe that all these are factors which must be taken into account in any comparative study or in any plan for labor relations in a new undertaking in either part of Ireland, especially if it is to be set up by a foreign corporation.

These workers are organized in a multiplicity of unions which neither legislative attempts nor hard work on the part of Congress has succeeded in reducing to any extent. There are 97 unions operating in the Republic, 77 of them affiliated to Congress, and 91 in the North, of which 40 are affiliated. Many in both areas are tiny by any standard.

Some unions operate wholly in the Republic, some wholly in the North; and a few of the Republic-based unions also operate in the North — including the biggest of all, the Irish Transport and General Workers' Union (I.T. & G.W.U.). A number of unions based in Britain operate in Ireland, some in the whole of Ireland, some only in the Republic, and some only in the North. The num-

---

called the World Confederation of Labour. But in February 1969 the AFL-CIO severed its ties with the International Confederation of Free Trade Unions.

[40] Analyses vary slightly according to interpretations made. E.g., is the Civil Service Alliance, for some 29 individual unions, to be taken as one or 29? The latter approach was adopted in the 1961 survey (*Trade Union Information*, July 1961) and the former in 1967. Data from the several sources tend to differ.

[41] As against in 1966: Sweden 56 percent, Britain 43 percent, Netherlands 36 percent, Japan 34 percent, West Germany 32 percent, United States 25 percent, France 23 percent. *Trade Union Information*, Feb-Mar. 1967, p. 2.

ber of members of British-based unions is 260,000 or 43 percent of the total number of Irish trade unionists. But it should be noted that Irish sections of British-based unions are usually, but not always, affiliated to the Irish Congress of Trade Unions.

Fifty-six percent of the total in the Republic are in the six largest unions, and the I.T. & G.W.U. alone represents 38 percent (140,000). Of the remainder, 45 organize 76,500 manual workers, and this includes 26 craft unions with 30,300 members (though pure craft unionism is breaking down); while there are 46 mainly white-collar unions with 83,500 members, including 19 in the Civil Service with 19,200 in membership. Only six of these 97 unions have memberships exceeding 10,000, and only 31 have more than 2,000.

The 77 unions in the Republic affiliated to Congress have 341,300 members, or 94 percent of the total. Of the 20 unaffiliated organizations, four are manual workers' unions (2,000 members), nine are Civil Service (7,100 members), and seven are other white-collar organizations (13,300 members). Only two unaffiliated unions, both white-collar, have memberships over 2,000 and 10 of them have fewer than 250 each.

Twenty-seven of the unions operating in the Republic have head offices in Britain. These unions have 50,600 members, or 14 percent of the total. The rest are based in the Republic itself. Of these, 49 are Civil Service associations, 29 of whom form the Civil Service Alliance.

Forty-three percent of the trade union membership in the North is in three unions, the Amalgamated Transport and General Workers' Union, with London headquarters, alone having 33 percent (82,400). There are 37 other manual workers' unions (83,700) and 51 mainly white-collar (57,300). Only 23 unions in Northern Ireland have more than 2,000 members, but their membership constitutes 90 percent of the total. Only four of them have more than 10,000 members, but these have 54.5 percent of the total membership.

The 40 unions in the North affiliated to I.C.T.U., have 85 percent of the total (i.e., 209,600). Only six of those not affiliated have more than 2,000 members, and 28 have fewer than 250 each. Twenty-eight of the unaffiliated organizations are of teachers, civil servants, and other public-service employees.

Seventeen of the unions operating in Northern Ireland have head offices there, five are headquartered in the Republic, and 69 are based in Britain. Of these 91, 28 also have members in the Republic.

Apart from surveys carried out by I.C.T.U.'s Research Service from trade union sources, statistics on trade unions and their memberships are available annually in the Republic from two sources. The Registrar of Friendly Societies makes returns of the number of registrations and certifications made under the Trade Union Acts, 1871 to 1952,[42] and the Department of Labour reports on the number of negotiating licenses issued under the Trade Union Act, 1941.[43]

Neither set of returns is complete. Unions based outside the country and those in the public service, along with some other bodies, are exempt from the registration requirements. All other Irish unions must be registered as a condition precedent to being licensed. Fifty-eight workers' unions were registered in 1965, and, apart from employers' unions, i.e., associations which come within these provisions also, nine would not usually be classed as unions at all. Seventy-six workers' unions are licensed, as are a number of employers' organizations.

In Northern Ireland the only equivalent returns are those of the Registrar, there being no licensing requirements for bodies that wish to engage in collective bargaining there. Seventy-eight were registered in 1966, and some of these were sections of other unions.

Like Britain, Ireland, both in the North and South, has no uniform pattern of craft unions, general unions, or industrial unions.[44] Craft unionism is breaking down into mixed unions of craftsmen and their assistants or into more general unions. Some unions are solely white- or blue-collar, while others organize both. Some are all-Ireland unions, some are international unions (British-based), and some are district or local unions. Because of recognition requirements in the two civil services, some are solely civil service. There is one wholly women's union. There is no overt organization on a religious basis, though one finds instances of unions or individual branches which are, for one reason or another, composed mainly or entirely of members of one religious group or another.

There is no apparent tendency toward a reduction in the number of unions, the occasional amalgamation being offset by the formation of new unions by breakaway or otherwise. In the Republic,

---

[42] See text accompanying notes 67-81 *infra*.

[43] *Ibid.* Membership returns are required only every three years, and the due years vary from union to union.

[44] See: O'Mahony, Industrial Relations In Ireland: The Background, 22 (Paper No. 19 of the Economic and Social Research Institute, Dublin 1964); Daly, *Industrial Relations: Comparative Aspects, With Special Reference to Ireland*, p. 108 (1968). Compare Research Paper No.5 of Royal Commission on Trade Unions and Employers' Associations. (1967).

union mergers are impeded by the provisions of the law on amalgamations, which are difficult to meet.[45] The former Congresses in Ireland, and, since 1958, I.C.T.U. have spent much time and effort in attempts to secure rationalization of the structure of the movement. A special Committee on Trade Union Organization was set up by Congress in 1961; but lack of any real power in the national center and the age-old range of loyalties, vested interests, and disinclination to give up sovereignty have frustrated any significant achievement. Despite a great deal of thought and effort on its part, the work of the Committee was suspended in 1967.[46]

More progress has resulted from I.C.T.U. promotion of the establishment of Industrial Committees and Trade Union Groups for the various industries[47] in the Republic, and these are particularly well established in the state-controlled enterprises such as the transport board (C.I.E.), the Electricity Supply Board (E.S.B.), and the Irish Peat Development Authority (Bord na Móna). Industrial Committees are intended to provide for regular consultation among unions in each industry on matters of common interest within the industry.[48] Trade Union Groups are intended to provide for coordination of policies and joint negotiation by the unions in each employment.[49]

Both a governmental attempt and voluntary efforts on the part of the unions themselves have received a setback from the law. An early rationalizational attempt in the Trade Union Act, 1941, resulted in a holding that Part III of the Act was contrary to the constitutional guarantee of the right of association in Article 40 of the 1947 Constitution.[50] Efforts at rationalization through collective agreements received a jolt when the Supreme Court outlawed the closed shop, and all efforts to enforce it, in the *Educational Company* case.[51]

---

[45] See Trade Union Amendment Act, 1876, and Trade Union Act, 1917, discussed in Shillman, *Trade Unionism and Trade Disputes in Ireland,* p. 7 (1960). British and Northern Ireland law has been modified to facilitate mergers and transfers, Trade Union (Amalgamations, etc.) Act, 1964, and Trade Union (Amalgamation, etc.) Act (Northern Ireland), 1965. See full discussion in Grunfeld, *Modern Trade Unionism,* pp. 236-48 (1966). Similar legislation is promised in the Republic.

[46] See Report of the Executive Council for 1967-68, p. 12, and the Annual Reports, 1961-67. See also the report of the (governmental) Commission on Vocational Organization of 1944.

[47] See Report of the Executive Council for 1967-68, pp. 20, 39, and the Annual Reports, 1961-67.

[48] See 1961 and 1962 Annual Reports for functions and constitution.

[49] *Ibid.*

[50] In *N.U.R.* v. *Sullivan and I.T. & G.W.U.,* [1947] I.R. 77, 91.

[51] *Educational Co.* v. *Fitzpatrick,* [1961] I.R. 343, 345, 370. See also "Trade

Even these Congress-sponsored trade union negotiation groups have produced reactions from smaller or less aggressive unions. The English-based Amalgamated Society of Locomotive Engineers and Firemen (A.S.L.E.F.) recently notified its Irish members of its intention to withdraw from Ireland, primarily because the practice of group negotiation by the C.I.E. group of unions prevented it from adequately looking after their interests. Yet it would appear that C.I.E., and apparently any other state enterprise in a similar position, could not refuse to negotiate with an individual union under the decision in *Federation of Rail and Road Workers* v. *G.S. Ry.*[52]

The Minister for Labour now seeks such rationalization by suggesting group negotiating licenses in his current proposals for reform of trade union and industrial relations law. The unions, understandably, have rejected them, and Congress has withdrawn from the negotiations on reform of these branches of law largely over this issue.[53] The Minister's proposal to provide for group negotiating licenses could run into similar constitutional difficulties, as did Part III of the 1941 Act, if they should exclude negotiation by individual unions. Indeed, it is not altogether clear that even the current single-union negotiating license provisions in that Act are constitutional.

Little thought appears to have been given by the government and other advocates of enforced mergers to their effect on the democratic content of trade unionism and so on other democratic institutions and democracy itself in Ireland. The price of rationalization may be too high and the loss of efficiency may be more acceptable to a society which wishes to preserve its democracy. But it is not unknown for governments and others to want strong centralization in the trade union structure in order to incorporate the movement as an instrument of control over the work force as a means of implementing government policies.

Internally, trade unions in Ireland, like those in Britain, are usually based on branches each covering all members in a geographical area, and not on the workplace, though plant-based branches resembling American single-plant affiliated local unions are sometimes found. Branches may be tiny or large. Some have full-time officials; in others, full-time officials are not found outside the headquarters, however large the branches or other organs of the union. The amount of power vested in a branch varies immensely, but gen-

---

Union Issues" in *Report of the Committee on the Constitution, December 1967,* pp. 41-43 (Dublin: Stationery Office. Pr. 9817).

[52] (1942) 8 IRISH JURIST REP. 33.

[53] See, e.g., Report of the I.C.T.U. Executive Council for 1967-68, pp. 5, 43.

erally it is not extensive. In large unions, branches are grouped geographically under area, district, or regional councils, and in a very large union, like the A.T. & G.W.U., there may be a hierarchy of these.

Some unions are federations of smaller or local organizations, while others are the results of mergers or of transfers of members from other unions. In both cases the constituents or sectional successors of former unions often have autonomy in varying degrees, and a single union may have six or seven different categories of members, differentiated by sectional lines or by union social security benefits to which entitled. Sectional interests may be catered for by sectional subdivisions, often with a considerable degree of autonomy on matters peculiar to the section, at branch or other level, including the national. This sectional division, just as much as interunion rivalry, may produce demarcation or jurisdictional difficulties inside the same organization.

There is no Irish counterpart in either the Republic or Northern Ireland to the American Landrum-Griffin Act. Machinery for resolving disputes between members or between members and officials varies tremendously from union to union. It is nonexistent in some. In most unions there is a hierarchy of appeals culminating in the national executive or, in some instances, in the periodic delegate conference. The flaw in most of these is that the scales are heavily weighted against the individual member — education, ability, financial means, official entrenchment. Indeed, the practical inability in many unions to secure the elementary rights guaranteed by the Rule Book is probably the most important defect in trade unionism in Ireland (and Britain) today. Occasionally a union provides appeal to a committee composed wholly of lay members, as in the case of the Amalgamated Union of Engineering and Foundry Workers.

The Irish Congress of Trade Unions has made a notable attempt to provide an independent forum for the settlement of such disputes or complaints. Part VIII of the Constitution provides for an Appeals Board to hear such cases, but its terms of reference are limited (appeals by individual members are restricted to cases of expulsion), and in practice few cases have been dealt with by the Board since its inception in 1963.[54] Its report is published annually, but separately. It is debated in private session, and neither the report nor the discussion on it appear in the regular Annual Report of I.C.T.U.

---

[54] See 1963 Annual Report, p. 216.

As in Britain,[55] there is no legal right to union membership in either part of Ireland, and as yet there has been no opportunity to see whether the courts would extend the analogy of *Nagle* v. *Fielden*[56] to the trade union field, at least in a closed- or union-shop situation in Northern Ireland. The right-to-membership provision in Section 35 of the Trade Union Act, 1941, being in Part III, ceased to have effect when that part was declared unconstitutional in the *N.U.R.* case, and the provision has not been reenacted. The effect of Section 13 of the same statute was held by the Supreme Court not to give any right to admission to membership.[57]

Express union security provisions or practices, in whatever form, have not been particularly common in Ireland — though there has been no study of their incidence such as that made by Dr. McCarthy in Britain.[58] However, they were outlawed in the Republic by the decision in the *Educational Company* case mentioned earlier as unconstitutional infringements of an implied right to remain unorganized, which was held by the Supreme Court to be a "necessary correlative" to the stated guarantee of the right to organize.[59]

In Northern Ireland, as in Britain, the general view is that such provisions are lawful; [60] but the question is not beyond doubt.[61]

Professor O'Mahony concludes of the Irish industrial relations system as a whole that "it has a certain inner logic of its own." [62] Apart from those sponsored by Congress, in which the activities of the Northern Ireland Committee as a coordinating body should not be overlooked, interunion cooperation takes place in formal multi-sided bodies, through formal agreements and working relationships between organizations, and in a multitude of informal joint activities at locality and plant level.

The main general feature is that interunion cooperation at

---

[55] See, generally, Rideout, *The Right to Membership of a Trade Union* (1963).

[56] [1966] 1 All E.R. 689, in which the English Court of Appeal held that the Jockey Club, which held a monopoly of issuing licenses to work as a racehorse trainer, could not arbitrarily refuse licenses to qualified applicants. See *Report of the Royal Commission on Trade Unions and Employers' Associations,* p. 1066 Cmnd. 3623 (1968) also cited herein as Donovan.

[57] *Tierney* v. *A.S.W.,* [1959] I.R. 254, 278. The N.U.R. case is discussed in the text accompanying note 50, *supra.*

[58] McCarthy, *The Closed Shop in Britain* (1964).

[59] *Educational Co.* v. *Fitzpatrick,* [1961] I.R. 343, 345, 370. See Congress Reports 1962, p. 75, and for each year since, under title *Trade Union Law.*

[60] See Grunfeld, *Modern Trade Union Law,* pp. 24-26 (1966); Donovan, pars. 1065-67.

[61] See McCartney, in Kahn-Freund (ed.) *Labour Relations and the Law,* pp. 155, 165 (1965).

[62] O'Mahony, *Industrial Relations in Ireland: The Background,* (1964).

branch level is organized on a geographical basis by local or district Trades Councils, e.g., the Belfast and District Trade Union Council and the Dublin Trades Council. These have lost some of their former influence and scope of activity because of lack of funds and the recent development of other forms of coordination. At plant level there may be formal union cooperation among local officials, but the usual pattern is agreement on common programs by shop stewards elected by members of each individual union or by all the members of the section of the plant, irrespective of union. Shop stewards' committees do much of the organizing and the bargaining at plant level. No study has been made of the shop steward in Ireland to parallel those carried out for the Donovan Commission, [63] but the general position is similar in the larger enterprises, though apparently much less so in the Republic.

The presence of so many unions, in particular the general and mixed ones, naturally causes much competition for membership and consequent disputes over recruitment and organizational spheres. In the absence, throughout Ireland, of a statute comparable to the National Labor Relations Act, prevention and control of interunion strife is sought through interunion agreements and cooperation among local officials and application of Part VII of I.C.T.U.'s constitution, [64] which is very similar to the Bridlington (no poaching) Declaration of the T.U.C. and provisions in the Standing Orders of the Scottish T.U.C.[65] The Executive Committee of Congress or its Disputes Committee (in Northern Ireland, the Northern Committee) may investigate any dispute between affiliates which arises or threatens to do so. The ultimate sanction is expulsion from Congress, though it is usually in the form of indefinite "suspension." Despite its modest size and severe financial limitations, the loss of the remarkably capable and extensive Congress services may be quite important to the small and medium-sized affiliate. The stigma of expulsion or suspension undoubtedly would be the operative sanction in most instances. However, it is doubtful that Congress could afford to expel one of its few large affiliates, e.g., the I.T. & G.W.U., if it were recalcitrant. Such interunion disputes which have come to the attention of Congress and the action taken on them are reported in its Annual Reports.

---

[63] Research Papers Nos. 1 (1966) and 10 (1968), Royal Commission on Trade Unions and Employers' Associations.

[64] Printed at the back of each Annual Report of Congress; see, e.g., p. 389 of the 1967 report.

[65] The Bridlington Agreement of 1939 which was designed to eliminate interunion "poaching" or "raiding" among British T.U.C. affiliates is discussed at length in Grunfeld, *Modern Trade Union Law*, pp. 215-28 (1966).

Demarcation or jurisdictional disputes, the "who does what?" issues, are similarly in the spheres of both interunion agreements and local cooperation, and of Congress activity under Part VII of its constitution. There are no provisions in the legislation of either part of Ireland like those in the Taft-Hartley Act concerning jurisdictional strikes.[66] The Demarcation Tribunal (or Northern Committee) of Congress again may investigate any such dispute or threatened dispute, and the ultimate sanction is the same. The reports of this tribunal are published annually. It is noteworthy that while it is not uncommon for poaching disputes to reach the Annual Reports, there are few published references to demarcation controversies. Mergers, interunion agreements, and union-management agreements have virtually eliminated demarcation problems in the major Belfast shipyards, an industry once plagued by them. In other spheres of employment it is clear that such problems and stoppages which result are often as much a sign of poor management, or ineffectual management tactics, as of protective or restrictive employee practices.

Employer Associations

There is an unexpectedly large number of employer associations in Ireland — something like two dozen in the Republic alone, judging by the annual reports of the negotiating licenses issued. Some are national in operations, others are local. The Retail Grocery, etc., Association (RGDATA) has easily the largest number of members, but the members of the Federated Union of Employers (F.U.E.) employ a vastly greater number of employees, and it is by far the most important so far as labor relations are concerned. F.U.E. has 10 geographical and about 80 industrial branches and nominates employer delegates to the I.L.O. On the instigation of the F.U.E., 12 employer organizations and some of the state enterprises formed a committee for joint consultation and coordination of employers' policies when the National Employer-Labour Conference was formed by I.C.T.U. and the F.U.E. in 1961.

Recently there has been a proposal to form one overall employer association in the Republic. In the North there are small local organizations in various industries; but the Confederation of British Industries has established a regional office in Belfast, and this is becoming the focal point of all local employer associations.

---

[66] Cf. *NLRB* v. *Radio and Television Broadcast Engineers*, 364 U. S. 573, 47 LRRM 2332 (1961).

Regulation of Labor Unions
and Employer Associations

In both parts of Ireland, as in Britain, any workers' union or employer association which satisfies the definition of a "trade union" in the Trade Union Acts, 1871-1913, may register as a trade union under the 1871 Act.[67] In the Republic such an organization must register with the Dublin registry and in Northern Ireland with the Belfast Registry. It may, alternatively, apply for certification as a trade union. The law in both respects is the same as in Britain, [68] but since both options are voluntary and the law merely confers privileges which many unions regard as unimportant and duties that are burdensome the incidence of registration or certification is not high in the United Kingdom. Some that operate throughout the British Isles register at one or more registries but not at others, either in ignorance of or disregard for the effects.

In the Republic, however, registration is of major importance to many home-based unions. This is not because of any consequence of the 1871 Act but because of the licensing requirements of the 1941 Act.

All "bodies," labor unions and employer associations, with head offices in the Republic, other than those scheduled in that Act as excepted [69] or excepted by ministerial order,[70] are required to take out negotiating licenses in order to be entitled to carry out collective bargaining, [71] and a prerequisite is that they must be registered as unions in Dublin.[72] Among those excepted are all foreign-based unions — whether registered, certificated, or neither — so long as they are trade unions under their native law.[73] Individual

---

[67] The Donovan Commission has recommended that employer associations be excluded from the term "trade union," which would then be confined only to combinations of employees. Employer associations whose principal activity is regulation of industrial relations would then become "registered employers' associations." Donovan, pars. 803, 806.

[68] See Grunfeld, *Modern Trade Union Law*, Ch. 3 (1966). "The reason why trade unions representing more than 10 percent of the total of trade unionists prefer not to register may partly be that under the Trade Union Act 1913 any unregistered trade union may apply for a certificate that it is a trade union within the statutory definition; which certificate, when granted, is conclusive evidence of that fact." Donovan, par. 791.

[69] Trade Union Act, 1941 (as amended by the Trade Union Act, 1942), Sections 6 (3) and (4).

[70] *Id.*, Section 6 (6)

[71] *Id.*, Section 6 (1). Collective bargaining for the purposes of this legislation is spelled out as "negotiations for the fixing of wages or other conditions of employment."

[72] *Id.*, Section 7(1) (a).

[73] *Ibid.*

employing bodies and recognized unions of civil servants and teach-ers [74] headquartered in the Republic are the principal excepted or-ganizations. Other excepted bodies are Wages Boards and regis-tered [75] bodies of employees which negotiate with their own employ-ers only. In addition, all bodies that require a negotiating license must lodge a deposit [76] with the High Court in Dublin. The amount of the appropriate deposit has been reduced for home-based unions by a ministerial order to one quarter of the amounts given in the schedule to the 1941 Act.[77] Judgment debts are paid out of these de-posits, if necessary.[78]

Monetary penalties are prescribed in subsection 6(2) of this statute; but a more serious sanction is that, by subsection 11(1), the immunities given by Sections 2, 3, and 4 of the Trade Disputes Act, 1906, the principal protections given to individuals involved in trade disputes and, subject to qualifications, to unions in any tort action are confined to "authorized trade unions" [79] holding negotiating li-censes and their members and officials.[80] However, neither sanction appears to have been resorted to in practice.

The granting of a negotiating license is mandatory on the Min-ister for Labour so long as he is satisfied that the applicant is an "authorized trade union"; but he may revoke a license where he is satisfied that this condition has ceased to be fulfilled.[81]

Licensed unions which are registered under the 1871 Act are obliged by Section 12 of the 1941 statute of the Republic to include in their rules provisions specifying the conditions for entering and leaving membership, and such a union must maintain a register of members which may be inspected at its offices. These are in addi-

---

[74] I.e., recognized by the Ministers for Finance and Education, respectively.

[75] I.e., registered under Section 6(4) of this act and not under the form of reg-istration available under the 1871 Act.

[76] Trade Union Act, 1941. Sections 7(1)(b), 14, 15.

[77] First by Section 8 of that statute, until the last war emergency period ended; then by annual enactment from 1947 until made permanent by the Trade Union Act, 1952.

[78] Trade Union Act, 1941, Section 16.

[79] Defined as one which fulfills the conditions in Section 7(1), i.e., is registered under the 1871 Act, or foreign union not required to register, and has lodged its deposit, in other words, a union holding and entitled to hold a negotiating license. Since the interpretation of "trade or industry" in the 1906 Act would be likely to exclude civil servants and teachers from its protection anyway, this exlusion would appear to be aimed at unofficial bodies of other workers or at other home-based unions which have failed to register.

[80] Since an individual person is not a "body," though a body may be a "per-son," the licensing provision and consequently the first penalty would not appear to apply to an individual employee negotiating on his own behalf, but the second one would if he were not a member of such an authorized and licensed trade union.

[81] Trade Union Act, 1941, Sections 10 and 17, respectively.

tion to the requirements of the 1871 Act. Unions that hold negotiating licenses, but are exempt from registering under the 1871 Act, are subject under Section 12 of the 1941 Act to obligations akin to those in the earlier statute, in addition to those which are imposed on registered unions, so the net effect is much the same.

COLLECTIVE BARGAINING AND AGREEMENTS

In Ireland there have been no research studies of the bargaining process and the bargainers to parallel those made elsewhere; [82] but the pattern appears to be broadly similar, both North and South, to that in Britain.[83] On a skeleton of basic national agreements, much of the reality of what is in the pay packet is added by bargaining at enterprise, plant, or work-place level, but there is so much diversity of practice that even this broad generalization should not be pushed too far. The current situation is largely the result of decades of pragmatic approach. There is national bargaining covering all industries and trades for certain types of craftsmen. There is plant bargaining, particularly in the single-firm industries, both state-controlled and private. There is industry-wide bargaining, and there is area bargaining, which is largely predominant in the older industries and is much less likely to be found in the newer industries and commercial enterprises.

Joint Councils of employer and union representatives, on Whitley lines, both in the form of merely consultative bodies and of negotiating bodies are to be found at plant level and at industry level, in state employment and in private. The distinction between the two functions tends in practice to become blurred. In the Republic the Labour Court facilitates the establishment of such Joint Industrial Councils (J.I.C.'s) and provides chairmen, secretaries, and facilities for meetings for those Councils which register with the Court. The main condition for such registration is the embodiment of a peace obligation in the rules of the Council.

As with other collective agreements, those made by J.I.C.'s may be made enforceable on all employers in the industry or district by registering them with the Court under the provisions of Part III of the Industrial Relations Act, 1946; but few are. I discuss the process of registration later in this paper. One important difference from the scene in Britain is that the smallness of scale in Ireland

---

[82] But see O'Mahony, *The Economics of Industrial Relations* (1965); McAuley, "Collective Bargaining and Industrial Disputes in Ireland," in *Statistical & Social Inquiry Society of Ireland* — paper delivered on April 14, 1967.

[83] E.g., see the Research Papers prepared for the Donovan Commission; Flanders, *The Fawley Productivity Agreements* (1964).

probably produces much less gap between the top, of both unions and employers, and the shop floor. Consequently there is more involvement of full-time union officials in labor-management relations, including bargaining. With so many tiny unions the top is often on the shop floor anyway.

The contents of the agreement vary greatly, too. With a state-provided concept of social security, unions rarely include such matters in their claims. National industry and area agreements usually relate only to the basic features of employment — wages, hours, overtime. Escalator clauses are rare. The specific detail of these and other aspects of employment are added by plant bargaining. Formal enterprise and plant-negotiated agreements tend to be a good deal more comprehensive and are naturally more strictly observed than industry or area agreements. Most are open ended, though phased fixed-term productivity agreements for two or three years are becoming more common.[84] However, a vast number of day-to-day matters are regulated by the custom and practice of the firm, very often the result of informal shop-floor agreement. Though "rights" or "grievance" issues are often catered for in "procedure" clauses, there is insufficient provision for reference to independent arbitration, and unnecessary stoppages do result. Quite a number of agreements, however, provide for a reference to the Labour Court in case of disagreement, and even where there is no such express provision disagreements are often referred there anyway. Indeed, there is justification for the complaint that negotiators on both sides, in order to avoid the responsibility for the outcome, too often resort to the Court before making any real attempt at negotiation. There is little resort to private arbitration, and there is nothing to resemble the labor arbitration of the American scene. If there is one thing shared by most unionists and most employers it is a desire to keep the lawyers from ordering their affairs, including their agreements.

In the Republic, the roughly annual or biennial series of wage claims have become more formalized since the end of the last war and are referred to as "rounds," [85] the current one being the eleventh. These rounds have occurred at intervals of anywhere from four to more than 18 months, depending on a variety of factors — rise in cost-of-living index, government tax policy, economic recession, improved economic position — and agreements concluded as

---

[84] Dr. Patrick J. Hillery, Minister for Labour, 234 DAIL EIREANN DEBATES 1568, May 21, 1968. Cf. Research Paper No. 4 (1967) prepared for Donovan Commission.

[85] For an account of this development see McAuley, *op. cit.,* note 82 *supra;* the Minister for Labour, 226 DAIL DEBATES 1426, 234 DAIL DEBATES 1567 (1968).

part of them have had durations of six to 24 months. About half of them resulted from agreements between the two former trade union centers and since 1959 between I.C.T.U. and the F.U.E. and other employer associations. In several cases these joint discussions were encouraged by government action. The government actually initiated the discussions of 1964 by stating that improved economic conditions justified an increase in wages and salaries. As would be expected, the years in which claims took place under the umbrella of such overall national agreements in the main produced few industrial disputes, and those in which such agreements were not concluded, especially in the periods of the seventh and eighth rounds (mid-1959 to mid-1962), produced a crop of stoppages. Not so the 1964 agreement.

Outside the national norms set by such agreements, there have been no consistent front runners among the unions or groups of workers in setting the pace for increases, but the usual pattern has been for manual workers to obtain settlements first and white-collar workers later. On the other hand, there are clear leaders within certain industries. As the Congress Industrial Committees and its Trade Union Groups in various employments succeed in developing coordinated policies, there is likely to emerge more planning in trade union strategy and tactics in making and processing claims.

In the first half of the period, when catching up on losses in real increases caused by war-time wage control in the face of cost-of-living increases, earnings appear to have risen almost wholly because of the "round" increases, i.e., by overall national pattern-setting, while in the second half (since about 1959) there has been a larger factor of wage drift. This has been due to full employment in Britain, with whom there is a common labor market, causing pressures in some Irish employments, and to higher bonuses as productivity increased. The great importance of the Labour Court in concluding overall national agreements and in settlement of individual claims, as well as in the whole field of labor, management, and state relations in the Republic, needs to be stressed. However, the extent to which claims and settlements are influenced by prevailing rates of wages and earnings and employment conditions in Britain is also a major factor, and there has been a broad, long-term maintenance of the relationship between Irish and British rates.

Other than to a minor extent in the Irish Republic, [86] there is no legislation in the British Isles concerning the legal status of the collective agreement, contrary to the situation in the United States

---

[86] In the provisions for enforcement of a collective agreement registered with the Labour Court. See Industrial Relations Act, 1946, Part III.

and a number of continental European countries.[87] The collective agreement is neither defined nor is its legal status prescribed. Consequently, since it is not a term of art, all types of all agreements resulting from collective bargaining are within the term, whether they be in writing, oral, or even implied, however formal or informal, and irrespective of the status of the parties in the union or employer hierarchy.

The problems of its legal status, and there are many, are left to the common law — both regarding its status as between the parties who made it and as to its effect, if any, on the individual worker's contract of employment. Though the law is the same in the whole of Ireland as in Britain, views as to what it is are diametrically opposed on a major aspect.

There has been little dispute about the law relating to the application of the collective agreement to the individual's contract, though much remains unclear about just whether, when, and to what extent the terms of a particular collective agreement will be embodied into it. Those questions, however, are connected with the extent to which a particular court would be prepared to go in implying collective terms into the latter contract, and are not determined by legal rules. Nevertheless, because of somewhat dubious authority, too little attention has been paid to the problem of whether a union negotiates as principal, as agent for its members or some part of them, or as both, in general or in particular instances. Too little attention has been paid also to other theories as to the legal status of the labor contract such as state and federal courts in the United States produced before the advent of the Labor Management Relations Act, especially Section 301.

On the other hand, in recent years there has been a rapidly growing refusal to accept the traditional view that, as between the parties to them, collective agreements are usually not contracts. The traditional view is that such agreements are merely gentlemen's agreements binding only in honor and therefore not enforceable in any court.[88] The opposed view is that there is no reason in principle to regard such agreements as "gentlemen's," since they are much more akin to ordinary commercial contracts than to mere social or domestic agreements.[89] It is rare in practice to find a collective

---

[87] See Kahn-Freund (ed.), *Labour Relations and the Law*, Part One (1965).
[88] *Id.* at 21-39; Donovan, pars. 1053-54.
[89] See McCartney, in Kahn-Freund, *op. cit.*, note 87 *supra*, p. 40. The most recent survey of British theories of the contractual nature of collective agreements is by Norman Selwyn: "Collective Agreements and the Law," 32 M.L.R. 377 (July 1969). Mr. Selwyn criticizes the decision of Mr. Justice Geoffrey Lane in *Ford Motor Company, Ltd.* v. *Amalgamated Union of Engineering and Foundry Workers*

agreement that expressly indicates in any way that it is not to be enforceable in the courts, and some in fact give every indication that they were regarded by the parties as legal documents, e.g., by being stamped. Nor is the problem of nonenforceability of those which fall under Section 4 of the Trade Union Act, 1871, nearly so great in application as is often thought, in view of the vastly more frequent and often very important agreements made with individual enterprises. Those, not being made with employers' unions, are unaffected by Section 4, and therefore that obstacle to enforceability has no application.

However, this does not dispose of the problem of legal enforceability, whether one sees enforceability as a panacea for the ills of stoppages in breach of agreements or as an undesirable and unworkable interference with industrial practices.[90] A large number of such agreements in the British Isles are drafted in language which the parties say they can understand (until a dispute arises about interpretation or until they are asked just what a particular part means) but which is so vague that the agreements should be held to be void for uncertainty. C.I.E. recently terminated its union agreements in order to have them so drafted as to remove this obstacle to enforcement.[91]

Under Section 33 of the Industrial Relations Act, 1946, of the Republic, the Labour Court is empowered, on the application of any person or of a court of law, to interpret any registered employment agreement or to decide on its application to any particular person. Its interpretations are conclusive in any court.

Breaches of such agreements are offenses punishable by fine; additional fines are specified for continuing an offense. By Section 32, a union representing workers affected by the agreement may complain if it thinks any employer to whom the agreement applies, either as a party to it or by its extension under Section 30 of the Act, is failing to observe its terms. If the Court regards the complaint as well founded it may order the employer to do whatever in its opinion is necessary to comply with the agreement. If such a union promotes, or assists out of its funds, any strike which its executive committee knows to be in contravention of a registered agreement, an employer or employers' union affected by the agreement

---

and Others, [1969] 1 W.L.R. 339, discussed earlier in this volume by Robert Copp and Professor Cyril Grunfeld.

[90] See Donovan, pars. 458-519, pars. 1053-54; pp. 279-81.

[91] On voidness of collective agreements for uncertainty, see Donovan, par. 472; on C.I.E. matter see I.C.T.U. Annual Report 1966, pp. 94, 291; Irish Times of June 22, 1965.

may lodge a complaint also. In successful complaints the Court may direct the union to stop assisting the strike out of its funds (e.g., by paying strike pay), and it may cancel the registration of the agreement. However, if such a strike continues after the Labour Court's direction and union members whose rates and conditions are not the subject of the strike are unable to work or decline to do so (the picket line is usually given high respect in the Republic), the payment of strike benefits to them is not regarded as assisting in the strike.

There are a number of procedures in both Northern Ireland and the Republic for extending the terms of collective agreements to employments other than those of the employer parties. First, general statutes provide for the award to unorganized or weakly organized employees in particular industries of rates of pay, hours, and paid holidays similar to those agreed between employers and unions in that industry or district. Second, awards by a general adjudication body may be extended when based on claims that the terms and conditions observed by a specific employer are lower than those generally prevailing in the industry or district. Third, when the Fair Wages Resolution applies the relevant collectively agreed rates to the employees of contractors or others covered by it.

In both parts of Ireland the old Trade Boards procedure of 1909, in modern form, is in operation. In Northern Ireland, this is achieved by Wages Councils under the Wages Councils Act (Northern Ireland), 1945; in the Republic, by Joint Labour Committees under the Industrial Relations Act, 1946.

By this method a tripartite board of union, employer, and independent representatives is established for each specific industry or part industry in which it is considered that collective bargaining is insufficient or nonexistent, because the industry is not, or is inadequately, organized.

The boards hear union claims and make awards that are binding as minimum conditions on all employers in that industry or district of it. The awards of such Wages Councils [92] in the North are confirmed by Wages Regulation Orders of the Minister for Health and Social Service. In the Republic the awards of the Joint Labour Committees, whose powers are more extensive than Wages Councils, are confirmed by Employment Regulation Orders of the Labour Court. [93] Enforcement by inspection and prosecution is in each

---

[92] For text of Wages Councils Act, 1959, see Wedderburn, *Cases and Materials on Labour Law*, pp. 366-70 (1967).

[93] See Mortished, *The Industrial Relations Act,* 1946, III PUBLIC ADMINISTRA-

case by the responsible Minister, and, since the Order becomes a term of his contract, the worker can sue for unpaid wages — though in practice this is a virtually useless remedy.

There are other minimum wage statutes, e.g., Agricultural Wages Acts, in both jurisdictions, but they are not in the form of extension procedures. There is no universal statutory minimum wage in either jurisdiction, though one is being actively sought by unions currently.

In the Republic the extension procedure is operated through the Labour Court [94] under the Industrial Relations Act, 1946, and is available only where the recognized terms and conditions are included in an "employment agreement" made between a union and an employer or employee association, [95] or at a meeting of a registered Joint Industrial Council (J.I.C.), and registered with the Labour Court. Among the conditions for registration are the following: Registration may be effected by any party to it but must be with the consent of the other party or by substantial consent if there is more than one other party. In turn, the parties must be substantially representative of employers and employees. The agreement itself must provide a procedure for settlement of disputes and a peace obligation until such procedure has been exhausted, and it must be in a form suitable for registration. The extent to which registration has taken place is very small, only 41 agreements having been on the register at the end of 1965.

Once registered, its terms apply to every worker and employer in the industry, or district of it, to which the agreement relates. Enforcement is by complaint by the aggrieved worker's union to the Court, which, if satisfied, will direct the employer to observe the conditions of the agreement, on penalty of prosecution and fine. As its terms become part of the individual contract of employment, the worker can sue for breach also, but this is practically ineffectual.

INDUSTRIAL CONFLICT: CONCILIATION, ADJUDICATION, AND ARBITRATION

Labor Disputes

Northern Ireland has a population of just one and a half mil-

---

TION IN IRELAND 75 (1963); Part IV of the Act; O'Mahony, *Industrial Relations in Ireland: The Background,* pp. 70-73 (1964).

[94] Industrial Relations Act, 1946, Part III. O'Mahony, *op. cit,* note 93 *supra,* 62-67 (1964).

[95] Such employer associations must, of course, hold negotiating licenses under the 1941 Act. Agreements made at J.I.C. meetings are not otherwise enforceable,

lion and an employee labor force of 473,800, [96] while the Republic's population is 2,880,800 and the employee labor force is 650,000.[97] Because of the importance of small-scale agriculture there is an unusually large number of self-employed persons as well, both North and South, but they are outside the realm of labor disputes. In Ireland, self-employment in industry, labor-only subcontracting ("grip" or "lump" working), and other forms of self-employment which in Britain have assumed prominence in the building and construction industry, and are appearing in others, [98] have not yet developed to an extent that would influence the employment figures. On the other hand, such practices are an appreciable factor in strikes.

In a country with as small a work force as this, a dramatic effect is produced on the statistics by the presence in one year, or the absence in another, of a single large stoppage of work. There is, therefore, considerable fluctuation in the picture as seen from one year to another, and the average over a fairly lengthy period of years has to be taken to get an average impression at all. Such long-term averages may themselves be misleading due to the great changes in the factors conducive to disputes, not least the economic condition of the country, which are likely to have taken place during it.

In the Republic, the available statistics are superficially more dramatic. For the three years 1964 to 1966 the numbers of days lost annually per employee due to disputes were given for 16 countries by the I.L.O.[99] The Republic's figure is 1.6 working days lost per employee, making the Republic the highest of the 16 countries in time lost because of strikes. In this same period, Italy was next with 1.17 working days lost per employee; the United Kingdom lost 0.19 working days annually per employee, while the United States lost 0.87 working days.

Without further examination this would indicate a strike-prone work force in Ireland. But the lost time has usually, in fact, been concentrated in a single or a few large disputes. In 1964 no less than three quarters of the total lost time was due to a single strike,

---

and Congress has decided to seek amendment of Part III to make them enforceable, e.g., 1962 Annual Report, pp. 167-68.

[96] In June 1965. See *Economic Report on 1965,* Economic Section of Cabinet Offices, June 1966 (H.M.S.O.), Belfast; Northern Ireland Digest of Statistics, March 1966.

[97] 1961 Census.

[98] See report of the Phelps Brown Committee on problems associated with these practices. Cmnd. 3714 (H.M.S.O.), London (1968).

[99] See Donovan, par. 363. See also commentaries in *Trade Union Information,* July 1966, pp. 9-10; December 1966, 12; and April 1967, pp. 8-9. The March issues of the *Irish Statistical Bulletin* give the annual figures for the Republic.

one of nine weeks in the building industry in Dublin. Similarly, in 1965 about three fifths of the total was due to a 10-week strike in printing in Dublin, and another one fifth to a strike and lockout in the nationalized transport industry (C.I.E.). From 1961 to 1966 an average of only 3 1/2 percent of all employees in the Republic were involved in lost-time disputes, compared with 6 1/2 percent in the United Kingdom, 13 percent in Australia, 15 percent in France, and 23 percent in Italy. Lost time due to disputes in 1966 greatly exceeded that of 1965, and the total was due mainly (about 75 percent) to four strikes: one in Dublin docks, one in the E.S.B., one in C.I.E., and an all-Ireland 13-week bank strike.

The figures for 1967 in the Republic were the lowest since 1962, due to the absence of any large dispute, while in the first five months of 1968 the time lost exceeded the total of 183,000 days for the whole of 1967. This again was the result of two disputes, one over pay in the nationalized electricity supply industry (E.S.B.), and the recognition dispute with the E.I. Company, a subsidiary of General Electric.[100] The E.S.B. has a history of disputes, and a formal enquiry into the causes under the chairmanship of the director of the Institute of Economic and Social Research is proceeding at present.

McAuley's analysis [101] of Labour Court and Central Statistics Office reports for the 10 years 1956-1965 produces other interesting data which give a somewhat different picture from the analysis of the last five years of the period. In the 10-year period, some 80 percent of all stoppages lasted less than three weeks. Disputes concerning economic interests, used in a broad sense, accounted for about 40 percent of all stoppages, 68 percent of all workers involved in stoppages, and 73 percent of all time lost as a result. One thing on which all are agreed is that a few major strikes account for a large proportion of the time lost each year.

A notable factor is that a high proportion of stoppages, including major ones, were due to differences in interpretation of agreements entered into by the parties to the dispute. The 1964 building-trades stoppage was a trial of strength to determine whether the 10th Round nationally agreed wage formula precluded other kinds of claims. So also were the 1965 stoppage in printing and the 1966 bank strike.

---

[100] Report of the Minister for Labour, 234 DAIL DEBATES 1563-65, May 21, 1968.

[101] McAuley, "Collective Bargaining and Industrial Disputes in Ireland," *Journal of the Statistical & Social Inquiry Society of Ireland,* paper read on April 14, 1967. Mr. McAuley is Statistics and Economics Officer of the Federated Union of Employers.

Grievance issues appear to account for no less than a third of all strikes, though the number of workers involved is relatively small and the loss of time about 10 percent of the total.

Governmental Services for
Resolution of Labor Disputes

The private arbitration system is little developed in Ireland, though there are instances in both North and South.

The two governments provide a similar range of facilities for preventing disputes and ending those which have broken out, but they do so in different ways. There is very little compulsory adjudication or arbitration [102] in either part of the country, but the services of governmental mediators and an independent tribunal for the hearing of disputes are provided for those who voluntarily use them, and power for inquiries to be conducted into serious disputes is available also.

The Northern Ireland techniques for governmental involvement in labor disputes is virtually identical with that in Britain. In Northern Ireland the Conciliation Service of the Industrial Relations section of the Ministry of Health and Social Services provides skilled civil servant mediators, either on request of the parties to a dispute or on the initiative of the Ministry. On the enactment of the Terms and Conditions of Employment Act (Northern Ireland) 1963 with its extension procedure, an Industrial Court was established on a permanent basis under the Industrial Courts Act, 1919. [103] It is tripartite with a highly qualified counsel as president, and under the 1963 Act it may force an employer or a trade union to arbitrate an issue. The issues are broadly economic and do not involve individual employee grievances. Its arbitration awards are made on "claims" reported to the Ministry by a union or employers' association and not by individuals, although the awards are enforceable only as implied terms of individual workers' contracts. This jurisdiction may not be exercised in connection with terms and conditions covered by any other statutory provision, including Wages Councils.

The Industrial Court also acts as a voluntary adjudication or

---

[102] In this paper I use the term "arbitration" for procedures where the result is binding on the parties to the dispute, whether by operation of law or their prior acceptance, and "adjudication" for all other procedures where there is a trial of the issue and an award or recommendation.

[103] The 1963 enactment and the Conciliation and Arbitration Act 1896 both provide for the use of private conciliators or arbitrators, but this is not often done. See Sams, "Securing Proper Observance of Terms and Conditions of Employment," in Recent Developments in Labour Law, 7 N.I.L.Q. reprint pamphlet, pp. 7, 8 (1968).

arbitration body on request from both parties to a dispute and adjudicates on references to it by the Northern Ireland government of complaints of violation of the Fair Wages Resolution and other matters. Its voluntary adjudication decisions are not necessarily enforceable; but in the latter case administrative sanctions will be applied by the government agency concerned.

Other disagreements on an increasing range of matters in Northern Ireland come within the compulsory jurisdiction of the Industrial Tribunals, originally constituted to determine disputes over the amount of levy an employer had to pay under the Industrial Training Act (Northern Ireland) 1964. Though their jurisdiction now extends to questions of payment of Selective Employment Tax, of notice or pay in lieu of notice that an employee is entitled to receive under the Contracts of Employment legislation, and to other matters, the bulk of their business is the settlement of disputes over payment of redundancy compensation.[104] Its jurisdictions are compulsory, i.e., at the suit of a single party, which may be the government, and are binding.

Disputes between the civil service unions and the Northern Ireland Government may be referred to a Civil Service Arbitration Tribunal established under Ministry of Finance authority on agreed terms of reference; but there are no other governmental tribunals in the labor relations field other than for the police.

Public exposure of the issues in a major dispute can be conclusive in promoting a settlement, and the Minister may order a formal and usually public inquiry under the Industrial Courts Act, 1919. The Court of Inquiry device is used sparingly, in order not to blunt its powerful effect by familiarity. Alternatively, the Minister may order a more informal investigation under the Conciliation and Arbitration Act, 1896.

The Labour Court, established in the Republic under Part II of the Industrial Relations Act, 1946, consists of a full-time chairman, a deputy chairman, two members nominated by Congress and two by the F.U.E. All are appointed by the Minister for Labour, but their conditions of appointment and the restrictions on their removal are intended to ensure their independence of the government.

The Court has its offices in Dublin and normally sits there, with occasional hearings at provincial centers. It may sit in divisions and may utilize assessors. It has power to summon witnesses, to take evidence on oath and to require the production of documents,

---

[104] Contracts of Employment and Redundancy Payments Act (Northern Ireland) 1965.

all on penalty of fine. Its procedure may be informal or formal and is often inquisitorial since a main function is to investigate disputes.

In order to relieve its members from outside pressure, the Court issues only one recommendation or award and gives no indication of division of opinion. Section 17 provides that there shall be no appeal from any decision given within its jurisdiction; but the Supreme Court has held that this applies to its statutory jurisdiction only and not to any consent jurisdiction. Prohibition does not lie against it in respect of its main jurisdiction under Section 67.[105]

The Labour Court combines both a conciliation service and adjudication and arbitration machinery within its framework, under the Industrial Relations Acts 1946 and 1955. Proposals for extension of its powers and scope have been made by the Minister for Labour, and he recently announced that legislation was being drafted.[106]

The services of the Court are activated either on application by one of the parties to a dispute or by the Court itself taking the initiative to intervene. It may do so whenever a trade dispute exists or is apprehended, subject to the limitations in Sections 67 and 71 of the 1946 Act. The limitations in Section 67 exclude certain employments from its scope, such as workers in the electricity supply industry, who come within the scope of the tribunal established under the Electricity Supply Board (E.S.B.) (Superannuation) Act, 1942, to deal with their disputes. The Labour Court may not intervene unless requested by that tribunal.[107] In other cases listed in the section the Court may not intervene of its own accord unless it is of the opinion that the dispute is likely to cause a stoppage of work.

Before the Court attempts to adjudicate on a dispute it usually seeks to mediate through one of its permanent conciliation officers, either to effect a permanent settlement or to obtain a temporary solution pending adjudication by the Court. The conciliation officers are civil servants in the Republic, as they are in the North.

The definition of "trade dispute" in Section 3 is wide enough to enable the Court to investigate virtually any difference between

---

[105] *Branigan* v. *Keady,* [1959] I.R. 283; 291. Supreme Court reversing Haugh J.

[106] On May 21, 1968, 234 DAIL DEBATES. For a review of the work of the Labour Court to the end of 1965 see *Trade Union Information,* December 1966, pp. 2-5.

[107] A major dispute in that industry in 1961 was referred to the Court by the Minister and provoked an outcry from members of the E.S.B. Tribunal. Another occurred in 1965 and the Court intervened at the request of I.C.T.U. despite the initial objections of the E.S.B. based on the statutory position. See *Annual Report of the Labour Court for 1965,* p. 4.

employers and workers and between workers and workers also. It is clear from the text of the rest of the Act that licensed unions of employers and employees are both included in this definition. In its adjudications the court is charged to investigate the issues and "to make a recommendation setting forth its opinion on the merits of the dispute and the terms on which, in the public interest, and with a view to promoting industrial peace, it should be settled, due regard being had to the fairness of the said terms to the parties concerned and the prospect of the said terms being acceptable to them." [108] Reconciling these often diametrically opposed criteria is quite difficult. But there has been a high rate of acceptance of its recommendations, [109] and it is held in general high regard by both sides of industry.

Section 70 gives opportunity for the Court to refer a dispute to one or more arbitrators or to sit itself as an arbitration body, if all the parties to the dispute consent. The parties, especially the unions, rarely do, and there were only 39 such consents to the end of 1965, 23 of them in the last 10 years.

Section 71 provides a power which appears to have been even less frequently used. It applies to situations in which a stoppage has actually occurred and the dispute is not being promoted or assisted by any workers' union. By precluding the Court from "investigating," i. e. adjudicating on, a stoppage to which a workers' union is a party, the draftsmanship of the section appears to add a further limitation on the Court's powers to the apparently exhaustive list of limitations in Section 67. Nevertheless, it does, as in the E.I. dispute itself.

In investigating such an instance the Court must first advertise in the local newspapers its intention to take evidence about the stoppage. Having heard evidence from anyone concerned with the dispute who wishes to testify, the Court may make either a recommendation (nonbinding), as in other investigations, or an award.[110] Such an award binds every employer within its application for three months from the date on which it is made. It is an offense punishable by fine for him to employ or agree to employ, during that period, any worker under conditions inconsistent with its terms.

The effect of this provision is wider than might appear at first

---

[108] Industrial Relations Act, 1946, Section 68(1).

[109] An average of around 85 percent of all its recommendations over the years. See its Annual Reports; McAuley, *op. cit.,* note 101 *supra.*

[110] Award must not be inconsistent with the terms of "a registered employment agreement." Section 71 (2) (c) (iii). Does this mean any such agreement, or only one applying to that industry? The section does not indicate.

sight. By Section 3, for the purposes of this Act "trade union" is confined to a body which holds a negotiating license, so that a stoppage by workers organized in a union without a negotiating license is as much within its compass as a stoppage by those who are unorganized. Mortished, the first chairman of the Court, thought this applied also to unofficial stoppages by members of a union which has a negotiating license, and his view has been quoted by other writers.[111] But the way in which such terms as "promoting or assisting" have been interpreted in unemployment benefit legislation leaves room for doubt. Though "trade dispute" is defined, "stoppage of work" is not. Does it include a "work to rule," which stops the plant even though there is no breach of contract?

The penalty does not apply to the workers, so there is no compulsion on them to return to work other than the knowledge that for three months they cannot get the employer to pay more than the award; but it will be remembered that they and their unlicensed unions are deprived of the protection of Sections 2, 3, and 4 of the 1906 Act.[112]

Though most of the adjudication of labor disputes in the private sector of the economy, and much of that in the public, is centered on the Labour Court, the government in the past has kept the civil service and some state-controlled industries from its purview. As a result, employees in the civil service, the Electricity Supply Board, and other public bodies come under other conciliation and arbitration tribunals, ranging from voluntary ones in the national air lines and elsewhere to statutory ones for the police[113] and for employees of the Electricity Supply Board.[114]

The Industrial Relations Act, 1946, having repealed the Conciliation and Arbitration Act, 1896, and the Industrial Court Act, 1919, provided power for investigations by the Labour Court in labor disputes, but did not provide for the Minister to order other kinds of general inquiry or investigation. However, the techniques of public inquiry have been activated recently, following a recommendation of the National Industrial Economic Council (N.I.E.C.), and currently inquiries into labor relations in the E.S.B. and in Bord na Móna are taking place under "general Ministerial powers." [115]

---

[111] Mortished, op cit., note 93 supra, at p. 84.

[112] By the Trade Union Act, 1941, Section 11.

[113] Section 13 of the Garda Siochana Act, 1924, which parallels the 1919 Act in the United Kingdom.

[114] E.S.B. (Superannuation) Act, 1942, Section 9.

[115] Minister for Labour on May 21, 1968, 234 DAIL DEBATES 1566.

Direction of Reform in the Republic

Parallel to the developing demand in Britain for standard fast and effective grievance procedures[116] has been a similar realization in the Republic of the needless loss of time caused by disputes of right, in the sense not only of individual grievances but of general differences on economic issues, believed of fundamental principle, in interpretation of national or other agreements.[117] This has produced a demand for a tribunal to decide rights issues and also has led to incorporation into new-type productivity "contracts," which appear to be a feature of the 11th Round [118] of binding grievance procedures.[119] The trends on both sides of the Irish Sea have been influenced, of course, by developments in this field at the fiftieth and fifty-first sessions of the I.L.O. in 1966 and 1967, and the "Recommendation of the Examination of Grievances within the Undertaking" of the latter session. Provisions establishing such a tribunal in the Republic will no doubt appear in the Minister's Bill for the reform of industrial relations law.

Though the Donovan Commission gave less attention to grievance procedures in general and proposed a different solution [120] from that in the Republic of Ireland, there has been special concentration recently in both countries on unnecessary disputes caused by management dismissals for alleged cause.

Again, both owe much to the I.L.O.'s recommendation on the subject (No. 119 of 1963). In 1966 the Federal Union of Employers and I.C.T.U. established a joint committee to consider what to do about the problem,[121] but the report has not yet been made.

Redundancy payments legislation belongs largely to a consideration of manpower policies, but it has played an important part in avoiding disputes over dismissals, especially large-scale ones in the United Kingdom. There, opposition to laying off men and demands

---

[116] See, e.g., Donovan, pars. 452-57, and Royal Commission Research Papers nos. 2 (Parts I and II); 8 (Study No. 2); 10, p. 23.

[117] E.g., the National Employer-Labour Conference proposals for subcommittees on grievance procedures and on communication within the undertaking, 1964, and subsequent developments through the Irish National Productivity Committee. See I.C.T.U. Annual Reports, 1964; 1965, p. 61; 1966, p. 72; 1967, p. 85.

[118] See I.C.T.U. Annual Report 1967, 239; 1968, 44.

[119] Particularly those with the nationalized airline (Aer Lingus), with Roadstore (a major firm in the building and construction industry) with Guinness, with the Dublin Port & Docks Board, with Esso, and with John Jameson & Son Ltd. See 234 DAIL DEBATES 1567-68 (1968). The Aer Lingus agreement is reproduced in *Trade Union Information*, December 1966, pp. 10-11.

[120] Donovan, pars. 530-44; 1056-60. See also the British Ministry of Labour's report "Dismissals Procedures" (H.M.S.O.), London, 1967.

[121] I.C.T.U. Annual Report 1967, p. 93.

for work sharing, which previously had often produced major stoppages, were translated by the lump-sum compensation into redundancy-payments mindedness in trade union officials and their members alike. However, indications are that the honeymoon period of redundancy compensation is over, and that attention is turning again to preventing layoffs.

The Irish Republic enacted somewhat similar legislation, [122] effective January 1968, and can expect a somewhat similar experience despite differences in principle in their scheme.

Part of the same legislation in the United Kingdom [123] has provision for minimum periods of notice, ranging from one week to four, to be given employees. Though far less than the periods of notice required in some European continental countries, this could reduce the number of disputes somewhat. There is much merit in the standard contractual provisions in American labor agreements that forbid discipline, suspension, or discharge of employees, "except for just cause," and provide for enforceable reinstatement orders. But the private arbitration system that underpins these employee protections is unknown in Ireland and elsewhere in Europe and is not likely to develop there. No legislation on notice or unjust dismissals has been introduced in the Republic, but it may be expected soon, following proposals by the Department of Labour in 1968.

---

[122] Redundancy Payments Act, 1967.
[123] Contracts of Employment and Redundancy Payments Act (Northern Ireland) 1965, the close equivalent of the Contracts of Employment Act 1963 and the Redundancy Payments Act 1965 in Britain.

PART V

Wages and Employment Benefits in Western Europe and the United States

This part is concerned first with comparisons of methods of remunerating workers for their labors in the United States and Western Europe. A number of preliminary questions intrude. What is the interplay between the private process of negotiating employment and related benefits through collective bargaining, or their establishment by unilateral employer action, and the political process of enacting legislation to the same end? Are there greater efficiencies in the acquisition and consumption of goods and utilization of services when these are purchased mainly through the contents of the wage or salary check or when such goods and services are made available by tax-supported and government-administered benefits, grants, allowances, or subsidies? Peter Henle, Chief Economist of the U. S. Bureau of Labor Statistics, warns, *inter alia,* of likely error in viewing European labor costs solely in terms of comparative average weekly take-home pay.

Samuel C. Silkin, Q. C., M. P., discusses the rationale of the current British Prices and Incomes Policy. Freely conceding that such a policy inhibits freedom of private wage determination through collective bargaining, he seeks to justify wage and price controls as a short-term mechanism to rectify immediate national economic problems.

Within an EEC context, Dr. Leo H. J. Crijns analyzes the potential conflict between national or Community economic and social goals and the privacy of wage determination. He asserts that the initiative for disruption is reciprocal; that just as the results of private wage negotiations may block governmental attainment of articulated social and economic aims, so too may inadequate governmental policy and action frustrate constructive collective bargaining.

Dr. Julius Rezler discusses the uses of the official British Prices and Incomes Policy to encourage "productivity bargaining" and de-

305

scribes American experiences in official peacetime prices and incomes policies and in productivity bargaining.

Finally, Dr. G. M. J. Veldkamp narrates and analyzes the obstacles to harmonizing social security systems of the EEC nations to accommodate to the free mobility of workers in the Common Market. As complex as might be the present difficulties in such harmonization efforts, the acceptance of the United Kingdom, the Irish Republic, Denmark, and Norway will introduce more variations of domestic social security systems and thus there will be more hurdles to scale. Some of the Loyola conferees sought to push Dr. Veldkamp into advocacy of a single Common Market social security system with standardized employer contributions and uniform character and scale of benefits. But his diplomatic experience stood him in good stead and he went no further, even "off the record," than the conclusions expressed in his article.

TRENDS IN LABOR COMPENSATION: UNITED STATES AND WESTERN EUROPE

By Peter Henle

In increasing numbers, business firms have been crossing national boundaries to establish subsidiaries, working partners, and affiliates. The effect has been a much closer knitting together of the economies of the United States and Western Europe. This changing economic ownership has been one factor producing changing national and international policies affecting trade, tariffs, and investment.

U. S. firms operating in Western Europe employ 2.5 million workers with an annual payroll of nearly $9-billion, and these numbers have been growing. These figures tell the importance of having available adequate information comparing employee compensation and labor costs in the United States and Western Europe. Such information is necessary to meet the needs of individual companies with foreign investments, and to guide public and private decisions involving questions of international trade and balance of payments.

The purpose of this paper is to lay the groundwork for an understanding of the compensation problems encountered by American firms operating in Western Europe. To begin with, the concept of compensation will be defined. Second, basic information on trends and current practices in the United States will be presented. Finally, comparisons of compensation practices and expenditures among the countries of Western Europe and the United States will be made.

THE COMPENSATION CONCEPT

What is meant by "labor compensation"? Do we mean basic wage rates or weekly earnings? Do we mean a worker's total income? Or an employer's total labor cost?

The word "compensation" has no universally accepted definition. In the United States, it generally means total payments to employees — straight-time wages plus wage supplements, or "fringe benefits." To many Europeans the very word itself is misleading, suggesting indemnities for injury. Instead, they use the phrase "total remuneration" to refer to the combined cost of wages and supplementary employee benefits.

The Concept in the United States

In this country, the concept of "total compensation" is based on employer expenditures. These may be cash payments directly to employees or indirect payments on behalf of employees for insurance premiums or into special funds. Compensation is not considered in terms of direct income of workers and thus avoids the thorny problem — particularly difficult in international comparisons — of placing a price tag on certain indirect benefits received by workers. The cost to the employer is the basic consideration.

However, compensation is not equivalent to total labor cost, which includes additional employer expenditures for such items as training, recruitment, and certain welfare services.

Direct payments to employees constitute the overwhelming share of total compensation in the United States. (See table below.) Such direct payments consist not only of straight-time pay for time worked but also include other types of direct payments. In 1966, almost 90 percent of total private nonfarm compensation was in the form of direct payments — almost 81 percent as straight-time pay for all time worked, and 9 percent divided among various supplementary payments. The two most significant groups of direct supplementary or "fringe benefit" payments are:

Paid leave. This includes payments to employees for various types of paid leave — vacations, holidays, military duty, and personal reasons such as funeral leave.

Premium pay. Payments by employers for work performed at specific times or under specific conditions — for overtime, work on holidays, shift differentials, and hazardous work.

Indirect payments by American employers amounted to 10 percent of total compensation in 1966, and were divided almost equally between the two following types of supplementary or "fringe benefit" payments:

Private employee benefit plans or payments for various welfare benefits — pension, health, life insurance, unemployment. This group also includes profit-sharing and thrift plans or savings plans.

Government programs with benefits financed, at least in part, by employer payments. Typical are employers' taxes under the Old Age, Survivors, Disability and Health Insurance system (or Social Security System, as it is commonly known), taxes for unemployment insurance, and required payments for workmen's compensation.

Percent Distribution of Compensation for All Employees in the Private Nonagricultural Economy, 1966, United States

	Total nonagri- cultural	Total manufac- turing
Total expenditures	100.0	100.0
Direct payments	89.9	89.2
Straight-time pay (all time worked)	80.6	78.2
Supplements or "fringe"	9.3	11.0
Paid leave	5.6	6.3
Vacations.............	3.1	3.5
Holidays..............	1.9	2.2
Other leave	.6	.6
Premium pay	2.4	3.5
Nonproduction bonuses	1.2	1.3
Indirect payments	10.1	10.8
Legally required	5.1	4.9
Social Security	3.1	3.0
Unemployment Insurance ...	1.1	1.1
Other	.9	.8
Private benefit plans	5.0	5.9
Life, health insurance	2.1	2.6
Pensions	2.5	2.9
Other	.4	.4

International Standards

The need for internationally comparable concepts and data on this question was recognized at the ILO's Eleventh International Conference of Labour Statistics in October 1966. Members from 34 countries as well as representatives of the European Economic Community and the High Authority of the European Coal and Steel Community discussed varying labor-cost concepts and compensation practices.

Despite many differences among countries, certain basic agreements were reached. The resolution which was adopted stated that "for purposes of labour-cost statistics, labour cost is the cost incurred by the employer in the employment of labour." While this is hardly a startling conclusion, in effect it represents agreement that, whether called "total compensation" as in the United States or "total remuneration" as in Europe, the underlying concept is identical.

This meeting also identified specific components of labor cost as "direct" or "indirect" and listed them in some detail under 10 major headings in the International Standard Classification of Labour Cost as:

Direct Labour Costs

I. Direct Wages and Salaries.
II. Remuneration for Time not Worked.
III. Bonuses and Gratuities.
IV. Food, Drink, Fuel and Other Payments in Kind.

Indirect Labour Costs

V. Cost of Workers' Housing Borne by Employers.
VI. Employers' Social Security Expenditures.
VII. Cost of Vocational Training.
VIII. Cost of Welfare Services.
IX. Labour Cost Not Elsewhere Classified.
X. Taxes Regarded as Labour Cost.

The range of items included as labor cost is far broader than the concept of total compensation or total remuneration with which this paper is primarily concerned. Thus, several items listed under indirect costs — training and welfare services, for example — usually would not be considered as a part of total compensation.

U. S. EXPERIENCE

Since the end of World War II, the level of U. S. compensation has risen markedly — in terms of both straight-time wages and wage supplements. Moreover, supplementary wage payments — or fringe benefits — have increased far more sharply than the basic wage rates. As a result, although still less than in most of Western Europe, wage supplements have become a constantly rising proportion of total compensation in this country.

Not too long ago, almost all of the "return to labor" in the United States was in the form of straight-time pay. In 1935, the year the Social Security Act was passed, the amount spent on supplementary wage payments or "fringe benefits" was less than 1 percent of wages. Today, direct and indirect wage supplements account for over 20 percent of total compensation expenditures in the private nonagricultural economy.

Fringe benefits for the blue-collar worker did not begin to develop until after 1939. During World War II, the government's wage stabilization program accelerated this development because "fringes" were not controlled as strictly as wage rates. The 1950s witnessed a phenomenal growth in employee benefit plans, and this trend continued in the 1960s. In 1966 and 1967, eight out of every 10 major collective bargaining settlements involved new or liberalized fringe benefits. Changes in health and retirement plans were made in 70 percent of settlements. New or liberalized provisions for pension plans appeared in roughly half the settlements, while paid vacations were affected in slightly more than 30 percent of the cases.

Although the emphasis in this country has been on the development of benefits through collective bargaining or unilateral employer action, statutory action also has been involved. The first type of employee benefit generally available was achieved through state laws on workmen's compensation developed about 1910. Federal social security programs and a law mandating premium pay for overtime work were adopted during the 1930s. The growth of private pension plans has been assisted by special tax legislation and regulations. In the mid-1960s, Medicare and Medicaid health programs for the aged and needy were added to the basic federal social security program.

Medicare and Medicaid serve to illustrate a relatively recent trend in this country toward stregthening — and adding to — legislation providing employee benefits. At the same time, in a shift of emphasis in the other direction, many European collective bargaining agreements increasingly include provisions dealing with wage supplements.

Two of the major types of fringe benefits which have grown so rapidly since World War II merit discussion — paid leave and private employee benefit plans.

Paid Leave

Paid leisure represents a post-World War II phenomenon for most workers in this country. A 1940 study disclosed that only about one fourth of union members were eligible for annual vacation, and for most of these the maximum vacation period was one week. Although major holidays were frequently observed throughout industry, the practice of providing holiday pay for hourly rated employees was quite rare.

Today, three out of four major bargaining agreements provide a maximum vacation of four or more weeks. A sizable number of agreements made in 1966 and 1967 provided a basic vacation allowance of five weeks or longer and some called for six weeks of vacation after 30 years of service. Similarly, about 90 percent of the workers covered were entitled to paid holidays. Thirty percent of the agreements granted eight days, and another 20 percent nine days or more.

It is interesting to note that more holidays are being fitted to the desire for longer periods of leisure. For example, the day before Christmas is a holiday (or half holiday) in almost one third of all major agreements, the day after Thanksgiving in over one sixth. Some agreements simply provide for additional holidays, designated annually to fit the mutual convenience of workers and employers. To provide more three-day weekends, Congress enacted legislation in June 1968 that would move four of the traditional American holidays to specifically designated Mondays — to become effective in 1971.

Private Employee Benefit Plans

Just as the development of paid leave reflects the worker's search for leisure, the growth of private benefit plans reflects his search for greater economic security. If government programs had fully met the need for greater economic security against the hazards of illness, old age, and unemployment, private employee benefit plans would never have attained their present importance. But in each case — whether it be social security, unemployment insurance, or medical care — government programs have provided only the fundamentals of protection to all citizens, or have been confined to a particular group of citizens (the elderly in the case of Medicare, for example).

Health and Other Insurance Plans

Health insurance for employees and dependents is perhaps the most rapidly changing fringe item. In this area no national program was developed through legislation until the 1965 amendments to the Social Security Act introduced Medicare and Medicaid — and, as work-related benefits, these apply only to workers still on the job who are over 65.

Today, nine out of every 10 urban plant workers in this country are covered by formal provisions for life, hospitalization, and surgical insurance paid for — at least in part — by the employer. Most plans provide protection also for dependents of employees. About eight out of 10 such workers are protected by medical insurance and some form of sickness and accident insurance or sick leave. Six out of every 10 are covered by accidental death and dismemberment insurance, and over four out of 10 by major medical or catastrophe insurance.

Just as prevalent as hospital benefits are death benefits, which are usually provided through group life insurance. Over 90 percent of all urban plantworkers have such protection, and coverage increasingly is being extended to laid-off workers. Retired employees are also frequently covered, and — to a lesser extent — the workers' dependents. Although the amount of coverage varies widely, the median is around one year's earnings.

Most of the expansion of health and insurance plans has been financed by the employers. Life, hospitalization, and surgical insurance and retirement plans currently are provided to over 60 percent of plant workers in the United States without any part of the cost being deducted from the worker's wages.

Pension and Retirement Plans

The expansion of retirement plans is among the major developments in the labor compensation structure of this country since World War II. Between 1950 and 1966, the number of employees covered by private plans grew from almost 10 million to 26-1/2 million and the amount of benefit payments from $370-million to $3.7-billion annually.

The level of retirement benefits continues to rise, but most workers under negotiated plans must still look to federal Social Security for the greater part of their retirement income. However, the emphasis in the public program is necessarily placed on basic retirement benefits for all members of the labor force. Although it provides the worker with low earnings a relatively larger benefit than the worker with higher earnings, the amount is still small. Consequently, the need continues for supplementary private pension plans to yield a more satisfactory level of retirement income.

In 1967, nearly three out of every four plant workers in metropolitan areas were covered by private retirement plans, compared to two out of three in 1960. In the main, pension plans do not require worker contributions; in fact, about 85 percent of plant workers under private retirement plans in 1967 did not have to contribute toward these plans.

The Current Situation

The worker of today obviously is better off than his counterpart of 20 years earlier. During the first postwar decade, 1947-1957, employee compensation per man-hour rose 37 percent in real terms; that is, after adjusting for price changes. The next decade, 1957-1967, witnessed a continued substantial rise, but not quite as large — 28 percent. In terms of wages and salaries alone, the growth during both decades is smaller and the slackening after 1957 more pronounced. In contrast, the value in real terms of wage supplements more than doubled in both decades (see table below).

Increase in Real Employee Compensation per Man-Hour

	Total (%)	Wages and salaries (%)	Supplements (%)
All private nonfarm			
1947-1957	37	34	121
1957-1967	28	20	131
All manufacturing			
1947-1957	45	41	98
1957-1967	26	21	86

The first economy-wide survey[1] of total compensation shows that in 1966 all nonfarm employees received an average of $3.40 per hour. Manufacturing employees received an average of $3.67 an hour and nonmanufacturing employees $3.23.

About 81 percent of total compensation in 1966 was in the form of straight-time pay for all hours worked. Another 9 percent was for direct wage supplements; 5-1/2 percent for paid leave, 2-1/2 percent for premium pay, and over 1 percent for nonproduction bonuses. The remaining 10 percent of total compensation was in the form of indirect wage supplements, with legally required benefits accounting for 5 percent and private benefit plans the other 5 percent.

For employees in manufacturing, the distribution of direct payments differed somewhat from that for all employees. Straight-time pay accounted for a somewhat smaller share of total compensation and wage supplements a somewhat larger share, chiefly because more compensation was received from premium pay, paid vacations, and private employee-benefit plans (see table, p. 309).

---

[1] *Employee Compensation and Payroll Hours in the Private Nonagricultural Economy, 1966;* U.S.D.L. 8902, August 22, 1968.

EUROPEAN COMPENSATION PRACTICES

As in the United States, European compensation or remuneration practices are set by a combination of collective bargaining, legislation, and custom. However, supplementary wage benefits developed earlier in Europe. Also, while collective bargaining has played the dominant role in securing employee benefits in the United States, legislation has determined prevailing practice more frequently in most European countries. For these reasons, wage supplements or fringe benefits are a more important share of compensation in many European countries than in the United States. Many benefits common in other countries do not exist at all, or occur only infrequently, in this country. To complicate the situation further, supplementary benefits differ markedly among the various countries.

One way of viewing the differences in compensation practices is to consider a hypothetical employee who is given his choice of country in which to work — the United States or one in Western Europe. Suppose he is paid the same basic weekly wage in terms of purchasing power no matter which country he chose. Suppose further that his supplementary compensation — or fringe benefits — vary with the prevailing practice of the country selected. On this basis, what country would he prefer?

It would not be an easy choice. From an employee's point of view, no single country appears to be most liberal with respect to all types of fringe benefits. The decision undoubtedly would depend upon the requirements of the individual's job, his own personal preferences among the many supplementary benefits, and whether he was near the beginning or the end of his working life.

If he were interested in accumulating additional income and was willing to work overtime to do so, he would lean toward the United States because none of the Western European countries requires by law — as does the United States — the payment of time and one-half for all overtime hours over 40. In France, a premium of 25 percent must be paid for the first eight hours of overtime; this rises to 50 percent for all hours over 48. In the United Kingdom, Belgium and the Netherlands, a 25-percent premium is usually paid for the first two hours of overtime daily and 50 percent thereafter. The statutory premium is 25 percent in Germany, but many collective agreements provide for overtime pay up to 50 percent. In Italy, the statutory premium is only 20 percent for the first two hours and 30 percent for additional hours, but in practice the rate is usually higher.

If, on the other hand, our mythical worker were more interested in leisure, he would be facing a dilemma. In most European countries, the standard workweek remains above 40 hours, with some averaging as high as 46. On the other hand, practices with respect to vacations and, in particular, holidays provide greater leisure. The European standard, generally based on legislation, provides higher minimum vacations, but many American workers have been able to achieve vacation arrangements above the European standard through collective bargaining.

On both continents, the length of the vacation may vary depending on age and length of service and also may differ for blue- and white-collar workers. The legal minimum in Germany is 15 working days up to age 35 and 18 working days thereafter. Many collective agreements provide for longer periods, based mainly on seniority. About three fourths of all workers in France receive a four-week vacation, three weeks of which are required by law. Depending on continuous service, blue-collar workers in Italy usually receive from 12 to 18 days and white-collar workers from 15 to 30 days. And practically all workers in the United Kingdom receive a minimum of two weeks.

No matter how successfully American workers may have bargained for vacations, very few receive the equivalent of what is provided by legislation in Belgium — a vacation bonus which doubles the worker's earnings during his vacation period. Such bonuses are also often provided in the Netherlands and have been obtained by some unions in Germany.

With respect to paid holidays, Italy provides the most — 16 by law plus an additional day that is specified in most collective agreements. German workers are legally given from 10 to 12 paid holidays, with the exact number set by each state. Workers in France have 11 national holidays, but usually are paid only for five; Belgian workers receive 10 legal holidays; and workers in the United Kingdom generally are entitled to a minimum of six.

When it comes to the various types of social security or insurance programs, the European social security system generally provides broader protection than in this country. Supplementation of statutory old age, medical, and health benefits varies from country to country, but is generally not as great as in the United States. Family allowances are unknown in the United States, but are included in the social security systems of the United Kingdom and Common Market countries, with the method of financing varying by country.

Also, European workers often are entitled by law to other benefits, some of which are not common in the United States. Italian workers receive a Christmas bonus equal to one month's earnings. Employers in Belgium also frequently grant annual bonuses, sometimes in return for no-strike agreements. Italian employers are required by law to increase wages and salaries as the cost-of-living index rises, and cost-of-living increases are also usually provided in Belgium, France, and Luxembourg.

Presented with these assortments of supplementary benefits, our mythical employee understandably might be quite indecisive if he were asked to choose a country for its supplementary benefits. Perhaps business firms are sometimes equally confused in planning their compensation programs for plants in Western Europe.

INTERNATIONAL COMPARISONS

Bearing in mind these differences in compensation practices as well as the glaring deficiencies in available data, what useful conclusions can we draw from comparing the level and trend of compensation in the United States with Western Europe?

Ideally, data should be available to permit comparisons over an extended period of time covering all elements of compensation for the total economy, as well as for specific industries. Such statistics are needed on a per-hour and per-unit-of-output basis. Realistically, we shall have to settle for incomplete data generally covering limited groups of employees over limited periods of time. Often, the information is for wages only, without supplements, and certain supplements are included as wages in some countries but not in others.

Nonetheless, data are available and, with all their limitations, are useful as guides for making international comparisons of compensation. We shall begin with some observations concerning the simplest measure available, average hourly earnings, move on to international comparisons of the ratio of supplements to total compensation, and then to one of the most difficult but essential of all measures — unit labor costs.

Average Hourly Earnings

Obviously, data on average hourly earnings for production (wage) workers in manufacturing are a very incomplete indication of total compensation in view of their limited coverage and exclusion of many wage supplements. Yet only by focusing on such a narrow indicator is sufficient data available for comparisons over time.

The relevant data are given in the table below. It indicates that in 1967 wage earners in manufacturing averaged $2.83 in the United States. Converted to U. S. currency units at official exchange rates, the average was $1.15 in Germany, $1.05 in Belgium, $1.02 in the Netherlands, 84 cents in France, 68 cents in Italy, and $1.35 for male wage earners and 78 cents for female wage earners in the United Kingdom. (A combined figure for both sexes is not available for the United Kingdom.)

Average Hourly Earnings of Wage Earners in Manufacturing in the United States, United Kingdom, and Common Market Countries, 1957 and 1967, and Percent Change in Average Hourly Earnings, Consumer Prices, and Average Hourly Real Earnings, 1957-67

Country	Average hourly earnings in national currency units			Average hourly earnings in U.S. dollars, 1967
	Currency unit	1957	1967	
United States....	dollar	2.05	2.83	2.83
Belgium	franc	27.1 [2]	52.3 [3]	1.05
France	new franc	2.015	4.13 [2]	.84
Germany (F.R.)..	DM	2.09	4.58	1.15
Italy	lira	207.	425. [3]	.68
Netherlands	guilder	1.56	3.68 [3]	1.02
United Kingdom:				
Men	pence	65.3	116.0	1.35
Women........	pence	38.0	66.6	.78

Country	Percent change, 1957-1967			1967 official exchange rates (currency units per U.S. dollar)
	Average hourly earnings (in national currency units)	Consumer prices	Average hourly real earnings [1]	
United States....	38.0	18.7	16.3	–––
Belgium	93.0	25.0	54.4	50.0
France	104.5	60.5	27.4	4.937
Germany (F.R.)..	119.1	26.1	73.8	4.0
Italy	105.3	41.2	45.4	625.
Netherlands	135.9	40.	68.5	3.62
United Kingdom:				
Men	77.6	32.5	34.0	85.7 [4]
Women........	75.3	32.5	32.3	85.7 [4]

[1] Nominal earnings adjusted by the change in consumer prices.
[2] Estimated by projecting the rate of change in adjacent years.
[3] Estimated from data for part of 1967.

[4] Exchange rate prior to November 1967 devaluation.

Source: *Bulletin of Labour Statistics* (Geneva: International Labor Office) and national publications.

From 1957 to 1967, average hourly earnings of wage earners in manufacturing increased by a moderate 38 percent in the United States, compared with increases of over 75 percent in the United Kingdom, 90 percent in Belgium, 105 percent in France and Italy, 120 percent in Germany, and 136 percent in the Netherlands. However, these increases in average hourly earnings do not represent equivalent advances in workers' purchasing power, as they have not been adjusted for price increases. In Germany and the Netherlands, where the rises in consumer prices were relatively moderate, real earnings increased by approximately 70 percent during the decade. For other European countries, the increase in purchasing power — as measured by average hourly earnings alone — was less; but in no country was it as low as the 16 percent for the United States.

Hourly earnings figures converted to a common currency unit at official exchange rates are inadequate indicators of either total hourly compensation or total labor costs. Earnings statistics generally include basic wages, premium pay, and paid leave for wage earners — but exclude similar payments to salaried workers, payments of various welfare benefits, payroll taxes paid by employers, and other employer costs usually considered part of total compensation. Such figures consequently are inadequate guides to the payments by employers to labor as a factor of production and throw little light on inter-country differences in total compensation or unit labor costs.

Total Compensation

On the question of international comparisons of total compensation, definitive answers will have to await more complete data, but some important clues are provided by a recently published study of the Swedish Employers' Confederation.[2] According to this study, the proportion of indirect labor costs to total labor costs ranges from a low of 12 percent in Great Britain and 17 percent in the United States to a high of about 50 percent in Italy. In France, indirect costs account for 41 percent of total costs, while the ratio is about 32 percent in Belgium, the Netherlands, and Germany. The figures in this study relate to industrial enterprises (mining, manufacturing, and construction) and represent averages for the years 1958-1963.

These figures may be misleading in at least one important re-

---

[2] *Direct and Total Wage Costs for Workers, International Survey, 1958-66.* Swedish Employers' Confederation, Statistical Bureau, Stockholm, October 1967. It should be noted that the definition of "direct" costs used in this study does not quite match that used in the United States since it excludes paid leave. Also, the study refers to total labor costs which include many expenditures such as training and recruitment costs which are not part of total compensation as generally defined.

spect. In measuring government programs of wage supplements, general revenue financing is not counted as part of total compensation or labor costs, while payroll taxes are included. Thus, the low proportion of fringe to total costs in the United Kingdom — only 12 percent — is undoubtedly due in part to the fact that the National Health Service Insurance Plan is financed from general revenues rather than from payroll taxes. Similarly, family allowances in France are financed entirely by payroll taxes, while such allowances in Germany are financed from general revenues.

Unit Labor Costs

For a number of years the Bureau of Labor Statistics has prepared unit labor cost indexes for manufacturing in the major industrial countries. From 1957 to 1967, for all employees, unit labor costs rose only 11 percent in the United States but substantially more in Western Europe — from 23 percent in Italy to about 45 percent in France and the Netherlands. These figures are presented in the table below on both a national-currency and a U. S. dollar basis. The French devaluations of the late 1950s, for example, have the effect of converting a 47-percent increase on a national-currency basis to only a 13-percent advance on a U. S. dollar basis.

Percent Change in Unit Labor Cost in Manufacturing in the United States, France, Germany (F.R.), Italy, the Netherlands, and the United Kingdom, 1957-67

Country	National currency basis		U.S. dollar basis [1]	
	All employees	Wage earners	All employees	Wage earners
United States [2]	11.4	4.6	11.4	4.6
France	47.2	n.a.	13.3	n.a.
Germany (F.R.)	34.6	23.9 [3]	41.4	30.1 [3]
Italy	22.5 [4]	6.1	22.5 [4]	6.1
Netherlands	44.3	n.a.	52.6	n.a.
United Kingdom	31.7	23.1 [3]	29.3	20.9 [3]

[1] Adjusted for changes in the official or commercial exchange rate.

[2] Data based on Department of Commerce, Office of Business Economics output data.

[3] Data for 1967 estimated on the basis of the 1966-67 change for all employees.

[4] Data for 1967 estimated on the basis of the 1966-67 change for wage earners.

Source: *Unit Labor Cost in Manufacturing, Trends in Nine Countries, 1950-65*, as amended (U.S. Department of Labor, Bureau of Labor Statistics, Bulletin 1518, 1966).

A different picture emerges if unit labor costs are computed for wage earners alone. On this basis, manufacturing unit labor costs in the United States increased less than 5 percent between 1957 and 1967 even though average hourly earnings rose 38 percent during the same 10 years. Figures are not available for all the other European countries but those for which we do have data show a larger rise than in the United States — substantially greater in the United Kingdom and Germany but only slightly greater in Italy. For all three countries, unit labor costs for wage earners increased less than for all employees.

These figures, indicating changes in unit labor costs over time, are useful for determining whether labor costs in the United States are increasing or decreasing in relation to other industrial countries. They do not reflect country differences in the level of unit labor costs. Such absolute comparisons are much more difficult to develop largely because of differences in the final output of industries in different countries, since labor-input (and thus cost) requirements vary greatly from one product to another.

The Iron and Steel Industry

The Bureau recently released its first comparison of absolute unit labor costs in a study[3] relating to the primary iron and steel industry of the United States and the three largest steel producing countries of Western Europe — France, Germany, and the United Kingdom. The study is based on 1964 data, the latest year for which the necessary information is available, but trends in the four countries since then indicate little relative change in the ratios developed for 1964.

The study compares output per man-hour and hourly labor cost as well as unit labor cost in the United States and the three European countries, providing information on the relative standing of the four countries in each of these respects. Since data limitations prevented the development of precise comparisons, the results for the countries of Western Europe are presented as ranges of high to low estimates in the table below.

---

[3] *An International Comparison of Unit Labor Cost in the Iron and Steel Industry, 1964: United States, France, Germany, United Kingdom*, BLS Bulletin No. 1580, 1968.

Iron and Steel Industry:[1] Hourly Earnings, Labor Costs, Productivity, and Unit Labor Costs in the United States, France, Germany, and the United Kingdom, 1964

Country	Average hourly earnings of wage earners [2]	Average hourly labor costs [2]	
		Wage earners	All employees
United States ...	$3.43	$4.36	$4.63

	(Index: U.S. = 100)					
	Maxi-mum	Mini-mum	Maxi-mum	Mini-mum	Maxi-mum	Mini-mum
France	22.2	22.2	32.1	31.7	34.6	33.9
Germany (F.R.) ..	33.5	31.5	38.8	36.8	38.9	36.5
United Kingdom..	33.8	32.9	30.7	30.0	29.6	28.7

Country	Man-hours per ton of output for all employees	Unit labor cost per short ton for all employees
United States ...	12.70	$58.77

	(Index: U.S. = 100)		
	Maximum	Minimum	Maximum	Minimum
France	208.0	195.0	71.9	66.3
Germany (F.R.) ..	184.5	158.0	71.7	57.8
United Kingdom..	216.7	199.5	64.1	57.4

Exchange rate: U.S. dollar = 4.90 new francs, 3.977 deutsche marks, 0.3584 pounds.

[1] As defined in the United States except that wire and wire products are excluded in the United Kingdom and wheels and axles in Germany.

[2] Covers hours worked only. Average hourly earnings include direct wage supplements except pay for time not worked; labor costs include both direct and indirect supplements as well as other employee costs.

Source: *An International Comparison of Unit Labor Costs in the Iron and Steel Industry, 1964: United States, France, Germany, United Kingdom* (U.S. Department of Labor, Bureau of Labor Statistics, Bulletin 1580, 1968).

Using the midpoints of these ranges permits review of the relations among the four major steel-producing countries, starting with data on average earnings and building step by step to a comparison of unit labor costs. In 1964, average hourly earnings of wage workers in the U. S. iron and steel industry were $3.43. Average hourly earnings in Germany and the United Kingdom were about one third the U. S. level, and in France one fourth the U. S. level.

The addition of supplementary benefits and other employment costs yields a total hourly labor cost figure of $4.36 per wage earner in the United States. Hourly labor cost per wage worker was 38 percent of the U. S. level, in Germany, 32 percent in France, and 30 percent in the United Kingdom.

When hourly costs for salaried workers are added, total labor cost in the United States in 1964 increases to $4.63. The addition of salaried worker costs increases the relative labor-cost level in France to 34 percent of the U.S. figure. However, the relative cost in Germany remains at 38 percent of the U.S. level and declines slightly to 29 percent in the United Kingdom.

Based on hourly earnings of wage earners alone, the French iron and steel industry appears to have a competitive advantage over both Germany and the United Kingdom. Based on total hourly labor costs for all workers, the United Kingdom has the advantage. But, in all three European countries, hourly costs are still well below the U. S. level.

The lower hourly-labor-cost advantage in these countries, however, is partially offset by higher man-hour requirements per ton of output. About twice as many man-hours were required per ton of output in France and the United Kingdom as in the United States; Germany required about 75 percent more man-hours than the United States.

Taking into account the greater man-hour requirements in Europe, unit labor cost in the three European countries — adjusted for differences in product mix — was approximately two thirds the U. S. cost. Unit labor cost was 69 percent of the U. S. level in France, 65 percent in Germany, and 61 percent in the United Kingdom. Thus, the European countries have a major labor cost advantage over the United States, but this advantage is far less than that indicated by average hourly earnings figures alone. The contrast is particularly great for France. France has the lowest average hourly earnings figure among the three European countries, but unit labor costs appear somewhat greater in France than in the other two countries.

Let me add a further caution on the use of these figures. The study compares direct labor costs only — not total production cost per unit of output. Although labor costs are a sizable part of total cost in the iron and steel industry — about 40 percent in the United States and between 20 and 30 percent in the three European countries — material and other costs represent a larger proportion of total costs. Consequently, differences in unit labor costs do not imply similar inter-country differences in other costs of production. Moreover, the fact that unit labor costs average higher in the United States than in Western Europe by no means implies that this is true for every steel-mill product or for every plant in each country.

CONCLUSION

In dealing with a complex set of relations, figures can provide insight but they can also create confusion. Consider the implications of certain of the international comparisons cited. The figures on manufacturing unit labor cost show that by this test, U. S. costs have risen far less than costs in most Western European countries during the past 10 years. Seemingly this would indicate that U. S. manufactured products would be more competitive in third markets than their European counterparts. Yet we know that this is not true. The answer, or a major part of it, lies in the growth of European manufacturing capacity. In 1957, such capacity was limited, and most European manufacturers were pressed to meet domestic demand in their home countries. Ten years later, after considerable expansion of capacity, they are more interested and aggressive in selling to customers across their borders. Although U. S. unit labor costs may have risen less during the decade on a percentage basis, the absolute level of U. S. costs, as illustrated by the recent study of the iron and steel industry, is still substantially above that of the Western European producers. The result is an increasing flow of the more competitive steel products from Western Europe to the United States.

Thus, as the discussion on compensation proceeds, it is useful to keep in mind both the value and the limitations of the statistics.

PRICES, INCOMES, AND PRODUCTIVITY:
A POLICY FOR BRITAIN

By Samuel C. Silkin

In some 70 years Britain has had a favorable balance of payments less than a handful of times. Yet the perpetuation of unfavorable balances has become Britain's economic Achilles heel and the political Achilles heel of successive governments. What creates this paradox?

The short and simple explanation is that before the 1939-1945 war the returns from Britain's foreign investments were sufficiently massive to provide a comfortable cushion against the excess of expenditure over earned income. The dark days after Dunkirk altered all that. Britain ended the war with her overseas portfolios sadly depleted and with an accumulation of sterling debts which have come to be known as "the sterling balances." The overseas portfolios still exist. But today the margin between solvency and insolvency is far narrower. The "business of Britain" can no longer be run at a recurrent loss. Every crisis — a bad monthly balance, a dock strike, a Middle East war — is likely to panic the sterling creditors into calling for their money; and so the value of the pound drops in a wave of selling, and the fear of devaluation creates a vicious circle.

Any British government today, of whatever political color, is like a juggler balancing a number of tennis balls. If one is dropped, the others are likely to come bouncing down. What then is this balancing art which the juggler has to perform? First and foremost, he must balance his payments; and hence his export orders must exceed in value his imports. Next, he must control cost inflation; for if he cannot achieve this, his exports will cease to be competitive. Then his act must be constantly throwing up growth; for without growth of productivity and production he cannot satisfy the constant need for increased investment. It is that increase which will produce more competitive exports and the rising living standards to provide the essential incentive to the producers. Finally, he must keep a constantly watchful eye on that tennis ball which it is easiest to forget and neglect: the living standards of the nonproducers — the retired, the widowed, the sick, the disabled, the rentiers, the unemployed, the redundant, the unemployable. For if he fails to watch these, political failure will be the inevitable reward of his juggling.

It matters not how brilliant is the juggler's technique, how light his touch, and how sure his eye. He will not succeed unless he can control that which affects each one of his tennis balls — prices, incomes, and productivity. A rise in money incomes without a corresponding or greater rise in productivity will reduce competitiveness and so affect the balance of payments. An exorbitant rise in prices will hit the living standards of the nonproducers and will encourage pressure for the producers to demand a corresponding increase in incomes for themselves. A failure to achieve greater productivity will inhibit investment and so restrict growth.

Every British government for at least a decade has recognized the need for a prices, incomes, and productivity policy. Only the present British Government has grasped the nettle; it took some time to gain the courage to do so and it is still not certain whether its hold is firm. This is not surprising to those who understand the traditions of the British trade union movement and those of British industry. The British trade union movement has been built upon the struggle of labor against capital. The traditions of the Tolpuddle martyrs and the "dockers' tanner" die hard. The more far-sighted union leaders realize that today their struggle is more one of trade against trade, worker against consumer, than between laborer and capitalist; but this philosophy is less popular than an appeal to traditional emotions. British industry also tends to look to the past to see a shimmering mirage of riches built upon free enterprise in contrast to the reality of a planned and controlled economy. Thus British industry and British trade unionism alike have tended to join together as the last refuge of free bargaining in a controlled society.

In October 1964, when it had just achieved power, the Wilson Government optimistically believed that control of incomes could be achieved by voluntary agreement among government, industry, and unions. Industry would see the value of planned growth; the unions would accept restraint provided that its management was manifestly equitable. At first the dream seemed to be approaching reality. The unions and industry joined in a common declaration of intent. The need for restraint was recognized. This great success turned out, alas, to be a paper tiger. The euphoria which it created was translated in reality into increases of income at more than twice the rate of increases in productivity. The seamen's strike of the summer of 1966 drove the last nails into the voluntary policy's coffin. In July 1966, less than six months from its return with a much enlarged majority, the Wilson Government was compelled to slow down drastically the pace of consumption and to recognize that an incomes policy could only be achieved by legislative sanction.

The "July measures" took effect. Well into 1967 both incomes and prices remained steady; but the disinflationary effect of those measures did little or nothing to encourage the third partner in the trinity — productivity. The British economy achieved the stability of the static. True, the balance of payments turned in Britain's favor — but at the expense of unemployment, of reduced consumption, of lesser demand for imported consumer goods. It was a precarious stability; and when in the autumn of 1967 the dockers, who for over half a century had been campaigning for a guaranteed working week, at last achieved it, they showed their gratitude by a strike which produced the worst monthly trade figures for years, another call on the sterling balances, and eventually the November devaluation.

The statutory prices and incomes policy of 1966 had been timed to run a year. As I have shown, it was successful while it lasted; the dock strike could not be fairly attributed to it. But once it ended, the pent-up pressure for money increments burst out. In a few months money incomes rose by more than the percentage increase in a whole year of voluntary restraint. Thus was demonstrated the weakness of a statutory incomes policy; once the statutory control ends, the floods take control.

The Wilson Government now has its third — and many would say its last — chance. Devaluation fortunately coincided with slack in employment and newly built factories waiting for tenants. Thus the hope of an export-led boom was higher than in the days when factories were busily producing goods for home consumption and vacancies far outnumbered unemployed. In those easy days before the "July measures" why should a motor-car manufacturer make 20 dollars profit on his motor car in Asia when he could make 250 dollars profit at home? Devaluation turned the tables. If British prices could be held, it gave a great opportunity to divert production towards exports.

"If Britain's prices could be held" — but that meant once again a stringent control of money incomes. This time the Wilson Government took no half measures. A budget of unexampled severity drastically reduced purchasing power at home. Military commitments abroad — the largest drain on British-held foreign currency — were savagely reduced, a measure that was necessary but unpopular with many friends of Britain. A new Prices and Incomes Bill was introduced, this time giving the government power to hold up not only salary and wage increases but prices, rents, and company dividends.

The 1966 Prices and Incomes Act incurred fierce resistance, especially from the left-wing of the Labour Party. Its 1968 successor has incurred even tougher opposition. Ranged against it are the Conservative Opposition, basking in the confidence of by-election victories and tempted thereby to discard the cautious approach of its liberal wing led by Maudling in favor of an outright policy of Powellist laissez-faire; the unions and their representatives in Parliament; and the solid core of Labour left-wingers who have become known to some of their colleagues as "the total abstainers." In face of this combined opposition the Wilson Government could have been forgiven for dragging its feet; but it did not do so. The sole concession to its critics was to make this second piece of legislation temporary like the first.

The new legislation is designed to fit into the post-devaluation policy. By the time the Act expires, that policy will have succeeded or it will have failed. If it has failed, it will be too late for the Wilson Government to start afresh. Some other administration will have to solve the problem — to balance the tennis balls.

From what I have said it will be seen that in Britain prices and incomes policy, even though based, as it is today, on a foundation of productivity (for only genuine productivity increases will be held to justify increases in money incomes), still lacks a fundamental philosophy. It is a policy of hand to mouth, designed to remedy immediate problems, to provide the vital substratum for an essential economic policy of change and growth. But what of the future? There are many, like myself, who believe that in the modern society free union-employer bargaining no longer makes sense. For this there are two reasons. First, experience has shown that whatever national agreements are made, shop bargaining is bound to sap the basis of the national agreement — particularly in times of acute labor shortages. But secondly the immense fruits of technological advance cannot justly be left to benefit a single industry, whether the benefit is drawn by employers, employees, or both. Today the consumer must have a powerful voice in the division of economic gains. I am pleased to find so many of my observations in this paper confirmed by the June 1968 Report of the Royal Commission on Trade Unions and Employers' Associations, which recommends the encouragement of collective bargaining procedures designed to protect the ultimate interests not only of the worker but of the consumer also. This is the only route to a fair and sensible incomes structure that is compatible with a free society.

WAGES AND INCOMES POLICY IN THE EEC

By L. H. J. CRIJNS

The six EEC nations share the same five fundamental economic and social aims, which are as follows:

(a) Adequate economic growth.

(b) Internal monetary equilibrium, or price stabilization.

(c) External monetary equilibrium, or balance-of-payments equilibrium.

(d) Full employment.

(e) An equitable distribution of national wealth and income.

In the several nations there may be varying emphasis in existing programs for attainment of these objectives. Priorities may be altered at certain times or in certain circumstances. Some objectives may conflict with others at a given moment. However, these occasional variations do not alter the basic aim, in each of these countries and at the community level, to realize these goals simultaneously and optimally. The main responsibility for doing so lies with the government of each member country, and, at the EEC level, the Community institutions share such responsibility with member governments.

A second essential fact is that in the six EEC countries the representatives of management and labor are free to fix wages and other working conditions in their joint agreements. This private autonomy is also recognized at the EEC level.

INTERPLAY OF COLLECTIVE BARGAINING AND OTHER FORMS OF ECONOMIC DECISION-MAKING

National aims and privacy of wage determination are not always in balance. At a given time, management and labor may be pursuing a wage policy that makes it virtually impossible for the government currently to attain the five basic economic and social objectives detailed above. If, for instance, they fix wages at a level that makes it impossible for the increase in wage costs per unit of output to be offset by an equivalent reduction in other cost factors or by a reduction in profits, the automatic result is higher prices. Price increases engender deterioration of an industry's ability to compete in foreign markets, deficits in current account, cutbacks in productive investment, a shortage of potential jobs, and unemployment. Price rises may induce flights of capital and lower economic growth, hardships for people on fixed incomes, wild speculation, and the like. Inflation may even go so far as to necessitate revision of the official exchange rate or a substantial restriction on the movement of goods and services — in short, it may mean disruption of the economic process as a whole.

But the converse is also possible. A government may pursue a policy that prevents the two sides of industry from achieving and maintaining reasonable wage policies. An increase in prices may very well result, not from an excessive rise in wage costs per unit of output (cost push), but from too flexible a monetary policy. For example, a massive expansion of credit may produce undue liquidity compared with the growth of national product. Price increases may be induced by a budget policy involving high government expenditure without a simultaneous and proportionate reduction in the growth of private consumption and of productive investment in the private sector. Lack of discipline in nonwage incomes, such as prices, profits, dealers' margins, rents, and charges for public and private services, may also serve as inflationary pressures. In these cases, inflation results not from an increase in wage costs per unit of output but rather from excessive aggregate demand (demand pull). When such pressures are manifest, it is unreasonable to expect disciplined behavior from labor and management. Discipline then should rather be asked of governmental authorities, monetary institutions, and those making private economic decisions unrelated to collective bargaining.

NEED FOR COOPERATION

Although a theoretical distinction can be made between cost-push inflation and demand-pull inflation, in practice the two nearly always occur together — though to varying degrees and perhaps with a difference in timing, with one leading and the other following. A remedy is unattainable without the exercise of discipline by all concerned. Otherwise, none will achieve his aim and all will be dissatisfied. High levels of investment, large wage increases, and heavy expenditures by governments, separately applied, are important and desirable means to raise living standards. But when they are all applied at once, the economy is put under heavy strain and is endangered. There is an old and wise saying to the effect that you cannot do everything at the same time. What is possible and what is desirable should be discussed jointly and then put into effect. To put it another way, labor and management have a continuing moral responsibility for the simultaneous and optimum realization of the five economic and social aims. while the state must pursue an economic and social policy that will enable management and labor to administer reasonable wage policies. Communication and cooperation at all times and at all levels of unions, managements, and government are the keys to achieving a correct balance between the exercise of public and private power in the making of essential economic decisions.

INFORMAL GOVERNMENTAL INTERVENTION IN EEC NATIONS

In the EEC countries the need for reasonable discussion and cooperation between the government and the two sides of industry has been increasingly felt. In France, Belgium, Italy, West Germany, and Luxembourg, the governments have no means of direct formal intervention in wage negotiations, and in the Netherlands the existing system is now under examination. The governments have, however, sought in various indirect ways to exert their influence. They have tried warnings, exhortations for restraint, appeals to objectivity or a return to a scientific basis, memoranda from national bank presidents or economic advisory councils, and meetings behind the scenes with leaders of employers' and workers' organizations (particularly representatives of the growth industries). They have undertaken a kind of "hidden persuasion," such as manipulation of wages and other labor conditions in public and semipublic undertakings in those countries, as in France and Italy, where this form of enterprise plays a major role. They have awarded major projects to firms on condition that the builder or supplier observe certain standards in the matter of wages. Letters have been sent by prime ministers to business leaders. Mediators have been employed to push the negotiations in a specific direction. Sometimes they have even tried threats. But practice has shown that such indirect measures yield no suitable solutions. Indeed, the opposite effect is sometimes produced because tempers become even more heated and the positions of the negotiating parties become further hardened.

INADEQUACY OF CLASSIC METHODS

It has been found that use of the classic instruments of economic policy — monetary and tax policies — do not furnish a real answer either. Restriction of monetary demand by higher taxation, cuts in government expenditures, increases in the discount rate, credit controls, and the like certainly affect the labor market and hence wages and prices, but the link is not as close as was originally thought. The prices of many goods are not as flexible as is often assumed. There are, after all, such things as monopolies, restrictive agreements, and resale price maintenance. Wages, moreover, are no longer formed on the model of atomistic competition but through bilateral monopoly. It must be accepted that a conscious effort to restructure wages will fail and that wages can no longer be reduced. Admittedly, my last observation is true only of contractual wage rates and is not true about actual wages, since wage drift adjusts itself when demand falls and actual hours worked decline with the reduction of overtime. Furthermore, in the pluralistic society we inhabit, pressure groups and opposing forces all want to see their shares of the cake increased, or at least not reduced. Rightly or wrongly, they rely on the idea that when one group gets a rise the rest must get a rise too. What is more, a recent Community survey seems to indicate that the Philips curve does not apply for all EEC countries in the years 1955-1965; the link between the increase in nominal wages and the employment rate suggested in this curve is not as close as was thought.

In any case, a correlation between wages and the employment rate is an inadequate base for a stabilization policy. First, it is difficult to indicate the proper manpower reserve that corresponds exactly to specific wage increases that are compatible with price stabilization. Second, it seems impossible to manipulate monetary and tax policies in such a way as to attain and maintain with exactness the desired equilibrium. There is a great risk of overstepping the mark and getting into worse trouble by triggering a cumulative process of contraction. Moreover, although a temporary effect may perhaps be achieved in this way, the real question is whether the desired effect is achieved in the rather longer-term battle against creeping inflation. Nor can it be overlooked that some wage increases are needed to promote structural developments, such as the transfer of workers from low-wage industries to more prosperous high-wage industries. Such monetary inducements increase the average level of wages. And is it not the case that workers' organizations are more or less forced from time to time to squeeze out substantial wage increases, if only to keep their members under control? But for regular wage increases in amounts acceptable to their constituencies, the trade unions simply could not exist. Lastly, in wage negotiations the reaction to the changing economic situation comes after a time-lag. This time-lag contributes appreciably to the scale of economic fluctuations. If the economy is to be stabilized with a view to regular growth, for instance, wage policy will have to be linked to a medium-term economic policy and not be made so dependent on short-term changes in circumstances.

There is another and greater disadvantage connected with the application of monetary and tax measures. These classic instruments of policy have a negative influence on employment and economic growth. It should be evident that healthy economic growth calls for a high employment rate, for unemployment means a loss of productive hands and must inevitably produce less growth than full employment. The argument that a certain percentage of unemployment increases labor productivity because the worker is threatened with losing his job is shortsighted. Both politically and socially, a high level of employment is a very good thing. It creates a climate of optimism in which risks are more likely to be taken. In an atmosphere of growth there is more business investment. Labor organizations then do not oppose rationalization, mechanization, automation, and technological progress. Structural shifts are easier to make. Slowing or halting economic growth produces failure to carry out infrastructure investments, imposes restrictions on scientific research and education and vocational training, and produces high interest rates and restriction of productive investment in the private sector.

The great danger of traditional stabilization policy through monetary and tax measures is that monetary success in combating inflation may be achieved at the expense of lower economic growth, with the result that in the medium term it is even more difficult to fight inflation. It is my view that in a booming economy with high growth rates many problems can be solved more easily than in a stagnant economy.

To sum up, it is being increasingly recognized that governments must exercise prior influence on the movement of wages and incomes if the optimum level of employment and substantial economic growth compatible with monetary stability are to be achieved. But the many disadvantages in an *ex post facto* resort to the traditional instruments of monetary policy and tax policy are obvious. The problem is to make coordinated and balanced use of various instruments in the field of monetary and credit policy, capital market policy, budget policy, and incomes policy.

INCOMES POLICY

I do not speak of wages policy. We cannot confine our attention to wages alone. In the first place, this would not make economic sense. Nonwage incomes such as prices, profits, dividends, interest, rents, and charges for certain services must also be included in discussions between governments and the two sides of industry. It would be a psychological error to limit control mechanisms only to wages, because we would thereby lose the support of the trade unions. It is essential to a proper income policy that the burden should be carried by all sides. Nor should we restrict ourselves to primary incomes. Secondary incomes must also be taken into account. Discussion should cover the redistribution of national income by means of tax policy, subsidies, transfers, social security, and the like. Finally, there should also be consultation on how wealth can be distributed more fairly — arrangements for granting premiums on savings, profit sharing, return on investment, and fair shares in the increase in wealth. In brief, we are concerned not with wage policy in the strict sense but with all-around income policy.

The objective of income policy should be to influence the formation, distribution, and allocation of income in a way that will facilitate optimum realization of the five general economic and social aims in each country. This will be possible only if income policy is integrated with general economic and social policy not so much in the short term as in the medium term. The central points in medium-term economic policy are an optimum relation between consumption and investment. Such a relationship determines future economic growth and employment. It encompasses wage elements that contribute to consumption and those that do not. At the same time national consumption should not exceed national resources, so that internal and external monetary balance is attained. All of these are decisive factors in attaining a fair distribution of national income and at the same time a fairer distribution of wealth.

If we are to have consultation and cooperation between governments and the two sides of industry over income policy as part of the general medium-term economic and social policy, one or more institutional bodies should be set up. The kinds of joint bodies that are the most appropriate should be left to consultation between those concerned. Adequate high-quality statistical and other material should be made available to such consultative bodies in ample time, so that government, management, and labor can each play its role as efficiently as possible. It must be stressed that forecasts must be made for the medium term in the form of alternatives or variants, thus furnishing one of the major conditions for proper and fruitful consultation.

A dozen observations are in order:

1. In income policy there will have to be cooperation between Community institutions and representatives of the six member governments on the one hand and representatives of management and labor on the other. This is needed if the five general economic and social aims, which are already accepted by everyone at the Community level, are to be realized simultaneously and optimally. None of the EEC countries can now lead an insular existence. Each of them is becoming increasingly dependent on the trend in the EEC and therefore less and less capable of pursuing an independent national policy. Wage policy in the Netherlands has made this abundantly clear. Even if the necessary discipline is being exercised in a given country by both sides of industry, the monetary authorities, the government, and the business world, it is still possible to suffer from external cost push or external demand pull. There must be discipline at the Community level also. Another example relates to employment. The desperate attempt to maintain specific wage norms when there is severe strain on the labor market was shown to be impossible in the Netherlands. Employment policy must be coordinated at the European level. Another example is what is known in Germany as "Vermögensbildung in Arbeitnehmerhand" and in France as "une politique des patrimoines," where the purpose is essentially to give workers a share in their firm's increased profit. If there is no Community coordination, one country or another risks a flight of capital; in other words, reasonable distribution of wealth is possible only if there is joint consultation at the Community level.

These are enough examples to show the need for coordination of income policies of the six countries at the Community level. Such coordination would seem to follow automatically from the actual or planned withdrawal of certain aspects of general economic policy from the jurisdiction of the member countries, or from plans for fuller coordination or harmonization at the Community level. Characteristic are the elimination of customs duties within the Community (completed as of July 1, 1968) and the definitive introduction of a common tariff on imports from outside the Community, the common agricultural policy, the common transport policy, and the free movement of workers and capital within the Community. Other examples are freedom in the Community to set up in business or to supply services, the common competition policy, tax harmonization (recently begun with the introduction of a common turnover-tax system), coordination of economic policy, monetary policy, budget policy, science policy, and Community policy on industrial concentration generally. Finally, there is the medium-term economic policy.

All these policies have an influence on income. In order to achieve overall impact, other elements such as wage and income policy must be taken into account.

2. Coordination at Community level of the classic forms of economic policy — monetary and tax policies — will not provide an adequate solution to the problems we are concerned with, any more than it does in the member countries individually. Here too, monetary and credit policy, budget policy and capital market policy will have to be coordinated with income policy.

3. Income policy will have to extend not only to wages but also to nonwage incomes, especially profits. It must also relate to secondary incomes. A policy on wealth will also have to be developed within the framework of such an income policy.

4. Income policy must be integrated with the medium-term economic policy that is now being formulated at the Community level and for which a first program was adopted in February 1967 by the Council. The aim of this program is to coordinate the general economic and social policies of the six member countries. Within this framework, coordination of income policies will have to be given a central place, as indicated in the second program recently submitted to the Council.

5. Medium-term economic policy will have to include forecasts in the form of alternatives to leave room for consultation and cooperation between Community bodies and governments on the one hand and management and labor on the other.

6. If consultation and cooperation are to be fully used, there should be an institution at the Community level where those concerned could regularly exchange information and consult each other with a view to reaching gentlemen's agreements where possible. There could perhaps be something along the lines of a Community labor board — rather like the Dutch "Stichting van de Arbeid," but tripartite. The underlying idea is that management and labor should remain independent in their wage-negotiating positions, but prepared to enter voluntarily into reasonable consultation and cooperation.

7. An essential element in this form of cooperation is that adequate statistical and other material should be available when needed, so that the major components of the current and expected general economic trend can be discerned. Without this there can be no proper consultation.

8. Employers' and workers' associations will have to adjust their structures so that negotiations at the Community level can be

carried on by representatives who are willing and able to use all their authority and influence in their organizations to ensure that any gentlemen's agreements reached will as far as possible be implemented.

9. What concrete action should be taken, what material conditions should be established, and what criteria should be adopted so as to put into practice the ideas decided upon are matters for which I have no ready answer. This would require closer investigation. Or would it perhaps be possible to start cooperating immediately and *then* to try to find step by step the best course to follow? In fact, the "Stichting van de Arbeid" was set up in the Netherlands before it was known how it should function exactly. Its functions were worked out in practice.

10. An income policy, as here advocated, is in no way designed as a means of intervening directly in the process of wage and profit determination. Its purpose is to have an overall influence on the course of events through informed consultation, and thus to make it easier for the authorities, monetary institutions, the business world, and labor to reach decisions on medium-term economic policy in general and income policy in particular. Such procedures would make it possible for the Community to achieve at one and the same time all five of our basic economic and social aims.

11. An income policy of this kind cannot be constructed within a few years. It will take a long time, and a great number of difficulties and teething troubles will have to be overcome. However, I believe it is worthwhile to begin to tackle these problems promptly.

12. Whether the political and social and psychological climate in the six member countries and at the Community level is such that a step of this nature can be taken in the short term is a question I do not and cannot answer. Time alone will tell.

RELEVANT EEC STATISTICAL TABLES, 1958-1966

I. Average nominal gross wage income per year per wage earner (gross wages and salaries paid out per worker, including employers' contributions to social security) rose in 1958-1966 by approximately:

Luxembourg	50%
Belgium	65-70%
Germany	85%
France, Netherlands	100%
Italy	110%

II. Prices (cost of living or retail prices; rents excluded for Luxembourg and Belgium, included for the other countries) were up in 1958-1966 by approximately:

Luxembourg	15%
Belgium	20%
Germany	22%
Italy	32%
Netherlands	33%
France	36%

III. Average real gross wage income per year per wage earner (excluding employers' contributions) rose in 1958-1966 by approximately:

Luxembourg	30%
Belgium	40%
France, Netherlands	45%
Germany	50%
Italy	55%

The increase in real net wage income per year per wage earner is not known but will be rather less than the increase in gross wage incomes, because employers' social security contributions and taxes have increased everywhere.

IV. Macroeconomic labor productivity (real gross national product per wage-earner) rose in 1958-1966 by approximately:

Belgium, France	25%
Netherlands	25-30%
Germany, Italy	35%
Luxembourg	no information

V. Unit labor costs rose in 1958-1966 by approximately:

Belgium	30%
Germany	35-40%
France, Netherlands	50%
Italy	55-60%
Luxembourg	no information

VI. Wage costs per worker per hour worked in all industries, including mining and construction (in Belgian Francs):

	1959	1966
Luxembourg	60	88
Belgium	43	76
Germany	40	80
France	40	68
Italy	32	63
Netherlands	34	74

These figures show that the gap between the highest and lowest in 1959 was about 100 percent but had dropped by 1966 to about 40 percent. If Luxembourg (where the steel industry predominates) is excluded, the difference between the highest and the lowest was about 35 percent in 1959 and about 27 percent in 1966.

RECENT WAGES AND INCOMES POLICIES BASED ON PRODUCTIVITY IN THE UNITED KINGDOM AND THE UNITED STATES

By Julius Rezler

In the United States and the United Kingdom the role of productivity as a major factor in wage determination has received increasing attention. Productivity and wages have always been closely related economic factors. For the greater part of economic history, at least until World War II, a long-term relationship existed in Western Europe and the United States between real wages and productivity. Productivity had operated as an autonomous factor underlying the market forces. During and after World War II, this long-term relationship was disrupted for three main reasons: first, the existence of a tight labor market, particularly in the economies of Western Europe, which upset the balance between supply and demand in favor of the labor supply factor; second, the strong market power of trade unions; third, sporadic wars in Korea, the Middle East, Algeria, and now in Vietnam. These wars disturbed the balance in the product market and caused an inflationary pressure from the demand side.

The weakening of the autonomous effects of the productivity factor on the process of wage determination has recently stimulated some deliberate efforts by economic policymakers in the United States and Western Europe to restore the link between wage movements and productivity trends through an official income or wage policy. Efforts to find a yardstick for noninflationary wage determination have been intensified in response to prevailing inflationary trends in most of the Western European economies and in the United States since World War II. Arthur M. Ross, former Commissioner of the Bureau of Labor Statistics, observed: "As wage increases have accelerated, widespread fears of inflation have developed in financial and governmental circles. As a result, leading officials have been urging wage restraints, . . . and advocating that wage increases be limited, in some fashion or other, by increases in productivity."

The growing interest in productivity as a determinant of wages has not been limited to government officials. Managements in America and Western Europe have also been concerned with productivity and wage relations lest their products be priced out of world markets. Businessmen have realized that comparative labor costs, a major factor in competitiveness, are determined not only by the hourly wage rates and added fringe benefits, but also by the productivity trends prevailing in foreign markets. The comparative levels of labor productivity existing in the United States and in some West European economies in 1960 serve as a helpful introduction. Measuring productivity by output per manhour at U.S. relative prices, productivity exhibited the following percentages of U.S. productivity: Belgium and the Netherlands, 62; Germany, 58; United Kingdom, 56; France, 55; and Italy, 41.

A brief conceptual clarification is in order before an analysis of actual developments in the application of productivity to wage determination may be undertaken. To avoid terminological confusion, distinction should first be made between the term "productivity" as used in the marginal productivity wage theory of the neoclassical school of economics, and physical or gross productivity as it is understood in the present macro-economic context. In neoclassical wage theory, productivity represents the increment that each subsequent unit of a productive factor adds to the revenue of the firm, and, of course, particular emphasis is placed upon the productivity of the marginal unit.

In the context of this discussion, productivity means the efficiency with which material and human resources are converted into products. Quantitatively speaking, physical or gross productivity is expressed in the ratio between total output and total input and is usually measured by indexes of output per man-hour. As Kendrick has said, "This is a partial productivity measure since it is a ratio of output to only one class of input, although labor is the most important input." In the United States, the output-per-man-hour indexes are regularly computed and published by the BLS for individual industries and for the whole national economy.

That physical productivity is measured in terms of the labor input does not mean that manual labor is the only or even the main cause of productivity gains. Economists universally agree that introduction of new equipment based on advanced technology is the most important single cause of productivity increases. It is closely followed by innovations in the organization of production and administration, and in management techniques.

In the United Kingdom and in the United States, the productivity concept has been applied to the process of wage determination in two principal ways. The oldest and most frequently used method of tying compensation to productivity is incorporated in the term "incentive payments," in which there is an immediate and direct relationship between the amount of compensation earned by a worker and his own productivity. Incentives represent the application of the productivity concept to compensation at the micro-economic level, since an increase in compensation depends on upward changes in the individual productivity of the worker. The system of incentive wage payments is formulated in such a way as to encourage a maximum increase in the worker's productivity.

The second major method of applying the productivity principle to compensation relates changes in wage payments to the average physical productivity either already realized or to be anticipated in a company, in an industry, or in the national economy. Here the relationship between productivity and compensation is neither direct nor immediate; the yardstick is no longer the workers' own productivity but the industrial or the national average.

Trends in incentive payment systems vary substantially in the major industrial nations. In the United Kingdom, the relative importance of incentives has increased. Mangum reports that "The percentage of wage earners on payment by results was 34 percent in 1938, 37 percent in 1947, and 42 percent in 1961." On the other hand, due partly to the opposition of trade unions in the United States and partly to the advance of automation in the United States and the Soviet Union, the use of incentives in those two countries has declined. For example, in the Soviet steel and iron industry the percentage of piece-rate workers in 1936 was 79.2 percent, whereas in 1961 it was less than 52 percent. Similar trends appear in the Soviet coal industry. In the United States the percentage of factory workers on incentive payment declined from 31 percent in the early 1950s to approximately 25 percent in the mid-1960s.

The coupling of upward wage movements with productivity trends prevailing in the national economy is applied differently in the United States and in the United Kingdom. Therefore, I separately survey wage and productivity developments in the two countries.

With the emergence of a persistent inflationary trend in the second half of the fifties, labeled cost-push inflation, the attention of American government officials turned increasingly to the behavior of the cost factors, primarily to labor costs and profits. The idea of connecting wage and price movements with productivity trends appeared officially first in the Economic Report of the President for 1957. It was suggested that "Negotiated wage increases and benefits should be consistent with productivity prospect and with the maintenance of a stable dollar." In the next year's Report of the President, business management and labor leaders were admonished that movements in prices and wages that go beyond overall productivity gains are inconsistent with stable prices. The Economic Report in 1959 restated the proposition that "increases in money wages and other compensation not justified by the productivity performance of the economy are inevitably inflationary."

President Kennedy left to the Council of Economic Advisers the detailed spelling out of the macro-economic application of the productivity concept to wage determination under the term "guide posts for non-inflationary wage and price behavior." The Report of the Council in 1962 proposed as a general rule that hourly labor compensation should advance in accordance with the increase in trend productivity. Trend productivity was defined as the annual average percentage change in output per man-hour in the entire economy during the latest five years. In the 1962 Report, no specific estimate of that trend was given. However, in the 1964 Report the now-well-known 3.2 percent was accepted as trend productivity in the American economy between 1959 and 1964. In its 1966 Report, the Council of Economic Advisers specifically recommended that 3.2 percent should be the general guidepost for noninflationary wage determination. The guideposts were not considered a rigid yardstick; the Council listed a number of situations in which deviations from the guideposts in upward or downward direction could be exercised.

How did the guidepost policy succeed in this country? Statistical data concerning wage movements suggest that between 1962 and 1966 the policy was successful. In those years average wage settlements exceeded only slightly the trend productivity of 3.2 percent. But examination disclosed that forces other than the guideposts were also responsible for the comparative wage stability. Critics of the guideposts attributed this achievement to the high rate of unemployment prevailing in the early sixties. They seem to have been right because when the rate of unemployment subsided to around 4 percent, the floodgates that had contained inflationary wage movements were broken through. In the past two years, average wage increases have greatly exceeded trend productivity in the American economy.

Decline in unemployment was only one of the factors defeating the guidepost policy. The opposition of management and organized labor, the two primary parties involved in wage determination, proved to be a more decisive factor in its downfall. A number of influential American business organizations have objected to the guidepost policy from its very inception for various reasons. Primarily, they considered it an uninvited government intervention into private economic relations. But they were against the guideposts on technical grounds, too. For example, General Electric Company attacked the guideposts on two accounts: first, the correctness of the so-called trend productivity was questioned. It was contended that this was nearer to 2 percent than to the 3.2-percent figure propounded by the Council of Economic Advisers. General Electric also felt that the challenges of competition from abroad and unemployment at home called for wage increases that were less than the increase in the nation's productivity.

Standard Oil of Indiana contended that there was no definite mathematical relationship between productivity and wage levels. Furthermore, it asserted that the guideposts imposed formula bargaining on employers and that formulas are inflexible by nature.

While labor and management representatives usually take diametrically opposing views on the issues emerging in industrial relations, in the case of the guideposts they found themselves in the same camp. Labor objected to them for different reasons. The unions complained that private collective bargaining ought not to be obstructed by government intervention. They also resented the one-sided effects of the guidepost policy, which was supposed to control price changes as well as wage movements. While the second objective was achieved, at least between 1962 and 1966, the retail price index moved upward at an accelerating rate. In 1967 the retail price increase was 3.5 percent and in 1968 it reached about 5 percent. Labor leaders contend that a 3.2-percent raise in wages would not even make up for the erosion in real wages. We all know that the guideposts have been entirely discarded and collective agreements providing wage increases of 5 to 6 percent have become commonplace.

Has the United Kingdom fared better with the application of the macro-economic productivity concept to wage determination? According to Professor Knowles of Oxford, productivity was only one of the principles of wage determination in the United Kingdom in the past, and it operated haphazardly and imperfectly. The results of a study conducted by Nicholson and Gupta support the conclusion of Professor Knowles. They compared the trend in productivity with that in men's hourly earnings in almost 100 industries between 1948 and 1954, and found insignificant correlation between the two. If productivity did not have a major influence on British wages after World War II, then what were the factors that shaped the British wage system before the present experiments with productivity wage bargaining? According to students of the British labor economy, the tight labor market and the structure of collective bargaining exerted the greatest impact on wage determination, at least up to the early sixties.

The tightness of the British labor market is evident from its low unemployment rate. Between 1957 and 1966, this rate fluctuated between 1.6 and 2.6 percent. But the structure of collective bargaining also contributed to the upward movement of wages. In the British industrial relations system, wages are usually established in two steps: first on an industry-wide basis through negotiations between an employers' association and a national union, and then at the local level. Approximately 450 national agreements were in force in the early 1960s. These agreements, however, established only the so-called minimum wages, and the actual wage rates, which might considerably exceed the national minimum, were determined at the local level by shop stewards and the plant managers. As a consequence of this two-tier system of wage determination, the phenomenon of wage drift has become a major problem of British industrial relations. The "wage drift" is the difference between the minimum wages established in the national agreements and the actual wage compensation arrived at locally. In some cases it may be as large as 50 percent.

Because of the tight labor market and the wage drift, the restraint of inflationary wage and price movements has become a major concern of the British economy. Among the various remedies sought and tried, politicians and economists paid growing attention to a wage policy that would establish some relationship between wage movements and productivity trends.

The first step toward such a policy appeared to be the creation of a Council on Prices, Productivity and Incomes by the Conservative Government in 1957, with the idea of arranging a link between the rate of wage increases and the growth in overall productivity. In its fourth report in 1961, the Council made some further move toward a wage policy based on productivity trends by suggesting the use of a formula that would rest on the anticipated growth in productivity rather than the already realized gains. In 1962, Selwyn Lloyd, Conservative Chancellor of the Exchequer, sent a message to the Trades Union Congress seeking its reaction to a national wage policy that would hold average wage increases within an anticipated 2.5-percent annual increase in national productivity. The TUC did not respond positively to this suggestion.

The Labour Government, elected in 1964, continued to pursue

a policy of applying the productivity concept to wages. In 1964 the government issued a "Joint Statement of Intent on Productivity, Prices, and Incomes." To carry out the policy inherent in the statement, a National Board for Prices and Incomes was established. Although the Board lacked power to enforce its decisions, it proclaimed a noninflationary wage increase norm that was based on an anticipated trend of 3 percent in productivity.

Paralleling attempts of the Conservative and Labour Governments to formulate a new wage policy embodying the productivity concept, some developments in collective bargaining aim in the same direction. A novel method, denoted "productivity bargaining," has evolved in the private and public sectors of British industrial relations. According to a researcher for the Royal Commission on Trade Unions and Employers' Associations, "Productivity bargaining may be described as an agreement in which advantages of one kind or another, such as higher wages or increased leisure, are given to workers in return for agreement on their part to accept changes in working practice or in methods or in organization of work which lead to more efficient working." Removal of excessive overtime, relaxation of intercraft demarcation, and greater flexibility in hours of work are some examples of concessions made by workers in return for higher wages. The first major agreement that granted wage increases in return for the elimination of restrictive work rules which stood in the way of increasing productivity was concluded at the Esso Refinery at Fawley in 1960. This pioneering agreement has been followed by an increasing number of similar agreements that established a direct relationship between wage increases and measures to advance productivity. A 1966 study by the Fabian Society listed more than 50 agreements resulting from productivity bargaining.

In the meantime, there have been further developments in the national wage policy. At the instance of the Labour Government, which was concerned with a rapidly rising wage level, the Prices and Incomes Act was passed in 1966. The Act provided for a six months' wage freeze and a further six months' wage restraint. An immediate increase could be granted, however, where there was a bona fide productivity agreement. The National Board for Prices and Incomes, to which was entrusted the administration of the new wage policy, drafted certain guidelines for productivity agreements which may provide wage increases under the Act. The first one stated: "It should be shown that the workers are making a direct contribution toward increasing productivity by accepting more exacting work or a major change in working practices." According to the third guideline, "An accurate calculation of the gains and costs should normally show that the total cost per unit of output will be reduced."

Despite these strict measures, the trend toward higher wages continued in 1967. Preliminary figures show that there was an increase of more than 6 percent in hourly wage rates. To avoid further cost-push inflation, the Wilson government in 1968 secured an amendment to the 1966 Incomes Act under which the government was given power to delay the effective date of wage and price increases for up to 12 months. Under the Prices and Incomes Act, productivity agreements remained the principal loophole for immediate wage increases.

What are the main differences between the American guidepost policy and the British application of the productivity concept? The American guideposts were based on past productivity trends while the British wage policy considers the anticipated productivity gains. The British policy appears to be two-dimensional in contrast with the single dimension of the American guideposts. While the official American wage policy was based entirely on productivity trends appearing in the national economy, the British income policy considers productivity movements in the national economy as well as in individual industries and companies. For example, British productivity agreements like the one at Esso are based not on the national average but on productivity gains to be realized in a particular company. With a few exceptions, notably in the longshore industry and at Kaiser Steel, Americans have not paid much attention to the kind of productivity bargaining that is gaining acceptance in Great Britain.

Are inflationary dangers inherent in a situation where a national wage policy based on macro-economic productivity trends is operated simultaneously with incentive systems that rely on the individual productivity of the workers involved? In such cases, workers paid on individual or group incentives may receive productivity wage increases in two ways: a general increase based on the average productivity gains anticipated or realized in the national economy, and another based on their own productivity, which is a contributing factor to the national productivity. Further research is needed concerning the compatibility of national productivity wage policies with incentive systems.

Author's Recommended Reading List

Douty, H.M., "Productivity Bargaining in Britain," *Monthly Labor Review*, Vol. 91 (May 1968), pp. 1-6.

Flanders, Allan, *The Fawley Productivity Agreements* (London: Faber, 1964).

Jones, Ken, and Golding, John, *Productivity Bargaining* (London: Fabian Society, 1966).

Kendrick, J.W., "Productivity, Costs and Prices: Concepts," in *Wages, Prices, Profits and Productivity* (New York: American Assembly, 1959), pp. 249-260.

Knowles, K.G.J.C., "Wage Structure and Productivity in Great Britain," in *Labor Productivity* (eds. Dunlop-Diatchenco) (New York: McGraw-Hill, 1964), pp. 249-260.

Maddison, Angus, "Comparative Levels and Movements of Labor Productivity in Western Europe," in *Labor Productivity, op. cit.*, pp. 126-139.

Mangum, G.L., "Are Wage Incentives Becoming Obsolete?," *Industrial Relations*, Vol. 2, No. 1, (October 1962), pp. 73-96.

Nicholson, R.J., and Gupta, S., "Output and Productivity Changes in British Manufacturing Industry, 1948-54," *Journal of the Royal Statistical Society*, 1960.

Rees, Albert, "Patterns of Wages, Prices, and Productivity," in *Wages, Profits and Productivity* (New York: American Assembly, 1959), pp. 11-36.

Ross, A.M., "Prosperity and British Industrial Relations," *Industrial Relations*, Vol. 2, No. 2 (February 1963), pp. 63-94.

Council of Economic Advisers, *Annual Report* in 1962, 1964, 1966 (Washington, D.C.: U. S. Government Printing Office).

General Electric Company, "Another Look at the 'Wage Guideposts,'" *Relations News Letter,* August 13, 1963.

National Board for Prices and Incomes, *Productivity Agreements,* Report Number 36 (London: Her Majesty's Stationery Office, 1967).

Royal Commission on Trade Unions and Employers' Associations, *Productivity Bargaining,* Research Papers 4 (London: Her Majesty's Stationery Office, 1967).

TOWARD HARMONIZATION OF SOCIAL SECURITY IN THE EEC

By G. M. J. Veldkamp

In their origins, the social security systems of most countries — especially those which can boast of a history extending over more than half a century — show clear traces of both national and international influences. In seeking international sources of inspiration one looks for a relationship with Bismarckian laws. In more modern systems the concepts of the Beveridge Reports are often perceptible. The establishment of specific social security standards have been influenced by international agreements, sometimes on the initiative of the countries concerned and sometimes within the framework of international organizations such as the International Labour Organization, the Council of Europe, the European Economic Community, the European Coal and Steel Community, and Euratom.

Traces of national influences are especially marked in social legislation in general and social security law in particular.[1] Such influences are apparent in the debate at the various internal levels that surrounded the passage of social legislation. The subject matter of such legislation differed widely from country to country. Often the local character of the social ills sought to be remedied made for the enactment of provisions understandable only to the initiated.[2] Other national variations were caused by deliberate choice between a regulated and an unregulated system. Other historical differences are based on internal economic potential or preference, greater or lesser attention to specifics in legislative draftsmanship, promptness of compliance with enacted laws, and sometimes variations in the tempo of imposed compliance.

When consideration is given to the variations of these interna-

---

[1] I do not consider it necessary to give a detailed definition of the term "social security law." In this paper I am mainly concerned with social insurance law and legislation directly related to it. The family-allowances scheme for self-employed persons in the Netherlands is financed entirely from the general funds, but I treat it as coming under social security law. I do not conceive social security law as broadly as does a recent study by J.J.M. van der Ven, "Sociale zekerheid als maatschappelijk verschijnsel" (Social Security as a Social Phenomenon), in *Sociaal Maandblad Arbeid 1967*, p. 152 *et seq.* — that is to say, broadly enough to use the term as comprising both labor standards and social security legislation.

[2] M. G. Levenbach, "Het Nederlandse in onze arbeidswetgeving" (The Influence of the Dutch character in our Labor Legislation), in M. G. Levenbach, *Arbeidsrecht* 1951, p. 283.

tional and national influences over the years, it is readily seen how in most countries social legislation in general, and social security legislation in particular, acquired a fragmentary character and patchwork appearance.

For the taxpayer and the beneficiary, social security legislation has become an untraversable labyrinth. It is understandable that in many countries there should be a desire for a simplified, systematically compiled, and comprehensible body of law on the subject. But one still hears it said in a number of countries that, while harmonized, or even "equalized" or unified, social security legislation is desirable, the goal is utopian.[5]

DIFFICULTIES IN HARMONIZING SYSTEMS

It is difficult to achieve internal harmonization, equalization, or unification within the national systems of social security in the various countries of Western Europe. It is a much harder task to integrate the social security systems of different countries of the EEC, even if the governments of the six countries concerned were to set about it wholeheartedly and unqualifiedly. Indeed, the difficulties experienced at the national level in harmonizing or equalizing social security systems become multiplied, even apart from the manifest fiscal and economic obstacles, when the process is transposed to the international plane.

The governments concerned do not respond with much enthusiasm to pressures for overall harmonization of social security systems. Their objections have a realistic basis. The intensity of the challenge to certain acquired rights in the spheres of politics and social policy is a matter of common knowledge. Fears concerning the opposition of social pressure groups to any idea of relinquishing such rights are real and substantial. Let me cite a few examples which come within the broader orbit of social legislation.

The German arrangement for co-management and the Work Promotion Law,[4] debated and introduced in 1968, also embodies the legal machinery for unemployment insurance. Other illustrations are the recent French legislation on division of wealth increment, the French, Belgian, and Italian system of family allowance, the

[5] Cf. M. G. Levenbach, *40 Jaar Arbeidsrecht* (40 Years of Labor Legislation) (1966); W. Herschel, "Gesetzbuch der Arbeit, Heute?" (A Code of Labor Legislation — Today?) in *Arbeits — und Sozialrecht*, p. 1440 (1959); and Francesco Santoro-Passarelli, *Il diritto dell'economia* (Economic law), p. 19 *et seq.* (1950).

[4] "Entwurf eines Arbeitsförderungsgesetzes (AFG)" (Work Promotion Bill), Drucksache 484/67.

Dutch disablement insurance and the four nationwide insurance schemes, and the Luxembourg provisions concerning compulsory wage indexing in collective labor agreements. It is clear that much time will pass before the interested social pressure groups will formally yield their rights. Should harmonization proceed over their protests, then perforce the most favorable aspects of social legislation prevailing in the six Community countries will be adopted as the criterion. The price of harmonization is upward movement of all social security systems involved. The demands for harmonization thus may be just as impracticable as might be pressures for a harmonized taxation system incorporating what from the taxpayer's standpoint would be the most favorable parts of the legislation of each of the various countries concerned.

Must harmonization then be dropped as a goal? If anybody feels that what I have said thus far is a defeatist introduction that negates the desirability of harmonization, I should like quickly to disabuse him of this notion. While I firmly maintain that we must aim at harmonization, I have deliberately advanced some of the major drawbacks because I believe that recognition of these difficulties can instill in us a sober realism regarding the provisional and definitive tasks involved. I firmly insist that unless within measurable time European integration produces a European unitary state with unified legislation for all citizens living in its territory, a program of harmonization resulting in full unification or equalization is unattainable.[5]

As the Common Market develops further socially and economically, I favor efforts, within the limits of the possible and the desirable, to harmonize the various social security systems. I stress the words "within the limits of the possible and the desirable." For not every kind of harmonization is desirable and not every kind possible. The speed of movement to the consensual optimum, socially desirable in quality and range and economically possible, depend upon the degree of social and economic development — of social and economic progress, if you prefer — in the several EEC countries. Against the background of these socio-political and socio-economic facts of life are a number of considerations involving applicable law.

Rome Treaty

The Rome Treaty establishing the European Economic Community concerns itself in detail primarily with measures in the eco-

---

[5] This means, therefore, that both delegation through decentralization and deconcentration and autonomous rulemaking within unified legislation might result in differentiation of one type or another.

nomic field. It contains few provisions on social questions. Articles 48 and 51 relate to the free movement of workers within the Community, the exchange of young workers under a common program, and the measures necessary in the field of social security to bring about the free movement of workers.[6] In the same connection, Article 121 sets out rules concerning the implementation of common measures, particularly as regards social security, for the migrant workers referred to in Articles 48 to 51. Article 119 contains provisions on equal pay for equal work performed by men and women workers. Article 120 concerns the maintenance of the existing equivalence of holidays-with-pay schemes. Articles 123 to 128 embody rules regarding the European Social Fund and the general principles to govern the application of a common policy on vocational training. Finally, there is a special protocol concerning overtime in France.

That the Treaty contains so few concrete provisions in the social sphere is not in itself surprising. The authors' overriding preoccupation was the establishment of an economic union. In order to enable the economic union — with its corollary of free movement of workers — to function as efficiently as possible, *ad hoc* arrangements had to be made, and the concrete provisions on social matters were drafted accordingly. The view adopted was that everything likely to result in artificial distortions of conditions of competition must be settled in the Treaty and that provisions concerning social conditions and social policy were something distinct from the objective of establishing economic union and thus unnecessary. Not all differences in social conditions, labor costs, and the like hamper the functioning of an economic union. On the contrary, it might have been cogently argued that if conditions in the social sector were to be equalized on a large scale, the effect might be to destroy the objectives of the economic union because these include ensuring that production is carried on where it can be done most efficiently; that cost conditions ought to reflect scarcity conditions as accurately as possible.

Yet these considerations do not alter the fact that the provisions of the Treaty on a number of concrete subjects are of lesser importance than the provisions of Articles 117, 118 and, in my view, 122 also. Article 122 states that in its annual report to the European

---

[6] What it is customary to call the coordination of social security as distinct from the harmonization of social security; in the former case, the various national systems are as a general rule left intact. See also T. Koopmans, "Tenuitvoerlegging van gemeenschapsrecht door de Nederlandse overheid-sociale verzekering" (Implementation of Common Law by the Dutch Authorities-Social Insurance), *Transactions of the Vereniging voor Administratief recht, LX*, p. 26 (1968).

Parliament, the EEC Commission must devote a special chapter to the development of the social situation in the Community. It further provides that the European Parliament may ask the Commission to draw up reports on special problems regarding the social situation. Reporting is one of the Commission's major tasks. A skillfully worded report can show clearly where harmonization has been neglected without good reason or where an existing form of harmonization has been impaired. The task laid on the Commission by Article 122 can be closely related to the substantive specification of Articles 117 and 118.

Article 117 expressly postulates the principle of social harmonization in its declaration that the Member States recognize the necessity for promoting improvement of workers' living standards and labor conditions through general levelling-up. It proceeds directly to say that the Member States consider that this process will be accomplished in three ways, namely through the functioning of the Common Market, which will make for the harmonization of social systems, through the procedures laid down in the Treaty, and through correlation of legislative and administrative provisions.

Article 118 is the most important declaration on social policy. While this article lays considerable stress on the autonomy of the Member States in this field, it asserts that, without prejudice to the other Treaty provisions and in line with its general objectives, the Commission has the task of promoting close cooperation among the Member States in the social field. Seven types of social legislation, including social security, are listed by way of illustration. To this end the Treaty requires the Commission to work in close collaboration with the Member States by carrying out studies, making formal recommendations, and organizing consultations on problems arising at the national level or affecting international organizations. Before issuing recommendations, the Commission must consult the Economic and Social Committee. Articles 117, 118, and 122 actually embrace the entire field of social policy.

It is not an exaggeration to say that social policy has been assigned a subordinate place in the Rome Treaty, despite the declared and fundamental aim of the Common Market ultimately to raise living standards. As the preamble to the Treaty puts it: "constantly improving the living and working conditions of their (the signatory states') peoples." [7] The declared aim does not alter the limited role accorded to social policy in the Treaty. The limitation is not fortuitous. If it were, and if the Member States desired a vigorous social

---

[7] Cf. H. ter Heide, "De Europese Integratie" (European Integration), in *1966 Reports of the Vereniging voor de Staathuishoudkunde,* p. 123.

policy, geared in particular to harmonization or equalization of the social security systems, it would not be difficult to interpret the Treaty in such a way that a solid legal basis for such a common social policy would be found. But that is not the position. An examination of the events leading up to the signing of the Treaty reveals that social policy was an extremely controversial issue from the outset. Originally it was France that pressed for the inclusion of social harmonization among the Treaty aims. This was not because of any denial of the priority of economic union. On the contrary, France's desire for social harmonization stemmed not from social considerations but from a belief that thoroughgoing social harmonization (especially with regard to equal remuneration for men and women, the financing of social insurance, and hours worked and payment for overtime) was one of the major conditions for the removal of artificial restrictions on the proper functioning of the Common Market. While it might be argued that such beliefs were fallacious, or at least inadequate, because social charges cannot be dissociated from other normal cost factors, such as primary wage costs and capital costs,[8] it still would not follow that the factors in question would not distort competition. Inequalities in the financing of social security alone may seriously affect market competition.

The differences in concepts necessitated a compromise formula regarding social policy in the Treaty so as to accommodate the two viewpoints urged during the preliminary work on the drafting.[9] The first of these was that social charges are artificial costs which distort competition and must accordingly be harmonized. The second view was that social charges are — chiefly because they are so closely related to wages — natural costs which are determined by the place of business, do not distort competition, and therefore need not be harmonized. The first attitude was expressed mainly by France. The second was advanced by Germany. There was also the significant background factor at work that social policy was at the time felt to be within the exclusive province of the national authorities.

I share the opinion of Wohlfahrt and his colleagues, footnoted in the two preceding paragraphs, that, in conformity with the overall concept of the EEC Treaty, social charges must ineluctably be deemed to be artificial costs and should therefore be treated as such, that is to say, in the same way as the taxes imposed on a product.[10]

---

[8] E. Wohlfahrt, U. Everling, H. J. Glaesner, R. Sprung, *Die Europaische Wirtschaftsgemeinschaft* (The European Economic Community), p. 363 (1960).
[9] *Id.* at 367.
[10] *Id.* at 364. Cf. Articles 95 and 96 of the Treaty. Under the provisions of

It is true that the compromise formula in Article 117 tended to meet the view that social charges distort competition when it predicted that the functioning of the Community would automatically result in an equalization of the living and working conditions of labor in the various Member States. But the other view finds support in assertions that the Member States are in agreement as to the necessity of promoting improvement of the living and working conditions of labor and thus encouraging "upward equalization." However, no obligation to proceed further in this direction is assumed other than the provisions of Article 118, which are open to so many constructions.

A will was not then present, nor is it today, to establish such a far-reaching obligation either as economic policy or as social policy and social law. The difference between these two approaches, as I see it, lies in the fact that, where economic policy is concerned with social security, only the level of social charges and the method of financing them are relevant, whereas from the angle of social policy and social law, the relevant factor is the building up of the social security system as such, both materially and with regard to underlying criteria.

In view of these facts it is necessary to examine ways of steering a course between Scylla and Charybdis so as to arrive at an optimum solution in the light of the limited Treaty provisions.

EEC Commission v. Council of Ministers

I must point out that the EEC Commission has wanted to go further in this matter than the governments of the six Community countries and that, through its powers under Article 118, it wanted to give impetus to European social policy, both in the direction of harmonization and in substantive benefits. The Commission's activities in this field have not always met with the approval of all the Member States. Divergence between the Council of Ministers and the Commission gradually developed into an impasse in that the Council expressly dissociated itself from the activities undertaken by

---

Article 95, a countervailing levy may be imposed on an imported product to bring the fiscal charge on the product into alignment with the fiscal charge on like domestic products through indirect taxation in the broadest sense of the term. Conversely, a drawback may be allowed on exports. The provisions of Articles 95 and 96 are designed to achieve equality in fiscal levies for the purposes of conditions of competition, in other words, to prevent a specific distortion as a result of tax policy. According to Wohlfahrt et al, note 8, supra, the same treatment, or a different treatment which nevertheless has the same effect, should be applied to social charges.

the Commission under Article 118. For a long time no special meeting of the Council on Social Questions took place.

In the second half of 1966, when I was acting chairman of the
Social Council set up within the Council of Ministers, I made an
attempt to end this unsatisfactory situation by activating matters
through a memorandum — in the nature of things a compromise
document — designed to prepare the ground for a discussion in the
Council. This discussion brought about agreement on December 19,
1966.

The best way to feel the extent of the crisis of confidence,
which lasted until the end of 1966, is to consider the wide divergence of ideas on social policy for the European Community. This
issue raises fundamental questions: Is there any need for a European social policy? What should be the role of the Council of Ministers, the Commission, the European Parliament, the Economic and
Social Committee, the national governments, and the two sides of
industry in this field? Which subjects should be given priority?
What are the procedures that must be followed? In what community
instruments should the results, if any, be reflected? [11]

The principal criticism directed to the Commission by the various governments was that it was prone to go beyond its powers
under Article 118. According to some critics, instead of fostering
close cooperation among the Member States, the Commission sought
to compel social harmonization by bringing pressure to bear on the
two sides of industry, in particular the trade unions, and the national parliaments. Thus some groups expressed a desire to curb the
Commission's freedom of action drastically in two ways. First, it
was urged that the Commission should be allowed to study particular subjects only after it had been formally empowered to do so by
or in the Council. Secondly, the proposal was made that consultation of the two sides of industry by the Commission should be limited only to the subjects thus authorized and only by those bodies
that had been provided for in the Treaty or set up subsequently by
a decision of the Council.

In my memorandum, I left no room for doubt that from a legal
standpoint both these demands were unacceptable. In both respects,
I asserted, the Commission possesses its own rights, which are not

---

[11] L. H. J. Crijns, "De sociale politiek van de Europese Gemeenschap" (The
Social Policy of the European Community) in *De Christelijke werkgever*, April
1967, No. 4, p. 211 *et seq.* See also J. D. Neirinck, "Social Policy of the EEC Commission," *Collegium Falconis, Louvain* (1967).

inhibited by Article 118 or any other Treaty article.[12] Since I felt that experience had clearly shown that little could be achieved with mere formal and legalistic references, my memorandum advocated a more pragmatic approach, a sort of gentlemen's agreement, under which the Commission would have to be prepared, pursuant to Article 118, to concentrate primarily — and this included consultation with the two sides of industry — on matters which it knew to be of interest to the Member States. Such an agreement would mean that the governments of the Member States would for their part be willing to give their full backing to the implementation of relevant proposals for cooperation, which would open up possibilities for more specific forms of harmonization. On this basis, the Council reached agreement on December 19, 1966. The various points that relate to the harmonization of social security are dealt with in detail later in this paper.

To evaluate the various problems surrounding the harmonization of social security systems, it is necessary to distinguish the extent and manner of the financing of such systems and their administrative structure for determining benefit eligibility wherein the numbers and classes of recipients naturally constitute an important factor. If anything is to be achieved in the harmonization of these two major aspects of social security, there will have to be an examination of the Treaty provisions to see what can be done within their framework.

Under Article 117 of the EEC Treaty, harmonization of social systems can be pursued along three lines — first, through the functioning of the Common Market; second, through the procedures outlined in the Treaty; and third, through the correlation of legislative and administrative provisions. The functioning of the Common Market does not present a question of wielding a legal instrument. The contrary is true of the two other methods. Utilization of the procedures contemplated by the Treaty requires interpretation and application of all provisions relating directly or indirectly to workers, particularly Articles 48 to 51, Article 118, and Articles 123 to 128. The correlation of legal and administrative provisions involves specifically Articles 100 to 102.[13]

Emphasis upon these particular articles does not mean that I do not attach importance to other articles in the Rome Treaty, such as for instance, Articles 38 et seq. (common agricultural policy), 74 et seq. (common transport policy), 104 (high level of employment),

---

[12] There was a momentary misunderstanding in some trade union circles that the compromise would have prejudiced these rights.

[13] Wohlfahrt et al., op. cit., note 8, supra, p. 366.

and 105 and 145 (coordination of general economic policies). All of these have substantial social significance.

Some people are enraged by the expression "social harmonization." They construe harmonization as meaning complete equality materially and formally. This interpretation is a serious misunderstanding of the term. Advocates of harmonization do not contemplate complete equalization. The reach of harmonization inferable from the Treaty is modest. It is my opinion that the term "harmonization" means nothing more or less than bringing all systems into alignment with each other and comprises a whole range of possibilities. If four out of six countries have an old-age pension scheme and the two others do not, the introduction of such a scheme in these two countries means that a certain degree of harmonization has been effected because all the countries concerned now have an old-age pension scheme. If all countries have a system of old-age insurance but some of them have a number of specific restrictions, the abandonment of these restrictions means that in this case too, despite all other remaining differences, a measure of harmonization has taken place. If a number of countries guarantee a "social minimum" for a specific sector in their social security legislation and the other countries decide to do the same, this may be said — even though the social minima themselves are different — to constitute harmonization. If a major legal concept can be standardized in the otherwise differing insurance laws of the countries concerned, here again we would have an example of harmonization.

Need for Gradual Approach

Anybody who thinks that social harmonization can be achieved overnight by means of a large-scale reorganization is making a mistake. Whoever takes his time and seeks to effect seemingly minor harmonizations will find that a gradual approach is quite fruitful. There are good reasons for proceeding gradually and along pragmatic lines.

Time is on the side of harmonization because the method afforded by Article 117 requires time to make its effects felt. The view that harmonization of social systems is assisted by the functioning of the Common Market itself is being borne out.[14] The range of insured persons in the Community has been widened considerably since 1958, differentiated according to insurance branch, categories

---

[14] Ph. van Praag, "Harmonisatie en egalisatie in EEG-verband van de verschillende sociale verzekeringssystemen" (Harmonization and Equalization of the Various Social Insurance Systems in the EEC), *Sociaal Maandblad Arbeid,* p. 606 (1966).

of persons, and country. A particularly notable feature has been the extension of the scheme to the self-employed.[15] There has also been an evening up in the ratios between the total amount of social security benefits and the national income, namely from 13.4 to 17.4 percent in 1960 to 17.7 to 19.5 percent in 1965. From these figures it may be concluded that the range is from one sixth to one fifth of the national income, with a tendency towards alignment. Should the variations become still smaller and eventually be eliminated, it could legitimately be said that, despite all differences, social security had been harmonized in the material aspect. But this in itself would not solve the problem. For there would remain the question of harmonizing benefits per head of population.

The influence exercised by contacts in the Council of Ministers, committees, and working groups is demonstrable. These afford opportunities of promptly ascertaining intentions and developments in other countries and arriving at the right interpretation from first-hand data. I know from experience what an exemplary effect is thus obtained.

There is another reason for proceeding gradually. As I have already shown, social security systems have assumed a labyrinthine aspect on the national level. International comparison of the various national social security systems is in itself becoming more difficult as it becomes more detailed. It requires time and care to make an accurate comparison based on a precise interpretation of concepts. It also takes time to ascertain which measures can be accomplished quickly and which only at a much later date.

In this connection, it seemed desirable to me in 1966 that the

---

[15] Van Praag, *op. cit, supra*, p. 608, states, for instance, that in 1958 the proportion of the total EEC population which was covered by health insurance legislation amounted to 75 percent; by 1963 it had risen to about 85 percent and has since increased further. Van Praag points out that the expansion has been to a large extent accounted for by self-employed persons. Thus the following classes have been brought within the ambit of national health insurance: retail tradesmen and craftsmen (Italy); self-employed farmers (France and Luxembourg); aged persons (France); self-employed persons in general (Belgium), under a law on the application of old-age insurance; self-employed persons in the crafts sector (Italy); and traders, industrialists, and members of the professions (Luxembourg). In the Netherlands, the self-employed have been brought under the law concerning old-age, widows', and orphans' pensions. On the other hand, the author shows that in the financing of social insurance there is still a difference between two groups of countries. In Germany, Belgium, and Luxembourg, State contributions have been maintained at a high level (between 19.3 and 24.2 percent of the funds in 1958 and between 22 and 22.5 percent in 1965). The relevant proportion has been low in France and the Netherlands (7.1 to 9.8 percent in 1958 and 6.7 to 7.3 percent in 1965). In the case of Italy, it was at about the same level as in France and the Netherlands in 1958. By 1965 it had risen in Italy to 22.6 percent as a result of the provisional fiscal measures in the field of social security.

Council and the Commission should reach agreement on a strategic approach that would incorporate a fundamental methodological view. I suggested that the Commission should first concentrate, under Article 118, on three matters all of which lie mainly within the sphere of social security. The Council of Ministers concurred, adding to these three questions a number of other ones which are important but are not here discussed.

The field of social security would be investigated in these respects:

(1) A systematic inquiry would be made into the desirability, necessity, and possibility of a harmonization of the concepts and definitions employed in the various social systems, particularly those relating to social security;

(2) There would be extensive studies concerning social benefit costs and the extent of apportionment of such cost between employers and workers and the public treasury;

(3) An inquiry would be made into the possibility of ratification by the Member States of conventions on minimum social security standards that have been drawn up within the framework of other international organizations.

In my opinion, these three inquiries will enable justice to be done to both major aspects of social security, the economic aspect and that of social policy and social legislation.

The second of the studies initiated, although it contains implications affecting social policy and social legislation in view of the charges which are borne by the insured themselves, is concerned primarily with vital economic policy that seeks to prevent distortions in such matters as common agricultural prices. On the two other points I feel that some further explanation is called for. It will be noted that the first inquiry is confined to the desirability, necessity, and possibility of harmonizing concepts and definitions. No mention is made of any systematic inquiry into the desirability, necessity, and possibility of harmonizing the actual benefits. For clarity, in the rest of my discussion I shall distinguish between "material harmonization" and harmonization of standards and principles.

The term "material harmonization" refers chiefly to the scope of the insurance with regard to volume and sphere of operation. How far harmonization is desirable and possible in this respect depends on both economic and social factors. An ideal social security system affording the most satisfactory protection possible against all social risk is not to be found in any of the six Community countries. The systems of EEC nations have a variety of gaps. In the gradual

.development of an optimum social security system in any nation, allowance must be made for financial and economic factors on the one hand and social factors on the other. Financial and economic factors must be taken into account because the introduction of new social benefits and the revision of existing benefits make demands on economic and financial resources. Although such measures restrict opportunities for spending primary income, they either bring about an increase in costs, which is passed on in prices, or else limit industrial profits. New or improved social benefit programs may cause higher governmental expenditures. Such expenditures either curtail spending for other purposes or lead to increased taxation. The most rational course for introducing new or improved social benefits would be to secure their financing from expansion of productivity. Such methods would avoid undesirable inflationary impulses and prevent adverse influences upon the development of private savings.

All the countries concerned have heeded these considerations, though insufficiently, in the course of the years. Attention to such precautions means that all social benefit aims cannot be fulfilled at the same time. Sometimes the introduction of a new or improved type of social insurance is retarded by general economic pressures, as reflected in the following criteria: an adequate level of employment, balance-of-payments equilibrium, a reasonable level or growth of investments, a fair distribution of income, and stable prices.

In view of the limited resources available, the various countries of the EEC have repeatedly been confronted with the question of priorities for improvements. Thus the social problems dealt with in the expressed political aims of each nation may be clearly seen.

The choice of economic and social priorities as regards volume and sphere of operation has not been the same in every country.[16] Moreover, the economic conditions for the development of the social security system have not been propitious in all countries at the same time. Thus it is clear why there is a difference in volume and sphere of operation. Even if there were a general will to reduce or eliminate the existing material differences through harmonization, the varying rates of economic growth and social preference in each nation inhibit efforts to standardize.

The differences are great. This is seen if, for instance, the French and Italian family allowances are compared with the corre-

---

[16] E.g., W. Clausen, in *Kein Verlass auf Vater Staat, Soziale Sicherheit heute und morgen* (No Reliance on the State Bountiful; Social Security Today and Tomorrow) (1967), is of the opinion that, with increased prosperity, the extent of social security benefits could be limited because the population, being better off, could itself bear elementary risks.

sponding rates in Germany and the Netherlands. Or when the optimum disability benefit for wage earners in the Netherlands is compared with that in other countries, where victims of industrial accidents receive distinctly more favorable treatment than persons who have been unable to work for a long period through causes not connected with employment. In the field of old-age and widows' and orphans' benefits, too, there are considerable differences. The situation varies from favorable to very unfavorable, an example of the latter being the absence of a satisfactory widow's benefit in France. While I do not lay too much stress on the *de facto* differences, I would point out that there are particularly marked differences in the sphere of operation. Whereas in practically every country the family-allowances system either covers or is on the way to covering the entire population, the other forms of benefit show appreciable differences in the extent of protective coverage.

Although exchange of information and acquaintance with the situations and initiatives of other nations may influence social preferences, it must suffice here to trace the trend in material harmonization that results from the functioning of the Common Market. Where this is favorable, in both economic growth (structure) and stability of such growth (economic situation), conditions are created for the necessary improvement of social security. In medium-term programming, of course, attention could be given to this aspect in relation to the other aims of the economic, financial, and social policies of the Community countries, which would appear to be the intention in the third program with regard to medium-term economic policy.

In discussing harmonization of principles, I have chiefly in mind general legal concepts and principles that include such matters as definitions, forms of delegation, administrative regulations for the implementation of laws, rules of procedure, and enforcement regulations.

In this field manifestly there is a great deal of uncharted territory concerning comparison and harmonization of laws. Although these are not spectacular aspects, they are nonetheless highly important ones. Moreover, harmonization of principles encounters far fewer financial, economic, or political obstacles. It is desirable that such comparative studies should open up the way to harmonization of legal techniques. In turn these efforts could be employed as catalysts for further-reaching forms of harmonization.

Another subject of study concerns the possibility of ratification by the Member States of conventions on minimum social security standards which have been drawn up within the framework of other international organizations. While there are conventions on social security standards that some Community countries have not yet ratified, an inquiry within the EEC into this question may have the effect of stimulating the ratification of all, or at least a number, of these conventions. Thus, harmonization will be furthered.

To my notion the most important instruments concerning harmonization of social security systems are:

ILO Convention No. 102 on minimum social security standards, ratified by all EEC countries except France;

ILO Convention No. 118 on equality of treatment for nationals and foreigners in the field of social security, ratified by Italy and the Netherlands;[17]

ILO Convention No. 121 on benefits in the case of employment injury, ratified by the Netherlands only, although Belgium and Luxembourg have initiated the ratification procedure;

European Social Charter, ratified by Germany and Italy, although the ratification procedure has been initiated in Belgium, Luxembourg, and the Netherlands;

European Code on Social Security and Protocol, ratified by the Netherlands only, although the ratification procedure has been initiated by Belgium, Italy and Luxembourg.

In my discussion thus far, I have not dwelled at any length on the rules concerning the free movement of workers within the Community because the regulations promulgated in connection with Articles 48 to 51 and 121 of the Treaty in the field of social security systems[18] are concerned to a far greater degree with individual disputes than with harmonization of social security systems.[19] In that respect the regulations are comparable with the system embodied in ILO Convention No. 118 concerning equality of treatment for nationals and foreigners and with most of the bilateral conventions concluded between countries in the field of social security. In addition, particular attention focuses on rules concerning the nondiscrimination principle, the *pro rata temporis* principle, and the export-of-acquired-rights principle. While inequalities affecting migrant workers between legislation in the mother country and legislation in the country of migration do not alone demand administrative har-

---

[17] Also relevant here are the bilateral conventions concluded between Belgium and Greece and between Belgium and Turkey; between Germany and Greece and between Germany and Turkey; between France and Greece; and between the Netherlands and Greece and between the Netherlands and Turkey.

[18] Of particular importance here are Regulations 3 and 4.

[19] Cf. J. Mannoury, *Hoofdtrekken van de sociale verzekering* (Principal Features of Social Insurance), p. 206 (1968); see also T. Koopmans, *op. cit.*, note 6, *supra*, p. 27.

monization, it cannot be gainsaid that equality would aid administration in the consequent simplification of claim-settling procedures.

As a consequence of the free movement of workers, nationals of the six Community countries are quickly aware of the effects of social security systems in other countries. Where these systems offer them better social treatment, the migrant workers will let this be known in their own countries. Such communications may lead to social and political action. Where this holds good for individual workers, it applies with all the more force in the case of trade union leaders from the various countries who have contacts with each other at the European level. Nor can we underestimate the significance of the contacts set up at a high official level in the Administrative Committee for Social Security, to which important tasks are assigned by the provisions of Regulations 3 and 4.

MEANS OF HARMONIZATION

In the foregoing I have endeavored to outline as objectively as possible a variety of impediments to the harmonization of social security systems, and I have sought to demonstrate the limited possibilities for such action. I have also called attention to the need to utilize to the full such possibilities, where they exist, and I have attempted to provide an understanding of the strategy which should be employed, as mapped out by the Council of Ministers in December 1966. I deem it a matter of satisfaction that since that date there has been no deviation from the agreed course. I now propose to examine in detail the instruments which can be used either to widen the limited possibilities or to carry out harmonization measures within them as they now stand. It is therefore necessary to distinguish between *jus constituendum* and *jus constitutum*.

To start with *jus constituendum*, I should like to refer to my argument that if all the Member States were determined to harmonize social security systems in the best possible manner, extensive interpretation of the Treaty might well facilitate more rapid progress than is now planned. This does not alter the fact that social policy has received scant treatment in the Treaty. The only way to change this situation is to change the Treaty itself. An *ad hoc* amendment is clearly out of the question. But it might be within the abilities of European workers' and employers' organizations and of the national parliaments and the European Parliament to bring strong pressure to bear on the governments, now that the Executives have been duly merged, for the merging of the Treaties. Such Treaty mergers would offer draftsmanship opportunities for a new chapter on social policy more in keeping with the ultimate aim of the Treaties than the present one.

To particularize, the existing provisions could be supplemented by rules relating to minimum social security standards, such as those found in ILO Convention No. 102, the European Code on Social Security, and the European Social Charter. These new provisions could be put into operation in accordance with a certain time schedule. A degree of social security harmonization could be incorporated as one of the Treaty aims in more explicit terms than at present. I emphasize "a degree" of harmonization because in my opinion full-scale harmonization can never be the ultimate goal. In this connection the expression in Article 3(e) of the ECSC Treaty "gradual harmonization in an upward direction" could not be used as it stands. But the wording used should make it unequivocally clear that social security harmonization must be carried out to the greatest possible extent and should also prescribe procedures for ensuring that efforts are actually directed to that end. Let there be no misunderstanding. I do not advocate following a course prejudicial to the economic development of the Communities. But if the economic development of the Communities affords scope for such measures, I do urge positive efforts toward harmonization of social security systems, not only from an economic view but also in social policy and social law. I do not argue for equalization, because it is my view that, subject only to compliance with minimal standards, national preferences and differences must be allowed to continue.

It is well to distinguish between those existing instruments which are and those which are not expressly designed to promote the creation of Community standards of law. As already noted, Article 117 declares that the alignment process will result primarily from the functioning of the Common Market itself. But the functioning of the Common Market is not something that is merely inherent, or derived alone from the free play of economic and social forces. It is something that is influenced by the Community's whole policy.

Just as overall economic and financial policy in the individual countries today seeks to create conditions for vigorous and balanced economic growth, there is also required a similar European policy for the development of the Common Market. Furthermore, and precisely for the purposes of social policy — and the need for social security harmonization is an integral part of this social policy — such a European policy for expansion and balanced growth must be supported. Another factor of major importance is the provision of information by means of reports. The more data the Commission offers concerning the *de facto* differences and the possibilities and difficulties surrounding the elimination of the differences, the easier will it be to find a way of removing superfluous variations. To this end, the investigations and studies which the Commission is empowered to undertake pursuant to Article 118 are of vital significance. And the more agreement the Commission and the Council of Ministers can reach on that point, the more likely are effective results. While here the inquiry strategy resolved upon in 1966 assumes an important place, it is still more important that in the future there be no straying from strategic points. The overall problem of social security harmonization has so many facets that it is easy to stray from the main thoroughfares, and whoever does this finds himself wandering aimlessly in a maze.

Use of the instruments specifically designed to promote the creation of Community legal standards requires investigations, studies, and discussions concerning social security harmonization. The more systematically and carefully such inquiries are carried out, the more effective are likely to be the efforts to arrive at Community legal standards. In connection with the establishment of such standards, I must distinguish between the instruments afforded by the EEC Treaty for this purpose and the instruments afforded by separate conventions between the Member States where the standards in question cannot be established on the basis of the Treaty. As I see it, the instruments embodied in the Treaty are supplemental to the opinions issued by the Commission under Article 118 and the Council's recommendations, the directives provided for in Article 100, the recommendations provided for in Article 155, and the preliminary decision of the Court of Justice referred to in Article 177 of the Treaty.[20] Article 100 declares that the Council of Ministers, acting by means of a unanimous vote on a proposal of the Commission, must issue directives for the correlation of those legal and administrative provisions applying in the Member States which have a direct bearing on the establishment or functioning of the Common Market. The question is, therefore, whether aspects of social security harmonization may be deemed to have a direct relationship to the establishment or functioning of the Common Market.

A great deal of weight is carried by recommendations made by the Commission and by the Council. I must distinguish between recommendations which do not relate directly to the harmonization of social security systems but are of significance in this respect and recommendations which directly concern the harmonization process.

---

[20] Cf. Van Praag, *op. cit.*, note 14, *supra*, p. 608.

The first type may be said to comprise recommendations on overall economic and financial policy, such as those relating to short-term and medium-term economic policy, and recommendations having a bearing on policy to be followed with regard to particular sectors, such as agriculture and transport.[21] These recommendations will be concerned far more with the economic and political aspects of "material harmonization," in the field of both financing and benefits, than with the harmonization of principles and the like. I feel rather apprehensive about recommendations relating to policy for individual sectors that give rise to separate social security policies for each sector in a Community context. This counters the tendency towards the general application of social security systems which is taking place in most of the countries concerned.

Even though recommendations of a general or economic character as a rule are concerned not with harmonization but with policy coordination, the relative autonomy of the various social security systems and the policy to be applied to them must not be overlooked lest a situation arise in which social security is accorded bottom priority in such recommendations.

Recommendations relating directly to social security harmonization may be a direct result of the studies referred to previously and may provide for step-by-step fulfilment of certain aspects of such harmonization. Recommendations to this end have already been issued, such as the European Commission's recommendation of July 23, 1962, to the Member States concerning the compilation of a Community list of occupational diseases; that of July 20, 1966, concerning conditions for compensation of victims of occupational diseases; and the draft resolution of 1966 concerning a common definition of disablement to support claims for disablement benefit, upon which the European Parliament issued an opinion at its session in January 1968.

Another instrument which can be used for the establishment of Community standards of law is the judgment rendered by the Court of Justice in the form of a preliminary decision, as provided by Article 177 of the Treaty.[22] The decisions made by the Court on such

---

[21] As part of the common agricultural policy or the common transport policy, it is even permissible to lay down regulations and directives or to give instructions in principle regarding social questions too. The problems involved are not dealt with here.

[22] T. Koopmans, "Het Hof van Justitie van de Europese Gemeenschappen en de Sociale Verzekering" (The Court of Justice of the European Communities and Social Insurance), *Sociaal Maandblad Arbeid* (1966), and G. Lyon-Caen, in a paper quoted by Van Praag, *op. cit.*, note 14, *supra,* and read at Brussels on February 20, 1967.

matters — which differ from the directives and recommendations in that they do not create any Community law but interpret what has already been established under this head — are aimed at preventing Community law from being interpreted and applied in different ways in different countries. They are binding upon domestic courts. While they play no part in the interpretation of the national legal and administrative provisions, they may nevertheless indirectly influence this process. An instance is provided by the Court's judgment (Case 75/63) holding that the applicability of Article 19 of Regulation No. 3 , concerning social security for migrant workers, is not limited to migrant workers in a narrow sense. This judgment has had significant practical effects in the case of wage earners spending their holidays as tourists in another Member State. Pursuant to unanimous agreement reached between the government representatives in the Administrative Committee as a result of this judgment, each Member State issued directives for the application of the relevant provisions, with the result that insured persons who are not actually migrant workers but, for reasons other than the carrying on of their wage-earning activities, are temporarily staying in the territory of a Member State other than that in which they have their residence may submit claims under the provisions of article 19, par. 1, of Regulation No. 3.[23]

Steps at the National Level

Up to this point I have viewed the problems involved in the harmonization of social security primarily from the angle of the EEC and the EEC Treaty. Apart from each nation's contribution towards the functioning of the Community, what can be done at the national level with regard to the desirable harmonization? A theoretical distinction might be made between two possible contributions. The first would consist of amendments to municipal laws which would eliminate differences from the laws of most of the other countries. The second would be to refrain from making any amendments to the local laws which would increase such differences. A question would arise whether the latter inhibition should be carried so far that, for sake of harmonization, improvements in local social security laws should be thwarted because they had not yet been enacted in other countries. I believe this question should be answered in the negative.

---

[23] See *Vierde Jaarverslag betreffende uitvoering van de verordeningen inzake de sociale zekerheid van migrerende werknemers* (Fourth Annual Report Concerning Implementation of the Regulations on Social Security for Migrant Workers), Jan.-Dec. 1962, par. 24.

With regard to a concrete contribution from the municipal laws, I should like to mention four matters in which the harmonization aspect appears. The first of these is the gradual elimination of all wage and income ceilings in Dutch social insurance for all categories of employed and self-employed persons, with the exception of medical-treatment insurance, under the Health Insurance Funds Law, in respect of normal risks such as medical and surgical treatment by family doctors, specialists, and hospital treatment during the first year. In justification of the abolition of wage ceilings, especially in sickness-benefit insurance and redundancy and unemployment-benefit insurance, it is emphasized that, apart from considerations of general social policy, in this way a degree of harmonization with the systems of the other EEC countries can be obtained. In this connection, attention should be given to the study carried out within Benelux on aspects of social security legislation which lend themselves to harmonization, wherein the abolition of the wage ceiling is highlighted. To judge by the report, the measures enacted in this field by the Dutch authorities are applauded by the other Benelux countries. On May 25, 1964, the Benelux Committee of Ministers endorsed the report's findings.

The second matter concerns recent discussion in the Netherlands on the abolition of family allowance for the first child. In view of the rising trend of social insurance charges, especially in the field of medical treatment, ways are being sought to achieve some retrenchments in social insurance to ensure that first things come first in the determination of social priorities.[24] In this connection, the Government has asked the Social and Economic Council for an opinion concerning abolition of family allowance for the first child. In the suggestions which I advanced on the subject, I gave due weight to the argument that even if the level of the family allowance is left out of account, harmonization of the family allowance laws within the EEC will be rendered easier if the allowance is granted as of the second child rather than the first. In the past, I have advocated gradual elimination over a period of five years of the allowance for the first child.

The third matter concerns the constant pressure that has been exerted from various quarters in the Netherlands for an increase in the state contribution to social insurance. Attention is called to the fact that the corresponding contributions are in general higher in

---

[24] See Veldkamp, *De Sociale Zekerheid opnieuw beschouwd in perspectief* (Social Security Reappraised at Long Range) (1967), also published in *Sociale Triptiek*, 1968. For a condensed survey, see my articles "Aspecten van de hedendaagse Nederlandse sociale verzekering" (Aspects of Present-day Social Insurance in the Netherlands), I and II, *Revue Belge de Sécurité Sociale* (1968 and 1969).

the other EEC countries. I do not contend that the mere ironing out of differences in this respect would be likely to equalize conditions of competition in the field concerned, because in any case it would be necessary to know the funds from which the state contributions were being financed.

To come to the fourth matter, I have in mind the desirability of requiring an insured person to bear a certain proportion of the risk in medical-treatment insurance and what this proportion should be. Although in the Netherlands a number of groups — some of them in Parliament — have paid lip service to the introduction of such a measure, they have hitherto been emphatic in their rejection of concrete proposals on the subject. Nor have any opinions yet been expressed by the official advisory bodies which have been consulted by the government in this connection. Precisely because this is a field in which a question of restricting rights arises, it would appear to be worthwhile to make a comparison with what has been done elsewhere in the EEC before enacting any relevant measures.

Needless to say, the problem of the contribution, and in this case the negative contribution, to harmonization of social security systems also crops up when it comes to reviewing and extending these systems at the national level. I maintain that the governments concerned, when submitting proposals to the national parliaments on the subject, should provide as detailed information as possible on the arrangements in operation in the other EEC countries. Thereby due account may be taken of the various points of agreement and difference and of the possible narrowing or broadening of the differences through revision or extension of social security systems.

I further maintain that for the time being, apart from necessary social improvements, everything possible should be done to avoid increasing disparities among the various nations. I believe, however, that, as long as important social needs have not been satisfied and the growth in the national prosperity makes it possible to satisfy them, there must be no delay in remedying this situation within the framework of the desirable harmonization of social security systems.

As far as the Netherlands is concerned, I have in mind principally the full-scale introduction of the Law on Industrial Injury Insurance, effective July 1, 1967. Under this law, there is no longer any distinction between disablement as a result of an industrial accident and disablement not so caused. For all workers who are incapacitated for a protracted period, adequate loss-of-earnings insurance benefits and rehabilitation facilities have been established.

I also have in mind the disablement insurance scheme for persons other than wage earners which is still being set up. I refer also to the introduction on January 1, 1968, of the General Law on Special Sickness Costs, which provides for insurance of the entire population against severe medical risks, including long periods of treatment in hospitals. Finally I have in mind important activities which still must be carried out to secure adequate pensions for aged persons and widows and orphans in addition to or in connection with General Old-Age Insurance and General Widows' and Orphans' Insurance. Naturally, I consider that in the implementation of these projects due heed must be given to the experience of other EEC countries. Quite naturally I am in favor of an exchange of views on the subject with other EEC countries and with the Commission in order to ensure that, within the framework of the desired extension, aspects of social security harmonization are as far as possible accorded the attention which they merit.

CONCLUSION

I began my survey by pointing to the considerable difficulties involved at the outset in harmonization of social security systems in the EEC countries, quite apart from varying national attitudes. I then examined the relevant aspects of social security harmonization in an EEC context. I believe that, despite all the difficulties and all the restrictions which there may be at the present time, we can nevertheless say that harmonization of the social security systems can be accomplished. The *de facto* trend is towards alignment. At policy level, agreement has been reached on a strategic method of investigation. Moreover, the Commission's activities have been directed to carrying out the necessary inquiries. All this begets a moderate amount of optimism, which must not, however, divert our minds from sober appraisal of the tasks ahead.

Author's Recommended Reading List

Querido, Arie, *The Development of Socio-Medical Care in the Netherlands* (New York: Humanities Press, 1968).
Windmuller, John P. *Labor Relations in the Netherlands* (Ithaca: Cornell University Press, 1969).
Employer's Liabilities Under Social Service Legislation in the Countries of the European Common Market. S.A. C.E.D. — Samson N.V. 7 Rue Ph. de Champagne, Brussels 1, Belgium.

Part VI

Utilization, Mobility, and Training of Manpower in Western Europe

Wage levels and manpower availability are interdependent. Despite pieties like the Clayton Act declaration that "the labor of a human being is not a commodity or article of commerce," labor markets do exist and wages are determined to a significant degree by the market forces of supply and demand. In this part, Professor John C. Shearer, among other things, cautions American firms against optimistic assumptions that higher levels of job skills and better work habits will generally be found among available West European workers than among their American counterparts. He shows that the European experience parallels the American in the coexistence of large-scale unemployment with extensive manpower shortages because of the inadequacy of industrial training methods. He contrasts the more mature official European manpower programs with the belated and fragmentary American efforts to cope with unemployment and skill shortages.

Professor Louis F. Buckley supplements Professor Shearer's analyses with his own observations as a manpower administrator and academic researcher. Allan Flanders discusses a reservoir of trained manpower resources, idle because of management timidity and trade union rigidity. Guy Nunn analyzes the present edge that employers in the United States have over European employers in the costs of arranging employee layoffs of even short duration. He suggests that the costs of layoffs to American employers will increase in the near future through collective bargaining provisions comparable to European specifications for long notice of job termination or suspension. P. P. Fano discusses the manpower difficulties and policies of Italy, the EEC nation with the greatest labor surplus. Dr. G. M. J. Veldkamp concludes this part with an analysis of manpower problems in the EEC countries and argues that attempts at national solutions in the Six must prove futile; the answers, he believes, will be found in Community-wide programs of short-term, medium-term and long-term character.

In the seminars much of the commentary was aimed at two

pervasive manpower issues: First, are there any data evidencing long-term success in retraining employees of obsolete skills in new skills not likely to be soon rendered obsolescent? For example, Mr. Flanders observed that British coal miners could easily be retrained to become bus fare collectors, but he noted also that local carrier transportation in Britain was moving increasingly to one-man operation. Second, should new industry be encouraged to move to economically outmoded areas, or should employees and their families be transported to existing or new industrial areas? From seminar discussion it appeared that these problems are as vexatious in Western Europe as they are in the United States.

MANPOWER ENVIRONMENTS CONFRONTING AMERICAN FIRMS IN WESTERN EUROPE

By John C. Shearer

Manpower considerations relevant to the operations of firms in Western Europe, or, indeed, in any other part of the world, may be conveniently divided into two broad areas: first, the manpower environment *external* to a given firm, and second, the manpower environment *internal* to that firm. The first deals with national, regional, or even local manpower policies and circumstances concerning which any individual firm has little direct influence, but which affect firms and, therefore, necessarily influence their decisions. The second deals with the manpower policies and practices which a firm pursues with respect to its own operations. I shall comment on both areas, and, where relevant, I shall compare certain Western European circumstances with corresponding ones in the United States.

THE EXTERNAL MANPOWER ENVIRONMENTS

The most noteworthy difference between national manpower policies in the United States and those throughout Western Europe is that manpower considerations are far more basic to overall economic and social policies in the latter countries. In fact, manpower policies characteristically dominate the broader economic and social policies of many of the Western European countries. This has been true for most of them since the end of World War II and, in some instances, much earlier. Nominally, the United States, too, accepted the standard and fundamental national goal of a high level of employment with the passage of the Employment Act of 1946. This manpower policy, which is the central national goal in most Western European countries, has never attained in the United States the prominence which it has enjoyed across the Atlantic. Whereas this goal in Western Europe has generally been the paramount national goal, to which other national goals have been subordinated, this has not been true in the United States despite persistently much higher levels of unemployment than the Western European countries have experienced in the postwar period.

In considering national manpower policies it is important to consider them as they relate to the most important overall national goals. These goals have been very similar for the United States and for the Western European countries. Of course, the relative importance of these goals may vary among countries and over time for a particular country. These goals are:

1. Full employment, which we have already described.

2. A high and sustained rate of growth of gross national product.

3. Stable prices.

4. Balance of payments equilibrium.

5. Freedom from direct controls on wages, prices, and corporate earnings.

Both theoretical economic analysis and empirical observations of the experience of many countries clearly indicate that tradeoffs must take place in the pursuit of these goals. For example, substantial progress toward the first two of these invariably acts to the detriment of the third and fourth goals. A dominant concern for the goal of price stability, on the other hand, must usually be purchased at the cost of uncomfortably high levels of unemployment. A number of Western European countries and, to some extent, the United States have moved closer to direct controls on wages and prices in an attempt to avoid setbacks with respect to the third and fourth goals in the face of substantial progress on the first and second.

In addition to the much higher priority given by Western European countries to the full employment objective, the following major differences with the United States might be noted. The rapid growth objective is emphasized more in Europe than in the United States and is often explicitly incorporated into their national policies. Probably no Western European nation attaches as much importance to price stability as does the United States. Except for a few countries such as England and the Netherlands, which are much more dependent on foreign trade than is the United States, our country gives the balance of payments objective higher priority than do the European countries. Although direct controls on wages and prices are very rare in any of these countries, several of them have adopted quasi-mandatory national "incomes policies" to restrain wage and price increases.

While the full-employment goal is the central manpower goal for the Western European countries, other manpower goals relate closely to it and to all other broad national goals. In the case of the United States the list of national goals must be expanded to include another central manpower goal: the equality of educational, economic, and social opportunities for all citizens.

The "rule of thumb" quantities often associated with these overall economic goals for Western European countries are a maximum of 2 percent unemployment, a minimum of 4 percent growth in real GNP per year, and a maximum of 2 percent annual increase in consumer prices. Depending upon the growth of the labor force, a 4 percent increase in GNP implies an increase in productivity per manhour of about 3-1/2 percent per year. This number, therefore, becomes the desirable limit on increases in real wages and the basis for national "incomes policies." These are more systematic and more effective cousins of the abortive efforts by the United States to encourage voluntary compliance with wage-price "guideposts" of about the same magnitude. In the case of the United States, however, the magnitudes of the other goals differ considerably. In this country we experienced a seven-year period (1958-1964) with annual rates of unemployment in excess of 5 percent, and as high as 6.8 percent (1958), without anything remotely resembling a consequent political crisis. We generally assume in this country that full employment is achieved at about the 4 percent unemployment level, and, indeed, we become somewhat alarmed with respect to the other national goals when unemployment falls below that level as it has for the past two years. The usual estimate of "frictional" unemployment in the United States, that is, unemployment due mainly to the normal movement of workers between jobs, is 3 percent. Because of differences in the nature of the economic institutions, and in the composition and mobility of labor forces, this figure is generally estimated at about half or less of our 3-percent figure for most European countries.

Very low levels of unemployment, especially during the present decade, have been the dominant manpower fact of life for almost every Western European country, as shown in the table below. For the six-year period 1960-1965 none of the cited 11 Western European countries experienced as heavy unemployment as did the United States, and for almost every country throughout the 10 years (1957-1966) unemployment rates were consistently and considerably below ours. Recent investigations of the comparability of unemployment measures used by European countries with those used in the United States indicate generally rather insignificant differences.

The extremely tight labor markets in several of these countries, and especially West Germany, the Netherlands, France, Sweden, and Norway, and to a somewhat lesser extent the United Kingdom, invariably have considerable impact upon the national manpower situation and consequently upon that confronting individual firms. In general, European nations have sought to alleviate the infla-

General Level of Unemployment of Selected Countries
(Percent of Labor Force)

Country	1957	1958	1959	1960	1961	1962	1963	1964	1965	1966
Austria	4.7	5.1	4.6	3.5	2.7	2.7	2.9	2.7	2.7	2.5
Belgium	3.9	5.5	6.3	5.4	4.2	3.3	2.7	2.2	2.4	2.7
Denmark	10.2	9.6	6.1	4.3	3.9	3.3	4.3	2.9	2.4	2.6
Finland........	––	––	2.2	1.5	1.2	1.2	1.5	1.5	1.4	1.5
France	0.8	0.9	1.3	1.2	1.0	1.1	1.4	1.1	1.3	1.4
Germany (Federal Republic)	3.4	3.5	2.4	1.2	0.8	0.7	0.8	0.7	0.6	0.7
Italy	8.2	6.6	5.6	4.2	3.5	3.0	2.5	2.7	3.6	3.9
Netherlands	1.2	2.3	1.8	1.2	0.9	0.8	0.9	0.8	0.9	1.2
Norway	1.4	2.3	2.2	1.7	1.2	1.4	1.7	1.4	1.2	1.1
Sweden	1.9	2.5	2.0	1.4	1.2	1.3	1.4	1.1	1.1	1.4
United Kingdom.	1.6	2.2	2.3	1.7	1.6	2.1	2.6	1.8	1.6	1.6
United States ...	4.3	6.8	5.5	5.5	6.7	5.5	5.7	5.2	4.5	3.8

Source: International Labor Office, *Bulletin of Labour Statistics* (Geneva: ILO, 1967—Second Quarter), Table 4, pp. 21-26.

tionary consequences of these very tight labor markets by policies directed at improving the efficiency of potential and actual labor force participants. They have been greatly concerned with improving the preparation of new entrants to the labor force through the continual development and revitalization of educational and training programs, the improvement of the efficiency of employment services, and the retraining of workers whose skills become outdistanced by technological changes. Many countries have made concerted efforts for many years to draw more heavily upon "labor reserves" — especially women, older persons, and the handicapped.

Many of the Western European countries embarked on major national programs of training, retraining, and improved efficiency of employment services immediately after World War II, often in response to the special needs of rebuilding war-devastated economies and of reintegrating war veterans and refugees into productive activities. It was not until 1962, with the passage of the Manpower Development and Training Act, that the United States embarked upon similar national policies. As in Western Europe, the main emphasis of these programs initially was to reduce bottlenecks caused by shortages of certain skills. In the case of the United States, however, the emphasis has shifted dramatically in recent years to a concentration on bringing the hard-core unemployed, the "disadvantaged," into the economic mainstream.

Before we consider some of the national manpower policies of

Western European countries, I should emphasize again that for virtually all of them the integration of manpower policies with other economic and social policies has been much more fully developed than is the case in the United States, and that manpower objectives, and especially that of full employment, usually take precedence over other economic and social goals. For example, in some European countries the manpower authorities can, on their own initiative, commence public-works projects as a means to maintain full employment.

National manpower policies for all countries have three basic and interdependent aims: to develop the abilities of. the people to their full potential, to encourage the development of jobs that will best utilize these abilities, and to match people and jobs. In addition to their long-established programs of occupational education and apprenticeship, most European countries have now incorporated the training and retraining of adults as permanent parts of their manpower activities. In most instances, such training and retraining activities are not limited to the unemployed, but are used also to upgrade the skills of employed persons. This is particularly important in preventing and reducing manpower bottlenecks caused by shortages of needed skills.

Although it is difficult to do so with certainty, most countries make concerted efforts to anticipate future demand for manpower by occupation as a guide to the preparation of workers for future employment needs. One key input to estimates of future demand for most of these countries is the widespread practice, which is a legal requirement in a few countries such as France, for employers to notify the national employment service of anticipated layoffs. Even where there is no legal requirement to do so, it is usual in many countries for employers to provide such notification, often 60 days ahead of time. In Sweden employer organizations have voluntarily entered into agreements with the National Labor Market Board to give such advance notice of pending layoffs.[1] These "early warning systems" enable employment services, and the training facilities with which they cooperate closely, to prepare displaced men for other employment with a minimum of dislocation.

The employment services in most Western European nations are much more heavily involved in placement, training, and related activities than is true in the United States federal-state employment service system. In a few countries, such as France, the official em-

---

[1] Margaret S. Gordon, "Retraining Programs — At Home and Abroad," *Proceedings of the Seventeenth Annual Meeting of the Industrial Relations Research Association* (Madison, Wis., 1965), p. 133.

ployment service is the sole legal placement agency and requires the registration of all job seekers and of all job vacancies. No worker may be laid off until the Ministry of Labor has given its approval, which often depends on local labor market conditions.

It is standard practice in Western Europe for adults to receive training allowances of 80 to 90 percent of their previous earnings plus a family allowance and compensation for necessary travel expenses and training materials. These training allowances average considerably more than do those in our MDTA programs. Typical rates of placement of 80 to 100 percent soon after such training or retraining are much higher than for comparable programs in the United States.[2]

Serious national concern about the great and increasing disparities in the concentration of wealth, economic opportunities, and population between major metropolitan areas and other areas is just now beginning in the United States. It results largely from the widespread urban rioting, which has shocked this nation into an awareness of the major social and economic *diseconomies* consequent to continuing urban concentration. Our newly expressed national concern with over-concentration and our previous insensitivity contrast sharply with the long history of such concern in many European countries. Their heedfulness of geographically more balanced growth and employment led to a series of government investigations in Great Britain in the early 1930's which resulted in the Special Areas Development and Improvement Act of 1934 and the Special Areas Reconstruction Act of 1936. These laws provided financial inducements for industry to locate in seriously distressed areas, but because of widespread unemployment at that time, they were not very successful.[3]

In 1937 a Royal Commission on the Distribution of the Industrial Population conducted a general study which identified the regional imbalances of industrial employment as major causes of persistent high levels of unemployment in some areas. When high unemployment rates persisted after World War II in such areas despite low overall unemployment rates, the Distribution of Industries Act of 1945 was enacted to enable the Board of Trade to offer financial assistance and other inducements to businesses to locate in depressed areas. The Town and Country Planning Act of 1947 ex-

---

[2] *Ibid.*, p. 135.
[3] William H. Miernyk, "British and Western European Attitudes Toward Unemployment," *Lessons in Foreign Labor Market Policies* (Washington, D.C.: U.S. Senate, Subcommittee on Employment and Manpower, Eighty-eighth Congress, Second Session, 1964), p. 1393.

tended this authority and required Board of Trade approval for the erection of new facilities of 10,000 square feet or more in order to discourage industrial growth in already congested areas and to stimulate it in areas of labor surplus. Despite strong objections that this would lead to an uneconomic distribution of industry and to international competitive disadvantage, a major national study showed that higher initial costs of production of "deconcentrated firms" tended to be eliminated soon, as workers got experience in their new occupations.[4]

Subsequent British legislation, such as the Local Employment Act of 1960, has strengthened the Board of Trade's key role in implementing the national policy of moving jobs to people rather than people to jobs. During the first two years under the 1960 Act, the Board of Trade engaged in 362 projects which provided 85,000 new jobs for a total government expenditure of approximately $209,000,000, or an average outlay of $2,460 per job. Unemployment in the developing districts declined by more than 5 percent between 1961 and 1962 while at the same time overall unemployment in Britain grew substantially, from 1.6 percent to 2.1 percent.[5]

For Great Britain and for the many other Western European countries which seek to influence the development of uncongested areas as a specific antidote to urban congestion, the general principle of such subsidies is that they be on a "once and for all" basis. They look to development, generally around specific centers or nuclei which will be fundamentally economic, that is, which will make long-run contributions to national output after benefiting from public assistance in overcoming real, or merely apparent, initial disadvantages of decentralized locations. Adherence to these principles necessarily rules out continuing subsidies to support uneconomic operations.[6]

The orientation of development policies around specific regional development centers has been pursued furthest perhaps in Italy, Holland, and France and least in Belgium, Britain, and Germany. In the case of France, this emphasis is coupled with major efforts not only to discourage firms from locating in congested areas, especially Paris, but also to induce firms already there to vacate crowded metropolitan areas and to relocate in uncongested areas. The negative measures include the withholding of building permits and the

---

[4] *Ibid.,* p. 1395.

[5] *Ibid.,* p. 1396.

[6] U.S. Department of Commerce, Area Redevelopment Administration, *Area Redevelopment Policies in Britain and the Countries of the Common Market* (Washington, D.C.: U.S. Government Printing Office, January 1965), p. 6.

imposition of high tax rates based on the space used. Positive measures include special premiums paid to firms to demolish or vacate quarters in crowded urban areas and to move outside. Firms are induced to move to job-shortage areas by direct subsidies, loans, interest subsidies, free plant sites, and tax exemptions.

Similar measures are employed by other Western European countries, most of whom seem quite intent upon attaining a better geographic balance of economic opportunities and population than has the United States. Even little Luxembourg, with an area of 999 square miles, encourages development in that half of the grand duchy which is less congested. The largest and most comprehensive program for regional development in Western Europe concerns the Italian South, on which the Italian government has spent, on the average each year, a sum equal to about 3 percent of the 1961 total gross capital formation in the country during the period 1950-1965 in order to promote the development of that depressed area.[7]

Curiously, even in some of the countries which have most heavily subsidized the deconcentration of industry and the development of distressed areas, the location decisions of their nationalized industries seem peculiarly uninfluenced by these national policies, perhaps because they are ineligible for such subsidies.

Despite the strong emphasis on moving jobs to workers rather than workers to jobs, the Western European countries provide generous relocation allowances to workers willing to move from job shortage areas to those of plentiful employment. Most of these programs have been in effect for a considerable length of time. The United States has only recently begun offering modest levels of relocation allowances on an experimental basis.

Foreign Workers

One of the major innovations of the Treaty of Rome of 1957, which established the European Economic Community, was its provision for a free market for manpower throughout the six countries. Implementation of this aspect of the Treaty has sought, with only limited success, to develop interchangeable social security systems to facilitate the free movement of workers across national boundaries.[8] The very tight labor markets which have persisted for most Western European countries have resulted in considerable flows of foreign workers from countries outside the EEC to The Six and to other

---

[7] *Ibid.*, p. 4.
[8] See Veldkamp, *Toward Harmonization of Social Security in the EEC,* p. 351, *supra.*

Western European countries with serious manpower shortages. Those countries which have experienced the most rapid technological and economic growth and which, despite increases in productivity, have required additional manpower for many years have constituted very strong magnets for intra-European migration. The most important of these countries are Germany, Switzerland, France, Belgium, Luxembourg, and, to a lesser extent, Great Britain and Sweden. Particularly for Germany and Switzerland, immigration has long been an indispensable contributor to their economic development. Germany in recent years has employed almost one million foreign workers. Approximately one worker out of 22 has been a foreigner. In Switzerland, the proportion has been one out of every three in recent years.[9] The European countries from which the foreign workers come are those characterized by high rates of population increase accompanied by low rates of economic growth. Foremost among sending countries have been Italy, Spain, Portugal, Greece, and Turkey. Some of these countries, such as Italy and Spain, which have recently been experiencing increased growth, are now trying to reclaim some of their emigrated skilled manpower.

Most of the foreign workers, who have been so important to the manpower supply of many Western European countries, are at low skill levels. They provide the basic manpower which frees nationals for upgrading to higher-skilled positions. The bulk of the foreign labor force has been transient. There have been circular flows of workers to and from the home countries.

Although I have found no specific evidence on this point, it is possible that a falling off of the European economic boom might present countries which have been heavily dependent on foreign labor with new problems similar to those which have begun to dominate the manpower policies of the United States, that is, problems of how to provide meaningful opportunities for "disadvantaged" workers. With the high levels of support for displaced workers through unemployment compensation, training and retraining allowances, etc., it is possible that significant numbers of newly redundant foreign workers might elect to stay in their host countries rather than return to their much poorer countries of origin. If so, they will constitute groups of low-skilled, unemployed aliens who may become "hard core" groups similar to the "native alien" groups that are of such concern to the United States.

---

[9] Flavia Zaccone Derossi, "On Migrations for Economic Reasons in Europe," *Official Documents of the Conference* (European Population Conference) (Strasbourg: Council of Europe, September 1966), p. 2.

THE INTERNAL MANPOWER ENVIRONMENTS

Our concern here will be chiefly for the foreign or multi-national corporation operating in Western Europe, with particular reference to United States firms. We shall explore some of the manpower circumstances relating to their internal operations particularly as they relate to the policies and practices that typify their home-country manpower activities.

In their development of manpower policies and techniques, firms in the United States have sought mainly to achieve the fundamental objectives of the efficient recruitment, development, allocation, motivation, and utilization of the human resources associated with the enterprise. Much of this development has been in response to the rapid growth of powerful unionism, which has succeeded in winning costly concessions from even the largest, strongest, and most militantly anti-union firms. Such worker gains have obliged these and other firms, whether unionized or not, to formulate policies and practices which seek maximum returns for the concessions granted. Manpower policies and practices, then, have basically the economic objective of relating the human resources of the enterprise to other factors of production in ways that will maximize their economic returns. American unions have been clearly the most economically, or business, oriented of any of the world's unions and have concentrated much more heavily than have others on the direct pressuring of employers to obtain economic and job-related improvements. The consequent increases in labor costs have obliged firms continuously to seek more efficient management of their increasingly more costly human resources.[10]

The general manpower approach of most United States companies, then, seeks to formulate and implement those policies which will enable them to manage most efficiently their costly human resources. Policies concerning recruitment seek to identify and attract to the firms those persons at all levels who are potentially most able to contribute to its success. Toward this end, firms have developed sophisticated mechanisms and made heavy expenditures. Outstanding examples are the extensive systems for annual recruiting of graduates of colleges and technical schools and the highly developed techniques for interviewing and testing applicants at all occupational levels. Any successful company makes massive investments in the development of its manpower to higher levels of knowledge and skill

---

[10] John C. Shearer, "Industrial Relations of American Corporations Abroad," *International Labor,* ed. Solomon Barkin *et. al.* (New York: Harper and Row, 1967), pp. 111-112.

appropriate to the firm's present and anticipated needs. These investments are made through in-company educational and training programs, apprenticeship programs, on-the-job training, and many other means. Many investments are made by firms in conjunction with educational institutions, for example, in extended management and executive training programs on university campuses. The allocation of employed manpower to most effective employment within firms is closely tied with their efforts to upgrade human knowledge and skills and with their concern for the most effective motivation of workers at all levels of the organization. The design and administration of various types of incentive systems constitutes an important manpower area that is rich in innovations and experimentation, all designed to promote more efficient job performance. These incentive systems usually involve nonmonetary elements such as the visual evidence of increasing prestige through office size, location, and furnishings, as well as the monetary elements of increasing compensation in relation to performance, bonus and stock option plans, and promotion in recognition of demonstrated competence.

The authority of American management over the utilization of the knowledge and skills of its work force is more limited than its authority in many other areas of the management of its manpower. Union pressures and work rules and practices limit unilateral management authority and impose another dimension upon the management task: the necessity to reach accommodation with union organizations many of whose interests are at variance with those of management with respect to the terms and costs concerning the utilization of its work force.

Despite frequent and strong divergences of interest between American management and unions, these two groups, and the governmental agencies that relate to them, share a fundamental consensus, particularly in their acceptance of capitalism, as the basis for all their dealings. This acceptance of capitalism by American unions is fundamental to the development of our approaches to manpower affairs. This is, however, almost the only country in the world where a strong system of unionism has accepted, almost without reservation, capitalistic institutions as the basis of national economic organization. In this important respect, as in many others, the foreign milieu in which American multi-national corporations operate is inevitably very different from that of the parent organization in the United States.[11]

One of the most significant differences confronting American

---

[11] *Ibid.*, p. 113.

firms in Western Europe is the more widespread public regulation of management prerogatives in manpower management. Perhaps the most notable example is in the universal legal protection of workers against layoffs. In the United States reductions in work force are made simply, routinely, usually with very little notice, and, until recently, almost without cost to the firm. In Western Europe layoffs are costly, complex, restricted by law as to required notice, and, indeed, are sometimes actually impossible by virtue of administrative ruling or union pressure. For example, Italy requires up to three months' notice to employees plus a severance allowance of one month's pay at the employee's highest wage for each year of service.[12] The Ministry of Labor of France closely monitors contemplated layoffs or plant closings. The Ministry must approve each layoff and will often withhold such approval in the face of substantial local unemployment.

Habit and tradition play stronger roles in manpower management in Western Europe than in the United States. This is perhaps most noticeable in the strong, although usually unofficial, opposition of unions in many countries to technological change. Despite persistently tight labor markets, with the consequent relative ease of securing alternative employment, the introduction of labor-saving machinery such as fork-lift trucks was a slow, painful, and costly process in Great Britain after World War II. In the United States major labor-saving innovations are made continually in most industries with little opposition from even the strongest of our unions. Only in relatively recent years have some American unions negotiated "cushions" for those displaced, despite the fact that our overall unemployment levels have been much higher than those in Europe.

American firms operating in the very different environments abroad usually try to transplant their home-based manpower policies and practices, which they may or may not modify in response to the different circumstances abroad. There are many instances where American firms have successfully adapted their manpower programs and many other instances where they have failed to do so, often with costly consequences to the firms. For example, in the area of motivation of personnel at all levels, most American firms have developed imaginative and rational systems of incentives, including job evaluation and wage and salary administration systems, which strongly promote higher levels of performance. Some firms have found, however, that the application of some techniques, such as annual performance reviews as the basis for salary increases, violates

---

[12] Industrial Relations Counselors, *Facts on Europe* (New York: Industrial Relations Counselors, 1966), p. 60.

local values, which impede their operation as intended. In Italy, for example, it is unacceptable to pass over an individual for annual increases merely because of his unsatisfactory performance. When a system imported from the United States proves inappropriate, it behooves the American firm to devise new approaches to attain the thwarted objective.

The uniquely American casualness with respect to laying off workers causes great difficulty for American firms in some European countries even when they follow scrupulously the severe legal restrictions. For example, a pharmaceutical firm in Rome laid off 350 employees and precipitated a takeover of the plant by protesting workers. There have been about 20 such cases in Italy in recent years despite the fact that such occupation of a factory is a crime. The authorities generally do nothing to help managements regain control of their plants. As is often the case, this firm was obliged to rescind the mass layoff and to deal individually with each case. For those workers who could be induced to resign voluntarily, the company had to provide, in addition to the statutory severance pay, indemnification of 900 hours' wages or three months' salary.[13]

There are also important areas of manpower policy and practice where United States firms have not applied to their foreign operations the attention and imagination which they have successfully applied for many years to similar problems at home. Although American firms have generally been leaders in management practices wherever they have operated in the world, they have often abdicated leadership in the manpower area and have passively accepted some of the least advantageous patterns of their environments. In the manpower field, just as fully as in the fields of organization, technology, production, finance, and marketing, American firms should be able to use their innovative strengths to advantage in environments often quite different from the United States. For example, the expertise which American firms have developed over the years in the recruiting of college and technical graduates could well be applied to fuller development of such techniques in other countries.

Other areas that warrant further development abroad are the identification and development of the most promising supervisory, managerial, and executive talent for future leadership roles. In many European environments upward mobility is strongly influenced by family, social, or political status, the particular school background, and other ascriptive criteria. American firms are usual-

---

[13] *Ibid.*

ly well advised to reject this aspect of their overseas environment in favor of the full application of rational criteria for rewards and advancement, such as periodic performance reviews, integrated with appropriate salary administration programs, which they have usually developed to a fine art in their domestic operations. Especially when operating in tight labor markets, and the markets for top-quality high-level manpower are invariably the tightest of these labor markets, firms must, in their own interest, concentrate their attention and innovative skills on the most effective recruitment, development, and utilization of their work forces. The further application overseas of many of the policies and techniques which they have successfully developed in their domestic operations, when imaginatively adapted to their overseas environments, can make substantial contributions toward this end.

The "Brain Drain"

Although many Western European countries are heavy importers of relatively unskilled, blue collar workers from poorer surrounding countries, they are heavy exporters of the most valuable manpower — high-level human resources — that is, the engineers, scientists, technicians, and managers who are invariably the most important inputs to any organization's efforts. The United States is a very strong "magnet" for these high-level human resources. A total of approximately 16,000 engineers, natural scientists, and social scientists entered the United States for permanent residence during the three-year (fiscal) period 1962-1964. The trend has been upward during and after that period. Of this three-year total, 67 percent were engineers (the largest group being electrical engineers), 29 percent were natural scientists (largely chemists), and 4 percent were social scientists (primarily economists). Of this three-year total of 16,000 high-level immigrants, 20 percent were born in the United Kingdom, 12 percent in Canada, and 8 percent in Germany.[14] In 1966, of 9,875 scientists, engineers, and physicians who immigrated to the United States, over 36 percent came from Europe.[15]

Although I have no data on the brain drain specifically from United States subsidiaries in Western Europe, it is clear that even if actual losses are small the total reservoir of high-level manpower

---

[14] National Science Foundation, *Scientists and Engineers from Abroad, 1962-64* (Washington, D.C.: U.S. Government Printing Office, 1967), p. ix.

[15] U.S. House of Representatives, Research and Technical Programs Subcommittee, Committee on Government Operations, *The Brain Drain into the U.S. of Scientists, Engineers, and Physicians* (Washington, D.C.: U.S. Government Printing Office, 1967), Table IV, p. 4.

from which United States firms can draw in Western Europe is significantly reduced. Because the new U. S. Immigration Act replaces geographic quotas with occupational preferences, depending upon United States needs, it will surely stimulate substantially the already heavy brain drain from Western Europe and make it still more difficult for American firms to recruit top talent there. This will be especially difficult in countries which graduate far smaller proportions of young people from university programs than is true in the United States. For example, in the United Kingdom the proportion of young people graduating from college is only about one tenth of that in the United States.

The Counter "Brain Drain"

An unusual opportunity is available to American firms that operate abroad for recruiting often uniquely qualified high-level manpower. Many of the firms whose international operations I have studied complain of the lack of university training in Europe and elsewhere in certain areas of great importance to American business, especially in management and industrial administration, and of the lack of familiarity of foreign graduates with U. S. business practices. At the same time, large numbers of students from the very countries in which U. S. firms are heavily concentrated abroad are studying relevant subjects at U. S. colleges and universities.

In the school year 1966-67, of somewhat more than 100,000 foreign students in U. S. colleges, over 14,000 were from Europe. Of these more than 3,000 came from the United Kingdom, about 2,200 from Germany, over 1,200 from France, almost 900 from Italy, over 700 from the Netherlands, almost 700 from Norway, and so on. The majority of these were graduate students. Almost 17 percent of the 14,000 students from Europe were studying engineering (especially electrical engineering), almost 16 percent were in the social sciences (especially economics), almost 14 percent were in physical and life sciences, and about 9 percent were studying business administration.[16] Many of these areas are among those that are most sought after by progressive American firms.

Despite the scarcity of such skills in Europe, very few of the firms that I have studied use their highly developed college recruiting machinery in the United States to identify and recruit foreign students in our universities for home-country positions.

---

[16] Institute of International Education, *Open Doors 1967* (New York: Institute of International Education, July 1967), Table II, pp. 22-23.

CONCLUSIONS

The external manpower environments in Europe are characterized by great national concern for full employment and related manpower objectives. This concern tends to dominate other national economic and social goals. Whether for these reasons or because of exogenous influences, the full-employment goal has been more than attained in most European nations with consequent serious shortages as the major manpower fact of life for more than the past decade. The immigration of unskilled blue collar workers has been an essential ingredient to the continued economic growth of a considerable number of these countries. When faced with circumstances of this sort, it is obvious that firms must intensify their efforts for maximum efficiency in the recruiting, training, allocation, and utilization of their manpower. Many of the techniques which have been developed in the United States, such as sophisticated and sensible systems of incentives, could be imaginatively adapted to the needs of these very tight labor markets.

With respect to the key human resources, high-level manpower, firms face a very different situation. Here the scarcities are not mitigated by immigration of talent but rather are aggravated by a very substantial, consistent, and worsening brain drain of engineers, scientists, technicians, administrators, and executives from these countries, especially to the United States. I feel that this loss of high-level manpower has far more serious implications for firms than do the very tight labor markets for blue collar workers. I also feel that American firms can do a great deal about this with respect to their own key people. American firms are experienced at designing systems of incentives, both monetary and nonmonetary, to facilitate the recruitment, development, and retention of their top talent. Effective merit review and salary programs are often augmented by bonus, stock option, and retirement programs which unashamedly seek to reduce the likelihood that key personnel will be attracted away. Many of these same techniques could be used specifically to counteract the strong magnetism of opportunities in the United States. Parenthetically, as more firms become truly multi-national operations, the international interchangeability of scientists, engineers, and executives will render national designations within these firms less and less meaningful.

I urge those firms which have not yet done so to apply the energy and imagination that has long characterized their college recruiting activities in the United States to the incorporation into these activities of purposeful recruiting of foreign students for opportunities in their home countries. The able foreign student trained in the United States will usually have a considerable advantage working in his home country for an American firm. This natural advantage should be exploited much more fully by firms seeking the best talent with the most appropriate training than has been the case in the past.

EMPLOYMENT, UNEMPLOYMENT, AND MANPOWER POLICY IN WESTERN EUROPE

By Louis F. Buckley

In the first part of this paper, I shall discuss the major factors involved in an analysis of supply and demand for labor and the employment and unemployment situation in Western Europe. In the second part, I shall explain the major manpower policies that have been developed to meet the problems encountered by employers and workers in adjusting to labor market conditions in Western Europe.

LABOR MARKET ANALYSIS

Since availability of qualified workers is one of the most important factors to be considered in determining the location of a business establishment and continuing its efficient operation, consideration first will be given to the patterns and trends to be found in an analysis of the European labor force. These data also have important implications in evaluating the market demand for products.

Labor force patterns and trends in any country reflect to a great extent the changing size and composition of its population as well as the extent to which the population participates in the labor market.[1]

Population Trends

The long-term trends of life, work life, and years spent outside the labor force have each shown marked increases both in Europe and in the United States. American and French scholars find that in their respective countries, the same conclusions must be drawn: "Despite the reduction in age of entry and earlier retirement, work life expectancy has continued to increase under the important influence of declining mortality."[2] At age 20, the average number of remaining years of life in the United States is 49.6 for males and 56 for females. These averages are greater in a number of European

---

[1] Seymour L. Wolfbein, *Employment and Unemployment in the United States*, (Chicago: Science Research Association, 1964), p. 1.

[2] *Ibid.*, p. 125, quoting P. Depoid, "Tables Français concernant la population masculine (1906-46)," *Bulletin of the International Statistical Institute*, Part IV, 1951.

countries, including the United Kingdom, Italy, Germany, France, and Sweden.[3]

Total Population

Total population, which is the basis for analyzing labor force trends, has increased and will continue to increase in Europe at a rate of growth about half that of the United States.[4] The population increase between 1965 and 1970 will vary between 2 and 5 percent for practically all European countries. The Netherlands and Portugal resemble the United States, with anticipated increases of 6 to 8 percent. This trend is expected to continue for the period of 1965 to 1980. While the average increase will be 11 percent between 1965 and 1980, which will be half the U. S. rate, Germany and Austria will be well below the average, with rates of 5 and 7 percent, respectively. On the other hand, there will be four countries with increases above the average: Norway, 15 percent; Ireland, 17 percent; Portugal, 21 percent; and the Netherlands, 25 percent.[5]

Population of Working Age

Projections of size of the population of working age 15 years ahead are much more reliable than forecasts of the total population, since everyone who will be over 15 in 15 years' time has already been born.

The population of working age (15-64 for men and 15-59 for women) is expected to increase between 1965 and 1980 about 8 percent in Europe compared to about 22.5 percent in the United States. From 1965 to 1975, the population of working age will decrease in Germany and Austria, barely increase in Sweden and the United Kingdom, and rise from 3 to 4 percent in Switzerland, Denmark, and Italy. The increase will be around 7 percent in France, Norway, Ireland, Spain, and Greece. The Netherlands and Portugal rates of about 13 percent will approach the 15-percent rate of the United States.[6]

Comparison of the population of working age with the total population shows a perceptible difference between European countries and Canada and the United States. In the latter, the pop-

---

[3] United Nations, *Demographic Yearbook*, 1966, p. 580.

[4] International Labour Office, *Employment and Economic Growth* (Geneva: 1964), p. 6.

[5] Organization for Economic Co-operation and Development, *Demographic Trends* (Paris: 1966), p. 20.

[6] *Id.,* p. 25

ulation of working age will rise at about the same pace as the total population; in contrast, growth in European countries will be slower in the population of working age. The divergence is wider for females than for males, and it widens for both sexes up to 1975. At that point it narrows for females and for both sexes combined, but for males alone remains the same in 1980 as in 1975.[7]

These overall relationships will vary considerably among countries. Spain, France, Greece, and Portugal resemble the United States in that from 1965 to 1980 their population of working age is expected to rise at about the same rate as their total population. On the other hand, in Germany and Austria the population of working age will fall, and in the United Kingdom and Sweden it will rise very little between 1965 and 1975. After 1975, the gap will tend to become narrower in Germany and Austria.[8]

Age Structure of the Population of Working Age

The young adult population (15-44 years) constituted approximately 68 percent of the working-age population in European countries combined and in the United States in 1965. This combined proportion for European countries is not expected to change during the next 15 years, whereas there will be a marked increase in the United States. However, wide differences exist and are anticipated in individual countries.[9]

In 1965, the percentage of young adults in the population of working age in Sweden, Norway, United Kingdom, Switzerland, Ireland, Austria, Germany, and Denmark varied from 64.5 to 66.6 percent, respectively. In the United States, France, Netherlands, Italy, Spain, Greece, Canada, and Portugal, the corresponding percentages vary from 68.8 to 72 percent, respectively. By 1980, the percentages are expected to cluster between 66 and 70 percent except in Portugal, the Netherlands, the United States, and Ireland, where they will exceed 70 or even 71 percent.[10]

Supply of Labor—the Labor Force

In addition to the population trends, the studies of the Organization for Economic Co-operation and Development (OECD) take into account the effect of migration. As a result of the natural increase in population, of immigration, and of the increase in female

---

[7] *Ibid.*
[8] *Ibid.*
[9] *Id.,* p. 31.
[10] *Id.,* p. 36.

labor market participation, the United States will have by far the largest growth in active population or labor force, almost 30 percent, between 1965 and 1980. The Netherlands and Switzerland will show the largest increases in Europe with increases of 21 and 16 percent, respectively. The increase in Switzerland will be chiefly attributable to the predicted large volume of immigration. Increases by 1980 of from 10 to 14 percent are expected in Norway, Spain, Portugal, and France. Increases of from less than 1 to 4 percent are expected in Greece, Austria, Germany, Italy, and the United Kingdom, while no increase is forecast for Sweden.

The Labor Force Sex Composition

In 1965, women constituted about 34 percent of the labor force in France, the United States, and the United Kingdom. The percentage was higher in Germany (36 percent), Sweden (37 percent), and Austria (40 percent) and lower in Spain (20 percent), the Netherlands (23 percent), Norway (23 percent), and Portugal (26 percent). The rates of increase of women in the labor force between 1965 and 1980 are expected to be as follows: Spain, 46 percent; United States, 36 percent; Switzerland, 13.5 percent; Ireland, 20.6 percent; the Netherlands, 14 percent; Norway, 13.7 percent; France, 13.8 percent; Portugal, 10 percent; United Kingdom, 5 percent; and Greece, 1 percent. A decline of 2 to 3 percent in the number of women in the labor force is expected for Germany, Austria, Italy, and Sweden.[11] The increase in the number of men in the labor force from 1965 to 1980 is expected to be 25 percent in the United States, 17 percent in Switzerland and the Netherlands, and 11 to 13 percent in Ireland, France, and Portugal. A slight increase of from 3 to 8 percent is forecast for Austria, Germany, Spain, Italy, Norway, United Kingdom, a small decline for Sweden, and no change for Greece.

In 1965, the labor market participation rate for males varied from 88.4 percent in Italy to 100 percent in Portugal, compared with 90 percent in the United States. The rate for women showed an even greater variation, from 24.6 percent in Spain to 60.9 percent in Austria, compared to 48 percent in the United States. It is relatively high in Sweden (58.9 percent), United Kingdom (54.5 percent), and Germany (53.3 percent) and low in Greece and Ireland (40.9 percent), Italy (36.3 percent), Norway (32.2 percent), Netherlands (29.9 percent), Portugal (35.5 percent), and Switzerland (42.2 percent).[12]

---

[11] *Id.*, p. 60.
[12] *Id.*, p. 72.

The domestic labor supply of a number of European countries, including France, Germany, Switzerland, Belgium, Netherlands, Sweden, and Denmark, has been expanded by inflows of approximately five million workers from Italy, Spain, Portugal, Yugoslavia, Greece, and Turkey during recent years. The 1967 recession closed this migration to Northern Europe and resulted in a return flow of some of these workers.[13]

Educational Background of Labor Force

In European countries compulsory full-time schooling usually ranges in duration from seven to nine years. The compulsory school period is terminated at age 14 in Austria, Denmark, United Kingdom, France, and the Netherlands and in a few of the German states. The age is 15 in most of the German states. In the past, the middle schools and secondary education took in about 5 to 10 percent of the children. Attendance at these schools has increased by more than 50 percent during the past 10 years in most countries. The percentage going to these schools varies from 50 percent in France to 25 percent in Germany.[14] In the United States, 72 percent go on to secondary school.[15] In Germany, 81 percent of young persons leaving school go into apprenticeship programs. The percentage of young people age 20 to 24 attending college is as follows: United States, 43 percent; France, 16 percent; Germany, 8 percent; and United Kingdom, 5 percent.[16]

Demand for Labor

We now turn to the demand side of the labor market and consider the major changes that are taking place in the industrial and occupational patterns of demand.

Changing Industrial Patterns

The absolute as well as the relative numbers of workers engaged in agriculture have been falling in European countries, although the decline has varied in given periods. The actual decline in numbers in agriculture began in Great Britain before the end of the 19th century, while it appeared in the United States about 1910, in

---

[13] Robert C. Doty, "Europe's Migrant Workers are Facing Job Crisis," *New York Times*, Feb. 27, 1967, pp. 1, 5.

[14] International Labour Office, *European Apprenticeship* (Geneva: 1966), p. 25.

[15] *The Christian Science Monitor*, Oct. 20, 1966.

[16] "The Outlook," *Wall Street Journal*, May 27, 1968, p. 1.

France and Italy about 1921, and in Germany after 1940. The decline has been very large in some countries recently: 30 percent in Germany between 1954 and 1960; 31 percent in Italy from 1954 to 1961; and 29 percent in Sweden in 10 years.[17]

The percentage of the labor force in agriculture has declined to 3.8 percent in the United Kingdom, 5.5 percent in the United States, between 10 and 11 percent in Germany and Italy, and 13 percent in Sweden. It is higher in Italy (24 percent), Ireland (35.2 percent), Spain (34 percent), Portugal (42 percent), and Greece (54 percent). The rate of decline has been marked in countries like Italy, where it changed from 28 percent in 1961 to 24 percent in 1966, and in Spain, where it changed from 41 to 34 percent.[18]

In the agricultural countries undergoing industrialization, especially Greece, Italy, Portugal, Spain, and Turkey, manpower leaving agriculture almost exactly matched manpower entering the industry sector. As a result of the recent rises in employment in commerce and the services in European countries where industrialization has made the greatest progress, the service sector now absorbs all the manpower released by the relative shift from agriculture and even triggers a relative shift from industry. In the United Kingdom, as in the United States, employment in commerce and services increased at the cost of a relative shift from industries producing goods.[19]

Women make up a larger percentage of the total employed in commerce and services in most European countries than in the United States. In Sweden and France, for example, they constitute between 54 and 56 percent, compared to 48 percent in the United States.[20] However, with the exception of the United Kingdom and Sweden, the percentage of the female staff working part time is lower than in the United States.[21]

While the percentage of women in the labor force has increased in the United States, Great Britain, and France, there has been a marked decrease in employment of women in Italy. In addition to the massive exodus of women from the land induced by mechanization of farms, there has been a decrease in the number of women employed in the textile industry and the ready-to-wear clothing

---

[17] International Labour Office, *Employment and Economic Growth* (Geneva: 1964), p. 10.

[18] International Labour Office, *Yearbook of Labor Statistics* (Geneva: 1967), pp. 112-123.

[19] Maurice Lengelle, *The Growing Importance of the Service Sector in Member Countries,* OECD (Paris: 1966), p. 11.

[20] OECD, *Manpower Problems in the Service Sector* (Paris: 1966), p. 51.

[21] *Id.,* p. 77.

trade. Many of the farm women, especially those over 30 years of age, have not been able to adjust themselves to factory work. Also, the economic prosperity in Italy has lowered the age of marriage. Although 65 percent of the women in the 20-to-25 age group are employed, only 30 percent of those over 30 are employed in contrast to 48 to 50 percent, respectively, in the United States and Britain.[22]

There are marked differences in employment within each of the broad industrial sectors and between countries. In the service sector in recent years, for example, the greatest increases have taken place in business services in Sweden (9 percent), in medical and health services in France (8.4 percent), and in the educational services in France (6.7 percent). The increase in trade has been the greatest in France (4.8 percent).[23] Within manufacturing, we find both rapidly growing and rapidly contracting industries. Between 1953 and 1960, for example, employment in textiles fell by 21 percent in Sweden and by 30 percent (cotton textiles only) in the United Kingdom. During this period employment in electrical machinery increased by 17 percent in Sweden and by 34 percent in the United Kingdom.[24] There were marked declines in hard-coal-mining employment from 1958 to 1963 varying between 17 and 51 percent in Italy, Belgium, France, Germany, and the United Kingdom.[25] Among other branches of industry affected by declining employment are shipbuilding and railways.[26]

Changing Occupational Patterns

As in the United States, there have been important changes in the types of jobs within industries, with resultant expanding and declining occupations, as employment in service industries has grown. The most important change is the relative and in some cases absolute decline in "blue-collar" occupations and the increase in "white-collar" jobs. Although this trend lags in time behind the United States, where employment in professional, technical, administrative, clerical, and sales occupations has expanded to 42 percent of total employment, these occupations have expanded, for example,

---

[22] Walter Lucas, "Fewer Women Hold Jobs in Italy," *The Christian Science Monitor,* Sept. 28, 1967, p. 14.

[23] Maurice Lengelle, *The Growing Importance of the Service Sector In Member Countries,* OECD, (Paris: 1966), p. 156.

[24] International Labour Office, *Employment and Economic Growth* (Geneva: 1964), p. 11.

[25] International Labour Office, *Redundancy Procedures in Selected Western European Countries* (Geneva: 1966), p. 13.

[26] *Ibid.,* p. 39.

to 33 percent in the United Kingdom and Sweden, to 29 percent in Germany and France, and to 25 percent in Italy.[27]

Unemployment

Unlike the United States, where unemployment fluctuated between 5 and 6.8 percent from 1958 to 1964, a period characterized in the United States by cyclical change, most European industrial countries had unemployment rates from 1958 to 1967 which varied only within narrow limits and remained below 3 percent of the labor force. This group included Germany, France, the Netherlands, Sweden, and the United Kingdom.[28] The rate in Germany was less than 1 percent from 1960 to 1966 and less than 2 percent in Sweden during this period. In Italy, which had a rate similar to that of the United States of almost 7 percent in 1958, a steady decline was experienced to less than 3 percent in 1963. Since then the unemployment rate has varied between 3 and 4 percent in Italy.[29]

The number of unemployed rose in 1967 in every industrialized European country but Italy. The number of jobless more than doubled in 1967 in West Germany, Denmark, Finland, and Luxembourg. France, Belgium, Greece, Norway, the Netherlands, and Sweden all registered increases of more than 30 percent. The increase in unemployment in industrialized countries was attributed to the slackening of economic expansion or the extreme slowness of recovery.[30] Despite the increase, rates in 1967 were still lower than in the United States in countries such as France, Germany, Great Britain, and Sweden.

It appears in July 1968, however, that the recession of 1967 is coming to an end in most European countries. The German outlook is very encouraging, with new orders for machinery up sharply. Reports indicate an increase in production of 6 to 11 percent in capital-goods industries. Output of automobiles in the first quarter of 1968 was 39 percent greater than a year earlier. German economists are reported to anticipate a 5 percent or better rate of expansion. The growth rate of close to 6 percent reached by Italy alone in Europe in 1967 seems likely to be repeated this year. Reports indi-

---

[27] International Labour Office, *Yearbook of Labour Statistics* (Geneva: 1967), pp. 222, 225, 231, 239, 241.

[28] International Labour Office, *Employment and Economic Growth* (Geneva: 1964), p. 19.

[29] Arthur F. Neff and Rosa A. Holland, "Comparative Unemployment Rates," *Monthly Labor Review,* April 1967, p. 18-20, and International Labour Office, *Bulletin of Labor Statistics* (Geneva: 1968, 1st Qtr.), p. 27.

[30] "Industrialized Countries' Jobless Generally Rose in '67, I.L.O. Says," *New York Times,* Feb. 9, 1968, p. 4.

cate that Italy has ample reserves of labor, no serious inflation, and a strong balance of payments. Despite social and political problems, a growth rate of 4.5 percent is expected in France and between 3 and 4 percent in Great Britain. Trends in the smaller countries of Europe, including Sweden, indicate an average growth rate of 4 percent.[31]

Conclusion and Implications

The relatively small increase in total population and the even smaller increase in population of working age, especially young adults, in many western European countries is of concern since it is reflected in a correspondingly small increase in the labor supply. It raises a particularly serious labor-shortage problem in countries like Germany, the United Kingdom, and Sweden. Women constitute about the same percentage of the labor force as in the United States in a number of countries such as France, Germany, the United Kingdom, and Sweden. Margaret S. Gordon has concluded that shortages of labor and difficulty in curbing inflationary trends are the main factors that might cause economic growth to be retarded.[32]

Employers from the United States will have to adjust their hiring standards for technical, professional, and managerial staff to the relatively few college graduates in Europe. The "brain drain," with about 13,000 European professional and technical workers migrating each year to the United States, has further aggravated this situation.[33] Adjustments will also have to be made in the requirement for hiring of the equivalent of a high school diploma. Employers will find, however, that the labor force in most of Europe is usually well trained, highly literate, and exceptionally productive.

The supply of labor from the agricultural sector is no longer sufficient to meet the expanding demand of manufacturing and service industries for labor in a number of countries. Manufacturers are encountering increasing competition in employment expansion from the service sector, especially with respect to women. Supplies of labor, however, exist in sections of countries where industry is declining, such as in the mining areas. As demand shifts from the blue-collar to the white-collar occupations, employers are finding it increasingly difficult to obtain qualified employees with the educa-

[31] "When Europe Looks Ahead Now," *U. S. News and World Report,* June 17, 1968, pp. 54-55.

[32] Margaret S. Gordon, *Retraining and Labor Market Adjustment in Western Europe,* Manpower Automation Research Monograph No. 4, 1955, p. 15.

[33] "U. S. Penetration in European Markets," *Editorial Research Report,* Jan. 1968, p. 74.

tional background needed. The foreign supply of workers for northern countries from southern European countries diminishes as these latter countries become more industrialized and unemployment is reduced.

For a number of years the maladjustment between supply and demand, especially in northern Europe, has been one of an excess of demand over the available supply of labor. Consideration will be given in the remainder of this analysis to the manpower policies developed to meet this problem.

LABOR MARKET POLICY

Full employment and labor shortages have resulted in the evolution of an active manpower policy for the development and utilization of human resources in Western Europe. Professor Shearer's excellent paper in this volume incisively makes these points. The form and extent of comprehensive manpower programs have varied between countries. In many countries, representatives of labor and management participated in the formulation of policy.

An active or positive labor market policy involves a program of policy-making and initiative by the government or some other central authority, which is integrated with fiscal and monetary policy to promote the smooth functioning of the labor market. An active labor market policy has also been defined in terms of the measures adopted to correct the imbalances of manpower that exist because of fluctuations in supply and demand in rapidly expanding societies.[34]

The role of the central government in manpower activities has expanded in Western Europe. Professor Richard A. Lester emphasizes that the recognition of the importance of improving the quality of the labor force through education and training and the growing realization of the need to integrate economics and manpower policies have encouraged such expansion.[35]

Human Resource Development

Although the Western European countries have not extended their secondary and higher education to the degree that we find in the United States, some observers believe that most countries are superior in providing a uniform basic education of good quality and in

---

[34] OECD, *The Public Employment Services and Management,* 1965, p. 24, and Alfred Green, *A Study and Appraisal of Manpower Programs,* 1963, p. 3.

[35] Richard A. Lester, "National Manpower Administration and Policies," in *International Labor* edited by Solomon Barkin and others (New York: Harper & Row, 1967), p. 208.

the avoidance of illiteracy. This is due to some extent to the homogeneity of population, the small geographic areas involved, and the strong central governments. Beatrice G. Reubens, however, cites the extensive new program in Sweden providing education, housing, and vocational training for local gypsies as an example of government response to the problems of a minority. Professor Ruebens also believes that Britain's black children receive compulsory education of the same quality and learn as well as comparable white children.[36]

General Education

The period of compulsory education is being extended in most countries to 15 and 16 years and the programs are being expanded. Business studies, for example, have been made available to 14- and 15-year-olds in secondary schools in Britain. Although the age for leaving school will not be raised to 16 by statute until the early 1970s, more students are staying on voluntarily in Great Britain. Universities are expanding in Britain, and 80 percent of the university population are "first generation" students whose parents left school at 14 or 15. The Confederation of British Industry (CBI) raised funds from industry for the support of the London and Manchester postgraduate business schools. Management training facilities have expanded enormously in Britain since 1964. Although British industry needs many more scientists every year than are being turned out by the universities and technological colleges, the OECD recently reported that only the United Kingdom in relative terms approached the United States in its output of pure science graduates. This report stated that both France and the United Kingdom produced as many people with doctor's degrees in pure science as the United States in relation to the number of people in each age group.[37]

By 1973, the Swedish education system will have undergone a complete change, with compulsory school attendance until 16 and a maximum class size of 25 pupils in the lower grades. The study of English will be compulsory for the fourth, fifth, and sixth years, and all students in the ninth year will spend three weeks' training under actual working conditions regardless of whether they plan to go on eventually to a university. Greater emphasis will be placed in the

---

[36] Beatrice G. Reubens, "Lessons for the United States from Western Europe," *Proceedings of the 1967 Annual Meeting of the Industrial Relations Research Association*, p. 309.

[37] Melita Knowles, "Britain Turns to the Classroom for Technological Upgrading," *Christain Science Monitor*, May 15, 1968, p. 6.

Swedish secondary schools on economics and other social sciences, natural sciences, and technology.[38]

A recent OECD report noted that one reason for the "brain drain" from Europe is that European countries do not utilize their graduates as fully as does the United States.[39] It is reported that 50 percent of German scientists interviewed in the United States said they would like to return home. The number of their wives holding this view was even greater.[40] European scientists and engineers employed in the United States would appear, therefore, to be a good source of recruitment for American firms establishing branches in Europe.

Vocational Training

Emphasis is placed in the European Economic Community on expanding vocational training and in bringing the levels of training among the member states to a common standard by instituting training programs. The Division of Vocational Training in the European Economic Community has determined that the number of workers in the Community who do not obtain some form of vocational training is quite small — 4 to 5 percent — except in Italy. In Germany and France the rate is even less — 1.5 percent. Most of the period of vocational education in Germany is spent within the industrial enterprise, while in Belgium the candidate stays in school. In France and Italy about 40 percent of vocational training takes place within industry, and the remainder is provided in the schools. In the Netherlands, only about 15 percent is done by industry.[41]

Apprenticeship, as well as middle-school and secondary education, is expanding in the West European countries, while employment without training has been gradually losing ground. In Germany, where there has been an absolute decrease in the number of young people going into apprenticeship, the proportion of newly registered apprentices has increased to over 80 percent of the young persons leaving school.[42] The number of offers from places in which training is provided is often greater than the available supply of trainees. Employers, pressed by skilled-worker shortages and com-

---

[38] "School Reform Hits Sweden," *Christian Science Monitor*, October 8, 1966, p. 7.

[39] Richard Lewis, "Europe Is Closing Technological Gap," *Chicago Sun-Times*, May 12, 1968, p. 34.

[40] "West Germany Seeks Ways to Narrow Technological Gap," *Christian Science Monitor*, October 20, 1966, p. 3.

[41] Mark J. Fitzgerald, *The Common Market's Labor Programs* (South Bend: University of Notre Dame Press, 1966), p. 39.

[42] European Apprenticeship, Geneva, CIRF Publications, ILO 1966, p. 26.

peting for the most capable persons leaving school, have been willing to make substantial investments in the training of youth.

In most countries the trend both in the new apprenticeable trades and in the choices made by young persons is toward longer periods of training. The period of apprenticeship for skilled trades is around three years in Germany, the Netherlands, and France, while in the United Kingdom five years is required in the majority of trades and four years in the building trades.[43] There has been an overall trend away from artisan-trades apprenticeships and towards training in the industrial trades and commerce. This is particularly evident whenever commercial and clerical occupations are in the trade list.[44] There is a trend toward broad and basic training suitable for a number of specializations. The manufacturing and service industries currently hold the dominant position in the recruitment of apprentices.

Although apprenticeship candidates may not be generally as well qualified as in the past, studies indicate that the levels of knowledge and skill attained in training today are in many cases superior to those of a few years ago. Many recruits in the past were intellectually overqualified for their trades. Today such persons are remaining in school to continue their education.[45]

Employers and their organizations and trade unions are taking a greater interest in promoting vocational training. Studies indicate that restrictive practices, which once were fairly common, have largely disappeared. Fear of unemployment and of competition from apprentices as cheap labor is not as evident as in the 1930s.[46]

It is my impression that the schools and apprenticeship programs in a number of European countries are doing a better job of preparing youth, especially for entrance jobs in industry, than we are doing in the United States. The educational programs there seem to be better designed to meet the needs of industry. There is some doubt in my mind, however, as to whether the school programs are adapting themselves rapidly enough to the changing needs of a shift to white collar employment.

Retraining

The term "retraining" includes vocational training for unskilled adults, retraining for persons with obsolescent skills, and re-

---

[43] *Id.,* p. 58.
[44] *Id.,* p. 61.
[45] *Id.,* p. 183.
[46] *Id.,* p. 186.

fresher training for those whose skills have not been used recently or require adjustment to technological change.[47]

The need for retraining programs to increase the employability of the unemployed, has not been evident in Western Europe in recent years because of the tight labor market conditions. As a result, there has been a decline in these programs in some countries, including Germany and the Netherlands. However, in other countries, such as Belgium, France, Great Britain, and Sweden, training programs have been expanded in order to meet skilled-worker shortages and to increase productivity.[48]

Margaret S. Gordon emphasizes the problems involved in expanding retraining in a tight labor market when the supply of unemployed individuals available for training is disappearing. She notes, however, that it is possible to introduce measures to induce employed persons to enter programs to upgrade their skills, and to draw trainees from the unemployed, married women, young men emerging from military service, the disabled, and seasonal workers.[49]

Some countries, such as France and the United Kingdom, maintain large government training centers, while others, such as Germany, Sweden, and the United States, hold classes wherever space can be found, as in public school buildings.[50]

Government retraining is limited to the unemployed except in France and Belgium, where there is a substantial enrollment of persons who have voluntarily left employment in order to upgrade themselves.[51] In Belgium, France, and the Netherlands, 80 percent or more have been trained for the building or metal trades. In Italy most adult trainees, are men. A substantial majority of them also have been trained for the building and metal trades. In Sweden, Germany, and the United States, training is provided in a number of different types of occupations, and the proportion of women enrolled is substantial.[52] Special efforts are also made to offer training for disadvantaged groups, such as elderly women in Sweden and older persons supported through emergency programs in West Berlin.[53]

---

[47] Margaret S. Gordon, *The Comparative Experience with Retraining Programmes in the United States and Europe,* Reprint No. 287, Institute of Industrial Relations, University of California, Berkeley, 1966, p. 255.

[48] *Id.,* p. 259.

[49] *Id.,* p. 260.

[50] *Id.,* p. 261.

[51] *Id.,* p. 262.

[52] *Id.,* p. 263.

[53] *Id.,* p. 264.

Sweden is an outstanding example of a nation that has succeeded in expanding a training program. The Swedish Government is approaching its goal of retraining of about 1 percent of the labor force annually. An equivalent goal in the United States would require the training of some 700,000 to 750,000 workers each year, compared to actual enrollment of only 286,000 in the fiscal year ending June 1967.[54] Consideration is being given to extending the training activity in Sweden to other than the unemployed or underemployed to cope better with acute shortages of trained manpower. A recent government report in Sweden recommended that industry assume a larger share of training responsibilities. As an incentive to such private training, a governmental grant is proposed for the trainee and the enterprise providing the training.[55]

The British Industrial Training Act of 1964 has a number of features which are of particular interest to Americans. This act emphasizes an industry rather than an occupational approach on the assumption that each industry should be responsible for its own organized training. A second noteworthy aspect is the requirement that educators be included in the administration of the act. The objectives of the act are to insure an adequate supply of trained workers, to improve the quality of industrial training, and to share the cost of training more evenly among firms. The act applies to all industries and to all levels within industry, including management and supervisory training as well as skilled, semiskilled, and unskilled workers, and to persons of all ages.[56]

Industrial Training Boards (ITB) for individual industries are established under the act by the Minister of Labour (now Minister of Employment and Productivity) and include representatives of employers, employees, and education. These boards make certain that facilities are provided to meet the needs of the industry and establish standards of training. The boards impose a levy on all employers in the industry to cover training costs and to make grants to companies with board-approved training arrangements.[57]

With the increase in unemployment in Great Britain during the year prior to July 1968, emphasis is being placed by the government on the retraining of unemployed workers, and the government has granted funds to the ITB for grants to industry for retraining

---

[54] *Id.,* p. 259, and *Manpower Report of the President,* 1968, p. 307.

[55] *Modern Swedish Labor Market Policy,* Stockholm, The National Labor Market Board, 1966.

[56] Gary B. Hansen, *Britain's Industrial Training Act.* Washington, D. C. National Manpower Policy Training Task Force, 1967, pp. 27-30.

[57] *Id.,* pp. 31-34.

the unemployed for occupations at the semiskilled level. The interest of the ITB is not in the unemployed as a special group needing assistance. Instead, its objective is job-oriented training as a means of making job performance more efficient in order to meet the skilled-manpower shortages. Gary B. Hansen believes that the present thinking in Britain is that the Industrial Training Boards have obligations to provide adult retraining for the separate industries, while the problem of unemployment is and should be a governmental responsibility.[58]

In view of the interest in the United States in governmental programs to stimulate training within private industry, one must note the main incentives offered by European governments for this purpose. Governmental subsidies are used: (a) to cover expenses such as loss of worktime and use of materials and equipment, as in Austria; (b) to reimburse the employer for the wages of instructors, as in Britain and France, or for allowances to trainees, as in France, Germany, and Sweden; (c) to compensate for the difference between the productivity of trainees and that of fully trained workers, as in Austria and the Netherlands; (d) to encourage training to advance regional development, as in Britain and Sweden; and (e) to foster training instead of dismissal of workers when technical changes take place, as in France. In some countries, governments enter into contracts with private firms to pay part of the operating expenses involved in programs conducted by industry.[59]

Manpower Allocation

The tight labor market that existed prior to 1967 in Europe has given rise to such programs as the expansion of the employment service to reduce frictional and structural unemployment, incentives to workers to increase mobility, and measures to increase the supply of labor.

Public Employment Service

In his paper Professor Shearer has stressed the matching of people and jobs as one of the three basic aims of national manpower policies. He also pointed out that government employment services in most West European nations are much more heavily involved in placement, training, and related activities than is true in the United States.

[58] *Id.*, p. 63.
[59] "Foreign Governments Increasingly Stimulate Training Opportunities for Adults in Industry," *Labor Developments Abroad,* May, 1968, p. 7.

Tripartite administration of the employment service by employers, workers, and government at the national and local levels exists in countries like Germany and Sweden. Professor Leonard Adams, of Cornell University, commented on this aspect of employer relationships with the public employment services as follows: "Those countries which seem to have the public service most acceptable to employers (for example, Sweden and West Germany) have experienced not only employer and worker participation in policy making and operation, but also active cooperation in the building of the organization itself and in providing it with the support, financial and otherwise, so essential to attainment of the desired goals."[60]

Although the public employment service in France is the sole legal placement agency and requires the registration of all job seekers and of all job vacancies, a recent study concludes that, despite these powers, "the employment service lacks any comprehensive listing of vacancies, and most workers seem unwilling to use the labor exchanges of the employment service."[61] In contrast to France and Italy, where the public employment service has a formal monopoly, the number of private, fee-charging employment agencies in Great Britain has grown with increased labor shortages. In Germany, Sweden, and the Netherlands only specially authorized and closely supervised placement agencies are allowed to co-exist with the public employment service.

Employers use the government employment service more extensively in most European countries than in the United States, where the penetration rate is estimated to be around 16 percent. It has been estimated that public exchanges make about one third of all placements in Great Britain and Sweden and from 35 to 50 percent in Germany. In a small country like Belgium the penetration rate of the public employment service does not rise above 5 or 6 percent because contacts between employers and job seekers are comparatively easy to establish.[62]

The public employment service makes a substantial contribution to the allocation of manpower in some European countries through vocational guidance. I was particularly impressed with the effective manner in which this function is being carried out in Germany, where the employment service has a monopoly in vocational

---

[60] Leonard P. Adams, *Industrial and Labor Relations Review,* Oct. 1967, p. 125.

[61] U. S. Department of Labor, Manpower Administration, *Manpower Policy and Programs in Five Western European Countries.* Manpower Research Bulletin Number 11, 1966, p. 12.

[62] *The Public Employment Services and Management,* Final Report of the International Management Seminar, Paris, OECD, 1966, pp. 34, 44, 53, and 101.

guidance. Information on occupations and the training required is made available to young German students and to their parents. For example, very attractive calendars carrying pictures depicting different occupations are provided for school classrooms. These are supplemented with informational material for teachers on each occupation. Other printed materials, lectures, films, demonstrations, and conferences with parents and students are used extensively. Where training is not available in a particular occupation for the school leaver in his home area, the vocational guidance service can provide financial assistance to enable him to go where training is available.

The functions of the public employment offices are coordinated with overall manpower policy to a greater extent in Europe than in the United States. The placement offices in several countries, for example, can offer a number of incentives, such as travel grants, to stimulate both geographic and occupational mobility. Contrary to policies of some large American cities, where efforts are made to keep industry from moving elsewhere, the trend in Europe is to encourage relocation of industry and workers in development areas away from the cities. Many of these plans, as in Great Britain, are administered by the employment exchanges. They involve much more planning than we are accustomed to in the United States. I was impressed in Germany by the sight of the new industries moving into areas where coal mines were being mechanized and where workers were trained for industrial employment as they were being dismissed from employment in the mines.

Labor Reserves

Professor Shearer has discussed in his paper the use of foreign workers as a source of labor in tight labor markets. With an increase in unemployment he believes it is possible that significant numbers of redundant foreign workers may remain in their host countries and constitute groups of low-skilled "hard core" unemployment similar to our "group" type of unemployment in the United States. If the unemployment problem in the country of origin of these workers continues to decline as they become more industrialized, as is the case of Italy, it would appear that many such workers would have an incentive to return home. Furthermore, it appears to me that unemployment will not become a long-standing or serious problem in the countries which have used foreign workers extensively, since they have thus far demonstrated their ability to maintain full employment in the long run.

West European countries, for the most part, have not experienced the type of "group" or "hard core" unemployment to the same extent as the United States. Beatrice Reubens estimates that about two million workers are covered in Western Europe under a quota system requiring employers to employ certain physically and mentally disabled persons.[63] German legislation requires, for example, each employer with more than 15 employees either to hire a quota of severely disabled workers or to make payments into a fund used to finance rehabilitation centers. In Great Britain, employers with at least 20 employees are required to employ a quota of disabled persons.[64] In Sweden, the Rehabilitation Service provides placement for the hard to place, including alcoholics, gypsies, refugees, and those with criminal records in addition to those suffering more standard disabilities. It also affords vocational training, adjustment courses, and sheltered work of various kinds to these disabled and disadvantaged persons. Over 75,000 different cases are handled annually; the U. S. equivalent would be over 1.5 million cases a year.[65]

Seasonal unemployment has been reduced in some European countries, such as Germany, thus eliminating a source of labor for nonseasonal industries in off-seasons.[66]

Professor Shearer has mentioned that many countries have made efforts to draw more heavily upon "labor reserves." Greater consideration probably should be given to the use of older workers and women in coping with shortages of workers. It must be recognized, however, that the participation rate of male workers between 55 and 59 years of age is already greater than in the United States in most of the West European countries other than France. The opposite is true, however, with respect to women in this age group. Since the participation rate for women in 55-59 age bracket is considerably lower in Western Europe than in the United States, employers should heed this source of labor supply. Because the overall labor market participation rate for women is relatively high in most countries, attention possibly should be centered in attracting more older women to the labor force, especially by offering more part-time employment. A committee reporting on labor market policy in

[63] Beatrice G. Reubens, "Lessons for the United States from Western European Experience with the Hard-to-Place." Industrial Relations Research Association, *Proceedings of the Twentieth Annual Winter Meeting,* 1967, p. 312.

[64] U. S. Dept. of Labor, Manpower Administration, *Manpower Policy and Programs in Five Western European Countries,* Research Bulletin No. 11, 1966, pp. 22, 33.

[65] Beatrice G. Reubens, *op. cit.,* note 63, *supra,* p. 311.

[66] Jack Stieber, "Implications of West European Manpower Programs for the United States," *Proceedings of the Annual Winter Meeting of I.R.R.A.,* 1967, p. 303.

Sweden, for example, emphasized that a higher participation rate among married women would require more part-time jobs.[67] Some European countries have done a much more effective job of establishing programs for taking care of children of working mothers than we have done in the United States. I was much impressed with the progress made in Sweden in attracting almost 40 percent of their women to the labor market through Labor Market Board training and placement activities and through the use of such devices as the establishment of day nurseries in cooperation with other interested public agencies.

Conclusion

This brief review of some of the many labor market policies in effect in European countries shows that, despite the emphasis placed upon resolving manpower problems, much more needs to be done if industry is to overcome the challenge of labor shortages. This is based on the assumption that the actions taken to combat the slowdown in expansion experienced recently will be effective in restoring full employment and even overemployment where it previously existed. It is recognized, however, that because of the complicated international trade factors involved, there is some uncertainty as to how soon this will be accomplished in Great Britain.

I agree with the emphasis placed by Professor Shearer on the need for firms to concentrate their attention on the most effective recruitment, development, and utilization of their work force. It appears to me that the conclusions reached by Professor Shearer relating to the recruitment of nationals for high-level posts in underdeveloped countries in his paper at the 1964 meeting of the Industrial Relations Research Association may be applicable to some extent to our present discussion. He indicated then that the scarcity confronting most firms he studied resulted less from tight labor markets than from their own inefficiency in finding and generating national manpower resources. He concluded that "the selection of nationals for high-level posts is generally done by the Americans abroad and is either a 'seat of the pants' operation or one based vaguely on selection criteria borrowed without modification from the parent company."[68]

Professor Shearer also stresses in this book the need for imag-

---

[67] *Modern Swedish Labor Market Policy,* The National Labor Market Board, Stockholm, 1966, p. 87.

[68] John C. Shearer, "The Underdeveloped Industrial Relations of U.S. Corporations in Underdeveloped Countries," *Proceedings of the Industrial Relations Research Association,* 1964 Annual Meeting, p. 63.

inatively adapting policies and techniques developed in domestic operations to their overseas environments. In my observation of the operation of public employment offices in European countries, I was surprised to find in some of the countries the traditional division between male and female employment service departments. I was in England at the time the employment service broke with tradition by eliminating the practice of separating the sexes for employment interviews. There was strong objection being raised to participating in interviews conducted by members of the opposite sex. I note that a Swedish Committee recommended recently that a similar change be made in Sweden.[69] I cite this as an example of the necessity of adjusting an employment technique to a foreign environment.

In view of the serious problems involved in finding additional manpower, it would appear that firms also will place great emphasis on mechanization of operations. Professor Shearer has referred to the opposition of unions in many countries to technological change. It would appear to me that this opposition should diminish if the full employment which has characterized many European countries for so long a period is quickly restored following the increase in unemployment in the past year. Furthermore, the desire for shorter hours by workers in an overemployment economy should further reduce the opposition of workers to technological change. I found labor leaders whom I interviewed in Germany stressing this latter point in maintaining that they welcomed more mechanization.

Employers will find that in many countries it will be necessary to develop short-term and long-term plans for manpower recruitment and development to coincide with overall government planning. It will be necessary for employers to supply more information, such as job-vacancy data, advance notice of layoffs, and forecasts of manpower requirements, than they have done in the United States. They will find such data helpful in developing their own manpower programs, which in some countries will have to be related to governmental investment-credit and production plans.

Finally, employers no doubt will take advantage of the efforts being made to close the statistical gap. The inadequacies and the delays in issuing data, as well as the difficulties involved in their interpretation because of lack of uniformity of classification and of collection methods, has made it difficult for employers to use published data in planning manpower policies. Most European nations are taking action to improve their statistical services, since more ade-

---

[69] *Modern Swedish Labor Market Policy, op. cit.,* note 67, *supra,* p. 86.

quate data are needed by them for governmental planning. It should also be recognized that, in some cases, Europeans are providing data not available in the United States, such as the number of job vacancies. Much of the impetus for improved and more uniform and current statistics comes from such international organizations as the Economic Commission for Europe, the Organization for Economic Co-Operation and Development, and the International Labour Office. J. Russell Boner recently reported that much of the effort to improve statistics involves reporting the raw data in a more meaningful form. Mr. Boner cites a German report for the second half of 1967 which showed a rising ratio of unemployed to job vacancies. When these figures were adjusted for seasonal factors, the data indicated just the opposite — that an economic recovery was under way.[70]

More attention is being given to manpower research in the universities in Europe, as is also the trend in the United States. I note, for example, that the Office of the Chancellor of the Swedish Universities, after studying the question of special university departments or institutions for labor market reserarch, has recommended the establishment of an institute closely attached to the University of Stockholm. It is my understanding that the proposal passed by the Riksdag anticipates that this institute will develop into an important instrument for a general activation and coordination of the research and training activity in manpower conducted in different quarters. It is interesting to note, especially in view of the sponsorship of the 1968 Loyola University conference, that the head of the institute in Sweden will have a seat and vote in the faculty of social sciences as well as in the faculty of law on questions that concern the institute's field of activity.[71]

Author's Recommended Reading List

Adams, Walter, ed., *The Brain Drain* (New York: Macmillan, 1968).
Barkin, Solomon, ed., *Technical Change and Manpower Planning Coordination at Enterprise Level* (Paris: OECD, 1967).
Fitzgerald, Mark J., *The Common Market's Labor Program* (Notre Dame: Notre Dame University Press, 1966).
Lorwin, Val Rogin, ed., *Labor and Working Conditions in Modern Europe* (New York: Macmillan, 1967).
Meyers, Frederic, *Training in European Enterprises* (Los Angeles: Institute of Industrial Relations, University of California, 1969).

---

[70] J. Russell Boner, "Closing the Statistical Gap," *The Wall Street Journal*, February 12, 1968, p. 26.
[71] *Modern Swedish Labor Market Policy, op cit.*, note 67, *supra*, p. 101.

Page, G. Terry, *The Industrial Training Act and After* (London: Deutsch, 1967).

Routh, Guy, *Occupation and Pay in Great Britain, 1906-1960* (New York: Cambridge University Press, 1966).

Smith, Anthony D., *The Labor Market and Inflation* (New York: St. Martin's Press, 1968). •

International Manpower Seminar (Washington: U.S. Department of Labor, 1967).

"Report on West Germany," *Current History,* May 1968, entire issue.

Symposium on Manpower and the War on Hunger (Washington: U.S. Department of Labor, 1968).

HIDDEN MANPOWER RESOURCES

By Allan Flanders

Professor Shearer in his paper drew an initial distinction between the external and the internal manpower environments of the firm. I first take this up to bring out what has been one of the great paradoxes in British economic life after the war — a paradox which the nation and indeed most of those intimately concerned have taken a very long time to appreciate. It can be put quite simply: An acute labor shortage may be registered in the external manpower environment of a firm by the current state of the labor market, and the firm's internal manpower environment can register a considerable labor surplus. This constitutes the paradox: shortage of the same labor in the one environment and a surplus in the other.

This is possible because, although full employment has become a compelling national goal in Britain, it is quite compatible, in practice, with very serious underemployment on the job. These two things not only merely can co-exist, as we know for certain in Britain; they are also connected, as I hope to show.*

Now, the great difficulty about surplus in the internal manpower environment is that it may not be visible, certainly not visible to society at large; and possibly not to management, either. For many years in Britain, even in situations where labor was utilized perhaps at the most to an extent of 30 percent as in extreme cases like the national newspapers, top management was unaware of this because it did not seek the relevant information. So the problem was unquantified. Even when the Donovan Commission's Report deals with utilization of labor, it suffers from the poverty of quantitative evidence on a broad scale. Most of the evidence has to be put together from those firms that have sought to establish the facts in this respect, and they are a small minority.

When you bring this paradox into your consideration of manpower problems, it gives them a new dimension, a dimension which can alter policies in various ways. One may refer to underemployment on the job as constituting hidden manpower resources. The policy question is how to tap them. In Britain this question is of the utmost importance, in the first place, because of our demographic trends. One of the very useful decisions taken by our old Ministry of

---

* Ed. Note: "Labor-Management Relations and the Democratic Challenge," p. 487 *infra*.

Labour, now Department of Employment and Productivity, was to set up a Manpower Research Unit, which has published to date seven reports. The first, *Pattern of the Future*, appeared a few years ago. It tried with the help of demographic and other data to foresee future trends in labor supply. The conclusion was that, between 1968 and 1973, the growth of our working population would slow down very substantially while the total population would continue to grow at much the same rate as before. The very slow increase in the active labor force over the period suggested that a situation of overall shortage was much more likely to occur than one of surplus, so that the strain on manpower resources could well be more severe than over the previous five years. The strain depends, of course, also on the monetary and fiscal policies that the government finds itself forced to pursue in relation to the balance of payments. Nevertheless, from a national point of view, the tapping of hidden reserves of manpower lying within the firms' internal environment is a matter of great urgency.

It is also important from the point of view of the firm; and, let me add, from the point of view of the individual worker, because of one thing I am sure from my own observations when I was working on the shop floor in industry. No man likes to have his time treated by management as if it were unimportant. That is an affront to his dignity as a human being. This is true even though labor under-utilization may sometimes be due to certain restrictive practices enforced by unions or work groups. They may serve to protect him, but the individual worker rarely enjoys these situations if they lead to enforced idleness.

I saw this illustrated when I was going through the publishing house of one of our leading newspaper and printing organizations, which shall be nameless. In showing me around, they hustled me through one particular room where a lot of chaps were sitting in their overcoats and drinking tea, some playing cards. Later I asked who they were. They were "redundant workers," it appeared, and the agreement said that they should not lose their jobs until they had found alternative employment. So for more than a year a slowly dwindling number had been coming along for the night shift to fill in their time. I said: "Isn't this very demeaning for them? Why don't they go home?" I was told that the union had insisted upon their clocking in because it would otherwise create an unfortunate precedent. Surely that kind of life and treatment must be demeaning for the individual; it makes him less than a man. So I am concerned with the problem of under-utilization — not just as an economist, but also from a social point of view.

But how do you tap these hidden reserves of manpower? I know only one short answer: You have to negotiate the changes that will release the supply. You cannot enforce them when they depend on gaining the consent of unions and their members. This is where productivity bargaining comes into the picture. It is essentially a method of negotiating union agreements to bring about a more efficient utilization of labor.

Now this is not just a matter of eliminating featherbedding, make-work practices, and the like. It goes much further than that. One of the great sources of underemployment on the job in Britain has undoubtedly been the ever-rising levels of regular overtime, much of which is unnecessary except to make up the pay packet. Another source has been incentive pay systems that are no longer systems or incentives. The modernization of payment systems in Britain could lead to a vast improvement in labor utilization. In short, a whole variety of changes in working practices and pay structures are at stake here, but they are all changes that have to be negotiated.

Finally, I would like to say a few words about a very important subject in the British setting, our experience with the Industrial Training Act of 1964. This measure was a complete break with tradition. In the past, if anything was to be done at a social level to improve training, there had to be conversations between employers and unions, and any results had to be voluntary results. The use of compulsion was barred, although everybody knew that the standards of industrial training in many places were a scandal. This Act was a very interesting innovation as a mixture of compulsion and inducement. In addition to increasing the supply of properly trained people, by raising the level of training, the Act was intended to spread the costs of training more evenly among firms. It is best to try to do these things through industrial machinery, by setting up industry training boards which fully involve the parties in the process. But no less important in the Act was the one element of compulsion it brought in, a compulsory levy. This meant that firms developing adequate training programs could be paid for these programs out of the sums collected from the levy, while those firms who did no training paid the levy and got nothing back. In this way inducement was underpinned by one element of compulsion.

I was talking a few weeks ago to the chairman of the Engineering Training Board, which is the most important one both in view of the size of the industry and also because this Board happens to have the highest levy and, therefore, the most funds for development. I was amazed at the progess the Board had made. So little of this information ever reaches the public. Apart from things that I knew about, the reorganization of the standards of training on the basis of modules, or clusters of different skills which could be put together in different ways, I realized for the first time that the Board was developing a counselling service for firms on quite a large scale. They were going into firms, of course at the firms' request, with their own officers to look at the firms' training needs and to advise them. And not merely to advise them on their training programs, because you cannot consider training in isolation from everything else. So an instrument was being forged for noncompulsory intervention. Firms were turning to the Board when they had not the resources of their own to secure new training systems and support. I believe this will be a very important lever in raising our standards of training.

It does not solve the problem of access to jobs, however. When you have trained, skilled people — and this also applies to those coming out of the government training centers, whose intake has recently been very substantially increased — will they get jobs? Or will the craftsman say, "You can't come in," as they do in some cases; or, "You can only come in as a dilutee in spite of your expert training, and that means if there is any redundancy you are first out before any man who has served his time." I see no solution to this problem again except through negotiation.

Resolution here does not depend primarily on changing our union structure. The problem is not one of craft unions. They hardly exist any more. An organization like the Amalgamated Engineering and Foundry Workers Union is not a craft or a multicraft union in the sense that its boundaries are drawn according to crafts. It organizes in practically every industry in the country, and unskilled as well as skilled workers. The problem is one of craft attitudes and they are deep-seated. There exists a craft culture, you might say; you find that on the shop floor, and you have to change it on the shop floor. You cannot go along to a union and say, "Please change your craft culture, your craft attitudes for us," because the union cannot deliver. If management is to begin to change these attitudes it must show that they are a liability to the men themselves, and the employer must offer them a more attractive alternative. Above all, it must get to work where the real pressures lie, among the craft groups on the shop floor. This is in fact another aspect of many of our major productivity bargains. It is a particularly intractable problem in negotiations, but they have demonstrated that it is not insoluble.

MANPOWER UTILIZATION IN WESTERN EUROPE AND THE AMERICAN INVESTOR: A TEARLESS COMMENTARY

By Guy Nunn

I was seriously tempted, listening to the preceding four speakers, to ingratiate myself with all of you by simply applauding them and sitting down — which is probably a very sound response, even if somewhat demagogic. However, in the circles in which I travel, it is almost treasonable to decline an opportunity to make verbal noise. You've got to say something!

1. Professor Shearer's statement strikes me, in the overall, as sound in both its assumptions and its conclusions. I was especially grateful for the emphasis he put on the (comparative) U. S. derelictions in the area of manpower planning and our irresolute commitment to the goal of reasonably full employment — as well as for his recognition that the aggressive pursuit of constantly higher wages and improved fringes by American unions have made of rising manpower costs an often beneficial goad to higher efficiency and human resource utilization. Employers, in the main, are still astonishingly ungrateful to unions for this periodic contribution to corporate well-being.

2. As to the relatively higher costs to employers of layoffs in Western Europe, I would have several comments (none tearfully sympathetic to the American investor who might be vexed by them), with some of which, at least, Professor Shearer might agree:

a. Such costs are almost certainly going to be minor as compared with nonlabor costs of a layoff.

b. If they are a crucial risk to the investor, he probably shouldn't be there anyhow.

c. Such costs are relatively easy to plan for. They will normally, in any case, be less typical of the American-directed firm than of the European, for the American firm will be — or ought to be — in capital-intensive enterprises where labor costs in the overall are already relatively small, as a fraction of gross costs, and highly likely to decline rapidly with time.

d. For whatever consolation it may offer, American investors in European manufacturing may be certain that layoff costs in America will rise rather sharply over the next decade toward parity with European termination costs.

e. There are other consolations, already operative, which should, I believe, more than compensate the American investor for the relatively higher present cost of dumping his workers on the street. One is that he will not generally find his labor demanding wages commensurate with the productivity or profitability of the company involved. The high-efficiency producer in Europe is far less likely than his U. S. counterpart to a find a strong local union demanding a cut of the take geared to the profits of that particular firm. On the contrary, he is likely to find a wage-repressing ally in a national union center which is almost as unhappy as the employer's federation of the government at the prospect of serious breaches in industry-wide wage scales.

A Kaiser-Frazer vice president once told me that, a good many years ago, he decided to open a new assembly plant in Holland with a bit of a splash. To curry good will with workers and the public alike, as well as to minimize his labor-recruitment problem, he announced that the company would pay, across the board, about 30 percent over the then-prevailing metalworking scales. The first delegation to pound on his door in protest was not from the government or from his fellow members of the Employers' Association. It was from the Dutch metalworkers federation. He was rocking their boat, too. And, being a fellow with a certain reputation to sustain for being soft on labor, he retreated.

European unions, even where they are strong (and they are almost pitifully weak and divided in France and Italy), tend to pursue nationwide or, at best, industry-wide bargaining. They do so for reasons which are, for the most part, honorable, responsible, and, for all I know, correct. But one upshot is that wage scales tend — even in strongly unionized countries like West Germany — to be those which are easily digestible by the less efficient producers in any given industry, and national wage guidelines are relatively easy to enforce. A corollary to highly centralized wage bargaining (to which the government is usually a direct and conservative party) — and one that has certain cost implications of a reassuring nature for American investors — is a generally highly centralized trade union structure which tends to resist assertions of local autonomy, and which has such limited grass-roots structure that it rarely intrudes in local managerial prerogatives, which include the unilateral fixing of production standards.

I would hardly know how to begin to compute the probable

cost imposed on a typical stateside manufacturing operation by the necessity to carry hordes of company-paid union busybodies, in the form of shop stewards and committeemen (contract policemen with a presumptive mission to stick their noses into everything), but, large or small, it is a cost which the equivalent operation in Europe does not have to bear. It also is a cost which few unions show much disposition to inflict upon management.

I would like warmly to second Mr. Flander's observations concerning the unexploited interior labor resources of Western Europe (as well as in the United States), and to second his observations on incentives. My own union — and I think this is true of most non-craft unions in this country — is deeply unenthusiastic about incentive wages, and it frequently puzzles us that employers do not seem as generally to share that distaste. In the bulk of our incentive schemes, it becomes fairly apparent after a couple of years that the workers take control of them, and the incentive schemes can in fact be, as Mr. Flanders has suggested, disincentives. Workers tend to gear their output, even under the most lucrative incentive schemes, to their presumptions regarding future production demands, and frequently employers find themselves paying high per-hour costs simply because workers gear their output to their presumptions of what the gross requirements of the company are going to be over the period of the week or a month.

A further compensation for the vexations — to the American investor — of functioning inside highly regulated economic systems should reside in that very fact. The European market should, being so largely managed, be somewhat more predictable and somewhat more stable than the U. S. market. For that matter, John Kenneth Galbraith is hardly the first to have observed that our own economy is increasingly a managed one (although with somewhat less humane purposes than is generally the case in Western Europe), and the European investor with any experience in the United States will already be somewhat conditioned to having to function within a matrix of decisions, some of them apparently irrational, and practices imposed by others.

There is also the general likelihood that, while the American manufacturing investor in Western Europe will encounter skill shortages at least as acute as those now prevailing in the United States, he will — for some years to come — find such manpower as he can assemble (except possibly in Great Britain) measurably more docile and "company oriented" than is generally the case here. And while outcroppings of "irrational" opposition to the introduction of new techniques or patterns of production (as employers tend to view all such opposition) will doubtless continue to occur, these are far less likely to manifest themselves in new operations, and almost all such occurrences are, in essence, avoidable in any case. As Elton Mayo (followed by a host of more sophisticated industrial psychologists) started trying to tell us over three decades ago, an ounce of frank advance consultation and explanation is worth a pound of ingenious — but fear-creating — innovations, sprung full-blown.

For what it may be worth as a manpower consideration, the likelihood of strikes (France of May 1968 notwithstanding) seems measurably smaller in Western Europe for the next decade or two than in the United States. European unions are simply not equipped, either ideologically or economically, to sustain strikes of prolonged duration, and the tradition of industry-wide or national bargaining reduces the likelihood of local strikes against targets of special opportunity, no matter how tempting.

As to labor supply, again there is no gainsaying the problem, but common sense suggests that recruitment should, in the short run, be essentially no more difficult than in the United States. While the American manufacturer in Europe will probably begin at a level of technology markedly more sophisticated than that generally prevailing among his competition, with correspondingly higher demands on managerial training, we have only just begun to realize that the training process itself is as susceptible to automation and foreshortening as are production and distribution, and Europeans begin with at least the receptivity of Americans to accelerated education. (It would be my guess, in fact, that the level of effective literacy is somewhat higher in Europe, on the average, than in the United States.)

I am not familiar with the example cited by Professor Shearer of the pharmaceutical firm layoff and its consequences in Italy, but I do understand that in the world pharmaceutical industry as a whole, gross labor costs come to something like 3 percent, whereas promotion costs or sales costs independent of distribution costs come to about 5 percent. It strikes me that an equivalent saving might have been made simply by laying off their advertising firms rather than by laying off the workers. If layoff costs are, however, a truly crucial risk to the American investor in Europe, I would say he probably should not be there and probably will not be there long. If so fragile an investor is there, he is gambling with the lives of human beings. He should not try such experiments. Such costs should be relatively easy to plan against. They will normally, in any case, be rather less typical of the American-directed firm in Western Europe than of the European firm because, by and large, the American firm will be, or at least ought to be, in capital-intensive enterprises where unit labor costs are relatively small and are likely, with expectable increases in productivity, to decline in time.

As Professor Buckley's paper demonstrated, there is also a still partially untapped manpower reservoir in most European countries in the large number of women who have, as yet, not been drawn into the work force. These women can be expected to enter the labor market as family consumer desires widen and working class families accept the almost universal proposition that you cannot break into the middle class, as consumers, without at least two incomes per family.

I can only guess at the cost of labor turnover to the typical American firm — and it's hardly more than a guess that turnover should be lower in Europe, but it seems reasonable that it should be. The persistent housing shortage alone throughout Europe seems to be a powerful anti-mobility factor in the labor market. (In that connection, incidentally, any American firm that can contrive to accompany its recruiting with the possibility of improved housing is likely to find its recruiting problems disappearing overnight).

Czechoslovakia is not, politically, Western Europe as yet, but it would very much like to be. It claims the most intense labor shortages at every level, with women accounting for close to half the gross work force. There is a kind of black market in Czechoslovakia for skills, managerial and otherwise, but the only successful inducement which can currently be offered a man to change employers is larger or better living quarters for himself and his family. In Western Europe generally, employers have found themselves obliged to show a far greater interest in the provision of housing and transportation for workers than has typically been the case in the United States. No doubt this stems more from necessity than from benevolence, but it is a cost factor which many American enterprises in Europe will have to reckon with.

Finally, if the recent pattern of American expansion into Western Europe persists (namely, intrusion through merger with, or acquisition of, preexisting enterprises, rather than through the founding of new enterprises from scratch), the possible risks and traumas inherent in the manpower peculiarities of Western Europe are obviously greatly reduced.

MANPOWER PROBLEMS IN ITALY

By P. P. Fano

Until rather recently most of the Italian labor force worked on the land. Because the country is densely populated and does not enjoy an abundance of fertile soils, there was a great excess of agricultural population living in precarious conditions and under high rates of unemployment and underemployment. Italian industry, on the other hand, which had begun to develop later than in other West European countries, catered especially to the home market, under the protection of high tariff barriers, and offered but limited opportunity for employment.

This situation has gradually changed during the last 15 years or so, during which the Italian economy and its industry have been able to develop intensely and in many new directions. The Marshall Plan first gave impetus to the development of Italian industry. Subsequent advances were made possible by adoption of a free trade policy and the opening of the Common Market. And a significant factor in Italian industrial development is found in the initiative of its entrepreneurs and the adaptability and industrious qualities of its population.

The country is rapidly catching up with the economically most advanced nations, and many products of its industry are competing successfully on the world market.

Between 1958 and 1967 the volume of Italian industrial production increased 116 percent as against 70 percent in the European Economic Community as a whole (60 percent in Western Germany, 65 percent in France, 88 percent in the Netherlands, 53 percent in Belgium), 32 percent in the United Kingdom, and 75 percent in the United States. Gross national income of Italy increased during this period at an average rate of over 5.5 percent a year.

REDEPLOYMENT OF MANPOWER

The transformation of the economic structure of the country has been most vividly reflected in the changes that have occurred in the distribution of its manpower resources. From 1951 to 1967 the number of agricultural workers declined from 8.2 million to 4.4 million, while workers in industry increased in number from 5.8 to 7.6 million. During the same period there was also a marked increase in the number of people employed in the tertiary or service sector. The labor force of Italy numbers about 20 million out of a population of nearly 53 million.

The transition from a predominantly agricultural to an industrial economy and the grafting of modern cosmopolitan institutions onto the old parochial structures of the country have taken place too quickly not to raise challenging problems in practically every field. The redeployment of the labor resources of the country is among these problems. It causes the greatest preoccupations on account of its vast economic and social implications. During the last eight years, 2.3 million agricultural workers have left the land at the average rate of 287,500 a year. The flight from agriculture has occurred everywhere throughout the country, but has been and still is especially pronounced in the backward areas of the South, where the land is generally poor and can seldom afford stable employment and decent standards of living and where few alternative opportunities for employment are yet available. Most of the people of the South who abandon agriculture move to the central and northern regions of the peninsula, attracted by the hope of finding jobs where most of the economic potential of the country is concentrated. Others seek employment in the mining and industrial communities of the Common Market or go overseas to Latin America, Canada, or the United States.

This exodus has helped relieve the pressure of population in agricultural areas and provided a vital reservoir of manpower, albeit unskilled, when the expanding modern sectors of the economy of the country needed it most. On the other hand, if it were to continue unabated it would menace the South of Italy with virtual depletion of the manpower resources which are necessary to carry out the plans for the rehabilitation of that region.

Moreover, the ability of the densely populated industrialized regions to continue to absorb a vast influx of population is being limited by the saturation of their housing, educational, health, and transportation facilities and other social services. Limitations are also imposed by shrinking opportunities for employment due to widespread reorganization and concentration of enterprises and the introduction of labor-saving equipment and techniques. Official statistics indicate that during 1967 there was an average of 689,000 unemployed, corresponding to 3.5 percent of the total labor force.

These figures do not seem to point to an exceptionally high rate of idle manpower. But this impression is soon corrected if it is considered that the figures do not include several hundred thousand

migrants temporarily employed in the area of the the Common
Market, in Switzerland, and elsewhere who would not hesitate to
return to Italy at the first offer of a decent job. Nor do they include
over one million people, mostly unskilled woman workers, who have
recently abandoned marginal and precarious occupations in agriculture and are not officially classified as unemployed. There is also
an additional labor reserve in the urban areas composed of un-
trained women who are not in the labor market only because they
have no hope of getting a job. The conclusion is that the potential
manpower supply of the country is much larger than that which appears in the official statistics.

CONCERN WITH UNEMPLOYMENT

In a country like Italy, which, since time immemorial, has been
plagued by unemployment and underemployment — and only recently has succeeded in ameliorating this situation — the workers
are born with a virus in their blood which is called fear of losing
the job. In the United States this disease is rare if not unknown.
The very vastness of the land has permitted successive waves of population to conquer frontier after frontier and has provided jobs to
anyone who was prepared to work hard enough to exploit its almost
unlimited natural resources. In addition America is rich enough to
provide substantial unemployment compensation benefits to idle
workers. Italy has very few natural resources, is more densely populated than the United States, and is without frontiers to conquer.
Our idle citizen may only cross our national boundaries with his
emigrant visa.

In these circumstances, an American employer should not be
surprised by the fact that the Italian unions make special efforts to
protect the workers against dismissal and that there are agreements
signed by the employers' and workers' organizations providing for
compulsory advance union-management consultation on group dismissals and for advance notice and monetary and other benefits for
dismissed workers.

The elimination of unemployment is indeed the major objective
of the Italian economic policy, as outlined in the five-year program
of economic development. Paramount among the means for achieving this goal is a substantial increase in capital investments in industry throughout the country. Much of this allocation of capital is
directed to the Italian South, in order to create in that region a sufficient number of new productive jobs, retain its population, and

raise its standard of living to a level comparable with the rest of the country.

Measures are also contemplated to increase the productivity of agriculture to make it possible to narrow the gap between industrial and agricultural incomes and reduce the flight from the land. In the national development program, however, it is a fundamental premise that these aims will not be attained without a vast increase in the numbers of skilled workers at all levels. This, of course, is a problem which is challenging all expanding economies. Unfortunately, in Italy, the educational system and the vocational training facilities, like many other social institutions, were not prepared for the rapid advance of the economy and are still inadequate to meet the greater and more diversified demand for trained personnel.

RECRUITMENT PROBLEMS

Enterprises in all modern sectors of the economy have experienced difficulties in recruiting qualified personnel and have had to rely, quite often, on the innate ingenuity and adaptability of the Italians and upon internal training systems more than on the official educational curricula.

It is estimated that more than half the Italian labor force is made up of unskilled workers most of whom have had only a few years of elementary education. In industry, about one third of the workers are unskilled and, except for the younger generation, a large proportion of skilled labor and shop-floor supervisory staff has acquired its qualifications on the job rather than in regular training courses.

The basic system of vocational training, open to those who are 14 years of age and thus have completed the period of compulsory education, consists either of two-year courses for skilled workers or five-year courses for technical personnel of intermediate levels. Both types of courses are administered by the Ministry of Education and cover industry, commerce, and agriculture. There are, in addition, many other training and retraining facilities operated by public or private institutions under the auspices of the Ministry of Labor.

The larger corporations often have training facilities of their own, and modern vocational training centers have been set up, in the developing areas of the South, by the employer associations of both private and government-controlled industries to meet the demands of the new enterprises.

The value of the government or government-sponsored vocational training institutions — and they constitute the bulk of the training facilities of the country — varies a great deal, from the excellent to the mediocre. From a general viewpoint, the efforts of these institutions are scattered and their courses too often correspond poorly to the actual requirements of modern society and of the current labor market.

Scarcity of well-qualified instructors, educational planners, and administrators is one of the reasons for this situation. The other, as I have noted above, is the rate with which the demand made upon the education and training systems has increased in volume and changed in nature.

There are only two major institutions that specialize in management training. One is supported by private employers and the other by the government-controlled industries. The universities do not provide special courses in business administration.

The country is aware that this situation must be drastically improved, and the national program for economic development makes provision for the investment of over 5 percent of the national income in the years 1966 to 1970 for reform of the school system in general and of the technical and vocational training system in particular. Under the new system, vocational training will be divided into two periods, the first aimed at providing basic general education and vocational training of a multipurpose character and the second at furnishing specialized training for individual professions and trades. The program contemplates that the new system should be able, within five years, to qualify 1,150,000 young workers and retrain 440,000 unemployed and 300,000 agricultural workers leaving the land.

Comparing the composition of the labor force of 1961 with that which should obtain in 1981 as a result of the strengthening of the school and vocational training systems, the national economic development program forecasts that the volume of unskilled labor should decline from 52.7 percent to 15.3 percent of the total labor force, the proportion of skilled workers should increase from 31.2 to 51.6 percent, and that of supervisors and foremen should rise from 12.5 to 26.1 percent. During the same period, administrative and managerial personnel trained in the secondary schools and in the universities should grow from 3.6 to 6.6 percent of the total labor force.

Few steps of practical value have been taken so far to determine the occupations given priority in training to cope with trends in the labor market and to solve the related questions of vocational counseling and vocational guidance. These problems have been the object of a good deal of research. It has been suggested in various quarters, official and unofficial, that a major role in these areas should be played by the employment service, whose reform is under consideration.

The employment service is administered as a public service by the Ministry of Labor and operates in the field through provincial employment offices whose functions do not go much beyond the matching of offers and demands for labor and the collection of employment statistics. Representatives of the employers' and workers' organizations are associated in a consultative capacity with both the central and the peripheral machinery of the service. As a general rule, workers must be hired through the official employment offices, but direct employment is permitted in certain cases, including the hiring of persons for executive positions. Moreover, employers are permitted by the official employment offices to select workers possessing particular skills.

The two major problems which are under consideration regarding the reorganization of the employment service concern the extension of its functions to include manpower planning and vocational guidance and the demand of the trade unions for a greater share of responsibility in the placement of the workers.

In conclusion, I must admit that I have dwelt at least as much on things to come as on the present manpower situation. In asking your indulgence for this, I will say that Italy is like an old house inhabited by a modern family that is quite impatient of the inconveniences of the old structures and wanting to renovate them. If an American employer proposes to go to Italy, he should take that into consideration as well.

MANPOWER IN WESTERN EUROPE

BY G. M. J. VELDKAMP

Manpower problems of West European nations are influenced by rapid technical and economic changes in the industrial structure. The technical changes result from major developments in classic mechanization. Inventions in the field of electronics accelerate the pace of technical change.* The economic changes are largely the result of the forms of economic cooperation that have come from the creation and functioning of the European Community.

The technical changes of our day have inaugurated a second Industrial Revolution, which is still insufficiently recognized as such by industry and governments. The recognition lag may be a consequence of the experience of various European countries for many consecutive years with the phenomenon of overemployment. As a result the effects of industrial change upon employment have long remained concealed, just as in a flood tide much is hidden from the gaze which is clearly apparent at ebb tide.

When there was a recession several years ago in the economic and employment situation in Western Europe, the decline in gross employment in various countries was immediately apparent. But the structural nature of this recession was not immediately and universally recognized. Management and union representatives and members of the national parliaments appealed to the governments for emergency measures to aid industries concerned in keeping employment up to requisite levels. Although this is understandable, a careful analysis of the essential problems leads only to the conclusion that such efforts to increase employment in the sectors concerned are inadequate. It is, of course, desirable that the industrial divisions concerned be aided and their resistance and their fighting capacity in the competitive struggle be increased. But this only maintains the profitability of the sectors concerned and the contributions that they can make to national production and economic growth. Over the long run the need is for a high degree of improvement of efficiency by means of mechanization and automation. In this way large groups of employees are permanently excluded from employment opportunities in the affected industrial units.

---

*Ed. Note: "[E]lectronics is not an ordinary industry: it is the base upon which the next stage of industrial development depends." J.-J. Servan-Schreiber, *The American Challenge*, 13 (1968).

In some respects a comparison may be made with the first Industrial Revolution in the nineteenth century. While the first Industrial Revolution made a major contribution to economic growth, it was accompanied by a number of subsidiary social phenomena that caused large sections of the working population to suffer for decade after decade. Gradually the fullest possible employment became the goal in the various countries. Not only was full employment thereby created, but all groups of employees were enabled to share in the fruits of economic progress. Between the start of the Industrial Revolution and the achievement of this social equilibrium there was, however, a considerable time lag and great social distress.

Everything points to the fact that we are once again faced with such a situation. Now that economic recovery is an established fact in the various countries of Western Europe, it is clear that the structural employment discussed above has not risen despite the economic recovery. On the contrary, it must be expected that severe declines in employment will be experienced in sectors such as the textile industry, the ready-made clothing industry, the leather industry, the footwear industry, shipbuilding and the building trades. Agriculture now provides employment to 12 million persons in the six member countries of the EEC. Within a few years this number will have declined to substantially less than half because of further structural changes and mechanization.

A paradoxical element of the problem is the disturbed equilibrium between technical and economic development on the one hand and the degree of training of the other. It is obvious that technical and economic development can be pursued more quickly and flexibly on the side of capital goods than on that of manpower. After all, the situation is such that the employees in practically all occupations and from bottom to top have in fact been trained for occupations that they planned to practice all their lives. Modern industrial development continuously renders large numbers of occupations superfluous. One must conclude that an average working man in the years that lie before us will have to change his occupation two or three times in his working lifetime, even though he will have to work for a shorter time than in the past. However, his basic training is such that a switch to a new occupation is not easy. Not only did his basic training make no allowance for the possibility of change, but many workers simply are reluctant to accept the fact that their training has lost its utility. Within the framework of educational possibilities both inside and outside industry, all nations in Western Europe have not made it possible to absorb the ever-growing stream of industrial rejects, to inform and advise them, to train, retrain, and reskill them. Moreover, even if educational plans had been made, we still do not have available methods that would utilize penetrating sociological and psychological research.

However depressing it may be, we must say that we are not prepared for all this in Western Europe — and I venture to say that this is true of the whole industrial world. I drew attention to this in 1967 and 1968 during the International Labour Conferences in Geneva. Enormous scientific research to prepare for a tremendous socio-educative infrastructure will have to be set in motion. In my opinion the individual countries themselves are not capable of this. Such a program will require international cooperation.

In our quest for solutions we must bear in mind that continued acceleration of technical development should lead to an acceleration of economic growth. If the problem of unemployment is not to be made greater than it already is, technical development must be coupled with substantial shortening of working hours. One need not be prepared to go as far as certain futurists, who at present are predicting that a sabbatical year will soon be within everybody's reach (six years' work, one year's holiday), to predict that in the near future there will have to be a considerable reduction of working hours. While it is true that economic growth may be delayed thereby, such a reduction presents a bright side from the employment point of view. Developments in recent years have clearly demonstrated that availability of more leisure time leads to major changes in the pattern of life that create new needs calling for satisfaction and thus enlarge work opportunities.

We shall not be concerned with simple changes but with a complete revolution of the social pattern of life. While the pattern of life in the last 50 years was dominated by the rhythm of work, it seems likely that in the future it will be replaced by the rhythm of human development outside work. This will lead to the creation of numerous new occupations and jobs in the tertiary or service sector.

Both scientific research into the methods demanded by occupational labor mobility of the future and the socio-educative infrastructure that has to be created will be of a size matching the institutions in the field of medical science and the medical infrastructure. This means that not only will a large number of persons have to be trained for and placed in this new service sector, but also that there must be capital and subsidies in sizes comparable to what we now bear for medical services. Such financing naturally creates enormous problems — as the financing of medical provisions already does. A solution will have to be sought within the framework of the social security systems. For if the burdensome problems of future employment cannot be solved, the full burden of that unemployment — at least in a material respect — will fall upon the unemployment benefit provisions created within the framework of the systems of social security. Enormous sums are concerned here. It seems better to use these sums for the development and preservation of a system in which people can keep on working than merely to use these monies to make up the loss of income of people who have no work. In the first case, these monies have a long-range productive use, in the second case only a temporary, consumptive one.

This is a gigantic problem that faces the EEC nations. I have the impression that there is not a single country or selected group of neighboring nations that can solve this problem alone. Existing international organizations must enlist the world's best experts for the formulation of world-wide solutions.

PART VII

American Management
and Investment
in Western Europe:
Some European Views

Only European contributors appear in the discussion of American management and investment in Western Europe that follows. Samuel C. Silkin discusses the complicating factor that the American presence in Western Europe may create in the emergence of a United States of Europe, a cause to which he declares his dedication. Other contributors offer candid observations about errors of American companies that have set up operations in their countries. Throughout this part there is expressed not only a concern that American enterprise might ultimately dominate the economies of the host nations, but also the fear that their polities may be subjected to the extrajurisdictional reach of the government of the United States of America through mandatory prohibitions on trade with certain nations, compulsory contraction of overseas activity, compulsory repatriation of dividends earned in foreign operations, and the like. Executive Order No. 11387, promulgated by President Johnson on January 1, 1968, was viewed by some of the Europeans at the Loyola conference as an example of indirect interference by the American government in the political affairs of Western Europe.

AMERICAN INVESTMENT AND EUROPEAN CULTURES: CONFLICT AND COOPERATION

By Samuel C. Silkin

What has really stood out in what we heard and discussed at this conference is the tremendous variety of practices and laws among different European countries and the very long way which Europeans must go to attain that process of harmonization which has been achieved to a large degree in the United States. To those of us who, like myself, are painfully seeking to achieve the future United States of Europe, the deficiencies are evident.

Before dealing with the variations of one kind or another that have been disclosed, variations between the United States practices and those of Europe as a whole and the differences among the various countries in Europe, I want to discuss British attitudes toward U.S. investment and management in our nation.

I have no doubt that many Europeans in attendance at this gathering will, as I would wish to do, seek to encourage U.S. industry and U.S. capital to invest in the countries of Europe. But it would be quite wrong to leave the impression that everybody in Europe is aching to see more U.S. intervention, because this is not so. In my own country there has been opposition from some quarters. It is an opposition which is not unreasoning and unintelligent. It may perhaps be summed up by the resolution which the British Trades Union Congress passed in 1964. It said: "Whilst not deprecating bona fide foreign investment in British firms, Congress deplores the infiltration of foreign capital into British industry for the purpose of acquiring control of key sectors of the British economy."

That view is the attitude not only of many British trade unions but, in my experience, of many people throughout Europe who are rather afraid of the process which has been taking place — of American investment in Europe, not in native companies, but in American companies which are controlled from the United States. I think I remarked in the course of one of our seminars that there are those who, when asked who the superpowers of the world will be in the next generation, reply, "The United States, the U.S.S.R., and U. S. investment in Europe."

Now, I say this simply to point to the potential danger. It is one of which I am quite certain that the U. S. leaders themselves are very conscious. There are obvious pitfalls in such a situation which are inevitable when a very powerful capitalist nation seeks outside fields for investments and does so in areas that are fragmented and relatively weak. Among your leaders are some who have seen that danger and have been wise enough to take a long view and encourage the process of European integration that will bring about the future United States of Europe. This process is most likely to build some measure of parallelism between the strength of Europe and that of the two major powers today.

But the benefit to Europe from American investment may be diminished by internal corporate policies of American companies who set up plants in Britain and elsewhere in Europe. A memorandum issued in 1967 by the Draughtsmen's and Allied Technicians' Association (DATA), one of our somewhat left-wing but very definitely middle-income unions, says this, among other things, on the subject: "Finally, there is the question of trade union recognition. Many American firms have been, at first, reluctant to recognize trade unions, but eventually have conformed to British practice. There are, however, still significant exceptions. The one in the news at the moment is Roberts-Arundel of Stockport." The Association's report goes on to say that the Minister of Labour and the president of the Board of Trade have publicly announced that they will take steps to make firms which want to open business in this country very well aware of the traditions and requirements to which they must conform if they do so.

But the Association goes on also to say that the problem of trade union recognition is not confined to American firms. When I was thinking about this conference and taking advice from sources in London, I wrote to the Minister of Labour and to the president of the Board of Trade and asked for information they might be able to give me. Mr. Roy Hattersley, a minister at the Department of Employment and Productivity (formerly the Ministry of Labour) said, among other things, exactly the same as the DATA memorandum narrates, that difficulties of this kind are not confined to U.S.-controlled companies. Recognition problems, for example, have arisen not infrequently over white-collar employees in British firms, particularly in the banks. He drew attention to certain disputes which resulted in strikes against British firms which lasted quite a long time, and which showed similarities to the Roberts-Arundel dispute.*

---

* Ed. Note—In 1965 the Roberts Company of Sanford, N.C., a manufacturer of textile machinery, headed by Robert E. Pomeranz, bought out Arundel-Coult-

With his letter, he sent a memorandum giving the history of the Roberts-Arundel dispute, one that is very familiar to people in my country, but maybe is not so familiar to some here. Broadly speaking, the Roberts-Arundel dispute resulted from the engagement, by an American company newly operating in my country, of women to do work which previously had been done by men, without any consultation with the unions. When this led to a dispute, all the union members were dismissed and replaced by nonunion labor. This led to tremendous difficulties and picketing, demonstrational strikes, and so on. The efforts of the Ministry of Labour, as it then was known, a special Chamber of Commerce group and all

---

hard, a British firm in the same business. The new firm, Roberts-Arundel, Ltd., closed down four of the five acquired facilities and conducted operations with 145 shop employees in the factory at Southgate, Stockport. What ensued after October 1966, according to *The Times* of London (September 15, 1967), was "one of the most bitter industrial clashes of recent years."

The Economist (London), December 16, 1967, commented:

"Mr. Pomeranz was by his own admission . . . somewhat naive in his view of the difficulties of setting up in Britain. He obviously failed to find out how hard it is to get English people and English trade unions to change their way. But no advance research could have told him that by buying up the musty British firm of Arundel-Coulthard, seeking to close down four of its factories and concentrating production in one, he would also be running head-on into the struggle for leadership of Britain's most reactionary trade union. [This is a reference to the Amalgamated Engineering Union.]

"The politically motivated anti-Americanism of the local union leadership won wide support in some national newspapers."

But Roberts-Arundel antagonized not only the union and its adherents. According to a report headed "Years of violence over three women" in *The Times* of December 7, 1967, the American-owned company's failure to honor a dispute-settlement agreement reached in September "brought down the wrath of the Engineering Employers' Federation which stepped in on the side of the unions. Alarmed at the 'continuing deterioration of Anglo-American relations caused by the dispute,' a joint union-employers deputation met Mr. David Bruce, United States Ambassador, in London and asked his help. Mr. Bruce promised a thorough examination. Meantime, the picketing intensified and there were more clashes."

Dispatches in *The Times* impart some sense of the emotional pitch of the controversy. On February 23, 1967, there were two front-page reports: One described the violence of the previous day when "part of a 1,000-strong crowd of trade unionists got out of hand . . . After the rally the men went away chanting: 'Yanks, go home.' " The other story was headed: "Why Trouble Breaks Out Under U.S. Ownership." The following week counsel for eight demonstrators entered pleas of guilty to charges of use of threatening and abusive words, obstruction of the police, and obstruction on the street. Counsel advised the court that "the strikers' tempers had been more sorely tried in this than in most industrial disputes. There were three unusual features about the strike, he added. It was not usual, in a dispute, for strikers to be permanently dismissed and replaced with other labour; it was not usual for the employers to refuse to negotiate with the unions; and it was not usual for a dispute to last so long." (February 28, 1967) On September 2, 1967, a front-page story was headlined: "Police clubbed in factory siege. 3,000 chant 'Yankee ideas out.' 12 arrested."

See also 6 *British Journal of Industrial Relations* 116 (March 1968).

kinds of other people were brought in to try to solve this really relatively minor matter. They were dealing with only a hundred people or so. With good will and common sense, this could have been disposed of in a matter of a few hours. But, in fact, it led to token strikes by several thousand workers in other firms, and lasted for months. That is the kind of thing which it ought to be the aim of good industrial relations to avoid.

It is bad enough when you have major industrial warfare arising out of really important matters of principle. But when they arise out of relatively minor, unimportant issues, such as were involved in the Roberts-Arundel dispute, then something is seriously wrong. I think what really probably was wrong was simply a matter of ignorance by the company concerned of the practices, the traditions, the matters regarded as of importance in the United Kingdom, and an assumption that methods hallowed by tradition and supplemented by law in the United States must be right wherever they are exported.

One only has to look at the vast differences between U. S. practices and European practices, taking them as one, to see how fallacious that attitude is. Later I shall discuss the varieties of European practices.

U. S. — EUROPEAN DIFFERENCES

Let us then pick out a number of respects in which it seems to me, from the discussion we have had, that U. S. practice differs widely from European.

First of all, and in a way this is rather odd, the United States is traditionally the home of free enterprise and, indeed, many Americans boast of their reliance upon the idea of free enterprise. Yet in the field of labor law the United States is far more rigidly controlled than any European country. The control exercised by the laws of the central government and by the framework of administrative agencies and judicial supervision set up by American law is considerable. Of course, one consequence of that is the psychological effect. If you have a very rigid legal framework, then your attitude is very much, "Well, so long as I simply follow the law, I can't go wrong." If your statutory framework is a very loose one or a nonexistent one —and it comes very near to being nonexistent in the United Kingdom —then you cannot adopt that attitude. You have to look at each problem on its merits and adapt your methods to it. That may well be one explanation, at any rate, for the Roberts-Arundel dispute.

Second, as we have learned, in the United States, national or industry-wide bargaining, while applicable to a few industries, is much less prevalent than in Europe, and plant bargaining is much more common. Here again, of course, this necessarily induces a totally different attitude to the realities of collective bargaining, although the report of the Donovan Commission advocates more plant-level bargaining in Britain.

Third, the labor lawyer is much more familiar in the United States than in Europe. The American labor lawyer's is a significant and highly regarded profession. American unions and employers would hesitate to make any important decision affecting labor relations without reference to the advice of labor lawyers, whereas in Europe this is certainly not the case. When I visited Professor Kamin's home before this conference opened, I was quite impressed to find in his huge library not only a tremendous collection of volumes on labor relations and labor law, but two extensive sets of books. The first, *Labor Relations Reference Manual*, consisting of something like 70 volumes, reported every administrative decision and state and federal court judgment in the labor law field handed down since 1935. A weekly loose-leaf supplement to the bound volumes reported judgments announced as recently as the prior week. I must confess that I prefer our simpler literature in Britain, where in Professor Grunfeld's one-volume treatise, for example, I can find an analysis of every English labor statute and every significant labor case in which a judgment was ever delivered in our nation.

But the second set of books in Professor Kamin's library, *Labor Arbitration Reports*, of 50 or so volumes, impressed me much more than the other set. As he explained it, the *Labor Arbitration Reports* contain but a small sample, 5 percent or less, of the many grievance arbitration decisions since 1946 made by private arbitrators who function under the voluntary agreements of the parties to decide not basic disputes over the substantive terms of collective bargaining agreements, but rather employee claims of employer injustice such as discipline or dismissal without proper cause and other violations of the labor agreement. While I have had no opportunity fully to study the American grievance arbitration system, I understand that the arbitration procedure is contractually established in exchange for a peacekeeping arrangement during the life of the collective labor contract. As you well know, in Britain we are greatly concerned with unofficial strikes often called to correct employee complaints of maltreatment. Certainly, we ought to know more about the American system of grievance arbitration, and perhaps find it in some way adaptable to our industrial methods in the United Kingdom.

In my own country, lawyers are simply not trusted by the trade unions. This is the result of history which I certainly hope will disappear, but which we have to allow for. The Donovan Commission has allowed for it in its proposals, and it must be allowed for by our foreign guests when they come to invest and operate in our country.

Fourth, I think it has emerged in this conference that on a percentage basis union membership in the United States is relatively low compared with Europe, although I gather it is much more powerful and more concentrated where it does exist. American unions themselves are very much stronger than ours, but the field which is actually covered by unionism is not as great as in my own country or in many of the countries of Europe.

Fifth, I think it is right to say that in the United States the unions are strongly procapitalist. Their motives are not mixed. Their *raison d'être* is solely to get the most out of the benefits of production for their members. In the countries of Europe, as we have heard, this is not necessarily the case, though there are variations. In some countries unions are strongly political or religious or thoroughly allied to political parties. Even so, it is true that the union leaders regard it as their job to do the best they can for their members. Nonetheless, attitudes may well be affected to a degree by this political or religious connection. In England, at any rate, this has been so.

Sixth, I would say that on the whole in Europe, partly because of the great disparity between ourselves and the United States in technological advance and partly because of the effects of the war on some of our countries, we have got into a rut from which we have to be dug out. There is a greater need for rapid industrial change in Europe than there is in the United States. When the factor is added of the tremendous overpopulation that exists in some of our countries, at any rate, my own, the Netherlands, and some others, this may result in greater impediments to the mobility of labor.

Seventh, in contrast to the attitude towards labor relations law, when one comes to the field of social security and other fields which may have a bearing upon collective bargaining, there is a great deal more government intervention in Europe than there is in the United States. These are matters that have to be taken into account, sometimes very strongly, in labor negotiations in the United Kingdom and the EEC countries under discussion at this conference. The highly developed European social security and social legislation make a solid substratum to negotiations on wages and other matters.

Finally, and I am not by any means suggesting that these are exclusive and that there are not other differences, the United States appears to accept as normal or, at any rate tolerable, a substantially higher rate of unemployment than we would in Europe or in the United Kingdom. In the same context, you do not seem to be as concerned as we are in Europe with the consequences of what you call layoffs or what we call redundancies. Those two things go together very much. And, of course, they are also bound up with the previous distinction, in that it is in the field of redundancies and similar matters that European governments have intervened a great deal.

DIFFERENCES AMONG EUROPEAN COUNTRIES

Great as are the differences that emerge between the United States and Europe in this field, the differences within Europe itself are, I think, at least as great. I shall not conduct a survey country by country. But I have set out a very large number of differences which I think are of importance, differences which, as I observed earlier, we in Europe have got to try to reduce. If we are to become a united continent, we must harmonize our laws and our practices.

First of all, the number of unions in a particular country varies tremendously, from 600 or more in my own to a handful in some European countries. Bargaining may be with one union or with several, according to what the position is. As I noted earlier, in some countries unions are divided politically. In some, like my own, unions support a single party, and in others, as in Germany, they are not permitted to have party affiliations at all. Some countries place greater emphasis on the national collective bargaining and others more on the workplace bargain. In some countries the rules are explicitly written into statutory law or developed by court judgments in case-law jurisprudence much as in the United States. In others, again very much like my own, they are governed more by practice and custom. The rate of union membership varies considerably from the very high to the relatively low.

There is a very high degree of mobility in some countries. Italy is an example of that. Others are very much more stable from this point of view; workers are more difficult to move about. In my own country whatever steps we may be taking, and we are taking many to try to induce people to move, are not readily acceptable to the individuals and families concerned.

In some European countries there is a built-in right to join a union; in others there is not. In some there is the right to a closed shop, and in others it is illegal. In some there is a right to strike; in others that right is either doubtful, or at any rate qualified, at least in the sense that in some European countries the position of strikers differs according to whether the strike is legal or illegal.

Some countries have unions which are firmly controlled by the Communist Party and others do not. Here again, certainly in the long term, this may be a matter of importance.

Some countries in Europe have much more highly developed prices and incomes policies than others. Again, this can be of great importance. Social security differs in extent and degree. The level of unemployment differs between one European country and another, though none, I think, accepts the level which is regarded as acceptable in America.

Some have more immigrants than others, and in some the immigrant population is more transient than in others. In some countries, when there is a period of recession, the immigrants tend to move back to their countries of origin; whereas in my own country, while theoretically this may be a possibility, in practice it is highly unlikely that the West Indian or the Pakistani will return to his own country for the period of recession.

Some nations of Europe place a greater emphasis on regional development than others. Italy is a noteworthy example of that. Their fears and anxieties differ. As Mr. Fano graphically put it, "Some workers have the fear of unemployment born in their blood." And others, as in Germany, have a greater fear of inflation. These are questions of history which one cannot ignore. Some have excellent industrial training methods and others do not.

Finally, the degree of governmental intervention in the field outside labor relations varies greatly between one European country and another. It is perhaps right to say that the efforts of the EEC to harmonize governmental intervention in the social security field, discussed by Dr. Veldkamp, may bring a degree of equality; but this does not necessarily extend to other fields at the moment. Even within the EEC, there are differences of philosophy as to the permissible extent of governmental intervention in planning and economics. Those seem to me to be the principal differences among the European nations we have carefully examined at this conference.

SIMILARITIES IN EUROPEAN PRACTICES

When one comes to similarities in European attitudes and practices, first of all, the trade unions generally, whether they are political or not, whether they are Socialist, Communist, Catholic, or Protestant, are primarily concerned to do a trade union's job; that is, to look after the interests of the members of the organization rather than those of the community at large. This is not all black or all white. Union leaders are responsible people on the whole, and they understand economics probably as well as any other section of the community. They appreciate what are the national economic requirements, and they know that what may be good for their members in the short term may be bad in the long term. Therefore, on the whole, it is fair to say that they will generally respond to economic needs, unless the pressure from their own membership to act irresponsibly is too great for them to withstand.

Although I do not say trade unions are in any way allergic to American investment in European countries, they are, as I observed earlier, certainly allergic to control from across the Atlantic and, particularly, that kind of control which brushes aside local practices and traditions. They are generally apprehensive about widespread foreign ownership of key industries. In that context, they make a very clear distinction between foreign investment and foreign ownership and operation, such as U. S. companies maintain to a considerable extent in Europe.

Continuing with the similarities among European countries, there is an increasing tendency in Europe toward plant bargaining rather than national or industry-wide bargaining, although, as I said, this varies. That is the broad tendency, which seems to be increasing. If I may comment on that, it does seem to me to be a sensible approach rather analogous to the free retail price system, in that it enables the most efficient plants to give the highest benefits. The fixed industry-wide bargain, rather like resale price maintenance, has the disadvantage of penalizing the efficient by fixing prices or earnings, as the case may be, at the level of the least efficient. Therefore, I anticipate that the tendency toward plant bargaining is likely to spread still further in Europe.

White-collar employment and status are expanding all over Europe at the expense of blue-collar status, but generally white-collar unionism is expanding much more slowly than blue-collar unionism has in the past.

And, finally, on European similarities: On the whole, and this is certainly a generalization, I would say that in Europe social attitudes, rather than the law, govern practice in the industrial field. That is not to say, of course, that some countries do not have a close system of law.

FUTURE DEVELOPMENTS

That seems to be the position today. I look now briefly at the future. All European societies are changing. The EEC is seeking to work out common rules as to social security, tax laws, the status of companies, and the laws governing companies. In some fields they have been more successful than in others. The United Kingdom, as you know, is likely to be developing its industrial relations system in the light of the Donovan Report. And European nations generally — taking Europe in the broad sense — through the efforts of the Council of Europe in particular, and the Organization for Economic Co-operation and Development (OECD), are in the course of a strong movement toward harmonization of law and practice. I am certain this will continue irrespective of any question of the enlargement of the EEC, whether that comes sooner or later. I myself had the privilege recently of trying to persuade the European Ministers of Justice, in their conference in London, to support the idea of setting up a European Law Commission on a permanent basis to be charged with the task of harmonizing European law. This idea has been greeted with much interest. It is an illustration of the movement toward that unity of systems of law which is a critical ingredient in the United States of Europe, which will one day bring something of the philosophy and success of the new world back to the old.

Now, one asks oneself whether practice in the future is going to follow the realities of the situation or the forms. For example, industry generally is not concerned with how wage increases affect the various classes of workers who make up their labor force. Rather, managements generally are concerned with the totality of the wage increase and how they can absorb it into their costings and their price systems. We have the odd situation very often that in reality the collective bargain is between different classes of workers, between workers in one industry and another, or between competing groups of workers in a single plant or groups of workers within one plant who compare their wages with apparently similar groups in other establishments. Yet because of the way in which history has evolved, these interlabor controversies take the form of a battle between labor and capital, when in actuality capital itself is often not necessarily greatly concerned or involved. One wonders whether these realities will be recognized in time and systems will be devised which take the employer out of the battlefield and expose the real protagonists, the labor groups themselves, as they engage in the battle in opposition to one other.

There are changes that one may see taking place. It is fairly certain that they will have widespread repercussions. Where they are going to lead us, we cannot tell. One of the reasons why we cannot tell, I think, is that there is not nearly enough information and research in Europe. The thorough examination of the highly developed system of American labor relations by your academicians and practitioners sets a very high standard for Europeans. The graduate school programs in industrial relations in your institutions of higher learning, such as Loyola University of Chicago, University of Illinois, University of Chicago, University of California, Cornell University, and others, are something that our educational institutions in the United Kingdom could well emulate.

I am quite convinced myself that one of the most important results of this conference has been the spread of information, even the spread of knowledge about European practice, although we had to come across the Atlantic to the United States to achieve this. But I am equally certain that the knowledge which we have in Europe is nothing like enough.

As I thought about one or two of the topics that have been discussed, sometimes in detail, sometimes rather sketchily, in the course of our seminars, this has impinged itself upon my mind very strongly. For example, we in England have recently instituted our system of redundancy payments or severance pay. Perhaps it is too recent to know exactly what the effect of our system is going to be, but this is something that we must know in the future. How is it going to affect labor in a rapidly changing society where we are going over to the new technology which has made these payments a necessity? Which of the workers are going to be the ones to be dismissed and which are the ones that are going to be kept on? Will redundancy payments affect that? Will it affect the type of worker who is going to be put into the job of looking after the new and more technical mechanisms? These are matters that can only be discovered by research and experience. I do not think that *a priori* reasoning and planning will take one very far. Again, we have spoken about the growth of plant bargaining, and in that context I must mention also the very great growth in productivity bargaining. This is the hope for the future in Britain, and I have no doubt that it has very strong points in its favor. But what will be its effects on prices and incomes policy? In the course of the conference, I have noticed that there have been expressions of different views about national prices and incomes policy. This area is also something that we have to watch very carefully and study and do research upon.

We heard from my friend and colleague, Allan Flanders, about the tremendously important question of wasted manpower. Until I heard him I had not realized the real extent of it in my own country, and no doubt it exists in many others. But how much do we really know about this? Mr. Flanders said that where this is taking place even the managements themselves do not know about it. It must be, therefore, of primary importance to carry out research and to discover what the true limitations of so vital a factor may be. But, fortunately, I think the tendency is and will be for greater research. Here I am certain that American resources and experience can and should help in Europe, not only for the benefit of the American corporations but for that of Europe as well. You have a great head start on us in this field. In your coming to our countries and introducing your technological methods and advances and your management methods and advances, I hope that you will help us also to set on foot and to conduct our studies and researches and enable us to gain more information about what is actually happening in our own countries. Because something is absolutely certain, and that is, as Professor Kamin said in his first remarks to the conference, that this gathering would show up the difference between theory and practice. It is quite certain that it is vital to act in the light of practical experience rather than simply in the light of theory.

WHAT U.S. COMPANIES CAN DO

And so I come finally to my views on what U. S. companies can do to help Europe in this field. I think that they can study European practices and fit their own policies into those practices, even if the practices seem to them to be irritating or repugnant, because it is vital to the success of the partnership which is involved in the use of American capital and know-how and European labor. Those who operate American organizations in Europe should recognize and understand fully the fears and the prejudices which exist in Europe, whether rightly or wrongly, as a result of long years of history. Then, U. S. companies can and should incorporate their own best management ideas as well as their own best technological ideas. For example, Professor Shearer gave us the interesting idea of how U. S. companies might make use of methods of selection of management trainees by going directly to American educational institutions to find foreign students and by otherwise helping with resources for education and training in Europe, as they do here. This is a valuable way of helping us and helping themselves at the same time.

It is most important that U. S. companies should seek to fit their own investment into European regional policies. Of course, sometimes they may be compelled to do so, whether they like it or not, because of the strength of our legal systems in this respect. In England this is largely our position. We are forced to have very strong regional policies. But even where there is flexibility, U. S. companies would help considerably by fitting in, perhaps by providing homes for the workers in the areas where they seek to operate and generally, if necessary, by accepting some economic sacrifice in order to work in with the overall regional policies which are necessary. I hope that U. S. companies would be prepared to collaborate with European companies in technological advance. We, in Europe, in advance of or in default of expansion of the European Communities, which many of us hope to see achieved, are seeking to have at least technological cooperation. This is very difficult; it becomes more difficult when you have limitations ·of capital and investment such as we have seen in relation to our space program and other common projects which had to be slowed down or abandoned. Here American resources can be of great value.

U. S. companies should always seek to anticipate the changes likely to occur in the host nation. You have heard a lot about our Royal Commission on Trade Unions and Employers' Associations. I wonder whether Mr. Pomeranz of Roberts-Arundel even knew that it existed. He may have, for all I know, and I may be doing him an injustice. But the Commission's report is a document which is going to make profound changes in our industrial relations system. For those U. S. companies that are thinking of going into Europe or extending their European field, particularly coming to the United Kingdom, it would be very wise to anticipate what is likely to happen.

U. S. companies should constantly be on the lookout for the sort of innovations represented by the Fawley and the Ford labor agreements, which are admirable examples of compliance with the best principles which I have tried to enumerate. That is, they should show regard for the local circumstances and intelligently combine American management techniques and know-how with the realities of the local environment and conditions. I hope that they will seek to tap the untapped manpower resources that Allan Flanders spoke about wherever they can, by making use of female labor in occupations where that is appropriate, by full cooperation in training and retraining, and by generally regarding themselves as having come to us as part of us, and not as some sort of alien unit which is there simply to draw a return and never integrate into the country in which it operates.

And, above all, I hope that American companies entering Europe will not expect U. S. practices, such as the practice — no doubt, admirable and desirable in the U. S. — of recognizing only the majority union as the active bargaining union, to apply in Europe. If American practices are simply assumed to be in existence and to be followed in European countries, one has on one's hands another Roberts-Arundel dispute. I hope you will continue to train our brains rather than drain them; that you will familiarize yourselves with the available instruments that we have, such as the Industrial Training Board, and make the fullest possible use of them. I am certain that so long as U. S. companies follow the traditions of the best of them, traditions which involve throwing themselves into and regarding themselves as part of the life of the country into which they have put their capital, their investment, and their operative methods, these things will happen and the best results will follow. It is only if they regard themselves as something rather alien that trouble will follow.

AMERICAN INVOLVEMENT IN BELGIUM

By Roger Blanpain

Between 1959 and 1966, more than 2,364 foreign investments were booked in Belgium, totaling 57 billion Belgian francs and creating 43,829 new jobs. Of these investments 70 percent were from the United States. In 1967 alone new American investments were about 10.5 billion Belgian francs and constituted 80 percent of new foreign investment for that year in Belgium. These investments have taken place in the most dynamic sectors of the Belgian economy, the metal, chemical, and petro-chemical industries. Between 1961 and 1966, the growth rhythm of American investment in Belgium was 23.2 percent, against 16 percent in Western European countries in general. A complete picture of foreign investment is given clearly by the following statistics:

Foreign Investment by Industry
(In millions of Belgian francs)

Year	Metal	Petro-chemical	Textile	Others	Total
1959.....	604	1,830	20	4	2,458
1960.....	1,415	576	19	1,343	3,353
1961.....	1,504	4,216	201	803	6,724
1962.....	4,455	801	330	1,228	6,814
1963.....	2,548	1,590	250	1,056	5,444
1964.....	1,625	6,035	367	1,049	9,076
1965.....	10,479	6,063	917	548	18,007
1966.....	1,356	3,038	234	1,114	5,472
TOTAL	23,986	24,149	2,338	7,145	57,618

Investments by Germany, the Netherlands, France, Great Britain, United States
(In millions of Belgian francs)

Year	Germany	Netherlands	France	Great Britain	United States
1959.....	– – –	133	– – –	884	1,409
1960.....	412	62	85	462	2,318
1961.....	1,101	260	64	216	3,980
1962.....	203	464	9	252	5,700
1963.....	109	157	815	470	3,612
1964.....	4,069	194	174	370	3,476
1965.....	187	1,118	107	128	16,039
1966.....	38	1,641	117	228	2,496
TOTAL	6,119	4,029	1,317	3,070	39,030

REPORTS OF AMERICAN MANAGERS IN BELGIUM

Through the facilities of the Institute for Labor Relations of the University of Leuven, we made inquiry of principal managers of some major American companies located in Belgium and asked for comments on their experiences in several aspects of industrial relations. What appears below are their unedited answers.

Acceptance of the American Company by the Belgian Community

"The location of an American company here was strongly encouraged and heartily welcomed. All of our relations with the town officials have been most cordial and helpful. In fact, I sometimes feel they are more than a little proud to have an American company in their midst — probably because they have not had any before."

"In our case there has been absolutely no problem in acceptance by the community in which we have located. On the contrary the cooperation received from the local and provincial governments has been outstanding and we are very pleased with the location as well as with the acceptance by the community."

"On the whole the attitude of the Belgian unions has been very favorable to foreign investment. Sometimes there have been grumblings about companies situated in Belgium but directed by people at the other side of the ocean. This attitude can be attributed to two factors:

1. The nationalistic attitudes of a neighboring country, (France) and its press which also influences to a certain degree the thinking of certain Belgian union leaders;

2. The frequent tactic of the labor union which seeks a scape-goat when it meets with resistance to its demands.

"For the moment the Belgian unions are concentrating their attention on avoiding internal conflict and scrutinizing carefully how much the Flemish and the Walloon parts of Belgium get in new investments, irrespective of origin. Full employment is their main preoccupation."

Management — Union Relations

"Belgian conditions are fundamentally different from the American system. Contrary to our American experience of dealing with a single union as exclusive bargaining representative of the production and maintenance workers, in this country we must deal at the same time with two and sometimes three unions, all speaking for the same work group. We find the Belgian system in some ways better than the American system because we need not be concerned with the pressures of irresponsible and often leaderless minority factions whose discontents find outlet in disruption of production and other kinds of inarticulate unrest at the workplace."

"The main problem encountered in management-trade union relations arises from the fact that the trade unions in Belgium do not have legal status. As a result it is very difficult to obtain a binding agreement from the trade unions with whom we deal. A further major difference from the American system is the existence of national agreements which through royal decrees become law and therefore have to be followed by individual companies. As a result often local conditions cannot be taken into account, which result in a lack of flexibility in bargaining on the local level. In our particular case from time to time this has resulted in conflicts with the unions who had no understanding or did not want to understand local circumstances which required a deviation from national agreements. This is especially true with regards to new and highly mechanized industries which fall outside the average Belgian pattern. Concerning the works-council and the safety and health committee, we feel that their usefulness is greatly reduced because of the quality of the people who are elected to these committees. As a result the delegates contribute little to the solution of the problems encountered. The main advantage of these committees is their functioning as a means of explaining management viewpoints and decisions to the workers. In general I would say that the union climate in Belgium is less severe than in the United States. The main problem encountered in our plant is due to the fact that we are required to meet with union delegates who are not competent enough to deal with the problems which are encountered in our particular operations."

"We have during the last several years extensively bargained on the local level since we were faced with special circumstances unique to our type of enterprise. In general this has given satisfactory results. Our main difficulty has been that the bargaining had to be conducted with union delegates who were not sufficiently trained or not educated enough to understand the specific problems inherent in a highly technical enterprise."

"We have had only brief experience to date with trade unions, so that I cannot comment meaningfully on our experiences. We have however been affiliated with the G.I.C.R.A. (Groupement des Industries Chimiques de la Region Portuaire Anversoise), which is the trade bargaining association for the petrochemical industries in Antwerp. This Association comprises: Amocofina, Petrochim S. A., Union Carbide Belgium, Polysar (Belgium) N.V., Monsanto, Bayer, N.V., B.A.S.F., Polyolefins, and Amoco Chemicals. Through this Association in 1967 we concluded a collective bargaining agreement which will be effective through the end of 1968. Generally speaking, I would say this type of association promotes more exchange of data than we would normally have between American companies on the subject of dealing with unions. In fact, in the chemical industry in America this type of cooperative approach by employers would be unheard of."

Managerial Freedom

"I have generally found that there is more freedom in the right to manage here in Belgium than was the case in America. There has been no restriction placed on us to date on reasonable subcontracting, and especially on job transfers within the maintenance categories. There is a lot of flexibility in craft handling in our maintenance group. The workers themselves feel this is a proper way to do things, provided management is reasonable and does not downgrade the rate of pay. This attitude and the pride of craftsmanship that we find are very pleasant surprises for an American."

"In this respect our company has not experienced any problems or difficulties. We have never been confronted with any restrictions with regards to subcontracting, sales distribution, production, etc."

Expectation of Pay Scales by
Belgian Workers Employed by American Firms

"In our company we apply the same wage rates and salary levels that are average for industries of our type in Belgium. We have no reason nor inclination to pay higher wages or higher salaries than commensurate with the job and the performance of the individual."

"In all of our hiring practices we certainly have noticed that the Belgian workers do expect American firms to pay well. I have heard very little comment that our pay scales were not in favorable conformity with the higher levels of Belgian compensation."

Protective Labor Legislation

"There have been a lot of restrictive Belgian laws and practices which have made us staff the plant at a higher level than we would have done in the United States. For example, let me discuss vacation practices, overtime work and Sunday work.

"Vacations are sacred here. By law, two of the three weeks off must be allowed to be taken in the period from May to September. Despite the fact that we have had a start-up this year, almost all of our employees look askance at any idea that vacations could be deferred. Overtime is legal only for emergencies. The definition of 'emergencies' here means that the event must have happened. The likelihood of something happening is not enough. Thus any arrangement to schedule overtime for critical periods becomes illegal, but we have found out that if the amount does not exceed 5 percent, it will be winked at. Any work on Sunday requires an automatic grant of a day off within the next six days. Effectively this means that the maintenance complement that we can bring in on weekends on overtime is only half of what it could be during the week.

"The upshot of the above problems is that our maintenance staff is about 15 percent higher that it would be in the United States for exactly the same work complement. We also had to add a larger supervised shift maintenance group.

"With the combined effect of holidays, vacation periods and shift break days, we find that we need 4.6 men to man one position on a shift basis. Since our labor contract calls for a 40-hour week beginning December 1 this year, the requirement increases to about 4.8 men per position. This means that we require essentially a five-shift manning to maintain full shift operation. In the United States we would use four shifts and upgrade from the labor ranks to cover vacations.

"We have found that the pension system in the chemical industry in Antwerp is very progressive, and as Americans we are deeply envious of its complete portability. This and the legal contractual system make salaried workers relatively expensive. Because of these conditions, we have found that there is absolutely no substitute for taking a lot of time in hiring the salaried staff."

"In this respect the rules and regulations in Belgium are considerably more strict than those in the United States. For instance, it is required that each hourly worker be given at least two weeks' notice before layoff or dismissal. In the case of salaried personnel this period is considerably longer. This is a very considerable departure from the practices in the United States, where most people do not work under a contract with a dismissal clause. The Belgian system undoubtedly provides more job security, but it constitutes also a considerable restriction on management with regards to the most efficient use of personnel. Another point which is much more restrictive in Belgium is that overtime can only be applied after prior approval by the unions and the labor inspector. This is contrary to the practices in the United States, where overtime can always be applied, with the prior approval of the individuals involved. There need be only compliance with the premium-pay requirements of the Fair Labor Standards

Act or, if there is a labor agreement, compliance with its usually higher rates of premium pay."

In general it can be said that the labor situation is satisfactory for the establishment of American industry in Belgium. The most important differences concern the job security required by law in Belgium. Another point that is difficult to understand for American firms is the matter of acquired rights. This problem concerns customs which have developed over a period of time and which subsequently are considered vested rights by the employees and are frequently upheld in litigation.

SOURCES OF CONFLICT AND TENSION

The foregoing first-hand reports only tell a part of the story. Conflicts between American firms and Belgian unions are not infrequent. Most may be attributed to the normal power relationships between unions and managements. But others are directly related either to xenophobia or to outright failure of the American managers to understand the nuances of the Belgian environment.

In 1965 more than 5,000 workers at Genk struck Ford Motor Company for several weeks. The strikers published a "black book" which started with an introduction that may be fairly translated as follows: "In this report we want to denounce the introduction into Belgium of a kind of American capitalism that completely disregards our social legislation, our labor relations practices and our revered traditions." That labor dispute concerned the interpretation of the collective bargaining agreement and the role and functions of the union delegation.

The Ford Genk contract was made in 1962 for a five-year period. The principal clauses of the contract dealt only with the fixing of wages. Nothing else was negotiated except a willingness of the company to discuss the creation of a union delegation.

The conflict mainly concerned the question whether items not regulated in the contract could be subject to trade union action. It was the unions' position that they could discuss, bargain, and strike for all points that were not expressly foreclosed by specific contract language. This was not the view of the employer.*

Another main point of conflict concerned the union delegation. It was the union's contention that the shop stewards did not get enough credit hours and plant facilities consistent with Belgian customs and traditions. The delegates took the time they thought they

---

* Ed. Note: Cf. *Jacobs Manufacturing Company,* 94 NLRB 1214, 28 LRRM 1162 (1951), *enforced,* 196 F.2d 680, 30 LRRM 2098 (2nd Cir., 1952).

needed, as is usually done, but the company initially responded by withholding pay for such time. Finally the head delegates were suspended for spending excessive time away from work in union-delegation activity. Other disputed points were overtime and details of paid vacations.

In my view neither side of the Ford Genk dispute behaved reasonably or consistently with established Belgian labor practices. Thus, I believe that in the strike both the employer and the unions lost face and dignity.

Another case deserving mention involved a Belgian shoe manufacturing and leather firm which was taken over by an American company. The American purchaser decided immediately to automate the plant. An American industrial engineering consultant came over and said flatly that more than 50 percent of the work force would be dismissed. This American expert probably did not understand the extreme importance that Belgian workers attach to job security. No strike occurred because the issues were settled in the joint committee under heavy union pressure. A job security system was worked out, providing better employment guarantees that in almost any other sector of Belgian industry; assuring complete information and bargaining rights for the trade unions in case of dismissal; specifying longer notice terms with an additional maximum of four months' notice for blue-collar workers and an obligation to rehire previous employees to fill the first available openings.

Other difficulties arise from the fact that American companies are "American." A Belgian firm was taken over by an American firm; 60 percent of the invested capital was American participation. The Republic of Cuba (1967-1968) placed an important order with this firm for agricultural machines, of a total value of 125 million Belgian francs. But as a consequence of an American law compelling an embargo on Cuba, the American authorities forced the order to be cancelled. This direct interference in the Belgian economy because of American foreign policy has given rise to many angry remarks, even in the Belgian Parliament. Trade unions are quite concerned about consequent unemployment. And many Belgians now speak about economic colonization of Belgium.

Another problem arises when the American nonautonomous subsidiary branch of an international corporation is the first to suffer from economic recession. If the international corporation as a whole has less business, the first workers to be laid off or to be dismissed are in the European branches. This fact is also strongly resented in Belgium.

EUROPEAN COMMUNITY
TRADE UNION SECRETARIAT *

In his paper on Collective Bargaining in the European Economic Community, Dr. L.H.J. Crijns referrred to the Trade Union Secretariat of EEC. Owen Fairweather also comments briefly in this volume on the European Trade Union Secretariat (ECTUS). In his response to Mr. Belford, Guy Nunn of the United Automobile Workers touched upon the future role of international trade union collaborative efforts. Similarly, J. D. Neirinck has referred to EEC-wide collective bargaining in his article in this volume.

Since ECTUS has its headquarters in Brussels and its growing influence may be felt by American management in Belgium, in the other Common Market countries and in Britain and Ireland, it seems appropriate for me to report on ECTUS as of April 1969.

ECTUS was set up and is financed by the national free trade union confederations of the six Common Market countries. As always in Europe, there is no specific information available on its financial situation. There are no American affiliations. As yet ECTUS has no set of official rules and bylaws. Neither has there been any proclamation of a guiding policy or of an official ideology which may underly any of the actions of ECTUS. It is fairly obvious that the ECTUS program is based on the common elements out of the national programs of the participating confederations of free trade unions.

There are no formal links whatsoever among the European Regional Organization (E.R.O.), the International Federation of Christian Trade Unions (I.F.C.T.U.), and ECTUS. I.C.F.T.U. seeks to coordinate the activities of all free trade unions of the world. E.R.O. is a suborganization which does the same for all European trade unions. E.R.O. is to be compared with similar regional organizations of free trade unions in the Americas, Asia, and Africa.

ECTUS, the permanent secretariat of the European committee of free trade union organizations, includes some of the same national confederations as E.R.O. and aims at more than a mere coordinating of the national activities of the Common Market confederations of free trade unions. As appears from the 1962 Brussels Gen-

---

* Ed. Note: In a congress at The Hague on April 23-25, 1969, ECTUS was reorganized as the European Confederation of Free Trade Unions in the Community. André Klous of the Netherlands (N.V.V.) was elected as its first president and Theo Rasschaert of Belgium (F.G.T.B.) was chosen as the first secretary-general. The congress adopted a formal governing statute detailing organizational aims, governing structure, and internal procedures.

eral Assembly, from the 1964 Paris General Assembly, and from the 1966 General Assembly of the European Community Free Trade Unions organizations in Rome, ECTUS hopes to meet the European challenge with an appropriate autonomous program which would be more than a mere compilation of diverse national interests.

Collaboration exists between the international free trade unions, formally affiliated with ECTUS, and the Christian trade unions, which are not formally affiliated. Indeed, the Christian trade unions of EEC have their own parallel secretariat. The free trade unions favor the development of a single international labor movement representing all workers and reject the idea of trade union pluralism. But those are essentially ideological declarations behind which there exist close relationships with the Christian unions and active exchange of information and ideas for more effective collective bargaining.

But these observations refer merely to what presently appears in formal records. To demonstrate how rapid has been the movement toward European labor unity in the past two years, I shall discuss an article written by England's most renowned labor writer, Eric Wigham, who served as a member of the Royal Commission on Trade Unions and Employers' Associations. In May 1967,[1] in an article optimistically entitled "Britain's Entry the Kiss of Life for European Trade Unionism," Mr. Wigham discussed the consequences upon trade unions of Britain's joining the Common Market. At that time, Britain's application was pending and had not yet been blocked by President de Gaulle.

Anticipating the withdrawal of the AFL-CIO from the International Confederation of Free Trade Unions — this became a reality by action of the AFL-CIO Executive Council in February 1969 — Mr. Wigham proceeded to explore in depth the policies and operations of ECTUS and the manner whereby Britain's entry into the European Communities would bring about "a working trade union organization such as has never been known. From the days of Karl Marx the international movements have devoted most of their time to politics and bickering ...." Mr. George Woodcock, then general secretary of the British Trade Union Congress, and Mr. Harm Buiter,[2] then Secretary General of ECTUS, were said by Mr. Wigham to be convinced that ECTUS with full British membership "will be

---

[1] *The Times,* London, May 22, 1967, page 11.

[2] Mr. Buiter resigned in 1969 to become secretary-general of the International Confederation of Free Trade Unions. He was replaced as secretary-general of ECTUS by Theo Rasschaert.

something more like a national federation with members working together in practical ways to improve living standards throughout. Mr. Woodcock, when he went to see the ECTUS executive . . ., was delighted to find himself among men talking a common language on economic and industrial problems. This is what he had always wanted...."

The leaders of ECTUS, continued Mr. Wigham, "are not happy about their advisory position on the Common Market economic and social council because decisions are taken in obscure ways elsewhere before reaching the council and they look to the T.U.C. to help them to insist that decision-takers must be identifiable and accountable."

Since Mr. Wigham wrote his perceptive article, much has happened to make ECTUS a more significant organization. Prior to July 1967, the ECTUS executive committee was essentially only a private meeting of union representatives from the six member nations of the EEC. But starting in July 1967, the British Trades Union Congress, upon invitation, has been regularly sending its general secretary and a member of its General Council to the executive sessions of ECTUS. While the Irish Congress of Trades Union, which includes the unions of both Northern Ireland and the Republic of Ireland, has not yet received a formal invitation to attend the executive committee meetings of ECTUS, preliminary contacts have been made.[3]

In April 1969 there were even more significant developments. The EEC Commission at long last recognized the leftist, but dominant, labor organizations of Italy (CGIL, claiming 3,500,00 members) and France (CGT, claiming 2,500,000 members) as representative labor organizations that must be formally treated and dealt with in EEC affairs. At the same time, similar developments are reported in ECTUS, and exploratory discussions are going forward to achieve practical methods of collaboration. The European Committee of the International Metalworkers Federation is reported as the principal instigator of these movements.

The most important and effective organs of ECTUS are its subcommittees, which have been established to represent labor organizations in each industry separately. While there has not yet emerged from ECTUS anything of the magnitude of the World Automotive Federation which Guy Nunn describes elsewhere in this volume, the latter Federation is being regularly cited as an example

---

[3] See Beever, *Trade Unions and Free Labour Movement in the EEC* (PEP European Series No. 10, 1969).

to be followed. The regular interchange of economic data and collective bargaining experiences in the industrial subcommittees of ECTUS are already showing practical results. American managers in Belgium and elsewhere should keep careful note on these trade union developments.

AMERICAN MANAGEMENT IN THE UNITED KINGDOM

By Cyril Grunfeld

It was a revelation to me to learn at this conference about the attitude of multinational corporate management. I could not help feeling that it all boiled down, in a sense, to the simple and fundamental point that the law of life is adaptation. And it seemed to me that multinational corporate management, at least in what its representatives expressed here, had started from this viewpoint and used a similar kind of language in speaking about its host environment and the need to be sensitive to that environment and to adapt to it in order to get the best out of it.

I have been immensely struck and impressed — I hope you won't think I am being patronizing, because I am not — by the intelligence and the scientific attitude of American management in dealing with their problems overseas. I don't know what our management is doing — British companies have a lot of subsidiaries overseas — but we don't seem to bother to find out what they are doing, and they don't seem to bother to tell us what they are doing. Consequently, we don't know if they are getting into trouble or what is the efficiency of their overseas operations. We can best hope that our new business schools and our new Industrial Relations Research Unit will begin to discover these things about our own transnational operations. Perhaps they may even enter into an investigation of American operations in Britain, which, I understand, in not many years are going to account for at least 20 percent of British manufacturing.

As we all know, there are certain differences in national attitudes, like the acceptance by American trade unionism of capitalism. Having been brought up on a classical education, I had dinned into me the Socratic outlook that you never unquestioningly trust words, especially words like "capitalism." I would have liked to have asked just what it is that American trade unions accept. Can it mean a rejection of communism? By this test British trade unions also accept capitalism, but everyone seemed to think British trade unions do not accept capitalism, so acceptance of capitalism cannot really mean the rejection of communism.

Did it, then, mean the absence of an American political party based primarily on trade unionism and trade union support and finance? Or did it mean the acceptance of managerial prerogatives without any question? Some seem to suggest that is what it meant, whereas others suggest it was not that at all. There were cases in which managerial prerogatives in the United States were questioned. Did it mean the absence of any desire to alter the ownership of the means of production? If so, British trade unionism largely accepts capitalism, at least in the form of a mixed economy. Of course, the question then is, "Does American trade unionism accept a mixed economy?" Is America a mixed economy? The only answer I can give in the light of my present limited experience is that it does not appear to be an unmixed economy.

Be that as it may, there are differences of attitudes. And we heard Professor Gamillscheg discuss a little town in Germany, and Monsieur Mandereau told us about another little town in France where, for 400 years, everyone had the same name and over the generations the names were related to their work. Then the big American company comes in and takes over the little local company and later, for managerial reasons, closes it down. As Professor Gamillscheg pointed out, a sort of xenophobic paranoia results. If an American company closes a little local company for purely managerial reasons, the population starts saying that the Americans are doing this deliberately in order to pinch out an effective part of the local economy. What may be one exceptional case is subsequently cited in common conversation as the typical one.

In Britain too we see all these things. I hope Mr. Charles Pomeranz of Roberts-Arundel has learned something from his experience in Britain. But apart from these odd little examples, what impressed me was that the great American corporations and their managements are fully aware of these matters and quite clearly do not intend any more consciously to pursue courses that might fall into the same error. When you set up an operation in another country, you would not dream of not looking into its tax law, corporation law, and other aspects of its commercial environment, and it is clear that American management treats labor relations practices and law in exactly the same way today.

Now, of course, differences in the balance of industrial and political power in all the different countries necessarily arise from their different histories. And it may very well be that our refusal to tolerate American levels of unemployment is due to our different balance of industrial and political power; and this is something that American management has to and, I am certain, does accept. I am also certain that, within a country like Britain, American management accepts the importance and significance of preplanning of industrial changes that involve job security. I wonder if they accept the following also: The Redundancy Payments Act lays down that a person becomes entitled to redundancy pay if he is "dismissed." But then we have had situations in which good management, in accordance with the best redundancy procedures, which our Department of Employment and Productivity has now codified in a widely distrib uted booklet, gives as much advance warning of forthcoming redundancy as it can. And our worker goes trotting around and finds himself another job, and off he goes before the time comes for the final redundancy. Then in a case before the Industrial Tribunal, which went on appeal to the High Court, it was held that he was not entitled to redundancy pay because he had not been "dismissed." So good management, I now understand, are adopting the practice that when our worker goes around and gets his job and says, "Right, I've got my job, I'm going," good management gives him a letter saying, "We hereby dismiss you." And so he produces this, gets his redundancy pay, and, of course, the company concerned gets the rebate. You can get your rebate only if the worker was strictly entitled to his redundancy pay: It is a very technical statute, as I stated in my principal paper.

I do hope that American companies, under their management, may be adopting this English practice in order to bend the law for the sake of carrying out what was really the intention of the Act. But before you say, "Well, all right, we'll think about that, but surely you should be a little bit more efficient — you should engineer your law in Britain so that it carries out the policies you want it to carry out," may I hasten to add that we have now set up an inquiry into the working of this law, which will undoubtedly, in due course, be followed by remedial amendments so that the law will come into conformity with what we want; with its intention, the intention of the legislature to stimulate labor mobility.

PROBLEMS FACING MULTINATIONAL FIRM

Now I must indicate what seem to me to be three delicate areas where multinational corporate management may conceivably run into a little trouble in Britain. First of all, there is the question of developing research opportunities within the host country, opportunities for that country's own manpower, and indeed womanpower, which has been highly trained in particular on the scientific and engineering sides. There has been and still is a real apprehension in Britain lest American corporations remove their research facilities from Britain and locate them in the United States. People have spoken of the danger of American corporations turning the British into a nation of helots, who will do merely the assembly work but not the real brain work. This is a genuine and substantial fear since, of course, we do have highly trained people in the fields of science and engineering, and people of the highest originality of mind for whom we want to have opportunities in these fields within Britain rather than at the other end of the brain drain. This is a delicate area — so delicate that an odd rumor was put about when Chrysler, for all practical purposes, took over Rootes, that the British Government required Chrysler to enter into an undertaking not to remove its research facilities in Britain to the United States or elsewhere. Mr. John D. Wilson of Chrysler, our colleague at this conference, very kindly checked and discovered that there is no such undertaking at all. But the fact that such a rumor could go about indicates something of the measure of this apprehension.

The second point is the necessity for political neutrality within the host country. We introduced the Companies Act 1967, which requires companies of the larger kind, which will include a lot of the American companies or American-British companies, to reveal in their annual returns political contributions made in the course of the preceding year. To my mind, it would be ill-advised if an American company had to announce in this way that it had made a substantial contribution to the Labour Party, or even the Conservative or the Liberal Party. Of course, it does not mean that members of management are personally precluded from making such contributions. A law of that kind would be a most serious incursion into personal liberty. We are speaking now purely about corporate funds. It seems to me that might again be a delicate area. So far, there have been various announcements of contributions having been made by different companies to the Conservative Party, but all are British companies.

The third point concerns the need for political neutrality with regard to the external trade of the host country. This is a very tricky matter, especially as British businessmen, and I suspect European businessmen generally, are inclined at present to be even harder-headed on this aspect than American businessmen. We in Britain and our fellow Europeans are beginning to cast covetous eyes upon the vast untapped markets of Eastern Europe, Russia, and China. I am quite certain that we would not want to be restricted in exploiting these markets by the external foreign policy of the United States. This is a very delicate area. There probably will come a time when American businessmen will leap ahead of us into these markets. But, for the time being, governments have their policies, often transient policies, and I think we would be strongly disinclined to give way even to transient foreign policies in this matter. We had that relatively recent business about the selling of our old double-decker buses to Cuba, but I think we shall want to go further than that now. As you know, we are trying to negotiate what France and Italy have already negotiated with Russia, the creation of a complete motor-car assembly factory in Russia. Our hope is if we let the Russians get a real taste of the motor car, then no Russian government will be able to prevent the Russian people from demanding the importation of cars on a vast scale. I saw recently that the Russians have begun to lay a highway across Russia, and I thought, "That's it, that is the beginning, as it were, of the beginning." The motor car is the great leveler.

These, then, in my view are three sensitive areas: research opportunities, internal political neutrality, and external political neutrality so far as development of external trade is concerned.

I, and those I have spoken to, have been enormously taken by a particular aspect of the conference. It is this. No matter to whom one spoke, or who was speaking, or to whom one was listening, whether it was members of management or members of trade unions, academicians, union lawyers, management lawyers, or labor arbitrators, they all seemed to speak a common language of concepts and principles which they obviously had mastered in ways and places I am not quite certain of yet. Perhaps it occurred in your institutes of industrial relations or in your innumerable interprofessional and intraprofessional conferences; perhaps this common language is spoken because your system of labor relations is so highly structured legally that issues are all handled out on the surface publicly where they can be analyzed systematically. Whatever the reasons, all the Americans attending this conference seemed to be speaking this common language of concepts and principles.

This is something that I think is unknown in our country. It seems to me it would be tremendously important if we could only codify all these things — one would have in Britain too a set of superb managerial and union principles to deal with labor relations, subject always, of course, to those differences of national attitudes and of the balance of industrial and political power to which we have constantly made reference.

AMERICAN INVESTMENT IN ITALY

By P. P. Fano

American supranational corporations began to make significant investments in Italy in the second half of the 1950s. They were attracted in the main by the rising level of internal demand and the fast rate of economic expansion of the country. To a lesser extent they also came to Italy because of the fiscal and credit facilities granted to investors in the developing areas of the South.

In 1966 the total of direct foreign investments in the Italian industry was estimated to be about $2 billion, of which 20 percent were of U. S. origin. Twenty-two percent of direct foreign investment came from fellow Common Market countries and 48 percent from Switzerland. Foreign investors, including the Americans, have shown a marked preference for the modern sectors of the manufacturing industries and to a lesser extent for banking and trade. They have been generally inclined to create new enterprises rather than to buy existing ones and to keep a majority interest in the business in order to be able to control it.

American investments are particularly significant in the oil, chemical, pharmaceutical, engineering, electronic, and electromechanical idustries. Productivity in American-controlled enterprises is on the average higher than that of Italian firms in the same field, except in the production of electrical household appliances.

American-controlled enterprises have introduced to the Italian market new products which have since been widely adopted by Italian consumers and have contributed to the spread of modern technical commercial and managerial know-how, and, to a certain extent, also to the opening of foreign markets and to the raising of the level of employment. It is regrettable that they have not undertaken significant research activities in Italy.

Italian public opinion is generally rather well disposed to foreign investments, so long as the investors are prepared to conform with the laws of the country and refrain from the temptation of imposing practices which are in contrast with its basic ways of life. It can hardly be overemphasized that the observance of these principles is of special importance in the administration of labor-management relations. To many Americans the Italian system of industrial relations — different as it is from that of the United States — may be difficult to digest and it may look suspicious. But in Italy, as in any

473

other country, there are enterprises in which industrial peace is seldom broken and still others in which labor troubles are most frequent.

Professor Shearer has described in his paper the labor difficulties encountered by American pharmaceutical firms operating in Italy when they did not follow Italian law and custom with respect to redundant employees and other labor relations practices. On the other hand, industrial relations in the American-controlled sector of the Italian oil industry are considered to be a model of labor-management understanding and collaboration. Since both the pharmaceutical and the oil industry work within the same system of industrial relations, the conclusion I must draw from these contrasting experiences is that such difficulties as may occur are not built into the Italian system.

In the administration of labor relations, foreign enterprises are more vulnerable than national enterprises — if only because the latter are more familiar with the psychology of the workers and of their leaders and with the social environment in general. A special effort to comprehend these basic facts of life and to take them into account in dealing with labor problems may be bothersome, but will in the end pay very good dividends.

THE U. S. CORPORATION IN IRELAND

By J. B. McCartney

About a month before this conference opened, I received an urgent airmail letter from our Conference Director, Professor Kamin, containing one sentence: "Ireland needs this kind of publicity like it needs another famine." Enclosed was a cutting of a press service dispatch which appeared in the *Chicago Daily News* on June 7, 1968. The story was headed "Union Organizing Dispute Snarls Irish Bid for Capital." Representatives of both the company and the union discussed in the dispatch are in attendance at this conference, and so I have no reluctance to give them and this gathering the benefit of my investigation and observations of their recent difficulties, fortunately now temporarily resolved.

The news dispatch is quite brief, and I quote it in full:

"Dublin (UPI)—General Electric Co. and a major Irish labor union are locked in a battle that threatens to wreck Ireland's efforts to attract foreign capital.

"At issue is the refusal of a GE subsidiary, the Electrical Industries Co., to recognize the Irish Transport and General Workers Union as a bargaining agent for the company's 1,250 employes.

"The plant began manufacturing radio and television components in 1962, and has an annual payroll of about $2,500,000.

"Early this year the union mounted an organizational drive at the company, taking the issue directly to the employes in a referendum. More than 60 percent of the workers on March 14 voted against union representation, according to General Electric.

"Five days later the union picketed the plant. The dispute has escalated ever since. Pickets were extended to include employe transports and goods being ferried to and from the factory, which continues to produce.

"Calls to have the company's goods 'blacked' in other countries have been heard in union circles. Labor members of Parliament have demanded government action to force recognition of the union.

"It is a ticklish spot for the Irish government. On one hand it faces a restless labor front; on the other, the Republic's need of foreign capital investment.

"Labor Minister Patrick Hillary looked the other way as long as possible. When the row spread into the operations of Shannon Airport by means of pickets at a refueling station, Hillary called company representatives to his office.

"Discussions were brief and fruitless. The company maintained its position. It cited results of the plant referendum and underscored it by saying that only 200 of the 1,250 employes have honored picket lines.

" 'The issues at stake here are vital to labor everywhere in the world' said one union official, 'and the outcome is being watched in many places.'

" 'We are concerned only with the running of our business here in Shannon and with the settlement of this dispute in accordance with the wishes of a majority of our employes,' a company spokesman said.

"Other companies operating out of Shannon, many of them also U.S.-backed, are watching the battle with growing unease.

"No one is willing to predict the outcome. But there is real fear in Shannon that it could result in the withdrawal of American capital from an area needing it desperately."

This report is an oversimplified and inaccurate explanation of a complex situation. The reporting is unfair both to the Irish Transport and General Workers Union and to the General Electric management. Some American labor relations experts would get the impression from the dispatch that after losing an official election the union was illegally picketing against a certification of a nonexistent Irish Labor Relations Board, in violation of something like Section 8(b)(7)(B) of the American National Labor Relations Act. While the American Labor Act has no extraterritorial application, even to an American-owned enterprise operating in another land, in some way some expert readers might have moral reflexes condemning the union. On the other hand, other American labor law experts might get the impression that General Electric, even abroad, is the rogue elephant of American employers which sought to impose "Boulwarism" upon an Irish trade union and its members. Neither version is correct, as I shall show.

Of 1,250 employees in Electrical Industries Co. at Shannon, as of 1968, about 300 to 400 were members of the Irish Transport and General Workers Union. Contrary to the dispatch, the union did not make a postelection demand, in American terms, that the company "recognize the Irish Transport and General Workers Union as a bargaining agent for the company's 1,250 employees." To the contrary, the union's postelection claim was only to be permitted to act as bargaining agent for its own members and not for company employees who were not members.

The company's attitude was that it would not recognize the union as a bargaining agent for any employees, their own members included, unless a majority of all the employees wished to be represented by the union. In the latter case, the company would then recognize the union as the only bargaining agent for all employees, whether members of the union or not. A ballot was taken on this proposal, and the majority of the employees apparently did not wish to be represented by the union as a bargaining agent. The union was very critical of the actual wording of the question put on the ballot, but, be that as it may, the union maintained that when it agreed to the ballot it did so without prejudice to its claim to represent its own members.

After the election was held on March 14, 1968, with 404 employees voting to be represented by the Irish Transport and General Workers Union and 599 voting for the existing setup, the union, on behalf of its members, made certain demands upon the company in respect of wages and conditions of employment. It is not denied that the union was so instructed by its members. The company refused to agree to these demands.

Pickets were then placed on the premises, and legal proceedings were brought by the company in the High Court. The court granted an interlocutory injunction to restrain picketing on two general grounds — first, that the method of picketing was objectionable and exceeded that permitted by law, and second, that the demand as to wages and conditions was not genuine and that in fact the union was only trying to use this for the purpose of obtaining recognition.

While there was no evidence taken in the interlocutory proceeding and the High Court relied upon affidavits, on the issue of the method of picketing the trial judge was impressed by two uncontroverted affidavits. One described picket placards declaring: "Yankees, you can't dictate." The other affidavit concerned a statement by a union officer who addressed an American executive of the company "in a hostile way" and said: "You are a Yank. We don't want you here."

An appeal was taken by the union officials and employees who had been enjoined. The appeal was heard by the Supreme Court, a majority of which was satisfied (several opinions were given) that there was prima facie a trade dispute in being within the provisions of the Trade Disputes Act, 1906, namely, that relating to wages and work conditions. The court therefore discharged the injunction, though it issued a stern warning about the method of picketing.

Ó Dálaigh, C. J., in one of the majority judgments observed: "It will, however, be clear that all reference to racial origins is outside the protection of the 1906 Act . . . ." Walsh, J., in another of the majority judgments said:

> "In my view there can be little doubt but that the conduct engaged in by the defendants on the 19th March, that is, the first day of the strike, was grossly in excess of that permitted by law and that the interim injunctions were properly granted against such of the defendants as

were present. ... The use of words such as 'scab' or 'blackleg' are historically so associated with social ostracism and physical violence as to be far beyond anything which might be described as mere rudeness or impoliteness and go beyond what is permitted by law. In the present context the references made to the race or nationality of the employers could produce the same disorderly response and also go beyond what is permitted by law."

The other question — whether or not, where there is not a dispute with regard to wages or conditions, a dispute confined solely to the right of the employees to nominate their union as the bargaining agent can constitute a trade dispute — is left over for the full hearing of the action if it ever comes on in the High Court.

The company undoubtedly wished to have the general American system of one union representing all employees, or no union at all. The union naturally would have liked to represent every employee in the factory and perhaps induce all to become members, but in addition it quite naturally claimed the right to act as the selected spokesman of its own members.

Europeans accept, rather than find offensive, the notion of "members only" labor agreements. And indeed in the United States there is nothing at all illegal about members-only arrangements. As I understand American law, the members-only contract is simply not a bar to a representation petition filed with the National Labor Relations Board by a rival labor organization which desires to be the exclusive statutory representative.[1]

Moreover, an examination of actual American practice, even after passage of the original National Labor Relations Act in 1935, discloses that the members-only labor agreement was a frequently used device to avoid strikes and showdowns on exclusive-recognition controversies in the early days of the organization of American industrial unions. A noted American labor historian discusses in considerable detail the Taylor-Lewis agreement of 1937, whereby the new Steel Workers Organizing Committee (SWOC) was first recognized by the U. S. Steel Corp. The making of this agreement was "one of the critical junctures in American economic history. Not only did it ensure the existence of unionism in basic steel, but it provided inestimable assistance to the CIO in its drive to organize other industries."[2]

But it is also to be noted that this historic American labor agreement was precisely the type of agreement that the Irish Trans-

---

[1] *Appalachian Shale Products Co.*, 121 NLRB 1160, 42 LRRM 1506 (1958). But cf. *Hebron Brick Company*, 135 NLRB 245, 49 LRRM 1463 (1962).

[2] Galenson, *The CIO Challenge to the AFL: A History of the American Labor Movement 1935-1941*, 93 (1960).

port and General Workers Union sought in 1968 from the General
Electric Co.

> "In the agreement, which was signed on March 2, 1937,
> Carnegie-Illinois recognized the SWOC *as the bargaining agent for its
> members, while the SWOC agreed not to intimidate or coerce nonun-
> ion employees into membership.* Minimum daily wages were raised to
> $5, and a 40-hour week was established with time-and-a-half pay for
> all hours in excess of 8 per day or 40 per week. This was supplement-
> ed on March 17 with a series of collective agreements covering the
> several operating subsidiaries of U. S. Steel which contained, in addi-
> tion to the wage and hour clauses, provisions for paid vacations, sen-
> iority, arbitration or grievances, and other standard clauses." (Em-
> phasis supplied) [3]

Moreover, as I have already commented in my principal paper,
in the Republic of Ireland an employee has a constitutional right
not to be a member of the union, just as he has a constitutional
right to be a member. The great practical difficulty in this type of
case is that even if the union had won the election, whatever the
company or even the union might have decided to do, an individual
employee who was not a member of a union might elect to conduct
his own negotiations or indeed be represented by his lawyer or any
other adviser. It is doubtful that the Republic has any constitutional
method at present of accommodating the principle of exclusive representation reflected in Section 9(a) of the American National Labor
Relations Act.[4]

Nor was the situation improved at all by some other information which had been sent to the Irish Transport and General Workers Union by American trade unions describing their relations with
the General Electric Co.[5] Other factors in this case were that the
bulk of the workers in this factory came from rural areas and were
not particularly union-conscious and that the conditions of employment were remarkably good. That accounted for the fact that three
quarters or more of the workers regularly went to work despite the
presence of the picket line.

Yet, to my notion, General Electric should have been anxious
to deal with one union only, rather than with a multiplicity of unions. At the time of the dispute no other union apparently was interested in the Electrical Industries plant. It seems to me that General Electric should have moved to its own advantage to utilize this
reality. For example, in the national electricity board in the Repub-

[3] *Ibid.*

[4] *Educational Co.* v. *Fitzpatrick,* (1961) I.R. 343 (Injunction) and 345 (High
Ct.); 370 (Supreme Ct.); (1962) 96 I.L.T.R. 161 (Supreme Ct.); (1963) 97
I.L.T.R. 17 (Budd, J.).

[5] Especially the decisions of the trial examiner and the National Labor Relations Board in *General Electric Co.,* 150 NLRB 192, 57 LRRM 1491 (1964).

lic, there are something like 16 different unions catering to the employees, and that frequently gives rise to trouble because of the sensitivity of one union to the activities of another and often because of the desire of the unions to maintain their separate identities by asserting themselves.

In the E. I. matter, the company always had maintained contact with the union on an unofficial basis. They gave the Irish Transport and General Workers Union every encouragement to keep the workers happy. They met with union officials on this basis and wrote soothing letters to the union, which nonetheless did not make any concessions on the question of officially treating with the organization. This was probably exasperating for the union, which is accustomed to getting fairly blunt letters from Irish employers with whom they are in dispute. The unions on their side obviously have a vested interest also in seeing that it not be too clearly demonstrated that, in some cases at least, employees can exist happily without them. On the whole the approach of the E. I. Company to employees in Ireland at least appears to be somewhat paternalistic, and that is something that never really commends itself to unions.

The General Electric or E. I. dispute at Shannon in 1968 illustrates some, but not all, of the main points that the contributors to this section of the volume were asked by Professor Kamin to comment upon. What political problems are caused in the host country by American entry and operation? The first objection often raised — in the North as well as in the Republic — is that the host country has forfeited its sovereignty over its own internal affairs. These objections come as much from right-wing conservatives as from left-wing radicals or from the trade union movement. Although these are real issues discussed in both parts of Ireland, let me suggest that the Irish do not feel as strongly about it as do similar vocal elements in Britain — largely because neither in the North nor in the Republic do we possess very much real sovereignty.

As the General Electric case illustrates, there were feelings that American companies seek to import labor relations concepts which trample upon internal constitutional guarantees, such as the right to organize into labor unions and the correlative right to eschew union affiliation without effect upon the individual contract of employment. While the Republic of Ireland does not go as far as does Sweden, where both the right to organize and to bargain collectively are guaranteed,[6] any American corporation coming into the Republic

---

[6] See, generally, *Trade Union Situation in Sweden: Report of a Mission from the International Labour Office,* 1961. The basic Swedish law is stated in the Right of Association and of Collective Bargaining Act of 1936.

must take into account these deeply felt and often aggressively asserted constitutional rights. Disregard of these feelings provokes charges that Americans are trying to remake the political institutions of the Republic of Ireland.

There are complaints that come mainly from the Left about the influence of American foreign policy on the policy of the Republic of Ireland. As all of you know, the Republic's policy since its founding after the 1922 Treaty traditionally has been a neutral one. I cannot cite illustrations in the Republic or in the North of cancellation of orders based on some prohibition of American law. In the North, for example, our domestically owned shipbuilding companies fill orders for communist countries. But I can freely predict what would happen in Northern Ireland or in the Republic should a wholly owned American subsidiary company located in either part of Ireland be compelled by American law to reject or cancel an order from North Vietnam, Cuba, mainland China, Albania, or any Iron Curtain nation. There would be eloquent charges that the U.S. Government was interfering in the domestic affairs of the host nation by undermining the local economy, by deliberately creating unemployment, or by wilfully blocking the opportunities for expansion of the economy of the host country.

In the North, our unemployment rate is not as favorable as that of the United Kingdom as a whole or even of the Republic. While average unemployment is 2.6 percent for Britain as a whole and 5.4 percent in the Republic, in Northern Ireland it is 8 percent. There has been job erosion in traditional occupations such as shipbuilding, textiles, and agriculture. The Ministry of Commerce of Northern Ireland is aggressively seeking new companies to invest in our part of the world. Outright cash grants are offered for new buildings, plants, and machinery. The grants rise as high as 45 percent if the incoming enterprise will create reasonable employment in relation to total capital outlay. Notwithstanding these generous offers by the Northern Ireland Government to attract industry, an incoming employer from America or elsewhere would be seriously mistaken if he were to assume that his plant would become an enclave, immune from the surrounding political and cultural milieu.

The Industrial Development Authority of the Republic is perhaps even more assertive than the Northern Ministry of Commerce in its efforts to attract American investment. Government-sponsored industrial estates at Galway, Shannon Airport, and Waterford provide ready-built factories for renting on favorable terms. A manufacturer may purchase or build his own factory with the aid of grants. Grants may also be provided toward the cost of new machinery and for the training of workers. Projects established at Galway, Shannon, and Waterford enjoy a specific number of years of freedom from tax on profits for exports. The IDA is quite candid. The Republic cannot absorb the products of a new manufacturer. Therefore, the IDA solicits new industry which will manufacture anywhere at all in Ireland but export the product there produced.

To American companies in Ireland or thinking about investing there, I would counsel one thing above others. Our scale in Ireland is such that you can pick up a telephone and talk to a top official or indeed to a Minister with little difficulty.

Of course, I am not suggesting that law firms and management consultant firms are useless and superfluous in Northern Ireland or in the Republic. But it is still important for the incoming management to get on the ground and talk directly to the people. As we would put it, you will do far more in an evening's discussion over a pint of stout or a jar than you will over weeks of long-range study of charts and statistical tables.

Difficulties can be negotiated away. But merely because a major American corporation may have a larger annual turnover than the whole of the government of the Republic or the government of Northern Ireland does not justify an assumption that it can barge right through the trade union movement. On the ground, the trade unions can concentrate their strength and they are quite effective. Since I believe that American corporations come to Ireland essentially to make immediate and continuing profits and not out of charity or sentiment, it seems downright unwise to substitute bluster for negotiations. If you are going to negotiate away difficulties, you must ascertain what they are.

Personal contact is the best approach in Ireland for still another reason. There is very little that has been published on industrial relations law and practice in Ireland. The publication that will result from this conference will be quite helpful. For this reason I have sought in my principal paper to give as much factual information as possible rather than offer purely speculative discussion on nice academic legal problems.

When I return I shall recommend to both of the Irish governments that they do something about financing necessary labor relations studies and publications. The pretty, glossy publications and the beautifully illustrated advertisements put out both in color and in black and white by the Ministry of Commerce and the IDA are useful. But my attendance at this gathering persuades me that what prospective American investors in Ireland want to know are the detailed facts of life about labor relations of American corporations and other foreign-owned plants which are already in operation in Northern Ireland and in the Republic.

Labor-Management Relations and the Democratic Challenge

This volume concludes, as did the 1968 Loyola Summer Institute on Business and Law, with an independent discussion by Allan Flanders, then University Lecturer, University of Oxford, and now a full-time member of the newly created Commission on Industrial Relations. Mr. Flanders analyzes the informal power of plant work groups that may be more effective and more productive for the employees directly concerned than the formal power of the recognized labor union. While his data are based on British experience, Mr. Flanders believes that his thesis is applicable to all advanced industrial countries in Western Europe and North America.

LABOR-MANAGEMENT RELATIONS AND THE DEMOCRATIC CHALLENGE

By Allan Flanders

It is good practice to begin by defining one's terms. You will hardly need a definition of labor-management relations, but "democratic challenge" in the title of my address refers to the challenge to managerial authority coming today from the rising power and claims of separate work groups on the shop floor of industry. If I had been discussing this subject only a few years ago it would have been taken for granted that I meant the challenge coming from trade unions; that they were the thrusting democratic force in industry with which managements had to contend. I propose to argue that this assumption no longer holds or at least not to the same extent as in the past, because the work group is replacing the trade union. More than that, the work group is increasingly challenging the authority of trade unions as well as that of managements.

Naturally I can most easily develop my argument in the context of British institutions, especially in view of the very thorough inquiry into industrial relations undertaken by our Royal Commission on Trade Unions and Employers' Associations — the Donovan Commission — whose report was published in June 1968.[1] One cannot, of course, generalize from the experience of one country, yet the basic phenomenon is, in my view, common to all advanced industrial countries in both Western Europe and North America. What differ very much from one country to another are its consequences. They are affected by the existing structure of the industrial relations institutions in each country and, above all, by the legal framework of these institutions. It so happens that in Britain the consequences can be seen at their extreme.

Few people in Britain, outside of universities, talk about work groups. They talk instead about shop stewards, and since hardly a day passes when they do not read in the newspapers about an unofficial strike (our term for a wildcat stoppage), they are inclined to regard shop stewards as troublemakers. As the stewards are sup-

---

[1] *Report of Royal Commission on Trade Unions and Employers' Associations 1965-1968*, Cmnd. 3623 (London: Her Majesty's Stationery Office (H.M.S.O.), June 1968), hereinafter referred to as Report of Royal Commission. For a more critical appraisal than the author offers here, see the symposium of articles in the *British Journal of Industrial Relations*, Vol. VI, No. 3., November 1968.

posed to be union representatives inside the plant, and as their unions are invariably parties to agreements with employers which include a "peace obligation" until the agreed disputes procedure has been exhausted, trade unions are put in the dock and accused of irresponsibility for failing to discipline their erring members. It is then a short step to conclude that all would be well if only our collective agreements were legally enforced as contracts, as they are in most other countries, Unions and their members would behave more responsibly — so the argument runs — if they knew that strikes in breach of agreements would incur legal penalties. One of our two major political parties — the one at present in opposition — has made this a plank in its program,[2] and there was a widespread expectation that the Donovan Commission would endorse this proposal or advance alternative recommendations for punishing unofficial strikers. In fact, with a few dissenting voices among its members, it has done nothing of the kind. On the contrary, in one of the most brilliantly argued chapters of its report,[3] it has shown how great would be the practical and legal difficulties of putting into effect any of these proposals. Its reasons for coming out so strongly against any immediate legal enforcement of collective agreements are germane to my subject, but before I come to them let me stay with the topic of shop stewards and work groups.

POWER OF WORK GROUPS

One of the popular delusions about industrial relations is a belief that shop stewards have power of their own. The power they appear to have resides in the groups they represent. It is the sanctions at the command of work groups, sanctions they can impose on their members, and, still more, sanctions they can impose on management, which are the important factor in the situation. As to the latter, the instant stoppage is only one weapon in their armory. Cut-price industrial action, as it has been called, takes many forms, from work to rule and bans on overtime to a mere withdrawal of cooperation. A further mistake is to assume that this power is derived from trade unions. They may benefit from it, just as work groups benefit from the reinforcement of their position by external union organization, but, as a number of studies have shown, the strategic power of work groups depends mainly on factors connected

---

[2] *Fair Deal at Work, the Conservative Approach to Modern Industrial Relations* (London: Conservative Political Centre, April 1968).

[3] *Report of Royal Commission*, Chapter VIII, "The Enforcement of Collective Agreements," pp. 122-140.

with the technology of production. This is also their impersonal be-getter and one of the principal determinants of their behavior.

The increase in the autonomous industrial power of work groups over the past two decades appears to be a universal phe-nomenon in most developed countries. Clearly it is associated with conditions of full employment or, where these do not exist, with labor shortages in large sectors of employment and a weakening of management's ability to impose control and discipline by negative sanctions; that is, in the last resort, by threat of dismissal. This is part of the explanation in Britain, but it is by no means the whole of it. The power of the groups, and thus the authority of their spokesmen, has been built up, surprisingly enough, by management. In the national survey of workplace relations made by the Donovan Commission a structured sample of managers were asked whether, when they had a choice, they would prefer to deal with the shop steward or a full-time union official, if both were equally competent. Over two thirds preferred the steward to the official,[4] and an ear-lier, private inquiry raising a similar question yielded a higher pro-portion of three quarters.[5]

Management's chief reason for this preference was the stew-ard's "intimate knowledge of the circumstances of the case." But, as the Commission observes in its report, this "is as much a conse-quence of their preference as a cause of it. If managers choose to deal with shop stewards on an informal basis, full-time officers can-not be expected to acquire a detailed knowledge of the issues which arise in the factory."[6] This pattern of managerial behavior reflects the traditional preference on the part of many British employers for what, in our engineering industry, are known as "domestic settle-ments." Originally this preference arose as part of a policy to con-tain trade unions and safeguard managerial prerogatives by insisting that employers should be free to settle a wide range of matters with their own employees.[7] In the modern context of transformed power relations on the shop floor it has resulted in a steady growth of in-formal collective bargaining between members of management and shop stewards or other workers' representatives.

What is the character of this workplace bargaining? In my own evidence to the Donovan Commission I suggested that it had three

---

[4] W. E. J. McCarthy and S. R. Parker, *Shop Stewards and Workshop Rela-tions*, Royal Commission Research Paper No. 10 (London: HMSO, 1968), p. 3.

[5] H. A. Clegg, A. J. Killick, and Rex Adams, *Trade Union Officers* (Oxford: Blackwells, 1961), pp. 174-177.

[6] *Report of Royal Commission*, p. 28.

[7] See Arthur Marsh, *Industrial Relations in Engineering* (Oxford: Pergamon Press, 1965), pp. 16-18.

leading characteristics: that it was "largely informal, largely fragmented, and largely autonomous."[8] Taking each of these characteristics in turn, the informality of this bargaining implies that its results are rarely expressed in written agreements at all, let alone
signed agreements with the unions. Formal plant agreements, similar to those in the United States, are confined in the main to nonfederated firms in Britain, firms which are not members of an employers' association. Otherwise the results of workplace bargaining
take the form of oral understandings, of alleged management decisions arrived at after consultation with workers' representatives,
and of so-called "custom and practice." This informality, it should
be appreciated, applies as much to the procedural as to the substantive aspects of the bargaining process. Disputes procedures inside
the firm are usually ill-defined and inadequate. Even where they
have been put down on paper, they are often short-circuited in practice.

By fragmentation I mean that bargaining is conducted in such
a way that within the same factory different groups get different
concessions at different times. This can best be illustrated as cause
and effect of disorganized pay structures and degenerate incentive
pay systems. A study of payment by results recently undertaken by
our National Board for Prices and Incomes "found widespread dissatisfaction with the fluctuations and uncertainties in earnings" resulting from many conventional time-based piecework systems. They
found too, "considerable disenchantment with the constant and
time-consuming process of shop floor haggling, inversions of customary skill differentials, and lack of security so often associated with
these systems. They frequently give rise to anomalies in earnings between different jobs and skills, in many cases leading to competitive
bargaining between groups of workers."[9]

Lastly, there is the autonomy of most of this bargaining to consider. Neither trade unions nor employers' associations have any
control over it as a rule. Indeed, they often have little knowledge of
what is going on inside the plant until it leads to a stoppage of
work and they are asked to intervene. Most of their joint agreements concluded at industry level set minimum wages which are
substantially improved upon by local bargaining. Though they invariably claim to fix a "normal" working week, so many men work
so much overtime that they do not effectively regulate actual work-

---

[8] Allan Flanders, *Collective Bargaining: Prescription for Change* (London:
Faber and Faber, 1967), pp. 27-30.

[9] National Board for Prices and Incomes, Report No. 65, *Payment by Results
Systems*, Cmnd. 3627 (London: H.M.S.O., May 1968), p. 70.

ing hours either. Besides, there are many issues of industrial conflict arising at the place of work, on such matters as dismissal and discipline, for example, which are rarely mentioned in industry-wide agreements.

Autonomy, or lack of external control over workplace bargaining, is partly a result of its informality and fragmentation. One cannot control externally what is internally disorganized and uncontrolled. But there is more to it than that. As the Donovan Commission points out in its report, we now have in Britain virtually two different systems of collective bargaining at odds with each other. Our traditional system based on industry-wide agreements, has increasingly become a pretense, a mere house of cards, because it has been undermined by the rapid growth of workplace bargaining. The expectation of stability in the traditional system rested on the premise that regulation could be made effective and order preserved by the joint efforts of powerful trade unions on the one hand and equally powerful employers' associations on the other. In practice, national trade union organization has become progressively weaker, and that of employers' associations weaker still.

Recent changes in labor-management relations within the plant have two further important features resulting from the enhanced power of work groups. First of all, they cannot be described exclusively in bargaining terms. Even informal collective bargaining implies some discussion, compromise, and agreement between the parties. A noticeable feature of shop-floor developments in postwar Britain has been the extension of unilateral regulation by workers of their pay and work. These unilateral shop-floor rules have always existed to some extent, especially among craftsmen.* Today they are no more made the subject of discussion with management than were, say, the working rules of the printers' unions in the nineteenth century prior to their acceptance of collective bargaining. Management must tacitly accept them because it has no alternative. But such acceptance does not represent the same thing as an unwritten collective agreement. The serious problem of restrictive labor practices in Britain, to give them their familiar if somewhat biased title, is quite substantially a postwar product. Very few of these practices are to be found in union rule books or collective agreements. Some of them, it is true, have nineteenth-century craft origins, but many more are workplace conventions, which have multiplied and become

---

*Ed. Note: For an overview of make-work rules and policies in the United States, see Slichter, Healy and Livernash, *The Impact of Collective Bargaining on Management*, pp. 317-341 (1960); and Jacobs, *Dead Horse and the Feather Bird* (1962).

more stringent with the work groups' growing power. Understandably, these groups have used their sanctions to enforce regulations that would improve their bargaining advantage and protect their income and job security. The increasingly disordered context of their activities has made it all the more necessary for them to rely on their own efforts.

The other important point to be made about this challenge from below is that it has been extending the subjects of collective bargaining beyond the rather narrow range covered by formal union agreements in Britain. This is associated with another new factor in the situation which I have not touched on as yet: the rising level of expectations among workers — white collar as well as manual — about what industry owes them. The authors of a recent study of labor relations in our motor industry have argued that the increasing incidence of strikes in the industry reflects "a major change in manual workers' expectations."[10] This is not just a question of more money, although the expectation of regular annual increases in earnings is part of the pattern. Workers, they suggest, now expect that wages should be fair in comparative terms and, as a corollary, that workloads should be negotiable. Equally, they have come to believe that "performance of a job establishes property rights in it,"[11] and therefore no longer accept dismissal or other infringement of those rights without resistance. Setting aside the question whether this is a satisfactory explanation of the high incidence of strikes in certain car firms (which I doubt), the general proposition is persuasive. Given the accepted range of subjects for collective bargaining in the United States, many may think it strange that these expectations have not been met before. Be that as it may, the point I wish to emphasize is that the drive to modernize British collective bargaining is coming from the shop floor. It is here that new rights are being claimed and asserted that rarely figure in official union negotiations with employers.

There is evidence too that greater stability and security of earnings, associated sometimes with a rejection of the old status divisions between manual and staff workers, are emerging much more prominently in the workers' demands. In the large number of case studies that were made to prepare the Prices and Incomes Board's report on payment by results I was particularly interested in two firms in the North of England where the changeover from piecework to measured daywork resulted from shop stewards' initiative, although

---

[10] H. A. Turner, Garfield Clack, and Geoffrey Roberts, *Labour Relations in the Motor Industry* (London: Allen and Unwin, 1967), p. 336.
[11] *Ibid.*

their members had been gaining from the very high rate of earnings drift under the old payments system. Their main reasons for favoring the change appeared to be that they wanted their earnings to be more secure even if the rate of increase was likely to be slower; and they were fed up with all the fiddles of the piecework system and the heavy pressures it placed upon them.

RESPONSE OF MANAGEMENT

So far I have said nothing about the response of British management to these new facts of industrial life, although it has been a crucial factor in determining their outcome. One can summarize this response quite briefly. Management was ill-prepared in every conceivable way to cope with these facts constructively. At the end of the war and for a long time afterwards, the prevailing view — not confined to management circles — was that the appropriate institutional form for industrial relations at the place of work was joint consultation. Many joint consultative committees were set up — they were obligatory in the nationalized industries — and great hopes were placed in them. It was believed that they would promote a sense of common purpose in industry by giving the workers opportunities for participation in management, with management still retaining its right to make the final decisions. Collective bargaining was looked upon as an institution external to the firm in that the negotiations were conducted only with full-time union officials. This was the theory. In practice, the surviving joint consultative committees mainly became forums for informal bargaining.

Lower levels of management in particular could not afford to be unrealistic about the new-found power of work groups. If they disregarded it, it was brought to their attention by stoppages or the application of other sanctions disrupting production, for which they were likely to be blamed. Why should they threaten their own careers? Better to come to terms with power by making concessions or allowing practices to develop, such as rising levels of overtime which they knew to be unnecessary, in order to keep the peace. Only the members of top management could continue to live in a world of pretense. What was happening down below came to their notice only if it was reported and forced upon their attention, and no rewards were to be gained for doing that. This is one of the reasons why workplace bargaining remained informal. In a research paper prepared for the Donovan Commission it was pointed out that "some *de facto* concessions could not be written down because management, particularly at board level, would not be prepared to admit publicly that they had been forced to accept such modifications in their managerial prerogatives and formal chains of command."[12]

Apart from the mixture of ideology and pretense, which obstructed a clear view of the reality of labor-management relations at those levels of management where policy is decided, there were other factors hampering a constructive response to the changed situation. Few managers had the knowledge or training to develop and execute policies in labor relations demanding initiative and an acceptance of risk. Relations were therefore shaped more by drift than by design. Many a firm continued to believe that membership in an employers' association and readiness to observe formal union agreements, with perhaps some improved fringe benefits or welfare considerations, constituted a sufficient industrial relations policy. During and after the war, it is true, the total number of personnel managers steadily increased, but even the best of them were rarely in a position to form policy. There is a striking passage on this subject in the Donovan Commission Report:

> "If companies have their own personnel specialists, why have they not introduced effective personnel policies to control methods of negotiation and pay structures within their firms? Many firms have no such policy, and perhaps no conception of it. They employ a personnel officer to be responsible for certain tasks: staff records, selection, training, welfare, negotiation and consultation. Many of the older generation of personnel managers see themselves simply as professional negotiators. Even if a personnel manager has the ability to devise an effective personnel policy, the director responsible for personnel (if there is one), or the board as a whole, may not want to listen to him. Many firms had acquired disorderly pay structures and unco-ordinated personnel practices before they appointed a personnel manager, and the burden of dealing with disputes and problems as they arise has absorbed his whole time and energy."[13]

Much more could be said about the historical and social reasons for the present inadequacies of British management but, whatever the causes, the industrial relations consequences are not in doubt. In the main shop stewards were left to make the running and managements responded by yielding to pressures when it became costly to resist them. The immediate market expediency of getting and retaining enough labor and the immediate managerial expediency of avoiding stoppages and an interruption of production served as the main guides to action. Work groups and the shop stewards leading them could hardly be blamed for looking after their own parochial interests. Finding that militancy produced concessions, they

---

[12] W. E. J. McCarthy, *The Role of Shop Stewards in British Industrial Relations*, Royal Commission Research Paper No. 1 (London: HMSO, 1966), p. 27.
[13] *Report of Royal Commission*, p. 25.

pressed on. Managers and shop stewards alike found themselves involved in a feverish activity of petty haggling that perpetuated the situation and never alleviated the forces making it inevitable.

SIGNS OF CHANGE

To be fair, I have tended to dwell on the worst cases and consequently painted a darker picture than would be authentic for the generality of British industry. Nor is it any longer the case that companies are displaying no independent initiatives in labor relations. Over the past five years or so there have been significant signs of a change in outlook. One of these is the spread of productivity agreements. I wrote a detailed study of the first major example, the Fawley Agreements, negotiated in 1960 at Esso's largest oil refinery on Southampton Water.[14] Since then, other companies and industries have negotiated similar agreements. They have also been made the subject of a special report by the Prices and Incomes Board, which drew up a number of guidelines or basic rules for negotiators to follow in productivity bargaining.[15]

This is not an occasion for an extended discussion of productivity bargaining or the Labour Government's policy for productivity, prices, and incomes which has helped to push such bargaining into the foreground.[16] The one point I would like to make is that productivity agreements have not only been a means of raising labor

---

[14] Allan Flanders, *The Fawley Productivity Agreements*, (London: Faber and Faber, 1964).

[15] These guidelines were as follows:

1. It should be shown that the workers are making a direct contribution towards increasing productivity by accepting more exacting work or a major change in working practices.

2. Forecasts of increased productivity should be derived by the application of proper work standards.

3. An accurate calculation of the gains and costs should normally show that the total cost per unit of output, taking into account the effect on capital, will be reduced.

4. The scheme should contain effective controls to ensure that the projected increase in productivity is achieved, and that payment is made only as productivity increases or as changes in working practices take place.

5. The undertaking should be ready to show clear benefits to the consumer through a contribution to stable prices.

6. An agreement covering part of an undertaking should bear the cost of consequential increases elsewhere in the same undertaking, if any have to be granted.

7. In all cases negotiators should beware of setting extravagant levels of pay which would provoke resentment outside.

National Board for Prices and Incomes, Report No. 36: *Productivity Agreements*, Cmnd. 3311 (London: HMSO, June 1967), pp. 47-48.

[16] As I have argued elsewhere, the restraint imposed by incomes policy has helped to induce reform. See Allan Flanders, "The Case for the Package Deal," *The Times*, London, July 9, 1968.

productivity by gaining the unions' and their members' consent to changes in uneconomic working practices, such as excessive and unnecessary overtime or unduly rigid and outmoded job demarcations. Where they have taken the form of comprehensive plant or company agreements, they have also been an instrument for reforming management and collective bargaining because they have provided an answer to those shortcomings in intraplant relations that I have described. Productivity agreements have helped to overcome the excessive fragmentation of bargaining by their comprehensive character, and to replace informal understandings and custom and practice by signed, written agreements with the unions. Not least, they have diminished the autonomy of local bargaining in several ways. Their negotiation, for example, has forced full-time trade union officials to work closely with their stewards in a common cause. In some industries they have already brought about a revision of industry-wide agreements so that they provide a more realistic framework for plant negotiations. They have even induced a movement for the reform of employers' associations to get them to provide more in the way of positive services for their member firms in the shape of advice and guidance.

The effect of productivity agreements on management is possibly their most important long-term contribution to an improvement in economic efficiency and industrial relations. To quote the Prices and Incomes Board Report:

"Negotiating the agreements had two main consequences for management. First, the length and scope of the negotiations at all levels brought their negotiators into closer touch with the unions than before; and because far more managers were brought into the process than in conventional negotiations many of them were made closely aware for the first time of the consequences for industrial relations of technical and financial decisions. Secondly, the experience of applying the agreements, together with their provisions on overtime, flexibility, manning and so on has brought about nothing less than a revolution in managerial control over working hours and practices in many of the undertakings affected.

"In addition there have been changes in organization, in personnel and the provision of training. Generally speaking therefore, management is better informed and better organized than before the agreements."[17]

I am not suggesting that productivity agreements offer the only solution to the problem of diminishing the disorder that the rise in the power of work groups has caused. Comprehensive company and factory agreements have been negotiated to reshape chaotic wage

---

[17] *Productivity Agreements,* note 14, *supra,* p. 25.

structures with the help of job evaluation,[18] or to bring payment systems under firmer control by better measurement based on work study. New factories have been opened with agreements providing a stronger and more clearly defined institutional framework for regulating pay and work from the start. What I would claim, however, is that the particular significance that the productivity agreements have acquired on the contemporary British scene is due to the policy of drift which so many managements have followed in labor relations. These agreements are often a necessary step in the process of bringing unilaterally enforced "custom and practice" into the realm of joint regulation and formal collective bargaining. Their negotiation in fact forces management to face up to the paradox whose truth they find so difficult to accept: "they can only regain control by sharing it."[19]

One of the central problems, therefore, which the Donovan Commission faced was how to speed up this movement, already in being, for the reform of collective bargaining. They rightly decided with unanimity that the crux of the matter was to find ways to promote the negotiation of formal factory or company agreements with the unions. Such agreements alone, they concluded, could provide for "effective and orderly collective bargaining . . . over such issues as the control of incentive schemes, the regulation of hours actually worked, the use of job evaluation, work practices and the linking of changes in pay to changes in performance, facilities for shop stewards, and disciplinary rules and appeals."[20] Industry-wide agreements "should be limited to those matters which they can effectively regulate," although they could also, with advantage, set out guidelines to keep local bargaining within acceptable bounds.[21]

As the main initiative for change in this direction had to come from the boards of directors of companies, the Commission proposed two practical measures to accelerate reform. In the first place companies above a certain size should be placed under a legal obligation, enforced by a monetary penalty, to register collective agreements with the appropriate government department or explain why they had failed to negotiate them. Secondly, an Industrial Relations Commission should be set up to which problems arising out of the

---

[18] "The number of employees known to be covered by job evaluation in Britain is small as contrasted with the U.S.A. Our survey, however, has shown a growing interest and a rapidly expanding application of job evaluation." National Board for Prices and Incomes, Report No. 83, *Job Evaluation*, Cmnd. 3772 (London: HMSO, September 1968), p. 41.

[19] *Collective Bargaining: Prescription for Change*, note 8, *supra*, p. 32.

[20] *Report of Royal Commission*, p. 40.

[21] *Id.* at p. 263.

registration of agreements could be referred. This body would also have other functions. For example, it would deal with disputes over union recognition or inquire into the general state of industrial relations in a particularly strike-prone factory or industry.

CASE AGAINST LEGAL SANCTIONS

Part of the Donovan Commission's case for rejecting any immediate legal enforcement of collective agreements ties in with these recommendations and rests on the simple dictum of first things first. It would be stupid and unfair, the Commission argued, to start by enforcing existing (mainly industry-wide) agreements when they are so badly in need of reform. Indeed, such a step would create a disincentive against reform. But once collective bargaining has been reformed and, in particular, plants and companies have established satisfactory internal disputes procedures, legal enforcement may prove to be unnecessary. This question should be kept under review by the proposed Industrial Relations Commission. If, later, legal sanctions are thought to be necessary to ensure the observance of agreements, they should be "employed as an emergency device for use from case to case."[22]

Why such reluctance to turn to the law to enforce obligations? Because — and here we have the other part of the case against the use of legal sanctions — none of the parties in Britain really want to bring industrial disputes into the courts if they can avoid it, or lawyers *qua* lawyers into industrial relations. In most cases employers could already claim damages for breach of individual contracts of employment when unofficial strikes occur, but they rarely do. Similarly, the main reason why collective agreements are not treated as legally binding contracts is that this would be contrary to the intentions of the parties. In short, employers and trade unions generally prefer social to legal regulation and voluntary to compulsory collective bargaining; and *they* have to make the system work. One cannot sensibly redesign any industrial relations system *ab initio* and ignore the culture and the values of the people and organizations primarily involved. Change and continuity must be reconciled.

CONCLUSION

For my part I am convinced that in Britain we can maintain our longstanding preference for social regulation and voluntary agreements, which have many positive advantages, and yet solve our most

---

[22] *Id.* at p. 268.

urgent problems of restoring order and efficiency, provided trade unions and managements show themselves capable of responding to the democratic challenge of the work group. If they fail, I fear the alternative will be a massive degree of state intervention and regulation which nobody wants. Let me conclude then, by sketching out the kind of response required.

It cannot be denied that the present organization of British trade unions presents many serious obstacles. Their lack of control over the behavior of their shop stewards and the groups they represent is partly due to the complexities of trade union structure which, despite a new wave of mergers, still lead in most cases to multiunionism in the plant. When the members of one work group belong to three different unions like the 40 maintenance welders in my Fawley study, the point of absolute absurdity is reached. The absence of factory-based branches in many unions is another factor hampering union control. When a branch that is the basic unit in union administration consists of several small groups of members from a number of different factories and offices, it cannot have much influence on any of them, and the independence of work groups is enhanced.

But the most important factor in internal union organization is the low ratio of union officials to stewards and members. In the United Kingdom the average ratio is one official for every 3,800 members, as compared with 1,400 in the United States. We have in all about 3,000 full-time union officers and about 175,000 stewards or their equivalent.[23] On a rough calculation, shop stewards, because there are so many more of them, spend in total six to seven times more hours in servicing union members than do full-time union officers.[24] Small wonder that, when they conflict, the influence of the trade union may prove to be weaker than the influence of the work group to whom the steward is immediately responsible.

How could the pace of reform in trade union organization be forced? Not by legal compulsion, unless one is prepared to envisage a degree of state control that would make a mockery of free trade unionism. In the main it has to be induced, and the incentives are

---

[23] *Id.* at pp. 188-190.

[24] The Royal Commission's inquiry showed that the average number of hours per week spent by stewards on union business was six; four in working time or during breaks and two in the stewards' own. (Government Social Survey, *Workplace Industrial Relations*, (London: HMSO, March 1968), p. 16.) An earlier, less reliable, estimate of the average hours worked by full-time union officers was 57 per week (*Trade Union Officers*, note 5, *supra*, p. 90). This probably overstates the time they spend on union business, but accepting it the minimum figure in the above calculation holds.

most likely to come, as they have in the past, from changes in the organization of collective bargaining. At the 1966 Trades Union Congress, George Woodcock, its general secretary, told the full-time union officers who compose most of the delegates:

> "I will tell you flatly to your faces, you will go through the motions as unions and you will boast yourselves as unions, and already many of your members are getting three times as much as you have negotiated for them. . . . The trade union movement is being transformed, if not eroded, because of your lack of control already." [25]

The mode of growth of workplace bargaining in Britain has resulted in a pull down of authority in trade unions. It follows that the reversing of this trend will depend: *first,* on a more active involvement of the unions as unions in plant affairs, which is implicit in the conclusion of formal plant agreements; *second,* on a considerable increase in the number of full-time union officers that this in turn will necessitate; and *third,* on financing the increase by substantially higher union dues that union members will be more ready to pay when they see their full-time officers negotiating improvements for them along with their stewards. They seldom see them now, and when they do it is usually after a stoppage in a conflict situation, when the officials are trying to get them to return to work.

This brings me back to the most important theme in the Donovan Commission's report. In my own words, the Commission is saying that the responsibility for irresponsibility in industrial relations must be traced back to the board room, even though its effects may be displayed on the shop floor. Trade unions by themselves cannot initiate the necessary reforms in the structure and content of collective bargaining, although these offer the most promising approach by inducing them through situational pressures to reform their own organization. Boards of directors must first decide, particularly in the large companies, to put their own houses in order, to give industrial relations the priority it warrants in modern professional management. And let me add in parentheses that attitudes in the board room will also be the decisive factor in the reform of employers' associations. The Commission is not asking managements to be idealistic. First and foremost it is asking them to be realistic, to take a realistic view of existing power relations and of their own responsibilities to improve the economic performance of their companies.

For one thing is certain. The democratic challenge coming from the work group cannot be eliminated or suppressed, any more than could the earlier challenge coming principally from the trade unions.

---

[25] *Trades Union Congress Report* (London: 1965), p. 494.

The development of appropriate institutions within the company for a continuing reconciliation of the interests of different groups of employees so as to keep the inevitable conflict within reasonable bounds is a prime responsibility of management. Not that peace is the supreme aim. Peace comes as a byproduct of consistency, understanding, and fair treatment, which may demand a readiness to resist unreasonable demands. Nor is it only a question of attitudes. The most difficult problems are problems of managerial organization which, with the growth of scale, call for the highest expertise and the fullest use of the findings of social science.

From this point of view I have always argued that managements get the shop stewards they deserve. It may not be entirely true, but it is wiser for managements to act as if it were. The remarkable postwar paradox of British management is that, by insisting on the fiction of defending its earlier prerogatives, it has in fact merely succeeded in forfeiting them. In the extreme cases it has ended up by losing effective control over pay and work, and therefore over labor costs. Irresponsible management has proved to be ineffective management. Perhaps there is a simple moral to this, one which I suspect has fairly universal validity. Management should talk less about its rights and think more about its responsibilities.

APPENDIX 1

OTHER PARTICIPANTS IN THE
LOYOLA CONFERENCE ON BUSINESS AND LAW
Highland Park, Ill., July 7-12, 1968

Program speakers whose talks do not appear in this book:

C. C. MacArthur, Manager of Labor Relations
International Telephone and Telegraph Company
New York:
  "A Corporate View of Controlling Compensation Costs in Western Europe"

Jean-Louis Mandereau, Consul General of France
Chicago:
  "The French General Strike of 1968"

Jerrold L. Sager, Management Attorney
Chicago:
  "The American Management Lawyer in Western Europe"

Arthur Ll. Wilbraham, Management Consultant
Brussels:
  "Executive Compensation in Western Europe"

Other Participants in Plenary Sessions and Seminars:

William T. Aber, Personnel Manager
Travenol Laboratories International
(Baxter Laboratories)
Morton Grove, Ill.

Dr. Charles W. Anrod, Professor of Economics (Emeritus)
Loyola University of Chicago

Carole K. Bellows, Lawyer
Chicago

Carl Bevernage, Assistant to the Director
Institute for Labor Relations
University of Leuven Law School
Leuven

F. Virgil Boyd, Dean
School of Business Administration
Loyola University of Chicago

Lee M. Burkey, Union Attorney
Chicago

John Carroll, Chief Industrial Officer
Irish Transport and General Workers Union
Dublin

William Cavers, Regional Attorney
National Labor Relations Board
Chicago

Connolly Cole, Deputy Director
Industrial Development Authority of Ireland
Chicago

Rev. William C. Cunningham, S.J.
Assistant Professor
The Law School of Loyola University of Chicago

H. J. Hebden, Director
Personnel and Industrial Relations
Massey-Ferguson (United Kingdom) Ltd.
Coventry, England

503

Professor Jordan Jay Hillman
The Law School of Northwestern
     University
Chicago

Donald M. Irwin, Labor Economist
John Deere Company
Moline, Ill.

Malcolm S. Kamin, Management
     Attorney
Chicago

Arthur J. Kelley, Jr., Consultant
International Employee and Labor
     Relations
General Electric Company
New York

Fintan Kennedy, General Secretary
Irish Transport and General Work-
     ers Union
Dublin

William L. Lamey, Dean
The Law School of Loyola Univer-
     sity of Chicago

Arthur G. Leisten, Assistant Profes-
     sor
The Law School of Loyola Univer-
     sity of Chicago

William F. Lemke, Professor of
     Law
The Law School of Loyola Univer-
     sity of Chicago

Bert L. Luskin, Past President
National Academy of Arbitrators
Chicago

Arthur Malinowski, Associate Pro-
     fessor
Institute of Industrial Relations
Loyola University of Chicago

Kenneth C. McGuiness, Manage-
     ment Attorney
Washington, D. C.

Edward B. Miller, Management
     Attorney
Chicago

Brian O'Kelly, Consul General of
     Ireland
Chicago

George M. Oostdyk, President
Forge & Machine Workers Indus-
     trial Union
Cicero, Ill.

Arnold Ordman, General Counsel
National Labor Relations Board
Washington, D. C.

Henri Perdieus
Consul General of Belgium
Chicago

Joanne H. Saunders, Attorney
Wage and Hour and Public Con-
     tracts Division
U. S. Department of Labor
Chicago

Paul B. Schechter, Assistant
Legal Department
Chicago City College

Martin H. Schneid
Assistant to Regional Director
National Labor Relations Board
Chicago

Truman G. Searle, Management
     Attorney
Rochester, New York

A. C. Smith, Manager
Industrial Relations, Foreign Op-
     erations
Aluminum Company of America
     (ALCOA)
Pittsburgh, Pa.

John Stanek, Director of Survey
     Programs
Industrial Relations Center
University of Chicago

H. R. Templeton, Vice President
     — Industrial Relations
Taylor Forge, Inc. (Subsidiary Gulf
     + Western Industries)
Chicago

Solomon Tisdale, Auditor
Welfare and Retirement Plans of
     Local 189
Service Employees International
     Union
Chicago

Vincent F. Vitullo, Assistant Dean
The Law School of Loyola University of Chicago

John D. Wilson, Supervisor, Pension Plans
Chrysler Corporation
Detroit, Mich.

Minor K. Wilson, Attorney
Chicago City College

Wayne L. Wright, Manager
Components Industrial Relations
Texas Instruments, Inc.
Dallas, Tex.

APPENDIX 2

PERTINENT ARTICLES OF THE TREATY ESTABLISHING THE EUROPEAN ECONOMIC COMMUNITY (TREATY OF ROME, MARCH 25, 1957) *

PART TWO—BASES OF THE COMMUNITY

* * *

Title II. Agriculture

ARTICLE 38

1. The Common Market shall extend to agriculture and trade in agricultural products. Agricultural products shall mean the products of the soil, of stock-breeding and of fisheries as well as products after the first processing stage which are directly connected with such products.

2. Save where there are provisions to the contrary in Articles 39 to 46 inclusive, the rules laid down for the establishment of the Common Market shall apply to agricultural products.

3. Products subject to the provisions of Articles 39 to 46 inclusive are listed in Annex II to this Treaty. Within a period of two years after the date of the entry into force of this Treaty the Council, acting by means of a qualified majority vote on a proposal of the Commission, shall decide as to the products to be added to that list.

4. The functioning and development of the Common Market in respect of agricultural products shall be accompanied by the establishment of a common agricultural policy among the Member States.

ARTICLE 39

1. The common agricultural policy shall have as its objectives:

(a) to increase agricultural productivity by developing technical progress and by ensuring the rational development of agricultural production and the optimum utilisation of the factors of production, particularly labour;

(b) to ensure thereby a fair standard of living for the agricultural population, particularly by the increasing of the individual earnings of persons engaged in agriculture;

---

*The editor has selected only those provisions referred to by contributors to this volume, notably J. D. Neirinck and G. M. J. Veldkamp. The translation in English, taken from the document prepared by the publishing services of the European Communities for the convenience of English-speaking peoples, is entirely unofficial and has no legal authority. Valid versions of the Treaty are those drawn up, executed, and ratified in the four languages of EEC: Dutch, French, German, and Italian.

(c) to stabilise markets;

(d) to guarantee regular supplies; and

(e) to ensure reasonable prices in supplies to consumers.

2. In working out the common agricultural policy and the special methods which it may involve, due account shall be taken of:

(a) the particular character of agricultural activities, arising from the social structure of agriculture and from structural and natural disparities between the various agricultural regions;

(b) the need to make the appropriate adjustments gradually; and

(c) the fact that in Member States agriculture constitutes a sector which is closely linked with the economy as a whole.

* * *

Title III. The Free Movement of Persons, Services and Capital

CHAPTER 1. WORKERS

ARTICLE 48

1. The free movement of workers shall be ensured within the Community not later than at the date of the expiry of the transitional period.

2. This shall involve the abolition of any discrimination based on nationality between workers of the Member States as regards employment, remuneration, and other working conditions.

3. It shall include the right, subject to limitations justified by reasons of public order, public safety and public health:

(a) to accept offers of employment actually made;

(b) to move about freely for this purpose within the territory of Member States;

(c) to stay in any Member State in order to carry on an employment in conformity with the legislative and administrative provisions governing the employment of the workers of that State; and

(d) to live, on conditions which shall be the subject of implementing regulations to be laid down by the Commission, in the territory of a Member State after having been employed there.

4. The provisions of this Article shall not apply to employment in the public administration.

ARTICLE 49

Upon the entry into force of this Treaty, the Council, acting on a proposal of the Commission and after the Economic and Social Committee has been consulted, shall, by means of directives or regulations, lay down the measures necessary to effect progressively the free movement of workers, as defined in the preceding Article, in particular:

(a) by ensuring close collaboration between national labor administrations;

(b) by progressively abolishing according to a plan any such administrative procedures and practices and also any such time limits in respect of eligibility for available employment as are applied as a result either of municipal law or of agreements previously concluded between Member States and the maintenance of which would be an obstacle to the freeing of the movement of workers;

(c) by progressively abolishing according to a plan all such time-limits and other restrictions provided for either under municipal law or under agreements previously concluded between Member States as impose on workers of other Member States conditions for the free choice of employment different from these imposed on workers of the State concerned; and

(d) by setting up appropriate machinery for connecting offers of employment and requests for employment, with a view to equilibrating them in such a way as to avoid serious threats to the standard of living and employment in the various regions and industries.

ARTICLE 50

Member States shall, under a common program, encourage the exchange of young workers.

ARTICLE 51

The Council, acting by means of a unanimous vote on a proposal of the Commission, shall, in the field of social security, adopt the measures necessary to effect the free movement of workers, in particular, by introducing a system which permits an assurance to be given to migrant workers and their beneficiaries:

(a) that, for the purposes of qualifying for and retaining the right to benefits and of the calculation of these benefits, all periods taken into consideration by the respective municipal law of the countries concerned, shall be added together; and

(b) that these benefits will be paid to persons resident in the territories of Member States.

*   *   *

Title IV. Transport

ARTICLE 74

The objectives of this Treaty shall, with regard to the subject covered by this Title, be pursued by the Member States within the framework of a common transport policy.

ARTICLE 75

1. With a view to implementing Article 74 and taking due account of the special aspects of transport, the Council, acting on a proposal of the Commission and after the Economic and Social Committee and the Assembly have been consulted, shall, until the end of the second stage by means of a unanimous vote and subsequently by means of a qualified majority vote, lay down:

(a) common rules applicable to international transport effected from or to the territory of a Member State or crossing the territory of one or more Member States;

(b) conditions for the admission of non-resident carriers to national transport services within a Member State; and

(c) any other appropriate provisions.

2. The provisions referred to under (a) and (b) of the preceding paragraph shall be laid down in the course of the transitional period.

3. Notwithstanding the procedure provided for in paragraph 1, provisions which relate to the principles governing transport and the application of which might seriously affect the standard of living and the level of employment in certain regions and also the utilisation of transport equipment, shall, due account being taken of the need for adaptation to economic developments resulting from the establishment of the Common Market, be laid down by the Council acting by means of a unanimous vote.

PART THREE — POLICY OF THE COMMUNITY

Title I. Common Rules

CHAPTER 1. RULES GOVERNING COMPETITION

*   *   *

SECTION 3 — Aids Granted by States

ARTICLE 92

1. Except where otherwise provided for in this Treaty, any aid, granted by a Member State or granted by means of State resources, in any manner whatsoever, which distorts or threatens to distort competition by favoring certain enterprises or certain productions shall, to the extent to which it adversely affects trade between Member States, be deemed to be incompatible with the Common Market

2. The following shall be deemed to be compatible with the Common Market:

(a) aids of a social character granted to individual consumers, provided that such aids are granted without any discrimination based on the origin of the products concerned;

(b) aids intended to remedy damage caused by natural calamities or other extraordinary events; or

(c) aids granted to the economy of certain regions of the Federal Republic of Germany affected by the division of Germany, to the extent that such aids are necessary in order to compensate for the economic disadvantages caused by such division.

3. The following may be deemed to be compatible with the Common Market:

(a) aids intended to promote the economic development of regions where the standard of living is abnormally low or where there exists serious under-employment;

(b) aids intended to promote the execution of important projects of common European interest or to remedy a serious disturbance of the economy of a Member State;

(c) aids intended to facilitate the development of certain activities or of certain economic regions, provided that such aids do not change trading conditions to such a degree as would be contrary to the common interest.

Any aids to shipbuilding existing on 1 January 1957 shall, to the extent that such aids merely offset the absence of customs protection, be progressively reduced under the same conditions as apply to the abolition of customs duties, subject to the provisions of this Treaty relating to the common commercial policy in regard to third countries; and

(d) such other categories of aids as may be specified by decision of the Council acting by means of a qualified majority vote on a proposal of the Commission.

ARTICLE 93

1. The Commission shall, together with Member States, constantly examine all systems of aids existing in those States. It shall propose to the latter any appropriate measure required by the progressive development or by the functioning of the Common Market.

2. If, after having given notice to the parties concerned to submit their comments, the Commission finds that any aid granted by a State or by means of State resources is not compatible with the Common Market within the meaning of Article 92, or that such aid is applied in an improper manner, it shall decide that the State concerned shall abolish or modify such aid within the time-limit prescribed by the Commission.

If the State concerned does not comply with this decision within the prescribed time-limit, the Commission or any other interested State may, notwithstanding the provisions of Articles 169 and 170, refer the matter to the Court of Justice directly.

At the request of any Member State, the Council, acting by means of a unanimous vote, may, if such a decision is justified by exceptional circumstances, decide that any aid instituted or to be instituted by that State shall be deemed to be compatible with the Common Market, notwithstanding the provisions of Article 92 or the regulations provided for in Article 94. If the Commission has, in respect of the aid concerned, already initiated the procedure provided for in the first sub-paragraph of this paragraph, the request made to the Council by the State concerned shall cause such procedure to be suspended until the Council has made its attitude known.

If, however, the Council has not made its attitude known within a period of three months from such request, the Commission shall act.

3. The Commission shall be informed, in due time to enable it to submit its comments, of any plans to institute or to modify aids. If it considers that any such plan is not compatible with the Common Market within the meaning of Article 92, it shall without delay initiate the procedure provided for in the preceding paragraph. The Member State concerned may not put its proposed measures into effect until such procedure shall have resulted in a final decision.

ARTICLE 94

The Council, acting by means of a qualified majority vote on a proposal of the Commission, may make any appropriate regulations with a view to the application of Articles 92 and 93 and may, in particular, fix the conditions of the application of Article 93, paragraph 3, and the categories of aids which are exempt from this procedure.

*   *   *

CHAPTER 3. APPROXIMATION OF LAWS

ARTICLE 100

The Council, acting by means of a unanimous vote on a proposal of the Commission, shall issue directives for the approximation of such legislative and administrative provisions of the Member States as have a direct incidence on the establishment or functioning of the Common Market.

The Assembly and the Economic and Social Committee shall be consulted concerning any directives whose implementation in one or more of the Member States would involve amendment of legislative provisions.

ARTICLE 101

Where the Commission finds that a disparity existing between the legislative or administrative provisions of the Member States distorts the conditions of competition in the Common Market and thereby causes a state of affairs which must be eliminated, it shall enter into consultation with the interested Member States.

If such consultation does not result in an agreement which eliminates the particular distortion, the Council, acting during the first stage by means of a unanimous vote and subsequently by means of a qualified majority vote on a proposal of the Commission, shall issue the directives necessary for this purpose. The Commission and the Council may take any other appropriate measures provided for in this Treaty.

ARTICLE 102

1. Where there is reason to fear that the enactment or amendment of a legislative or administrative provision will cause a distortion within the meaning of the preceding Article, the Member State desiring to proceed therewith shall consult the Commission. After consulting the Member States, the Commission shall recommend to the States concerned such measures as may be appropriate to avoid the particular distortion.

2. If the State desiring to enact or amend its own provisions does not comply with the recommendation made to it by the Commission, other Member States may not be requested, in application of Article 101 to amend their own provisions in order to eliminate such distortion. If the Member State which has ignored the Commission's recommendation causes a distortion to its own detriment only, the provisions of Article 101 shall not apply.

Title II. Economic Policy

* * *

CHAPTER 2. BALANCE OF PAYMENTS

ARTICLE 104

Each Member State shall pursue the economic policy necessary to ensure the equilibrium of its overall balance of payments and to maintain confidence in its currency, while ensuring a high level of employment and the stability of the level of prices.

ARTICLE 105

1. In order to facilitate the attainment of the objectives stated in Article 104, Member States shall co-ordinate their economic policies. They

shall for this purpose institute a collaboration between the competent services of their administrative departments and between their central banks.

The Commission shall submit to the Council recommendations for the bringing into effect of such collaboration. . . .

*   *   *

Title III. Social Policy

CHAPTER 1. SOCIAL PROVISIONS

ARTICLE 117

Member States hereby agree upon the necessity to promote improvement of the living and working conditions of labour so as to permit the equalisation of such conditions in an upward direction.

They consider that such a development will result not only from the functioning of the Common Market which will favour the harmonisation of social systems, but also from the procedures provided for under this Treaty and from the approximation of legislative and administrative provisions.

ARTICLE 118

Without prejudice to the other provisions of this Treaty and in conformity with its general objectives, it shall be the aim of the Commission to promote close collaboration between Member States in the social field, particularly in matters relating to:

—employment,
—labour legislation and working conditions,
—occupational and continuation training,
—social security,
—protection against occupational accidents and diseases,
—industrial hygiene,
—the law as to trade union, and collective bargaining between employers and workers.

For this purpose, the Commission shall act in close contact with Member States by means of studies, the issuing of opinions, and the organising of consultations both on problems arising at the national level and on those of concern to international organisations.

Before issuing the opinions provided for under this Article, the Commission shall consult the Economic and Social Committee.

ARTICLE 119

Each Member State shall in the course of the first stage ensure and subsequently maintain the application of the principle of equal remuneration for equal work as between men and women workers.

For the purposes of this Article, remuneration shall mean the ordinary basic or minimum wage or salary and any additional emoluments whatsoever payable directly or indirectly, whether in cash or in kind, by the employer to the worker and arising out of the worker's employment.

Equal remuneration without discrimination based on sex means:

(a) that remuneration for the same work at piece-rates shall be calculated on the basis of the same unit of measurement; and

(b) that remuneration for work at time-rates shall be the same for the same job.

ARTICLE 120

Member States shall endeavour to maintain the existing equivalence of paid holiday schemes.

ARTICLE 121

The Council, acting by means of a unanimous vote after consulting the Economic and Social Committee, may assign to the Commission functions relating to the implementation of common measures, particularly in regard to the social security of the migrant workers referred to in Articles 48 to 51 inclusive.

ARTICLE 122

The Commission shall, in its annual report to the Assembly, include a special chapter on the development of the social situation within the Community.

The Assembly may invite the Commission to draw up reports on special problems concerning the social situation.

CHAPTER 2. THE EUROPEAN SOCIAL FUND

ARTICLE 123

In order to improve opportunities of employment of workers in the Common Market and thus contribute to raising the standard of living, a European Social Fund shall hereby be established in accordance with the provision set out below; it shall have the task of promoting within the Community employment facilities and the geographical and occupational mobility of workers.

ARTICLE 124

The administration of the Fund shall be incumbent on the Commission.

The Commission shall be assisted in this task by a Committee presided over by a member of the Commission and composed of representatives of Governments, trade unions and employers' associations.

ARTICLE 125

1. At the request of a Member State, the Fund shall, within the framework of the rules provided for in Article 127, cover 50 per cent of expenses incurred after the entry into force of this Treaty by that State or by a body under public law for the purpose of:

(a) ensuring productive re-employment of workers by means of:
—occupational re-training,
—resettlement allowances; and

(b) granting aids for the benefit of workers whose employment is temporarily reduced or wholly or partly suspended as a result of the conversion of their enterprise to other productions, in order that they may maintain the same wage-level pending their full re-employment.

2. The assistance granted by the Fund towards the cost of occupational re-training shall be conditional upon the impossibility of employing the unemployed workers otherwise than in a new occupation and upon their having been in productive employment for a period of at least six months in the occupation for which they have been re-trained.

The assistance granted in respect of resettlement allowances shall be conditional upon the unemployed workers having been obliged to change their residence within the Community and upon their having been in productive employment for a period of at least six months in their new place of residence.

The assistance given for the benefit of workers in cases where an enterprise is converted shall be subject to the following conditions:

(a) that the workers concerned have again been fully employed in that enterprise for a period of at least six months;

(b) that the Government concerned has previously submitted a plan, drawn up by such enterprise, for its conversion and for the financing thereof; and

(c) that the Commission has given its prior approval to such conversion plan.

ARTICLE 126

At the expiry of the transitional period, the Council, on the basis of an opinion of the Commission and after the Economic and Social Committee and the Assembly have consulted, may:

(a) acting by means of a qualified majority vote, rule that all or part of the assistance referred to in Article 125 shall no longer be granted; or

(b) acting by means of a unanimous vote, determine the new tasks which may be entrusted to the Fund within the framework of its mandate as defined in Article 123.

ARTICLE 127

On a proposal of the Commission and after the Economic and Social Committee and the Assembly have been consulted, the Council, acting by means of a qualified majority vote, shall lay down the provisions necessary for the implementation of Articles 124 to 126 inclusive; in particular, it shall fix details concerning the conditions under which the assistance of the Fund shall be granted in accordance with the terms of Article 125 and also concerning the categories of enterprises whose workers shall benefit from the aids provided for in Article 125, paragraph 1 (b).

ARTICLE 128

The Council shall, on a proposal of the Commission and after the Economic and Social Committee has been consulted, establish general principles for the implementation of a common policy of occupational training capable of contributing to the harmonious development both of national economies and of the Common Market.

*   *   *

PART FIVE — INSTITUTIONS OF THE COMMUNITY

Title I. Provisions Governing Institutions

CHAPTER 1. INSTITUTIONS

Section 1—The Assembly

ARTICLE 137

The Assembly, which shall be composed of representatives of the peoples of the States united within the Community, shall exercise the powers of deliberation and of control which are conferred upon it by this Treaty.

ARTICLE 138

1. The Assembly shall be composed of delegates whom the Parliaments shall be called upon to appoint from among their members in accordance with the procedure laid down by each Member State.

2. The number of these delegates shall be fixed as follows:

Belgium	14
Germany	36
France	36
Italy	36
Luxembourg	6
Netherlands	14

3. The Assembly shall draw up proposals for election by direct universal suffrage in accordance with a uniform procedure in all Member States.

The Council, acting by means of a unanimous vote, shall determine the provisions which it shall recommend to Member States for adoption in accordance with their respective constitutional rules.

ARTICLE 139

The Assembly shall hold an annual session. It shall meet as of right on the third Tuesday in October.

The Assembly may meet in extraordinary session at the request of a majority of its members or at the request of the Council or of the Commission.

ARTICLE 140

The Assembly shall appoint its President and its officers from among its members.

Members of the Commission may attend all meetings and shall, at their request, be heard on behalf of the Commission.

The Commission shall reply orally or in writing to questions put to it by the Assembly or its members.

The Council shall be heard by the Assembly under the conditions which the Council shall lay down in its rules of procedure.

ARTICLE 141

Except where otherwise provided for in this Treaty, the Assembly shall act by means of an absolute majority of the votes cast.

The quorum shall be laid down in the rules of procedure.

ARTICLE 142

The Assembly shall adopt its rules of procedure by a vote of the majority of its members.

The records of the Assembly shall be published in accordance with the provisions of its rules of procedure.

ARTICLE 143

The Assembly shall discuss in public meeting the annual general report submitted to it by the Commission.

ARTICLE 144

If a motion of censure concerning the activities of the Commission is introduced in the Assembly, a vote may be taken thereon only after a period of not less than three days following its introduction, and such vote shall be by open ballot.

If the motion of censure is adopted by a two-thirds majority of the votes cast, representing a majority of the members of the Assembly, the members of the Commission shall resign their office in a body. They shall continue to carry out current business until their replacement in accordance with the provisions of Article 158 has taken place.

Section 2 — The Council

ARTICLE 145

With a view to ensuring the achievement of the objectives laid down in this Treaty, and under the conditions provided for therein, the Council shall:

—ensure the coordination of the general economic policies of the Member States; and

—dispose of a power of decision.

ARTICLE 146

The Council shall be composed of representatives of the Member States. Each Government shall delegate to it one of its members.

The office of President shall be exercised for a term of six months by each member of the Council in rotation according to the alphabetical order of the Member States.

ARTICLE 147

Meetings of the Council shall be called by the President acting on his own initiative or at the request of a member or of the Commission.

ARTICLE 148

1. Except where otherwise provided for in this Treaty, the conclusions of the Council shall be reached by a majority vote of its members.

2. Where conclusions of the Council require a qualified majority, the votes of its members shall be weighted as follows:

Belgium	2
Germany	4
France	4
Italy	4
Luxembourg	1
Netherlands	2

Majorities shall be required for the adoption of any conclusions as follows:

—twelve votes in cases where this Treaty requires a previous proposal of the Commission, or

—twelve votes including a favorable vote by at least four members in all other cases.

3. Abstentions by members either present or represented shall not prevent the adoption of Council conclusions requiring unanimity.

ARTICLE 149

When, pursuant to this Treaty, the Council acts on a proposal of the Commission, it shall, where the amendment of such proposal is involved, act only by means of a unanimous vote.

As long as the Council has not so acted, the Commission may amend its original proposal, particularly in cases where the Assembly has been consulted on the proposal concerned.

ARTICLE 150

In case of a vote, any member of the Council may act as proxy for not more than one other member.

ARTICLE 151

The Council shall adopt its rules of procedure.

These rules of procedure may provide for the establishment of a committee composed of representatives of Member States. The Council shall determine the task and competence of that committee.

ARTICLE 152

The Council may request the Commission to undertake any studies which the Council considers desirable for the achievement of the common objectives, and to submit to it any appropriate proposals.

ARTICLE 153

The Council shall, after obtaining the opinion of the Commission, lay down the status of the Committees provided for in this Treaty.

ARTICLE 154

The Council, acting by means of a qualified majority vote, shall fix the salaries, allowances and pensions of the President and members of the Commission, and of the President, judges, advocates-general and registrar of the Court of Justice. The Council shall also fix, by means of the same majority, any allowances to be granted in lieu of remuneration.

Section 3 — The Commission

ARTICLE 155

With a view to ensuring the functioning and development of the Common Market, the Commission shall:

—ensure the application of the provisions of this Treaty and of the provisions enacted by the institutions of the Community in pursuance thereof;

—formulate recommendations or opinions in matters which are the subject of this Treaty, where the latter expressly so provides or where the Commission considers it necessary;

—under the conditions laid down in this Treaty dispose of a power of decision of its own and participate in the preparation of acts of the Council and of the Assembly; and

—exercise the competence conferred on it by the Council for the implementation of the rules laid down by the latter.

ARTICLE 156

The Commission shall annually, not later than one month before the opening of the Assembly session, publish a general report on the activities of the Community.

ARTICLE 157

1. The Commission shall be composed of nine members chosen for their general competence and of indisputable independence.

The number of members of the Commission may be amended by a unanimous vote of the Council.

Only nationals of Member States may be members of the Commission.

The Commission may not include more than two members having the nationality of the same State.

2. The members of the Commission shall perform their duties in the general interest of the Community with complete independence.

In the performance of their duties, they shall not seek or accept instructions from any Government or other body. They shall refrain from any action incompatible with the character of their duties. Each Member State undertakes to respect this character and not to seek to influence the members of the Commission in the performance of their duties.

The members of the Commission may not, during their term of office, engage in any other paid or unpaid professional activity. When entering upon their duties, they shall give a solemn undertaking that, both during and after their term of office, they will respect the obligations resulting therefrom and in particular the duty of exercising honesty and discretion as regards the acceptance, after their term of office, of certain functions or advantages. Should these obligations not be respected, the Court of Justice, on the application of the Council or of the Commission, may according to circumstances rule that the member concerned either be removed from office in accordance with the provisions of Article 160 or forfeit his right to a pension or other advantages in lieu thereof.

ARTICLE 158

The members of the Commission shall be appointed by the Governments of Member States acting in common agreement.

Their term of office shall be for a period of four years. It shall be renewable.

ARTICLE 159

Apart from retirements in regular rotation and the case of death the duties of a member of the Commission shall be terminated in individual cases by voluntary resignation or by removal from office.

Vacancies thus caused shall be filled for the remainder of the term of office. The Council, acting by means of a unanimous vote, may decide that such vacancies need not be filled.

Except in the case of removal from office referred to in Article 160, a member of the Commission shall remain in office until provision has been made for his replacement.

ARTICLE 160

If any member of the Commission no longer fulfils the conditions required for the performance of his duties or if he commits a serious offense, the Court of Justice, acting on a petition of the Council or of the Commission, may declare him removed from office.

In such case the Council, acting by means of a unanimous vote, may provisionally suspend the member from his duties and make provision for his replacement pending the ruling of the Court of Justice.

The Court of Justice may, on a petition of the Council or of the Commission, provisionally suspend such member from his duties.

ARTICLE 161

The President and the two Vice-Presidents of the Commission shall be appointed from among its members for a term of two years in accordance with the same procedure as that laid down for the appointment of members of the Commission. Their term of office shall be renewable.

Except in the case of an entire renewal of the Commission, such appointments shall be made after the Commission has been consulted.

In the event of resignation or death, the President and the Vice-Presidents shall be replaced for the remainder of their terms of office in accordance with the procedure laid down in the first paragraph of this Article.

ARTICLE 162

The Council and the Commission shall consult each other and shall settle by mutual agreement the particulars of their collaboration.

The Commission shall adopt its rules of procedure with a view to ensuring its own functioning and that of its services in accordance with the provisions of this Treaty. It shall be responsible for the publication of its rules of procedure.

ARTICLE 163

The conclusions of the Commission shall be reached by a majority of the number of members provided for in Article 157.

A meeting of the Commission shall only be valid if the number of members laid down in its rules of procedure are present.

Section 4 — The Court of Justice

ARTICLE 164

The Court of Justice shall ensure observance of law and justice in the interpretation and application of this Treaty.

ARTICLE 165

The Court of Justice shall be composed of seven judges.

The Court of Justice shall sit in plenary session. It may, however, set up chambers, each composed of three or five judges, in order either to conduct certain enquiries or to judge certain categories of cases in accordance with provisions to be laid down in rules for this purpose.

The Court of Justice shall, however, always sit in plenary session in order to hear cases submitted to it by a Member State or by one of the institutions of the Community or to deal with preliminary questions submitted to it pursuant to Article 177.

Should the Court of Justice so request, the Council may, by means of a unanimous vote, increase the number of judges and make the requisite amendments to the second and third paragraphs of this Article and to Article 167, second paragraph.

ARTICLE 166

The Court of Justice shall be assisted by two advocates-general.

The duty of the advocate-general shall be to present publicly, with complete impartiality and independence, reasoned conclusions on cases submitted to the Court of Justice with a view to assisting the latter in the performance of its duties as laid down in Article 164.

Should the Court of Justice so request, the Council may, by means of a unanimous vote, increase the number of advocates-general and make the requisite amendments to Article 167, third paragraph.

ARTICLE 167

The judges and the advocates-general shall be chosen from among persons of indisputable independence who fulfil the conditions required for the holding of the highest judicial office in their respective countries or who are jurists of recognized competence; they shall be appointed for a term of six years by the Governments of Member States acting in common agreement.

A partial renewal of the Court of Justice shall take place every three years. It shall affect three and four judges alternately. The three judges whose terms of office are to expire at the end of the first period of three years shall be chosen by lot.

A partial renewal of the advocates-general shall take place every three years. The advocate-general whose term of office is to expire at the end of the first period of three years shall be chosen by lot.

The retiring judges and advocates-general shall be eligible for reappointment.

The judges shall appoint from among their members the President of the Court of Justice for a term of three years. Such term shall be renewable.

ARTICLE 168

The Court of Justice shall appoint its registrar and determine his status.

ARTICLE 169

If the Commission considers that a Member State has failed to fulfil any of its obligations under this Treaty, it shall give a reasoned opinion on the matter after requiring such State to submit its comments.

If such State does not comply with the terms of such opinion within the period laid down by the Commission, the latter may refer the matter to the Court of Justice.

ARTICLE 170

Any Member State which considers that another Member State has failed to fulfil any of its obligations under this Treaty may refer the matter to the Court of Justice.

Before a Member State institutes, against another Member State, proceedings relating to an alleged infringement of the obligations under this Treaty, it shall refer the matter to the Commission.

The Commission shall give a reasoned opinion after the States concerned have been required to submit their comments in written and oral pleadings.

If the Commission, within a period of three months after the date of reference of the matter to it, has not given an opinion, reference to the Court of Justice shall not thereby be prevented.

* * *

ARTICLE 175

In the event of the Council or the Commission in violation of this Treaty failing to act, the Member States and the other institutions of the Community may refer the matter to the Court of Justice with a view to establishing such violation.

Such appeal shall only be admissible if the institution concerned has previously been invited to act. If, at the expiry of a period of two months after such invitation that institution has not stated its attitude, the appeal may be lodged within a further period of two months.

Any natural or legal person may submit to the Court of Justice, under the conditions laid down in the preceding paragraphs, a complaint to the effect that one of the institutions of the Community has failed to address to him an act other than a recommendation or an opinion.

ARTICLE 176

An institution originating an act subsequently declared null and void or an institution whose failure to act has been declared contrary to the provisions of this Treaty shall take the measures required for the implementation of the judgment of the Court of Justice.

This obligation shall not affect any obligation arising from the application of Article 215, second paragraph.

ARTICLE 177

The Court of Justice shall be competent to make a preliminary decision concerning:

(a) the interpretation of this Treaty;

(b) the validity and interpretation of acts of the institutions of the Community; and

(c) the interpretation of the statutes of any bodies set up by an act of the Council, where such statutes so provide.

Where any such question is raised before a court or tribunal of one of the Member States, such court or tribunal may, if it considers that its judgment depends on a preliminary decision on this question, request the Court of Justice to give a ruling thereon.

Where any such question is raised in a case pending before a domestic court or tribunal from whose decisions no appeal lies under municipal law, such court or tribunal shall refer the matter to the Court of Justice.

ARTICLE 178

The Court of Justice shall be competent to hear cases relating to compensation for damage as provided for in Article 215, second paragraph.

ARTICLE 179

The Court of Justice shall be competent to decide in any case between the Community and its employees, within the limits and under the conditions laid down by the relevant statute of service or conditions of employment.

*   *   *

ARTICLE 181

The Court of Justice shall be competent to make a decision pursuant to any arbitration clause contained in a contract concluded, under public or private law, by or on behalf of the Community.

ARTICLE 182

The Court of Justice shall be competent to decide in any dispute between Member States in connection with the object in this Treaty, where such dispute is submitted to it under the terms of a compromise.

ARTICLE 183

Subject to the powers conferred on the Court of Justice by this Treaty, cases to which the Community is a party shall not for that reason alone be excluded from the competence of domestic courts or tribunals.

ARTICLE 185

Appeals submitted to the Court of Justice shall not have any staying effect. The Court of Justice may, however, if it considers that circumstances so require, order the suspension of the execution of the act appealed against.

ARTICLE 186

The Court of Justice may, in any cases referred to it, make any necessary interim order.

ARTICLE 187

The judgments of the Court of Justice shall be enforceable under the conditions laid down in Article 192.

ARTICLE 188

The Statute of the Court of Justice shall be laid down in a separate Protocol.

The Court of Justice shall adopt its rules of procedure. They shall be submitted to the Council for unanimous approval.

APPENDIX 3

DIRECTORY OF ORGANIZATIONS AND AGENCIES CONCERNED WITH LABOR RELATIONS MATTERS

INTERGOVERNMENTAL ORGANIZATIONS

United Nations

United Nations Economic and Social Council
U. N. Plaza, First Avenue
New York, N. Y. 10017

United Nations Research Institute for Social Development
Palais des Nations
1211 Geneva 10, Switzerland

International Labour Organization (ILO)
154 rue de Lausanne
1211 Geneva 22, Switzerland

U. S. Branch Office of ILO
666 Eleventh Street, N. W.
Washington, D. C. 20001

International Institute for Labour Studies
154 rue de Lausanne
1211 Geneva 22, Switzerland

European Economic Community

Commission of the European Communities
23 Avenue de la Joyeuse Entrée
Brussels, Belgium

EEC Directorate General of Social Affairs
170 rue de la Loi
Brussels, Belgium

EEC Economic and Social Committee
3 Boulevard de l'Empereur
Brussels, Belgium

European Community Information Service
808 Farragut Building
Washington, D. C. 20006

Other

The Council of Europe
Place Lenôtre
Strasbourg, France

PRIVATE INTERNATIONAL ORGANIZATIONS

Employer Organizations

Council of European Industrial Federations
Conseil des fédérations industrielles d'Europe
3 Avenue Gribaumant
Brussels 15, Belgium

International Confederation of Senior Officials
Confédération Internationale des Corp de Fonctionaires
36 Boulevard Bischoffsheim
Brussels 1, Belgium

International Management Association
135 W. 50th Street
New York, N. Y. 10020

International Organization of Employers — IOE
98 rue de St. Jean
1201 Geneva, Switzerland

Union of Industries of EEC
Union des Industries de la Communauté Européenne — UNICE
4 rue Ravenstein
Brussels 1, Belgium

Employee Organizations

European Confederation of Free Trade Unions in the Community
(Formerly *Secretariat Syndical Européen* or European Community Trade Union Secretariat or ECTUS)
37-41 rue Montagne aux Herbes Potagères
Brussels 1, Belgium

International Confederation of Free Trade Unions — ICFTU
37-41 rue Montagne aux Herbes Potagères
Brussels 1, Belgium

International Confederation of Professional and Intellectual Workers
Confédération internationale des travailleurs intellectuels
1 rue de Courcelles
Paris 8e, France

International Metalworkers' Federation
54 bis Route des Acacias
Geneva, Switzerland

World Confederation of Labour (Formerly International Federation of Christian Trade Unions)
26 rue Juste Lipse
Brussels 4, Belgium

World Federation of Trade Unions
Nam. Curieovych 1
Prague 1, Czechoslovakia

World Union of Liberal Trade Union Organizations
Union mondiale des organisations syndicales sur base économique et social libérale
41 Badenerstrasse
Zurich 4, Switzerland

Other

European Association of National Productivity Centers
60 rue de la Concorde
Brussels 5, Belgium

European Movement
Mouvement européen
14 rue Duquesnoy
Bureaux 14-18
Brussels, Belgium

International Association for Social Progress
Association internationale pour le progrès social
47 rue Louvrex
Liège, Belgium

International Commission of Jurists
Commission internationale de juristes
2 Quai du Cheval-Blanc
Geneva, Switzerland

International Industrial Relations Association
154 rue de Lausanne
1211 Geneva 22, Switzerland

International Institute of Administrative Sciences
Institut internationale des sciences administratives
25 rue de la Charité
Brussels 4, Belgium

International Institute for Human Labor Problems
Institut international pour les problèmes humans du travail
9 rue Delvau
Namur, Belgium

International Juridical Institute
Institut juridique international
Permanent Office for the Supply of International Legal Information
6 Oranjestraat
The Hague, The Netherlands

International Society for Labour Law and Social Legislation
Société Internationale de Droit du Travail et de la Sécurité Sociale
4 place du Molard
Geneva, Switzerland

BELGIUM

Government

Ministry of Employment and Labor
Ministère de l'Émploi et du Travail
2 rue Lambèrmond
Brussels 1

Ministry of Social Security
Ministère de Prèvoyance Sociale
123 rue Royale
Brussels

Industrial Section
Belgian Consulate General
50 Rockefeller Plaza
New York, N. Y. 10020

Employer Organizations

Féderation of Belgian Industries
Fédération des Industries Belges
4 rue Ravenstein
Brussels 1

American Chamber of Commerce in
    Belgium
21 rue de Commerce
Brussels

Belgian National Federation of
    Chambers of Commerce and
    Industry
*Fédération Nationale des Chambres
    de Commerce et d'industrie de
    Belgique*
40 rue du Congrès
Brussels 1

Labor Organizations

*Fédération Générale du Travail
    de Belgique* (F. G. T. B.) (Al-
    gemeen Belgisch Vakverbond)
General Federation of Labor of
    Belgium
42 rue Haute
Brussels 1

*Confédération des Syndicats Chré-
    tiens* (C. S. C.)
Federation of Christian Trade Un-
    ions
135 rue de la Loi
Brussels 4

*Centrale Générale des Syndicats Li-
    béraux   de   Belgique*
(C. G. S. L. B.)
General Federation of Liberal
    Trade Unions of Belgium
69 Boulevard Albert
Ghent

Other

U. S. Embassy
27 Boulevard du Régent
Brussels

FRANCE

Government

Ministry of Social Affairs
127 rue de Grenelle
75 Paris 7

Secretary of State of Social Affairs
    in Charge of Employment
7 rue de Tilsitt
75 Paris 17

Ministry for Economic Affairs and
    Finance
93 rue de Rivoli
75 Paris 1

Employer Organizations

*Conseil National du Patronat fran-
    cais*
31 Avenue Pierre I de Serbia
Paris 16

Paris Chamber of Commerce
27 Avenue de Friedland
Paris 8e

Labor Organizations

Confédération Générale du Travail
(C. G. T.)
General Confederation of Labor
213 rue Lafayette
Paris 10e

Force Ouvrière
198 Avenue du Maine
Paris 14

Confédération Francaise Démocratique du Travail (C.F.D.T.) (formerly known as Confédération Francaise des Travailleurs Chrétiens ˚C.F.T.C. which survives as name of a minority group of the prior organization, see next entry)
26 rue de Montholon
Paris 9

Confédération Francaise des Travailleurs Chrétiens (C.F.T.C.)
56 rue du Fauborg Poissonnière
75 Paris 10e

Confédération Générale des Cadres (Union of supervisors, executive staff and technicians)
30 rue de Gramont
Paris 2e

Fédération de l'Education Nationale (Teachers' Union Federation)
10 rue Solférino
Paris 7e

Other

U. S. Embassy
Avenue Gabriel 2
Paris 8e

FEDERAL REPUBLIC OF GERMANY

Government

Federal Ministry of Labor and the Social Structure
Bundesministerium für Arbeit und Sozial Ordnung
5300 Düsdorf bei Bonn
Bonner Strasse 85

Employer Organizations

Association of German Chambers of Industry and Commerce
Deutscher Industrie-und Handelstag
Adenauerallee 148
Bonn

Confederation of German Employers' Associations
Bundesvereinigung der Deutschen Arbeitsverbände
Oberländer Ufer 72
5 Köln-Bayenthal

Federation of German Industries
Bundesverband der Deutschen Industrie
Habsburgerring 2-12
Cologne

Labor Organizations

German Confederation of Labor Unions
Deutscher Gewerkschaftsbund (D.G.B.)
Hans-Böckler-Haus am Kennedydamm
Postfach 2601
Düsseldorf

Metal Workers Union
Industriegewerkschaft Metall für die Bundesrepublik Deutschland
Untermainkai 70-76
Frankfurt-am-Main

Clerical, Technical and Administrative Workers
Deutsche Angestellten-Gewerkschaft — DAG
Karl-Muck-Platz 1
2 Hamburg 36

Federation of Civil Servants and Public Officials
Deutscher Beamtenbund
Kölner Strasse 157
532 Bad Godesberg

Police Union
Gewerkschaft der Polizei
Forststrasse 3a
Hilden

Other

U. S. Embassy
Mehlemer Avenue
Bad Godesberg

REPUBLIC OF IRELAND

Government

Department of Industry and Commerce
Kildare Street
Dublin 2

Department of Labour
Mespil Road
Dublin 4

Labour Court
Ansley House
Mespil Road
Dublin 4

Industrial Development Authority
Landsdowne House
Ballsbridge
Dublin 4

U. S. Offices of Irish Industrial Development Authority
1 East Wacker Drive
Chicago, Ill. 60601
and
405 Park Avenue
New York, N. Y. 10022

Employer Organizations

Association of Chambers of Commerce of Ireland
7 Clare Street
Dublin 2

Federated Union of Employers
8 Fitzwilliam Place
Dublin 2

Federation of Irish Industries
9 Ely Place
Dublin 2

Federation of Trade Associations
5 Upper Pembroke Street
Dublin 2

Irish Management Institute
Orwell Road
Dublin 14

Labor Organizations

Irish Congress of Trade Unions
Congress House
19 Raglan Road
Ballsbridge
Dublin 4

Irish Transport and General Workers Union
Liberty Hall
Dublin 1

Irish National Teachers Organization
35 Parnell Square
Dublin 1

Workers' Union of Ireland
29 Parnell Square
Dublin 1

Other

Economic and Social Research Institute
73 Lower Baggott Street
Dublin 2

Institute of Public Administration
57-61 Lansdowne Road
Dublin 4

Irish Council of the European Movement
27 Merrion Square
Dublin 2

Irish National Productivity Committee
14, St. Stephen's Green
Dublin 2

National Industrial Economic Council
72-76 St. Stephen's Green
Dublin 2

U. S. Embassy
42 Elgin Road
Ballsbridge
Dublin 4

NORTHERN IRELAND

Government

Ministry of Commerce (Includes Industrial Development)
21 Linenhall Street
Belfast 2

Ministry of Health and Social Services
(Includes industrial injuries benefits, industrial relations, conciliation and arbitration, administration of Wages Councils and Factories Acts, Contracts of Employment and Redundancy Payments legislation)
Dundonald House
Upper Newtownards Road
Belfast

British Industrial Development Office
British Consulate-General
845 Third Avenue
P. O. Box 3434
New York, N. Y. 10017

Employer Organizations

The Northern Ireland Chamber of Commerce and Industry
Chamber of Commerce House
22 Great Victoria Street
Belfast

Belfast Chamber of Trade
36 Victoria Square
Belfast 1

Labor Organizations

Amalgamated Engineering Union
110 Peter's Hill
Belfast 13

Amalgamated Transport and General Workers Union
17 Orchard Street
Londonderry

Electrical Trades' Union
279 Antrim Road
Belfast 15

National Union of General and Municipal Workers
40 North Street
Belfast

Ulster Teachers' Union
72 High Street
Dublin

Other

The Northern Ireland Economic Council
21 Linenhall Street
Belfast 2

ITALY

Government

Ministry of Industry and Commerce
Via Vittorio Veneto 33
Rome

Ministry of Labor and Social Security
Via Flavia 6
Rome

Employer Organizations

General Federation of Italian Industry
Confederazione Generale dell'Industria Italiana (Confindustria)
Piazza Venezia 11
00187 Rome

Northern Italy District Office
Via Brasa 3
20123 Milan

Associazione Sindicale Intersind
Via Aurora 29
00187 Rome

Associazione Sindicale per le Aziende Petrolchimiche e Collegate a Partecipazione Statale (ASAP)
Via Aurora 29
Rome

Labor Organizations

General Confederation of Labor
Confederazione Generale Italiana del Lavoro — CGIL
Corso d'Italia 25
00198 Rome

Italian Confederation of Trade Unions
Confederazione Italiana Sindicati Lavoratori — CISL
Via Po 21
Rome

Italian Union of Labor
Unione Italiana del Lavoro — UIL
Via Lucullo 6
Rome

Italian Confederation of Independent Trades Unions
Confederazione Italiana Sindicati Autonomi Lavoratori — CISAL
Via G. B. Vico 1
Rome

Italian Confederation of National Workers' Unions
Confederazione Italiana Sindicati Nazionali dei Lavoratiori — CISNAL
Via Aureliana 53
Rome

General Federation of Artisans
Confederazione Generale Italiana dell' Artigianato
Via Plebiscito 102
Rome

General Federation of Professionals and Artists
Confederazione Generale Italiana dei Professionisti e Artisti —CIPA
Via S. Nicola da Tolentino 21
Rome

Other

Institute for Industrial Reconstruction
Instituto par la Riconstruzione Industriale — IRI
Via Veneto 89
Rome

U. S. Embassy
Via Veneto 119-A
Rome

LUXEMBOURG

Government

Ministry of Social Security, Public Health and Family Affairs
102 Boulevard de la Petrusse
Luxembourg

Ministry of Trade and Foreign Affairs
5 rue Notre Dame
Luxembourg

Ministry of Labor
57 rue de la Petrusse
Luxembourg

Employer Organizations

Chambre de Commerce
8 Avenue de l'Arsenal
Luxembourg

Fédération des Industriels Luxembourgeois
8 Avenue de l'Arsenal
Luxembourg

Labor Organizations

Luxembourg General Confederation of Labor
Confédération Générale du Travail du Luxembourg — CGT
4 rue P. Hentges
Luxembourg

Luxembourg Confederation of Christian Unions
Confédération Luxembourgeois des Syndicats Chrétiens
13 rue Bourbon
Luxembourg

Other

U. S. Embassy
22 Boulevard Em. Servais
Luxembourg

THE
NETHERLANDS

Government

Ministry of Economic Affairs
Bezuidenhoutseweg 30
The Hague

Ministry of Social Affairs and Public Health
Zeestraat 73
The Hague

Employer Organizations

Netherlands National Committee of the International Chamber of Commerce
Prinses Beatrixlaan 5
The Hague

Federation of Netherlands Industry
Verbond van Nederlandsche Ondernemingen — VNO
Prinses Beatrixlaan 5
The Hague

Netherlands Federation of Christian Employers
Federatie van Katholieke en Protestants — Christelijke Werkgevers Verbond — FKPWV
Raamweg 32
The Hague
FKPWV is secreteriat for the following:
   Netherlands Federation of Catholic Employers
   Nederlands Katholiek Werksgevers Verbond
   Raamweg 32
   The Hague

and
   Federation of Christian Employers in the Netherlands
   Verbond van Protestants — Christelijke Werkgevers in Nederland
   Raamweg 32
   The Hague

Netherlands Society for Industry and Commerce
Nederlandsche Maatschappij voor Nijverheid on Handel
Florapark 11
P. O. Box 205
Haarlem

Labor Organizations

Netherlands Federation of Trade Unions
Nederlands Verbond van Vakvereinigingen — NVV
P. O. Box 8110
Amsterdam

Netherlands Catholic Trade Union Federation
Nederlands Katholiek Vakverbond — NKV
Oudenoord 12
Utrecht

Christian National Federation of Trade Unions in the Netherlands
Christelijk National Vakverbond in Nederland
Maliebaan 8-8a
Utrecht

Other

Foundation of Labor
Stichting van de Arbeid
Bezuidenhoutseweg 60
The Hague

Social Economic Council
Sociaal-Economische Raad
Bezuidenhoutseweg 60
The Hague

U. S. Embassy
Lange Voorhout 32
The Hague

UNITED
KINGDOM

Government

Department of Economic Affairs
Storey's Gate
London W. C. 2

Department of Employment and Productivity
8 St. James Square
London S. W. 1

Department of Social Services
10 John Adam Street
London W. C. 2

Commission on Industrial Relations
G. K. N. House
22 Kingsway
London W. C. 2

National Board for Prices and Incomes
Kingsgate House, Victoria Street
London S. W. 1

National Economic Development Council
Millbank Tower
London S. W. 1

National Joint Advisory Council
8 St. James Square
London S. W. 1

Regional Economic Planning Councils
Storey's Gate
London W. C. 2

Employer Organizations

Associations of British Chambers of Commerce
68 Queen Street
London E. C. 4

British Institute of Management
Management House
Parker Street
London W. C. 2

Confederation of British Industry
21 Tothill Street
London S. W. 1

Engineering Employers' Federation
Broadway House
Tothill Street
London S. W. 1

Labor Organizations

Trades Union Congress
23-28 Great Russell Street
London W. C. 1

Scottish Trades Union Congress
12 Woodlands Terrace
Glasgow C 3, Scotland

General Federation of Trade Unions
Centre House
Upper Woburn Place
London W. C. 1

Amalgamated Society of Boilermakers, Shipwrights, Blacksmiths and Structural Workers
Lifton House
Eslington Road
Newcastle-on-Tyne 2

Amalgamated Union of Engineering and Foundry Workers
110 Peckham Road
London S. E. 15

Electrical, Electronic and Telecommunication Union/Plumbing Trades Union
Hayes Court
Hayes, Bromley

National Union of General and Municipal Workers
Ruxley Towers
Claygate, Esher
Surrey

National Union of Public Employees
Civic House
Aberdeen Terrace
London S. E. 3

National Union of Teachers
Hamilton House
Mabledon Place
London W. C. 1

Transport and General Workers' Union
Transport House
Smith Square
London S. W. 1

Other

British Productivity Council
Vintry House
Queen Street Place
London E. C. 4

Fabian Society
11 Dartmouth Street
London S. W. 1

Political and Economic Planning
(PEP)
12 Upper Belgrave Street
London S. W. 1

U. S. Embassy
24-32 Grosvenor Square
London W. 1

UNITED STATES OF AMERICA

Government

U. S. Department of Labor
U. S. Department of Labor Building
14th Street and Constitution Avenue, N. W.
Washington, D. C. 20210

Equal Employment Opportunity Commission
1800 G Street, N. W.
Washington, D. C. 20506

Federal Mediation and Conciliation Service
U. S. Department of Labor Building
14th Street and Constitution Avenue, N. W.
Washington, D. C. 20427

National Labor Relations Board
1717 Pennsylvania Avenue, N. W.
Washington, D. C. 20570

Employer Organizations

Chamber of Commerce of the United States
1615 H Street, N. W.
Washington, D. C. 20006

National Association of Manufacturers
277 Park Avenue
New York, N. Y. 10017

Labor Organizations

American Federation of Labor and Congress of Industrial Organizations
815 Sixteenth Street, N. W.
Washington, D. C. 20006

International Brotherhood of Teamsters, Chauffeurs, Warehousemen and Helpers of America
25 Louisiana Avenue, N. W.
Washington, D. C. 20001

International Union of United Automobile, Aerospace and Agricultural Implement Workers of America
800 East Jefferson
Detroit, Mich. 48214

UAW International Affairs Department
1126 Sixteenth Street, N. W.
Washington, D. C. 20036

Other

American Arbitration Association
140 West 51st Street
New York, N. Y. 10020

Committee for Economic Development
711 Fifth Avenue
New York, N. Y. 10022

Industrial Relations Research Association
Social Science Building
Madison, Wis. 53706

Institute of Labor and Industrial Relations
University of Illinois
504 East Armory Avenue
Champaign, Ill. 61820

Institute of Labor and Industrial Relations
University of Michigan
Ann Arbor, Mich. 48104

Institute of Industrial Relations
Loyola University of Chicago
820 North Michigan Avenue
Chicago, Ill. 60611

Institute of Industrial Relations
University of California
Berkeley, Calif. 94720
or
9244 Bunche Hall
UCLA
Los Angeles, Calif. 90024

New York State School of Indus-
   trial Relations
Cornell University
Ithaca, N. Y. 14850

School of Labor and Industrial Re-
   lations
Michigan State University
East Lansing, Mich. 48823

The W. E. Upjohn Institute for
   Employment Research
709 South Westnedge Avenue
Kalamazoo, Mich. 49007

TOPICAL INDEX

A

Agricultural labor
—COPA, European agricultural employers association, and agricultural unions of EEC nations, agreement 64
—social policy, EEC Commission action program formulated in 1963 64
—working conditions, EEC Commission Joint Advisory Committee opinion 64
—working hours, harmonization of 64
American investment and European cultures
—conflict and cooperation 441
—Draughtsmen's & Allied Technicians' Assn. (DATA) memo 442
—European attitudes and practices, similarities in 448
—European countries, differences within 447
—future developments 450
—Roberts-Arundel dispute 442-444, 468
—U.S. companies entering Europe, need of familiarity with European operative methods 452
American Investment in Italy, Fano 473
American Management in the United Kingdom, Grunfeld 467
Automotive industry (See also Ford of Britain; General Motors Corporation; World Automotive Department)
—supranational corporations 13

B

Belford, John A.
—*The Supranational Corporation and Labor Relations* 3
Belgium
—agreements, how negotiated 76
—American involvement 455
——American company, acceptance by Belgian community 456

——Belgian workers employed by American firms, pay scales 458
——conflict and tension, sources of 460
——European Community Trade Union Secretariat, influence of 462
——management-union relations 457
——managerial freedom 458
——protective labor legislation 458
—cement industry, fixed-term agreement, no-strike clause 76
—collective bargaining 239
——at level of enterprise 246
——joint committees; establishment, composition 235, 236
—dismissals, terms of notices, employer compliance 218
—economy system 210
—enterprise level, representation 230
—enterprises and employed personnel, size (1965) 212
—female workers, average gross wages 211
—industrial disputes, settlement 249
—industry-wide bargaining 244
—institutionalized relations between employers and trade unions 229
—job security and guaranteed income, aspirations of employees 217
—labor force 214
——categories of employees (1965) 215
——leading personnel 216
——supervisors 216
—labor-relations system 219
—male workers, average gross wages 211
—manual workers 214
—national interindustry agreement 78
—national interindustry bargaining 243
—National Labor Council, function 238
—safety and health committee, employer's responsibility to establish 234
—social security costs, evolution of (1958-1968) 213
—strike
——freedom to 247

European Social Fund—Contd.

—retraining of all workers, not only jobless and underemployed 34

F

Fairweather, Owen
—*Western European Labor Movements
and Collective Bargaining—
An Institutional Framework*
69
Fano, P. P.
—*American Investment in Italy* 473
—*Manpower Problems in Italy* 429
—*The Italian Labor Movement and
Collective Bargaining* 99
Farming
—EEC farming, employment in, EEC
Commission study 51
Federal Republic of Germany (See West
Germany)
Flanders, Allan
—*Hidden Manpower Resources* 419
—*Labor-Management Relations and the
Democratic Challenge* 487
Ford of Britain
—Court of Inquiry, labor dispute 113
—equal pay for women 112
——reduction in male-female differential 113
—government conciliation and strike
settlement 117
—job evaluation, outside consultants,
use of 110
—job profiles and descriptions 111
—job ranking and grading 111
—labor dispute, Court of Inquiry 113
—major wage-structure-reform agreement of 1967 109
——original settlement, resistance to 116
—National Joint Negotiating Committee
110
—new wage structure negotiations
——labor relationships, description of
workings 109
——lessons learned 113
—1969 agreement, duration 118
—Procedure Agreement of 1958 110
—sewing machinist classification, evaluation 112
—strike, balance-of-payments impact of
loss of export income, re-
vised settlement 117
—wage structure
——condition in 1967 110
——female differential 112

—wildcat or unofficial strikers, Ford
principle in bargaining 113;
attempt to secure legal enforcement 117
—women, equal pay for 112
——reduction in male-female differential 113
France
—closed shop and union shop contracts,
legality 83
—devaluation and inflation 121
—general strike of 1968
——beginning of end of the strikes 129
——Common Market Relations, impact
on 135
——communist role 123, 124
——government role 125
——"Grenelle Protocol" 126; settlement after Grenelle 129
——gross national product, effect on
134
——illegal strikes, participators, liability for breach-of-contract
suits 138
——management, impact on 132
——national and plant-level negotiations 126
——power play 121
——right to strike, legality 137
——strategy of 136
——unspecified pay raises, negotiation,
CGT and CFDT joint an-
nouncement 126
—inflation and devaluation 121
—"Matignon Agreement" 119
—national or regional agreements, provisions 84
—"people's capitalism," development
of 85
—plant-level bargaining, different channels 86
—profit-sharing plan
——Minister of Labor's power to prescribe 85
——required by law 85
—strike, French model 155
—union membership 83
—wages, lowest in six-nation Common
Market 119
Frontier commuters
—EEC regulations, special regulations
supplementing 33

G

Gamillscheg, Franz
—*Outlines of Collective Labor Law in
the Federal Republic of
Germany* 253